A Reader in Medical Anthropology

Blackwell Anthologies in Social and Cultural Anthropology

Series Editor: Parker Shipton, Boston University

Drawing from some of the most significant scholarly work of the nineteenth and twentieth centuries, the *Blackwell Anthologies in Social and Cultural Anthropology* series offers a comprehensive and unique perspective on the ever-changing field of anthropology. It represents both a collection of classic readers and an exciting challenge to the norms that have shaped this discipline over the past century.

Each edited volume is devoted to a traditional subdiscipline of the field such as the anthropology of religion, linguistic anthropology, or medical anthropology; and provides a foundation in the canonical readings of the selected area. Aware that such subdisciplinary definitions are still widely recognized and useful – but increasingly problematic – these volumes are crafted to include a rare and invaluable perspective on social and cultural anthropology at the onset of the twenty-first century. Each text provides a selection of classic readings together with contemporary works that underscore the artificiality of subdisciplinary definitions and point students, researchers, and general readers in the new directions in which anthropology is moving.

A Reader in Medical Anthropology

Theoretical Trajectories, Emergent Realities

Edited by

Byron J. Good, Michael M. J. Fischer,

Sarah S. Willen, and Mary-Jo

DelVecchio Good

WILEY-BLACKWELL

A John Wiley & Sons, Ltd., Publication

Registered Office
John Wiley & Sons Ltd, The Atrium, Southern Gate, Chichester, West Sussex, PO19 8SQ, United Kingdom

Editorial Offices
350 Main Street, Malden, MA 02148-5020, USA
9600 Garsington Road, Oxford, OX4 2DQ, UK
The Atrium, Southern Gate, Chichester, West Sussex, PO19 8SQ, UK

For details of our global editorial offices, for customer services, and for information about how to apply for permission to reuse the copyright material in this book please see our website at www.wiley.com/wiley-blackwell.

Library of Congress Cataloging-in-Publication Data

A reader in medical anthropology : theoretical trajectories, emergent realities / edited by Byron J. Good ... [et al.].
    p. cm. – (Blackwell anthologies in social and cultural anthropology)
  Includes bibliographical references and index.
  ISBN 978-1-4051-8315-4 (hardcover : alk. paper) – ISBN 978-1-4051-8314-7 (pbk. : alk. paper)
  1. Medical anthropology. 2. Traditional medicine. I. Good, Byron.
    GN296.A567 2010
    306.4′61–dc22
                      2009054233

A catalogue record for this book is available from the British Library.

Set in 9/11pt Sabon
by SPi Publisher Services, Pondicherry, India
Printed in the United States

4   2012

Contents

Acknowledgments

The editors and publisher also gratefully acknowledge the permission granted to reproduce the copyright material in this book:

1   W. H. R. Rivers, "Massage in Melanesia," pp. 57–61 in *Psychology and Ethnology*. New York: Harcourt, Brace and Co., 1926.

2   E. E. Evans-Pritchard, "The Notion of Witchcraft Explains Unfortunate Events," pp. 18–32 in *Witchcraft, Oracles, and Magic among the Azande*. Oxford: Clarendon Press, 1976. © Oxford University Press. By permission of Oxford University Press.

3   Victor Turner, "Muchona the Hornet, Interpreter of Religion" pp. 131–50 in *The Forest of Symbols*. Ithaca, NY: Cornell University Press, 1970.

4   Irving A. Hallowell, "The Ojibwa Self and its Behavioral Environment," pp. 172–82 in *Culture and Experience*. New York: Schocken Books, 1955.

5   Rudolf Virchow, "The Charity Physician," pp. 33–6 in L. J. Rather, ed., *Collected Essays on Public Health and Epidemiology*. Canton, MA: Science History Publications, 1985 [1879]. Used by kind permission of the publisher: Science History Publications/USA, division of Watson Publishing International LLC, Sagamore Beach, MA.

6   Benjamin Paul, "The Role of Beliefs and Customs in Sanitation Programs," *American Journal of Public Health* 48 (1958): 1502–6.

7   Charles Leslie, "Introduction," pp. 1–12 *[modified]* in C. Leslie, ed., *Asian Medical Systems*. Berkeley: University of California Press, 1976. © 1976 University of California Press Books. Reproduced with permission of University of California Press Books in the format textbook via Copyright Clearance Center.

8   Byron J. Good, "Medical Anthropology and the Problem of Belief," pp. 1–24 *[modified]* in *Medicine, Rationality and Experience*. Cambridge: Cambridge University Press, 1994. Reprinted by permission of Cambridge University Press.

9 Arthur M. Kleinman, "Medicine's Symbolic Reality: On a Central Problem in the Philosophy of Medicine," *Inquiry* 16 (1973): 206–13. Reprinted by permission of the publisher (Taylor & Francis Group; www.informaworld.com).

10 Thomas J. Csordas, "Elements of Charismatic Persuasion and Healing," *Medical Anthropology Quarterly* 2/2 (1988): 121–42. Reproduced by permission of the American Anthropological Association from *Medical Anthropology Quarterly* 2/2 (1988), pp. 121–42.

11 Ellen Corin, "The Thickness of Being: Intentional Worlds, Strategies of Identity, and Experience among Schizophrenics," *Psychiatry* 61 (1998): 133–46.

12 Cheryl Mattingly, "The Concept of Therapeutic 'Emplotment'," *Social Science and Medicine* 38/6 (1994): 811–22. ©1994 Elsevier Science and Technology Journals. Reproduced with permission of Elsevier Science & Technology Journals in the format Textbook via Copyright Clearance Center.

13 Michael Jackson, "Myths/Histories/Lives," in *Minima Ethnographica*. Chicago: University of Chicago Press, 1998. Reprinted by permission of the publisher, The University of Chicago Press.

14 Janis Hunter Jenkins, "The State Construction of Affect: Political Ethos and Mental Health among Salvadoran Refugees, *Culture, Medicine and Psychiatry* 15 (1991): 139–65. With kind permission from Springer Science + Business Media: Culture, Medicine and Psychiatry, The State Construction of Affect: Political Ethos and Mental Health Among Salvadoran Refugees, 15, 1991, pp. 139–65.

15 Robert Desjarlais, "Struggling Along: The Possibilities for Experience among the Homeless Mentally Ill," *American Anthropologist* 96/4 (1994): 886–901. Reproduced by permission of the American Anthropological Association from *American Anthropologist* 96/4 (1994), pp. 886–901.

16 Lorna A. Rhodes, n.d. "Dreaming of Psychiatric Citizenship: A Case Study of Supermax Confinement."

17 Adriana Petryna, "Biological Citizenship: The Science and Politics of Chernobyl-Exposed Populations," *Osiris* 19 (2004): 250–65. Reprinted by permission of the publisher, The University of Chicago Press.

18 João Biehl, n.d. "Human Pharmakon: Symptoms, Technologies, Subjectivities."

19 Veena Das, "The Figure of the Abducted Woman: The Citizen as Sexed," in *Life and Words: Violence and the Descent into the Ordinary*. Berkeley: University of California Press, 2007. © 2007 by the University of California Press – Books. Reproduced with permission of the University of California Press – Books in the format Textbook via Copyright Clearance Center.

20 Miriam Ticktin, "Where Ethics and Politics Meet: The Violence of Humanitarianism in France," *American Ethnologist* 33/1 (2006): 33–49. Reproduced by permission of the American Anthropological Association from *American Ethnologist* 33/1 (2006), pp. 33–49.

21 Mary-Jo DelVecchio Good, "The Medical Imaginary and the Biotechnical Embrace: Subjective Experiences of Clinical Scientists and Patients," in J. Biehl, B. Good, and A. Kleinman, eds., *Subjectivity: Ethnographic Investigations*. Berkeley: University of California Press, 2007. © 2007 by University of California Press –

Books. Reproduced with permission of University of California Press – Books in the format textbook via Copyright Clearance Center.

22 Lawrence Cohen, "Where It Hurts: Indian Material for an Ethics of Organ Transplantation," *Daedalus* 128/4 (1999): 135–66. © 1999 by the American Academy of Arts and Sciences.

23 Aslihan Sanal, " 'RobinHood' of Techno-Turkey or Organ Trafficking in the State of Ethical Beings," *Culture, Medicine and Psychiatry* 28/3 (2004): 281–309.

24 Marca C. Inhorn, "'He Won't Be My Son': Middle Eastern Muslim Men's Discourses of Adoption and Gamete Donation," *Medical Anthropology Quarterly* 20/1 (2006): 94–120. Reproduced by permission of the American Anthropological Association from *Medical Anthropology Quarterly* 20/1 (2006), pp. 94–120.

25 Jim Yong Kim and Paul Farmer, Kim, "AIDS in 2006: Moving toward One World, One Hope?" *New England Journal of Medicine* 355/7 (2006): 645–7.

26 Michael M. J. Fischer, n.d. "Lively Biotech and Translational Research."

27 Hans-Jörg Rheinberger, "Beyond Nature and Culture: Modes of Reasoning in the Age of Molecular Biology and Medicine," in M. Lock, A. Young, and A. Cambrosio, eds., *Living and Working with the New Medical Technologies: Intersections of Inquiry.* New York: Cambridge University Press, 2000. Reprinted by permission of the publisher, The University of Chicago Press.

28 Hannah Landecker, "Immortality, In Vitro: A History of the HeLa Cell Line," in P. E. Brodwin, ed., *Biotechnology and Culture: Bodies, Anxieties, Ethics.* Bloomington: Indiana University Press, 2000. Reprinted by permission of Hannah Landecker.

29 Joseph Dumit, "A Digital Image of the Category of the Person," in G. L. Downey and J. Dumit, eds., *Cyborgs and Citadels: Anthropological Interventions in Emerging Sciences and Technologies.* Santa Fe, NM: SAR Press, 1997. Reprinted by permission. © 1997 by the School for Advanced Research, Santa Fe, New Mexico.

30 Kaushik Sunder Rajan, "Experimental Values: Indian Clinical Trials and Surplus Health," *New Left Review* 45 (2007): 67–88.

31 George M. Foster, "Medical Anthropology and International Health Planning," *Medical Anthropology Newsletter* 7/3 (1976): 12–18. Reproduced by permission of the American Anthropological Association from *Medical Anthropology Newsletter* 7/3 (1976), pp. 12–18, 1976.

32 Craig Janes, and Kitty K. Corbett, "Anthropology and Global Health," *Annual Review of Anthropology* 38 (2009): 167–83.

33 Pimpawun Boonmongkon, Mark Nichter, and Jen Pylypa, "*Mot Luuk* Problems in Northeast Thailand: Why Women's Own Health Concerns Matter as Much as Disease Rates," *Social Science & Medicine* 53 (2004): 1095–112. © 2004 by Elsevier Science & Technology Journals. Reproduced with permission of Elsevier Science & Technology Journals in the format Textbook via Copyright Clearance Center.

34 Paul Farmer, "The New Malaise: Medical Ethics and Social Rights in the Global Era," in *Pathologies of Power.* Berkeley: University of California Press, 2003. © 2003 by University of California Press – Books. Reproduced with permission of

University of California Press – Books in the format Textbook via Copyright Clearance Center.

35 Didier Fassin, "Humanitarianism as a Politics of Life," *Public Culture* 19/3 (2007): 499–520.

36 Byron J. Good and Mary-Jo DelVecchio Good: written especially for this volume.

37 Erica James, "The Political Economy of 'Trauma' in Haiti in the Democratic Era of Insecurity," *Culture, Medicine and Psychiatry* 28 (2004): 127–49. With kind permission from Springer Science & Business Media: *Culture, Medicine and Psychiatry* 28 (2004), pp. 127–49.

38 Mariella Pandolfi, "Contract of Mutual (In)Difference: Governance and the Humanitarian Apparatus in Contemporary Albania and Kosovo," *Indiana Journal of Global and Legal Studies* 10 (2003):3 69–80.

39 Sarah S. Willen, "Darfur through a Shoah Lens: Sudanese Asylum Seekers, Unruly Biopolitical Dramas, and the Politics of Humanitarian Compassion in Israel." Substantially modified version of a piece that appeared in French in *Cultures & Conflits* n°72, autumn 2008, as "L'hyperpolitique du 'Plus jamais ça!': demandeurs d'asile soudanais, turbulence gouvernementale et politiques de contrôle des réfugiés en Israël."

40 Angela Garcia, "The Elegiac Addict: History, Chronicity, and the Melancholic Subject," *Cultural Anthropology* 23/4 (2009): 718–746. Reproduced by permission of the American Anthropological Association from *Cultural Anthropology* 23/4 (2009), pp. 718–46.

Editors' Acknowledgments: The editors of this volume acknowledge the enormous support of Seth Hannah and Ken Vickery in assembling and editing these texts. We thank Rosalie Robertson and Julia Kirk, editors at Wiley-Blackwell, for their support, encouragement, and patience through this whole project. And we thank Parker Shipton, who years ago first encouraged us to edit a volume on medical anthropology that represents our understanding of the theoretical lineages of the field. We also thank Entang Wiharso for use of the striking image from his brilliant *Landscaping My Brain* for the cover of this volume. And we express our appreciation to the authors who agreed to have their work reprinted here or to appear for the first time in this *Reader*.

About the Editors

Byron J. Good is Professor of Medical Anthropology in the Department of Global Health and Social Medicine, Harvard Medical School, and the Department of Anthropology, Harvard University. He is author of *Medicine, Rationality and Experience: An Anthropological Perspective* (1994), and co-editor of eight books, including *Culture and Panic Disorder* (with Devon Hinton, 2009), *Postcolonial Disorders* (with Mary-Jo DelVecchio Good, Sandra Hyde, and Sarah Pinto, 2008), *Subjectivity: Ethnographic Investigations* (with Joao Biehl and Arthur Kleinman, 2007), and *Culture and Depression* (with Arthur Kleinman, 1985).

Michael M. J. Fischer is Andrew W. Mellon Professor in the Humanities and Professor of Anthropology and Science and Technology Studies at MIT, and Lecturer in Global Health and Social Medicine at the Harvard Medical School. He is author of *Anthropological Futures* (2009); *Mute Dreams, Blind Owls, and Dispersed Knowledges: Persian Poesis in the Transnational Circuitry* (2004), *Emergent Forms of Life and the Anthropological Voice* (2003); *Debating Muslims: Cultural Dialogues in Postmodernity and Tradition* (with Mehdi Abedi, 1990), *Anthropology as Cultural Critique* (with George Marcus, 1986), and *Iran: From Religious Dispute to Revolution* (1980).

Sarah S. Willen is Assistant Professor of Anthropology at Southern Methodist University. A former NIMH Postdoctoral Fellow in the Department of Global Health and Social Medicine at Harvard Medical School, she has taught in the Department of Anthropology at Harvard University. She is editor of *Transnational Migration to Israel in Global Comparative Context* (2007) and guest editor of a special issue of *International Migration* (2007). Her work also appears in *Cultures et Conflits* (2008), *International Migration* (2007), the *Journal of Middle East Women's Studies* (2005), and the *Harvard Review of Psychiatry* (with Antonio Bullon and Mary-Jo DelVecchio Good, forthcoming).

Mary-Jo DelVecchio Good is Professor of Social Medicine in the Department of Global Health and Social Medicine, Harvard Medical School, and the Department of Sociology, Harvard University. She edited *Culture, Medicine, and Psychiatry*, with Byron Good, from 1986 to 2004. Her publications include "Complex Engagements: Responding to Violence in Post-Conflict Aceh" (2009), *Postcolonial Disorders* (with Sandra Hyde, Sarah Pinto, and Byron Good, 2008), "The Biotechnical Embrace" (2001), *American Medicine: The Quest for Competence* (1995), and *Pain as Human Experience* (with Paul Brodwin, Arthur Kleinman, and Byron Good, 1994).

About the Cover Artist:

Entang Wiharso, an Indonesian-US-based artist, often examines humanity's duplicitous and contradictory nature by scrutinizing social relations in his visually provocative work. Described as an artist who can paint the uncertainty of identity honestly, Wiharso has exhibited internationally in such venues as the Kiasma Museum of Contemporary Art, Helsinki, Finland, the 51st Venice Biennale, and the 2006 Beijing Biennale. A Pollock-Krasner Grant recipient, whose work was most recently exhibited at the 2009 Prague Biennale and the 2009 Asian Art Biennale in Taipei, he has been recognized by the Indonesian Fine Art Foundation as one of his country's Top 10 Painters.

Introduction

Every society grapples with large questions of the meaning of illness, suffering, and death, and every culture has developed specialized bodies of knowledge, with practitioners or healers and distinctive therapeutic modalities aimed at managing the human body, treating illness, and providing care for those who suffer. Anthropologists have had a long-standing interest in how illness is understood and experienced, theorized and treated, in the diverse cultures and civilizations within which they work. Medical anthropologists have collaborated with physicians and public health specialists to improve the distribution and effectiveness of medical care, demonstrating the relevance of detailed understanding of local forms of medical knowledge and social organization. At the same time, anthropologists are often deeply influenced by the societies in which they work, by how individuals and societies cope with the most intimate moments of birth, sickness, and death, by therapeutic forms that provide important alternatives to biomedical conceptualizations of health and healing, and by the religious and spiritual traditions drawn on by individuals and communities throughout the life cycle and in times of crisis. Medical anthropology thus deals with many of the most vital issues that define what it means to be human.

At the same time, anthropologists increasingly live and carry out research in societies that are extraordinarily culturally diverse, with globalized media and competing cultural and religious claims, where the very categories "culture" and "community" are called into question. Some find themselves working amidst violence or in communities in various stages of post-conflict recovery, responding to health care needs in settings in which trauma is an everyday reality and humanitarian organizations, local NGOs and advocacy groups, and governmental facilities and military forces, interact in complex ways. Nearly all anthropologists work in societies with increasing access to high technology medical regimes, though often in partial and incomplete ways, and the "medical imaginary" (M. Good 2001; ch. 21, this volume) – a profound fascination with biotechnologies and therapeutics – is increasingly ubiquitous. Diseases and biotechnologies follow new structures of inequalities, no longer neatly tied to "developed" versus "developing" or high and low income nations, producing unthinkable existential dilemmas and new contradictions. Deeply indebted Indian women have to decide whether to sell a kidney to maintain their families. Individuals and families worldwide are forced to make decisions about mortgaging the future to pay for treatments for cancer or other diseases, which may or may not be effective. The language of human rights has increasingly entered this domain, with varied effects. Access to anti-retroviral drugs is increasingly seen as a human right for persons with AIDS, which has spurred a global movement to increase HIV treatment. At the same time, efforts to make psychotropic medications, often highly effective, available to treat mental illnesses may be seen as the imposition of Western categories fostered by drug companies. It is in this complex new world, unimaginable to the anthropologists of a previous era, that medical anthropologists now take on diverse roles as researchers, activists, health care providers, teachers, participants in international organizations, and collaborators with local institutions and organizations.

Any sourcebook or collection of essays in a field as diverse as this is necessarily a partial representation of a discipline, a personal reading of the field and a statement about where the authors feel the field has come from, where it is going, and which writing exemplifies the most interesting work in the field. David Landy's 1977 reader, *Culture, Disease, and Healing*, was organized around 14 substantive topics in the field, from "Paleopathology" and "Ecology and Epidemiology of Disease" to sections on "Obstetrics and Population Control," on the roles of patients and healers, and on medical systems in settings of social change. Thomas Johnson and Carolyn Sargent's 1990 reader was intended as a "handbook of theory and method," a set of essays aimed at summarizing particular topics and research methods current in the field at that time. And Peter Brown's 1998 reader, *Understanding and Applying Medical Anthropology*, is divided between essays distinguishing "biocultural" and "cultural" approaches to the field, and a set of chapters representing applications of medical anthropology to issues such as stigma and chronic illness, gender and women's health, and culture and nutrition.

Medical Anthropology: Theoretical Trajectories, Emergent Realities is intended as a source book of theoretically engaged writing in medical anthropology. Rather than representing the field in bimodal terms as biosocial versus cultural, or setting out sections on theory, methods, and substantive topics, this reader is organized around what we consider the most important theoretical frames that have shaped and continue to shape medical anthropology, along with the "emergent realities" – new biotechnologies, new epidemics, new forms of "postcolonial disorders," new forms of subjectivity – that medical anthropologists have struggled to make sense of using these analytic frames. In our view, medical anthropology has gone from being a largely a-theoretical practice-oriented discipline to one of the most deeply engaged theoretical subfields within anthropology. Our goal is to provide a guide to the field from this perspective. We bring together in each section of this book authors and essays that represent distinctive ways of thinking about and writing in medical anthropology, point out the theoretical lines of inquiry that link authors working within particular traditions, and illustrate the distinguishing elements of writings and theoretical perspectives across traditions.

In this book, we view the history of medical anthropology as a set of competing and complementary theoretical perspectives that have their own "trajectories," which might be sketched out in the broadest terms as follows. Medical anthropology emerged as a distinctive subdiscipline within social anthropology in the 1950s, led by a small group of committed anthropologists in schools of public health and at the Smithsonian Institute, collaborating with international health specialists working in Latin America and Africa. In the 1970s, the field began to take shape as a more central field within anthropology. Medical anthropology was reshaped as the "comparative study of medical systems," with a particular focus on Asian medical systems, and it developed a distinctive theoretical foundation linked to interpretive anthropology, symbolic studies, and phenomenology. During the 1980s, medical anthropology virtually exploded in size, as more anthropologists began working in clinical settings, strong interest groups developed within the Society for Medical Anthropology, and theoretical debates particular to the field took form and were engaged in new, specialized journals. In this period, medical anthropology came increasingly into conversation with diverse critical theories, post-structuralism, and gender studies, and medical anthropologists engaged in critical studies of medical knowledge and institutions and conducted ethnographic research focused on poverty and unequal distribution of disease and access to medical care.

The 1990s saw an infusion of interest in biotechnologies, as medical anthropologists and anthropologists working in STS ("science, technology and society" studies) brought a newly developing anthropology of science into conversation with medical anthropologists working on such issues as genetics, pharmaceuticals, and high-technology therapeutic regimens. At the same time, medical anthropologists became increasingly involved in clinical research within high-tech medical settings, working with clinicians, patients, and bioethicists to fashion new studies of the culture of medicine. Anthropologists and a generation of young anthropologist-physicians were also deeply involved in the development of a global health movement that was in full force by the end of the 1990s, moving medical anthropology from applied activities in international public health to activist roles in developing treatment programs in low income countries for previously untreated diseases – such as drug resistant tuberculosis and HIV/AIDS – and becoming advocates for the redistribution of health care resources, drawing on ideologies of human rights and social justice. And medical anthropologists, along with others in the field of anthropology, became increasingly involved in settings of conflict and post-conflict, playing roles both as participants in and critics of humanitarian organizations and conducting research in settings of violence and social breakdown.

Medical Anthropology: Theoretical Trajectories, Emergent Realities assumes this broad historical outline of the field of medical anthropology in the seven sections of the book. While this framework is broadly historical in shape, we do not view the sections as representing "stages" in the development of medical anthropology. We take the term "theoretical *trajectories*" seriously, tracing ideas and concepts that have come from some place and have on-going vital lives, analytic frames that have developed – and continue to develop – in conversation and debate both within given theorized positions and across them. It is this focus on what we describe as theoretically engaged medical anthropology that distinguishes this particular sourcebook. The essays in this reader are grouped to provide a map of the theoretical lineages critical to the development of the field and a guide to the central ideas and questions of the discipline. This collection represents how the editors have experienced and participated in the field, positions we have advocated and how we have taught medical anthropology over the years. And it represents a collection of what we consider to be examples of the best writing in the field. Omissions – of important substantive topics and many of our favorite authors and writings in the field – are dictated by the limits of a single volume and the goal of providing a selective view of the field.

The volume begins with a part entitled "Antecedents." Included is a small sample of classic essays standing in for a large body of work from early twentieth century anthropology on illness and healing in small, non-literate societies. Essays were selected both because of their enduring contribution to our thinking about how culture shapes illness and healing and because they represent theoretical traditions – rationalist and phenomenological positions – that have long influenced the field. We also include exemplars from early public health anthropology and the great German social medicine tradition, which represent two important strands in applied medical anthropology. And we include an early example of the Asian medical systems tradition which served as transition to the medical anthropology that emerged in the 1970s.

Part II, "Illness and Narrative, Body and Experience," is a collection of essays representing what has become known as interpretive or meaning-centered medical anthropology. This perspective, closely linked to what Arthur Kleinman (1973) called "the comparative study of medical systems," is grounded explicitly in semiotics and symbolic studies, in narrative theory, and in phenomenology. Interpretive medical anthropology, with its focus on meaning and illness experience, on the cognitive and psychological management of illness, on illness narratives and the narrative dimension of clinical transaction, and on the body, embodiment, and the life world of medicine provides a broad theoretical framework linking cultural or symbolic studies to illness and healing. It provides an explicit critique of the belief model of early public health anthropology, including the assumption that people adopt the cultural models of their society at face value, and a response to claims that medical anthropology was largely an a-theoretical, applied discipline. In conversation with critical theory, post-structuralism, psychological and psychoanalytic studies, and various postcolonial modes of writing, interpretive medical anthropology continues to be a creative source of humanistic writing, research, and teaching within medical anthropology.

By the early 1980s, diverse critical theories, including both Marxist-inspired writing and post-structuralism, had become increasingly influential within anthropology and ethnographic writing. Part III, "Governmentalities and Biological Citizenship," represents the coming of age of a body of work in medical anthropology that grew out of these influences. We have chosen not to include here the polemical debates about what constitutes a "critical medical anthropology," in which some argued that interpretive medical anthropologists failed to attend adequately to macrosocial forces and the play of power, or some of the earliest writings in medical anthropology influenced by Michel Foucault. Instead, we include essays that represent more recent efforts to draw on decades of writing about biopolitics, biosociality, governmentality, citizenship, and subjectivity, all a part of the post-structuralist vocabulary, in order to think through topics such as contemporary prison psychiatry, nuclear disaster, HIV treatment, communal violence, and migrant health.

Part IV, "The Biotechnical Embrace," brings together essays that explore both classic and unexpected sites of the emergence of the medical imaginary and the powerful force of the biosciences and biotechnical therapeutics in managing fundamental issues of life, birth, and death in late modernity. While this work grows out of earlier studies of the culture of biomedicine and the sociology of medical experimentation, these studies of the "biotechnical embrace" represent medical anthropology's encounter with "emergent realities" – the global trade in human organs, the deployment of reproductive technologies in a poor Islamic nation, the growing faith in biotechnical responses to the worldwide AIDS epidemic – all in the context of globalized therapeutic procedures. C. P. Snow's classic divide between the worlds of science and humanities (1959) is here refigured as the conjoining of technology and desire, as clinical narratives and the political economy of hope, technologies deeply invested with affect and loosed in the popular imaginary.

This focus carries over to Part V, "Biosciences, Biotechnologies," which more explicitly links writing from the history, philosophy, sociology, and anthropology of science to medical anthropology. In the 1990s, anthropology came to have an increasing presence in a field dedicated to exploring social and historical contingencies of scientific practice and knowledge. Sociologists of science often preferred to focus on the "hard" cases, on physics or bench research, rather than medicine to explore such contingencies. But a flourishing anthropology of science quickly spilled out of the laboratory, following the "social life" of emergent scientific objects – stem cell lines, medical images, molecules labeled as pharmaceuticals – into their diverse social worlds. This section represents the conjunction of medical anthropology and studies of science, technology and society, suggesting possible futures for work in this field.

Part VI, "Global Health, Global Medicine," juxtaposes a long trajectory of medical anthropology working in international public health with the emergence of a new global health movement at the opening of the twenty first century. On close observation, anthropologists working in international public health, whether earlier figures such as George Foster or the most prominent contemporary practitioners, share an interest in issues that are newly labeled "implementation sciences." It is little wonder, however, that leading anthropologist-physicians, Paul Farmer, Jim Kim, Didier Fassin, for example, prefer to see this new global health movement as linked genealogically to the social medicine tradition of Rudolf Virchow, with his clarion call for physicians to be the "natural attorneys for the poor" and his advocacy for medicine to serve as an applied domain of human rights and social justice. This section provides a small representation of what was in the past, and has yet again become, one of the most vital domains of medical anthropology.

Finally, "Postcolonial Disorders" represents another potential future for medical anthropology. The term "postcolonial disorders" bears twofold significance, referring both to a theoretical orientation and to a constellation of phenomena in which medical anthropologists are increasingly engaged – communal violence and post-conflict interventions, humanitarianism and new sites of global governance, displaced populations and cultures, and the continued social pathologies associated with colonial violence, displacement, and remembered trauma. Defined as social pathologies, these phenomena provoke new forms of therapeutic interventions, reproducing in some ways interventions of the colonial era. Bringing together a reflexive awareness of the place of colonialism in anthropology's constitution, with a commitment to link studies of subjectivity, the afterlife of the colonial, and new forms of disorder and intervention, the essays in this section represent another range of possibilities for a vital, theoretically informed medical anthropology.

REFERENCES

Brown, Peter
    1998   Understanding and Applying Medical Anthropology. Mountain View, CA: Mayfield Publishing Co.
Good, Mary-Jo DelVecchio
    2001   Biotechnical Embrace. Culture, Medicine and Psychiatry 25:395–410.
Johnson, Thomas M. and Carolyn F. Sargent
    1990   Medical Anthropology: A Handbook of Theory and Method. New York: Greenwood Press.
Kleinman, Arthur
    1973   Toward a Comparative Study of Medical Systems. Science, Medicine and Man 1:55–65.
Landy, David
    1977   Culture, Disease, and Healing: Studies in Medical Anthropology. New York: Macmillan Publishing Co.
Snow, C. P.
    1959   The Two Cultures and the Scientific Revolution. New York: Cambridge University Press.

Part I

Antecedents

Introduction
Setting the Stage: Historical Antecedents to Contemporary Medical Anthropology

So common is it for medical anthropologists today to work in societies with complex, interacting forms of high technology biomedicine, folk healers, alternative literate traditions, and diverse popular movements and forms of religious healing that it is easy to neglect the large body of anthropological writing on illness and healing in relatively small-scale societies. The indigenous societies of Africa, the Pacific, and the Americas studied by anthropologists of the nineteenth and early twentieth century were complex societies and civilizations, deeply involved in global transactions, most notably colonialism, though this was often obscured by anthropologists. However, these societies were extremely different from those studied by anthropologists today – and healing rituals had a special place in many of them. Studies of such rituals, as well as of indigenous healing specialists, are found throughout ethnographic writing that pre-dated medical anthropology. They are, however, among the most important sources from which medical anthropology draws, raising a host of issues and analytic strategies which remain important for re-thinking medicine from an anthropological perspective. This first section of readings provides a small sample of a rich set of historical writing about issues of illness, misfortune, and healing.

These early essays are selected to represent key theoretical positions – the rationality tradition of British anthropologists, the American phenomenological tradition, and a German social medicine perspective – that have continued to be important in debates within medical anthropology. In addition to providing classic essays useful to think with – about medicine's role in providing rational explanations for mysterious events, about healing as a social process – it is our goal to draw attention to the early antecedents of theoretical debates that have continued within medical anthropology to the present.

W. H. R. Rivers (1864–1922) was a physician, experimental neuro-psychologist, psychiatrist, and anthropologist, who has come to be known better through Pat Barker's fictional trilogy (1991, 1993, 1995) on Rivers' life than through his anthropological writings. Rivers was among the first of the physicians who have become ethnologists, and is sometimes claimed as a founder of medical anthropology. Rivers was recruited to be a member of the Torres Straits Expedition to the Pacific in 1898, where he conducted basic psychological experiments with local populations. He went on to travel widely on colonial scientific expeditions and became a specialist of Polynesian and Melanesian societies (Rivers 1914). His Fitz-Patrick Lectures to The Royal College of Physicians of London in 1915 and 1916, published as *Medicine, Magic, and Religion* (1924), are far more widely cited by medical anthropologists than actually read. The writing is archaic, embedded in discussions of the stages of evolution of societies toward "civilization," and largely non-ethnographic in the contemporary sense of the word. His arguments, however, are powerful. Writing on the "Rationality of Leechcraft," a term used to denote a domain of empirical medical knowledge, he argued, "The practices of these peoples in relation to disease are not a medley of disconnected and meaningless customs, but are inspired by definite ideas concerning the causation of disease" (1924: 51). The book is devoted largely to identifying and describing those ideas and the practices they inspired.

The 1926 essay included here, "Massage in Melanesia," demonstrates how apparently empirical practices such as massage "are inspired by definite ideas," which turn out not to be "empirical" as expected. Rivers uses the example to show that a clear distinction between the rational and the superstitious cannot be maintained, and that the evolutionary view that medicine evolved by "sloughing off" the superstitious is untenable. Ultimately, Rivers' clinical work on shell shock among World War I soldiers and his ethical reflections on curing soldiers in order to send them back to the front to die is far more gripping and contemporary than his ethnology. However, his discussion of how native medical systems provide causal frames for explaining illness and misfortune and his efforts to classify these explanatory systems were an early example of what came to be known as the rationality tradition within British anthropology.

E. E. Evans-Pritchard (1902–73), Professor of Social Anthropology at Oxford from 1946 through 1970, was a master ethnographer rather than expeditionary ethnologist. Working for extended time in several African societies, particularly the Azande, he provided the classic formulation of how witchcraft, along with oracles and sorcery, served as devices to explain the unknown. It is *what* is explained that is critical, he argued (1937). The Azande are aware that termites cause granaries to fall. What is to be explained is why a granary falls at a particular moment on a particular person, causing injury or death. Witchcraft, and by extension all systems of medical knowledge, serve to explain both how and why someone becomes ill. They serve as *theodicy*, Evans-Pritchard argued, ways of explaining why terrible misfortune and suffering occur in this world and why good persons suffer no less than the bad.

Within British anthropology, the claim that witchcraft and local healing beliefs were to be understood as particular modes of explanatory rationality, not so distant from a natural science, provoked a later set of vigorous debates about the nature of science and rationality (see Good 1994: 10–14, for a review). However, while beginning with a similar recognition that illness and misfortune call forth a search for underlying causes and efforts at healing, Victor Turner (1920–83) carried his work on Ndembu "medicine" and healing rituals, what he called "rites of affliction," in quite a different direction. "Disease among the Ndembu must be viewed not only in a private or idiographic but also in a public or social structural framework," argued Turner (1967: 359). Divination and therapy is a "process of making hidden and secret things visible and thereby accessible, if they are harmful, to redressive and remedial action" (303). But what is made visible is typically "interpersonal or factional disputes, many of which have long histories" (360), and rites of affliction are social dramas aimed at making evident the underlying social conflicts and resolving them through ritual actions that have their effects at the social level. While linked to explanatory frames, these rituals are forms of symbolic action, embedded in complex symbolic forms, analyzed with remarkable richness by Turner.

The American tradition, represented by A. Irving Hallowell's (1892–1974) essay, stands in sharp contrast to that of the British. Although Hallowell described how illness served the social function of sanctioning behaviors considered immoral or dangerous for the native Ojibwa people (Hallowell 1976 [1963]), his real focus was on the deeply cultural nature of the self and the "culturally constituted behavioral environment" of the Ojibwa, a phenomenal world occupied by spiritual and animal "persons" as well as human persons (Hallowell 1955: chs. 4 and 8). This for Hallowell was a world shaped by language and culture and fully embodied, incorporated into perceptual processes as Ojibwa children entered this cultural world, shaping their experience of space, time, causality and persons – structures of knowing and being in the world for philosopher Immanuel Kant and the European phenomenologists who followed, as well as Franz Boas and Sapir and Whorf and other American anthropologists. Culturally shaped explanations of illness are of course important within this world. But as Hallowell wrote, "*Explanation* means what is intellectually satisfying ... because it is deeply embedded in a culturally constituted world view" (1976 [1963]: 392). The importance of this explicitly phenomenological tradition for medical anthropology will be explored in Part II of this Reader. Hallowell's seminal essays remain critical sources for this tradition.

Hallowell quotes directly from University of Chicago anthropologist Robert Redfield, the teacher of Charles Leslie, whose Introduction to the book *Asian Medical Systems* (1976) is included next. Hallowell focused on Redfield's elaboration of "world view" as an analytic device for investigating culture from inside, a means for understanding the cultural world through embodied experience rather than local forms of rationality of members of a society. Leslie, on the other hand, drew on Redfield's analysis of "peasant societies" (Redfield 1956), those differentiated between "big traditions" with literate specialists, and local "little traditions" that make up folk cultures. Redfield developed this perspective for his work in Mexico; Leslie drew on it for his studies of medical traditions in India. And it was within this framework that he began to advocate for the comparative study of "Asian medical systems," literate traditions of Yunani (Greek), Ayurvedic (Indian/Sanskrit), and classical Chinese medicines. These were the "big traditions" of classical medicine, the writings, pharmacopeia, institutions, and practitioners that belonged to the "great civilizations" of Greece, India, and China.

The "Asian medical systems" approach was first elaborated in a workshop organized by Charles Leslie in 1971, supported by the Wenner Gren Foundation, that brought together historians, sociologists, anthropologists, classics scholars, and public health specialists. The 1970s saw a burgeoning interest in complex Asian medical systems. Arthur Kleinman and his colleagues organized a similar workshop on medicine in Chinese societies, supported by the Fogarty International Center (Kleinman et al., 1976), and this tradition has continued to be productive (Leslie and Young 1992; Bates 1995).

Kleinman's 1973 essay "Toward a Comparative Study of Medical Systems" made explicit the implications of the Asian medical systems approach for a new medical anthropology. His 1980 *Patients and Healers in the Context of Culture* provided a monograph-length study of such a medical system in Taiwan. And the oft-cited essay in the *Annals of Internal Medicine*, "Culture, Illness, and Care" (Kleinman, Eisenberg and Good 1978), provided a translation of these ideas for clinical practice.

The Asian medical systems approach thus provided a crucial bridge from the anthropological studies of illness and healing in small, "preliterate" societies to research in the kinds of socially and politically complex societies in which medical anthropologists work today. Contemporary biomedicine was viewed as one form of professional medicine practiced within a society, now understood as culturally shaped practices embedded in a larger medical system constituted by professional, folk, and popular domains. This broad agenda for a comparative study of medical systems has had a powerful influence on what medical anthropology has become.

We have also included two historical sources representative of the international public health tradition of medical anthropology and the "social medicine" tradition. Benjamin Paul (1911–2005) played a critical role in introducing behavioral sciences into public health teaching and research. Paul taught in the Harvard School of Public Health from 1946 to 1962, establishing a social science curriculum in 1951. His 1955 textbook, *Health, Culture and Community: Case Studies of Public Reactions to Health Programs*, stood for years as the most significant model for medical anthropologists working within international public health programs. He was an ethnographer of a Mayan community in Guatemala, where he began working in 1941 as a graduate student, and where he continued to visit until he was 89 years old. Although the "health belief model," for years a popular approach to applying anthropological research to international public health work, has by now been widely criticized, Ben Paul, as he was known to many generations of medical anthropologists, and George Foster were critical practitioners of an early form of medical anthropology, through which the discipline came into being.

Rudolf Virchow (1821–1902) is quite a different kind of ancestor of medical anthropology. Virchow was an activist physician of nineteenth century Germany, a pathologist of enormous scientific importance, a social epidemiologist, specialist in epidemics and infectious diseases, and a committed advocate for public health services and medical care for the poor (Virchow 1985 [1879]). He and his revolutionary colleagues, who manned the barricades in the 1848 German uprising, advocated for public provision of medical care for the indigent, prohibition of child labor, protection of pregnant women, reduction of working days for those in dangerous occupations, removal of toxic substances, and adequate ventilation of work sites (Eisenberg 1984: 526). His grand aphorism "Medicine is a social science, and politics nothing but medicine on a grand scale" (Waitzkin 2006:7) has been an inspiration to a new group of global health activists who, like Virchow, argue that medical science should draw its problems from concrete social concerns and that medical anthropology should be rooted in the struggle for social justice (see Part VI in this volume).

The final essay in this section, "Medical Anthropology and the Problem of Belief," drawn from Byron Good's 1994 *Medicine, Rationality and Experience*, demonstrates the relevance of the divide between rationalist, "belief"-oriented theories and the phenomenological tradition. This essay demonstrates how the logic of these positions has given rise to very different types of medical anthropology, criticizes the use of "belief" as a category of analysis in medical anthropology and public health, and argues for a medical anthropology grounded in a meaning-centered or phenomenological tradition.

REFERENCES

Barker, Pat
  1991   Regeneration. New York: Plume.
Barker, Pat
  1993   The Eye in the Door. New York: Dutton Books.
Barker, Pat
  1995   The Ghost Road. New York: Plume.
Bates, Don
  1995   Knowledge and the Scholarly Medical Traditions. Cambridge: Cambridge University Press.
Eisenberg, Leon
  1984   Rudolf Ludwig Karl Virchow, Where Are You Now That We Need You? The American Journal of Medicine 77:524–32.
Evans-Pritchard, E. E.
  1937   Witchcraft, Oracles and Magic among the Azande. Oxford: The Clarendon Press.
Good, Byron J.
  1994   Medicine, Rationality and Experience: An Anthropological Perspective. Cambridge: Cambridge University Press.
Hallowell, A. Irving
  1955   Culture and Experience. New York: Schocken Books.
Hallowell, A. Irving
  1976 [1963]   Ojibwa World View and disease. *In* Contributions to Anthropology: Selected Papers of A. Irving Hallowell, pp. 391–448. Chicago: University of Chicago Press.
Kleinman, Arthur
  1973   Toward a Comparative Study of Medical Systems. Science, Medicine and Man 1:55–65.
Kleinman, Arthur
  1980   Patients and Healers in the Context of Culture. Berkeley: University of California Press.
Kleinman, Arthur, Leon Eisenberg, and Byron Good
  1978   Culture, Illness and Care: Clinical Lessons from Anthropologic and Cross-Cultural Research. Annals of Internal Medicine 88:251–58.
Kleinman, Arthur, Peter Kunstadter, E. Alexander, and James Gale, eds.
  1976   Medicine in Chinese Cultures. Washington, DC: Fogarty International Center.
Leslie, Charles, ed.
  1976   Asian Medical Systems. Berkeley: University of California Press.
Leslie, Charles, and Allan Young
  1992   Paths to Asian Medical Knowledge. Berkeley: University of California Press.

Paul, Benjamin
    1955   Health, Culture, & Community: Case Studies of Public Reactions to Health Programs. New York: Russell Sage Foundation.
Redfield, Robert
    1956   Peasant Society and Culture. Chicago: University of Chicago Press.
Rivers, W. H. R.
    1914   The History of Melanesian Society, vol. 2: Percy Sladen Trust Expedition to Melanesia, Publication No. 1. Cambridge: Cambridge University Press.
Rivers, W. H. R.
    1924   Medicine, Magic, and Religion. The FitzPatrick Lectures delivered before The Royal College of Physicians of London in 1915 and 1916. London: Kegan Paul, Trench, Trubner & Co. Ltd.
Rivers, W. H. R.
    1926   Massage in Melanesia. *In* Psychology and Ethnology. New York: Harcourt, Brace & Co., Inc.
Turner, Victor
    1967   The Forest of Symbols: Aspects of Ndembu Ritual. Ithaca, NY: Cornell University Press.
Virchow, Rudolf
    1985 [1879]   Collected Essays on Public Health and Epidemiology, vols. 1 and 2, ed. L. J. Rather. Canton, MA: Science History Publications.
Waitzkin, Howard
    2006   One and a Half Centuries of Forgetting and Rediscovering: Virchow's Lasting Contributions to Social Medicine. Social Medicine 1:5–10.

1

Massage in Melanesia

W. H. R. Rivers

When I was working in the Solomon Islands with Mr A. M. Hocart,[1] it was our custom, whenever possible, to accompany the native medicos on their visits to their patients. On one of these occasions the treatment consisted chiefly of abdominal massage carried on, so far as I could tell, just as it would have been by a European expert. On questioning the woman who was the subject of the treatment, I learned that she was suffering from chronic constipation, and if the matter had not been gone into more fully, it might have been supposed that the Solomon Islanders treated this disease according to the most modern and scientific therapeutics. Further inquiries, however, brought out the fact that the treatment we had observed was for the purpose of destroying an octopus which, according to the native pathology, was the cause of the woman's troubles. She was said to be suffering from a disease called *nggasin*, caused by the presence of an octopus in her body, and an inquiry into the diagnosis revealed the belief that the tentacles of the octopus would pass upwards, and when they reached the head of the patient, would kill her. The object of the treatment was to kill the octopus, and the treatment had already been carried out for several days, so that the octopus, which had at first been very large, had now become small, and was expected soon to disappear altogether. This result, however, was not ascribed so much to the mechanical action of the manipulation as to the formulæ and other features of the treatment which accompanied the massage.

On another occasion I observed the treatment of a case of supra-orbital neuralgia. The brow was kneaded carefully for a time and then a fold of the skin was caught and a motion made as though something were being drawn through the skin. The invisible object called *tagosoro* was thus extracted and blown away. I asked the leech[2] to carry out the treatment for *tagosoro* on my own forearm, and kneading manipulations, exactly like those of our own massage, were carried out till, by a sudden movement he showed me how he would have caught the *tagosoro* if it had been there, and would have blown it away. Here again a superficial inquiry would have seemed to show the existence of a massage indistinguishable from our own, and applied to conditions to which, according to our ideas, it is well adapted. It was only through systematic inquiry that it was discovered that the ideas underlying the treatment were wholly different from our own, and that the whole process rested upon a magico-religious basis. My object in describing this feature of Melanesian therapeutics is as an example of a difficulty which confronts that department of the history of Medicine which attempts to deal with origins. A few years ago

W. H. R. Rivers, "Massage in Melanesia," pp. 57–61 in *Psychology and Ethnology*. New York: Harcourt, Brace and Co., 1926.

I should have had no hesitation in regarding this Melanesian practice as an example of the growth of a rational therapeutical measure out of a magical or religious rite. I should have supposed that the practices of the Solomon Islanders were originally designed to extract the octopus or the *tagosoro* from the body, and that it would only be necessary to slough off what we regard as the superstitious aspect of the practice to have a true therapeutical measure. I should have regarded the Melanesian practice as one which has preserved for us a stage in the process of evolution whereby medicine evolved out of magic and, as a matter of fact, I believe that the vast majority of my anthropological colleagues, at any rate in this country, would still be fully satisfied with this view.

Many students of anthropology, however, are coming to see that human institutions have not had so simple a history as this view implies, and that many of the cases, formerly supposed to show stages in a process of a simple and direct evolution, are rather the outcome of the blending of peoples and their cultures. The example I have described will show the possibility that Melanesian massage, as we now find it, may have had a very different history. It is possible that massage, much in the form in which it is found among ourselves and so many other peoples of the earth, was introduced into Melanesia by an immigrant people, and that the beliefs in the octopus or the *tagosoro* are merely the outcome of attempts to account for the success of the new treatment on lines suggested by the pathological ideas of the indigenous people. The process would be like that among ourselves when any new treatment, if sufficiently successful to attract attention, is explained according to the current pathology and therapeutics of the day. A case analogous to that of my Melanesian example would be the orthodox explanation of the success of Christian Science based on the pathological distinction between organic and functional diseases and the therapeutical ideas summed up in the term "suggestion." Before we accept Melanesian massage as an example showing us a stage in the evolution of a medical remedy out of a magico-religious rite, it is necessary to suggest the alternative hypothesis that it may

have been the result of a blend between an introduced therapeutical measure and an indigenous belief. According to this, disease is due to animals or other agents which have found their way into the human body.

I cannot attempt here to deal fully with the evidence which would enable us to weigh the two hypotheses against one another, for the subject can only be treated adequately in conjunction with the study of many other features of culture. I can now point only to two considerations. One is that true massage, such as is practised by ourselves, apparently exists in Polynesia. It is, of course, possible that deeper inquiry would show that, underlying Polynesian massage, there are ideas which give it a special character, just as we found to be the case with the massage of the Solomon Islands. But the way in which the Polynesians use massage as a restorative suggests that the massage of this people is a true therapeutical measure thoroughly comparable with our own practice. True massage thus seems to exist in the same part of the globe as the Solomon Islands. On the hypothesis of transmission, it may have been introduced into those islands by Polynesian castaways, who often found their way to the Solomon Islands, or more probably may have been brought to these islands by the same people who were responsible for its introduction into Polynesia.

A second consideration, to which it is very difficult to know how much weight to attach, is the extraordinary similarity of the massage of the Solomon Islanders to the true therapeutical practice. When I observed the massage applied to others and experienced its application to my own arm, the manipulations seemed to me to be like those of true massage rather than the result of an attempt to catch an animal or some less material agent. When we consider the intense conservatism of people of rude culture, their tendency for generation after generation to carry out operations in the traditional way, I cannot help feeling that the resemblance of their manipulations to those of true massage may be the perpetuation of the practice as it was originally taught to them, although the ideas underlying the practice have come to be very different from those of their teachers.

My object in this place, however, is not merely to introduce a curiosity nor to lay down any dogmatic view of its origin, but rather to point out a basic difficulty which confronts those who attempt to trace out the origins of medical beliefs and practices. Medicine is a social institution. It comprises a set of beliefs and practices which only become possible when held and carried out by members of an organized society, among whom a high degree of the division of labour and specialization of the social function has come into being. Any principles and methods found to be of value in the study of social institutions in general cannot be ignored by the historian of medicine. Here, as in other departments of human culture, the outstanding problem of to-day is to determine how far similar practices in different parts of the world have arisen independently, and how far they are the outcome of transmission from people to people. The fundamental importance of this problem is at last adequately recognized by the student of human culture, and I have ventured to use Melanesian massage as a means of calling attention to a problem which must be faced by all who attempt to study the origins and early history of medicine.

NOTES

1 As members of the Percy Sladen Trust Expedition.
2 Mr Hocart has suggested that this old word should be used as a technical term for the practitioners of the rude art, which can be called neither medicine nor magic, but lies somewhere between the two.

2

The Notion of Witchcraft Explains Unfortunate Events

E. E. Evans-Pritchard

I

Witches, as the Azande conceive them, clearly cannot exist. None the less, the concept of witchcraft provides them with a natural philosophy by which the relations between men and unfortunate events are explained and a ready and stereotyped means of reacting to such events. Witchcraft beliefs also embrace a system of values which regulate human conduct.

Witchcraft is ubiquitous. It plays its part in every activity of Zande life; in agricultural, fishing, and hunting pursuits; in domestic life of homesteads as well as in communal life of district and court; it is an important theme of mental life in which it forms the background of a vast panorama of oracles and magic; its influence is plainly stamped on law and morals, etiquette and religion; it is prominent in technology and language; there is no niche or corner of Zande culture into which it does not twist itself. If blight seizes the ground-nut crop it is witchcraft; if the bush is vainly scoured for game it is witchcraft; if women laboriously bale water out of a pool and are rewarded by but a few small fish it is witchcraft; if termites do not rise when their swarming is due and a cold useless night is spent in waiting for their flight it is witchcraft; if a wife is sulky and unresponsive to her husband it is witchcraft; if a prince is cold and distant with his subject it is witchcraft; if a magical rite fails to achieve its purpose it is witchcraft; if, in fact, any failure or misfortune falls upon anyone at any time and in relation to any of the manifold activities of his life it may be due to witchcraft. The Zande attributes all these misfortunes to witchcraft unless there is strong evidence, and subsequent oracular confirmation, that sorcery or some other evil agent has been at work, or unless they are clearly to be attributed to incompetence, breach of a taboo, or failure to observe a moral rule.

To say that witchcraft has blighted the ground-nut crop, that witchcraft has scared away game, and that witchcraft has made so-and-so ill is equivalent to saying in terms of our own culture that the ground-nut crop has failed owing to blight, that game is scarce this season, and that so-and-so has caught influenza. Witchcraft participates in all misfortunes and is the idiom in which Azande speak about them and in which they explain them. To us witchcraft is something which haunted and disgusted our credulous forefathers. But the Zande expects to come across witchcraft at

E. E. Evans-Pritchard, "The Notion of Witchcraft Explains Unfortunate Events," pp. 18–32 in *Witchcraft, Oracles, and Magic among the Azande*. Oxford: Clarendon Press, 1976. © Oxford University Press. By permission of Oxford University Press.

any time of the day or night. He would be just as surprised if he were not brought into daily contact with it as we would be if confronted by its appearance. To him there is nothing miraculous about it. It is expected that a man's hunting will be injured by witches, and he has at his disposal means of dealing with them. When misfortunes occur he does not become awestruck at the play of supernatural forces. He is not terrified at the presence of an occult enemy. He is, on the other hand, extremely annoyed. Someone, out of spite, has ruined his ground-nuts or spoilt his hunting or given his wife a chill, and surely this is cause for anger! He has done no one harm, so what right has anyone to interfere in his affairs? It is an impertinence, an insult, a dirty, offensive trick! It is the aggressiveness and not the eeriness of these actions which Azande emphasize when speaking of them, and it is anger and not awe which we observe in their response to them.

Witchcraft is not less anticipated than adultery. It is so intertwined with everyday happenings that it is part of a Zande's ordinary world. There is nothing remarkable about a witch – you may be one yourself, and certainly many of your closest neighbours are witches. Nor is there anything awe-inspiring about witchcraft. We do not become psychologically transformed when we hear that someone is ill – we expect people to be ill – and it is the same with Zande. They expect people to be ill, i.e. to be bewitched, and it is not a matter for surprise or wonderment.

I found it strange at first to live among Azande and listen to naïve explanations of misfortunes which, to our minds, have apparent causes, but after a while I learnt the idiom of their thought and applied notions of witchcraft as spontaneously as themselves in situations where the concept was relevant. A boy knocked his foot against a small stump of wood in the centre of a bush path, a frequent happening in Africa, and suffered pain and inconvenience in consequence. Owing to its position on his toe it was impossible to keep the cut free from dirt and it began to fester. He declared that witchcraft had made him knock his foot against the stump. I always argued with Azande and criticized their statements, and I did so on this occasion. I told the boy

that he had knocked his foot against the stump of wood because he had been careless, and that witchcraft had not placed it in the path, for it had grown there naturally. He agreed that witchcraft had nothing to do with the stump of wood being in his path but added that he had kept his eyes open for stumps, as indeed every Zande does most carefully, and that if he had not been bewitched he would have seen the stump. As a conclusive argument for his view he remarked that all cuts do not take days to heal but, on the contrary, close quickly, for that is the nature of cuts. Why, then, had his sore festered and remained open if there were no witchcraft behind it? This, as I discovered before long, was to be regarded as the Zande explanation of sickness.

Shortly after my arrival in Zandeland we were passing through a government settlement and noticed that a hut had been burnt to the ground on the previous night. Its owner was overcome with grief as it had contained the beer he was preparing for a mortuary feast. He told us that he had gone the previous night to examine his beer. He had lit a handful of straw and raised it above his head so that light would be cast on the pots, and in so doing he had ignited the thatch. He, and my companions also, were convinced that the disaster was caused by witchcraft.

One of my chief informants, Kisanga, was a skilled woodcarver, one of the finest carvers in the whole kingdom of Gbudwe. Occasionally the bowls and stools which he carved split during the work, as one may well imagine in such a climate. Though the hardest woods be selected they sometimes split in process of carving or on completion of the utensil even if the craftsman is careful and well acquainted with the technical rules of his craft. When this happened to the bowls and stools of this particular craftsman he attributed the misfortune to witchcraft and used to harangue me about the spite and jealousy of his neighbours. When I used to reply that I thought he was mistaken and that people were well disposed towards him he used to hold the split bowl or stool towards me as concrete evidence of his assertions. If people were not bewitching his work, how would I account for that? Likewise a potter will attribute the cracking of his pots during firing to witchcraft. An experienced potter need have no fear that his pots will crack as a result of error. He selects the proper clay, kneads it thoroughly till he has extracted all grit and pebbles, and builds it up slowly and carefully. On the night before digging out his clay he abstains from sexual intercourse. So he should have nothing to fear. Yet pots sometimes break, even when they are the handiwork of expert potters, and this can only be accounted for by witchcraft. 'It is broken – there is witchcraft,' says the potter simply. Many similar situations in which witchcraft is cited as an agent are instanced throughout this and following chapters.

II

In speaking to Azande about witchcraft and in observing their reactions to situations of misfortune it was obvious that they did not attempt to account for the existence of phenomena, or even the action of phenomena, by mystical causation alone. What they explained by witchcraft were the particular conditions in a chain of causation which related an individual to natural happenings in such a way that he sustained injury. The boy who knocked his foot against a stump of wood did not account for the stump by reference to witchcraft, nor did he suggest that whenever anybody knocks his foot against a stump it is necessarily due to witchcraft, nor yet again did he account for the cut by saying that it was caused by witchcraft, for he knew quite well that it was caused by the stump of wood. What he attributed to witchcraft was that on this particular occasion, when exercising his usual care, he struck his foot against a stump of wood, whereas on a hundred other occasions he did not do so, and that on this particular occasion the cut, which he expected to result from the knock, festered whereas he had had dozens of cuts which had not festered. Surely these peculiar conditions demand an explanation. Again, every year hundreds of Azande go and inspect their beer by night and they always take with them a handful of straw in order to illuminate the hut in which it is fermenting. Why then should this particular man on this single occasion have ignited the

thatch of his hut? Again, my friend the wood-carver had made scores of bowls and stools without mishap and he knew all there was to know about the selection of wood, use of tools, and conditions of carving. His bowls and stools did not split like the products of craftsmen who were unskilled in their work, so why on rare occasions should his bowls and stools split when they did not split usually and when he had exercised all his usual knowledge and care? He knew the answer well enough and so, in his opinion, did his envious, back-biting neighbours. In the same way, a potter wants to know why his pots should break on an occasion when he uses the same material and technique as on other occasions; or rather he already knows, for the reason is known in advance, as it were. If the pots break it is due to witchcraft.

We shall give a false account of Zande philosophy if we say that they believe witchcraft to be the sole cause of phenomena. This proposition is not contained in Zande patterns of thought, which only assert that witchcraft brings a man into relation with events in such a way that he sustains injury.

In Zandeland sometimes an old granary collapses. There is nothing remarkable in this. Every Zande knows that termites eat the supports in course of time and that even the hardest woods decay after years of service. Now a granary is the summerhouse of a Zande homestead and people sit beneath it in the heat of the day and chat or play the African hole-game or work at some craft. Consequently it may happen that there are people sitting beneath the granary when it collapses and they are injured, for it is a heavy structure made of beams and clay and may be stored with eleusine as well. Now why should these particular people have been sitting under this particular granary at the particular moment when it collapsed? That it should collapse is easily intelligible, but why should it have collapsed at the particular moment when these particular people were sitting beneath it? Through years it might have collapsed, so why should it fall just when certain people sought its kindly shelter? We say that the granary collapsed because its supports were eaten away by termites; that is the cause that explains the collapse of the granary. We also say that people were sitting under it at the time because it was in the heat of the day and they thought that it would be a comfortable place to talk and work. This is the cause of people being under the granary at the time it collapsed. To our minds the only relationship between these two independently caused facts is their coincidence in time and space. We have no explanation of why the two chains of causation intersected at a certain time and in a certain place, for there is no interdependence between them.

Zande philosophy can supply the missing link. The Zande knows that the supports were undermined by termites and that people were sitting beneath the granary in order to escape the eat and glare of the sun. But he knows besides why these two events occurred at a precisely similar moment in time and space. It was due to the action of witchcraft. If there had been witchcraft people would have been sitting under the granary and it would not have fallen on them, or it would have collapsed but the people would not have been sheltering under it at the time. Witchcraft explains the coincidence of these two happenings.

III

I hope I am not expected to point out that the Zande cannot analyse his doctrines as I have done for him. It is no use saying to a Zande 'Now tell me what you Azande think about witchcraft' because the subject is too general and indeterminate, both too vague and too immense, to be described concisely. But it is possible to extract the principles of their thought from dozens of situations in which witchcraft is called upon to explain happenings and from dozens of other situations in which failure is attributed to some other cause. Their philosophy is explicit, but is not formally stated as a doctrine. A Zande would not say 'I believe in natural causation but I do not think that that fully explains coincidences, and it seems to me that the theory of witchcraft offers a satisfactory explanation of them', but he expresses his thought in terms of actual and particular situations. He says 'a buffalo charges', 'a tree falls', 'termites are not making their seasonal flight when they are expected

to do so', and so on. Herein he is stating empirically ascertained facts. But he also says 'a buffalo charged and wounded so-and-so', 'a tree fell on so-and-so and killed him', 'my termites refuse to make their flight in numbers worth collecting but other people are collecting theirs all right', and so on. He tells you that these things are due to witchcraft, saying in each instance, 'So-and-so has been bewitched.' The facts do not explain themselves or only partly explain themselves. They can only be explained fully if one takes witchcraft into consideration.

One can only obtain the full range of a Zande's ideas about causation by allowing him to fill in the gaps himself, otherwise one will be led astray by linguistic conventions. He tells you 'So-and-so was bewitched and killed himself' or even simply that 'So-and-so was killed by witchcraft'. But he is telling you the ultimate cause of his death and not the secondary causes. You can ask him 'How did he kill himself?' and he will tell you that he committed suicide by hanging himself from the branch of a tree. You can also ask 'Why did he kill himself?' and he will tell you that it was because he was angry with his brothers. The cause of his death was hanging from a tree, and the cause of his hanging from a tree was his anger with his brothers. If you then ask a Zande why he should say that the man was bewitched if he committed suicide on account of his anger with his brothers, he will tell you that only crazy people commit suicide, and that if everyone who was angry with his brothers committed suicide there would soon be no people left in the world, and that if this man had not been bewitched he would not have done what he did do. If you persevere and ask why witchcraft caused the man to kill himself the Zande will reply that he supposes someone hated him, and if you ask him why someone hated him your informant will tell you that such is the nature of men.

For if Azande cannot enunciate a theory of causation in terms acceptable to us they describe happenings in an idiom that is explanatory. They are aware that it is particular circumstances of events in their relation to man, their harmfulness to a particular person, that constitutes evidence of witchcraft. Witchcraft explains *why* events are harmful to man and not *how* they happen. A Zande perceives how they happen just as we do. He does not see a witch charge a man, but an elephant. He does not see a witch push over a granary, but termites gnawing away its supports. He does not see a psychical flame igniting thatch, but an ordinary lighted bundle of straw. His perception of how events occur is as clear as our own.

IV

Zande belief in witchcraft in no way contradicts empirical knowledge of cause and effect. The world known to the senses is just as real to them as it is to us. We must not be deceived by their way of expressing causation and imagine that because they say a man was killed by witchcraft they entirely neglect the secondary causes that, as we judge them, were the true causes of his death. They are foreshortening the chain of events, and in a particular social situation are selecting the cause that is socially relevant and neglecting the rest. If a man is killed by a spear in war, or by a wild beast in hunting, or by the bite of a snake, or from sickness, witchcraft is the socially relevant cause, since it is the only one which allows intervention and determines social behaviour.

Belief in death from natural causes and belief in death from witchcraft are not mutually exclusive. On the contrary, they supplement one another, the one accounting for what the other does not account for. Besides, death is not only a natural fact but also a social fact. It is not simply that the heart ceases to beat and the lungs to pump air in an organism, but it is also the destruction of a member of a family and kin, of a community and tribe. Death leads to consultation of oracles, magic rites, and revenge. Among the causes of death witchcraft is the only one that has any significance for social behaviour. The attribution of misfortune to witchcraft does not exclude what we call its real causes but is superimposed on them and gives to social events their moral value.

Zande thought expresses the notion of natural and mystical causation quite clearly by using a hunting metaphor to define their relations. Azande always say of witchcraft that it is the *umbaga* or second spear. When Azande kill game there is a division of meat between the man who first speared the animal and the man who plunged a second spear into it. These two are considered to have killed the beast and the owner of the second spear is called the *umbaga*. Hence if a man is killed by an elephant Azande say that the elephant is the first spear and that witchcraft is the second spear and that together they killed the man. If a man spears another in war the slayer is the first spear and witchcraft is the second spear and together they killed him.

Since Azande recognize plurality of causes, and it is the social situation that indicates the relevant one, we can understand why the doctrine of witchcraft is not used to explain every failure and misfortune. It sometimes happens that the social situation demands a common-sense, and not a mystical, judgement of cause. Thus, if you tell a lie, or commit adultery, or steal, or deceive your prince, and are found out, you cannot elude punishment by saying that you were bewitched. Zande doctrine declares emphatically 'Witchcraft does not make a person tell lies'; 'Witchcraft does not make a person commit adultery'; 'Witchcraft does not put adultery into a man. "Witchcraft" is in yourself (you alone are responsible), that is, your penis becomes erect. It sees the hair of a man's wife and it rises and becomes erect because the only "witchcraft" is, itself' ('witchcraft' is here used metaphorically); 'Witchcraft does not make a person steal'; 'Witchcraft does not make a person disloyal.' Only on one occasion have I heard a Zande plead that he was bewitched when he had committed an offence and this was when he lied to me, and even on this occasion everybody present laughed at him and told him that witchcraft does not make people tell lies.

If a man murders another tribesman with knife or spear he is put to death. It is not necessary in such a case to seek a witch, for an objective towards which vengeance may be directed is already present. If, on the other hand, it is a member of another tribe who has speared a man his relatives, or his prince, will take steps to discover the witch responsible for the event.

It would be treason to say that a man put to death on the orders of his king for an offence against authority was killed by witchcraft. If a man were to consult the oracles to discover the witch responsible for the death of a relative who had been put to death at the orders of his king he would run the risk of being put to death himself. For here the social situation excludes the notion of witchcraft as on other occasions it pays no attention to natural agents and emphasizes only witchcraft. Also, if a man were killed in vengeance because the oracles said that he was a witch and had murdered another man with his witchcraft then his relatives could not say that he had been killed by witchcraft. Zande doctrine lays it down that he died at the hand of avengers because he was a homicide. If a man were to have expressed the view that his kinsman had been killed by witchcraft and to have acted upon his opinion by consulting the poison oracle, he might have been punished for ridiculing the king's poison oracle, for it was the poison oracle of the king that had given official confirmation of the man's guilt, and it was the king himself who had permitted vengeance to take its course.

In these situations witchcraft is irrelevant and, if not totally excluded, is not indicated as the principal factor in causation. As in our own society a scientific theory of causation, if not excluded, is deemed irrelevant in questions of moral and legal responsibility, so in Zande society the doctrine of witchcraft, if not excluded, is deemed irrelevant in the same situations. We accept scientific explanations of the causes of disease, and even of the causes of insanity, but we deny them in crime and sin because here they militate against law and morals which are axiomatic. The Zande accepts a mystical explanation of the causes of misfortune, sickness, and death, but he does not allow this explanation if it conflicts with social exigencies expressed in law and morals.

For witchcraft is not indicated as a cause for failure when a taboo has been broken. If a child becomes sick, and it is known that its father and mother have had sexual relations before it was weaned, the cause of death is already indicated by breach of a ritual prohibition and the question of witchcraft does not arise. If a man develops leprosy and there

is a history of incest in his case then incest is the cause of leprosy and not witchcraft. In these cases, however, a curious situation arises because when the child or the leper dies it is necessary to avenge their deaths and the Zande sees no difficulty in explaining what appears to us to be most illogical behaviour. He does so on the same principles as when a man has been killed by a wild beast, and he invokes the same metaphor of 'second spear'. In the cases mentioned above there are really three causes of a person's death. There is the illness from which he dies, leprosy in the case of the man, perhaps some fever in the case of the child. These sicknesses are not in themselves products of witchcraft, for they exist in their own right just as a buffalo or a granary exist in their own right. Then there is the breach of a taboo, in the one case of weaning, in the other case of incest. The child, and the man, developed fever, and leprosy, because a taboo was broken. The breach of a taboo was the cause of their sickness, but the sickness would not have killed them if witchcraft had not also been operative. If witchcraft had not been present as 'second spear' they would have developed fever and leprosy just the same, but they would not have died from them. In these instances there are two socially significant causes, breach of taboo and witchcraft, both of which are relative to different social processes, and each is emphasized by different people.

But where there has been a breach of taboo and death is not involved witchcraft will not be evoked as a cause of failure. If a man eats a forbidden food after he has made powerful punitive magic he may die, and in this case the cause of his death is known beforehand, since it is contained in the conditions of the situation in which he died even if witchcraft was also operative. But it does not follow that he will die. What does inevitably follow is that the medicine he has made will cease to operate against the person for whom it is intended and will have to be destroyed lest it turn against the magician who sent it forth. The failure of the medicine to achieve its purpose is due to breach of a taboo and not to witchcraft. If a man has had sexual relations with his wife and on the next day approaches the poison oracle it will not reveal the truth and its oracular efficacy will be permanently undermined. If he had not broken a taboo it would have been said that witchcraft had caused the oracle to lie, but the condition of the person who had attended the seance provides a reason for its failure to speak the truth without having to bring in the notion of witchcraft as an agent. No one will admit that he has broken a taboo before consulting the poison oracle, but when an oracle lies everyone is prepared to admit that a taboo may have been broken by someone.

Similarly, when a potter's creations break in firing witchcraft is not the only possible cause of the calamity. Inexperience and bad workmanship may also be reasons for failure, or the potter may himself have had sexual relations on the preceding night. The potter himself will attribute his failure to witchcraft, but others may not be of the same opinion.

Not even all deaths are invariably and unanimously attributed to witchcraft or to the breach of some taboo. The deaths of babies from certain diseases are attributed vaguely to the supreme Being. Also, if a man falls suddenly and violently sick and dies, his relatives may be sure that a sorcerer has made magic against him and that it is not a witch who has killed him. A breach of the obligations of blood-brotherhood may sweep away whole groups of kin, and when one after another of brothers and cousins die it is the blood and not witchcraft to which their deaths are attributed by outsiders, though the relatives of the dead will seek to avenge them on witches. When a very old man dies unrelated people say that he has died of old age, but they do not say this in the presence of kinsmen, who declare that witchcraft is responsible for his death.

It is also thought that adultery may cause misfortune, though it is only one participating factor, and witchcraft is also believed to be present. Thus is it said that a man may be killed in warfare or in a hunting accident as a result of his wife's infidelities. Therefore, before going to war or on a large-scale hunting expedition a man might ask his wife to divulge the names of her lovers.

Even where breaches of law and morals do not occur witchcraft is not the only reason given for failure. Incompetence, laziness, and ignorance may be selected as causes. When a girl smashes her water-pot or a boy forgets to close the door of the hen-house at night they will be admonished severely by their parents for stupidity. The mistakes of children are due to carelessness or ignorance and they are taught to avoid them while they are still young. People do not say that they are effects of witchcraft, or if they are prepared to concede the possibility of witchcraft they consider stupidity the main cause. Moreover, the Zande is not so naïve that he holds witchcraft responsible for the cracking of a pot during firing if subsequent examination shows that a pebble was left in the clay, or for an animal escaping his net if someone frightened it away by a move or a sound. People do not blame witchcraft if a woman burns her porridge nor if she presents it undercooked to her husband. And when an inexperienced craftsman makes a stool which lacks polish or which splits, this is put down to his inexperience.

In all these cases the man who suffers the misfortune is likely to say that it is due to witchcraft, but others will not say so. We must bear in mind nevertheless that a serious misfortune especially if it results in death, is normally attributed by everyone to the action of witchcraft, especially by the sufferer and his kin, however much it may have been due to a man's incompetence or absence of self-control. If a man falls into a fire and is seriously burnt, or falls into a game-pit and breaks his neck or his leg, it would undoubtedly be attributed to witchcraft. Thus when six or seven of the sons of Prince Rikita were entrapped in a ring of fire and burnt to death when hunting cane-rats their death was undoubtedly due to witchcraft.

Hence we see that witchcraft has its own logic, its own rules of thought, and that these do not exclude natural causation. Belief in witchcraft is quite consistent with human responsibility and a rational appreciation of nature. First of all a man must carry out an activity according to traditional rules of technique, which consist of knowledge checked by trial and error in each generation. It is only if he fails in spite of adherence to these rules that people will impute his lack of success to witchcraft.

V

It is often asked whether primitive peoples distinguish between the natural and the supernatural, and the query may be here answered in a preliminary manner in respect to the Azande. The question as it stands may mean, do primitive peoples distinguish between the natural and the supernatural in the abstract? We have a notion of an ordered world conforming to what we call natural laws, but some people in our society believe that mysterious things can happen which cannot be accounted for by reference to natural laws and which therefore are held to transcend them, and we call these happenings supernatural. To us supernatural means very much the same as abnormal or extraordinary. Azande certainly have no such notions of reality. They have no conceptions of 'natural' as we understand it, and therefore neither of the 'supernatural' as we understand it. Witchcraft is to Azande an ordinary and not an extraordinary, even though it may in some circumstances be an infrequent, event. It is a normal, and not an abnormal, happening. But if they do not give to the natural and supernatural the meanings which educated Europeans give to them they nevertheless distinguish between them. For our question may be formulated, and should be formulated, in a different manner. We ought rather to ask whether primitive peoples perceive any difference between the happenings which we, the observers of their culture, class as natural and the happenings which we class as mystical. Azande undoubtedly perceive a difference between what we consider the workings of nature on the one hand and the workings of magic and ghosts and witchcraft on the other hand, though in the absence of a formulated doctrine of natural law they do not, and cannot, express the difference as we express it.

The Zande notion of witchcraft is incompatible with our ways of thought. But even to the Azande there is something peculiar about the action of witchcraft. Normally it can be perceived only in dreams. It is not an evident notion but transcends sensory experience. They do not profess to understand witchcraft entirely. They know that it exists and works evil, but they have to guess at the manner in which it works. Indeed, I have frequently been struck when discussing witchcraft with Azande by the doubt they express about the subject, not only in what they say, but even more in their manner of saying it, both of which contrast with their ready knowledge, fluently imparted, about social events and economic techniques. They feel out of their depth in trying to describe the way in which witchcraft accomplishes its ends. That it kills people is obvious, but how it kills them cannot be known precisely. They tell you that perhaps if you were to ask an older man or a witch-doctor he might give you more information. But the older men and the witch-doctors can tell you little more than youth and laymen. They only know what the others know: that the soul of witchcraft goes by night and devours the soul of its victim. Only witches themselves understand these matters fully. In truth Azande experience feelings about witchcraft rather than ideas, for their intellectual concepts of it are weak and they know better what to do when attacked by it than how to explain it. Their response is action and not analysis.

There is no elaborate and consistent representation of witchcraft that will account in detail for its workings, nor of nature which expounds its conformity to sequences and functional interrelations. The Zande actualizes these beliefs rather than intellectualizes them, and their tenets are expressed in socially controlled behaviour rather than in doctrines. Hence the difficulty of discussing the subject of witchcraft with Azande, for their ideas are imprisoned in action and cannot be cited to explain and justify action.

3

Muchona the Hornet, Interpreter of Religion

Victor Turner

I first became aware of Muchona on a dusty motor road of packed red clay towards the end of a Northern Rhodesian dry season. In one direction the road ran to harsh, colorful Angola, in the other to the distant Copperbelt town of Chingola. Along it passed an occasional truck, mail van, or missionary's car, and many tough black feet, most of them going east to European mines and towns. On this day the road was almost empty in the hot late afternoon. Kasonda, my African assistant, and I had walked a few miles from our home village to a cluster of villages where we had collected census material. Now we were returning, gay with the millet beer and gossip that usually rounded off our more serious sessions. To make the miles go faster we played a game popular among Ndembu children: each of us tried to be the first to spot the budding *kapembi* shrubs with their frail red presentiment of the rains. Even Ndembu find it hard to distinguish this species from three others. Kasonda, of course, soon had a higher total than myself, for like all Ndembu he prided himself on his knowledge of the mystical and practical properties of the herbs and trees that flourish in this area.

We were so absorbed in our rivalry that we failed to notice a swart elderly gnome who was padding perkily beside us. He was evidently keenly observant, for he joined in our sport and soon took the lead. Kasonda told me he was a *chimbuki*, a "doctor," in several kinds of curative ritual, and "knew many medicines." I pricked up my ears, for ritual symbolism was my major interest. Each plant used in ritual stood for some aspect of Ndembu social life or belief. In my opinion a full interpretation of these symbols would lead me to the heart of Ndembu wisdom. Consequently, I seized the opportunity of asking the little man, whose name was Muchona, the meaning of some of the medicines I had seen doctors handle.

Muchona replied readily and at length, with the bright glance of the true enthusiast. He had a high-pitched voice, authoritative as a school-teacher's when conveying information, expressive as a comedian's when telling a tale. Kasonda found his manner and mannerisms both funny and irritating, as he tried to show me by giggling conspiratorially behind his hand whenever Muchona had his back to us. I did not respond, for I liked the doctor's warmth, and thus began Kasonda's bitter jealousy of Muchona. Kasonda was worldly, and a shade spiteful, *au fait* with the seamier side of Ndembu (and indeed human) nature. He took

Victor Turner, "Muchona the Hornet, Interpreter of Religion" pp. 131–50 in *The Forest of Symbols*. Ithaca, NY: Cornell University Press, 1970.

a rancorous zest in the struggles for headmanship, prestige, and money that were the bane of village life. Muchona, for all his battling against witchcraft and the moody, punitive dead, had a curious innocence of character and objectivity of outlook. I was to find that in the balance mankind came off well for Muchona. Between these men lay the gap that has at all times divided the true philosopher from the politician.

Muchona showed me his quality that first day when he pointed to a parasitic growth on a *mukula* tree (a red hardwood). "That plant is called *mutuntamu*," he said. "Do you know why it has that name?" Before I could confess my ignorance he rattled on:

Well, it is from *ku-tuntama*, "to sit on somebody or something." Now, hunters have a drum [a ritual] called *Ntambu*, an old word for "lion." In *Ntambu*, a hunter who has been unlucky and has failed to kill animals for many days, goes into the bush and finds a big *mukula* tree like this one. The *mukula* tree has red gum, which we call "*mukula's* blood." It is a very important tree for hunters, and also for women. For hunters it means "the blood of animals." They want to see this blood when they go hunting. Now this unlucky hunter puts his bow over his right shoulder and his axe into his right hand – for the right side is for men and the left side for women, who carry their babies on their left arm – and he climbs up the *mukula* bearing bow and ax. When he is high up, he stands with one foot on one branch and one foot on another. Then he shoots an arrow at a *mutuntamu* plant. His arrow goes in strongly. Then he cries, "I have shot at an animal." Then he says, "I have shot you, *Ntambu* spirit. Please bring me quickly to animals." After that he roars like a lion. Then he puts his strung bow over the *mutuntamu* branches and breaks them with the strength of the bowstring. He throws the broken twigs on the ground. They will later be mixed with other medicines for washing his body and his hunting gear. Just as the *mutuntamu* "sits on" the tree of blood, so must the spirit come and sit on the animal and blind it, in order that the hunter may kill it easily. He shoots *Ntambu* to show the spirit that he has found him out. He now wants *Ntambu* to help him, and not to trouble him any longer.

Now I had heard many other Ndembu interpret plant symbols before, but never so clearly and cogently as this. I was to become familiar with this mode of exposition, the swift-running commentary on unsolicited details, the parenthetical explanations, the vivid mimicry of ritual speech, and above all, the depth of psychological insight: "What hurts you, when discovered and propitiated, helps you."

Kasonda was whispering to me, "He is just lying." I could not heed him, for Muchona had already pointed out another tree and had begun to explain its ritual use and significance in a way that also compelled belief. I felt that a new dimension of study was opening up to me. Sympathy was quickly growing between us and when we parted we arranged to meet again in a few days.

Muchona did not come. Perhaps he hesitated to visit me, for my camp was in Kasonda's village, and it is probable that Kasonda had already hinted that he would be unwelcome there. Perhaps he had been performing curative rituals in distant villages. He was a restless man, seldom at home anywhere for long, like many another Ndembu doctor. Soon afterwards I also had to go away – to Lusaka, for a conference of anthropologists. For one reason or another I did not see him again for two months.

Meanwhile, I learned many details of Muchona's life which were common knowledge in his neighborhood. He did not live in the traditional circular village, but with his two wives occupied a couple of low huts near the motor road. He had seven children, the eldest of whom was a clerk at the government township, a well-educated youth by Ndembu standards. Kasonda insinuated that this tall son of a meager father was the by-blow of a youthful affair of Muchona's senior wife. The remark was pure malice. The alert intellect of the father was unmistakably reproduced in his son; and the son's achievement was reflected in his father's pride in him.

Muchona came from Nyamwana chiefdom, just across the Congo border. His mother had been a slave, taken by the Ndembu before British rule was firmly established. His maternal kin were widely scattered over Mwinilunga

District and adjacent areas in Angola and the Belgian Congo. The nuclear group of a Ndembu village is a small matrilineage; and no such nucleus had been formed by Muchona's kin. Later he was to complain to me that his two sisters in distant villages had ten children between them and that if they had come to live with him he could have founded a real village. He ignored the fact that Ndembu women customarily reside with their husbands after marriage and that, indeed, his own wives had left their brothers' villages to live with him. Poor Muchona had been doomed to rootless wandering from early boyhood. First of all he had lived in the village of his mother's captors. That village had split, and Muchona and his mother went with the dissident group. His mother was then transferred as a debt slave to yet another group where she was married to one of her owners. It seems that when he was a young man, Muchona bought his freedom and lived in the villages of several successive wives. However, he was never able to achieve a high secular status or an established position in a single village. These vicissitudes were both his curse and the source of his great ability to compare and generalize. Living as he had done on the margins of many structured groups and not being a member of any particular group, his loyalties could not be narrowly partisan, and his sympathies were broader than those of the majority of his fellow tribesmen. His experience had been richer and more varied than that of most Ndembu, though all Ndembu, being hunters and seminomadic cassava cultivators, travel considerable distances during their lives.

When I returned from Lusaka, I decided to pursue my inquiries into ritual esoterica very much further than before. In this quest I was assisted by the senior teacher at the local Mission Out-School, Windson Kashinakaji by name, Ndembu by tribe. Windson was a man of independent mind, obsequious to no European, arrogant to no villager. He was a keen but by no means uncritical student of the Bible. We often discussed religion together, and he became as eager as myself to learn the hidden meanings of Ndembu beliefs and practices. Most of his boyhood had been spent at a Mission Station behind a sort of spiritual *cordon sanitaire* against "paganism."

"I know the very man to talk about these hidden matters with you," he said after my return, "Kapaku. He has very many brains." Next day he brought Kapaku – none other than Muchona! Muchona, as fluid and evasive in his movements as wood smoke, had many names and Kapaku was one of them. It turned out that Muchona and Windson were neighbors, the one inhabiting a big house of sun-dried "Kimberley" brick, the other his pole-and-daub hut. Thus began an association that was to last eight months. Eight months of exhilarating, quick-fire talk among the three of us, mainly about Ndembu ritual. Sporadically, our colloquy would be interrupted by Muchona's doctoring trips, but most evenings after school Windson would stroll over to my grass hut and Muchona would rustle on its still green door for admittance. Then we would spend an hour or so running through the gamut of Ndembu rituals and ceremonies. Many I had seen performed, others I had heard about, and still others were now no more than old men's memories. Sometimes, under Windson's prompting, we would turn to the Old Testament and compare Hebrew and Ndembu observances. Muchona was especially fascinated by the fact that the symbolism of blood was a major theme in both systems. My method was to take a Ndembu ritual that I had observed and go through it, detail by detail, asking Muchona for his comments. He would take a symbol, say the *mudyi* tree which is the pivotal symbol of the girl's puberty ritual, and give me a whole spectrum of meanings for it.

Mudyi has white gum [latex]. We say that this is mother's milk. So *mudyi* is the tree of motherhood. Its leaves represent children. So when the women seize *mudyi* leaves and thrust them into the hut where the novice's bridegroom is sleeping, this means that she should bear many live and lovely children in the marriage. But the *mudyi* is also the matrilineage. For our ancestress lay under the *mudyi* tree during her puberty ritual; and women danced round her daughter, our grandmother, when she lay in that place of death or suffering. And our mother who bore us lay there. And the *mudyi* also means learning. It is like going to school today, for it stands for the instruction the girl receives in her seclusion hut.

Later, Muchona would relate the whiteness of the *mudyi* to the white beads that are draped on a miniature bow and placed in the apex of the novice's seclusion hut. "These beads stand for her capacity to reproduce, her *lusemu* – from *ku-sema*, 'to bear children or beget.' When the girl comes out of seclusion and dances publicly her instructress hides these beads in a pack of red clay on her head. No man but her husband may see these beads. She reveals them to him on her nuptial bed." Then he would discuss the meaning of the quality of whiteness which many symbols possess. "It means good luck, health, strength, purity, friendship towards other people, respect for the elders and for the ancestors; it means revealing what is hidden."

At other times, I would ask Muchona to describe a ritual from the beginning, whether I had seen it or not. Sometimes I would mention to him what other Ndembu specialists had said about its symbols. His accounts and glosses were always fuller and internally more consistent than theirs. He had evidently pondered long on the mysteries of his profession, critically comparing the explanations given him by those who had instructed him in the various cults in which he was an adept.

Windson's comments were usually to the point. His father had been a famous councilor in the court of a former subchief and from him as well as from the Mission School, Windson has acquired a flair for elucidating knotty questions. Although he was a product of modern change, he had never lost his deep respect for the now passing traditional order and its "reverend signors." At the time I knew him, he was, like other converts to Christianity, beginning to look askance at the privileged lives of certain of the white missionaries and to wonder whether the religion of his loved father was really such a farrago of deviltries as he had been led to believe. His major value for me lay in his ability to slow down Muchona's word-spates into digestible sentences and intelligible texts. For, as I have indicated, Muchona was an enthusiast, not only in talk, but, as I have seen him, in professional action as well – brisk, agile, full of prescience and *élan*. Windson spanned the cultural distance between Muchona and myself, transforming the little

doctor's technical jargon and salty village argot into a prose I could better grasp. When taking a text I made him repeat slowly word by word Muchona's staccato speech so as not to water down its vividness. After a while, the three of us settled down into a sort of daily seminar on religion. I had the impression that Muchona had found a home of some kind at last.

I also came to know a few of Muchona's peccadilloes. For example, his knock would now and then be ragged; he would totter into the hut, his greeting an octave higher than usual, and slump down on a stool. He would then boast that his real name was "Chief Hornet" (*Mwanta Iyanvu*). This was his weak pun on the title of the mighty Lunda potentate in the Belgian Congo from whose realm the Ndembu had come some centuries previously. This title, Mwantiyanvwa, was the most important name the Ndembu knew. Iyanvu was Muchona's "beer-drinking name" (*ijina dakunwa walwa*), and when he used it he had come from drinking warm honey beer, a heady brew bobbing with bees. "Like a hornet or a bee," he would say, "I stay near the beer calabashes, talking loudly, and stinging those who annoy me." Hereupon Windson would fix him with a stern look, relieved by a twinkle of amusement, and tell him to go away and stay away until he had become "Mwanta Muchona" again. So the mighty "Chief Hornet," bedraggled with beer, would creep out of the hut.

This was the Muchona at whom men might scoff – at whom some did scoff, although others who had been treated by him for illness took a different view. Along with other motives less altruistic perhaps, Muchona had a genuine desire to cure the ailing and help the unlucky by his magical therapy. For instance, he would often say when describing how he first came to learn some curative technique, "I dearly wanted to cure well by means of *Kaneng'a* [or *Kayong'u* or some other ritual]." *Kaneng'a* doctors are often feared, as well as invoked, for they are the authentic "witch-doctors" who fight off the attacks of those given to the use of black art against their kin and neighbors. There is an implicit threat in the very knowledge the *Kaneng'a* doctors possess about the ways of witches and sorcerers. Muchona himself practiced a modified form of *Kaneng'a*, exempt from most of its terrifying elements. Thus, while most *Kaneng'a* practitioners collected medicines from the interior of graves, and some would even brandish human thighbones while they danced, Muchona merely took grass from the surface of graves and leaves and barkscrapings from trees growing in a circle around them. It is difficult to deduce attitudes from the behavior of members of another culture, but I once attended a *Kaneng'a* of Muchona's in company with a South African artist from Natal who had seen Zulu doctors at work. Muchona was treating an unfortunate woman who was suffering from delusions as the result of puerperal fever. My friend was impressed by what he considered the "compassionateness" of Muchona's demeanor. Gone was the rather uneasy pertness and comicality of his usual manner; in its stead was an almost maternal air – kind, capable hands washing with medicine, a face full of grave concern. My friend commented on the "heroism" with which Muchona, at one phase of the ritual, ventured out alone into the ghostridden graveyard, far from the firelight, to exorcise the agencies of evil that were making the poor victim writhe and babble nonsense. He subdued his fear to his curative vocation.

The compassionate side of Muchona's nature also emerged in the form of comments he made from time to time during our sessions on the luckless spirits whom Ndembu call *ayikodjikodji*, "mischief-makers." These are the spirits of persons inimical to society for one reason or other: through their greed and selfishness, because they were sterile, because they loved to stir up trouble, and so on. At many rituals gifts of food and beer are offered to the ancestors and always a small portion is set aside for the *ayikodjikodji*, usually at the margin of the sacred site and far from the person being treated. Instead of emphasizing the outcast position of these entities, Muchona invariably called attention to the fact that despite their delinquencies in life these spirits were still entitled to be fed. "For were they not human beings once, men and women like ourselves? Wickedness is in the heart [literally "liver"] and few can change the hearts they are born with. We do not want the *ayikodjikodji* to harm the living, but once they lived in

the villages, were our kin." Other Ndembu brought out the propitiatory character of this rite in their interpretations; Muchona had mercy on the disreputable dead. Could it have been because he himself had to wander around the margins of respectable society that he felt fellowship with the despised and the rejected?

In our "seminars," Muchona seldom betrayed the emotional bases of his calling. A new and exhilarating intellectual dimension had opened up to him as well as to myself in our discussions of symbolism. At such times he had the bright hard eye of some raptor, hawk or kite, as he poised over a definitive explanation. Watching him, I sometimes used to fancy that he would have been truly at home scoring debating points on a don's dais, gowned or perhaps in a habit. He delighted in making explicit what he had known subliminally about his own religion. A curious quirk of fate had brought him an audience and fellow enthusiasts of a kind he could never have encountered in the villages. In this situation, he was respected for his knowledge in its own right. What has become of him since? Can he ever be again the man he was before he experienced the quenchless thirst for objective knowledge?

For Muchona, the homeless, was peculiarly susceptible to nostalgia. He had a recurrent dream which I translate literally to keep the smack of his speech. "I dream of the country of Nyamwana where I was born and used to live. I am where my mother died. I dream of the village which is surrounded by a palisade, for bad people raided for slaves. Streams which were there I see once more. It is as though I were walking there now. I talk, I chat, I dance. Does my shadow [*mwevulu* – the personal life-principle] go there in sleep?" Here the rational side of Muchona came uppermost, for he went on: "I find that place the same as it was long ago. But if I had really visited it, the trees would have grown big, grass perhaps would have covered it. Would there have been a stockade? No, it is just a memory." He shook his head lugubriously and said, lingering on each syllable, "Āká" (meaning "alas," with a flavor of "Eheu fugaces!").

Muchona appears to have had an exceptionally close relationship with his mother, even for an Ndembu. This emerges in three ways from the history of his inductions into many kinds of ritual. First, it is apparent in the fact that Muchona was initiated into the preliminary grades of certain cults along with his mother, who held the position of senior novice or patient – in Ndembu ritual one must suffer before one is entitled to learn how to cure. Secondly, one finds that after Muchona's mother died she became for him an agent of supernatural affliction in at least one ritual context. The spirits of one's kin in Ndembu society punish one for a number of reasons, but through punishment, bane may become blessing, for the conduct of a ritual to mollify the spirit gives the patient the right of entry into a tribal cult. Affliction may thus well be a blessing in disguise. Thirdly, Muchona's attachment to his mother appears obliquely in that dead male relatives on her side plagued him into the acquirement of *expertise* in a number of rituals from which women are debarred, such as hunting cults.

My relationship with Muchona was at a professional rather than a personal level; we maintained towards one another a certain reserve about our intimate affairs. I did not ask him direct questions about his past, especially where the delicate question of his slave origin was concerned, but I learned much about it indirectly from his long spoken reveries on rituals in which he had taken part. Now and then, to be sure, he would suddenly take Windson and myself into his confidence about some matter that was currently troubling him. In the main, however, the pattern of his personality, like that of a poet in his poems, expressed itself in his accounts and interpretations of ritual, and in the nuances of gesture, expression, and phrase with which he embellished them. In a sense, therefore, Muchona's ritual history is his inner biography, for in ritual he found his deepest satisfactions.

Muchona's mother had been an adept in many kinds of ritual, for among the Ndembu slavery does not debar a person from ritual eminence. She also encouraged her children to acquire ritual skills. Muchona had been initiated into three women's cults concerned with curing reproductive disorders. One of these, *Nkula*, is performed principally to cure

menstrual disorders, but also to remove frigidity and barrenness. Its dominant medicine is the red *mukula* tree, which Muchona had mentioned to me at our first encounter. Here the tree symbolizes the blood of birth or motherhood, and the aim of the ritual is to placate an ancestress who is causing the patient's maternal blood to drain away and not to coagulate around the "seed of life" implanted by her husband. At the esoteric phase of *Nkula*, a *mukula* tree is ceremonially cut down and then carved into figurines of infants which are medicated with red substances and put into small round calabashes, representing wombs. These amulets are then given to the patients to carry on strings adorned with red feathers until they bear "live and lovely children."

Muchona was inducted into the *Nkula* cult when he was about seven years old. His mother was principal patient. At her request he was given the role of *Chaka Chankula*, usually taken by the patient's husband or uterine brother, although sometimes a classificatory "brother" or "son" may be chosen. The idea behind these choices is that a male who occupies a social position in which he might be called upon to support the patient jurally and economically should enact a role symbolizing the protective and responsible aspects of the male–female relationship. In practice, however, it is indeed very seldom that a patient's own son becomes *Chaka*.

A *Chaka's* main task is to squat behind the patient, after she has been washed with medicines by the doctor, and then to lead her backwards, while she rolls her head round and round under the doctor's flat collecting basket, to a small hut built for the afflicting spirit behind her own marital hut. Then the *Chaka* pulls her into the hut, both of them with their backs to the entrance. Later they emerge in the same fashion and return to the ritual fire. Muchona displayed his interest in "etymological" interpretations – an interest, incidentally, very common among Ndembu – when he told me that *Chaka* was derived from *kwaka*, "to deliver a child," or, more accurately, "to catch it as it drops."

Only a circumcised male can perform the role of *Chaka* since uncircumcised persons are reckoned ritually impure. An uncircumcised boy, like a menstruating woman, is *wunabula-kutooka*, "one who lacks whiteness," and hence purity, good luck, and other qualities possessed by "whiteness." Again, an uncircumcised boy represents social immaturity, and a barren woman is also regarded as in some sense immature. As Muchona explained, "*Mukula* and *Nkula* both come from *ku-kula*, 'to grow up or become mature.' When a girl has her first menstruation she has grown up a little. When she has her first child she has grown up still more. Both of these occasions have to do with blood. After a boy is circumcised he sits, with others who have been cut, on a long log of *mukula*, the tree of blood. He has also grown up a little."

Another curious feature of *Nkula* should be noted here, for it may well have influenced Muchona's development as a doctor. In the role of *Chaka* a man is regarded as a midwife, in Muchona's case his own mother's, in contradiction to the strict Ndembu norm that only a woman may deliver another woman in childbirth. Since many *Yaka* (plural of *Chaka*) become *Nkula* specialists, and since such specialists are thought to cure reproductive disorders, the implication is that they are spiritual midwives. In addition, the *Nkula* patient is thought of as being ritually reborn into fruitful maturity, reborn that she too may bear. Muchona's desire to help the unfortunate by the only means known to Ndembu, leechcraft and ritual, may have found its first channel in this early indoctrination in his mother's *Nkula*.

Without being markedly effeminate in his deportment, Muchona always seemed more at ease among women than men. In my mind's eye I can still see him pleasantly gossiping with Kasonda's sister, both of them clucking their tongues at the misdeeds of their little world. This gay, full-blown woman had scant time for her scheming brother, whom she often scolded for his meanness to her. Muchona, to his credit, or perhaps through timidity, never to my knowledge said a word out of place about Kasonda, who himself had no hesitation in slandering Muchona behind his back. I fancy that Kasonda's sister more than once, in her imperious way, defended the tiny doctor against Kasonda's insinuations. Certainly, she

called him in to perform the *Kayong'u* ritual for her, a ritual I shall shortly describe, for Muchona's first induction into it was a critical point in his development. Muchona might be described as a Tiresias figure, in that he had considerable insight into feminine as well as masculine psychology, especially in the fields of sex and reproduction. It seems certain that he identified himself closely with his mother, even to the extent of speaking in an alto voice. A young man I knew in Kasonda's village used to speak in a similar way, copying his mother, until he went away to work in a European township. When he came back he possessed a rich baritone, but had acquired a stutter in the process of masculinization. Muchona never lost his shrill pitch.

He resembled Tiresias in another important respect, for he was a diviner as well as a doctor. Here again the secret influence of his mother can be seen at work. During her lifetime she had caused Muchona to be initiated into no less than four kinds of ritual. After her death Muchona believed that she came as a spirit to afflict him "in the mode of *Kayong'u*," and thus to make a diviner of him. *Kayong'u* is the name of a specific set of symptoms, of the spirit that inflicts them, and also of the ritual to cure the victim. It has two variant forms, one to cure the illness and the other to prepare the patient to be a diviner as well as to cure him. Women may suffer from *Kayong'u* and may be treated by the curative ritual, but they cannot become diviners. They may, however, carry out minor ritual tasks during subsequent performances of *Kayong'u*, if they have been cured. Muchona's mother had been, in this sense, a *Kayong'u* doctor.

Muchona's initiation into *Kayong'u*, and the events leading up to it, stood out in his memory with harsh clarity. He was in his early thirties at the time and was living with his recently acquired wife, Masonde, among his stepfather's kin on the Angolan border. Apparently it was just about this time that he emancipated himself from slavery. One pictures him then as a minuscule fellow with a needle-sharp and pin-bright mind. He must have already developed a streak of buffoonery to curry the favor of the bigger and better-born. He must already have been something of an intellectual prodigy for his society, half derided and half grudgingly admired – and entirely unable to belong.

He told me that for a long time he had intermittent attacks of "being caught by a very heavy sickness in my body; I found it hard to breathe, it was like being pricked by needles in my chest, and sometimes my chest felt as though it has been blown up by a bicycle pump." A diviner was consulted, and he diagnosed that Muchona was suffering from the sickness of *Kayong'u*. Furthermore, not one but three spirits had come out of the grave to catch him, two full brothers of his mother, and his father. He himself had dreamed of one of his uncles and of his father while he was ill. Both these spirits, he said, were urging him to become a diviner, for they had practiced that profession. He had also dreamed of his mother, significantly enough. "She came too," he told me, "but she was so weak that the diviner did not recognize her." It is typical of Muchona that he felt compelled to stress the novelty of his personal lot in religious matters. A whole battery of spirits, not merely a single ancestor, had singled him out for this arduous and dangerous profession.

The values and attitudes expressed and inculcated in Ndembu ritual leave their stamp on its subjects. Personality is shaped at the forge of ritual, especially where the ritual deals with life-crisis, serious illness or, as I believe in Muchona's case, with a severe psychosomatic disorder. Thus, an account of one phase of Muchona's *Kayong'u* and his interpretations of it may reveal something of the man.

Let us go back thirty years or so to the flaring ritual fire of green wood outside Muchona's hut in the dull dawn. All night he has been washed with medicine, shuddering convulsively to the *Kayong'u* drum rhythm, a plaything of the savage spirits within him. At the first faint light, the senior officiant, a hunter-diviner, who was Muchona's father's brother-in-law, brings a red cock to the sacred site and holds it up before the patient by its beak and legs. *Kayong'u* like *Nkula* and the hunting cults is a "red" ritual, full of red symbolism standing for killing, punishment, witchcraft, and in general, for violent breach in the natural and social orders. Muchona, in a

sudden spasm, leaps on the cock and bites through its neck, severing the head. Blood spouts out and Muchona "beats the bloody head on his heart to quieten his mind." Then the big doctor orders a goat to be beheaded. Its blood pours on the ground and Muchona laps it up where it puddles. The cock's head is placed on a pole called *muneng'a*, newly cut from the same species of tree from which ancestor shrines of quickset saplings are made, symbolizing ritual death and contact with spirits. The sun now rises and the doctor takes a hoe, a cupful of goat's blood, the hearts of the cock and goat, various "sharp" objects, and leads a procession of the doctors from the village into the bush. They go to a fork in the path and keep straight on instead of following either path. They find the principal medicine tree of the ritual, a *kapwipu* tree, which stands in this context for initial misfortune followed by success – a meaning it also possesses in hunting cults. They pray to the afflicting spirits and then heap up a mound of earth at the foot of the tree roughly in the shape of a crocodile, with legs and a tail. Next they conceal the various small objects, such as a knife, a razor, needles, a bracelet, and a string of beads under the mound, at the head, tail, and sides. Before concealing the razor and needle, the big doctor pricks the cock's and goat's hearts with them. Then they bring the drums and beat out the *Kayong'u* rhythm.

Now Muchona is led out of the village to the crocodile image and seated on its "neck" facing forward. The doctors question him on why he has come to *Kayong'u* and he gives the stereotyped responses regarded as appropriate. Next he has to divine where each of the objects has been concealed. He told me jubilantly that he was completely successful in this, that he seemed to know just where everything was hidden. Each time he answered correctly, he said, the women who had accompanied him to the sacred site trilled their praises aloud, "making me very happy." Suddenly, two doctors dart off to the village to hide something there. Muchona is led home where he begins searching and snuffling about to find what has been concealed. At length he says, "You have kept something here for the name of a dead man." He approaches the *muneng'a* pole, he claws up the earth near it. He shouts aloud, "The name of the dead man is *Nkayi* ["duiker"], for you have hidden a duiker horn here." Someone called *Nkayi*, he said, had recently died in the village. Then he explains to the doctors, showing off a little, one suspects, "A duiker-antelope is an animal of the bush. An animal lives in the bush, but a man lives in the village." He explained this to me by saying that while hunters seek out hidden animals in the bush diviners hunt out the secret affairs of men in villages. At any rate, according to Muchona, the big doctor is highly impressed and calls out, "This man will make a true diviner." All gather round Muchona and praise him, but he had to pay the doctors many yards of cloth, he added rather ruefully. Nevertheless, he had been cured of his malady. It had gone immediately. The spirits that had afflicted him henceforth helped him to divine and protected him from evil. Shortly after the performance, he apprenticed himself to a famous diviner and learned the difficult manipulative and interpretative techniques of that profession, many of which he went on to describe in a series of sessions.

Muchona's interpretation of the symbolism of *Kayong'u* was compounded of both traditional beliefs and his own deeper insights: "The cock represents the awakening of people from sleep; at dawn the cock begins to crow and rouses them. The goat too stands for waking up, for at dawn it begins to bleat when it runs after she-goats and it disturbs people with its sound. The *Kayong'u* spirit too awakens people it has caught. It makes them emit a hoarse breathing, like a cock or a goat." I have myself heard Muchona and other diviners make a deep asthmatic wheezing noise in the course of ordinary conversation. This is supposed to be the voice of the *Kayong'u* spirit inside them. The *Kayong'u* then endows its possessor with special alertness, with the power of the first light that follows the secretive night, full of witches and mysteries.

Muchona continued: "It is the power of the *Kayong'u* spirit that makes a man kill the cock with his teeth. It makes a person a little mad. When he is shuddering he feels as though he were drunk or epileptic. He feels as though he were struck suddenly in his liver, as if by

lightning, as if he were being beaten by a hoe-handle, as if his ears were completely closed, as if he could not breathe. He is stopped up. But he is opened when he kills the cock. From the killed animals he gets wakefulness, alertness, for he must be wide awake to become a diviner and seek out hidden things." The orifices of various senses – ears, nostrils, eyes – are stopped up during his ritual seizure; then the novice experiences a release, an access of heightened sensitivity. Again the curious parallel with Tiresias springs to mind for the Greek soothsayer was smitten with blindness before he attained insight.

Muchona said of the fork in the path:

When people come to a fork, they must then choose exactly where they want to go. It is the place of choice. Usually they have foreknowledge of the way to go. Everyone has such knowledge. But the diviner goes between the paths to a secret place. He knows more than other people. He has secret knowledge.

When the doctor pricks the hearts with needle and razor, he is representing the patient's pain. The patient must not feel it again because it has already been done in the hearts of the cock and goat. But if he becomes a diviner, he will again feel that pricking inside him – while he is divining. It is the thing which tells him to look at the *tuponya* [the symbolic objects shaken up in a basket whose combinations tell the diviner the cause of his client's illness or bad luck or how someone's death was brought about by a witch or sorcerer]. The diviner must be sharp like the needle, cutting like the knife. His teeth must be sharp to bite off the cock's head with one bite. He goes straight to the point in hidden matters. The crocodile in *Kayong'u* stands for divination because it has many sharp teeth, like needles.

A diviner can catch witches by *Kayong'u*, by its sharpness, and also by his divining basket. These help one another. A person who has *Kayong'u* is safe from witchcraft. Thus if someone tries to bewitch me, my three *Tuyong'u* [plural of *Kayong'u*] would kill that witch. For they are terrible spirits.

I have tried to sketch some of the factors that may have been responsible for making Muchona a "marginal man" in Ndembu society. His slave origin, his unimpressive appearance, his frail health, the fact that as a child he trailed after his mother through several villages, even his mental brilliance, combined to make him in some measure abnormal. His special abilities could not overcome the handicaps of his social marginality and psychical maladjustment. But he found some kind of integration through initiation into curative ritual and especially into divinatory status. For these, his outsider characteristics were positive qualifications. In a ritual context he could set himself apart from the battles for prestige and power that bedevil kinship and village relationships in Ndembu society. Ndembu ritual, like ritual everywhere, tends to assert the higher unifying values of the widest effective congregation. The doctor-diviner heals or judges by reference to commonly held beliefs and values which transcend the laws and customs of everyday secular society. Thus Muchona's very weakness and vulnerability in village life were transmuted into virtues where the maintenance of the total society was concerned.

The rich symbolism of oral aggression in *Kayong'u* points up a very different aspect of the diviner's role, and since Muchona set so much store by his occupancy of such a role it must have modeled many of his attitudes. In the past, a diviner had to ply a dangerous trade. I have been told of diviners who were shot or speared by the relatives of those they had declared to be witches or sorcerers. Moreover, they had to overcome by aggressive means much fear and guilt in themselves to reach decisions that might result in the death by burning of their fellow men. At its mildest, their profession entailed the probability of declaring in public that someone was a witch. No one but a diviner would do this, for as in all societies, the polite fiction prevails among Ndembu that social intercourse is governed by amity and mutual consideration. Only the diviner, fortified by ritual and protected by ferocious spirits that torment him while they endow him with insight, can publicly expose the hates that simmer beneath the outward semblance of social peace.

One feels, therefore, that there is an aspect of unconscious revenge against the social order in divination. In Muchona's case, one may speculate that beneath his jester's mask, and under his apparent timidity, he may have cherished hatred against those more securely placed in the ordered groupings of society. Such hatred may itself have given him a certain clairvoyance into tense relationships in the kinship and political systems. Forever outside the village circle, he could see the villagers' weak spots and foibles more clearly than most. His very objectivity could further his general revenge. Nevertheless, he may himself have felt unconscious fear that those he disliked plotted counter-retribution against him. This fear made him at once meek and comical in his daily doings. By playing the timorous fool he belittled his own powers and thus defended himself. Moreover, his fear may have had something to do with the fact that he invariably rationalized his ritual tasks as being for the good of society. The flower of altruism sometimes has twisted roots.

It was an undoubted fact that Muchona, popular with most elderly women, was disliked by many men. For example, when his junior wife's baby died, a child who he admitted to everyone was not his, men from a number of villages took pleasure in telling me that they suspected he had bewitched it to death. To discredit these damaging views, communicated to Muchona by innuendo, he took the trouble to make a wearisome journey of several score miles to his parents-in-law to report the details of the baby's illness and the remedial measures he had taken. He told me wryly on his return that they had taken fifteen shillings – a considerable sum for a village – from him as compensation for the child's loss to their lineage. Muchona, as the husband, was held responsible for the child's welfare. He said that they had taken no account of the money he had already paid a diviner to ascertain the cause of death, nor of the cost of treatment by a herbalist, also borne by Muchona himself. The diviner had declared him innocent of the child's death in the presence of his wife's kin, had indeed nominated as the sorcerer an important headman belonging to her lineage. If Muchona had been a tougher personality in secular affairs, he might have refused to pay compensation for an illicit child and have gotten away with it. As it was, he felt constrained to ingratiate established authority whenever he met it – or else to run away and build his hut in a different area.

There is another instance of Muchona's tendency to capitulate without a struggle to public pressure. One day, after he had been working with me for about three months, he strutted in wearing a suit of white ducks, paid for out of my cash gifts. He had informed everyone with some pride, I was told later, that his son Fanuel Muchona had given him the suit. Indeed, poor Muchona often tried to give the impression that Fanuel was more solicitously filial than he really was. It was soon discovered that Fanuel had only put his father in touch with the vendor, not given him the money for the suit. After our session, schoolmaster Windson said to me sadly, "That fine suit will make everyone jealous, for people will realize that you have been paying him well, and we Ndembu are a very jealous people."

Sure enough, a few days later Muchona came to us in his usual khaki rags, looking utterly woebegone. "What on earth's the matter?" I asked. He replied, "This is the last time we can speak about customs together. Can't you hear the people talking angrily in the village shelter? When I passed it on my way here, they were saying loudly, so that I could hear, that I was giving away our [tribal] secrets, and that I was teaching you witchcraft matters." I was distressed and a little hurt to hear this, for my relations with the villagers had always seemed extremely friendly. I said as much to Muchona, who went on, "No, it is not the people of this village, at least only a few of them, who are talking like this, but others who come to hear a case discussed in the village shelter. But the people of this village, especially one man – I name no names – say that I am telling you only lies. Before I came, they say, you heard only true things about our ceremonies, but now you just hear nonsense. But one thing I found wonderful. The village people call me a liar, the strangers say I am betraying secrets. Their reasons [for disliking me] don't agree, but they agree with each other!" I knew that it was Kasonda who called Muchona a liar, for he had hinted as much to my wife often enough, but Muchona was too

polite or too diplomatic to say so, for everyone knew that Kasonda and I had been friends of long standing.

When Windson heard this sorry tale, his expression grew bleak and precipitous, as I suspect it must often have done when he dealt with refractory schoolchildren. "I must have a word with some of these people," he said. "Most of them have children at my school." He turned to Muchona, "Don't take any notice of these troublemakers. They won't say another word." Nor did they. For Windson was not only deeply respected as a man of integrity, but he also had effective sanctions at his command. As village schoolmaster, he could recommend or fail to recommend children for Middle School education at the distant Mission Station. Village Africans in Zambia are well aware that a good education is a vital means to such upward social mobility as is available to black people. If the schoolmaster were to become unduly aware of acts of naughtiness on the part of certain borderline cases for promotion, he might well send in an adverse report. I don't think Windson would have done this, for he was a gentle, earnest, and not unkindly man, but a hint in the proper quarters that Muchona was not to be bothered again had a wonderfully sobering effect.

Windson had become uncommonly fond of Muchona in the course of our discussions. At first, he had tended to display a certain coolness, bordering on disparagement, towards Muchona's "paganism," but in a very short time he grew to admire the little man's intellect and his appreciation of the complexity of existence. Later still, Windson came to take positive pride in the richness and sonority of the symbolic system Muchona expounded to us. He would chuckle affectionately at Muchona's occasional flashes of dry wit.

One of those flashes came after we had spent a long session on a painful subject, the *ihamba*. In its material expression, an upper front incisor tooth of a dead hunter imbeds itself in the body of a person who has incurred the hunter's displeasure. The tooth is removed by means of a ritual procedure which includes confession by the patient and by his village relatives of their mutual grudges, and the expression of penitence by the living for having forgotten the hunter-ancestor in their hearts. Only after "the grudge has been found" will the tooth cease "to bite" its victim and allow itself to be caught in one or another of a number of cupping horns affixed to the patient's back by the doctor's principal assistant. After about a couple of hours, Muchona became very restive on his hardwood stool. Full of the zest of inquiry, I had become thoughtless and had forgotten to give him his usual cushion. Eventually he burst out, "You have been asking me where an *ihamba* goes. Well, just now I have an *ihamba* in the buttocks." I silently passed him his cushion. However, this was not all. We used to punctuate our deliberations pleasantly enough with an occasional cigarette. Today I had forgotten even to pass around the yellow pack of "Belgas." So Muchona said, "I have another *ihamba*." "What's that one?" "The angriest *ihamba* of all, the *ihamba* of drinking [i.e., smoking] tobacco." Like a true professional, Muchona could make innocuous quips about his craft.

Muchona normally took *ihamba* beliefs very seriously. He had been treated no less than eight times, he said, to gain relief from an *ihamba* that made his joints sore. Either because the doctors were charlatans – one tried to deceive him with a monkey's tooth – or more often because "the grudge was unknown," the *ihamba* remained to vex him. Several divinations had established to his satisfaction that the *ihamba* came from a mother's brother who had been taken while still a boy by Luba slave raiders many years ago. Later, his mother had learned that her brother had become a famous hunter and a wealthy man in Lubaland, having purchased his freedom there, but she never saw him again. Muchona believed that he held an undying grudge against his maternal kin, perhaps because he had not been captured but had been sold into slavery by them – who could tell so long afterwards? Muchona was being afflicted on account of this grudge. Since no one could now find out what it was, he felt he could never be cured of the biting, creeping *ihamba*. May we not see in this a projection of Muchona's own state? Did he

bear an unconscious grudge against his mother – displaced on to her unknown brother – for saddling her son with slavery? Did he not have the fantasy that even a slave could become great, as his uncle was reputed to have done? At any rate, in Muchona's phrasing of *ihamba* beliefs, he seemed to feel that he was in the grip of some irremediable affliction, that indeed his sickness was himself. Although suffering made him a doctor in many curative cults, he never became an *ihamba* specialist. One fancies that this one incurable trouble represented for him the deathless gnawing of his chagrin at being of slave origin and at not really "belonging" in any snug little village community.

No man can do justice to another's human total. I have suggested that in Muchona there was a deep well of unconscious bitterness and a desire for revenge against a society that had no secular place for him compatible with his abilities. Yet the small man had a big mind. He was only too sensitively aware of the undertone of derision and resentment with which many men regarded him. Although he was paramountly intellectual rather than warm-hearted, he tried on the whole to speak and act civilly and charitably; and he treated his patients with compassion. In our long collaboration he achieved an amazing degree of objectivity about the sacred values of his own society. Whether his outlook was radically altered by our threefold discussions I was not to know. All I do know is that shortly before I left his land, probably forever, he came to see me, and we had an outwardly cheerful drink together. Presently, he grew quiet, then said, "When your motor car sets out in the early morning do not expect to see me nearby. When someone dies we Ndembu do not rejoice, we have a mourning ceremony." Knowing Muchona as I did, I could not help feeling that he was not simply feeling sorry at the loss of a friend. What grieved him was that he could no longer communicate his ideas to anyone who would understand them. The philosophy don would have to return to a world that could only make a "witchdoctor" of him. Had not some kind of death occurred?

4

The Ojibwa Self and Its Behavioral Environment

Irving A. Hallowell

Although there is no single term in Ojibwa speech that can be satisfactorily rendered into English as "self," nevertheless, by means of personal and possessive pronouns, the use of kinship terms, and so on, the Ojibwa Indian constantly identifies himself as a person. Every individual knows who he is, where he is, and what kind of being he is; he entertains definite beliefs and concepts that relate to his own nature. Besides this, his language enables him to express such concepts as self-defense, self-glorification, self-deceit, self-command. Large areas of his most characteristic thinking, his affective experience, his needs, motivations, and goals are not thoroughly intelligible unless we take the content of his self-image into account.

I believe that the essential features of the self-image of the Ojibwa, in their full psychological reality, can best be communicated by indicating how they function as an integral part of the experience of an individual. To present the material in this form I have let an Indian, long deceased, speak in the first person, rather than attempt an abstract exposition. In order to cover as many aspects of the topic as possible and yet remain as close as possible to data collected in the field, I have attributed to my Indian speaker knowledge and experience derived from the statements of a number of different informants. Furthermore, the statements of my Indian speaker, which all appear between quotation marks, may be taken as a free translation of a possible Ojibwa text, since I have not used any English words that do not have a fairly good equivalent in Ojibwa. Beside this, Ojibwa terms for key concepts are cited. In brackets I have added my comments on particular points in order to highlight significant concepts and have sometimes gone into further elaboration.[1]

"When I was born I had a body, *mīyó*, and I had a soul, *òtcatcákwin*. My body came out of my mother's womb and when I was an old man it was buried in the earth [the body has a definitive existence in time]. I was not one of those people who knew what was happening before he was born. But my father did.

"I have heard some other old people say that they had heard babies crying constantly until someone recognized the name they were trying to say. When they were given this name they stopped crying. This shows that someone who had once lived on the earth came back to live again. [Reincarnation is possible, even if occasional. There are special cues in such cases:

Irving A. Hallowell, "The Ojibwa Self and its Behavioral Environment," pp. 172–82 in *Culture and Experience*. New York: Schocken Books, 1955.

the recall of prenatal memories; crying and babbling that only stops when the name of a deceased person is mentioned,[2] which indicates the importance of the personal name in self-identification. Another cue is the presence of a few gray hairs on the infant's head. In cases like this no personal identification may be made. Certain inferences are clear: the soul is independent of a particular body; it transcends the body in time; an implicit concept of the self is intimately connected with the idea of the soul. Self-objectification is clearly implied since self-awareness is even attributed to the foetus. The informant says that his father knew when he was going to be born. To the Ojibwa to know what is going to happen ahead of time is one of the signs of a "great" man, i.e., a man with unusual powers.]

"When I was living on the earth I had to be careful that nobody got hold of any part of my body. When my hair was cut I always burnt the part that was cut off. I was afraid that someone with power [magic] might get hold of it. If he wanted to, such a person could make me sick or even kill me. I didn't want to die before I had to. I wanted life, *pīmădazïwin*. But someone did manage to kill me by sending something towards me that penetrated my body. That's when you need a *nībakīwin-inï* [an Indian doctor who tries to remove the object by sucking as part of his ritual]. Sometimes he will suck out a shell, a piece of metal, or a dog's tooth and show it to you. Then you can live. But he couldn't cure me. He didn't have enough power. The person who killed me had more. [The body is intimately connected with the self, so intimately that physical possession of even a part of it is considered as endangering the self. The self can also be attacked by magically potent material substances projected into the body. In general, it may be said that bodily illness of any kind arouses great anxiety. The Ojibwa tend to be hypochondriacal. There are two points of interpretation that are relevant in this connection: Since serious illness, in many instances, is thought to be due to sorcery, it becomes a direct personal attack upon the self by an enemy. At the same time since illness, viewed from the standpoint of experience, involves the dysfunctioning of bodily processes, the bodily aspect of

the self assumes great importance. The further implication is that an attack on the body destroys the balance that should exist between soul and body in order to realize the Good Life, that is, life in terms of longevity, health, and absence of misfortune. Since self-awareness is given content in terms of a self-image defined by this dichotomy, anxiety may be aroused if either soul or body is endangered. In a positive sense this is why *pīmădazïwin* expresses a very central goal for the self – a level of aspiration towards which the self is motivated.[3]]

"When I died and my body was buried that was not the end of me. I still exist[4] in *djïbaiak-ing*, Ghost land or the Land of the Dead. [Existence of self is not coordinate with bodily existence in the ordinary human sense.] When I was dead people called me a *djïbai*, ghost. Some Indians have seen *djïbaiak* (plural) or heard them whistle. [In other words, a dead person has a form, a ghostly appearance that can be seen by the living and, without being visually perceived, may occasionally be heard by the living. Death involves metamorphosis because the body formerly associated with the soul has become detached from it and lies in the ground. On the other hand "I" *know* when "I" am a *djïbai*; self-awareness, personal identity, personal memories persist; there is a continuity of the self maintained.]

"It is a long hard journey to the Land of the Dead. To reach it you travel south.[5] [There are cases known in the past in which pagan Indians begged their Christianized relatives not to bury them in a coffin. They believed that they would have to carry it with them on the journey to the Land of the Dead, and they did not wish to be burdened with it. This journey is not conceived in "spiritual" terms at all; the "living" self can become emotionally disturbed by the anticipation of difficulties to be encountered by the "dead" self. It is plain that, psychologically, the behavioral environment of the self is all of one piece.]

"When I got there I found it to be a very fine place. The Indians who had died before me were glad to see me. Some of them had moss growing on their foreheads [like old rocks], they had died so long ago. I sang and danced with them. A few Indians have reached the Land of the Dead and then gone back to tell those who were alive what they saw there. [The dead in appearance are thought of anthropomorphically, not as disembodied spirits. They live in wigwams. But there are differences. In one account a youth visiting the land of of dead was offered food by his grandmother. It was decayed (i.e., phosphorescent) wood. When he refused, she said: "Naturally you are not truly dead. . . ." An essential point for emphasis is the continuation of a fundamental duality of essence. *Djîbaiαk* like *ànicinábek* have souls, and some kind of *form*. As will become more apparent later, this duality holds for *all* orders of animate beings.]

"If an Indian dies and a good medicine man starts after him quickly enough he may be brought back [i.e., his soul may be captured and returned to his body]. Then he can go on living as before. Once I saw Owl do this.[6] Tcètcebú was very ill. By the time Owl arrived where her father was encamped, she died. Owl tied a piece of red yarn around the girl's wrist at once [to enable him to identify her quickly in a crowd] and lay down beside her body. He lay in this position a long, long time. He was still; he did not move at all. Then I saw him move ever so little. The girl began to move a little also. Owl moved more. So did the girl. Owl raised himself up into a sitting posture. At the same moment the girl did the same. He had followed her to the Land of the Dead and caught her soul just in time. Everything has to have a soul in order to exist (as an animate being). I'm in the Land of the Dead now but I have a soul just as I had one before I came here. [Death involves the departure of the soul from the body; the soul takes up its residence in a new locale. There is metamorphosis. The body becomes inanimate and "selfless." The persistence of the self in conjunction with the soul in its new form is implied in the self-awareness attributed to ghosts.]

"If a conjurer, *djìsakîwininī*, has power enough he can bring a soul back from the Land of the Dead into his 'shaking tent.' I was called by a conjurer once because my son was ill and this man was trying to cure him. My grandchild went with me. When her mother, who was sitting with the other Indians outside the conjuring tent, heard her speak, she cried.[7] I had to tell about something wrong I had

done when I was living. This helped my son to get well.[8] [Under these circumstances the ghost has no usually perceptible form; only the soul is there. But functionally, a self continuous with a "living" existence is implied because personal memories of an earlier period in life are recalled.]

"When a person is sleeping anyone can see where his body is, but you can't tell whether his soul is there or not. Some conjurer may have enough power to draw your soul into his shaking tent while you are asleep. If he has the power you can't resist. Perhaps he only wants to have you talk to the people in his camp and tell them the latest news. But he may want to kill you. If your soul doesn't get back to your body then you'll be a *djîbai* by the next morning and have to start off to the Land of the Dead. I had a lucky escape once. I was only sixteen years old. A conjurer drew my soul into his conjuring lodge and I knew at once that he wanted to kill me, because I had made fun of his son who was a 'humpy' [hunchback]. I said 'I'm going out.' But the old man said, 'No! You can't go.' Then I saw my own head rolling about and the people in the lodge were trying to catch it. [The "people" were the guardian spirits, *pawáganak*, of the conjurer – superhuman entities.] I thought to myself that if only I could catch my head everything would be all right. So I tried to grab it when it rolled near me and finally I caught it.[9] As soon as I got hold of it I could see my way out and I left. Then I woke up but I could not move my legs or arms. Only my fingers I could move. But finally I managed to speak. I called out to my mother. I told her I was sick. I was sick for a couple of days. No one saw my sould go to and fro but I knew where I had been. I told my father about it and he agreed with me.

[It is quite clear from all this that the soul is detachable from the body and may occupy a different position in space. This is true both with respect to a dead person and a person asleep. It is also possible to infer with reasonable certainty that the soul cannot be conceptually dissociated from the self. Where a functioning self exists, there must be a soul. Where a soul exists there must be a self. In terms of an assumed dependent relationship the self-soul relation in Ojibwa thought logically parallels the self-body relation in our sophisticated thinking. We emphasize a certain kind of *physical* body or form as a necessary substratum for a functioning self. We are skeptics so far as any other kind of a structural substratum is concerned. On the other hand, the Ojibwa take it for granted that the soul is the only necessary substratum. Any particular form or appearance is incidental. Thus, various kinds of metamorphosis can be accepted so long as it is assumed that a soul continues to exist. What is particularly interesting to note, it seems to me, is that once we accept this assumption, it becomes more and more apparent that *functionally* the same generic attributes of the self as we understand it – and that we assume can only be manifested where a human bodily structure is present – are constant functions of the soul as thought of by the Ojibwa. The soul of the living or the dead knows who it is, what it is, where it is in space and time; it is conscious of past experiences, it has a capacity for volition, etc., irrespective of the form or appearance it may present to others at the moment. This interpretation is further illustrated by what follows.]

"There was a *djîbai* here who paid a visit to her grandfather. He was so very sad after she died. She visited him one day when he had put a mast up in his canoe and with a blanket for a sail was crossing a lake. She appeared to him as a little bird that alighted on the top of the mast. She didn't say anything but he knew who it was because he was a wise old man.[10] [The deceased – one of the very old people, *ketéänicinábek* – may be seen by a living person, not as a ghost but in the form of a bird. Metamorphosis is possible for a *djîbai*; in this case from ghost to bird.]

"The soul of a living person, too, after it leaves the body can look like an animal. A powerful medicine man can do a lot of harm because he can go about secretly at night. But you can see his body lying there in his wigwam all the time. A long time ago a friend of mine told me what he had seen.[11] He and his wife were living with an old man suspected of being a sorcerer. One night he thought the sorcerer was up to something. The latter lit his pipe and covered himself up completely with his blanket. My friend kept watch. After a long, long time had gone by, all of a sudden the sorcerer

threw off the blanket and fell over towards the fire. Blood was running from his mouth; he was dead. My friend found out what killed him. At the very same time that the sorcerer was lying under his blanket so quietly, in another part of the camp Pindándakwan was waiting with a gun in the dark beside the body of his son who had been killed by sorcery. A kind of 'fire' had appeared around the camp several times before the boy died. This night Pindándakwan saw the 'fire' coming again. It[12] made a circle around the corpse, which was covered by birch bark. He heard a voice saying, 'This is finished.' Then he saw a bear trying to lift the bark near the head of his son; he was going to take what he wanted.[13] Pindándakwan shot the bear and he heard a man's voice crying out. Both the sorcerer and the boy were buried the next day. Everyone thought the old man was a bad one. No one blamed Pindándakwan.

[This anecdote requires some lengthy comment, since it will enable us to penetrate further into Ojibwa thought and the basic premises involved. (a) It is obvious that there is not metamorphosis of the body of the sorcerer. The *mîyó* remains in the wigwam in its usual form. (b) Unlike the previous case where the soul was drawn from the body by the power of another person, here the soul leaves the body behind through a volitional act of the conjurer himself. In fact the Ojibwa would say that *he* left his body and point out that this was not the first time, since his reputation for wickedness implies this kind of behavior. And the "fire" had been seen at Pindándakwan's camp before. (c) It is likewise obvious that, in this case, the conjurer was not understood to be prowling around *dressed up* in a bear skin. This was John Tanner's interpretation, over a century ago, of similar stories. He writes: " . . . by some composition of gunpowder, or other means [they] contrive to give the appearance of fire to the mouth and eyes of the bear skin, in which they go about the village late at night, bent on deeds of mischief, oftentimes of blood."[14] This is simply Tanner's effort at an explanation intelligible to him. (d) I believe that all we need to say is that the self of the sorcerer was in Pindándakwan's camp. To say that *he* was there is the meaningful core of the whole situation; it was Pindándakwan's assumption that *he* would be there and he acted on this premise. In these terms the situation is as humanly intelligible to us as it is to the Objbwa. What is always difficult for them is to explain what we would call the *mechanism* of events, exactly *how* they occur. To them, this line of thought seems "pedantic." Explanation is never pursued in much detail at this level (which is actually the level of science). But to say that *he* (the sorcerer) had visited Pindándakwan's camp on several occasions, that *he* had killed Pindándakwan's son, that he was caught there on a particular night and killed by Pindándakwan in revenge is thoroughly meaningful to them. All they take for granted (as an implicit metaphysical principle) is that *multiform appearance* is an inherent potential of *all* animate beings. What is uniform, constant, visually imperceptible and vital is the soul. A sorcerer being a person of unusual power is able to leave his human body in one place and appear in another perceptible manifestation elsewhere. (e) There is an additional point to be noted. Inquiry revealed that Pindándakwan was known to have considerable power himself. Since he assumed it was a sorcerer prowling around and not an ordinary bear, he did not load his gun with an ordinary bullet. He mixed "medicine," *máckĭkĭ* (having magical potency), with his gunpowder. Just as it is thought possible to attack a person's ordinary body with intent to kill by projecting a material object with magical properties into it, in the same way the sorcerer, in the bodily appearance of a bear, could be directly attacked through his body, although something more than an ordinary bullet was required. (Under the circumstances there was no way of focusing the attack on his soul). In both instances the body is assumed to be a vulnerable point of attack. Since it is fairly clear that what death implies for the Ojibwa is the *separation* of the soul from its humanly-formed body, I believe they would agree that the soul of the sorcerer did not succeed in getting back to his human body. This explains why his body was seen to collapse. It could not resume its normal functioning without a soul. This is why Owl was in such a hurry to capture the soul of Tcètcebú. Not being able to reach his body in

time to resume living (which was, no doubt, part of the magic employed by Pindánadakwan), the sorcerer's soul was compelled to assume the form of a *ghost*. In a brief account of his puberty fast, to which our Indian speaker now refers, the reader will note another in which the *temporary* separation of the soul from the body occurs. To the Ojibwa there is nothing particularly unusual in such a personal experience. We lack autobiographical anecdotes, however, because there is a traditional taboo upon references to personal experiences during the puberty fast.]

"Long ago, when every boy used to go out alone into the woods to obtain his helpers his body remained in the *wazīsán* (nest) his father built for him.[15] If you had been there you could have seen his body for yourself. But his soul might have been elsewhere. One of his helpers might have taken him somewhere. That is what happened to me."

> When I was a boy I went out to an island to fast. My father paddled me there. For several nights I dreamed of an *ógīmä* (chief, superior person). Finally he said to me, "Grandson, I think you are now ready to go with me." Then *ógīmä* began dancing around me as I sat there on a rock and when I happened to glance down at my body I noticed that I had grown feathers. Soon I felt just like a bird, a golden eagle (*kĭnīu*). *Ógīmä* had turned into an eagle also and off he flew towards the south. I spread my wings and flew after him in the same direction. After a while we arrived at a place where there were lots of tents and lots of "people." It was the home of the Summer Birds. . . . [After returning north again the boy was left at their starting point after his guardian spirit had promised help whenever he wanted it. The boy's father came for him and took him home again].[16]

From this account it can be inferred that in addition to living Indians and deceased Indians, there are other classes of animate beings in the behavioral environment of the Ojibwa self with whom the individual comes into direct contact under certain circumstances. For it is apparent that the dreams of the puberty fast are interpreted as experiences of the self. The being that first appears as a human being and then is transformed into a bird is representative of a large class of other-than-human entities that maintain an existence independently of *änicinábek* and are more powerful than man. The eagle-man is not the bird one ordinarily perceives but belongs to the class of "owners" or "bosses." All animal species, such as the golden eagle, are thought to have a *kădɑbenīmíkuwat*. These "owners" are only perceived, however, in dreams or visions.

If we assume that dream experiences are interpreted by the Ojibwa as experiences of the self we then arrive at a very important deduction. The *pawáganak* are experienced as appearing in a specific form, that is, as having a bodily aspect, whether human or animal. Years ago I wrote in my notebook that Chief Berens, my most intelligent informant, said flatly that the *pawáganak* had "bodies" and "souls," but no "ghosts." Since *my* natural bias was to think of these *pawáganak* as "spiritual beings," I did not at first see the implications of the statement he had made. In our present discussion its full import is clarifying. The soul is the essential and persisting attribute of *all* classes of animate beings, human or nonhuman. But the soul is never a direct object of *visual* perception under any conditions. What can be perceived visually is only the aspect of being that has some form or structure. Consequently, it is not surprising to find that when the *pawáganak* appear in dreams they are identifiable in a tangible visual form. This *experiential* fact taken at its face value indicates, of course, that they, too, have a body as well as a soul. Structurally, they are the counterpart of man. On the other hand, it is *not* assumed that they have a uniform or stable appearance. Metamorphosis is always possible, as in the dream reported. It may be inferred, therefore, that there are inherent attributes which remain constant for different classes of beings. In the dream referred to the *being* that appeared was a *pawágan* of a certain kind and not a human being, even though he first appeared in a human form. This is just the reverse of the bad old sorcerer who was essentially human even though he appeared as a bear on certain occasions. This means, of course, that in the behavioral world of the Ojibwa, no sharp line can be drawn between animals, *pawáganak*, men, or the spirits of the dead on the basis of outward bodily aspect or appearance alone. Myths illustrate this, too, and unless we are aware of the point I have just made it is utterly impossible to apprehend their verdical nature from the Ojibwa point of view. Myths are sacred stories because they rehearse actual events in which the superhuman *pawáganak* are the main characters. These *pawáganak* are specially adept at metamorphosis. This is part of the dramatic interest of the myths. The Ojibwa are quite prepared to have the *pawáganak* manifest the same characteristic attribute in dreams. It is one of their essential attributes because metamorphosis, especially when volitionally induced, has the implication of "power." It is thought that the human being who is capable of metamorphosis has derived his power through the help of *pawáganak*. This is the only source of it. When he possesses it he, therefore, becomes superior to his fellow-men in this regard. They have to respect him even though they fear him. The only metamorphosis of *all änicinábek* is brought about by death. The dead, however, have more power than the living; consequently they are more like *pawáganak*, including the power of metamorphosis. But the *pawáganak*, who are eternal, do not die; they never become *djíbaiɑk*.

The only sensory mode under which it is possible for human beings to directly perceive the presence of souls of *any* category, and then under certain conditions only, is the auditory one. The chief context of this kind of experience is the conjuring tent where, as I have already pointed out, the souls of *djíbaiɑk* may be present and speak.[17] It is only infrequently that ghosts may be heard to whistle, perhaps in the neighborhood of a grave, where it is sometimes said they have been seen. It is from the conjuring tent, too, that the voices of *pawáganak* may be heard to issue. They cannot be seen. Thus from the standpoint of our central problem it is difficult not to draw the conclusion that, while according to Ojibwa dogma it is a soul that is present, even to them it is always an identifiable self – *pawáganak* or ghost – that speaks. For them *òtcatcák* defines the conceptual substratum of beings with self-awareness and other related attributes (speech, memory, volition, etc.) that we associate only with a stabilized anthropomorphic structure. When Ojibwa speak of their own dream experiences or those of others, when they refer to what has been heard in conjuring performances, it is assumed that one's own soul or that of some other being was present and not the body. But this fact does not have to be explicitly stated any more than we have to be explicit about the presence of the body in referring to self-related experience or to social interaction with other selves. What is implied by the Ojibwa and by ourselves is an indication of the differences between their self-orientation and ours. What is held in common is a self-concept that assumes certain generic human attributes, despite conceptual differences in the nature of the substratum of a functioning self.

Returning once again to the puberty dream I should like to stress the fact that once dreams, on this occasion or any other, are construed as experiences of the self, we can only conclude that metamorphosis can be *personally* experienced. It follows from this, too, that to anyone who has had such a dream, episodes in myth, or anecdotes like those in which the sorcerer figured, cannot appear as strange or fantastic occurrences. In a dream, too, the self may experience the separation of the soul from the body and mobility over large distances. Accounts of such mobility also occur in myth and in anecdotes connected with conjuring. I was told by one informant that he once attended a conjuring performance to which another conjurer, from two hundred miles away, was called. He said, "I was sleeping, but I heard you calling me." People in the audience asked for news and received replies to questions. Then the soul of the visiting conjurer sang a song and departed for home.[18]

In addition to metamorphosis and spatial mobility, the self may likewise experience events in its dream phase that transcend the temporal schema of waking existence. Our autobiographer, for instance, not only made the long journey to the Land of the Summer Birds during his puberty fast; he stayed there all winter and flew north with the other birds under the guidance of his *ógīmä* in the spring. It is self-related experiences of this nature that coordinate the world as dramatized in myth with the world as experienced by the self in certain phases of its existence. Myths are

understood as past experiences of super-human selves – the *pawáganak*. Dreams are among the past experiences of the self. Thus the world of the self is not essentially different from the world of the *pawáganak*. The cultural emphasis given to dream experience helps to unify the world of the self through *experience*. For anthropomorphic entities such as *wîsakedja* may appear in both myth and dream as may the Winds, Snow, Thunder Birds, and so on, in personified form. No wonder that certain "natural" objects belong to an animate rather than an inanimate gender in linguistic expression. Furthermore, all classes of *pawáganak* are linguistically integrated in the kinship terminology since, collectively, they are spoken of as "our grandfathers." And in the dream reported by our autobiographer the *pawágan* calls him *nózis*, "grandson."

The Ojibwa self is not oriented to a behavioral environment in which a distinction between human beings and supernatural beings is stressed. The fundamental differentiation of primary concern to the self is how other selves rank in order of *power*. "Is he more powerful than I, or am I more powerful than he?" This is a crucial question applying to all human beings as well as to the *pawáganak*. But the fundamental distinction is that while other Indians may be more powerful than I, any *pawágan* is more powerful than any Indian. The power ranking of different classes of entities is so important because events only become intelligible in terms of their activities. All the effective agents of events throughout the entire behavioral environment of the Ojibwa are selves – my own self or other selves. *Impersonal* forces are never the causes of events. *Somebody* is always responsible. This is just as true for past events as the myths demonstrate. For example, Wiskɑdjak, the "culture hero" was responsible for certain events in the past that led, among other things, to the distinguishing characteristics of certain animals as known today.

A further assumption is this: While power may be used for good or evil ends, most of the *pawáganak*, but not all, are beneficent. Human beings, too, for the most part use their power for beneficent ends. This is exemplified by all those who specialize in curative functions.

They have received their power to cure from the *pawáganak* and, in turn, they help their fellow men. At the same time superhumanly acquired power may be used for malevolent ends.

Since "magic" power, as we have seen, is the ultimate source of successful adaptation in every sphere of life – from hunting to defense against sorcery – and the ultimate source of this power rests in the hands of the *pawáganak*, the fundamental relationship of the Ojibwa self to the *pawáganak* is clearly defined. It is one of dependence and is the root of their deep motivational orientation toward these powerful beings. But there is a normative aspect of this relationship as well. I must fulfill certain obligations that my guardian spirits impose upon me. I may have to make certain sacrifices, perhaps material ones (*pagîtcîgan*). In the dream visit of W.B. to the *memengwéciwak* these were mentioned. There is a story told about a man who, after he was married, went off hunting all winter. He never spoke to his wife or had sexual intercourse with her. She left him in the spring. It turned out that he had been observing taboos imposed upon him in his puberty fast as a condition of a long and healthy life. "If she could only have held out three more moons," he said, "it would have been all right." He married again but did not follow the taboos. One of his children died, then his wife. A third wife died, too. This was all the result of his failure to live up to his side of the bargain with his *pawáganak*. Since all the relations between an individual and his *pawáganak* are based on dreams, their psychological reality is fundamental. It is what makes the puberty fast so important. The conceptual reality of all these beings the Ojibwa boy has been acquainted with from babyhood by listening to the myths recited on long winter nights becomes in the course of the fast a *personal* experience. If the puberty fast of the Ojibwa is crucial to them for living in their world, this same experience, viewed psychologically, is equally crucial for making their world a reality for the self.

NOTES

1   Victor Barnouw ("The Phantasy World of a Chippewa Woman," *Psychiatry*, XII [1949],

67–76.) cites verbatim the intra-uterine reminiscences of a Wisconsin Chippewa (Ojibwa) man and refers to specific examples of memories from early infancy on the part of other individuals.

2   I discovered that the occurrences of identical personal names, sometimes more than a generation apart in my genealogies, could be explained in every case by reincarnation. None of these people were living at the time of my inquiries.

3   See Irving Hallowell, *Culture and Experience* (University of Pennsylvania Press, 1955), Part IV, ch. 20, where this goal is discussed with reference to what has happened to the Ojibwa as a consequence of acculturation.

4   There is a term for existence that is applicable to any class of animate beings.

5   For details about the Land of the Dead and stories of visits there, see Hallowell 1955, Chap. 7.

6   For this case, and a reputed case of resurrection, see Hallowell 1955, Chap. 7.

7   For details and a full account of this episode see A. Irving Hallowell, *The Role of Conjuring in Saulteaux Society* (University of Pennsylvania Press; Oxford University Press, 1942).

8   For the role of confession in relation to illness see Irving Hallowell, *Culture and Experience* (University of Pennsylvania Press, 1955), chs. 14 and 16, and Irving Hallowell, "Sin, Sex and Sickness in Saulteaux Belief," *British Journal of Medical Psychology*, XVIII (1939): 191–7.

9   Even in this "dream" a bodily part of himself – his head – assumes vital importance. The dreamer gives himself "form."

10   See Hallowell 1995, Chap. 7.

11   What I have given here is a highly abbreviated version of a longer text (unpublished).

12   This reference to "fire" illustrates the allusive manner of Indian narration. The listener is supposed to know what is meant. What is referred to here is made explicit in another anecdote. "One night when I was asleep, I was suddenly awakened. My strength came to me and I managed to get on my feet and walk outside" [the narrator had been very ill and thought he knew who had sorcerized him].

13   "Right in front of me I saw something. It was a bear lying right outside the tent." [Wild

animals do not ordinarily come so close to any human habitation]. "I saw the flame when he breathed. I said to my wife very quietly: 'Hand me the axe.' She could not find it. The bear started to go. I tried to follow but I could not walk fast enough. I spoke to the bear. I said, 'I know who you are and I want you to quit. I'm good natured but if you come here again I won't spare you.' He never came back and after that I gradually got better." It is said that a sorcerer who kills a person in this way is bound to visit the grave. He cuts off the fingertips of the corpse, the tip of the tongue, and gouges out the eyes, and stores them in a little box for magical use. This is why Pindándakwan made a pseudo-grave for his son outside the wigwam. It was a deliberate "trap" for the sorcerer. Pindándakwan was an actual person who appears in my genealogies.

14 John Tanner, *Narrative of the Captivity and Adventures of John Tanner, etc.*, E. James (ed.), 1830, p. 343. Tanner was a white man captured by Indians as a boy. He lived with Ojibwa and Ottawa, learned their language and published his reminiscences in later life. For further information on bear walking and the attitude of contemporary Indians toward it, see R. M. Dorson, *Bloodstoppers and Bearwalkers. Folk Traditions of the Upper Peninsula* (Cambridge, 1952), pp. 26–29 and Notes, p. 278.

15 The Ojibwa boy, at puberty or before, sought tutelaries or guardian spirits: without their help no man could be expected to get much out of life or amount to anything. The "nest" referred to was a sort of stage constructed by laying poles across the branches of a tree about fifteen feet from the ground. The boy was expected to remain on this stage several days and nights without food or drink. He was only allowed to descend to the ground to urinate and defecate. This fast was the most crucial event in a man's life and to undertake it he has to be *pekize*, pure (without sexual experience). Failure to observe all preliminary conditions and the fasting regulations destroyed his chances of blessings from other-than-human entities – the *pawáganak* (literally, "dream visitors") – who were more powerful than human beings. The situation is often de-

scribed by the Ojibwa by saying that the *pawáganak* took "pity" upon the *kīgusámo*, the faster. It was through dreams or visions, while the body lay inert, that direct experience of these entities occurred.

16 This account was repeated to me by a man who said he had heard the dreamer narrate it when he was an old man. The conjuring tent consists of a barrel-like structure, covered with bark or canvas, that conceals the conjurer who kneels within. Those who witness the performance are outside this structure. Since the *pawáganak* reputedly are *inside* they, like the conjurer himself, are invisible to the audience without.

17 On the other hand, it is said that the *pawáganak* do have a visible aspect from inside the tent. They look like tiny stars or minute sparks. It is only under very exceptional circumstances, however, that any person except the conjurer ever has an opportunity to even peep inside the structure during the performance. Consequently, the sensory manifestation of the spirits is typically auditory, not visual.

18 See Hallowell, 1942, pp. 50–51.

REFERENCES

Barnouw, Victor
1949 "The Phantasy World of a Chippewa Woman," Psychiatry XII: 67–76.

Dorson, Richard Mercer
1952 Bloodstoppers and Bearwalkers. Folk Traditions of the Upper Peninsula. Cambridge, MA: Harvard University Press.

Hallowell, A. Irving
1939 "Sin, Sex and Sickness in Saulteaux Belief," British Journal of Medical Psychology XVIII: 191–7.

Hallowell, A. Irving
1942 The Role of Conjuring in Saulteaux Society. Philadelphia and London: University of Pennsylvania Press.

Hallowell, A. Irving
1955 Culture and Experience. Philadelphia: University of Pennsylvania Press.

Tanner, John
1830 Narrative of the Captivity and Adventures of John Tanner, ed. Edwin James. New York: G. & C. & H. Carvill.

5

The Charity Physician

Rudolf Virchow

Health care for the indigent or, in other words, the medical treatment of poor patients, as practiced up to now has involved two great wrongs: one against the patients, and the other against the physician.

The indigent were compelled to accept treatment by certain physicians assigned from above, as they had no choice other than to either remain untreated or to consult the physician approved by the authorities. The physicians, due to unlimited competition, were obliged to accept a position which withheld from them payment commensurate to their efforts.

And with it all the patients who had at their disposal such an assigned physician, and the physicians who had managed to obtain such an ungrateful position had to be thankful, as there were large parts of the land where patients searched in vain for a physician, and numerous physicians worn out by years of vain struggle against nepotism of all sorts in their futile endeavor to obtain even such a beggarly post.

These conditions were bound to embitter the poor as well as the physicians; both were bound to be gradually imbued by the conviction that they were the victims of false social principles. Society thus created its own enemies. The proletariat grew more restive day by day; confused ideas of human welfare

and human dignity began to stir in them and were exploited for purposes of generalized agitation on an ever increasing scale, an agitation allegedly endangering European civilization. But who can be surprised that democracy and socialism nowhere found more adherents than among the physicians or that, on the extreme left, it is physicians who frequently head the movement? Medicine is a social science, and politics is nothing more than medicine on a large scale.

Not enough that politically and socially both the poor and the physicians were driven into the opposition, very often their mutual relations also became most deplorable. Poor patients made demands on the physician who had been officially foisted on them that the rich would not have dared to make without promising very high rewards, and they faced him distrustfully, rudely and brutally in the bargain. While they not infrequently neglected and disregarded the physician's instructions and prescriptions, they nevertheless demanded from him utter dedication by day and by night, complete devotion of body and spirit. The physician on his part, burdened with the demands of his profession and no doubt with worries for his own living, lacking adequate means for the proper care of the patients, almost without any prospects of personal appreciation for the pains he was taking,

Rudolf Virchow, "The Charity Physician," pp. 33–6 in L. J. Rather, ed., *Collected Essays on Public Health and Epidemiology*. Canton, MA: Science History Publications, 1985 [1879]. Used by kind permission of the publisher: Science History Publications/USA, division of Watson Publishing International LLC, Sagamore Beach, MA exhausted and ill-humored, only too easily tended to neglect his charges, to counter their exaggerated demands with cold phlegm, and to search in a more profitable and grateful practice compensation for his privations. What would be simpler and more natural?

And what were the consequences of such a situation for the state? The number of the ill increased, as did the number of poor in general; the lower classes increasingly fell victim to diseases and epidemics. Their children either died prematurely, or developed in a stunted and crippled manner. Even though great individual wealth may have accumulated in the hands of some, national prosperity as a whole stood on an increasingly unstable foundation and an ever increasing army of inimical dispossessed grew up within society. The proletarian knows that he owns nothing, and if the financiers and statisticians prove to him even more brightly than did Mr. Thiers that the prices of the necessities have been falling in the past 50 years, of what use is this to those who completely lack the means of purchasing all these cheap and beautiful things? Had Mr. Thiers, the well-to-do bourgeois, whose father-in-law, if we are not mistaken, for so long a time was General Tax-Receiver in Lille, only looked around in that city, he would have soon found out who profited by the low prices. Statistical evidence furnished by two members of the Lille Board of Health, Mr. Gosselet and Mr. Loiset, would have shown him that from 25 children of the poor, only one reached the fifth year of life; that, when recruiting in 1841, 95 percent of the young men were rejected because of small size; and that, so as to find 300 able-bodied men, these had to be selected from 537 conscripts. Such figures demonstrate more than would thick volumes on property. They sufficiently prove that a state which tolerates such conditions is facing the greatest of dangers. Mortality, as well as physical and moral debilitation of the population, rise in direct proportion with impoverishment. It goes without saying that no state can long endure on such a basis. Working power is the source of national prosperity and the wish to work the expression of the moral state of the population. Therefore, peace and legality can be assured only in a state formed by individuals possessing

a certain degree of physical and moral power. That mortality, too, should be a measure of the security of public institutions in the civilized states seems at first sight a bit far-fetched. However, regardless of the fact that increase in mortality denotes abnormal conditions in national public life, which fact sooner or later must be implanted in the public consciousness of a people, there is a yet more direct danger in the rapid change of generations. The experience of various different countries, in particular the investigation of the Irish immigration in England, has shown that under such conditions births increase with shortness of life span. Generation rapidly follows on generation. All conservative elements disappear in the progressive break-up of the family in such ephemeral populations, who become indifferent to their short life. Thus, society nurtures in its bosom the proliferating seed of its destruction.

Perhaps we have dwelt on this point longer than was quite necessary in this context. But we shall have to return to it later, and we therefore wished to clearly illuminate dangers which threaten the community from a faulty organization of the care for the poor from the medical point of view.

If we now return to the physician for the poor, who should be one of the most essential members in the care for, and the welfare of the poor, and to his position with respect to the impoverished patient, we soon note a great difference in the requirements of different localities. In the cities, especially in the big cities, there is an over-accumulation of physicians, many of whom have nothing to do. In the flat country, especially in the eastern provinces, there is a great shortage in physicians. The iniquity is evident.

Mr. S. Neumann ("Die öffentliche Gesundheitspflege und das Eigenthum," p. 82) has already drawn attention to the favorable effect of the number of physicians on mortality rates, and to the error of believing that physicians increase mortality. In the eastern provinces of Prussia almost as many people die from acute internal diseases as from chronic ones, while the proportion in the western and central provinces is 1 : 2. From these figures public opinion immediately demanded that the number of physicians be increased in these areas and that they be assured of a sufficient income at public expense, since the poverty and ignorance of the inhabitants precluded any prospects of their making a living from their practice. That is how the idea of appointed district physicians arose, and it now only remained to be decided whether these physicians should be paid by the state or by the community. This is tantamount to proposing for the countryside and the small cities a repetition of the very conditions already existing in the large cities and in certain rural areas: certain physicians were to be forced on the patients.

The demands of some physicians, in the pursuit of their special interests, went still further; consequently they claimed that all physicians should be engaged by appointment. Without going into further detail on these questions which we will discuss in a later article, we here only want to refute those who, while they defend free practice and the free right of establishing such a practice anywhere, nevertheless demand definitely remunerated posts by the appointment of physicians for the indigent (as community or district physicians) everywhere.

We have already exposed above the practical disadvantages inherent in the system of appointed physicians for the poor as practiced up to now, on account of the element of coercion associated with it. But the erroneous principle of the system is at least as harmful. For if the health services for the poor so far have rather appeared to be an outflow of public beneficence, while the natural right to such health and welfare services transpired only incidentally, and while their political and economical character was totally denied, the health services for the poor were looked upon as an exceptional institution exclusively destined for a certain part of the population and established out of mercy or mere necessity. This was accepted because one's heart strings were touched, or because nothing else could be done in safeguarding one's own security, but one always waited until the poor had become utterly deprived. All their efforts to save themselves from sinking into total destitution were futile. First a man had to become a pauper and only then was he given, in a bureaucratic way, documents of legitimation which insured his poverty for ever. The derelicts must not only taste their misery to the last drop, they must also carry it in their pockets in black and white. Only then were they taken care of, and a special physician for paupers was procured for them in advance.

The practical disadvantage hence arises from mistaken principles, and it would seem here too, as always, that the reasonable also is the appropriate, or at least that the unreasonable is always inappropriate. If one truly wants to create a public health service as would follow from the legally acknowledged principle of equal rights for all, as we have shown before, one must also liberate the dispossessed from his extraordinary position, and as far as possible rescue him from the dependence in which he has fallen on account of his need. It is realized that this cannot be achieved through a public health service alone, but only if education and a measure of prosperity are attainable to the poor to a wider extent than up to now. But public health care must at least contribute to maintain that individual independence as far as possible. For this reason we do not wish to see any special physicians for the poor, whenever that is possible. In the great cities and in the well-to-do regions we certainly do not need any. In poor districts with a low population one can perhaps not do without appointed district physicians even though difficulties will arise there for them which will render their efficient functioning difficult.

We shall take up this subject at a later date.

REFERENCE

Neumann, S.
1947 *Die Öffentliche Gesundheitsflege und das Eigenthum*, Berlin: Riess.

6

The Role of Beliefs and Customs in Sanitation Programs

Benjamin D. Paul

Man is a biological and social animal; he is also a cultural animal. He is cultural in that he runs his life and regulates his society not by blind instincts or detached reason alone, but rather by a set of ideas and skills transmitted socially from one generation to the next and held in common by the members of his particular social group. Culture is a blueprint for social living. Man resides in a double environment–an outer layer of climate, terrain and resources, and an inner layer of culture that mediates between man and the world around him. By applying knowledge which comes to him as part of his cultural heritage, man transforms his physical environment to enhance his comfort and improve his health. He also interprets his environment, assigning significance and value to its various features in accordance with the dictates of his particular culture. Among other things, culture acts as a selective device for perceiving and understanding the outer world. Since cultures vary from group to group, interpretations of the physical environment vary correspondingly.

Ordinarily people are unaware that culture influences their thoughts and acts. They assume their way is *the* way or the "natural" way. Interacting with others in their own society who share their cultural assumptions, they can ignore culture as a determinant of behavior; as a common denominator, it seems to cancel out. An engineer can construct health facilities in his home area without worrying too much about the cultural characteristics of the people who will use the facilities. Sharing their habits and beliefs, he has in effect taken them into account. But in another country with another culture, his assumptions and those of the residents may not match so well. In parts of Latin America maternity patients of moderate means expect a private hospital room with an adjoining alcove to accommodate a servant or kinswoman who comes along to attend the patient around the clock. In parts of rural India the hospital should be built with a series of separate cooking stalls where the patient's family can prepare the meals, in view of cultural prohibitions against the handling of food by members of other castes. And of course the effect of cultural differences looms even larger where sanitation has to be built directly into the habit systems of people,

Benjamin Paul, "The Role of Beliefs and Customs in Sanitation Programs," *American Journal of Public Health* 48 (1958): 1502–6.

rather than into structures and plants that serve the people.

Anyone familiar with the operation of technical assistance programs knows about the kind of behavioral differences I have mentioned. Unfortunately, however, it is easy to misconstrue these observed differences. Three kinds of misinterpretation are common. The first is to suppose that "they" have more odd beliefs and habits, while we have less of them. We tend to see them as captives of blind custom and ourselves as relatively free from cultural peculiarities. The fact is that all men are creatures of their culture with its inevitable admixture of rational and nonrational elements. Cultures differ and rates of cultural change differ, but peoples do not differ appreciably in the degree to which their actions are influenced by their respective cultures. We are quick to apply the term "superstition" or the epithet "uncouth custom" to the other fellow's manner of thinking or behaving. We may be repelled by the custom of eating domesticated dogs and yet impatient with people who would rather go hungry than eat their cattle. Americans take offense at the odor of night soil in the settlements of Korea and other parts of eastern Asia; a Korean gentleman on his first visit to New York was asked by a friend how he liked the great city, whereupon he replied: "Oh, very well, but the smells are so bad!"[1] Measured by the standards of one culture the manifestations of another are bound to appear more or less arbitrary or bizarre. We need to realize that we have culture, too, and that our ways can seem as peculiar to others as theirs do to us.

Even allowing that our behavior as well as their bears the stamp of cultural conditioning, a second facile assumption is that our ways and ideas are more advanced than theirs, that they have yet to catch up with us. The trouble with this assumption is that it represents a partial truth: Some aspects of culture, notably scientific knowledge and technical skills, are indeed subject to measurement and relative ranking. But knowledge is not wisdom, and many aspects of culture, including language, esthetics, moral codes, and religious values, lie beyond objective rating for want of a culture-free standard of measurement. It is a mistake and an insult to imply, as we inadvertently do at times, that because some areas of the world are technically underdeveloped their people or their cultures are in general underdeveloped.

A third and particularly common shortcoming in our understanding of cultural differences is a tendency to view customs and beliefs as isolated elements rather than as parts of a system or pattern. The linkages between the parts of culture may be loose or tight and the connections are not always apparent upon first inspection, but it frequently turns out that people cling to a particular practice or belief not merely because it is familiar and traditional but because it is linked to other elements of the culture. Conversely, a change effected in one area of the culture may bring with it unexpected changes in other areas or may result in awkward dislocations, as the following illustration will indicate.

On the island of Palau in the western Pacific the pattern of living calls for frequent and large gatherings of people to celebrate or solemnize certain social events. In the old days, Palauan houses were large enough to hold many people. There were no partitions, and it was possible for each man attending a feast to receive his food in the order of rank and to sit in such a way as not to cause offense by turning his back on anyone. Since the last war, most Palauans live in small two- or three-room houses built in the Japanese or American style. They try to maintain the old customs but they have their troubles. Visitors overcrowd the small house and sit packed together on the floor. They must suffer the insult of having to look at a neighbor's back and must take their food in any order they can. The Palauans are incessant betel chewers – and spitters. The old houses had several doors and numerous floor cracks to accommodate this habit. The new buildings, especially the Quonset huts now being created for chiefs' dwellings and council chambers, have caused a minor crisis. The two Quonset doors are premium locations; knotholes in the plywood floors are too scarce to provide relief for the majority of chewers. Tin cans are coming in as spittoons, but these are in scarce supply.[2]

Housing customs and hospitality customs, once closely linked in Palau, are now in strained relationship. It should be stated parenthetically that social or cultural strains are not necessarily good or bad in themselves; depending on the case, they can lead to increased cultural disorganization or to an eventual reorganization of the sociocultural system on a new basis.

In some instances people strive to prevent cultural strain by resisting environmental and sanitary improvements. In rural India, fecal contamination of food and water by direct contact or contact through flies and rodents constitutes a difficult problem. The source of the trouble is the custom of defecating in the open fields. Use of latrines would go far toward solving the problem. Public health engineers and others working in India have devised special types of latrine adapted to the local squatting posture and designed to meet varied soil, climatic, and water supply conditions. Numerous latrines have in fact been installed, but follow-up studies reveal that only a small proportion are used regularly. Women in particular tend to avoid the latrines. Every morning and afternoon women go in groups to the field, not only to relieve themselves but also to take time off from busy domestic routines, to gossip and exchange advice about husbands and mothers-in-law, and to bathe with water from tanks located in the field. The linked habits of going to the fields for social gatherings and for toilet and bathing activities meet a strongly felt need for community living and relaxation from daily toil. In the women's view, defecation customs are usefully linked to other customs. In the view of sanitation specialists these customs are harmfully linked to a cycle of contamination and intestinal disease. To disrupt the contamination cycle the women are urged to use the new latrines. They shy away from following this advice, partly because doing so would disrupt an ensemble of customs they prefer to keep intact, and partly because their culture has given them little basis for comprehending the connection between feces and enteric diseases.[3]

I began by saying that culture mediates between man and his material environment. In an article analyzing the outcome of a rural sanitation program in a small Peruvian town, the author explains how perceptions of so common an environmental element as water are culturally screened:

A trained health worker can perceive "contamination" in water because his perceptions are linked to certain scientific understandings which permit him to view water in a specially conditioned way. The Peruvian townsman also views water in a specially conditioned way. Between him and the water he observes, his culture "filters out" bacteria and "filters in" cold, hot or other qualities that are as meaningful to him as they are meaningless to the outsider.

An important part of the local culture is a complex system of hot and cold distinctions. Many things in nature, including foods, liquids, medicines, body states, and illnesses are classified as essentially "hot" or "cold" or something in between, irrespective of actual temperature. Sick people should avoid foods that are very cold, such as pork. "Raw" water is cold and fit for well persons; "cooked" water is hot and fit for the sick. The times of day when water can be boiled are hedged in by limitations of time and fuel and further restricted by "hot" and "cold" considerations. Water is consumed mainly around noon. Water boiled later in the day and standing overnight becomes dangerously "cold" and must be reboiled in the morning. So it is useless to boil it at any time other than the morning in the first place. The patient efforts of a local hygiene worker to persuade housewives to decontaminate their drinking water by boiling it met with only limited success in the face of of these cultural convictions.[4]

It is interesting to note that the hot-cold idea system now widely current in Latin America apparently goes back many centuries to the humoral theory of disease expounded by Hippocrates and Galen and transmitted by Arabs to Spain and by Spaniards to the New World, where it retained a place in formal medical teaching until the 18th century.[5] Folk theories of medicine in contemporary rural India and in other parts of Asia indicate that the humoral theory spread in that direction, too, if indeed it did not have its origin somewhere in Asia. In the course of its travels the humoral theory underwent modification, so that its present form in Asia is not identical to the one in Latin America. It is remarkable that cultural complexes such as the hot-cold idea system should persist, however altered, through such long periods of time.

Objectively viewed, the cosmos and all its contents are morally neutral; nothing is good or bad in itself; it simply is. But man clothes his cosmos in a moral cloak. He evaluates it, holding some things to be good and others evil. Values, the fundamental bases for choosing between alternative courses of action, are a central part of any group's culture. Values differ, but these differences are less apparent than differences in language, dress, posture, rules of etiquette, or other overt features of the culture. Because values usually remain below the level of awareness, we are particularly apt to impose our own values upon others on the innocent assumption that we are merely helping them achieve better health. Members of our own middle class tend to make a virtue of tidiness, apart from its possible bearing on sanitation. Cleanliness is both a health measure and a cultural value. This distinction can be appreciated if we glance back through history to see the shifting value assigned to bathing and cleanliness from the time of the ancient Greeks. Such a review also illustrates the connectedness of the parts of culture.

Although they built no great baths, the Greeks valued athletic sports and despised the Persians for their false modesty in keeping the body covered. The Romans, taking over much of the Greek cult of the body, constructed enormous public baths where men of leisure spent hours daily. The early Christians set themselves against the established pagan religion and also against many of the attitudes and amenities inherent in Roman culture. Baths were construed as instruments of paganism and vice, as devices for softening the body rather than saving the soul. Before long, even minimum cleanliness by current standards was seen as the road to ruin. The ascetic saint was indifferent to filth; attention to personal cleanliness, especially on the part of a man, incurred the suspicion that one might not be too good a Christian.

Bathing occupied an important place, however, in the lives of Europeans during medieval times. As the vessel of the soul, the body needed to be preserved. The monastery of the early Middle Ages had its bathroom for friars and pilgrims. By the 13th century, public bathhouses had come into use in the cities, providing both steam and water baths along with haircuts and minor surgery. But the presence of food and drink, girls and music increasingly converted the bath-houses into places of amusement and eventually earned the opposition of the clergy. Moreover, the bathhouses became centers of infection when syphilis began to plague Europe at the end of the 15th century. Municipal bathing disappeared from the urban scene, private houses lacked baths, and the entire custom of bathing was condemned for reasons of morality and health.

Interest in bodily cleanliness was revived in the 18th century with the growth of enlightenment, the increase in comforts, the refinement of social manners, and the rise of the bourgeoisie. The lead in this direction was taken in countries where the new wealthy middle class became especially influential; hence the scrubbing of Dutch doorsteps and the proverbial Englishman with his portable bath. Today, in the United States, prosperity, democracy, and frequency of bathing have become linked values. Americans say that cleanliness is next to godliness, an indication that bathing and cleanliness are affect-laden values in contemporary middle-class culture as well as a means to better health. Yet even in the United States bathing is neither as old nor as general as people now assume. Ackerknecht reminds us that President Fillmore was as much attacked for buying a bathtub for the White House in 1851 as was Harry Truman in our time for his balcony.[6]

We might have more success in exporting our technical means for improving the world's health if we could manage to divest these means of the values and other cultural trappings that accompany their use in the American scene. It might then be easier to fit our technical means into foreign cultural contexts. To do this we need to become skilled in perceiving our own cultural contours and those of the country we strive to help. This is one of the reasons why instruction in cultural anthropology and other social sciences is rapidly being introduced into schools of public health.

NOTES

1   Moose, J. Robert
    Village Life in Korea, 1911.
2   Barnett, H. G.
    Innovation: The Basis of Cultural Change.
    New York: McGraw-Hill, 1953, p. 91.
3   Mimeographed material distributed by the
    Research-cum-Action Project in Environmen-
    tal Sanitation, Government of India Ministry
    of Health.
4   Wellin, Edward
    "Water Boiling in a Peruvian Town." In Health,
    Culture and Community: Public Reactions
    to Health Programs (Benjamin D. Paul, Ed.).
    New York: Russell Sage Foundation, 1955.
5   Foster, George M.
    Use of Anthropological Methods and Data in
    Planning and Operation. Pub. Health Rep.,
    68:848, 1953.
6   Ackerknecht, Erwin H.
    Personal communication.

7

Introduction to Asian Medical Systems

Charles Leslie

The health concepts and practices of most people in the world today continue traditions that evolved during antiquity. Ideas about the ways that body processes are thrown off balance by the improper consumption of "hot" or "cold" foods, or the ways that envy, fear, and other strong emotions generate poisonous substances by disturbing the body's equilibrium, are based upon humoral theories that were first elaborated in the classic texts of medical science several thousand years ago. These ideas, and others related to them, are held by the majority of Asians and by large segments of European and African society. Imported to the New World in colonial times, they still play an important role in Latin American communities.

Folk curers throughout the world practice humoral medicine, but in Asia alone educated physicians continue its learned traditions. Most notably in China and India, but also in Japan, Sri Lanka (formerly Ceylon), and other countries, the institutional forms of professional education and practice have been adapted to indigenous medical traditions. Research institutes, colleges, hospitals, professional associations, and pharmaceutical companies for Chinese, Āyurvedic, and Yunānī medicine coexist to a greater or lesser extent

with similar institutions for cosmopolitan medicine. Together with folk practitioners, physicians who utilize these institutions provide a major source of medical consultation for all classes of people. Asian medical systems thus provide fascinating opportunities both to observe directly practices that continue ancient scientific modes of thought and to analyze the historical processes that mediate their relationship to modern science and technology.

Three primary traditions of medical science were formulated in what Alfred Louis Kroeber called the *Oikoumenê* of Old World society. The Greeks used the word *Oikoumenê*, the inhabited, to refer to the entire range of mankind, but Kroeber redefined the term to designate the civilizations of Asia, Africa, and Europe that from ancient times to the present day have formed "a great web of cultural growth, areally extensive and rich in content" (Kroeber 1952:392). Ideas and products have been transmitted from one end of this network to the other for thousands of years, and yet stylistically distinctive traditions have continued to exist. The stylistic continuities that distinguish the civilizations of the *Oikoumenê* can be identified in their medical traditions. For example, in *Asian Medical Systems* (Leslie

1976), Manfred Porkert and W. T. Jones contrast fundamental styles of thought in Chinese and Western medicine, though they approach the subject from different methodological perspectives. Also, Gananath Obeyesekere and Alan Beals describe long-enduring South Asian forms of thought, in Obeyesekere's case by analyzing the popular culture of Āyurvedic physicians and their patients in urban Sri Lanka, and in Beals' essay by describing the habits of mind of peasant villagers in Mysore State, India, as they decide to use different kinds of therapy.

I will call the three main streams of learned medical practice and theory that originated in the Chinese, South Asian, and Mediterranean civilizations "great-tradition" medicine – a term derived from Robert Redfield's work on the comparative study of civilizations. Observing that the development of civilizations was characterized by the differentiation of great from little traditions, Redfield described this process as "the separation of culture into hierarchic and lay traditions, the appearance of an elite with secular and sacred power and including specialized cultivators of the intellectual life, and the conversion of tribal peoples into peasantry" (Redfield 1956:76). Illustrating the interdependency of great and little traditions, Redfield speculated that "the teaching of Galen about the four humors may have been suggested by ideas current in little communities of simple people becoming but not yet civilized; after development by reflective minds they may have been received by peasantry and reinterpreted in local terms" (*ibid*: 71).

The first point that I want to make about the great medical traditions is that they maintained their individual characters although they were in contact with each other. The integrity of the separate traditions needs to be emphasized to avoid the assumption that all significant early medical science originated in Greece (or India or China, for that matter). My second point will be that the three traditions nevertheless share general features of social organization and theory that allow us to describe a generic great-tradition medicine which can be contrasted with cosmopolitan medicine.

The Mediterranean tradition was comprehensively formulated by Galen in the second century. It continued in this form through the Middle Ages in Christian and Islamic societies, and was carried by the spread of Islam to Central Asia, India, and Southeast Asia. The system was called *Yunānī Tibbia* in Arabic, meaning Greek medicine, and it is still practiced under that name in Pakistan, India, Sri Lanka, and other South Asian countries. J. Christoph Bürgel (1976) emphasizes the Galenic character of Arabic medicine: it was not significantly influenced by South Asian theories, although Ali al-Tabari was familiar with Indian medical texts as early as the ninth century. Nor, according to Sir Joseph Needham (1970: 14–29), did knowledge of Chinese medicine notably effect the Galenic tradition, though a thirteenth-century Persian physician, Rashid al-din al-Hamadani, directed the preparation of an encyclopedia of Chinese medicine.

Knowledge of the South Asian and Chinese medical traditions was carried through the *Oikoumenê* from the nuclear areas of their development, just as the Mediterranean tradition was carried to distant societies. The South Asian system was called *Āyurveda*, meaning knowledge of life, or longevity. It was known in the Mediterranean region long before the translation of Greek texts into Arabic. Several Hippocratic authors recommended medications that they attributed to India, and Plato's theory of vision – that a fiery element in the eye joined with the corresponding element in things – resembled that of Āyurveda, as did some details of his conceptions of illness and of anatomy (Filliozat 1964: 229–237). The diffusion of Buddhism from India to China was certainly accompanied by exchanges of Āyurvedic and Chinese medical knowledge, yet Chinese medicine had no discernible effect on the development of Āyurveda, and Joseph Needham maintains that the overall influence of Indian on Chinese medicine was minor. Evaluating the relation of Chinese medicine to Greek and Arabic tradition, Needham writes: "It is really hard to find in it any Western influences" (1970: 18–19). On the other hand, Chinese medicine strongly affected medical institutions in Korea, Japan, and parts of Southeast Asia, and Āyurveda had a marked influence in Tibet, Burma, and Southeast Asia.

Although the three great medical traditions were relatively independent, they evolved in similar ways. They all became professional branches of scientific learning in the millennium between the fifth century BC and the fifth century AD. Professional standards for education and practice were achieved by appeals to the authority of Galen, Caraka, the *Nei Ching*, and other highly respected texts. Since rational theories and therapeutic formulas were elaborated in the texts far beyond the knowledge of laymen and folk curers, the ability to show acquaintance with them validated claims to a superior social position. Claims to high status were symbolically expressed in special modes of dress and deportment recommended by the texts, and they were rationalized by ethical codes that defined a physician's responsibilities.

Women were not educated in medicine, and the perspective of the classic texts was masculine. Practitioners ranged from physicians who had undergone long periods of training to individuals with little education who practiced a simplified version of the great tradition. Other healers coexisted with these practitioners, their arts falling into special categories: bone-setters, surgeons, midwives, snake-bite curers, shamans, and so on. But the complex and redundant system of learned and humble practitioners, of full-time and part-time practitioners, of generalists and specialists, of naturalist and supernaturalist curers, was ideologically simplified by the distinction elaborated in the texts between quacks and legitimate practitioners. The concern the texts show for this distinction indicates that society assigned learned physicians a lower social status than the one that they aspired to, and that their power to dominate the overall system of medical practice was limited.

The Chinese may have led in rationalizing medical services, for they developed an extensive bureaucratic system to instruct and examine physicians, along with what, according to Joseph Needham and Lu Gwei-djen, "can only be described as a national medical service" (1969:268). But in all of these societies, armies required organized medical services, rulers acted as patrons to medical scholarship, and

medical aid was a philanthropic enterprise appropriate to religious institutions and to wealthy individuals. Needham's discussion of Chinese priorities is directed toward correcting the biases that have caused Western writers on the history and philosophy of science to focus on why the Scientific Revolution occurred in seventeenth-century Europe. The framework in which this question is asked sometimes resembles that of a believer in witchcraft who confronts the death of an old man with the question, "Why did it happen on Tuesday?" The fact that the Scientific Revolution first occurred in Europe is taken by Europeans as *a priori* evidence that the Western tradition possessed a genius for scientific progress lacking in the Chinese and Indian traditions. Thus it is possible to question the orientation – shared by Needham as much as by those he criticizes – that makes temporal priority a predominant issue.

Besides resembling each other in the organization of practice, the great traditions of medicine were formulated from generic physiological and cosmological concepts. All of them were humoral theories: four humors in the Mediterranean tradition (yellow bile, black bile, phlegm, and blood); three humors in the South Asian tradition (*kapha*, *pitta*, and *vayu*, usually translated as phlegm, bile, and wind); and six humors in Chinese medicine (the *chii*, or pneuma, which were held in the sway of *yang* and *yin*). The humors were alignments of opposing qualities: hot-cold, wet-dry, heavy-light, male-female, dark-bright, strong-weak, active-sluggish, and so on. The equilibrium of these qualities maintained health, and their disequilibrium caused illness, whatever the number of humors. Equilibrium was regulated by an individual's age, sex, and temperament in dynamic relationship to climate, season, food consumption, and other activities. Diagnoses required skill in observing and correlating physical symptoms and environment. Therapy utilized physical manipulations, modification of the patient's diet and surroundings, and numerous medications. Some medications required elaborate preparation; others, valuable and esoteric substances such as herbs gathered from distant mountainsides, saffron, gold, precious stones, or parts of rare animals.

Finally, great-tradition medicine conceived human anatomy and physiology to be intimately bound to other physical systems. The arrangement and balance of elements in the human body were microcosmic versions of their arrangement in society at large and throughout the universe. Sir Charles Sherrington's description of the world view of Jean Fernel, a physician in sixteenth-century Paris, applies equally to Chinese or Hindu physicians: "The macrocosm fulfilling its vast circuits and epicycles of meticulous precision, its rising and its settings, its movements within movements, was an immense body fashioned after the likeness of man's body" (1955:61). This conception rationalized the relation of men to their environment by making preventive and curative medicine efforts to maintain or to restore cosmic equilibrium.

At the end of the Middle Ages, scientific research and forms of professional association in Europe began a development which led eventually to the worldwide traditions of cosmopolitan medicine. Mixed with new knowledge, humoral theories and practices continued to be taught through the nineteenth century, and remnants of humoral theory survive in research to the present day. For example, studies that classify people by their body types, and correlate this typology with variations in behavior or in susceptibility to illness, are in the humoral tradition. Practitioners in India who argue that ancient scientific theories can be employed in modern research are correct when they claim that studies of body types by European and American scientists use concepts that resemble fundamental ideas in Âyurvedic medicine.

The scientific theories and social organization of cosmopolitan medicine evolved progressively over several centuries without significant practical consequences for patients. They developed with the expansion of Europe, the rise of modern science, the Industrial Revolution, and other movements that since the Middle Ages have been transforming the *Oikoumenê* of Old World civilizations into a world order. Research on anatomy and physiology during the Renaissance and Reformation generated new methods of scientific work and discovered facts that seemed to invalidate ancient medical authorities (Nef 1967:286–298). Associations of practitioners and government agencies were formed to sponsor and regulate medical services. The institutional network for teaching, research, and publication expanded around the world and became more efficient. But the great advances in therapeutic effectiveness that have become the hallmark of cosmopolitan medicine — the germ theory of disease and new surgical techniques – were not initiated until the late nineteenth century, followed by twentieth-century progress in chemotherapy. These advances, by radically increasing the consequences of medical learning for social welfare, have accelerated the professionalization processes that are creating throughout the world medical systems based upon a standardized university education for physicians. Professionalization also involves special courses of training for dentists, nurses, and numerous paramedical workers; the bureaucratic organization of medical work, dominated by physicians and centered in hospitals; state responsibility for environmental medicine and for organizing or supervising medical services, with the distribution of authority throughout the system enforced by state powers to license and regulate all forms of medical practice.

Another feature of cosmopolitan medicine has been called its "preeminence." Eliot Freidson writes:

If we consider the profession of medicine today, it is clear that its major characteristic is preeminence. Such preeminence is not merely that of prestige but also that of expert authority. This is to say, medicine's knowledge about illness and its treatment is considered to be authoritative and definitive. While there are interesting exceptions like chiropractic and homeopathy, there are no representatives of occupations in direct competition with medicine who hold official policy-making positions related to health affairs. Medicine's position today is akin to that of state religious yesterday – it has an officially approved monopoly of the right to define health and illness and to treat illness. (1970:5)

The ways in which cosmopolitan medicine progressively subordinates other forms of practice are major variables for the comparative study of medical systems. A necessary condition appears to be the respect people in all social classes have for the recent capacity of this system to generate effective new therapies, and a necessary means is the use of state power to legitimize and extend its authority. Among the upper classes everywhere in the world, and among all social strata in industrial societies, doctors now play a crucial role in episodes of birth, illness, and death. And in law and popular culture, the theories and institutions of cosmopolitan medicine define standards of health and abnormality that shape the ways people think and feel about themselves and about the norms for social conduct.

Access to medical knowledge and to consultation with specialists is another critical variable for comparing medical systems. Peasants and tribal peoples as well as urban dwellers admire the technology of cosmopolitan medicine and are eager to adopt new medications. At the same time, the abrupt manners of most physicians and paramedical workers when they deal with rural and lower-class people are resented, and in communities where these specialists are outsiders, resistance to their authority usually expresses class conflict. In this situation, indigenous practitioners adopt whatever seems useful and is available to them from cosmopolitan medicine. Laymen consult these eclectic practitioners of traditional and modern therapies, and only in emergencies risk the possible humiliation, the expense, and the other difficulties of gaining access to fully trained practitioners of cosmopolitan medicine. The data, if not always the interpretations, of earlier studies support these generalizations.

What I have been calling cosmopolitan medicine is usually called alternatively "modern medicine," or "scientific medicine,"or "Western medicine." Translations of these terms are widely used in Asian languages, along with other labels: Dutch medicine, English medicine, allopathy, doctor medicine, and so on. Fred Dunn (1976) calls attention in his essay to the biases associated with this usage and suggests the new designation "cosmopolitan medicine," which I have adopted. Dunn's

skepticism about current habits of mind deserves elaboration.

The term "modern medicine," used in contrast to traditional medicine, encourages the user to confuse inferences from the modernity–traditionalism dichotomy with reality. For example, the dichotomy opposes the changing and creative nature of modernity to an assumed stagnant and unchanging traditionalism, but acquaintance with historical documents and with the contemporary medical institutions labeled "traditional" reveals that considerable change has occurred in the last century, and that medicine like everything else has been changing throughout the past. The dichotomy implies that practitioners of traditional medicine are uniformly conservative and reject opportunities to acquire new knowledge, and yet the limited evidence at hand indicates that the opposite situation prevails. Within the resources available to them, many folk practitioners are innovative, and they have certainly been eager to gain new skills. This has also been true among the educated urban practitioners of great-tradition medicine. In Japan the physicians who practice Chinese medicine must be qualified in cosmopolitan medicine. In China the extensive use of traditional medicine in a modern system of health services has attracted worldwide attention. The system of colleges, research institutes, and other facilities for humoral medicine in India has been created by entrepreneural practitioners of traditional medicine, and by their patrons in politics, industry, and other modern occupations (Brass 1972; Leslie 1973). Thus when the term "modern medicine" is used in describing systems that include a large component of traditional medicine, it evokes stereotypes that contradict reality. These stereotypes tempt the advocates of modernity to lapse unconsciously into a self-flattering rhetoric that fights windmills of recalcitrant medical ignorance and superstition.

The term "scientific medicine" is also misleading. It encourages the assumption that all aspects of cosmopolitan medicine are somehow derived from or conducive to science, but by any ordinary criteria many elements in this system are not scientific – for example, the politics of research funding or of professional associations, various routines of hospital administration, or the etiquette of doctor–patient relationships. A second and equally stultifying assumption is that all medicine other than cosmopolitan medicine is unscientific. By commonly recognized criteria, Chinese, Āyurvedic, and Arabic medicine are scientific in substantial degrees. They involve the rational use of naturalistic theories to organize and interpret systematic empirical observations. They have explicit, orderly ways of recording and teaching this knowledge, and they have some efficacious methods for promoting health and for curing illness. Of course, by other criteria, such as the degree of instrumentation and standardization of techniques, or the refinement of experimental methods, these systems are less scientific. In objective comparative research, judgments about the scientific character of medical theories and practices vary because multiple criteria exist for calling them scientific, and because most criteria specify elements that may be more or less well developed. Recognition of the need to evolve conceptual models and to record data for the complex analyses that this subject requires is discouraged by preemptively labeling one set of institutions "scientific medicine."

Finally, the term "Western medicine" is misleading for obvious reasons. The scientific aspects of Western medicine are transcultural. Ethnic interpretations of modern science are the aberrations of nationalistic and totalitarian ideologies or, in this case, a reflex of colonial and neo-colonial thought. Furthermore, the social organization of cosmopolitan medicine as I have described it is as Japanese as it is Western. Because modern science and professionalization processes are intrinsically cosmopolitan, Fred Dunn's phrase "cosmopolitan medicine" is appropriate. Still, Croizier Ralph (1976) tells us that the Chinese referred to their own tradition simply as medicine, and began self-consciously to call it "Chinese" only in modern times as they adopted the contrasting term "Western medicine." Since ethnographic and historical descriptions benefit by using categories of the cultures they describe, it makes sense to use these terms in writing about modern China. For similar reasons, descriptive accounts of other Asian medical systems may

continue to refer to Western medicine. But for comparative purposes another term is needed, and the model that I have outlined in the preceding pages is best referred to as "cosmopolitan medicine."

The picture I have drawn of the great medical traditions formed in the *Oikoumenê* of Old World civilizations, and of the recent full emergence of cosmopolitan medicine, brings the subject of *Asian Medical Systems* in view. Let me restate it briefly. In countries like the United States or Japan, cosmopolitan medicine is preeminent: its representatives dominate medical work and exercise unprecedented legal and cultural authority to define situations and make decisions during birth, illness, and death, as well as to shape norms for sexual conduct, child rearing, or questions of sanity. Although cosmopolitan medical institutions exist in every country, most people alive today continue to depend on humoral theories and practices. In large parts of Asia, educated practitioners still draw upon these traditions and, with folk practitioners, provide a major source of medical care. Thus, great and little medical traditions coexist to various degrees and in various ways with cosmopolitan medicine in China, India, Japan, and other countries. Analyses of these variations are avenues to understanding the role of scientific knowledge and professional organization in transformations of the human condition.

I have defined the subject of our essays in language suited to their scholarly spirit, but my tone has been too cool to indicate the nature of our enterprise. *Asian Medical Systems* began in a castle on a mountain in Austria. Ours was the fifty-third Burg Wartenstein Symposium sponsored by the Wenner-Gren Foundation for Anthropological Research. Our aim was to develop new lines of research in medical anthropology, some of which the Foundation had initiated in previous symposia (Galdston 1963 and Poynter 1969). Preliminary drafts of our essays were circulated prior to our discussions, which lasted from July 19 to 27, 1971. Lita Osmundsen, Director of Research for the Foundation, lifted the spirit of the Symposium by participating in it, and by orchestrating arrangements for it to proceed in elegant informality through meals and intermissions and entertainments. We were honored, too, by Raymond and Rosemary Firth, who visited the castle briefly during the Symposium.

Had we been members of a single discipline or nationality, our discussions might have generated more disputes than they did. Most of us arrived at Burg Wartenstein knowing nothing or very little about most other members of the Symposium. We had a great deal to learn from and about each other, and we spent no time at all drawing intellectual boundaries. Initially our focus was substantive rather than methodological. This will sound dull to methodologists, and downright anemic to polemicists for whom the good guys wear white hats and the bad guys wear black. In fact, as the Symposium progressed we returned continuously to conceptual differences that caused some of us to think that others of us were naive or dogmatic or fuzzy-minded. Our guide in clarifying these disagreements was the philosopher W. T. Jones, whose message was that we did not have to agree on most theoretical issues so long as we understood how we differed. It worked because he showed us our commonalities and analyzed our differences with authority and good humor.

I will describe some of the differences that emerged in our thinking about the systemic properties of "the medical system." We had not been asked to develop a particular model for this purpose, though the titles of the Symposium and of its various sessions and their constituent papers provided guidelines for our discussions. Mark Field and Edward Montgomery addressed the issue directly, but all of the papers reasoned from general concepts of the system that they were reporting. Since they have been revised for publication and speak for themselves in the following pages, I will describe our conceptual differences in a schematic manner.

In human affairs, concepts never simply name and describe things without implying or recommending evaluations of them. The preeminence of cosmopolitan medicine in a country like the United States causes laymen and specialists alike to identify its professional institutions with *the* medical system. All other practices are then considered to be irregular, and thus to be aberrations of the system or

altogether outside of it. To some members of the Symposium, the model of a uniform cosmopolitan medical system with a monopoly of legitimate practice seemed more scientific and efficient and therefore truer and more desirable than a pluralistic model, which from their perspective appeared to legitimize quack medicine, or at least to tolerate and romanticize medical ignorance.

In fact, medical systems are pluralistic structures of different kinds of practitioners and institutional norms. Even in the United States, the medical system is composed of physicians, dentists, druggists, clinical psychologists, chiropractors, social workers, health food experts, masseurs, yoga teachers, spirit curers, Chinese herbalists, and so on. The health concepts of a Puerto Rican worker in New York city, the curers he consults, and the therapies he receives, differ from those of a Chinese laundryman or a Jewish clerk. Their concepts and the practitioners they consult differ in turn from those of middle-class believers in Christian Science or in logical positivism. Yet the institutions of cosmopolitan medicine are so extensive, well organized, and powerful, that the concept of a single, standardized, hieratic medical system administered by university-trained physicians appears to be normative in American popular culture, as well as in law. Since this is not true in Asian countries, where the structures of learned and folk, of humoral and cosmopolitan medicine are coexisting normative institutions, members of the symposium who reasoned from a pluralistic model felt that they were more objective – because less chauvinistic – than those who assumed the norms of a cosmopolitan medical model.

Another disagreement that emerged at our conference is related to different conceptions of cultural organization. Some participants conceived the systemic qualities of "the medical system" by using concepts of standardization and consistency derived from the ideal of mass culture. When Asian respondents differed among themselves in classifying items of food as belonging to "hot" or "cold" categories, or simultaneously used medicines associated with different ways of defining a malady, their ideas and behavior were interpreted as having a low degree of systematization. Other members of the Symposium saw variations of this kind as an essential dimension of the systems under consideration rather than evidence that they were disorganized. They interpreted categories of food and illness, or of the causes of illness and kinds of therapy, as a rhetoric for defining situations, deciding what to do, and justifying one or another course of action. If the categories were fixed and inflexible they could not be used for these purposes.

A third source of disagreement concerned ways of drawing the boundaries of a medical system. Indeed, the format of the Symposium encouraged the use of conceptual models derived from three approaches to this problem, which for convenience can be labeled biological, cultural, and social.

From the point of view of the biological approach, all ideas and behavior that the trained observer finds relevant to interpreting patterns of health and illness are considered to be part of the medical system. Thus behavioral epidemiology, which would analyze such things as the relationships between customary diet or working habits and disease vectors, would be important for developing comparative studies of medical systems. This inclusive conception of the systems under study has the advantage of emphasizing research goals that will be useful to health planners trained in cosmopolitan medicine. By using the best current knowledge in ecology, nutrition, pathology, and other subjects, it provides standards for comparing the health conditions and the utility of health practices in different societies. In contrast, the cultural approach conceives the medical system to be composed of deliberate actions, by members of a society, to maintain or enhance health and to cure illness. This way of thinking about the system emphasizes categories of thought and traditions within the culture. It excludes many ideas, items of behavior, and ecological relationships that the first approach includes. It emphasizes such things as a mother's self-conscious efforts to promote her child's health by regulating its diet. The social approach to conceiving the medical system would exclude the mother's behavior and conceptions of health and illness until she decided to consult another individual recognized in her community as a specialist. This conception locates the system in the role relationships between people who have reputations as authorities in matters of health and illness, and between these specialists and laymen.

Though our differential preferences for one or another of these approaches did not logically entail disagreements, they did cause us to have different feelings about what was interesting or important in our discussions. But even those who shared a preference for one approach would differ on other grounds. For example, those who used the cultural approach would locate the systemic nature of a medical tradition in the coherence of its theories, and reason that it was the integrity of the theory that held practices together in a medical system. One might argue that Chinese medicine was an integrated system in the past, whereas contemporary physicians who were supposedly working in the tradition did not understand the theories as they were previously understood, or believe in them in the way that they were once believed in. Thus contemporary practices appeared to be an opportunistic or non-systematic set of behaviors. But another student of Chinese tradition would disagree with this conception of history and of the relationship between medical theory and practice; while a third might agree with the general concept but disagree about how to evaluate evidence that the theories of Chinese medicine are now misunderstood or disbelieved.

In general, it is fair to report that those members of the Symposium who focused on the historical continuities in Asian medical systems, and on the systemic qualities of contemporary great and little traditions, appeared "romantic" and "theoretical" to those who emphasized historical discontinuities and who argued that the pluralistic, structurally differentiated Asian medical systems show a low degree of systematization. Of course, the participants who thought that others were "romantic" felt that their own perspective was "realistic" and "pragmatic."

Although I have only briefly described the methodological issues that emerged during our conference, enough has been said to indicate their nature. Our collection of essays as a whole has been designed to show how the comparative study of Asian medical systems opens a new field of scholarship. Such a book required the skills of authors with diverse kinds of training. Those who have contributed to it are trained in history, sociology, anthropology, public health, pharmacology, epidemiology, cosmopolitan medicine, and philosophy. One is a practitioner of Chinese medicine, and two are the sons of Āyurvedic physicians. My task has been to define the subject and to indicate concepts that join our individual essays in a unified dialogue. Our work will have been well done if others find in it both something to correct and something to build upon.

REFERENCES

Brass, Paul
1972 "The Politics of Āyurvedic Education: A Case Study of Revivalism and modernization in India," in Lloyd and Susanne Rudolph, eds., *Politics and Education in India*. Cambridge: Harvard University Press.

Bürgel, J. Christoph
1976 "Secular and Religious Features of Medieval Arabic Medicine," in Charles Leslie, ed. *Asian Medical Systems*. Pp. 44–62. Berkeley: University of California Press.

Croizier, Ralph C.
1976 "The Ideology of Medical Revivalism in Modern China," in Charles Leslie, ed. *Asian Medical Systems*. Pp. 341–55. Berkeley: University of California Press.

Dunn, Fred L.
1976 "Traditional Asian Medicine and Cosmopolitan Medicine as Adaptive Systems," in Charles Leslie, ed. *Asian Medical Systems*. Pp. 133–58. Berkeley: University of California Press.

Filliozat, Jean
1964 *The Classical Doctrine of Indian Medicine*. Delhi: Munshi Manoharlal.

Freidson, Eliot
1970 *The Profession of Medicine: A Study of the Sociology of Applied Knowledge*. New York: Dodd, Mead.

Galdston, Iago
1969 *Man's Image in Medicine and Anthropology*. New York: International Universities Press.

Kroeber, Alfred Louis
1952 *The Nature of Culture*. Chicago: University of Chicago Press.

Leslie, Charles
1973 "The Professionalizing Ideology of Medical Revivalism," in Milton Singer, ed., *Entrepreneurship and Modernization of Occupational Cultures in South Asia*. Durham: Duke University Press.

Leslie, Charles
1976 *Asian Medical Systems*. Berkeley: University of California Press.

Needham, Joseph
1970 *Clerks and Craftsmen in China and the West*. Cambridge: Cambridge University Press.

Needham, Joseph, and Lu Gwei-djen
1969 "Chinese Medicine," in F.N.L. Poynter, ed., *Medicine and Culture*. London: Wellcome Institute of the History of Medicine.

Nef, John U.
1967 *The Conquest of the Material World*. Cleveland: World.

Poynter, F. N. L.
1969 *Medicine and Culture*. London: Wellcome Institute of the History of Medicine.

Redfield, Robert
1956 *Peasant Society and Culture*. Chicago: University of Chicago Press.

Sherrington, Charles
1955 *Man on His Nature*. Garden City: Doubleday (Anchor).

8

Medical Anthropology and the Problem of Belief

Byron J. Good

[...]

I begin with an intuition that there is a close relationship between science, including medicine, and religious fundamentalism that turns, in part, on our concept "belief." For fundamentalist Christians, salvation follows from belief, and mission work is conceived as an effort to convince the unbelievers to take on a set of beliefs that will produce a new life and ultimate salvation. Ironically, quite a-religious scientists and policy makers see a similar benefit from correct belief. Educate the public about the hazards of drug use, our current Enlightenment theory goes, get people to believe the right thing and the problem will disappear. Educate the patient, medical journals advise clinicians, and solve the problems of noncompliance that plague the treatment of chronic disease. Investigate public beliefs about vaccinations or risky health behaviors using the Health Belief Model, a generation of health psychologists has told us, get people to believe the right thing and our public health problems will resolve. Salvation from drugs and from preventable illness will follow from correct belief.

Wilfred Cantwell Smith, a comparative historian of religion and theologian, argues that the fundamentalist conception of belief is a recent Christian heresy (Smith 1977, 1979). I want to explore the hypothesis that anthropology has shared this heresy with religious fundamentalists, that "belief" has a distinctive cultural history within anthropology and that the conceptualization of culture as "belief" is far from a trivial matter.

A quick review of the history of medical anthropology will convince the reader that "belief" has played a particularly important analytic role in this subdiscipline, as it has in the medical behavioral sciences and in public health. Why is there this deep attachment to analyzing others' understandings of illness and its treatment as medical "beliefs" and practices, and why is there such urgency expressed about correcting beliefs when mistaken? To begin to address this issue, I first describe the general theoretical paradigm that frames what I have referred to as the "empiricist theory of medical knowledge." I will indicate its relationship to the intellectualist tradition in anthropology and to debates about rationality and relativism, showing how the language of belief functions within the rationalist tradition. At the end of this chapter, I review recent criticisms that have shaken the foundations of this paradigm, criticisms that suggest the need for an alternative

Byron J. Good, "Medical Anthropology and the Problem of Belief," pp. 1–24 *[modified]* in *Medicine, Rationality and Experience*. Cambridge: Cambridge University Press, 1994. Reprinted by permission of Cambridge University Press.

direction in the field. This discussion will serve to frame the constructive chapters that follow.

The language of clinical medicine is a highly technical language of the biosciences, grounded in a natural science view of the relation between language, biology, and experience (B. Good and M. Good 1981). As George Engel (1977) and a host of medical reformers have shown, the "medical model" typically employed in clinical practice and research assumes that diseases are universal biological or psychophysiological entities, resulting from somatic lesions or dysfunctions. These produce "signs" or physiological abnormalities that can be measured by clinical and laboratory procedures, as well as "symptoms" or expressions of the experience of distress, communicated as an ordered set of complaints. The primary tasks of clinical medicine are thus diagnosis – that is, the interpretation of the patient's symptoms by relating them to their functional and structural sources in the body and to underlying disease entities – and rational treatment aimed at intervention in the disease mechanisms. All subspecialties of clinical medicine thus share a distinctive medical "hermeneutic," an implicit understanding of medical interpretation. While patients' symptoms may be coded in cultural language, the primary interpretive task of the clinician is to decode patients' symbolic expressions in terms of their underlying somatic referents. Disordered experience, communicated in the language of culture, is interpreted in light of disordered physiology and yields medical diagnoses.

[...] The empiricist theory of medical language is grounded in what philosopher Charles Taylor (1985a, 1985b, 1989) calls "the polemical, no-nonsense nominalism" of Enlightenment theories of language and meaning. For seventeenth-century philosophers such as Hobbes and Locke, the development of a language for science required a demystification of language itself, showing it to be a pliant instrument of rationality and thought, as well as the emergence of a disenchanted view of the natural world. The development of such a natural philosophy and the attendant theory of language required the separation of "the order of words" from "the order of things," in Foucault's terms (1970), the freeing of the order of language and symbols from a world of hierarchical planes of being and correspondences present in Renaissance cosmology. What we must seek, Francis Bacon argued, is not to identify ideas or meanings in the universe, but "to build an adequate representation of things" (Taylor 1985a: 249). Thus, theories of language became the battle ground between the religious orthodoxy, who conceived "nature" as reflecting God's creative presence and language as a source of divine revelation, and those who viewed the world as natural and language as conventional and instrumental. What emerged was a conception of language in which *representation* and *designation* are exceedingly important attributes. [...]

This broad perspective has the status of a "folk epistemology" for medical practice in hospitals and clinics of contemporary biomedicine. A person's complaint is meaningful if it reflects a physiological condition; if no such empirical referent can be found, the very meaningfulness of the complaint is called into question. Such complaints (for example of chronic pain – see M. Good et al. 1992) are often held to reflect patients' beliefs or psychological states, that is subjective opinions and experiences which may have no grounds in disordered physiology and thus in objective reality. "Real pathology," on the other hand, reflects disordered physiology. Contemporary technical medicine provides objective knowledge of such pathology, represented as a straight-forward and transparent reflection of the natural order revealed through the dense semiotic system of physical findings, laboratory results, and the visual products of contemporary imaging techniques. And "rational behavior" is that which is oriented in relation to such objective knowledge.

[...]

Rationality and the Empiricist Paradigm in Anthropology

The empiricist paradigm is most clearly represented by the intellectualist tradition in anthropology, which was prominent in Britain at the turn of the century and reemerged under the banner of Neo-Tylorianism in an important set of debates about the nature of rationality during the 1970s.[1] Even a cursory examination will indicate how the rationalist position flows out of the "Enlightenment" tradition of anthropology, demonstrate the critical role of "belief" in this paradigm, and suggest why it has had such power within medical anthropology.

A central issue in the rationality debate has been discussion of the problem of "apparently irrational beliefs" (for example Sperber 1985: ch. 2). How do we make sense of cultural views of the world that are not in accord with contemporary natural sciences, it is often asked. Do we argue that members of traditional cultures live in wholly different worlds, and their statements are true in their worlds, not ours, or even that they cannot be translated intelligibly into our language? Advocates of a typical rationalist position hold that such relativism is essentially incoherent, and have often argued either that seemingly irrational statements must be understood symbolically rather than literally or that they represent a kind of "proto-science," an effort to explain events in the world in an orderly fashion that is a functional equivalent of modern science. The crucial interpretive problem, for this tradition, is how to answer a question stated explicitly by Lukes (1970: 194): "When I come across a set of beliefs which appear *prima facie* irrational, what should be my attitude toward them?" Given our claims that other forms of thought are rational, how do we make sense of beliefs that are obviously false?

For much of this debate, Evans-Pritchard's *Witchcraft, Oracles and Magic among the Azande* (1937) serves as the primary source. This book was the first and is arguably still the most important modernist text in medical anthropology. It has had enduring influence because of the wealth of the ethnography and the richness of its interpretation of witchcraft as an explanation for illness and misfortune. Which anthropologist can think of cultural responses to misfortune without conjuring the image of Evans-Pritchard's young lad stubbing his toe and blaming witchcraft for its failure to heal, or of the granary collapsing? To these misfortunes, the Zande explanation was clear. "Every Zande knows that termites eat the

supports [of the granaries] in course of time and that even the hardest woods decay after years of service," Evans-Pritchard reports. But "why should these particular people have been sitting under this particular granary at the particular moment when it collapsed?" Thus, although practical reasons explain the immediate causes of illness and misfortune, the Azande turn to witchcraft to answer the "why me?" question, to find an underlying cause in the moral universe and a response that is socially embedded and morally satisfying.

The Azande text has been the key for the rationality debate for another reason. Evans-Pritchard in this text was explicitly empiricist, and his work provided examples that serve as paradigmatic challenges to relativism. Take, for example, his analysis of the Zande autopsy to investigate witchcraft, which appears as a substance in the intestine of a witch. Since witchcraft is inherited by kin, an autopsy may be performed on a deceased kinsman to determine whether others bear the unwanted substance. Evans-Pritchard (1937: 42) describes the scene:

> Two lateral gashes are made in the belly and one end of the intestines is placed in a cleft branch and they are wound round it. After the other end has been severed from the body another man takes it and unwinds the intestines as he walks away from the man holding the cleft branch. The old men walk alongside the entrails as they are stretched in the air and examine them for witchcraft-substance. The intestines are usually replaced in the belly when the examination is finished and the corpse is buried. I have been told that if no witchcraft-substance were discovered in a man's belly his kinsmen might strike his accusers in the face with his intestines or might dry them in the sun and afterwards take them to court and there boast of their victory.

Evans-Pritchard's (1937: 63) interpretation of this dramatic scene is telling.

> It is an inevitable conclusion from Zande descriptions of witchcraft that it is not an objective reality. The physiological condition which is said to be the seat of witchcraft, and which I believe to be nothing more than food passing through the small intestine, is an objective

condition, but the qualities they attribute to it and the rest of their beliefs about it are mystical. Witches, as Azande conceive them, cannot exist.

He goes on immediately to argue that although mistaken, the Zande views serve as a natural philosophy and embrace a system of values which regulate human conduct. They are, however, mystical. "Mystical notions," he argues in the book's introduction (p. 12), are those that attribute to phenomena "supra-sensible qualities," "which are not derived from observation" and "which they do not possess." "Common-sense notions" attribute to phenomena only what can be observed in them or logically inferred from observation. Though they may be mistaken, they do not assert forces that cannot be observed. Both are distinct from "scientific notions." "Our body of scientific knowledge and Logic," he says (p. 12), "are the sole arbiters of what are mystical, common-sense, and scientific notions."

Evans-Pritchard assumes in this account that the meaning of Zande "medical discourse" – whether of witchcraft, oracles, or "leechcraft" – is constituted by its referential relationship to the natural order as reflected in empirical experience. Analysis in the rationality literature follows from this assumption; it frames Zande beliefs as propositions, then questions the verifiability and the deductive validity of their inferences. Since we know that witches cannot exist empirically, it is argued, the rationality of Zande thought is called into doubt. It follows that the anthropologist must therefore organize analysis in response to the following kinds of questions. How can a set of beliefs and institutions which are so obviously false (propositionally) be maintained for such long periods of time by persons who in much of their lives are so reasonable? How could they possibly believe that, and why haven't their beliefs progressed, that is come to represent the natural world more correctly? Do such beliefs imply that the Zande have a different "mentality" or different psychological or logical processes than we? Do they simply divide up the common-sense and religious domains differently than

do we (as Evans-Pritchard responded to Lévy-Bruhl)? Are some societies simply organized around views that are reasonable but wrong?

Not altogether obvious in Evans-Pritchard's text is the juxtaposition of "belief" and "knowledge." The book is devoted largely to Zande mystical notions – witchcraft and sorcery – and ritual behaviors, such as resort to the poison oracle. One chapter, however, entitled "Leechcraft," is devoted to their common-sense notions of sickness. The language of "belief" and "knowledge" mirror this distinction. The book begins: "Azande *believe* that some people are witches and can injure them in virtue of an inherent quality ... They *believe* also that sorcerers may do them ill by performing magic rites with bad medicines ... Against both they employ diviners, oracles, and medicines. The relations between these *beliefs* and rites are the subject of this book" (p. 21; my emphasis). On the other hand, the Leechcraft chapter argues: "Azande *know* diseases by their major symptoms" (p. 482). "The very fact of naming diseases and differentiating them from one another by their symptoms shows observation and common-sense inferences" (pp. 494–5). Thus, the book is organized around a distinction between those ideas that accord with objective reality [...] and those that do not; the language of knowledge is used to describe the former, the language of belief the latter. Evans-Pritchard's text transcends its empiricist formulation, in particular because of the subtlety of its analysis of Zande reasoning and the location of witchcraft in Zande social relations, but it makes explicit many of the assumptions found more generally in the rationality tradition and shared by much of the medical social sciences.

If Evans-Pritchard's work on the Azande is the classic modernist text on witchcraft and illness, Jeanne Favret-Saada's *Deadly Words: Witchcraft in the Bocage* (1980), first published in French in 1977, is surely the classic post-modernist ethnography on the topic. Favret-Saada's ethnography is a first-person account of her effort to investigate witchcraft in rural France. In the early months of her work, villagers referred her to a few well known healers who were often interviewed by the press, but the peasants themselves refused to discuss the matter with her. Witchcraft? Only fools believe in that!

> "Take an ethnographer," she begins (1980: 4). "She has spent more than thirty months in the Bocage in Mayenne, studying witchcraft ... 'Tell us about the witches', she is asked again and again when she gets back to the city. Just as one might say: tell us tales about ogres or wolves, about Little Red Riding Hood. Frighten us, but make it clear that it's only a story; or that they are just peasants: credulous, backward and marginal ...
>
> "No wonder that country people in the West are not in any hurry to step forward and be taken for idiots in the way that public opinion would have them be ..."

The book is an account of how she eventually found her way into the discourse of witchcraft. She was taken ill, beset with accidents, and sought the aid of a healer in the region, an unwitcher. She began to interview a man and his family, whom she had met when the man was a patient in a mental hospital. As they told her the details of his illness and who they suspected might be responsible, she realized that they saw her as a healer and now expected her to act on their behalf. Why else would she ask about such matters so explicitly? Only the powerful would dare to ask such questions. Simply by asking about their difficulties, she was seen to be entering into their struggle with an enemy wishing them harm, a life and death struggle in which she was now an advocate for their interests. Witchcraft, she came to see, was a battle of powerful wills, a fight to the death, a fight through the medium of spoken words. One could only talk about witchcraft from an engaged position – as one bewitched, as a suspected witch, or as one willing to serve as unwitcher. To engage in talk was to enter the struggle.

In Favret-Saada's account, the language of belief, the position of the ethnographer, and assumptions about the relation of culture and reality are radically different than in Evans-Pritchard's text. Science for Favret-Saada is not the arbiter between the empirically real and the mystical, as for Evans-Pritchard, but one of several "official theories of misfortune," backed by powerful social agencies: the School, the Church, the Medical Association. Language is not a set of neutral propositions about the world, which the ethnographer judges to be more or less empirically valid, but the medium through which vicious and life-threatening power struggles are engaged. The world of illness and witchcraft only opens to the ethnographer as she enters the discourse. And much of the text turns on ironic reflections on "belief" – the peasants' claims not to believe in witchcraft, even as they seek the help of the unwitcher; the mocking view of the authorities about those who do believe; and Favret-Saada's juxtaposition of the meaning of belief in her text and in that of Evans-Pritchard. For many ethnographers, as for the French press, the question is whether the peasants really believe in witchcraft, and if so, how they can hold such beliefs in today's world. But for those attacked by a sorcerer, for those peasants – and Favret-Saada herself – whose very lives were at stake, *belief* in witchcraft is not the question. How to protect oneself, how to ward off the evil attacks producing illness and misfortune, is the only significant issue to be addressed.

Much has changed in the world of anthropology between that of 1935 colonialist Africa and contemporary post-colonialist ethnography. Evans-Pritchard's confident positioning of himself as observer and arbiter of the rationality of the native discourse is largely unavailable to us today. And throughout the history and sociology of science, the confident recording of science's progress in discovering the facts of nature has also given way. I will return to these issues as the discussion proceeds, but the juxtaposition of Evans-Pritchard's and Favret-Saada's texts brings into focus the role of "belief" as an analytic category in the history of anthropology and in the study of such phenomena as witchcraft, provoking several questions. Why has the discussion of others' beliefs come to be invoked increasingly with irony? What is the role of belief in the empiricist paradigm, and why has that position begun to give way? Where does the disjunction between "belief" and "knowledge," which I noted in *Witchcraft, Oracles, and Magic* and which serves as the basis for

Favret-Saada's irony, come from? Why "belief," and what is at stake here?

The Problem of Belief in Anthropology

Rodney Needham's *Belief, Language and Experience*, published in 1972, is the classic examination of the philosophy of belief by an anthropologist. Needham explores in great detail assumptions about belief as mental state, asking whether philosophers have formulated this with adequate clarity to allow us to use the term in cross-cultural research, and asking whether members of other societies indeed experience what we call "belief." After an extraordinary review, he concludes both that philosophers have failed to clarify "the supposed capacity for belief" and are unlikely to do so, and that evidence suggests the term may well not have counterparts in the ethnopsychological language of many societies. Needham's analysis suggests that Evans-Pritchard's claim that the Azande believe some people are witches may be a less straightforward description of the mental states of Zande individuals than we usually presume. For the moment, however, I want to focus on another dimension of belief as anthropologists have used the term in cultural analysis.

Mary Steedly, an anthropologist who worked with the Karobatak people in Sumatra, tells how when she was beginning fieldwork she was often asked a question, which she understood to mean "do you believe in spirits?" (1993: ch. 1). It was one of those embarrassing questions anthropologists struggle to answer, since she didn't, personally, but respected and wanted to learn about the understandings of persons in the village in which she worked. After stumbling to answer the question for some months, she discovered her questioners were asking "Do you trust spirits? Do you believe what they say? Do you maintain a relationship with them?" Any sensible person believes in their existence; that isn't even a meaningful question. The real question is how one chooses to relate to them.

Anthropologists often talk with members of other societies about some aspect of their world which does not exist in ours and which we are comfortable asserting is not part of empirical reality. How is it that "belief" has come to be the language through which we discuss such matters – the Zande witches, or the three humors wind, bile, and phlegm in Ayurvedic medicine, or the four humors of seventeenth-century European and American medicine? Moreover, why have we in Western civilization given such importance to beliefs, such importance that wars in Christendom are fought over beliefs, that church schisms and persecutions and martyrdom revolve around correct belief? How is it that belief came to be so central to anthropological analysis, and what is implied by the juxtaposition of belief and knowledge?

By far the richest discussion of the history of the concept belief is to be found in the writing of Wilfred Cantwell Smith, the historian of religion, whose lectures when I was a graduate student set me to thinking about these matters. In two books completed during the late 1970s, Smith explores the relation between "belief" and "faith" historically and across religious traditions. He sets out not to compare beliefs among religions, but to examine the place of belief itself in Buddhist, Hindu, Islamic, and Christian history. Through careful historical and linguistic analysis, he comes to the startling conclusion that "the idea that believing is religiously important turns out to be a modern idea," and that the meaning of the English words "to believe" and "belief" have changed so dramatically in the past three centuries that they wreak profound havoc in our ability to understand our own historical tradition and the religious faith of others.

The word "belief" has a long history in the English language; over the course it has so changed that its earlier meanings are only dimly felt today (Smith 1977: 41–46; 1979: 105–27). In Old English, the words which evolved into modern "believe" (*geleofan, gelefan, geliefan*) meant "to belove," "to hold dear," "to cherish," "to regard as lief." They were the equivalent of what the German word *belieben* means today (*mein lieber Freund* is "my dear or cherished friend"), and show the same root as the Latin *libet*, "it pleases," or *libido,* "pleasure." This meaning survives in the Modern English archaism "lief" and the past participle "beloved." In medieval texts, "leve," "love," and "beleue" are virtual equivalents. In Chaucer's *Canterbury Tales,* the words "accepted my bileve" mean simply "accept my loyalty; receive me as one who submits himself to you." Thus Smith argues that "belief in God" originally means "a loyal pledging of oneself to God, a decision and commitment to live one's life in His service" (1977: 42). Its counterpart in the medieval language of the Church was "I renounce the Devil," belief and renunciation being parallel and contrasting actions, rather than states of mind.

Smith (1977: 44) sums up his argument about the change of the religious meaning of "belief" in our history as follows:

> The affirmation "I believe in God" used to mean: "Given the reality of God as a fact of the universe, I hereby pledge to Him my heart and soul. I committedly opt to live in loyalty to Him. I offer my life to be judged by Him trusting His mercy." Today the statement may be taken by some as meaning: "Given the uncertainty as to whether there be a God or not, as a fact of modern life, I announce that my opinion is 'yes'. I judge God to be existent."

Smith argues that this change in the language of belief can be traced in the grammar and semantics of English literature and philosophy, as well as popular usage. Three changes – in the object of the verb, the subject of the verb, and the relation of belief and knowledge – serve as indicators of the changing semantics of the verb "to believe." First, Smith finds that grammatically, the object of the verb "to believe" shifted from a person (whom one trusted or had faith in), to a person and his word (his virtue accruing to the trustworthiness of his word), to a proposition. This latter shift began to occur by the end of the seventeenth century, with Locke, for example, who characterized "belief" along with "assent" and "opinion" as "the admitting or receiving any proposition for true, upon arguments or proofs that are found to persuade us … without certain knowledge …" (Smith 1977: 48). In the twentieth century we have seen a further shift

as beliefs have come to mean "presuppositions," as in "belief systems."

A second shift has occurred in the subject of the verb "to believe," from an almost exclusive use of the first person – "I believe" – to the predominant use of the third person, "he believes" or "they believe." In anthropology, the impersonal "it is believed that" parallels the discussion of culture as belief system or system of thought. This change in subject subtly shifts the nature of the speech act involved – from existential to descriptive – and alters the authorization of the speaker.

Third, Smith observes that an important and often unrecognized change has occurred in the relation of belief to truth and knowledge, as these are historically conceived. Bacon wrote in 1625 of "the belief of truth," which he defined as the "enjoyment of it," in contrast to the inquiry or wooing of truth and the knowledge or presence of truth. Belief maintains its sense here of holding dear, of appropriating to oneself that which is recognized as true. By the nineteenth century, however, "to believe" had come to connote doubt, and today it suggests outright error or falsehood. Knowledge requires both certitude and correctness; belief implies uncertainty, error, or both. […] Smith's favorite illustration of the juxtaposition of belief and knowledge is an entry in the Random House dictionary which defined "belief" as "an opinion or conviction," and at once illustrates this with *"the belief that the earth is flat"*! Indeed, it is virtually unacceptable usage to say that members of some society "believe" the earth is round; if this is part of their world view, then it is knowledge, not belief!

Smith goes on to argue that our failure to recognize this shift in meaning has led to mistranslation of texts in the Christian tradition and ultimately to "the heresy of believing," the deeply mistaken view that belief in this modern sense is the essence of the religious life rather than faith. *Credo,* in the Latin, is literally "I set my heart" (from Latin *cordis* or heart [as in cordial] and **-do* or **-dere,* to put). *Credo in unum Deum* was correctly translated in the sixteenth century as "I believe in one God," when it meant "I formally pledge my allegiance to God," Whom we of course all acknowledge to be present in the world. Today, it is a mistranslation, suggesting that the Credo consists of propositions the veracity of which we assert. This is historically inaccurate and profoundly misrepresents the traditional ritual acclamation. Equally importantly, for the comparativist, the misplaced focus on beliefs as the primary dimension of religious life has led to mistranslations and misunderstandings of other religious traditions, and in Smith's view, to the great failure to explore the *faith* of others in their historical and communal contexts, even to make faith a central category in comparative research.

Smith's argument about the importance of placing the study of faith rather than beliefs at the center of comparative and historical studies of religion has important implications for the study of illness experience. My interest at this time, however, is the place of "belief" in the history of anthropology, and what the use of the term tells us about the anthropological project. In what way does Smith's analysis of belief relate to the use of the term in anthropological writing? What is the history of believing in anthropology? How is the use of "belief" related to the epistemological assumptions of anthropologists?

From my initial explorations, it would appear that the term "belief" as it is employed in anthropology does indeed connote error or falsehood, although it is seldom explicitly asserted. A quick scan of the typical volumes on an anthropologist's shelf will provide many examples. My own favorite, paralleling Smith's discovery in the Random House Dictionary, comes from Ward Goodenough's little book, *Culture, Language and Society* (1981). In a discussion of "propositions" and the nature of reasoning cross-culturally, he provides the following example from the German ethnologist Girschner, to illustrate the "reasonableness" of members of other cultures.

Consider, for example, the following comment by a Micronesian navigator, defending his *belief* that the sun goes around the earth (Girschner, 1913 ...)

I am well aware of the foreigner's claim that the earth moves and the sun stands still, as someone once told us; but this we cannot

believe, for how else could it happen that in the morning and evening the sun burns less hot than in the day? It must be because the sun has been cooled when it emerges from the water and toward setting it again approaches the water. And furthermore, how can it be possible that the sun remains still when we are yet able to observe that in the course of the year it changes its position in relation to the stars? [emphasis added] (Goodenough 1981: 69).

Quite reasonable, even if mistaken: that is how the beliefs of others seem to be.

The juxtaposition of belief and knowledge is most evident in the intellectualist writing of turn-of-the-century British social anthropology. An example from a classic text in medical anthropology will be particularly instructive. W. H. R. Rivers' *Medicine, Magic and Religion* was published in 1924, the first major comparative study of medical systems by an anthropologist–physician.[2] The book is designed to show how concepts of disease vary cross-culturally, but focuses largely on beliefs about causation of disease. Rivers uses "believe" largely in the third person or impersonally; the object of belief is almost exclusively propositions; and these propositions are, from Rivers' point of view, counter-factual. For example, he writes (1924: 29):

Thus, in Murray Island, in Torres Straits, disease is believed to occur by the action of certain men who, through their possession of objects called *zogo* and their knowledge of the appropriate rites, have the power of inflicting disease. Thus, one *zogo* is believed to make people lean and hungry and at the same time to produce dysentery; another will produce constipation, and a third insanity.

His attitude is made clear several pages later, when he discusses the rationality of such beliefs. "From our modern standpoint we are able to see that these ideas are wrong. But the important point is that, however wrong may be the beliefs of the Papuan and Melanesian concerning the causation of disease, their practices are the logical consequence of those beliefs." This view is conveyed more subtly, however, and with far more profound implications at the end of the book. The conclusion is devoted to illuminating the role of belief in the practice of

Western medicine. Whereas in earlier chapters of the book, the word "believe," along with "ascribe," "regard," and "attribute," appears on nearly every page of discussion of the medical concepts of others, the word "believe" does not appear in the final fourteen pages of the book. Here the word "knowledge," and cognates "recognize," "realize," "acknowledge," and "awareness," are used to describe Western medicine. Rivers could not have more clearly stated his judgment.

This juxtaposition of what others believe to what we know is not only true of intellectualist writers such as Tylor, Frazer, and Rivers. Close reading of the Evans-Pritchard text shows that he uses "belief" and its cognates to far greater analytic advantage than his predecessors, focusing on the coherence of a set of ideas. "All their beliefs hang together," he writes (1937: 194), "and were a Zande to give up faith in witch-doctorhood he would have to surrender equally his belief in witchcraft and oracles." The study of folk "logics" is an important part of the repertoire of cultural analysis, and Evans-Pritchard was a master of this genre. Nonetheless, his analysis framed culture as beliefs, and these were juxtaposed to knowledge – grossly in the introduction of the book, then in a subtle and nuanced way throughout this classic text.

The subtle or explicit representation of belief and knowledge as disjunct continues to be found in anthropological writing up to the present time. It is most explicit in rationalist writing and subsequent discussions of relativism. A final example from Dan Sperber's book *On Anthropological Knowledge* (1985), which proposes to "outline an epistemology of anthropology" (p. 7), will illustrate. The central chapter in the book is entitled "Apparently Irrational Beliefs." It begins with an extract from Sperber's field diary during his research in Ethiopia, when an old man, Filate, comes in a state of great excitement to tell Sperber that he has learned of a dragon – "Its heart is made of gold, it has one horn on the nape of its neck. It is golden all over. It does not live far, two days' walk at most ... " – and asks him if he will kill it. Since Sperber had respect and affection for old Filate, and since Filate was too poor to drink and was

not senile, Sperber was left to puzzle how such a person could actually believe in dragons and about how to reconcile his respect for Filate with "the knowledge that such a belief is absurd."

Sperber's analysis of this problem leads him directly to the usual arguments about the nature of rationality. How are we as anthropologists to interpret cultural beliefs – be they about dragons or the role of witchcraft in causing illness – that are "apparently irrational," that is, not in accord with how we know the empirical world to be? Are such beliefs to be taken as literal or "symbolic"? If they represent literal claims about the nature of the empirical world, why have such systems not given way in the face of empirical experience? In Evans-Pritchard's words, why do the Azande practitioners not "perceive the futility of their magic" (1937: 475)? And what is the alternative? A strong relativist claim that the Azande world and ours are incommensurable, that so different are they that we cannot translate between our world and theirs? Sperber follows through these arguments; he ridicules the view that the mind "actively creat[es] its universe" (Douglas 1975: xviii), as deriving from a "hermeneutico-psychedelic subculture" (Sperber 1985: 38), and develops a detailed analysis of different types of propositional beliefs. In the end, he concludes that old Filate's belief was only "semipropositional" and was "not factual," that is, that it was not a kind of belief intended to really represent the way the world is and not clear enough to be stated in propositional terms that could be falsifiable. Thus his solution is that the old man really didn't believe in the dragon after all, that it was only a kind of fantasy to entertain himself and ultimately the anthropologist.

My intent is not to join the rationality debate and the technical issues it raises here, although these questions serve as the stimulus for many of the concerns of this book, nor to speculate on old Filate's motives. Here my intention is to raise meta-level questions about the role of "belief" in anthropology. How does it happen that the "apparently irrational beliefs" provide the paradigmatic problem for a central tradition in anthropology? Any human science, historical or anthropological, must deal with problems of translation, of differing world views and understandings of reality, of course. But how does it happen that "irrational beliefs" becomes the central, paradigmatic issue?

Surprisingly, there seems to be little analysis of the history of the concept "belief" in anthropology. It is constantly employed, a kind of Wittgensteinian "odd job word," but often used with little self-consciousness. The word almost never appears in indexes, even when it is employed throughout a text, and thus its use is not easy to trace. It is beyond the scope of this discussion to attempt such a history, but a brief review of anthropological texts suggests several hypotheses.

First, the juxtaposition of "belief" and "knowledge" and the use of "belief" to denote (or at least connote) counter-factual assertions has a long history in both anthropology and philosophy. This is contrary to what might be expected for both disciplines – for anthropology, because our primary goal has been to make understandable other societies in a non-judgmental way; for philosophy, because much of modern epistemology is designed to investigate the grounds for true belief.

Second, belief as an analytic category in anthropology appears to be most closely associated with religion and with discussions of the so-called folk sciences. "Belief" is most closely associated, that is, with cultural accounts either of the unknowable or of mistaken understandings of the "natural world," where science can distinguish knowledge from belief. In medical anthropology, analysis of "beliefs" is most prominent in cultural accounts of those conditions (such as infectious diseases) for which biological theories have greatest authority, and least prominent for those forms of illness (for example psychopathology) for which biological explanations are most open to challenge.

Third, the term belief, though present throughout anthropological writing, appears with quite varied frequency and analytic meaning in different theoretical paradigms. For example, it seems far less central in American anthropology, with its background in nineteenth-century German historicist theorizing,

than in British social anthropology, in particular in the rationality literature.

Fourth, the representation of others' culture as "beliefs" authorizes the position and knowledge of the anthropological observer. Though differing in content, anthropological characterizations of others' beliefs played a similar role in validating the position of the anthropologist as the description of native religious beliefs did for missionaries. However, the rising concern about the position of the anthropologist vis-à-vis members of the societies he or she studies has produced a "crisis" in ethnographic writing (Marcus and Fischer 1986: 8) and a generalized epistemological hypochondria, and this change in the relationship of anthropologist to the "Other" can be traced in the increasingly self-conscious and ironic uses of the term "belief."

Fifth, despite such post-modern hypochondria in some regions of the contemporary social sciences, the term "belief" and its counterparts continue to be important odd job words not only in the cognitive sciences, where culture is closely linked with states of the mind, but in fields such as the medical social sciences, where the conflict between historicist interpretations and the claims of the natural sciences is most intense. Examination of the concept thus has special relevance for medical anthropology.

These are rather crude hypotheses. However, they reflect my conviction that it was fateful for anthropology when belief emerged as a central category for the analysis of culture. This formation of anthropological discourse was linked to the philosophical climate within which anthropology emerged, a climate in which empiricist theories and sharp conflicts between the natural sciences and religion were prominent. It was also rooted in anthropologists' traditional relations to those they studied, framed by the superiority of European and American science and industrial development and by the colonialist context of research. Given the semantics of the term, that is the *meaning* "belief" had taken on by the late nineteenth century and continues to have in the twentieth century, the analysis of culture as belief thus both reflected and helped reproduce an underlying epistemology and a prevailing structure of power relations.

A Shaking of the Foundations

Anthropology's greatest contribution to twentieth-century sociology of knowledge has been the insistence that human knowledge is culturally shaped and constituted in relation to distinctive forms of life and social organization. In medical anthropology, this historicist vision runs headlong into the powerful realist claims of modern biology. Enlightenment convictions about the advance of medical knowledge run deep, and although faith in medical institutions has given way to some extent, medicine is a domain in which "a salvational view of science" (Geertz 1988: 146; cf. Midgley 1992) still has great force. No wonder that discussions of "the problem of irrational beliefs" so often cite medical examples.

Nonetheless, the foundations for a comparative, cross-cultural study of illness, healing and medical knowledge which is based in the empiricist paradigm have been profoundly shaken in recent years. Geertz concludes his chapter on Evans-Pritchard in *Works and Lives* (1988), noting that the confidence that shines through Evans-Pritchard's writing, as well as through Lévi-Strauss's *Tristes Tropiques* (1955), is simply not available to ethnographers today. Our relationships with those we study have changed profoundly, and our confidence in our own view of reality, even in the claims of the natural sciences to simply represent the empirical world, has been seriously undermined. This change is represented by increasingly ironic reflections on terms such as "rationality" and "belief" in anthropology, feminist studies, and the sociology of science, and by the proliferation of new approaches in medical anthropology.

Several aspects of the empiricist paradigm relevant to comparative medical studies have become especially problematic, pushing our field in new directions. First, positivist approaches to epistemology and the empiricist theory of language have come under sustained criticism in philosophy, the history and sociology of science, and anthropology. Whichever authors one invokes – Thomas Kuhn, Michel Foucault, Paul Feyerabend, Hilary Putnam, Richard Rorty, or a generation that grew up with these figures – older theories of the relationship between language and empirical reality now seem dated. Rationality and relativism no longer neatly divide the field. Increasingly, social scientists and philosophers have joined in investigating how language activities and social practices actively contribute to the construction of scientific knowledge (e.g., Latour 1987).

[. . .]

Second, the normative dimensions of the empiricist paradigm seem increasingly unacceptable. It is not that any of us doubt that the biological sciences have made astounding advances in understanding human physiology, but we are no longer prepared to view the history of medicine as a straightforward recording of the continuous discovery of the facts of nature. Given the rapidity of change of scientific knowledge, as well as subaltern and feminist critiques of science and its authority, claims to "facticity" have been seriously undermined. The role of science as arbiter between knowledge and belief is thus placed into question. Critical analysis has replaced celebration as the idiom of the history and sociology of science.

[. . .]

Third, the place of the ethnographer as objective, scientific observer – both in research and in ethnographic texts – seems less and less available to us today. Evans-Pritchard could assume such a position in his writings on the Azande only by ignoring his own relation to the colonial authorities, Favret-Saada (1980: 10) suggests that even Evans-Pritchard, while conducting field research, could situate himself outside of Zande witchcraft discourse – beyond possible charges of being a witch himself, for example – only because the Azande granted him the title "Prince without portfolio," which served as a kind of exemption from the claims of the discourse and thus protected him. Whatever the case for Evans-Pritchard and witchcraft, the position of today's anthropologist is increasingly contested. [. . .] In medical anthropology, arbitrating between belief and knowledge suggests positioning ourselves within what Favret-Saada calls "the official theories of misfortune," backed as they are by powerful social agencies. Finding a stance both as researcher and in the ethnographic text is thus increasingly difficult. The position implied by the language of belief is often untenable.

Finally, a variety of more technical analyses of belief suggests problems with the empiricist program, challenging the utility of "belief" as an analytic category, even questioning the existence in other societies of "beliefs" in our sense of the word (see Stich 1983; cf. Tooker 1992; Hahn 1973). A view of culture as propositional, mentalistic, voluntaristic, and individualistic – for example, of medical beliefs as rational propositions about the world, held in the minds (or brains) of individuals, and subject to voluntary control – is an elaboration of a particular folk psychology; such a view reproduces an ideology of individualism that matches poorly with much of what we know about the real world.

[...] Thus, despite powerful authorization by biomedicine and the biological sciences, the empiricist program in medical anthropology is deeply problematic [...] How we situate ourselves in relation to the underlying theoretical issues at stake here is extremely important for how we conceive a program for medical anthropology. How we situate our research in relation to biomedical categories and claims, the nature of authority we grant to biological and medical knowledge, the problems we see as central to the field, and the way we define the project in which we are engaged are all strongly influenced by our stance on these issues. Medical anthropology is one of the primary sites within anthropology where alternative responses to the confrontation between historicism and the natural sciences are being worked out.

[...] All medicine joins rational and deeply irrational elements, combining an attention to the material body with a concern for the moral dimensions of sickness and suffering. In his Marett Lecture in 1950, Evans-Pritchard argued that "social anthropology is a kind of historiography" that "studies societies as moral systems ..." In all societies, even in the modern world with overarching moral orders no longer intact, serious illness leads men and women to confront moral dimensions of life. It is after all a central task of "the work of culture" (Obeyesekere 1990) to transform human misery into suffering, and to counter sickness with healing. Biomedicine, as other forms of healing, is of special interest because it combines the empirical or natural sciences with this primal task. It is the privilege and the obligation of medical anthropology to bring renewed attention to human experience, to suffering, to meaning and interpretation, to the role of narratives and historicity, as well as to the role of social formations and institutions, as we explore a central aspect of what it means to be human across cultures.

NOTES

1 Key texts in this debate include Wilson (1970), Horton and Finnegan (1973), Hookway and Pettit (1978), Hollis and Lukes (1982), Leplin (1984), and Doyal and Harris (1986). See also, for example, A. Rorty (1988), Sperber (1985), Shweder (1984), Taylor (1985b: 134–51) and Tambiah (1990).
2 I am particularly grateful to Theresa O'Nell for her help in analyzing this text.

REFERENCES

Douglas, Mary
1975 *Implicit Meanings: Essays in Anthropology.* London: Routledge & Kegan Paul.
Doyal, Len, and Roger Harris
1986 *Empiricism, Explanation and Rationality. An Introduction to the Philosophy of the Social Sciences.* London: Routledge and Kegan Paul.
Engel, George L.
1977 The Need for a New Medical Model: A Challenge for Biomedicine. *Science* 196: 129–36.
Evans-Pritchard, E. E.
1937 *Witchcraft, Oracles and Magic among the Azande.* Oxford: Oxford University Press.
1950 [1962] Theories of Primitive Religion (The 1950 Marett Lecture). In *Essays in Social Anthropology.* London: Faber and Faber.
Favret-Saada, Jeanne
1980 Deadly Words. *Witchcraft in the Bocage.* Cambridge: Cambridge University Press.
Foucault, Michel
1970 *The Order of Things. An Archaeology of the Human Sciences.* New York: Random House.
Geertz, Clifford
1988 *Works and Lives. The Anthropologist as Author.* Stanford, CA: Stanford University Press.

Good, Byron J., and Mary-Jo DelVecchio Good
1981 The Semantics of Medical Discourse. In Everett Mendelsohn and Yehuda Elkana (eds.), *Sciences and Cultures. Sociology of the Sciences*, vol. V, pp. 177–212. Dordrecht, Holland: D. Reidel Publishing Company.

Good, Mary-Jo DelVecchio, Paul E. Brodwin, Byron J. Good, and Arthur Kleinman (eds.)
1992 *Pain as Human Experience: An Anthropological Perspective*. Berkeley: University of California Press.

Goodenough, Ward
1981 *Culture, Language and Society*. Menlo Park, CA: Benjamin/Cummings.

Hahn, Robert A.
1973 Understanding Beliefs: An Essay on the Methodology of the Statement and Analysis of Belief Systems, *Current Anthropology*, 14: 207–29.

Hollis, Martin, and Steven Lukes
1982 *Rationality and Relativism*. Oxford: Basil Blackwell.

Hookway, Christopher, and Phillip Pettit
1978 *Action and Interpretation. Studies in the Philosophy of the Social Sciences*. Cambridge: Cambridge University Press.

Horton, Robin, and Ruth Finnegan
1973 *Modes of Thought: Essays upon Thinking in Western and Non-Western Societies*. London: Faber.

Latour, Bruno
1987 *Science in Action. How to Follow Scientists and Engineers through Society*. Cambridge, MA: Harvard University Press.

Leplin, Jarrett
1984 *Scientific Realism*. Berkeley: University of California Press.

Lévi-Strauss, Claude
1955 *Triste Tropique*. Paris: Plon.

Lukes, Steven
1970 Some Problems about Rationality. In Bryan R. Wilson (ed.), *Rationality*, pp. 194–213. New York: Harper and Row.

Marcus, George, and Michael Fischer
1986 *Anthropology as Cultural Critique. An Experimental Moment in the Human Sciences*. Chicago: University of Chicago Press.

Midgley, Mary
1992 *Science as Salvation: A Modern Myth and its Meaning*. London: Routledge.

Needham, Rodney
1972 *Belief, Language and Experience*. Chicago: University of Chicago Press.

Obeyesekere, Gananath
1990 *The Work of Culture: Symbolic Transformation in Psychoanalysis and Anthropology*. Chicago: University of Chicago Press.

Rivers, W. H. R.
1924 *Medicine, Magic, and Religion*. London: Kegan Paul, Trench, Trubner & Co. Ltd.

Rorty, Amélie Oksenberg
1988 *Mind in Action: Essays in the Philosophy of Mind*. Boston, MA: Beacon.

Shweder, Richard A.
1984 Anthropology's Romantic Rebellion against the Enlightenment, or There's More to Thinking than Reason and Evidence. In R. Shweder and R. LeVine (eds.), *Culture Theory*, pp. 27–66.

Smith, Wilfred Cantwell
1977 *Belief and History*. Charlottesville: University of Virginia Press.

Sperber, Dan
1985 *On Anthropological Knowledge*. Cambridge: Cambridge University Press.

Steedly, Mary Margaret
1993 *Hanging Without a Rope: Narrative Experience in Colonial and Neocolonial Karoland*. Princeton: Princeton University Press.

Stich, Stephen P.
1983 *From Folk Psychology to Cognitive Science. The Case Against Belief*. Cambridge, MA: MIT Press.

Tambiah, Stanley Jeyaraja
1990 *Magic, Science, Religion, and the Scope of Rationality*. Cambridge: Cambridge University Press.

Taylor, Charles.
1985a *Human Agency and Language. Philosophical Papers 1*. Cambridge: Cambridge University Press.

1985b *Philosophy and the Human Sciences. Philosophical Papers 2*. Cambridge: Cambridge University Press.

1989 *Sources of the Self. The Making of the Modern Identity*. Cambridge, MA: Harvard University Press.

Tooker, Deborah E.
1992 Identity Systems of Highland Burma: "Belief," Akha *Zan*, and a Critique of Interiorized Notions of Ethno-Religious Identity, *Man*, 27: 799–819.

Wilson, Bryan R. (ed.)
1970 *Rationality*. New York: Harper and Row.

Part II
Illness and Narrative, Body and Experience

Introduction

In 1973, Arthur Kleinman published a brief but remarkably prescient essay entitled "Medicine's Symbolic Reality." (The paper is all the more remarkable for being Kleinman's first publication.) Kleinman (1973a: 208) used Wittgenstein's metaphor of natural language as being like "a maze of little streets and squares, of old and new houses," in contrast with the "straight regular streets and uniform houses" of scientific language, to argue that a new interest in "the relation of medicine and science to culture" was beginning to "radically remake our understanding of medicine." He called for a cross-cultural, "comparative study of medical systems" that would recognize the powerful role of language as mediating between the scientific and the human dimensions of medicine, a study of medicine as a "social and cultural enterprise" (208) and a "form of symbolic reality" (212), a "system" of "ordered, coherent … ideas, values, and practices embedded in a given cultural context from which it derives its signification" (208).

Throughout the 1970s and continuing to the present, anthropologists have taken up Kleinman's challenge to study the "maze of little streets and squares" that make up medical cultures and practices in diverse settings, in the process elaborating a broad theoretical program of "interpretive medical anthropology," drawing on closely related philosophical and analytic traditions committed to understanding culture in terms of symbolic meanings and embodied experience. First, working within the broad tradition of American anthropology and semiotic and symbolic analyses of the 1960s and 1970s, medical anthropologists began to systematically investigate local medical systems as "symbolic realities" in Kleinman's terms (1973a, 1973b, 1980), to explore the cultural "meaning of symptoms" (B. Good and M. Good 1980), the "semantics of medical discourse" (B. Good and M. Good 1981), and "semantic networks" (B. Good 1977; Bibeau 1981). Referencing Geertz's classic phrase "the interpretation of culture" (Geertz 1973) and the philosophic tradition of hermeneutics (see Ricoeur 1981; Taylor 1985), this new generation of medical anthropologists saw medicine as consisting of a set of "interpretive practices" (B. Good 1994) that constitute illness as a particular form of reality and as the site of potential interpretive conflict (B. Good, Herrera, M. Good and Cooper 1985). Kleinman (1973a, 1980) drew special attention to the "cognitive management" of illness, to the role of classificatory schemes and "explanatory models" available in all medical systems, and cognitive anthropologists, particularly Linda Garro (1986a, 1986b, 1988, 2003), used formal techniques to investigate the structure and distribution of medical "knowledge" and the relation of cultural models to care-seeking.

Second, medical anthropologists drew on cultural phenomenology to explore how illness is constituted as social, intersubjective, and experiential "realities" and how it becomes the object of therapeutic attention, with "the body" serving as "existential ground of culture and self" (Csordas 1994a). Whether as the "clinical construction of reality" of biomedicine (Kleinman, Eisenberg and Good 1977) or the discursive production of sorcery or witchcraft as sources of illness in contemporary France (Favret-Saada 1980), culture and symbolic practices were understood to play a critical role in producing distinctive modes of experience associated with disease, even "creating the form disease takes" (Kleinman 1973a: 209). Particular attention was given to "the body" as the often invisible agent and object of experience that emerges into awareness with disability (Frank 1986) or pain (Scarry 1985; M. Good, Brodwin, B. Good and Kleinman 1992). Illness, Pandolfi (1990, 1991) wrote, is history "written on the body," and "embodiment" emerged as a key paradigm in medical anthropology (Csordas 1990, 1994a, 1994b) and in humanistic writing (Benner 1994; Charon 2006). A classic essay by Scheper-Hughes and Lock (1987) demonstrated how an analytic of the body could be extended to a critical analysis of links between oppressive social forces and embodied experience.

Third, medical anthropologists in this tradition increasingly explored the fundamental role of narrative in medicine, illness, and healing. Influenced by a broad "narrative turn" in the social sciences, medicine, and psychiatry (e.g., Schafer 1981; Bruner 1986; Sarbin 1986; Brody 1987; Kleinman 1988; Hunter 1991; Kaufman 1993), medical anthropologists began exploring how stories make sense of and shape illness experience (Early 1982, 1985; Price 1987; Garro 1994; B. Good 1994). This notion was extended to the joint construction by physicians, patients and families of "clinical narratives" that organize therapeutic action and the experience of care (B. Good and M. Good 1994; M. Good et al. 1994; Mattingly 1998; M. Good and B. Good 2000; Mattingly and Garro 2000). Drawing in particular from writings on the phenomenology of reading and reader response theory (Iser 1978; Ricoeur 1981), medical anthropologists explored how illness experience is "emplotted" (Mattingly this volume; Garro 1994; B. Good 1994; M. Good 1995), how therapeutic narratives are structured to shape and manage desire, and how technologies are drawn into the "economy of hope" (M. Good 2001, 2008).

This tradition of interpretive medical anthropology, linking phenomenology, narrative studies, and semiotics, and more recently psychoanalysis and post-structuralist studies, continues as a lively tradition until today. In Part II, "Illness and Narrative, Body and Experience," we include seven examples representing a range of this work. The section begins with Kleinman's classic essay, "Medicine's Symbolic Reality," referred to above. In the second essay, Thomas Csordas elaborates one line of argument in Kleinman's essay (1973a: 208) – that "meaning and efficacy ... have always been inseparable from medical healing" – and develops a general theory of healing rooted in cultural phenomenology that links efficacy to rhetorical practices and the powerful relationship of language and the body (cf. Csordas 2004 for a monograph-length development of this argument). The third essay, by Ellen Corin, extends phenomenological methods in another direction. Drawing on the classic tradition of European phenomenological psychiatry, combined with intensive ethnographic research, Corin explores the lives of persons suffering with schizophrenia in Montreal. Her research, aimed at determining why some persons are frequently rehospitalized while others are able to live continuously in the community, comes to the startling conclusion that rehospitalization is closely linked with efforts to be reintegrated into the community, while those who develop a style of "positive withdrawal" are, paradoxically, able to remain in the community. From this she raises more general questions about how some societies make available religious and therapeutic spaces for withdrawal, and about the role North American values play in producing relapse for persons suffering severe mental illness (Corin 1990, 2007).

The essay by Cheryl Mattingly takes on in brief form the issues raised in her 1998 monograph, *Healing Dramas and Clinical Plots*. Mattingly's rich ethnographic writing links a very difficult and mundane aspect of medical practice – occupational therapists' work with persons suffering severe physical and neurological losses – with a broad and deeply philosophical theorization of narrative practices. She demonstrates that "therapeutic emplotment" is critical to this mundane work, providing sense at the site of the breakdown of meaning, placing therapeutic work within larger time horizons, and, when successful, establishing the desire and motivational structures necessary for patients to carry on in the face of nearly unbearable losses.

The last three essays in this section illustrate new directions for interpretive medical anthropology. First we excerpt a small section from *Minima Ethnographica* by Michael Jackson, a leading theorist and fine ethnographic writer in the phenomenological tradition, in which he explores the place of memories of colonial trauma in the collective suffering of an Aboriginal community in Australia. Jackson's writing has served as an important resource and guide for medical anthropologists working in the phenomenological tradition. Second, we include an analysis by Janis Jenkins that links traumatic emotions and embodied experience of Salvadoran refugees to the United States to the state construction of a political ethos of terror that organized those embodied emotions. We conclude this section with a fascinating essay by Robert Desjarlais, based on research with homeless men and women in a Boston shelter, in which he deconstructs the category "experience," arguing that the mode of being-in-the-world of many persons who are homeless lacks the qualities we usually associate with experience – reflexive interiority, hermeneutical depth, and narrative flow. He thus unsettles the very category "experience" used broadly within the interpretive tradition, including in his own earlier writing, suggesting this term is far from neutral and that it describes a very particular mode of subjectivity rather than serving as a natural category for investigating cross-cultural difference. These three essays in particular point ahead to the final part of this book on "postcolonial disorders."

REFERENCES

Benner, Patricia, ed.
  1994   Interpretive Phenomenology: Embodiment, Caring, and Ethics in Health and Illness. London: Sage.
Bibeau, Gilles
  1981   The Circular Semantic Network in Ngbandi Disease Nosology. Social Science and Medicine 15B:295–307.
Brody, Howard
  1987   Stories of Sickness. New Haven: Yale University Press.
Bruner, Jerome
  1986   Actual Minds, Possible Worlds. Cambridge, MA: Harvard University Press.
Charon, Rita
  2006   Narrative Medicine: Honoring the Stories of Illness. Oxford: Oxford University Press.
Corin, Ellen
  1990   Facts and Meaning in Psychiatry. An Anthropological Approach to the Lifeworld of Schizophrenics. Culture, Medicine and Psychiatry 14:153–88.
Corin, Ellen
  2007   The "Other" of Culture in Psychosis: The Ex-Centricity of the Subject. In João Biehl, Byron Good, and Arthur Kleinman, eds., Subjectivity: Ethnographic Investigations, pp 273–315. Berkeley: University of California Press.
Csordas, Thomas
  1990   Embodiment as a Paradigm for Anthropology. Ethos 18:5–47.
Csordas, Thomas, ed.
  1994a   Embodiment and Experience: The Existential Ground of Culture and Self. Cambridge: Cambridge University Press.
Csordas, Thomas
  1994b   The Sacred Self: A Cultural Phenomenology of Charismatic Healing. Berkeley: University of California Press.
Csordas, Thomas
  2004   Healing and the Human Condition: Scenes From the Present Moment in Navajoland. Culture, Medicine And Psychiatry 28(1):1–14.
Early, Evelyn
  1982   The Logic of Well-Being: Therapeutic Narratives in Cairo, Egypt. Social Science and Medicine 16:1491–7.
Early, Evelyn
  1985   Catharsis and Creation: The Everyday Narratives of Baladi Women of Cairo. Anthropological Quarterly 58:172–81.
Favret-Saada, Jeanne
  1980   Deadly Words: Witchcraft in the Bocage. Cambridge: Cambridge University Press.
Frank, Gelya
  1986   On Embodiment: A Case Study of Congenital Limb Deficiency in American Culture. Culture, Medicine & Psychiatry 10:189–220.
Garro, Linda
  1986a   Intracultural Variation in Folk Medical Knowledge: A Comparison between Curers and Non-Curers. American Anthropologist 88:351–70.
Garro, Linda
  1986b   Decision-Making Models of Treatment Choice. In Sean McHugh and T. Michael Vallis, eds. Illness Behavior: A Multidisciplinary Model, pp 173–88. New York: Plenum Press.
Garro, Linda
  1988   Explaining High Blood Pressure: Variation in Knowledge about Illness. American Ethnologist 15:98–119.

Garro, Linda
1994   Narrative Representations of Chronic Illness Experience: Cultural Models of Illness, Mind, and Body in Stories Concerning the Temporo-mandibular Joint (TMJ). Social Science and Medicine 38:775–88.
Garro, Linda
2003   Narrating Troubling Experiences. Transcultural Psychiatry 40:5–43.
Geertz, Clifford
1973   The Interpretation of Cultures. New York: Basic Books.
Good, Byron
1977   The Heart of What's the Matter: Semantics and Illness in Iran. Culture, Medicine and Psychiatry 1:25–58.
Good, Byron
1994   Medicine, Rationality and Experience: An Anthropological Perspective. Cambridge: Cambridge University Press.
Good, Byron and Mary-Jo DelVecchio Good
1980   The Meaning of Symptoms: A Cultural Hermeneutic Model for Clinical Practice. In Leon Eisenberg and Arthur Kleinman, eds. The Relevance of Social Science for Medicine, pp 165–96. Dordrecht: D. Reidel Publishing Co.
Good, Byron and Mary-Jo DelVecchio Good
1981   The Semantics of Medical Discourse. In Everett Mendelsohn and Yehuda Elkana, eds., Sciences and Cultures. Sociology of the Sciences, vol. V, pp. 177–212. Dordrecht: D. Reidel Publishing Co.
Good, Byron and Mary-Jo DelVecchio Good
1994   In the Subjunctive Mode: Epilepsy Narratives in Turkey. Social Science and Medicine 38:835–42.
Good, Byron, Henry Herrera, Mary-Jo DelVecchio Good, and James Cooper
1985   Reflexivity, Countertransference and Clinical Ethnography: A Case from a Psychiatric Cultural Consultation Clinic. In Robert Hahn and Atwood Gaines, eds., Physicians of Western Medicine, pp. 177–92. Dordrecht: D. Reidel Publishing Co.
Good, Mary-Jo DelVecchio
1995   American Medicine: The Quest for Competence. Berkeley: University of California Press.
Good, Mary-Jo DelVecchio
2001   The Biotechnical Embrace. Culture, Medicine and Psychiatry 14:59–79.
Good, Mary-Jo DelVecchio
2008   The Medical Imaginary and the Biotechnical Embrace: Subjective Experiences of Clinical Scientists and Patients. In João Biehl, Byron Good, and Arthur Kleinman, eds., Subjectivity: Ethnographic Investigations, pp 362–80. Berkeley: University of California Press.
Good, Mary-Jo DelVecchio and Byron Good
2000   Clinical Narratives and the Study of Contemporary Doctor–Patient Relationships. In Gary Albrecht, Ray Fitzpatrick, and Susan Scrimshaw. The Handbook of Social Studies in Health and Medicine. London: Sage.
Good, Mary-Jo DelVecchio, Cynthnia Schaffer, and Stuart Lind
1994   American Oncology and the Discourse on Hope. Culture, Medicine and Psychiatry 14:59–79.
Good, Mary-Jo DelVecchio, Paul Brodwin, Byron Good, and Arthur Kleinman, eds.
1992   Pain as Human Experience: An Anthropological Perspective. Berkeley: University of California Press.
Hunter, Kathryn
1991   Doctors' Stories: The Narrative Structure of Medical Knowledge. Princeton: Princeton University Press.

Iser, Wolfgang
    1978   The Act of Reading: A Theory of Aesthetic Response. Baltimore: Johns Hopkins
    University Press.
Kaufman, Sharon
    1993   The Healer's Tale. Madison: University of Wisconsin Press.
Kleinman, Arthur
    1973a   Medicine's Symbolic Reality: On the Central Problem in the Philosophy of Medi-
    cine. Inquiry 16:206–13.
Kleinman, Arthur
    1973b   Toward a Comparative Study of Medical Systems. Science, Medicine and Man
    1:55–65.
Kleinman, Arthur
    1980   Patients and Healers in the Context of Culture. Berkeley: University of California
    Press.
Kleinman, Arthur
    1988   The Illness Narratives. New York: Basic Books.
Kleinman, Arthur, Leon Eisenberg, and Byron Good
    1978   Culture, Illness, and Care: Clinical Lessons from Anthropologic and Cross-Cultural
    Research. Annals of Internal Medicine 88:251–88.
Mattingly, Cheryl
    1998   Healing Dramas and Clinical Plots. The Narrative Structure of Experience. Cam-
    bridge: Cambridge University Press.
Mattingly, Cheryl and Linda Garro, eds.
    2000   Narrative and the Cultural Construction of Illness and Healing. Berkeley: University
    of California Press.
Pandolfi, Mariella
    1990   Boundaries inside the Body: Women's Sufferings in Southern Peasant Italy. Culture,
    Medicine and Psychiatry 14:255–73.
Pandolfi, Mariella
    1991   Memory within the Body: Women's Narrative and Identity in a Southern Italian
    Village. In Beatrix Pfleiderer and Gilles Bibeau, eds. Anthropologies of Medicine, pp. 59–68.
    Heidelberg, Germany: Vieweg.
Price, Laurie
    1987   Ecuadorian Illness Stories: Cultural Knowledge in Natural Discourse. In Dorothy
    Holland and Naomi Quinn, eds. Cultural Models in Language and Thought, pp. 313–42.
    Cambridge: Cambridge University Press.
Ricoeur, Paul
    1981   The Narrative Function. In Paul Ricoeur. Hermeneutics & the Human Sciences, pp
    274–96. Cambridge: Cambridge University Press.
Sarbin, Theodore, ed.
    1986   Narrative Psychology: The Storied Nature of Human Conduct. New York: Praeger.
Scarry, Elaine
    1985   The Body in Pain. The Making and Unmaking of the World. New York: Oxford
    University Press.
Schafer, R
    1981   Narrative Actions in Psychoanalysis. Worcester: Clark University Press.
Scheper-Hughes, Nancy, and Margaret Lock
    1987   The Mindful Body: A Prolegomenon to Future Work in Medical Anthropology.
    Medical Anthropology Quarterly 1:6–41.
Taylor, Charles
    1985   Human Agency and Language. Philosophical Papers I. Cambridge: Cambridge
    University Press.

9

Medicine's Symbolic Reality
On a Central Problem in the Philosophy of Medicine

Arthur M. Kleinman

'Our language can be seen as an ancient city: a maze of little streets and squares, of old and new houses, and of houses with additions from various periods; and this surrounded by a multitude of new boroughs with straight regular streets and uniform houses'. (Ludwig Wittgenstein, Philosophical Investigations, *trans. by G. E. M. Anscombe (Blackwell, Oxford 1968), p. 8.)*

Wittgenstein's winsome metaphor for scientific language ('straight regular streets and uniform houses') against ordinary language ('maze of little streets ... of old and new houses') applies quite aptly to a traditional distinction in medical theory: medicine deals with two kinds of reality, 'scientific' and 'ordinary'; or put differently, it is both a biophysical and a human science. Modern medical theory has concerned itself almost entirely with the wide, well-designed and clearly mapped suburban avenues of the former, particularly in the study of disease, its biological substratum, and its determinants, effects, and control. Often the biophysical root of modern medicine has been used as the basis for a general critique of the whole of medicine; an example of which is the great amount of consideration given to the precise definition of such abstractions as illness and health, a largely unprofitable endeavor which has characterized much of what could be called the philosophy of medicine. Only recently has there been more than superficial and somewhat embarrassed attention given to medicine as a socio-cultural

system, as a practice and a human reality. Obviously, it is this archaic root of medicine which strikes us as most like the twisting, narrow, unmapped streets and clutter of old and new houses of the ancient inner city, Wittgenstein's analogy for the messy and poorly understood, yet crucial, social and individual aspects of language. Likewise these sides of medicine, which are now appreciated for their enormous importance, though not at all clearly understood, present a challenge to the modern theoretical structure of medical science, a structure based largely upon knowledge limited to medicine's biophysical reality.

Recently, the pendulum has swung away from the theoretical disinterest and even scorn shown by entrenched medical empiricism for medicine as a human science to a kind of theoretical chaos, as various social and behavioral science theories are stretched and forced to fit an elusive medical subject. Even though no sound theoretical integration or systematic critique of this enterprise has yet been forthcoming, there is general agreement that the socio-cultural

Arthur M. Kleinman, "Medicine's Symbolic Reality: On a Central Problem in the Philosophy of Medicine," *Inquiry* 16 (1973): 206–13. Reprinted by permission of the publisher (Taylor & Francis Group; www.informaworld.com)

approach is beginning to radically remake our understanding of medicine and, accordingly, we find the traditional dichotomy in scientific medicine undergoing marked change. Here again, the quotation from Wittgenstein, who apropos of our subject did speak of the similarity between philosophical investigations and medical healing, is most relevant, since he was writing about language as a mediating reality, and, as we shall attempt to adumbrate below, the realm of symbolic reality would appear to mediate between medicine's dual roots so as to form a bridging or unifying reality, which itself becomes a central problem for medical theory.

All of this is the result of several new perspectives on medicine, and for that matter science generally, which have focused their attention upon the relation of medicine and science to culture.[1] Moreover, these historical, anthropological, sociological, psychiatric, and medical field studies have begun to unify their interests around a common theme, the comparative study of medical systems: that is, appreciation for the structure and significance of medicine as a health care system in different cultural settings and historical contexts.[2] Recent developments in the sociology of knowledge, linguistic theory, and structural and symbolic analyses have made important contributions to the reconstruction of given medical systems, which in turn have been compared, either in part or as total structures, historically and cross-culturally.[3] This approach has produced a remarkable body of research findings and offers a phenomenology of medical practice. It is my intention to bring certain of these findings to bear upon the question of medical reality. In briefly doing so, I hope to demonstrate that the study of medicine as a social and cultural enterprise represents not only a fundamental breakthrough in our understanding of medicine, but also openly invites broad philosophical enquiry into medicine, something that has been strangely and seriously lacking in the past.

No matter what the perspective – diachronic or synchronic – medicine is always found to constitute a system. The medical system is an ordered, coherent body of ideas, values, and practices embedded in a given

cultural context from which it derives its signification. It is an important part of the cultural world and as such is structed, like any other segment of social reality, by the regnant body of symbolic meanings. The medical system forms an indissoluble and hierarchical whole in which healing acts are closely linked with ideas about disease causation and models for classifying disease. The whole is oriented toward the problem of effectively dealing with illness. From this view point, healing is not the outcome of diagnostic acts, but the healing function is active from the outset in the way illness is perceived and the experience of illness organized.

Medical systems function along the lines of the cultural dialectic, relating and treating both individual and social realities. In fact, the patient for most medical systems has traditionally been both the individual and his nexus of social relations. The acts of ordering, naming, interpreting, and offering therapy for illness are aspects of symbolic reality common to both the sick individual, the healer, and their society. Medical systems employ different explanatory models and idioms to make sense of disease and give meaning to the individual and social experience of illness.[4] Meaning and efficacy, until the very recent advent of biomedical technologies which actually control biochemical, physiological, and psychological processes, have always been inseparable in medical healing. Medical systems may be crudely characterized as expressions of the cultural loci of power which they utilize to explain and control illness.[5]

A given medical system in its socio-cultural context does considerably more than name, classify, and respond to illness, however. In a real sense, it structures the experience of illness and, in part, creates the form disease takes. Disease occurs as a natural process. It works upon biophysical reality and/or psychological processes, as the case may be. But the experience of illness is a cultural or symbolic reality. The experience of illness involves feelings, ideas, values, language and non-verbal communication, symbolic behaviour, and the like. What is perceived as illness in one culture may not be so perceived in another. We know a great deal today about typing and labeling of diseases, less so about symptom choice and culturally specified disease forms, and just enough about how illness behaviour is learned and socialized to know that socio-cultural factors are of enormous importance. More than that, we know that symbolic communication forms a pathway of sorts between social and cultural events and psychophysiological reactions.[6] Psychosomatic pathology has been well described, but we are just learning about sociosomatic pathology. The line begins to blur between ordering the experience of illness and shaping illness per se. I do not mean merely that psychiatric disorders or psychosomatic diseases are in this sense symbolic phenomena, but any disease – smallpox, leprosy, syphilis, hypertension, cardiovascular disorders, cancer, etc. – is in part a cultural construct. Disease derives much of its form, the way it is expressed, the value it is given, the meaning it possesses, and the therapy appropriate to it in large measure from the governing system of symbolic meanings.

Medical knowledge is intended to be effective. This can be seen in the way diseases and their therapies are taxonomized. Medical classificatory schemes are most often *not* objective descriptions of empirical reality. Rather they reflect healing concerns and the theoretical biases of given cultural and medical ideologies. Classification of disease is, in fact, the first therapeutic act. Classificatory schemes are intended to domesticate and make known a 'wild' and unknown phenomenon, which threatens the very idea of social order and personal stability, and transform it into something known, named, and thus manageable. In this sense, ideas of witchcraft as a random and highly malignant explanatory model are not at all badly matched with diseases such as endemic malaria and the pneumonia-diarrheal complex of disorders of infants, which are random and highly malignant. Some diagnostic systems are entirely symbolic, relating specific illnesses to specific therapies.[7] Though much of what we are describing for medical cognitive systems pertain for the most part to traditional forms of medicine, there are certainly a number of modern equivalents as students of social

deviance and those studying the sociology of medical knowledge, for example, are wont to point out.[8]

The ring of medicine's symbolic reality is made complete in the question of healing. Healing is an elemental social function and experience. It is equally as primary as the gift or exchange relationship, and comprises one of the fundamental forms of symbolic action, native to all societies. Even a surface examination of healing makes us aware that medicine begins as a radical form of humanism.[9] Traditionally, medical systems have not made a distinction between healing efficacy and provision of meaning for the personal and social experience of sickness. Efficacy, itself, is a cultural construct. The healing dialectic has been considered effective when the bonds between the sick individual and the group, weakened by disease, are strengthened, social values reaffirmed, and the notion of social order no longer threatened by illness and death; or when the individual experience of illness has been made meaningful, personal suffering shared, and the individual leaves the marginal situation of sickness and has been reincorporated in health or even death back into the social body. Healing is the end-point of the medical system, the successful reordering and organizing of the disease experience and, where possible, its control. Though it is clear that morbidity and mortality statistics, as well as empirical measures of therapeutic effectivity, do not measure healing efficacy, little is known about what personal and social standards of healing efficacy are in modern society, yet these should be crucial concerns for modern medicine.

Within the form of symbolic reality structured by the system of medical care, healing has a position situated at the strategic interface between the cultural systems, the system of social relations, and the individual. Healing occurs along a symbolic pathway of words, feelings, values, expectations, beliefs, and the like which connect cultural events and forms with affective and physiological processes. Psychosomatic and sociosomatic correlates are implicit in all medical healing relationships. Feelings and physiological responses are in some way linked to socio-cultural reality via early socialization and learning. Language and other symbolic forms are the most obvious bridge. In this way, medicine's biological and cultural roots are connected; the formal barriers between these realities begin to dissolve if we penetrate medicine's thoroughgoing symbolic reality. We reiterate that this symbolic structure is present not only in therapy, where it plays a patent role of mediation, but also in the social construction and cognitive mapping of illness; in other words it is to be found at all levels of the medical system.

In studying medicine as a human science this symbolic realm of ideas and actions becomes a fundamental problem with considerable practical and theoretical importance. The specific issues questioned are remarkably different from those emerging out of a concern with medicine's biophysical aspects, without disparaging the clear importance of the latter. Indeed, these issues come much closer to giving us a long-awaited general theoretical critique of medicine. What are real health needs of individuals, communities, or populations? What are the purposes of clinical care? What is the nature of clinical interpretation and knowledge? What is medical healing? How are medical ideologies constructed and how do they relate to political ideologies and social phenomena? How are social sources of power tapped for explanation and therapy? These questions are of particular significance for developing countries, where health structures are being remade. But certainly, they bring our study of modern medicine to a deeper level; they expose the infra-structure of medical knowledge and practice; and they call into question the interests and values which stand behind medicine.[10] If we consider medicine on the plane of symbolic reality, we rapidly come to think of the medical system as structured somewhat like a language; we may even think of 'medemes' (similar to phonemes and morphemes) in the comparative study of medicine, essential units of medical meaning which form the elements of medical systems and whose relational arrangements result in the unique configuration of different kinds of medicine. This analogy suggests that we might be able to describe in a general way basic relational

principles responsible for the structuring of given medical systems. To do so requires an understanding not only of medicine as a system, but particularly of a given medical system's cultural and historical contexts.

Our general medical model confronts the tremendous distortion and abridgement of traditional purposes in contemporary technological medicine: increasing technical control has been accompanied by the separation of efficacy from meaning, progressive dehumanization of the healing function, so much so that we are seeing traditional healing activities surface in the wider social structure just as they are disappearing from clinical practices, and systematic attempts to restrict medicine's symbolic reality to a single discipline, psychiatry, peripheral to the central core of medical research interests and practices. Ironically, medicine, one of the first human sciences and in some ways a paradigmatic one, is in the tragic process of emancipating itself, via technicalization of all of its problems, from this vital source.

The study of medicine as a cultural system returns our attention to the artificial and unfortunate separation of medicine into two distinct areas, only the first of which has heretofore qualified for scientific investigation. We have briefly tried to show that we must reconsider the 'maze of little streets' of the ancient city, medicine taken as a human reality, if we are to arrive at any general understanding of medicine, or have some success with the tangle of importunate problems besetting modern medicine. Since Plato, there has been a persistent and more or less unspecified ideal in the West of an anthropological medicine, a kind of medical science and practice that would be concerned unashamedly with such problems as human nature and other critical aspects of philosophical anthropology, a medical science conceived of in radically human terms, just as medical systems have traditionally been structured, and taking its place as an essential part of the human sciences. Though such an enterprise has nowhere been realized, we now seem to have before us a 'royal road' for systematically exploring medicine in these terms; comparative studies in medicine offer enormous support for the appreciation of medicine as a form of symbolic reality, a new direction which has already begun to challenge modern medical theory and which could well become a central problem for a philosophical reconsideration of medicine.

NOTES

1 A leading example of the comparative social study of science is Everett Mendelsohn and Arnold Thackray (Eds.), *Science and Human Values* (Humanities Press, New York, 1972). No single volume is yet available that satisfactorily reviews the comparative social study of medicine, rather one must turn to a number of outstanding articles in different areas.

2 The reader is referred to the following paradigmatic studies of different systems of medicine: for traditional Chinese medicine, Pierre Huard and Ming Wong, *Chinese Medicine* (World University Library, New York 1968); for primitive medicine, Victor W. Turner, *The Forest of Symbols* (Cornell University Press, New York 1967); for folk medicine, John M. Ingham, 'On Mexican Folk Medicine', *American Anthropologist*, Vol. 72, (1970), No. 1, p. 76; for ancient Greek medicine, Pedro Lain Entralgo, *The Therapy of the Word in Classical Antiquity*, ed. and trans. by L. J. Rather (Yale University Press, New Haven 1970); for modern medical systems, Eliot Freidson, *Profession of Medicine* (Dodd, Mead & Co., New York 1970); for culture contact and transformations between traditional and modern systems of medicine, R. C. Croizier, *Traditional Medicine in Modern China* (Harvard University Press, Cambridge, Mass. 1968), Charles Leslie, 'Modern India's Ancient Medicine', *Transaction*, Vol. 6 (1969), No. 8, p. 46, and Alexander Alland, *Adaptation in Cultural Evolution* (Columbia University Press, New York 1970). Recently, the Wenner-Gren Foundation has conducted an interdisciplinary conference on the comparative study of Asian systems of medicine, which is soon to be published. In October 1973 the first of several international conferences on the comparative study of medical systems will be held at the University of Washington and will deal with Chinese medicine and scientific medicine in China, as well as theoretical issues in comparative medicine; it is to be followed by a conference on African medical systems.

3 On the sociology of knowledge, see Peter Berger and Thomas Luckmann, *The Social Construction of Reality* (Doubleday, New York 1967); and Burkart Holzner, *Reality Construction in Society* (Schenkman, Cambridge, Mass. 1968), both of which are made relevant for medicine in Freidson (1970). On the relation of modern linguistic developments to the study of medical systems, see Claude Levi-Strauss, 'The Effectiveness of Symbols', *Structural Anthropology* (Doubleday, New York 1967), pp. 181–202; and S. J. Tambiah, 'The Magical Power of Words', *Man*, Vol. 3 (1968), No. 2, p. 175. Examples of symbolic and structural analyses applied to medicine are found in: Clifford Geertz, 'Ethos, World-View and the Analyses of Sacred Symbols', in Alan Dundes (Ed.), *Every Man His Way* (Prentice-Hall, Englewood Cliffs, New Jersey 1968); Victor W. Turner, 'The Syntax of Symbolism', *Philosophical Transactions of the Royal Society of London*, Series B (1966), 251, p. 295; and Nur Yalman, 'The Structure of Sinhalese Healing Rituals', *Journal of Asian Studies*, Vol. 23 (1964), p. 115. For modern ethnographic approaches to medical systems, see: Charles O. Frake, 'The Diagnosis of Disease among the Subanum of Mindanao', *American Anthropologist*, Vol. 63 (1961), No. 1, p. 113; and L. B. Glick, 'Medicine as an Ethnographic Category', *Ethnology*, Vol. 6 (1967), p. 31. Historical and cross-cultural comparisons of elements of medical systems are exemplified by Michel Foucault, *Madness and Civilization* (Mentor Books, New York 1965); and Mary Douglas, *Purity and Danger* (Pelican Books, Baltimore 1970). Alland (1970) attempts to compare whole medical systems in his evolutionary framework. General comparisons of Asian, African and Western medical systems are found in: Robbin Horton, 'African Traditional Thought and Western Science. I', *Africa*, Vol. 37 (1967), No. 1, p. 50; Pierre Huard, 'Western Medicine and Afro-Asian Ethnic Medicine', in F. N. L. Poynter (Ed.), *Medicine and Culture* (Wellcome Institute Publications, London 1969); and T. A. Lambo, 'Traditional African Cultures and Western Medicine', in Poynter, *Medicine and Culture*.

4 See Horton (1967).

5 Glick (1967), p. 34.

6 Cf. Heinz Werner and Bernhard Kaplan, *Symbol Formation* (Wiley, New York 1967),

pp. 15–54; K. I. Platnov, *The Word as a Physiological and Therapeutic Factor* (Foreign Language Pub. House, Moscow 1959), pp. 16–38; and Marcel Mauss, 'Les Techniques Du Corps', *Sociologie et Anthropologie* (Presses Universitaires de France, Paris 1950).

7 Victor W. Turner, 'Lunda Medicine and the Treatment of Disease', *Rhodes-Livingstone Museum Occasional Papers*, Vol. 15 (1964), pp. 4–5.

8 Freidson (1970), pp. 205–23.

9 See Pedro Lain Entralgo, *Doctor and Patient* (World University Library, New York 1969).

10 Cf. Jürgen Habermas, 'Knowledge and Human Interests: a General Perspective'. Appendix to his *Knowledge and Human Interests* (Beacon Press, Boston 1971).

10

Elements of Charismatic Persuasion and Healing

Thomas J. Csordas

[...]

The problem of *efficacy* appears repeatedly at the center of debate about religious healing practices. Although other reviewers have chosen to treat the diverse and voluminous literature on this problem (cf. Bourguignon 1976; Dow 1986; Moerman 1979), my purpose here is to develop an approach that is sensitive to incremental and inconclusive effects that define the lowest threshold of efficacy. It is by now commonplace to observe that efficacy is contingent on the nature of the problems addressed by different forms of healing, how those problems are defined in cultural practice, and what counts in cultural terms as their successful resolution. Given these observations, however, we are left with a lack of analytic specificity to the concept.

A first step is to be aware of which of three aspects, implicit in most discussions of healing practice, is the focus of analysis. The first is *procedure*, or who does what to whom with respect to medicines administered, prayers recited, objects manipulated, altered states of consciousness induced or evoked. The second aspect of healing practice is what we may call *process*, referring to the nature of participants' experience with respect to encounters with

the sacred, episodes of insight, or changes in thought, emotion, attitude, meaning, behavior. Third is *outcome*, or the final disposition of participants both with respect to their expressed level of satisfaction with healing, and to change (positive or negative) in symptoms, pathology, or functioning.

Of these three elements, therapeutic procedure has been treated exhaustively in many empirical studies and comparative works (Frank 1973 [1961]; Prince 1980). Therapeutic outcome has only recently begun to be treated systematically by anthropologists (Finkler 1985; Kleinman and Sung 1979; Kleinman and Gale 1982). However, therapeutic process as defined here has been virtually neglected, and relegated to the status of a "black box." This neglect may originate in a failure to distinguish between prototypical cases for ritual analysis, such as rites of passage (Turner 1969) and ritual healing. What is typically called process in anthropological studies of such rites conforms more to what we are calling procedure. Following this convention, studies of religious healing have been based on descriptions of healing rituals and interviews with ritual specialists, and have included little explicit attention to the phenomenology of the

Thomas J. Csordas, "Elements of Charismatic Persuasion and Healing," *Medical Anthropology Quarterly* 2/2 (1988): 121–42. Reproduced by permission of the American Anthropological Association from *Medical Anthropology Quarterly* 2/2 (1988), pp. 121–42. Not for sale or further reproduction.

transformative process as lived by participants. Moreover, while most studies acknowledge that ritual healing is religious, participants' experience of the sacred is seldom explicitly documented, with the result that it is often difficult to determine the contribution of the *religious* dimension of religious healing (Csordas 1987a).

Moreover, whereas the condition for efficacy in rites of passage is social consensus about a biological inevitability (puberty, death) or a social fait accompli (marriage), efficacy in a situation of affliction is not so straightforward a matter. Rites of passage fail only under extraordinary circumstances, while the results of ritual healing are immensely variable in any circumstance. Yet ritual healing is often described in such a way that its results must be seen as inevitable and definitive: it is either invariably successful (Kleinman and Sung 1979) or fails to do what it claims (Pattison, Lapins, and Doerr 1973). Given this situation, analysis has not been able to define satisfactory empirical conditions of efficacy that can also account for much healing that may be partial, incremental, and inconclusive. I suggest that these conditions may be found in the experiential dimension of ritual healing.

A fruitful analysis of therapeutic process can begin with the common ethnographic observation that a primary effect of religious healing is to alter the meaning of an illness for the sufferer (Bourguignon 1976). Frank (1973 [1961]) pointed the direction toward understanding this change by defining healing as a form of persuasion that alters a person's "assumptive world." Compatible with Frank's insight is the work in interpretive anthropology that analyzes ritual as performance (Csordas 1983; Kapferer 1979, 1983; Schieffelin 1985; Tambiah 1977, 1985). This work raises issues of subjective experience among ritual participants, impacts of utterance and action carried out within specific ritual genres, and performative transformation of context as well as of meaning. However, while interpretive scholarship has been able to highlight changes in assumptive worlds, it is generally more attuned to issues of language and rhetoric than to either clinical issues or to the concrete experience of

participants. The analysis I shall present attempts to balance interpretive and clinical interests, while staying as close as possible to experiential data.

Catholic Pentecostalism and Charismatic Healing

The healing system examined here is that of the Catholic Charismatic Renewal, a movement within the Roman Catholic Church. The movement is characterized by its integration of Pentecostal elements into Catholicism. Among these are Baptism in the Spirit (an experience of being infused with the power and blessing of God through His Holy Spirit), speaking in tongues or glossalalia (a kind of pseudolanguage lacking a semantic component and used primarily as a form of prayer which expresses praise to God), and the healing ministry (prayer accompanied by the laying on of hands for the relief of physical, emotional, or demonic illness). Since its beginning in 1967, this movement has spread into the general Catholic population and includes members from working, middle, and professional classes (Csordas 1980; McGuire 1982).

Catholic Pentecostals are organized either in "prayer groups" affiliated with particular parishes or in more highly structured intentional organizations known as "covenant communities." The principal ritual event is the prayer meeting, characterized by the coordinated use of several genres of ritual language (Csordas 1987b). Initiation seminars introduce new members to the "life in the Spirit" and integrate them into prayer group activities.

Catholic Pentecostals participate in the late 20th-century shift among Christians from emphasis on suffering and self-mortification as an imitation of Christ, to emphasis on the possibility and benefit of divine healing as practiced by Jesus in the gospels (Favazza 1982). The processes of healing and spiritual growth are linked, because illness is typically regarded as an obstacle to spiritual growth. Healing is therefore considered necessary for all persons in the process of spiritual growth, and spiritual growth is in turn conducive to good health.

The healing system is holistic in that it aims in principle to integrate all aspects of the person, conceived as a tripartite composite of body, mind, and spirit.

The tripartite concept of the person is the basis for three distinct but interrelated types of healing: *physical healing* of bodily illness, *inner healing* of emotional illness and distress, and *deliverance* from the adverse effects of demons or evil spirits (Csordas 1983). Physical healing is the simplest in form, in which laying on of hands and, in some instances, anointing with blessed oil accompany prayer. Healing ministers pray for relief from illness, success of medical treatment, lessening of side effects from medication, or release from suffering through death. Inner healing may be aimed at removing the effects of a particular life trauma, or it may be a review and reinterpretation of an individual's entire life history in light of the "healing presence of Jesus." Supplicants are frequently exhorted to forgive others for past wrongs. Vivid imagery often accompanies inner healing, either as a revelation of some repressed experience or as a confirmation that healing is taking place. In deliverance, a supplicant is relieved of oppression by evil spirits. Demons in this instance typically do not have complete control over a person in such a way as to require the formal Church rite of exorcism, but are nevertheless regarded as having a detrimental effect on the person's life and spiritual growth. Evil spirits identified or "discerned" by either the healing minister or the supplicant are dispatched by a "prayer of command" in the name of Jesus Christ. While healing ministers tend to specialize, most recognize the necessity at times of using all three forms in varying combinations.

Charismatic ritual healing occurs in a variety of settings. Large group-healing services originated at the periodic conferences in which movement participants assemble on a national or regional basis both to show their strength and unity and to worship and teach. In the decade from the late 1970s to the late 1980s these conference sessions evolved into the public healing service, in which healing ministers of some reputation attract Catholics who may not otherwise participate in the Charismatic Renewal. Healing prayers or petitions for self and others may also occur in a segment of smaller weekly prayer meetings. Following these prayer meetings, prayer for individual supplicants may be conducted in a separate "healing room" by a specially chosen team of healing ministers from within the group. More intensive group healing also occurs in smaller day-long or weekend retreats and "days of renewal." Private sessions may be arranged with an experienced healing minister or healing team. Some of those who practice in the private setting also have professional training in counseling or psychotherapy and integrate these practices with ritual healing. In addition, private healing prayer sometimes occurs over the telephone. Finally, healing prayer for oneself or others may be practiced in the solitude of private devotion.

Methods

The discussion presented here is based on a larger study of therapeutic process in Catholic Pentecostal ritual healing. Of the 75 healing ministers interviewed in the first phase of the research, six were recruited to participate in an intensive phase, in which their private healing sessions were observed and recorded. Healer recruitment was based on willingness to participate, a reputation within the movement as experienced and reliable, and an adequate case load. Healing ministers participated in recruitment of subjects, making initial contacts to determine their willingness to participate. Both to protect individuals who may have been particularly vulnerable and to enhance healer-researcher rapport, healing ministers were given discretion in determining which individuals to exclude.

For each person recruited, up to five healing sessions were recorded on cassette tape with the researcher present. During a subsequent interview, each participant was asked to identify the most important or meaningful event within the session. These events were played back, and commentaries were elicited for each person, using an adapted form of the Interpersonal Process Recall (IPR) method developed by psychotherapy process researchers (Elliott 1984, 1986). An additional background interview covered basic life history and medical/psychiatric history, nature and level of involvement in the Charismatic Renewal, and attitudes and expectations of religious healing. In order to confirm presence or absence of psychiatric disorder, this interview included an adapted and shortened form of the Schedule of Affective Disorders and Schizophrenia (SADS).

Both individuals whose cases are presented here were followed from beginning to end of their involvement with one of the participating healing ministers. They represent precisely the kind of incremental and inconclusive process that I suggested above as characterizing the lowest limits of therapeutic efficacy in ritual healing, and it is for that reason they were chosen as the focus of this analysis. Before discussing them, however, I shall introduce the healer with whom I followed these cases.

A Minister of Charismatic Healing

Father Felix, an experienced Charismatic healing minister, is a 60-year-old Catholic priest, ordained as a member of a religious order in 1952. He holds a Doctorate of Ministries with concentrations in psychology and counseling and has been an assistant supervisor of a program for priests in Clinical Pastoral Education (CPE). In 1975, as part of an assignment as director of pastoral care at a Catholic medical center, he was asked by the executive administrator to coordinate a Charismatic healing ministry within the hospital. Although he had been aware of Charismatic prayer groups, he had previously taken no interest; thus his involvement in Catholic Pentecostalism began with his consent to become active in Charismatic healing. Since then he has remained active in the healing ministry, leading public healing services and workshops and conducting private healing sessions.

Catholic Pentecostals believe that the power to heal stems from "spiritual gifts" ("charisms" in theological terms) granted by God. As Father Felix continued to work as both a counselor and healing minister, he asked God for "the gift of discernment to be able to know what to pray for. Because a lot of people are coming in. There's a lot of stuff that's unconscious; they

can't get in touch with it." *Discernment* – divinely heightened intuition – is understood as a divinely inspired ability to understand people, problems, and situations. Father Felix recounts two incidents in which he felt the granting of this charism was confirmed. In the first, while praying with a parish priest, he spoke about problems that were so uniquely relevant to the priest's situation that the latter thought his parishioners had already spoken to Father Felix about them beforehand. In the second, he discerned that he should ask someone else in the healing group to lead a vocal prayer while he prayed silently with his hand on a priest's back. During the prayer his hand became extremely hot. This heat was also perceived by the supplicant, who later mentioned that he had cancer in his back at the spot where Father Felix had "discerned" that he should place his hand. For Father Felix, the fortuitous placement of his hand was a manifestation of discernment, while the heat was a sign that healing was taking place. Since then, Father Felix has relied strongly on this gift in his healing practice.

Father Felix holds private healing encounters in one of the counseling rooms at the monastery where he resides. The session begins with a period of light talk or counseling, during which the priest typically inquires about changes that may have occurred since the previous session. He then places a straight-backed chair in the center of the small room, asks the supplicant to be seated there, and anoints the person's forehead with holy oil. He stands behind the person with one hand on her head and another on her shoulder, praying silently for approximately five minutes. During this period he often receives "discernment" about the person and the problem. Afterwards he asks the person about any experiences she might have had during the prayer. After this second brief period of conversation and counseling, the session ends, seldom having lasted more than a half hour.

Father Felix strongly believes in the necessity of "getting to the source" of a problem in order to heal it. From his experience, two important sources of people's problems are evil spirits and previous generations. To eliminate the influence of evil spirits he uses deliverance prayer, and to eliminate that of previous generations he uses the mass for healing of ancestry. Each of these will be briefly described.

In the Catholic Pentecostal healing system, evil spirits typically are named after emotions or behavioral patterns; Anxiety, Depression, Lust, and Rebellion are all common spirit names. Father Felix agrees with most other Catholic Pentecostal healers interviewed that spirits attack individuals at their most vulnerable points, whether these be the propensity for committing a particular type of sin or the lasting effects of traumatic experience. No one can be completely possessed by Satan unless he makes a conscious decision or pact; all other spiritual afflictions are in the form of oppression or harassment in a particular domain of life experience. Father Felix also allows for human sources of negative emotions in the absence of demonic influence, however, and it is a matter for discernment whether a person plagued by depression or lust is in fact under attack by the spirit of Depression or Lust. Among the most common spirits in his experience is Fear-of-Being-Found-Out, which causes such thoughts as "if only people knew the things I did or I think, I'd have no friends." Another very common spirit is Devaluation, akin to Self-Hatred, which causes "low self-image and self-esteem."

Father Felix's typical mode of deliverance is to pray silently as follows: "By the power of the Word of God, Jesus Christ, and by the power of the Sword of the Spirit I sever forever all negative spiritual, emotional, psychic, or physical negative influences that are bothering my sister [or brother]." Following this general prayer he specifically addresses whatever evil spirits may be present: "You, dark binding forces, I command you in the name of Jesus Christ to be separate one from the other, to be without communication and to be rendered powerless. You have no more power over this person. He [or she] belongs to Jesus Christ." He then silently commands individual demons by name, as their presence is revealed to him through discernment. He does not necessarily inform supplicants that there are evil spirits involved, but instead waits for a sign in their speech or behavior that confirms his discernment. Yet in withholding this divinely inspired knowledge,

he sometimes tells the supplicant that he has discerned things that may hurt if told. In this way he establishes a role both of wise protector and empowered healer who is in direct contact with the sacred.

In addition to private healing sessions, Father Felix often says a "healing-of-ancestry mass" in the home of the supplicant. Beforehand, he asks the person to prepare a family tree going back as many generations as possible, noting any important events or health problems, such as suicide, alcoholism, mental illness, or abortion. He then "prays over" the genealogy for discernment about the individuals represented. The principle enacted in this ritual is that illnesses or adverse effects of traumatic experiences can be passed "through the blood line" to successive generations. Part of a person's healing can include the healing through prayer of individual forebears who died without having been healed. In some respects this practice is akin to praying for the souls of the dead, but it goes a step farther in actually trying to *heal* the dead. When this is accomplished, the chain of negative influence is "severed," and the person is freed of the affliction.

This is a brief description of the Charismatic healing ministry as practiced by a single person. While it is well within the bounds of Catholic Pentecostal healing practice as delimited by the research described above, several contextualizing remarks are in order. First, while it is quite common for priests and members of religious orders to practice ritual healing, many Charismatic healing ministers are laypersons. Second, while some healing ministers have had professional training in counseling or psychology, most have had none. With respect to procedure, Father Felix makes less use of guided imagery than do many Charismatic healing ministers, although he encourages spontaneous mental imagery. On the other hand, he makes great use of deliverance, which many healing ministers avoid because of the perceived danger of dealing with powerful evil spirits. Finally, performing the mass for healing of ancestry in supplicants' homes appears to be a practice unique to Father Felix, and provides him with an opportunity to observe family dynamics in a way that is typically reported only of healers in small-scale traditional societies.

Two Cases of Charismatic Ritual Healing

Case 1

Margo is a 27-year-old woman, third youngest of nine children, who lives with her parents, three of her sisters, and one sister's three-year-old daughter. She is concurrently under treatment with a psychiatrist (psychopharmacologist) and in therapy with a psychologist, but she has been frustrated by the failure of both medication and therapy. The diagnostic portion of her interview confirmed panic disorder and major depression as her principal problems. She and her mother both report that one of her sisters, who lives at home, suffers from schizophrenic illness.

Margo's illness began in 1985, two years before recourse to the healing minister. She had dropped out of nursing school after doing less well than she had hoped, and had returned to full-time work as a hospital administrative assistant. She felt overworked and preoccupied by this stressful job. At the same time she felt that she was "losing" most of her previous friends as they got married, so that her social life had become "flat." After six months she "burned out" and took a transfer to a lower-status, less stressful job. Her first panic attack occurred two months after the transfer.

Difficulties of family life appear to have contributed to the problem. She regards her parents' marriage as very poor, characterized by frequent loud arguments. She describes her father as critical, cruel, and authoritarian, to the point of physically abusive discipline when his children were young. She is very close to her mother and older sister, but feels a need to distance herself from emotional overinvolvement and establish an independent life. She reports developing, one year prior to the onset of her illness, overt hostility and hatred for a previously close sister who had "ruined her own life" and moved back into the family home after having had a baby with a man she did not marry. An additional factor in her distress appears to be the accidental death of a brother some years earlier. Given this constellation of patterns and events, a major area of intense anxiety for her is relationships with men. Through psychotherapy she has come to associate this anxiety with a lack of opportunity to develop a sense of trust for others.

Margo is a practicing Catholic, and was involved in Charismatic prayer groups for a period of months several years prior to her illness, but for no clear reason she ceased attending. Since the onset of her illness, however, Margo has frequently attended public healing services and is on the mailing lists of two influential Charismatic healing ministers. At these services she often experiences "resting in the spirit," a form of motor dissociation in which a person, at the touch of the healing minister, falls in a peaceful, relaxing, and rejuvenating swoon as the "power of the Holy Spirit" overcomes her. Yet Margo had been disturbed in one of these services when the healer declared that she was being healed. On inquiry, the healer explained that her "gift of discernment" revealed that the healing process had already started. Margo reported being confused and baffled, since "if the healing has already started, personally I don't feel any different."

Margo called Father Felix to ask for help, and he advised that she attend his public healing service. At that event she requested prayer for severe depression, and the priest instructed his assistants to pray for expulsion of a "spirit of Darkness." He then suggested that she come to him for private healing sessions. At the initial session he recounted previous situations of successful healing, and stated that he felt she could be healed quickly. He "corrected" her idea that prayer would be more successful if she made her mind blank while he prayed, explaining that she should expect spontaneous mental imagery to emerge from her unconscious during the course of prayer and that God did not need her assistance for the prayer to be successful. He also "corrected" her view that she should cease weekly psychotherapy while undergoing ritual healing.

During the second session, Margo told Father Felix of a disturbing experience she had had repeatedly for several months prior to the onset of her illness. As she was drifting off to sleep, she "could feel another presence in my room. I could feel someone actually sit down on the end of my bed." She had never mentioned this to her psychiatrist or psychologist, for fear that they would think her crazy. Father Felix agreed that she was right not to have told them, but that he himself was quite familiar with such experiences: it was an evil spirit. This confirmed what she had suspected, and reassured her that it was a phenomenon with which Father Felix could deal.

During the period of silent prayer, perhaps in response to Father Felix's advice to allow thoughts to come to her mind, Margo experienced a series of ideas "coming from all directions." Three issues emerged: the difficulties she experienced in her past administrative job, whether or not to change doctors (she had been told that everything had been tried yet nothing seemed to help), and a disappointing relationship with an older man. The latter situation was one in which the man, who lived in a different city, had courted her for a period of time until she discovered that he was married. She cared for him, but was very angry, and felt conflict about her desire to be with him in spite of a conviction that it would be morally wrong to do so. None of these issues was subsequently discussed with the healer. Father Felix simply told Margo to make note of what came into her mind during prayer because "it would be important" for her.

A final event that unfolded over two sessions had to do with the priest's advice that one can verbally address negative emotions and command them to leave in the name of Jesus Christ. This event was explicitly identified as most significant by Margo in a subsequent interview. She interpreted the advice to mean that the problem is "all in the way that you're thinking." Invoking God indicates that He does not want her to feel as she does, and if she has the strength and faith to say "leave" in His name, the negative emotions of anxiety and depression should go.

During the following session, Father Felix discovered that this technique had not been successful in achieving the goal of changing her attitude. The following key exchange took place:

M: I had thoughts like, you know, I'm slowly going to wither away. Almost like having some form of cancer. It doesn't leave me. It haunts me. It never leaves me. It won't go away. I can't get rid of it. I don't know how to get rid of it. It's driving me crazy. It's driven me crazy. It's overtaken my whole life. And I . . .

FF: What did I tell you last time? I guess you forgot. About taking authority over these things within yourself. You take authority in the name of Jesus Christ, and you command them to just get the heck out. They have to obey.

M: I have said that to myself at different times. Like this whole past week while I was at mass. I had the tremors and the shakes real bad. You know, the fears around other people being there, whatever. And I kept saying that to myself over and over again.

FF: What did you say?

M: I kept saying, you know, "In the name of Christ, leave me, leave me." Trying to force the way that I thought into another direction, more positive. And . . .

FF: Let me clue you in to something. If you say, for instance, "In the name of Jesus," right? There's an evil spirit that calls itself "Jesus" . . . but it's a false Jesus. You've got to remember that. Some people get caught up – it's like conjuring up a spirit, and they're confronting the evil spirit [that] calls himself "Jesus." So I always use the name "Jesus Christ" or "Jesus of Nazareth," you know? *That* Jesus. Oh, yeah, hundreds of [Spanish-speaking] people call themselves Jesus.

In this interaction (identified as significant by Margo herself), the directive to specify the name Jesus Christ was more than a move by the healer to cover the technique's lack of success. For the failure to command one's emotions indicates in the logic of the healing system that more than one's emotions are involved. A powerful force must be standing in the way, blocking the path to healing. In a follow-up interview, Margo acknowledged surprise at learning both the subtlety of the religious technique and the demonic cause of her problem. She recalled Father Felix's original invocation of the "spirit of Darkness" during her first public healing service. She intimated that she had always "thought [about her problem] along those lines" and that the idea of evil forces being involved "struck home." With respect to how this interaction helped her, she responded that it was "to give me courage and more strength, and more faith. Faith-wise, to know that this is not of God. And how prayer can build your faith. It can build your strength."

In addition to having a home mass for healing of ancestry. Margo attended a total of three private sessions with Father Felix. Instead of going to her fourth session, she kept an appointment with her psychopharmacologist, who decided that since no other treatment had worked, she should be admitted for electroconvulsive therapy (ECT). She indicated that she would have resumed the sessions after discharge, but this was precluded by Father Felix's departure for a long sabbatical.

Case 2

Ralph is a 25-year-old man who has finished high school and spent a short period in college. He now lives with his parents and brother, a year his junior, and is under medical and psychiatric treatment for a variety of problems. The diagnostic portion of our interview confirmed a complex situation revolving around a primary diagnosis of paranoid schizophrenia originating from serious drug abuse; obsessive-compulsive disorder with onset at age 14; probable dysthymic disorder (a mild form of clinical depression); symptoms of agoraphobia, panic disorder, and simple phobia (fear of heights); epilepsy related to a probable brain lesion; and asthma.

In 1983, approximately four years before Charismatic healing, Ralph had had a major psychiatric hospitalization following a drug overdose. His inpatient experience was traumatic and appears to have been the occasion on which his principal complaint began: extreme "nervousness" in social situations for fear people are thinking negatively about him, in particular that they are thinking he might be homosexual. Since the advent of these fears, he has been unable to hold a job and finds it nearly intolerable to be in a group of people.

Another major source of distress is his brother, who in the past has also been under psychiatric care. He cannot tolerate his brother, who is highly abusive to their parents, so the two have taken turns living with their grandfather in a nearby town. Ralph appears to have a close relationship with his father, but he feels that his mother is critical and habitually makes him feel guilty even in small daily events. His primary pleasure comes from listening to recorded music and from writing poetry in a style that he considers similar to that of Kerouac and Ginsberg, though he finds it extremely difficult to write creatively under the influence of his antipsychotic medication.

Ralph's religious background includes exposure to the Charismatic Renewal when he was 16, when he attended a prayer group for about a month with his mother. During this time he had the experience of "Baptism in the Holy Spirit" and became familar with speaking in tongues and other Charismatic practices. He currently claims not to believe in God, but even so, admits that religious themes consistently emerge in his poetry. The encounter with Father Felix was initiated by Ralph's mother, who thought that, as a psychologist, he could best advise the family about a psychiatrist's recommendation that Ralph submit to electroconvulsive therapy (ECT). Father Felix responded that if Ralph saw him on a regular basis he would not need ECT. Ralph entered the situation expecting counseling for his main problem of social nervousness, and only when the sessions began did he realize they consisted primarily of healing prayer.

Hopes were raised after the first session, during which Ralph experienced warmth emanating from the priest's hands and the sensation of purple rings expanding concentrically in his visual field while his eyes were closed. Father Felix interpreted the vision in terms of Catholic liturgical symbolism, in which purple represents death. He concluded that something negative within Ralph was dying. More important for Ralph, the sense of a benign presence accompanied him for two days after this initial session. This experience encouraged him to attend mass with his grandfather, where he felt his eyes rotating upward in their sockets (nystagmus). One of Ralph's greatest fears is that this occasional phenomenon will occur in public, and its occurrence during the mass prompted him to feel betrayed by God. In subsequent sessions he again experienced heat and color, but the sensations progressively declined in intensity. In addition, although he had prayed silently along with Father Felix during the first few sessions, he ceased this participation in the final ones.

Ralph's post-session interviews reveal his perception of the therapeutic process as unsatisfactory. Two types of comments indicate that the healer at times either overinterpreted or misunderstood Ralph's experience in ways that weakened the rhetorical impact of the healing.

One of Father Felix's overinterpretations occurred when he was trying to convince Ralph that by dwelling on his nervousness he would perpetuate it, just as someone who repeats to himself "don't think about the color green" is in fact thinking about green. During the period of prayer with laying on of hands which followed this conversation, Ralph saw the color green in addition to his usual purple. Father Felix attributed significance to this, pointing out that green is the color of hope in liturgical symbolism. Ralph rejected the interpretation, attributing his vision of green to the suggestion planted by the previous advice, rather than to divine inspiration. In another example, Father Felix asked if he could invite two women from the local Charismatic prayer group to help him in the healing prayer in order to expose Ralph to female influence, which he felt was inadequate in his client's life, and apparently also in response to Ralph's fear of being thought a homosexual. Ralph's response to this therapeutic move was to list a variety of women he knew, rejecting the idea that his exposure to female presence was deficient. Finally, Father Felix attempted to portray as positive Ralph's uncharacteristic attendance at mass and visit to a restaurant with his grandfather. Ralph's response was that he had attended mass only once, and that going to a restaurant never made him as nervous as did being in a group of people.

In addition to these overinterpretations, Father Felix appears to have misunderstood Ralph on a number of occasions. In a segment during which the two discussed whether Ralph's nervousness would prevent him from attending a party, Father Felix stated that he thought mingling with people would be just the thing Ralph needed. In response to Ralph's statement that he was too nervous, the healer said that if you think nervous, you'll be nervous. Ralph objected, "No, I'm not thinking nervous, I *am* nervous!" In the follow-up interview, he stated specifically that he felt misunderstood, and that with paranoia one cannot simply tell oneself to do something. In another segment Ralph mentioned that his father encouraged him to "be like him" and not care what others think. Father Felix interpreted this as an expression of the father's insecurity, indicating that he did not feel in control of his life and really did care about others' opinions. In the follow-up interview, Ralph took exception to this, arguing that his father had made this statement only once or twice, in the context of encouraging Ralph, and wasn't guilty of "denial." He felt that Father Felix's basic point about people in general was correct, but that he was inaccurate in attributing such denial to his father. Finally, in a session when Ralph stated that no changes had occurred since the previous session, Father Felix turned to the researcher and asked if in fact I could not observe any changes. Ralph interpreted this attempt to solicit impressions of observable behavioral change as an outright contradiction of his report of no internal experience of change. He stated that this made him angry, although it "didn't have anything to do with the praying" as a form of treatment.

In spite of this apparent willingness to separate the religious effects of the prayer from the perceived missteps of the healing minister, successive overinterpretations and misunderstandings appear to have undermined the therapeutic process. Ralph terminated his involvement after five sessions and a healing-of-ancestry mass. Subsequently, Father Felix met in several sessions with the father, praying ostensibly for the second son with the father as "proxy." In private, however, he admitted he was simultaneously praying for the father himself, who he felt had an overly critical and negative manner. The priest felt that the man's manner was somewhat ameliorated through healing, and the family also reported that their second son had become less wrathful and abusive. However, the father soon terminated his sessions with Father Felix as well.

In an interview two months following his termination, Ralph described interactions with a new psychiatrist, who was skeptical of the diagnosis of paranoid schizophrenia and who had successfully hypnotized Ralph into not feeling nervous on a recent date with a woman. He tended to discount the apparent similarity between the peaceful feeling of being prayed over with eyes closed and being placed in light trance and was hopeful about his new course of treatment.

Incremental Change, Inconclusive Success

Much of the literature on religious healing implies that ritual necessarily and definitively accomplishes, at least in its own terms, what it sets out to do. Far from being definitive, the effects of healing in the two cases presented here are incremental and inconclusive. Both are close to what we could call limiting cases, beyond which the relevance of any idea of efficacy becomes questionable. Even so, the case descriptions indicate that the healing experience was more satisfying for Margo than for Ralph, since he rejected the process and she wished to continue it. This contrast in behavior suggests the need for an interpretive approach sensitive to subtle but important modulations of meaning and experience in the therapeutic process. In an earlier analysis based on retrospective accounts of Charismatic healing, I proposed that therapeutic process in ritual healing be analyzed in terms of participants' predispositions, their experience of empowerment, and their experience of transformation (Csordas 1983). Following cases prospectively has allowed a reformulation of these elements in more precise terms. Thus, we will examine the two cases in light of these elements of therapeutic process.

Disposition of participants

The term "disposition" is fortuitous in that it has the dual meaning of a prevailing

mood or tendency and of the act of disposing or arranging in an orderly way. In other words, under this heading we are looking not only at psychological states, such as expectancy or "faith to be healed," but at the disposition of persons within the healing process vis-à-vis social networks and symbolic resources.

While neither client was very active in the Charismatic movement, Margo was more familiar with religious healing through attendance at prayer meetings and public healing services and had no questions about basic religious belief. In addition, her mother was oriented toward Charismatic spirituality and subscribed to the leading Catholic Pentecostal magazine. In spite of strong disappointment at a healing service in which she was told that her healing had already begun, Margo's positive disposition within the process was expressed in her gratitude for having been singled out for one-on-one healing sessions with Father Felix and in her openness to his instructions. She accepted his injunctions both to be open to spontaneous images from her unconscious during prayer and to conceive of her anxiety and depression as "diminishing" from day to day. Her positive disposition was enhanced by the reassurance that an apparition at her bedside, about which she had never told her secular therapist, was not a sign of mental illness but a frequent and fully understandable manifestation of an evil force. Finally, in one session she took the initiative of asking the priest if he had spiritually "picked up" or "discerned" anything particular about her problem while he prayed over her. This anticipation of divine empowerment in fact caught Father Felix by surprise, but he was able to summarize several "fears" about which he had been "led" to pray, thus reinforcing Margo's already strong disposition.

Ralph, in contrast, entered the process with ambivalence: he expressed agnosticism but acknowledged a preoccupation with religion that emerged both in his poetry and even occasionally in praying by repeating the name "Jesus." Like Margo, he had been exposed to the practices of the Charismatic Renewal, although he had not been involved for at least eight years and then only briefly. In addition, he had entered healing under the assumption that his sessions with Father Felix would consist not of prayer but of counseling. Nevertheless, his disposition during the process was favorable enough that he prayed along with the priest during the first several sessions. Yet this level of participation diminished, with the final result that he discounted the healing process as cultlike.

Experience of the sacred

The human capacity to attend to the world as sacred, other, and powerful has been documented repeatedly by phenomenologists of religion (Eliade 1958, 1959; van der Leeuw 1938). Each healing system attends to the human condition differently, elaborating a repertoire of ritual elements that constitute legitimate manifestations of divine power. Within a particular healing system, we are concerned with individual variation in experience of the sacred that may influence the course of therapeutic process.

Margo's experiences of concrete empowerment included periodic "resting in the Spirit" at other healing services before entering the series of sessions with Father Felix. With the priest, instruction to be open to unconscious material resulted in the spontaneous experience of three significant aspects of her problem, "rushing at her from all directions." Both the motor dissociation of resting in the Spirit and the spontaneous imagery are examples of concrete, embodied experience of the sacred. Ralph's experience of progressively diminishing empowerment began with a distinct experience of abandonment by the transcendent presence that had initially been evoked in the healing prayer. The significance of this event never came to Father Felix's attention during the sessions; hence, he did not have the opportunity of dealing with it in the context of Catholic Pentecostal belief and practice. In short, this experience of the sacred was not incorporated into the therapeutic process for Ralph, and the intensity of his experience of power as presence, heat, and color progressively diminished. It is also possible that the priest's attempt to attribute symbolic meaning to the emergence of green in Ralph's visual field further

undermined the evocation of the sacred, since Ralph himself attributed the experience to the power of suggestion rather than to divine power.

The most striking difference between the two cases is that Margo's experiences had more sacred content that pertained immediately to her situation, as opposed to Ralph's vague sense of divine presence, heat, and color that received only minimal interpretation by the healing minister. The observer might surmise that the healer could have worked with this experience either by interpreting it as a mystical companion who could protect the young man from pathological nervousness in social situations or by using it as an experiential wedge into Ralph's agnosticism, thereby facilitating greater disposition toward healing. Father Felix might also have taken the occasion to induce behavioral and attitudinal transformation through his stated priority of getting to the "root" of Ralph's problems. Instead, any potential content of Ralph's experience remained unelaborated as insight, interpretation, or direction. It is unclear whether this did not occur because the healer was unaware of Ralph's experience of "presence" or because such a strategy would be unacceptable.

Margo's experiences of empowerment were substantially different, rich in biographical meaning (sudden emergence of thoughts about her job, doctor, and former boyfriend). For her, the experience was a moment not of abstract but of concrete transcendence. As pointed out by Kapferer, "A ritual fixed in a transcendent moment is empowered to act on contexts external to the performance and to transform them in accordance with the rearrangement or reordering which the transcendent moment of the rite expresses" (1979: 17). Unless the concrete rhetoric within such moments is identified, the phrase "in accordance with" posits no more than an abstract homology between elements of ritual and elements of a distressed life. The concrete experience of the sacred is not an experience of "the supernatural" but a transformed way of attending to the human world. For Margo but not for Ralph, the link between transcendence and the reordering of life was forged in the biographical content of her transcendent moment.

Negotiation of possibilities

A principal task of therapeutic persuasion and healing is to create alternatives by changing the "assumptive world" (Frank 1973) of the afflicted. Different healing systems may conceive the alternatives as new pathways, as a means of becoming unstuck, or of overcoming obstacles, as a way out of trouble, or in terms of a variety of other metaphors. They may use ritual or pragmatic means and may encourage activity or passivity, but the possibilities must be perceived as real and realistic.

The first possibility elaborated for Margo concerned her attitude toward medical treatment. She was persuaded that instead of cooperating with the effects of prescribed medication through a positive attitude, she had been expecting them to fail, and so they had. An extension of this line of thinking was her mother's conjecture that the doctor's unexpected decision to try ECT may have been an effect of the healing prayer.

The second possibility was elaborated through Margo's new understanding of the role of evil spirits, placing "spiritual power" alongside "illness" as a way to make sense of a frustrating life situation. This alternative was provided along with the reassurance that an unsettling apparition was not a sign of insanity but the manifestation of an evil spirit. She was later persuaded that the technique of "commanding her emotions" was not only a way to invoke divine power but also a way to instill some sense of control over emotions she experienced as uncomfortable and alien. The attribution of the technique's ineffectiveness to interference by an evil spirit not only "raised the stakes" to a cosmological level, but confirmed her feeling that anxiety and depression were alien to her natural state.

The story for Ralph can be summed up more briefly. There were simply no possibilities generated for him in the healing process. As with Margo, Father Felix offered methods – relaxation, developing a positive attitude, attending social events – but Ralph never perceived them as realistic.

Actualization of change

What counts as change, as well as the degree to which that change is seen as significant by participants, cannot be taken for granted in comparative studies of therapeutic process. This insight is all the more important for this discussion, where no definitive outcome exists and where our concern is to define minimal elements of efficacy.

The principal evidence for incremental change in Margo's healing is her report of a decision to share her troubles with a younger sister-in-law. While a reason for this decision did not explicitly emerge in follow-up interviews, it can be suggested that the healer's discourse on "Fear-of-Being-Found-Out" may have planted the idea of seeking support from others rather than attempting to hide her difficulties from them. Attributing her former behavior to a fear that is not only negative but may also represent the activity of an evil spirit is in this instance the key feature of the rhetoric of transformation. Whereas the desire to hide her distress had led to increasing social withdrawal, its linkage to the idea of an evil spirit now motivated Margo to make her distress itself the occasion for social engagement.

Failure to actualize change in Ralph's healing is evident in his explicit rejection of whatever Father Felix offered as evidence of therapeutic change. Attending mass with his grandfather was discounted because it only happened once, going to a restaurant with his grandfather was not significant because he customarily did such things without consequence anyway, and another person's opinion about whether he had changed was discounted both because he had no indication from others that this was so and especially because what mattered to him was that *he* felt no different. When the researcher asked whether his recent lack of trouble with uncontrolled eye movement was a possible result of healing prayer, Ralph did not reject the possibility outright but greeted it with ambivalence, precluding its classification as an experience of transformation. The healer's perception of a positive change in Ralph's father doubtless had minimal effect, since father and son already had a close relationship. Similarly, the parents' report of change in his brother had minimal effect, since strained relations between brothers persisted to the point where they were unable to live in the same house.

In sum, the therapeutic process for Margo was characterized by an initially positive disposition; experiences of divine power with discrete, intelligible content; the elaboration of viable possibilities; and significant, if incremental, changes. Ralph exhibited ambivalent disposition, diminishing empowerment, nonrecognition of possibilities, and rejection of change, with a strong perception of being misunderstood by the healing minister. In these terms, healing was more successful for Margo than for Ralph, and the analysis thus sheds light on the different modes in which the two terminated their sessions. Ralph left the religious healing process to find apparently greater satisfaction from a psychiatrist/hypnotist, with no sense of continuity from his Charismatic healing encounter. Margo, who was initially demoralized about psychiatry and psychotherapy, left the healing process to try an additional inpatient psychiatric treatment and probably would have continued religious healing if the priest had not left the area for an extended period.

Discussion

While moving in the right direction, this analysis still does not establish the significance of these transformations in comparison to what clinical thinking would call a cure. What is striking in the examples presented is their incremental character, with no guarantee that they will be permanently integrated into the person's life. The incremental and open-ended process of religious healing may prove to be an essential characteristic that requires some religious cures to be "symbiotic" (Crapanzano 1973): perhaps there is no therapeutic outcome, only therapeutic process. Catholic Pentecostal healing can include the symbiotic goal, encouraging supplicants to incorporate religious meaning and inhabit a religiously defined community. Yet in the sociocultural setting of late 20th-century North America, we may readily discern factors that contribute to the fragmentary and inconclusive nature of the healing process which do not pertain in the traditional societies from which the bulk of ethnographic knowledge comes.

First, consider Father Felix's attempt to draw the families of Margo and Ralph into the healing process through the healing-of-ancestry mass. If there is anything unique about Father Felix's healing practice in comparison to that of other Catholic Pentecostal healing ministers, it is his practice of entering the home and mobilizing family support through participation in this event. Most Charismatic healing is based on the model of the individual encounter, and it is not unknown for a woman to be in the healing process to the displeasure of her husband. Even when the healer takes the initiative in mobilizing social support, his authority is not such that he can intervene in the way sometimes described for traditional healers. Margo's father was pointedly absent from her ancestry mass, as was Ralph's brother from his. Ralph's father participated enthusiastically in several private sessions of his own with the priest, but he discontinued them without resolution, simply failing to make another appointment. Thus social support, often cited as one of the hallmarks of ritual healing, is by no means automatic. Support from the family and support from the community of religious believers are not identical or necessarily even compatible. Support from either may be less emphatic than might be expected from the cases commonly reported in the ethnographic literature.

Consider, in addition, the ease with which people may enter and leave the healing process in these examples. In cross-cultural perspective, this kind of mobility among healing resources seems to be a function of both the number of resources available and the exclusivity of each healing form. Finkler (1985) observed a distinction among Mexican Spiritualists between those who were devotees and those who made casual or periodic use of Spiritualist healing; Crapanzano (1973) noted a similar distinction between Hamadsha devotees who experienced a symbiotic cure and others who received a "one-shot" exorcistic cure. As Catholic Pentecostalism has developed over the past two decades, its healing forms have become more accessible to those with only a marginal exposure to the movement. Like Ralph and Margo, they are less likely to become involved in a total "symbiotic cure" and will more likely experience the kinds of incremental transformations documented here. Thus, little understanding will result if research is directed toward definitive therapeutic *outcome*, rather than toward the ambiguities and partial successes (and failures) embedded in therapeutic *process*.

Furthermore, if their diagnoses are correct, Ralph suffers from a serious schizophrenic illness characteristically associated with psychotherapeutic failure, while Margo's problems of depression and panic typically respond well to a variety of psychotherapeutic interventions. Research in traditional societies is often complicated by the fact that the anthropologist does not have comparable diagnostic information; on the other hand, research in contemporary society can be complicated by the fact that the informant *does* have this information. Ralph's rejection of Father Felix's comment, "If you think nervous, you'll be nervous," was based on his conception that clinical paranoia cannot simply be banished by a change of attitude. In contrast, Margo's willingness to tell about her experience of an apparition only to the priest and not to her psychotherapist was based on her concern that she might receive a diagnosis that to her was worse than depression and panic disorder.

One might say that the religious healing encounters of both supplicants were conditioned by previous encounters with mental health professionals, in terms both of knowledge about their conditions and, especially for Margo, of insights gained from previous psychotherapy. This interpretation would represent ethnographic myopia, however. More accurate for both Margo and Ralph, religious healing was an interlude in a history of encounters with the mental health establishment. Herein lies both the clinical and anthropological significance of these cases: anthropologically, in terms of how the interaction of both religious and clinical meanings shape the illness experience; and clinically, in terms of how the religious encounter may influence the trajectory of the illness. How did Ralph's previous hospitalization and interaction with mental health professionals affect the encounter with Father Felix, and how did the experience with Father Felix influence Ralph's subsequent encounter with the psychiatrist using hypnotherapy? Margo was seeing both a psychiatrist and a psychologist before meeting Father Felix, who suggested that she switch to a Christian psychotherapist while she continued with healing prayer. In the end she appeared committed to both psychiatric treatment and religious healing. But were these independent commitments or did, for example, religious healing influence Margo's willingness to submit to ECT?

The clinician should find this kind of information valuable, but it is not likely to be volunteered by the patient. Like Ralph and Margo, both of whom refused to permit me to contact their physicians, many of those who have recourse to religious healing undoubtedly believe they are better off not informing their physicians unless or until some dramatic change occurs for which they want medical documentation of a miraculous healing. Medical prejudice – real or perceived – against religious conviction may create a critical blind spot in the clinical picture of the large number of people who find religious healing congenial.

In concluding, we should allow a final word to Father Felix, who was himself disappointed that more noticeable and quicker results had not been achieved in either case. He attributed the difficulty with Ralph both to the supplicant's resistance and to his own failure to include more of a counseling component alongside healing prayer. He also saw Margo's main problem as a negative family environment and her inability to achieve independence from it.

Conclusion: Therapeutic Process and the Theory of Healing

The method adopted in this study of examining disposition, religious experience, possibility, and incremental change as elements of therapeutic process contrasts with studies that emphasize the global role of psychological mechanisms such as suggestion, catharsis, placebo effect, or regression in service of the ego (Calestro 1972; Sargant 1973; Scheff 1979; Torrey 1972). These studies tend to discourage detailed analysis of therapeutic process in the experience of individual persons, since if healing can be accounted for by a nonspecific mechanism, all that need be specified is how that mechanism is triggered. Even when more specificity is given, as in Scheff's (1979) proposal that a mechanism of distancing is essential to the mechanism of catharsis, analysis tends to discount the nature of distress and the differential effects of healing across individuals. We cannot definitively say, for example, that the technique of commanding her emotions constituted distancing for Margo, and even if we can, the effect may have been more cognitive than cathartic. A similar point applies to invocation of "altered states of consciousness" in explaining the effects of healing. These states cannot be treated like mechanisms such as catharsis or suggestion. Their nature must be defined in cultural as well as psychophysiological terms, and their place within healing systems must be specified.

In staying close to the experiential data, this method also contrasts with other more globally stated conceptions of the healing process. For example, Dow (1986) describes the healing process as one in which symbols from the mythic realm are "particularized" in meaning for an individual supplicant. The symbols are then "manipulated" by a healer to mediate or "transact" between the hierarchical levels of society and self. In addition, emotions are "attached" to the symbols to transact between levels of self and soma. In the case of Margo it is certainly possible to label the spirit of Darkness as a transactional symbol to which the healer attaches the emotion of depression; it could just as easily be described as a quality predicated by the healer on an inchoate pronoun (Fernandez 1974), or as a management of meaning by the healer, who is acting as a spiritual broker defining the conditions of the supplicant's participation in the religious group (Kapferer 1976). In short, a model is needed that can specify conditions for change, criteria for a job well done by the healer, and cultural repertoires of significant patient experience.

While Dow states that the healer "persuades" the patient that the mythic symbols are relevant to his or her condition, he does not explain how such persuasion occurs and creates a disposition to be healed. Elements of religious experience are judged by Dow to be "therapeutic preludes," the purpose of which is to establish a therapeutic relationship based on paradox; transcendence (Kapferer 1979) and experience of the sacred (Csordas 1987a) play no part. Finally, the relationship among social, self, and somatic levels is characterized as analogous to that of a "thermostat," such that "it is possible to affect processes in the self and unconscious-somatic systems through the manipulation of symbolic parameters at the social level" (Dow 1986:63). The thermostat analogy is entirely too mechanistic. What is needed at this stage in the development of a theory of healing is specification of *how* therapeutic process effects transformation in existential states.

An approach grounded in participants' own experience and perceptions of change may arrive at a more pragmatic conceptualization of healing as a cultural process. This should be a goal not only on a conceptual, theoretical level but also on the level of interaction between medical and sacred aspects of complex health care systems, as illustrated by the two cases analyzed here. Having chosen a type of religious healing that is formally and experientially different from psychotherapy, yet sufficiently similar for systematic comparison, I suggest the possibility of a theory of the healing process that will not only include other, more seemingly exotic forms but also permit a rethinking of healing in cosmopolitan biomedicine.

REFERENCES

Bourguignon, Erika
  1976 The Effectiveness of Religious Healing Movements: A Review of the Literature. Transcultural Psychiatric Research Review 13:5–21.
Calestro, Kenneth
  1972 Psychotherapy, Faith Healing, and Suggestion. International Journal of Psychiatry 10:83–113.

Crapanzano, Victor
1973   The Hamadsha: A Study in Moroccan Ethnopsychiatry. Berkeley: University of California Press.

Csordas, Thomas J.
1980   Building the Kingdom: The Creativity of Ritual Performance in Catholic Pentecostalism. Ph.D. dissertation, Department of Anthropology, Duke University.
1983   The Rhetoric of Transformation in Ritual Healing. Culture, Medicine, and Psychiatry 7:333–75.
1987a   Health and the Holy in African and Afro-American Spirit Possession. Social Science and Medicine 24:1–11.
1987b   Genre, Motive, and Metaphor: Conditions for Creativity in the Ritual Language of Catholic Pentecostalism. Cultural Anthropology 2(3):445–69.

Dow, James
1986   Universal Aspects of Symbolic Healing: A Theoretical Synthesis. American Anthropologist 88:56–69.

Eliade, Mircea
1958   Patterns in Comparative Religion. Rosemary Sheed, transl. Cleveland: World Publishing.
1959   The Sacred and the Profane. William Trask, transl. New York: Harcourt, Brace, and World.

Elliott, Robert
1984   A Discovery-Oriented Approach to Significant Events in Psychotherapy: Interpersonal Process Recall and Comprehensive Process Analysis. In Patterns of Change. Laura Rice and Leslie Greenberg, eds. Pp. 249–86. New York: Guilford Press.
1986   Interpersonal Process Recall (IPR) as a Process Research Method. In The Psychotherapeutic Process. Laura Greenberg and William Pinsoff, eds. Pp. 180–211. New York: Guilford Press.

Favazza, Armando
1982   Modern Christian Healing of Mental Illness. American Journal of Psychiatry 139:728–35.

Fernandez, James
1974   The Mission of Metaphor in Expressive Culture. Current Anthropology 15:119–45.

Finkler, Kaja
1985   Spiritualist Healers in Mexico. South Hadley, MA: Bergin and Garvey.

Frank, Jerome
1973   [1961] Persuasion and Healing. Baltimore: Johns Hopkins University Press.

Good, Byron, et al.
1982   Reflexivity and Countertransference in a Psychiatric Cultural Consultation Clinic. Culture, Medicine, and Psychiatry 6:281–303.

Kapferer, Bruce
1976   Transaction and Meaning: Directions in the Anthropology of Exchange and Symbolic Behavior. Philadelphia: Institute for the Study of Human Issues.
1979   Introduction: Ritual Process and the Transformation of Context. Social Analysis 1:3–19.
1983   A Celebration of Demons: Exorcism and the Aesthetics of Healing in Sri Lanka. Bloomington: University of Indiana Press.

Kleinman, Arthur, and Lilias Sung
1979   Why Do Indigenous Practitioners Successfully Heal? Social Science and Medicine 13B:7–26.

Kleinman, Arthur, and James Gale
1982   Patients Treated by Physicians and Folk Healers: A Comparative Outcome Study in Taiwan. Culture, Medicine, and Psychiatry 6:405–23.

McGuire, Meredith
1982   Pentecostal Catholics: Power, Charisma, and Order in a Religious Movement. Philadelphia: Temple University Press.

Moerman, Daniel
1979   Anthropology of Symbolic Healing. Current Anthropology 20:59–80.

Noll, Richard
1983   Shamanism and Schizophrenia: A State-Specific Approach to the 'Schizophrenic Metaphor' of Shamanic States. American Ethnologist 10:443–59.

Pattison, E. Mansell, Nikolajs A. Lapins, and Hans A. Doerr
1973   Faith Healing: A Study of Personality and Function. Journal of Nervous and Mental Diseases 157:397–409.

Peters, Larry
1981   Ecstasy and Healing in Nepal: An Ethnopsychiatric Study of Tamang Shamanism. Malibu: Undena Publications.

Peters, Larry, and Douglas Price-Williams
1980   Towards an Experiential Analysis of Shamanism. American Ethnologist 7:398–418.

Prince, Raymond
1980 Variations in Psychotherapeutic Procedures. *In* Handbook of Cross-Cultural Psychology, Vol. 6. Harry C. Triandis and Juris G. Draguns, eds. Pp. 291–349. Boston: Allyn and Bacon.

Sargant, William
1973 The Mind Possessed. New York: Lippincott.

Scheff, Thomas
1979 Catharsis in Healing, Ritual, and Drama. Berkeley: University of California Press.

Schieffelin, Edward
1985 Performance and the Cultural Construction of Reality. American Ethnologist 12:707–24.

Tambiah, Stanley
1977 The Cosmological and Performative Significance of a Thai Cult of Healing. Culture, Medicine, and Psychiatry 1:97–132.
1985 [1981] A Performative Approach to Ritual. *In* Culture, Thought, and Social Action. pp. 123–66. Cambridge: Harvard University Press.

Torrey, E. Fuller
1972 The Mind Game: Witchdoctors and Psychiatrists. New York: Emerson Hall.

Turner, Victor
1969 The Ritual Process: Structure and Anti-Structure. Chicago: Aldine.

van der Leeuw, Gerardus
1938 Religion in Essence and Manifestation. J. E. Turner, transl. London: Allen & Unwin.

11

The Thickness of Being
Intentional Worlds, Strategies of Identity, and Experience Among Schizophrenics

Ellen Corin

The construction of knowledge builds on the dialectical tension between researchers' categories and the reality they aim to describe. Although categories are progressively refined and honed, they remain bound by an initial intellectual frame of reference that predetermines what deserves attention within a given reality, for which our categories never suffice. In relation to psychiatry, Jaspers (1963) reminded us decades ago that reality, especially human reality, always transcends our knowledge of it and that knowledge always depends on, and is bound by, the methods used to access it. This process is inherent to knowledge, but researchers often forget that their knowledge is only part of the whole picture. Like the blind men in the fable who build a whole, imaginary picture of the elephant based on what they touch (trunk, tusk, tail, leg), researchers tend to make generalizations from results obtained with their research instruments.

In recent years, challenges associated with the heterogeneity of outcome in schizophrenia and the limitations of current knowledge to explain this phenomenon have led to the exploration of new approaches and avenues of thinking. Some researchers have explored the hypothesis that personal and interpersonal strategies for dealing with symptoms could significantly alter the course and outcome of

schizophrenia and have argued for the need to reintroduce subjectivity and experience into psychiatric research and practice (Ciompi 1984, 1989; Strauss 1985). Other studies have tried to grasp the "thick" dimension of the experience and its dynamics through alternative research methods, including life histories (Carpenter 1987; Estroff 1989; Fabrega 1989; Hatfield 1989; Strauss 1989). These studies have resulted in significant breakthroughs, reminding us above all that patients undergo tremendous suffering and are often actively engaged in trying to cope with this debilitating experience. However, authors tend to consider experience a "transparent reality," where meaning is directly accessible. It is still uncommon for researchers in psychiatry to consider other philosophical and social sciences' perspectives for the renewal or deepening of our common understanding of experience and subjectivity.

Recent anthropology has been dominated by a rise in critical trends that question the possibility of access to other people's lived worlds. Authors are now aware that knowledge of other cultures is always colored by the observer's own cultural belonging and intellectual orientations and by academic debates (Crapanzano 1992; Clifford and Marcus 1986). In his reflections for justifying and grounding an anthropology of experience,

Ellen Corin, "The Thickness of Being: Intentional Worlds, Strategies of Identity, and Experience among Schizophrenics," *Psychiatry* 61 (1998): 133–46.

Bruner (1986) emphasized that experience is by definition self-referential and therefore, only accessible to the individual. Access to the expression of experience is possible, but the relationship of experience to its expression is always partial and dialectical: experience is not just "being there," unrelated to its expression and context. Other authors have defended the idea that parts of experience always remain obscure to the actors themselves and require various levels of interpretation (Bibeau and Corin 1995). For example, individuals are constrained by the limitations of language and by their own alienation from subjective experience; experience can be revealed through silences, contradictions or inconsistencies which permeate lived experience as well as by the explicit content of discourse. Experience cannot be reduced to its conscious dimension or to what is expressed in discourse.

Experience and Its Horizon

Half a century ago, European phenomenological psychiatrists perceived psychiatric disorders to be problems affecting the basic coordinates of the being-in-the-world experience. However, they relied on a non-empirical notion of experience developed by philosophers such as Husserl, Heidegger, and others. In reaction to the formalism of neo-Kantian thinkers, Husserl argued for a return to "phenomena" per se, regardless of categories and learning. This implies bracketing the stock of knowledge and theories constitutive of science and of a commonsense understanding of the world, suspending a sense of co-belonging to the world where meaning is taken for granted. This "phenomenological reduction" approach intends to give access to the essence of things, beyond their empirical manifestations which always depend on a network of interpretations and purposeful actions. What is then revealed is not what is sensually perceptible but rather the basic structures through which the perceptible becomes understandable.

Husserl was particularly interested in discovering the essence of human consciousness and of human experience understood as a way of situating oneself within the world. Within this context, "experience" is a basic, "intentional" position toward the world. "Being there" in the world is by necessity "being in" space and time, and "being with" in a shared world. Building on these perspectives in their approach to psychiatric disorders, European psychiatric phenomenologists understood psychiatric disorders as expressing a basic alteration of the subject's intentional position toward the world. They attempt to describe the kind of presence in the world manifest through psychiatric symptoms and to describe alterations which characterize the main categories of psychiatric disorders (Binswanger 1970; Blankenburg 1991; Tellenbach 1979).

This contradicts what mainstream North American psychiatry used to call phenomenological. Although they both intended to eliminate biases introduced by theories and explanations, North American psychiatry relies on an empirical, objectivist notion of phenomena which must be observed from the outside, whereas European phenomenological psychiatrists prefer "diagnosis by penetration" which transcends the empirical surface of phenomena to reach understanding of the deep structure of the "being-in-the-world" expressed through phenomena. Empirical everyday discourses and behaviors provide access to "experience," but this experience cannot be reduced to it, because it is beyond facticity and empiricism. Diagnosis by penetration requires a dialectical to and fro between attention to the empirical reality of existence, and the constituents and foundations of experience. Blankenburg (1991) writes that a phenomenological attitude "eliminates nothing"; it studies everyday existence, from "chatting" to "humble, even despised states of things."

However, it is difficult to apply this perspective to research, mainly because of the nonempirical nature of the referred experience. European phenomenological psychiatry is a clinical discipline aimed above all at animating and orienting the clinical encounter. It can only be used in research in an analogical, transposed way. Research strategies and methods must be designed to help analyze the basic structure of the patient's being-in-the-world experience.

Analytical perspectives developed by Ricoeur (1986) in hermeneutics present interesting parallels with the phenomenological approach to experience and provide inspiration for research strategies. Ricoeur denounced the limitations of "empathy" which assumes a direct and unmediated communication from experience to experience. For Ricoeur, empathy is an illusion and a seductive trap; it is inescapably contaminated by personal expectations and desires, which we tend to project on the other's world, and by ideology. A specialist in text analysis, Ricoeur presents hermeneutics as an analytical method which combines detachment and communication, with both a critical stance assuming the distancing associated with science, and the reestablishment of a relationship of co-belonging between researcher and his object of study, inescapable in human sciences. The basic structure of the text must be interpreted through analyzing recurrences and contradictions, sets of opposites and combinations which hold the text together. There must be a dialectical relationship between "understanding," or "integrating within oneself the structuring work of the text," and the discovery of codes underlying the structure of the text.

From that perspective, listening to the patient's experience in his or her own words and developing an empathetic relationship with him or her remains a minimum but inadequate requirement. On the one hand, empathy is best perceived as a project or an aim rather than as a real possibility. On the other hand, the empathetic understanding of the patient's experience in his or her own words (Ratey, Sands, and O'Driscoll 1986) must be complemented by an attempt to gain access to the underlying premises and coordinates of his or her life-world. Analysis must involve both careful attention to the details of the person's daily life and an attempt to understand the basic structure of their experience.

The Life-World of Nonrehospitalized Schizophrenics in Montréal

The general objective of a research study carried out in Montréal was to contribute to clarifying the pitfalls and the limitations of deinstitutionalizing psychiatric patients and, more particularly, to understand what contributes to community tenure for people who have been diagnosed with schizophrenia. Our main hypothesis was that deinstitutionalization from psychiatric institutions is paralleled by a process of "social deinstitutionalization" through which patients are not allowed to resume normative social roles and are therefore pushed back toward the psychiatric institution and at risk for readmission. The hypothesis therefore focused on the impact of sociological processes of stigmatization and marginalization of the experiences and lives of schizophrenic patients.

More generally, we were also interested in understanding how subjectivity and experience are transformed in schizophrenia and how individuals affected by schizophrenia attempt to rearticulate their relationship with themselves and the world. We wanted to examine to what extent certain types of transformation of the experience may be associated with better outcome.

Methodological markers

The purpose and methods of the Montréal study have been presented more extensively elsewhere (Corin 1990; Corin and Lauzon 1992). I focus here on elements of methods which are particularly relevant to the approach of experience as mentioned previously.

The study involved 45 male patients diagnosed as schizophrenic more than 5 and less than 15 years ago. Selection criteria included a principal diagnosis of schizophrenia and a relative stability of diagnosis. All were between 25 and 50 years old and lived in the catchment area of the Douglas Hospital, a lower middle and working-class residential area. We divided them into three groups according to their rehospitalization history over the previous 4 years: patients without rehospitalization (15), those rehospitalized once or twice (17), those rehospitalized three or more times (13). Statistical tests allowed us to verify the comparability of the three groups according to sociodemographic variables, age of first contact with psychiatry, stability of diagnosis, and initial symptomatic picture. According to what the available data allowed us to judge, we have no reason to believe that patients differed on these dimensions at the first onset of their illness. Further comparisons of the three groups showed that patients differ significantly in the number of days hospitalized, in the use of psychiatric emergency services and outpatient clinics, and in the number of oral prescriptions of psychotropic drugs. It can therefore be said that our initial dividing criteria cover different ways of relating to the psychiatric system.

Open-ended interviews elicited four dimensions of relating to the world. The social network and social support system were reconstructed with an instrument adapted from the "expanded genogram" by Garrison and Podell (1981). Responses allowed us to draw a cognitive map of social relationships and to code their structural and interactional features. The relationship to social roles was explored with an instrument adapted from Serban (1981). We also explored patients' perceptions of their family dynamics and of their position within the family. Finally, we reconstructed the patients' last days and week and used these data to explore the spatio-temporal coordinates of their life-world; this permitted a comparison between the cognitive representation of social links derived from the expanded genogram and patients' interactive daily behavior. At each of these four levels, we explored not only behaviors but also perceptions, expectations, and values which gave us access to subjective life-worlds. In order to explore further the patients' experience of themselves, we also examined their self-descriptions and self-characterizations.

Patients were met between three and six times in a place where they felt safe enough to speak to us: at home, in a restaurant or other public place, sometimes in a psychiatric clinic. We were afraid that lengthy and repeated interviews might be considered intrusive or burdensome. On the whole, however, patients seemed to enjoy the opportunity to talk about themselves, to share worries and questions with us. We always tried to respect their rhythm and the boundaries they wanted to protect.

Instruments were structured enough to allow the data collected to be comparable across interviews, and flexible enough to give access to what was meaningful for each patient who could take the interviewer along unexpected avenues. This style of interviewing shed light on the concrete and symbolic strategies patients resorted to for inhabiting their world and giving meaning to their experience.

Findings discussed in this paper are derived from a comparison between the two extreme groups of patients: those nonrehospitalized and those frequently hospitalized over the last 4 years. Data were coded and intergroup comparisons were done through chi-squares with Yates correction. This revealed some features associated statistically with one or both groups of patients. We then examined further the meaning of these discriminant features by locating them within the context of larger associative chains within which they were embedded for each of the two groups. For that purpose, we identified all other variables statistically correlated ($r \geq 50$) with these discriminant features in each group and their own associations. This procedure laid out the significant texture of indices within each group of patients. It indicated that a similar feature can be associated with opposite connotations and meanings, depending on the group of patients. For example, both groups contrasted with the third one by a very low index of contacts with siblings ($p < .005$). In the frequently hospitalized group, however, this feature was associated with a negative evaluation of the relationship with siblings and corresponded with a feeling of not receiving any support from them. In the nonrehospitalized group, little contact with siblings was complemented by low expectation for more contact ($p < .02$) and by an absence of support from siblings ($p < .01$); moreover, low expectation for more contact with siblings was statistically correlated with infrequent contact with them and a perceived positive relationship with siblings. This procedure therefore revealed that the significance of a particular variable cannot be decided "objectively" or a priori, and that elements must be located within their specific semantic texture.

In order to identify the general structure of the being-in-the-world experience underlying the empirical data, we qualified the significant variables as a function of the orientation they indicated with regard to the social field: toward (+), outward (−), or neutral (0). This revealed that social integration in the two groups is mainly differentiated by features describing the patient's basic personal stance towards the world, which cuts across the areas of social life under consideration.

This first level of analysis, aimed at comparing the two groups of patients, was complemented by analyses at an individual level. Here, we began to examine the specific pattern of variables coded in a single narrative. A qualitative analysis of the content of these narratives provided important information for the further understanding of the meaning of structural orientation abstracted through quantitative techniques and for examining how they translate on a daily life level. It shed light on the imaginary and symbolic aspects of the relationship schizophrenic patients develop with themselves and the world.

The basic coordinates of an intentional world

Group comparisons indicated that both groups revealed a relative paucity of interpersonal relationships with family members and their social network, as well as global marginality regarding normative social roles. However, data on perceptions and expectations reveal that this shared feature has two different frames of meaning.

The frequently hospitalized patients express a feeling of being "kept out of things" at the interpersonal level while at the same time demanding more attention from others; they also perceive themselves as being excluded from family life: from contact with kin, friends, and neighbors, from family activities and from everyday family life. In the area of social support, they see themselves in an asymmetrical subordinated position, receiving more support than they give; they also perceive their parents as having no positive expectations of them. At the level of social roles, they tend to be convinced of the value of interpersonal roles,

even if they remain ambivalent towards their desires and expectations regarding their personal involvement in these roles. In general, the frequently hospitalized patients therefore appear to be characterized by a discrepancy between an intentional stance, which remains oriented positively toward the relational and social field, adhering to some extent to a normative ideal of social integration, and a sense of being marginalized or excluded from this field.

With regard to the nonrehospitalized patients, a globally similar "objective" situation seems to be perceived as proceeding from a personal movement and as being part of a global style of relating to the world. They mention having less contact during their reconstructed days even if their accessible social network appears to be of similar size. They perceive themselves as receiving and giving less support to other people. As for the categories of people they mention, nonhospitalized patients attach great importance to friends as significant individuals, as support people, and meet them more often in their daily life; it could be hypothesized that friends are less intrusive than family and kin, and pose less of a threat to the relatively withdrawn position they take toward the world. The frequently hospitalized patients also mention positive relationships with friends, but in their case, friends are not mentioned as significant others and do not appear to compensate for a general feeling of experienced exclusion and marginality. In the area of social roles, the nonrehospitalized patients tend to express a global detachment toward the importance of interpersonal and instrumental social roles as well as an apparent lack of desire or expectation of being involved in these roles. This analysis of quantified data pertaining to various areas of life therefore reveals recurrences that indicate contrasting structural stances toward the world.

An examination of the individual patterns of data collected with each of the nonrehospitalized patients reveals that a dominant withdrawn position is always slightly compensated by "relating" elements in spheres which vary from person to person and which permit them to perceive themselves as continuing to be articulated to the world in spite of, or through, their withdrawal. We have therefore qualified their position toward the world as "positive withdrawal."

The qualitative aspect of the patients' narratives and the data concerning their daily routine allow a better qualification of this "positive withdrawal" by providing access to the "subjective thickness" of the patients' world. Nonrehospitalized patients' narratives emphasize the positive value attached to withdrawal and its role in the significant reframing of a lonely position.

For example, a nonrehospitalized patient describes himself as quite uncommunicative: "I do not go out a lot. I rather stay at home. I wait for time to go by. When I want peace, I go to my room, on my bed. I meditate, I listen to music, I listen to the vibrations of the home's silence. I want calmness, to be with myself, then to evolve internally." Another person, for whom the psychiatric hospital represented protection, a shelter from other people, and who is now member of a charismatic group, says: "It is slow, I go quietly, I want to master things"; (to a question asking if he likes to be alone): "Yes, it is better to think, to pray." A patient who describes his past life as overly busy and hectic, comments: "When I left the hospital, I settled things with myself, I almost tried to withdraw into myself, I needed to retire, to be alone occasionally." A few individuals describe their withdrawal as an intentional strategy aimed at counteracting a tendency to fuse too much with the others. For example, a very active person who has created his own religious group, who has a number of followers and is involved in many activities, says: "I never did put my trust in others. One needs to keep a secret side. One cannot, one does not have to say everything"; (to a question asking if he likes to be alone): "Yes, because then I rest, I clear out my body entirely." The first person quoted below explains that he also tends to be overly talkative with neighbors, especially about religious matters, and comments: "I am not centered enough on the inside to be at peace with myself. I would like to find an inner peace."

Generally speaking, withdrawal is described as enabling the person to find inner peace, to settle things with oneself; in solitude, one is left with oneself, one is able to move at one's own rhythm, one takes the time to master things, to advance slowly, to think.

A second trend emanating from the narratives is the important role played by religious signifiers for a considerable portion of nonrehospitalized patients. Reference to a broadly defined religious frame allows them in some way to "inhabit" their private world, to protect and reinforce their withdrawal by giving it a positive value. Religious signifiers tend to be borrowed from marginal religious groups or to remain expressed in global terms without reference to particular religions. Individuals also tend to privilege some of the religious group's signifiers, to reinterpret them in accordance to their own life and to mix them with other kinds of signifiers (like those pertaining to astrology or to extraterrestrial beings). This gives the impression that their belief system is a kind of personal collage of a variety of beliefs rather than resulting from strict adhesion to an existing system. Religious signifiers appear to play a number of functions involving the reshaping of the inner experience of oneself, the elaboration of a sense of self-worth, providing the feeling of being part of a meaningful world, of being embedded within an interpersonal frame.

The analysis of the patients' daily routine reveals the central importance attached by most nonrehospitalized patients to frequenting public spaces like small restaurants, corner shops or shopping centres. For some of them, this gives a structure and a rhythm to their spatial and temporal world. It also enables them to relate to other people while not directly interacting with them and keeping distance. Some patients inhabit these spaces in a more intense affective way, through the development of privileged and often imaginary relationships with waitresses who sometimes appeared to them to be especially sensitive and attentive toward them.

It can therefore be said that nonrehospitalized schizophrenic patients appear to be particularly skillful at developing a position on the margin of our common world, simultaneously elaborating and protecting a space for withdrawal that allows them to reconnect with themselves and to construct an intimate and private space, to maintain or to draw symbolic or imaginary links with the outside world. Individuals are simultaneously in and out of the social field, detached rather than excluded, inhabiting an inner space of withdrawal rather than being trapped in it.

Living at the margins

Patients' narratives reveal how distancing and relating elements are interwoven in their lives, how a stance of positive withdrawal is negotiated and can be the main organizer of the existence.

Mr. H. lives with his mother, has no friends, and displays general disinterest in interpersonal roles, such as those of husband or father. He describes himself as having acquired a spirit of freedom yet at the same time, his time frame is carefully scheduled and one of his main endeavors is to impose discipline on himself. Each day, his morning is taken up looking for work and preparing himself for possible work: reading newspapers for job offers, going to the employment office, practicing with a typewriter. He insists, "I have a schedule, a timetable." The second half of the day, he strolls through the innercity streets and in shopping centers "to see people." He has a girlfriend whom he met in a shopping center "for helping psychological development." Listening to him, one gets the impression that this very schedule in itself gives a frame and meaning to his life. It is interesting to notice that the area where he concentrates much of his energy is related to the source to which he actually attributes his problems: an excess of tension due to his former work. He seems to be able to confront and control his original anxiety by introducing it at the core of his life and in neutralizing it through rigid organization that resonates with the general detachment he expresses throughout the interview.

Another nonrehospitalized patient, Mr. E., has no girlfriend nor any other friends; he only has some contact with patients he met in the psychiatric hospital or in prison, about whom he says, "We have things in common." He goes several times a day to a corner shop, always the same one. He spends his energy

resisting the pressure of his family environment which he experiences as hypernormative and rejecting. He opposes the value his parents attach to work and the success that comes through work and justifies the value of being on welfare on the basis of his religious values: "For my family, welfare is sin. I could not live being rich; living wealthy is sin." At the same time, he is aware of being "humiliated" by his mother and grandmother because he is on welfare. He expresses a similar personal distancing regarding interpersonal roles; marriage is only important for men unable to manage at home alone, not for him. His intentional and ethically grounded opposition toward his parents' values can be understood as a positive reshaping of his perceived marginality toward his family environment which he presents as highly cohesive: "My father had my mother. I had my sisters; my father didn't want me to be in contact with my mother. I was always alone. ... My six sisters were doing everything alike." At the same time, when discussing his own values, he continues to share his parents' wishes; "to succeed," as for his mother, and "to be happy," as for his father. It is interesting to note that the religious idiom he has chosen to resist them is in some way their own, as they went successively through various conversions; from Catholicism to the United Church, to Evangelism and to Pentecostalism. Pentecostalism is his own current religion.

In a third example, Mr. I. is divorced and his wife refuses to allow him to go out with their child. He describes himself as having lost all hope for the future; he feels indifferent, with no interests. However, in his fantasy life, he is the best, admired by everyone while at the same time not taking himself seriously. He has no friends apart from a brother-in-law he sees every 3 months. His social life is organized around regular visits to two restaurants where he has been going for the last 4 years and where he knows the waitresses. He came alone to Montréal at the age of 19 from a remote rural area of Québec where his father was a lumberer. His symbolic way of resituating himself within a significant frame of belonging is to read an etymological dictionary with regularity, as his father did. "Without the dictionary," he says, "I would feel lonely." He also mentions the role God plays in his life, even though he does not practice nor pray nor ask God for things. He says that he often thinks of God and believes in him, due to a special experience he had years ago when "light took on a different quality."

In a last case, intense involvement in a biblical school and charismatic groups provide Mr. C. with an important interpersonal and supportive environment and with a significant source of social feedback which helps him to adjust his speech and behaviors according to what is socially acceptable. This sense of belonging contrasts with a double alienation from his family milieu – because they live in another part of the province and because he has always felt excluded and underestimated by his family, especially by his mother who has "always considered him as her inferior" and by his relatives who always treated him as a child. He recalls how insecure he felt when he first arrived alone in Montréal. Although he is afraid of the idea of work, because of past experience where he felt ridiculed, belonging to the religious group provides him with the hope of doing some missionary work later and provides him with a frame through which he can articulate a vague sense of having something to give to other people. More immediately, religious beliefs give him a great sense of release: "Light comes in you."

Each narrative reveals how the respondents' sense of current alienation toward the world has progressively evolved from a complex and difficult life history. Life strategies have to be understood as attempts to renegotiate a place in the world and as restorative processes; they tend to be expressed in an idiom borrowed from their past and current social environment. Some seem more skillful than others in reassuming and reshaping a conflicting life history within their current existence. A few of the nonhospitalized patients we interviewed remained much more embedded in fusional and dependent relationships or in a sick role, their distancing toward the world appearing essentially restricted to a stance of intentional detachment toward normative social roles. In fact, two of the three patients corresponding to this picture relapsed the year following the research.

The construction of a narrative identity

One section of the open-ended interview aimed at grasping how patients perceive and describe themselves. Classical methods for studying self-perceptions propose a list of qualifiers from which respondents have to choose the one that best describes them. This method assumes that self-perceptions can be subsumed under a few discrete attributes and that they possess a well-defined, constant meaning that is the same for respondents and researchers. In our study, we preferred to ask the patients to qualify themselves using three different terms of their choice and to comment on their significance and importance for them.

At first glance, the meaning associated with certain expressions like "I am a biker," "wholehearted," "acting crazy/playing the fool," and "mixed up" is difficult to decide. In some cases, the meaning of the words appears straightforward, but an apparent discrepancy between the common meaning of the expression and the positive or negative value associated with it suggests that it could possess a specific meaning for the respondent; for example, "a guy who wants to make his way out" is rated negatively by a frequently hospitalized patient.

The analysis took into consideration the kind of stance evoked by the qualifiers (for example, personal attributes versus interactional processes) as well as patients' comments. Particular attention was paid to the stylistic dimension of the discourses. Detailed results have been presented elsewhere (Corin and Lauzon 1994). These data provide additional access to the set of meanings which constitute the patients' life-world described above. In the examples here, the terms or expressions patients use for characterizing them are indicated in brackets and are followed by what was actually said. FH designates a response given by a frequently hospitalized patient and NR, a response by a nonrehospitalized patient.

Self-descriptions confirm the degree of tension experienced by the frequently hospitalized patients between a normative definition of personhood and a sense of personal inadequacy and failure. For them, ideal life is expressed in terms of typical social roles; individuals express a deep desire to conform to a "normal way of life", while at the same time feel that this ideal remains beyond their grasp. (FH: "a normal man"): "I am normal but I do not lead a normal life. I should like to get married, to have children, to have a normal life. ... A normal woman will not go out with a guy who has been in a psychiatric hospital." (FH: "uncertain"): "I am apprehensive about my future. Will I end up alone, without a wife, without children, alone in the street? I would have liked to succeed, to have a wife, children." Sometimes, the feeling of inadequacy gets blurred under an expansion of the positive aspects of the self-image. (FH: "would like to be rich"): "A guy who works, in excellent health, with a good position, with responsibilities, who invests in real estate." (FH: "smart"): "Able to think, reasoning, know wrong from right; having your own way of saying words. ... If you were smart, you could be a genius, have a good IQ, have no problem with the speech of language." A feeling of doubt can also be expressed through the direct juxtaposition of a second qualifier that contradicts the first one (the FH patient who mentioned "smart" and quotes as a second qualifier "hyper"): "I talk quick, I don't give the person a chance, I should control myself. A person who's too hyper, they have to give him something to calm him down. He can't control his speech."

Nonrehospitalized patients do not refer as much to normative images of personhood. When they express the feeling of a discrepancy between their self-perception and others' image of themselves, they appear more confident in the value of their own perception, even if a kind of uncertainty always remains. (NR: "intelligent"): "I understand things faster. I know I behave normally; I try to behave normally; I look intelligent. I find myself very intelligent; it doesn't show but me, I know it."

Self-descriptions also confirm the value the nonrehospitalized patients attach to a withdrawn position. They are often aware of the cultural or social abnormality of this mode of being but it does not deter them from valuing it. (NR: "little self-confidence"): "I don't affirm my personality. I would like to find an inner space which could give me self-confidence. To put my confidence in God will help me." (NR: "calm"): "Most people need to speak. I can spend hours without saying a word. Sometimes, it is a bad thing because if one become too calm, one does not have feelings anymore. ... May be I am too calm sometimes but I like myself better too." (NR: "solitary"): "I do not communicate much. ... I know that I am more solitary than normal and that it is negative in people's eyes. I need to withdraw, to be alone occasionally."

At another level, responses of patients in both groups confirm the crucial role played by others' gaze in the construction of their self-image and the importance of the intermediary space between self and others. Notions of reputation, trust, and respect are emphasized in this context. (FH: "want to make my way out"): "I still have difficulty in commanding respect." (NR: "just"): "It gives me a chance of stability; people can trust me." (NR: "honest"): "People respect you if you are honest."

The value associated with this kind of public self-image brings out by contrast the damage inflicted by a pervading feeling of being stigmatized, sometimes at the level of physical appearance, or of not being recognized for personal qualities or efforts. (FH): "Maybe it's true that it is visible when I walk down the street." (NR): "Most people are offensive, people look at you, they stare at you ... because it shows that I am not somebody who has a steady job." Psychiatric labeling and what it evokes at the subjective level plays an important role in this perceived process of marginalization. Some frequently hospitalized patients feel totally trapped within a psychiatric world, which is a source of suffering and discouragement. (FH: "tired"): "I am tired being in psychiatry ... a feeling of discouragement. The doctor told me that I will have to take medications for the rest of my life. Some mornings, I tell myself that I would rather die than to feel like that." Nonrehospitalized patients appear to be more able to distance themselves from this characterization and to counteract it at a personal level. (NH: "Not capable of taking care of myself"), "I need help; day care, psychiatrist, doctor. There are two sides; you can learn from being in the hospital. It's hard to find a job. I am sick, mentally and physically; this brings lack of confidence in everything. I think I am wasting my time here (a day care center). (NR: "intelligent"): "In the hospital, it is as if you were not intelligent when they see you; they do not let you express your thinking." Nonrehospitalized patients also seem to be more able to neutralize others' comments. (NR): "I don't worry about what other people may think." (NR): "The others, I have never cared what they think."

Self-descriptions also reveal a general openness toward others for nonrehospitalized patients. This seems to accentuate the perceived importance of the "positive" dimension of "positive withdrawal" and indicate that withdrawal could concern an intentional retreat from close interpersonal relationships without precluding a broader openness to the world. Whereas the frequently hospitalized patients stress the value of normal social roles, the nonrehospitalized patients express a desire to feel part of an interpersonal space and to diffuse its potential hostility. (NR): "To act as a conciliator." (NR): "To go towards people, to try to speak first." (NR): "To gather around people who speak the truth, who are honest with you." (NR): "I would like to please people." (NR): "I would like to make other people happy." This kind of explicit intersubjective orientation is not as clearly expressed by the frequently-hospitalized patients.

An analysis of the stylistic characterization of the patients' self-descriptions allows a better understanding of the strategies used by individuals who have been diagnosed as schizophrenic in their contact with reality. These stylistic strategies can be described as language games which play on the semantic and grammatical dimensions of the discourse.

An infrequent but impressive first type of language game that can be found in all groups of patients is an ability to shift from one level of meaning of a word to another, from a literal to a figurative one, from a static to dynamic

significance of a term. Some patients deconstruct the conventional use of a word associated with a particular context of speech and appear to "reopen" the language from within. A first example involves a frequently hospitalized patient who characterizes himself as *entier*. This French word means literally "entire" or "whole"; however, it also has a figurative sense, "forthright" or "self-willed," which would normally be the one built upon for characterizing somebody. In his comment however, this person prefers to use the term in its literal sense – intact or whole, for describing the physical integrity of his body, his true masculinity – he then moves toward asserting his integrity or sanity: "That means that I am a man, I lack nothing. I think I have all my faculties, but there were periods where I was amnesic … to have all your limbs, not to be missing an intestine. In other words, I am all my own." In another example, a nonrehospitalized patient qualifies himself as "acting crazy," which he uses first in its derivative sense as it would be appropriate in the context of self-definition; he then comes back indirectly to its literal sense in expressing a deep, anxious questioning regarding madness: "I will take the first step towards others, try to be the first one to speak. I always try to make a joke of everything; it is not easy to be funny. You have to try to guess the character of the person with whom you are; I try to figure out why I found myself in a psychiatric hospital with the loonies, as they are called."

At a similar semantic level, nonrehospitalized patients introduce new valency into a word or they introduce an idea of intentionality within a seemingly negative feature, revealing their private attempt to reframe a problematic character into a positive dimension of life. (NR: "easily anxious"): "I am too focused on what goes around me to be at peace with myself; going through such ordeals leads me to evolve." (NR: "lazy"): "You don't take life too seriously, you relax better." (NR: "conceited"): "In my dreams, I am the best. It encourages me rather than being discouraging."

At a more "grammatical" level, nonrehospitalized patients tend to redefine a static attribute as an active one, indicative of an intentional stance. (NR: "simple"): "I make things simple. I don't make a big fuss over unimportant things. I am a peacemaker. I am able to stop verbal arguments." (NR: "sentimental"): "To have sentiments towards the person that you're with."

Finally, nonrehospitalized patients appear better able to inscribe their present situation within a historical frame; they may describe their present style of being as progress or view themselves as embedded in a dynamic movement toward greater participation in the world. (NR: "calm"): "In normal life, one has to live with a certain amount of stress. Before becoming ill, I earned my life with stress. ... In the last 10 years, I have dropped out. ... I accept myself as calm and tranquil. ... When I came out of the hospital, I came to terms with myself." (NR: "sincere, frank"): "I have changed enormously. Now, I see qualities rather than defects in people." (NR: "likes to communicate with people"): " ... like the Beatles, the people who are nice, who have something to say." (The same: "likes change"): "Generally, social change, change of people, of society in general."

Self-narratives enlighten the extent to which people who have been diagnosed as schizophrenic feel intimately marked by their contact with psychiatric services and by the others' gaze. They also confirm the tragic dimension of this process, especially for the frequently hospitalized patients who feel trapped in a sick role and a sense of their inadequacy. The few examples presented here illustrate the range of strategies patients use to distance themselves from a static, "naturalistic" characterization of themselves and, more particularly, the private, significant, and sometimes poignant ways nonrehospitalized schizophrenics attempt to infuse intentionality into their self-image. This echoes European phenomenological psychiatrists' descriptions of the way some long-term patients seem to have learned to "flirt" with psychosis, to play with it (Blankenburg 1991), the way they attempt to escape both the feeling of a static temporality and their timeless characterization as "schizophrenics" and to restore a valued sense of self and of their existence (Maldiney 1986). Their "language games" evoke what Good (1994) has described as the "subjunctivizing" function of certain styles of illness narratives which allow them to explore the indeterminacy of reality and keep open a network of potential perspectives.

The combination of the importance of the others' gaze in self-perceptions and of its general stigmatizing valency on the one hand, and the expression of an intentional movement toward others by nonrehospitalized patients on the other, suggests that "positive withdrawn" orientation of their life-world could also have in part a defensive and protective value in addition to expressing an intentional stance toward the world.

The thickness of being

Although we began this research with a sociological perspective that emphasized the role of external determinants in schizophrenic patients' ability to remain within the community, data led us in another direction. They indicate the central role played by a personal stance adopted toward the world and illustrate how it permeates various aspects of patients' life. This invites us to reevaluate the very notion of coping and to expand it on the basis of a broader approach to the notion of experience.

In building on the approaches to experience developed by European phenomenological psychiatry and on the analytical strategies developed by Ricoeur, we have explored how empirical details of daily life refer to a basic intentional position toward the world and how that position is expressed and clarified through the facticity of existence. Data collected in Montréal illustrate how the surface elements of the patients' discourse refer to a more basic, nontransparent way of being-in-the-world: concrete behaviors and discourses reveal simultaneously a basic alteration of their subjective world, which could be related by hypothesis to the disorder, and the patients' personal response to it, in a particular social environment; they illustrate the individuals' attempt to reinstate this experience within a space of liberty. Understanding evolved in a constant to and fro between concrete details of their empirical lives and the underlying structure of their being-in-the-world. Data also indicate the potential value of a style of discourse and behavior that appears able to "reopen" the experience while at the same time remaining in tune with the basic features of the person's life-world.

In our research, the set of structural opposites and similarities in the data on "social integration" indicate the strategic value attached to a position of positive withdrawal toward the world; the content of the patients' discourses indicates the network of meanings associated with such a position. Self-descriptions reveal the range of discursive and stylistic strategies resorted to by nonrehospitalized patients for evading a static, assigned definition of themselves and for reintroducing some space of "subjunctivization," freedom and play within their perception of themselves in a certain world. Fragments of life narratives illustrate in how many ways nonrehospitalized patients attempt to negotiate a position at the margin of the common world, simultaneously inside and outside, and to reshape a generally painful and conflicting life trajectory.

This article also illustrates the need to conjugate different perspectives for understanding the subjective intentional world of people diagnosed as schizophrenic and their attempt to reconstruct a viable life-world. Each of them offers but an imperfect and partial image of the individuals' subjective appraisal of themselves and of the world. Taken together, they illustrate the "thickness" of this experience, its paradoxical and multidimensional character, its embeddedness within multiple texts and referents.

As a general feature, the patients' life-world develops in the shadow of suffering, ambiguity and perceived marginality within a larger social and cultural world. One wonders how much the life strategies patients try to construct on their own, through a precarious and solitary bricolage, are constrained by social and cultural features that appear to echo some central cultural characteristics of North American societies. On the one hand, achievement, performance, and conformity are valued, and differences or discrepancies are subject to a wide range of normalizing techniques that tend to dominate the philosophy of rehabilitation and psychoeducation; people who "do not fit" and cannot be integrated in the dominant paradigm tend to remain "unseen," almost socially nonexistent and are left to a parallel life which

has few links to mainstream society (Corin 1986). On the other hand, if autonomy and self-coherence are valued, cultural norms and our postmodern ethos leave little room for the creation of spaces of solitude to mature and retreat temporarily from society, to allow inner growth, self-gathering, and personal development (Janicaud 1987). Moreover, the general stigmatization attached to psychiatric disorders converges with a pervading economic marginality and pushes people who have been diagnosed as schizophrenic toward a space of alienation which hinders their restorative attempts. One could hypothesize that this social and cultural context pervades and channels personal strategies and accentuates the withdrawn dimension of positive withdrawal; it over-determines its significance. Different cultures or societies might favor another form of articulating the psychotic experience and give it a different texture which could contribute to shaping the further evolution of problems.

REFERENCES

Bibeau, G., and E. Corin
From submission to the text to interpretive violence. In G. Bibeau and E. Corin, eds., *Beyond Textuality. Asceticism and Violence in Anthropological Interpretation* (pp. 3–54). Mouton de Gruyter, 1995.

Binswanger, L.
Analyse existentielle et psychanalyse freudienne. Gallimard, 1970. (Originally published in 1947)

Blankenburg, W.
La perte de l'évidence naturelle. Presses Universitaires de France, 1991. (Originally published in 1971)

Bruner, E. M.
Introduction. In V. W. Turner and E. M. Bruner, eds., *The Anthropology of Experience* (pp. 3–30). Urbana: University of Illinois Press, 1986.

Carpenter, W. T.
Approaches to knowledge and understanding of schizophrenia. *Schizophrenia Bulletin* (1987) 13(1):1–8.

Ciompi, L.
Is there really a schizophrenia? The long-term course of psychotic phenomena. *British Journal of Psychiatry* (1984) 145:636–40.

Clifford, J., and G. E. Marcus, eds.
Writing Culture. The Poetics and Politics of Ethnography. University of California Press, 1986.

Corin, E.
Centralité des marges et dynamique des centres. Anthropologie et Sociétés (1986) 10 (2): 1–21.

Corin E.
Facts and meaning in psychiatry. An anthropological approach to the lifeworld of schizophrenics. Culture, Medicine and Psychiatry (1990) 14:153–88.

Corin, E., and G. Lauzon
Positive withdrawal and the quest for meaning: The reconstruction of experience among schizophrenics. Psychiatry (1992) 55 (3):266–78.

Corin, E., and G. Lauzon
From symptoms to phenomena: The articulation of the experience in schizophrenia. Journal of Phenomenological Psychology (1994) 15 (1):3–50.

Crapanzano, V.
Hermes' Dilemma & Hamlet's Desire. On the Epistemology of Interpretation. Harvard University Press, 1992.

Estroff, S.
Self, identity and subjective experience of schizophrenia: In search of the subject. Schizophrenia Bulletin (1989) 15(2):189–96.

Fabrega, H. J.
On the significance of an anthropological approach to schizophrenia. Psychiatry (1989) 52 (1):45–65.

Garrison, V., and J. Podell
"Community support systems assessment" for use in clinical interviews. Schizophrenia Bulletin (1981) 7(1):101–8.

Good, B. J.
Medicine, Rationality and Experience. An Anthropological Perspective. Cambridge University Press, 1994.

Hatfield, A. B.
Patients' accounts of stress and coping in schizophrenia. Hospital and Community Psychiatry (1989) 40(11):1141–5.

Janicaud, D.
Haute solitude. Nouvelle revue de psychanalyse (1987) 36:9–20.

Jaspers, K.
General Psychopathology. Manchester University Press, 1963.

Maldiney, H.
Daseinsanalyse: phénoménologie de l'existant? In P. Fédida, ed., Phénoménologie, psychiatrie, psychanalyse (pp. 9–26). Édition G.R. E.U.P.P.

Ratey, J. J., S. Sands, and G. O'Driscoll
The phenomenology of recovery in a chronic schizophrenic. Psychiatry (1986) 49:273–89.

Ricoeur, P.
Du texte à l'action. Essais d'herméneutique, II. Le Seuil, Collection Esprit, 1986.

Serban, G.
Adjustment of Schizophrenics in the Community. SP Medical and Scientific Books, 1981.

Strauss, J.
Subjective experience of schizophrenia: Toward a new dynamic psychiatry. II. Schizophrenia Bulletin (1989) 15(2):179–87.

Strauss, J. S.
Negative symptoms: Future developments of the concept. Schizophrenia Bulletin (1985) 11 (3):457–60.

Tellenbach, H.
La mélancolie. Presses Universitaires de France, 1979. (Originally published in 1961)

12

The Concept of Therapeutic 'Emplotment'

Cheryl Mattingly

This paper rests upon a single claim: We make as well as tell stories of our lives and this is of fundamental importance in the clinical world. Narrative plays a central role in clinical work not only as a retrospective account of past events but as a form healers and patients actively seek to impose upon clinical time.

Narrative analysis is not new to medical anthropology. Most notable are the provocative and illuminating examinations of patients' representations and experiences of illness as revealed by the illness narratives they tell [1–4]. However, the argument made here departs radically from the way narrative has been understood, not only within medical anthropology but in anthropology as a whole. Narrative has been studied as a mode of discourse – as text or as performance. Even narrative theorists within the clinical community who argue for the narrative structure of experience also attend to stories as discourse. Schafer for example, speaks of "storied" lives but examines only those stories that are told, rather than analyzing social action itself [5]. In this paper, however, the material analyzed is taken from field notes of a clinical interaction rather than the therapist's or patient's story of that interaction [6]. The narrative structure of clinical time is not a script, as Holland and Quinn [7] speak of, for it is created within the clinical interaction, improvised from the available resources at hand and tailored, quite specifically, to context.

To say that narratives are lived before they are told, or even to say that there is something narrative-like about the structure of lived experience, is to make a contentious claim. Within formal narrative theory, the overwhelming assumption is that all narratives are 'fictions', that is, they construct a world rather than refer to one [8–10]. This anti-mimetic position, so fundamental to postmodernism, has been developed even within disciplines whose business is to tell 'true stories' about events that 'actually happened', i.e. history and anthropology. Within history, Hayden White has been central in claiming that history is also fiction [10, 11]. In anthropology, the fictional quality of ethnography has become a tenet of the 'reflexive' position and has been especially persuasively argued by the historian Clifford [12–14].

The question of how narrative discourses distort the world they purport to describe is both interesting and important. However, the basic modern and postmodern premise that all narrative *as form* is necessarily distortion because our temporal existence lacks the coherence of a unity with beginning, middle and end fails to recognize an underlying homology between life in time and narrative structure. Philosophers from two rather disparate camps have considered the narrative structure of lived experience, moral and political philosophers reinvoking pre-modern moral traditions, such as MacIntyre [15, 16] and Arendt [17], and phenomenological and hermeneutic philosophers who follow Husserl, Gadamer, and Heidegger. The most notable of these contemporary theorists are Ricoeur [18–20], Carr [21], Olafson [22], and also Arendt [17]. In developing a notion of therapeutic emplotment, I rely heavily upon these two philosophical strains. Drawing from five years studying and working with occupational therapists, including a two year ethnographic study of occupational therapists in an acute care hospital, I claim that these healers actively struggle to shape therapeutic events into a coherent form organized by a plot. They attempt to emplot clinical encounters by enfolding them into larger developing narrative structures. The notion of emplotment clearly reflects an etic framework far removed from medical discourse, imported from literary theory, philosophy of history and phenomenology. And yet, for occupational therapists at least, the language of narrative has been provocative as a vehicle for seeing practice in a new way [23–5].

Emplotment

Most simply, emplotment involves making a configuration in time, creating a whole out of a succession of events [18, 20]. What we call a story is just this rendering and ordering of an event sequence into parts which belong to a larger temporal whole, one governed by a plot. E. M. Forster visualized plot as "a sort of higher level official" concerned that everything which happens is marshalled appropriately so that it makes its contribution to the whole [26]. Particular actions then take their meaning by belonging to, and contributing to, the story. This "making a whole" is also making meaning such that we can ask what the point or thought or moral of the story is [10, 20].

The term 'emplotment' has had a history which has enlarged its meaning. It was originally coined by literary critic Northrop Frye [27] to describe four archetypal plot structures for construing experience – romance, tragedy, comedy and satire. Any narrative was necessarily 'emplotted' within one of these archetypal forms, Frye suggested. Hayden White then argued that history explains events by placing them within a coherent archetypal plot. Historical narratives are organized in terms of specific plot structures, what might be called 'explanation by emplotment'. Historical explanation, in White's view, is aesthetically grounded, gaining its plausibility and coherence by its placement within an archetypal narrative form. The poetics of plot do the decisive explanatory work. It is the plot which makes individual events understandable as part of a coherent whole, one which leads compellingly toward a particular ending [10, 28].

But the notion of emplotment is developed most intriguingly by the hermeneutic philosopher Paul Ricoeur. Ricoeur calls upon it to make the more radical phenomenological claim that the structure of human temporality itself, of life in time, is fundamentally related to the structure of narrative because both of these are tied to the structure of the plot. In his essay, 'Narrative Time', Ricoeur states that: "narrativity and temporality are closely related – as closely as, in Wittgenstein's terms, a language game and a form of life. Indeed, I take temporality to be that structure of existence that reaches language in narrativity and narrativity to be the language structure that has temporality as its ultimate referent" [18, p. 165]. He goes on to say that the narrative structure most associated with temporality is the plot [18, p. 167]. This argument is systematically elaborated in his subsequent three volume *Time and Narrative* [20, 29, 30].

My own use of the term emplotment differs from the above discussions for I carry this term directly into the arena of social action. Frye and White are concerned with emplotment as it pertains to the form of texts, quite specifically written narrative texts. Even Ricoeur, though considering the phenomenology of time, focuses upon texts rather than social actions. His use of the term emplotment is developed through considering the narrative structures of fiction and history rather than the more chaotic and improvisational realm of everyday activity. Ricoeur hedges on the extent to which life in time does indeed take on a coherence provided by a plot, preferring instead Wittgenstein's metaphors of close kinship and the game. In bringing this term to a study of therapeutic intervention, I reinterpret Ricoeur's claim, arguing that narrativity, and particularly the work to create a plot out of a succession of actions, is of direct concern to the actor in the midst of action.

Applying the notion of narrative plot to an analysis of therapeutic time raises a host of problems not addressed by theorists of narrative. Most significant, such an analysis must consider the fragile and shifting nature of any emplotment in time. How do we speak of emplotment as something made and unmade as time unfolds? How do we characterize social interactions as more or less narratively configured, taking into account those minimally narrative times when the actors find themselves lost, when there seems to be no 'point' to what they are doing, or when no ending appears desirable, when there is just one damn thing after another? Such an analysis must also consider the social nature of action for narrative time is multiply authored. How do we think of emplotment when there is no single author to a story created in action? How do actors, with their own individual perspectives, desires, commitments to a future, manage to create a sense that they are in the same story together? If there is no one storyteller, what does it mean to think of stories that are created? Even the notion of a 'life story' is a misleadingly individualistic construct, as though we lived our stories by ourselves. These questions are understandably neglected in discussions of emplotment among narrative theorists who inevitably foreground the written text.

Creating Stories in Time

When we tell stories, we intensify and clarify the plot structure of events as lived, eliminating events that, in retrospect, are not important to the development of that plot – which do not, as we say, contribute to the ending. However,

action, too, demands that we plot. We are motivated, as actors, to create stories while in the midst of acting. Locating ourselves within an intelligible story is essential to our sense that life is meaningful. In any situation we, as actors, have a narrative interest in constructing an 'untold story' out of discrete episodes. We have a need not only to make sense, as Goffman [31] says, but to *create sense* out of situations. A fundamental way we create sense is by shaping the 'one thing after another' character of on-going action into a coherent narrative structure with a beginning, middle and end. The told narrative, Ricoeur argues, builds on action understood as an as yet untold story. Or, in his provocative phrase, "action is in quest of a narrative" [20, p. 4]. Other philosophers, most notably Alisdair MacIntyre and David Carr, make very explicit claims about the narrative structure of lived time. Carr takes it that "narrative is our primary (though not our only) way of organizing our experience of time" [21, pp. 4–5]. He further states "that narrative structure pervades our very experience of time and social existence, independently of our contemplating the past as historians" [21, p. 9].

The interest in coherence and order is only one motive for attempting to play out a situation in such a way that a narrative (a desirable one, the right kind of one) can be told. Being an actor at all means trying to make certain things happen, to bring about desirable endings, to search for possibilities that lead in hopeful directions. As actors, we require our actions to be not only intelligible but to get us somewhere. We act because we intend to get something done, to begin something, which we hope will lead us along a desirable route. And we act with what Kermode [32] calls the "sense of an ending." Because we act with the sense of an ending and because we care about that ending, we try to direct our actions and the actions of other relevant actors in ways that will bring the ending about. We try to make actions cumulative [22]. Because we plot, as actors, the structure of lived experience already contains a (partly) plotted shape. Even if our actions are taken up, reworked and redirected by the responses of other actors, we still have some success some of the time in working toward endings we care about. And sometimes we are even able to negotiate with other actors so that we can move in directions cooperatively, cumulatively.

Six features of narrative time

The notion of plot, and of emplotted time, is most understandable by reference to its opposite – linear or serial time. In arguing for the fundamental role of plot in ordering our remembrances of times past and even our understanding of times present, Ricoeur and White contrast emplotted time to chronological time. A succession, that structure of linear time, of clock time, of one thing after another, is transformed by a plot into a meaningful whole with a beginning, middle and end. Any particular event gains its meaning by its place within this narrative configuration, as a contribution to the plot. This configuration makes a whole such that we can speak of the point of a story. Yet this is an always shifting configuration for we live in the midst of unfolding stories over which we have a very partial control. Life in time is neither predictable nor highly controllable. We are readers as well as makers of our lives and the stories we think we are living through are subject to surprises, twists of the plot we never even imagined. We may find ourselves at any one point contemplating an array of foreseeable endings, uncertain which will come to pass, scarcely knowing which we ought to desire. The actor's commitment to a plot does not translate into the capacity to bring about a particular plot. In what follows, I consider this configuring of singular events into plot episodes in the practice of occupational therapy. I look at a single encounter between an occupational therapist and a head injured patient as the creation of a therapeutic narrative, built in improvisational fashion from the actions of two characters. In turning occupational therapists, I consider the clinical utility of transforming linear clinical time into narrative time.

What is there to say about time demarcated by plot, by a beginning, middle and end, that distinguishes it from time marked linearly, one moment simply succeeding the next? Or even from time marked predictably, one moment progressing smoothly to the next? One way to answer this question is by looking at the way narrative time is structured when stories are told. For if there is a basic homology between lived time and time structured within narrative discourse, as I am claiming, an analysis of how time is organized in the told story should make key aspects of lived time visible. I propose six features of narrative time.

The principles of this sextet are as follows.

(a) Narrative time is configured

Events belong to an unfolding temporal whole, an evolving movement toward a telos. But the telos is not located in the literal ending, as a final stage of an action sequence. Rather, it emerges through the figure as a whole, the form of beginning, middle and end. This figure may be an intricate webbing of multiple figures, like the many smaller forms that comprise a complex dance. While built upon the relation of part to whole, no plot simply subsumes the parts such that they are merely episodes contributing to a single coherence. Narrative depth derives from a part-whole structure where episodes have their own authority; they, too may be memorable. A single glance in a single moment can have its own unforgetable character, conveying an image that sweeps across the surface of all other events, and is never simply swallowed in a larger action chain. Narrative form is based on the vividness of events in themselves as well as on their contributions to the plot.

(b) Action and motive are key structuring devices

Narrative time is human time, one might say, time in which human actions are represented as central causes for the outcome of events. Multiple actors with multiple motives are operating upon the same stage and through their interactions, narrative time is created.

(c) Narrative time is organized within a gap

Narrative time is that place of desire where one is not where one wants to be, where one longs to be elsewhere. Another way of saying this is that movement toward endings dominates the experience of time.

(d) Narratives show how things (and people) change over time

While change is central, not all change is narrative. In narrative, the movement from one time to the next is not linear; it is full of tricks and reversals.

(e) Narrative time is dramatic

Conflict is omnipresent. There are obstacles to be overcome in reaching one's desired object. Enemies must be faced, risks taken. One almost never hears the story of how things went without a hitch from beginning to end, just as planned. Stories are told about difficult, even frightening situations. Desire must be strong because danger is also present and one faces danger only when one wants something badly. In this time marked by conflict, there is an implicit dialogue of points of view played out by the key actors, or even, by the same actor when the narrative scene moves inward.

(f) Endings are uncertain

Narrative time is marked by suspense, by surprise, by the recognition that things may turn out differently than one wants or anticipates.

Narrative Time in the Clinic

Occupational therapists help disabled persons readapt to their lives after illness or injury. They belong to a rather unusual profession in the specialized world of the clinic, for they address an almost limitless range of dysfunctional problems which can arise with disability. They define their task as helping persons regain function, as far as possible, in the major occupations of their life, including work, play and what they call 'activities of daily living', meaning self-care skills. There is a certain fluidity from the ridiculous to the sublime, from the trivial to the essential, as therapists shift from playing endless games of checkers with spinal cord patients or teaching cardiac patients the cross-stitch, to engaging patients in intense discussions about why they should not just give up and die. Often profound discussions interweave, even appear

to depend upon, the homely 'treatment modality' of turning magazine pages with a mouth-stick or taking a trial run manoeuvre in and out of the hospital gift shop with the new wheel-chair. It is not always easy to identify the significant therapeutic encounter and the profound is not always displayed in words. The most mundane acts, putting socks on, eating spaghetti with an adaptive fork, easily become invested with symbolic meanings. I witnessed many a backgammon game in the spinal cord unit, for instance, in which winning the game by 'going home' came to have multiple meanings.

Fleming [33] has called occupational therapy a "common sense practice in an uncommon world." Within the non-ordinary world of the clinic, therapists ask patients to engage in a range of humdrum daily activities that characterize common life outside the clinic. They traffic in the habitual, the tacit knowledge of the able-bodied who heedlessly open doors, take showers, and turn on their computers. The holism of the profession is reflected in the equipment therapists call upon to carry out their treatment. Occupational therapy treatment rooms contain tables with mats (for re-learning sitting balance and other body training), wheelchairs, splints of all sizes and shapes, a hodge podge of non-clinical looking paraphernalia which belongs to adaptive kitchens and adaptive bathrooms, as well as closets crammed with games and arts and crafts materials. Although therapists do not always start out to do so, they very often end up negotiating with patients about what dysfunctional problems therapy will address in terms of the very deepest issues of how a patient's life story will be remade to accommodate to a new body. (Shall a therapeutic goal after a severe stroke be relearning handwriting in order to continue one's law practice? Or, adapting one's golf clubs and relearning golf in order to discontinue one's law practice and retire early to Florida?)

Chronic illness and suffering often generate a narrative loss, as well as a physical loss, the fracturing of a life story as patients restructure lives in new ways to accommodate disabled bodies. Simply devising an appropriate treatment plan tends to propel the therapist into worrying about how to insert therapy in some meaningful way into a life which is in radical transition. Like many other therapies, occupational therapy is a vulnerable profession in the sense that therapeutic efficacy depends not only upon what the therapist independently does *to* the patient, but on what patient and therapist are able to do together in therapy. If the patient does not view therapy as valuable, it will not be valuable. Patients and therapists need to come to some shared view about how to live as a disabled person, or at least they need negotiate a shared view about what role therapy can play in facilitating a life with disability. Often this does not happen, and therapeutic time becomes a place of struggle between therapist and patient, or is perceived by the patient as yet another forgettable and useless way to spend an hour in the hospital. Therapeutic success depends in part upon the therapist's ability to set a story in motion which is meaningful to the patient as well as to herself. One could say that the therapist's clinical task is to create a therapeutic plot which compels a patient to see therapy as integral to healing. At a more radical level, the task is to create a plot in which the 'ending' toward which one strives invokes a sense of what it means to be healed when one will always be disabled.

In the following example, an occupational therapist works to emplot a series of actions in a single therapeutic session, weaving them into a meaningful whole. The session illustrates the difference between treatment as mere sequence, just one medical intervention after another, and treatment structured narratively, one thing building upon another. In this example, there is a shift mid-session from a series of interactions in which therapeutic time looks like a linear succession of discrete acts ungrounded in context or in a picture of the patient, to the narrative shaping of therapeutic interaction in which therapeutic time has been emplotted by the clinician's picture of how to create a significant therapeutic experience for a patient.

The episode is familiar in the practice of occupational therapists. It is an everyday instance of a therapist's efforts to create a meaningful experience of the patient which foreshadows a larger therapeutic story, even a whole therapeutic process, in which she hopes to engage the patient. Or, as occupational therapists would phrase it, this episode illustrates the common task of getting a new and unconvinced patient to 'buy in' to therapy.

The analysis is based upon field notes. An interview was also done with the therapist but not the patient about what occurred in the session. No claim is being made that the therapist's efforts at emplotment *necessarily* yielded a meaningful experience from the patient's point of view or that the patient's way of making sense of the session mirrored the story told below. Nor did the therapist speak of plots and stories, a language entirely foreign to the conceptual framework of occupational therapy. She did speak, however, of her concern to motivate the patient, to give him a picture of what therapy would be like, and to solicit his interest and cooperation in future treatment. My claim is that the therapist can be seen to make a number of interventions which are directed to setting a certain sort of story in motion, and that the patient's observed responses strongly indicate a willingness to take up the therapist's storyline at critical junctures, at least for the space of this initial session. One of the most interesting features of therapeutic emplotment is that while it can be guided by the therapist, it cannot be dictated. The 'untold story' that unfolds is not created by any simple imposition of a preplanned treatment script but structured from unanticipated responses by the patient to the therapist's interventions.

The Tour

The session begins in the hospital room of Steven, a 20-year-old who has only awakened from a coma a few days earlier [34]. Steven is between 1 and 2 months post trauma from a car accident where he suffered a brainstem contusion. He cannot talk but communicates through signalling and writing. The occupational therapist, Donna, has seen this patient only twice before but very briefly since he was not yet ready for an 'OT' (occupational therapy) session.

As Donna comes into Steven's room, a physical therapist and a nurse are getting ready to transfer from his bed to a wheelchair. This is the first time he has been out of bed since the accident and he is reluctant to get up. Donna brings a student occupational therapist with her and they join the others around Steven's bed. So, as the session opens, Steven lies in bed surrounded by four medical professionals. During the first several minutes he is simultaneously treated by each of them. He is: (a) given a shot; (b) introduced to the student occupational therapist who puts on his sneakers; (c) has his lungs listened to by the physical therapist; and (d) asked questions about his height by Donna.

The occupational therapists, nurse and physical therapist have previously decided that he needs to stand up and then spend an hour sitting in a wheel chair. They are all there at the same time to help in transferring him from bed to wheelchair. The patient cannot speak but he is given a pad and marker and writes notes to them. Donna and the physical therapist tell him they realize he does not want to get out of bed. When given a pad and marker, he writes "Be careful of my back." All four professionals work together to stand him up. They give him instructions about how to help, for example, "Don't forget to put your elbow down and lean" or "Lift up your head. Straighten up your knee. Bring the right foot up." Two of the professionals congratulate him on how well he has done. The physical therapist does some more checking of his breathing while one of the occupational therapists tries to help him get more comfortable in the chair and asks him questions about pain. (Most of the questions directed at him are yes or no questions to which he simply puts thumbs up for yes, thumbs down for no.) The nurse and physical therapist then leave the room while the two occupational therapists stay behind.

The initial medical checking of Steven and the transfer to the wheelchair form a sequence of actions with little narrative integrity. This is most evident during the first minutes of medical check where each professional is doing something different, paying as little attention as possible to what the others are doing. The patient is treated primarily as an injured body, and is often referred to as "he," as in, "He is writing with his right hand. Was he a lefty? That's good writing." The professionals are primarily doing 'to' the patient rather than 'with' him. Minimal cooperation is required

on his part during this phase. Neither do the professionals need much cooperation from one another since the tasks they are carrying out are quite discrete and distinct from one another. They make no effort to build on what the others are doing because accomplishing their task does not require cooperative action. They are quite simply carrying out a pre-planned set of fairly isolated activities. Their tasks are certainly neither meaningless nor formless and the physical therapist in a minimal sense 'emplots' her actions by informing the group, including the patient, that his breathing capacity is improving and he now has the ability to help transfer himself to the wheelchair. She thus places his immediate responses within a temporal context that refers to backward ("That was so much better than yesterday.") and suggests a future based on steady physical improvements.

This bare chronicling can be contrasted with the more fully narrative emplotting which subsequently occurs between Donna and Steven. When the nurse and physical therapist leave, the following dialogue ensues. Donna hands Steven a comb and says "Try to comb your hair." He does not want to do it and hands her back the comb. She then tells him this will help him improve balance; It's a kind of exercise. She says, "It's good for balance practice." At this explanation, he combs, but with great effort. When he stops, Donna points to places he has missed. "Try here," she says, "Nurses can't do back here when you are lying down." As she touches spots on the back of his head for him to comb she says, "I'll guide you a little bit." She compliments him several times as he is combing. "Great job." "Nice." "Great."

Finally, they are done. The patient motions for paper. He writes, "Mirror." The therapist gets a mirror and sets it up on a table so he can see, correcting the angle just right. She asks him jokingly, "Going to make yourself look good for your girlfriend?" He signals for paper again. This time he writes, "Want to go for a ride." The therapist agrees enthusiastically. "Great! You want to check out your new place." Their tour begins. She takes him directly to the main occupational therapy room and she wheels him in. "This is the OT room. You will be spending a lot of time here," she tells him. She points to the mat and tells him that they will be working together there. She says, "You will learn to strengthen your trunk."

As they are about to leave, Steven expresses discomfort and Donna stops to investigate. He indicates that he has pain in his left shoulder when he moves his head. The therapist supports his arm and begins moving it. She explains the movements she is doing, asking him to hold and then let his arm go again. She notes, "Your left shoulder seems OK but that pain makes you not want to move it. But moving it is good. Moving will get it stronger and reduce the spasm."

They leave the occupational therapy treatment room, and the patient writes, "I want more of a tour before I go back to bed." The therapist says, "You've got it. This is University Hospital." As they wheel down the hospital corridors the therapist says. "Today is Friday. Saturday and Sunday I am not here. But as you get stronger, your family will take you out."

They come to a large window looking out over the city. The therapist stops to let him look out. She says, "Do you recognize the Prudential?" He motions for paper and writes, "Open window." She explains that the windows can't be opened, which she also demonstrates to him by going over to the window. She takes him past the nursing station and looks around to find any nurses who know him. The patient writes, "Is Beth here?" Beth comes out and they have a quick, warm conversation. The nurse tells him she's glad he is up. He writes down "Please visit" on a note to her. Then the occupational therapist and the patient proceed on their tour for a few more minutes. The therapist asks him if he is getting tired. He indicates yes, thumbs up. As they return to his room the therapist asks, "Do you remember which is your room?" The patient indicates thumbs up when they reach his room. And there ends the session.

(a) Creating figures in time

Emplotment of this session begins when Donna asks Steven to comb his hair. He does not want to do it. She persists, handing him back the comb and giving him a biomedical sounding rationale – improving balance – that

apparently satisfies him enough to accept the comb and do the task. When he finishes and she asks him to continue combing, pointing out missed places, she subtly changes the meaning of the task from a balance activity to a self-care activity by telling him that "Nurses can't do back here when you are lying down." It may be more accurate to say she adds a meaning, giving the activity a polysemic character. Hair combing becomes both a balance support exercise and self-care. And she decides to extend the task so that by the end he has not just carried out an exercise, he has, in fact, combed his hair. By the end of this activity, he seems to accept this meaning because he asks for a mirror to see himself, as one might do after combing one's hair but not after doing an exercise for balance practice. The therapist builds on his request by not only getting him a mirror but in carefully adjusting it for better viewing while simultaneously joking to him about fixing himself up for his girlfriend.

Donna emplots her actions and his by defining them as part of a therapeutic story she wants to carry out. The meaning of combing his hair as preparation for being seen by others, a meaning he acknowledges by asking for a mirror, is given emphasis by the therapist's joke. If you are able to comb your hair, her joke implies, you can feel ready to be seen by people you care about.

The patient initiates the next phase of the session by requesting to go for a ride. Again the therapist not only agrees but builds on his request by announcing to him the meaning of his request. She tells him he wants to check out his new place. She thereby turns a ride, which might have meant going up and down the hall, into a chance to see his new surroundings, a chance to see and be seen.

By the point where the ride begins, a "sense of an ending" is also emerging. Discrete actions are coming to take on a unity; a figure in time is being sketched. For this whole session plays upon the theme of reentry into the public world. The therapist builds on her success at getting the patient to comb his hair, which succeeds not only in that he does it but in his subsequently asking to see a mirror and then to go for a ride. In her response to both his requests she not only enthusiastically agrees but explicitly marks them as requests to move out into the world. She "reads" them as moves within a story of reentry, and does so aloud so that the patient hears her interpretation. To his request for a mirror she replies by joking about his girlfriend, signifying that he is getting ready to be seen. She interprets his second request for a ride as his wanting to see and in seeing, to take ownership, to "check out his new place." She "emplots" his requests with a plausible but strong reading of the desires motivating them.

And she emplots his requests through her actions as well, not only bringing him a mirror but adjusting it, not only taking him for a ride but giving him a tour which includes stopping by the occupational therapy treatment room and stopping at the nurse's station to find a nurse he is friends with. She is personalizing the hospital. She is showing him "his" particular version of the hospital, the version that includes a visit to a friend and the occupational therapy room where he will be working with Donna to get stronger.

She also uses his request for a ride to give herself the possibility of showing him what he will be doing with her. While both gaze toward the mat in the occupational therapy room, she quite literally points to a future story. She sketches, in the barest phrase, what kind of story they are in. In this prospective story they work together and he becomes stronger. She reiterates this same prospective story when he complains about his shoulder. She says that working, even working in pain, will make him stronger: "That pain makes you not want to move it. But moving it is good, will get it stronger and reduce the spasm."

She uses his requests as places of possibility to indicate a second story in which work, though it will take time and cause pain, will finally make him stronger. At this juncture of the session, the plot thickens. Two subplots are interwoven and embedded into a more complex causal chain. The first story of reentry, of return home, of freedom from an immobile body and an institutionalized existence, is connected to a second story about work and pain. The first story offers the hopeful ending. The second, however, emphasizes the difficult path which the patient will have to travel if he is to attain that ending. For before there is the return home, there is work, work which may be unpleasant, painful, work he may not want to do, but then there is strength and along with strength, there is the possibility of seeing and being seen, of reentering what Arendt [35] describes as the public world of appearing. Arendt takes it that our urge to appear, to see and be seen, is essential to what it means to be human. She writes, "To be alive means to be possessed by an urge toward self-display which answers the fact of one's own appearingness. Living things make their appearance like actors on a stage set for them" [35, p. 21].

The figure of the session, then, opens with the patient combing his hair, rather against his own wishes, and ends with a hospital tour. By the end, everything that has happened, from the initial taking of the comb to the end of the tour, becomes an extension or elaboration of a story of making himself presentable and thus reentering the public world. And by doing the tour after he combs his hair, the therapist also extends the meaning of that hair combing. What can look trivial to him becomes the very thing that makes it emotionally possible for him to leave his room for the first time.

One thing after another becomes, in narrative logic, one thing because of another. In what Kenneth Burke [36] calls a "temporizing of essence," earlier events become the causes of later events. Because the session links one small activity – hair combing – to another activity which the patient requests and clearly cares about, leaving his room for the first time, the session becomes an argument in story form about why occupational therapy activities should matter to this patient. The therapist is saying, through the experience, that something that might seem to him small for a large amount of effort on his part is really worth the trouble because it makes it emotionally possible for him to feel presentable and venture into the more public world of hospital hallways.

(b)   Human time and the centrality of motive

Story time is human time rather than physical time; it is shaped by motive and intention. To see myself as in a story, or a series of stories, is to see my life in time as stretching out toward possibilities (both hopeful and fearful) which I have some influence in bringing about. Even in serious illness, constrained by a physical body largely out of my control, my illness story concerns how I and the other actors who surround me respond to the physical press of disease and deformity. Narrative time differs from biomedical time because it is actor-centered rather than disease centered. While from a purely physical or biomedical perspective, the 'main character' in illness is the pathology, from a narrative perspective the main character is the person with the pathology [37].

Stories need not provide complex psychological accounts of intentions but they do foreground the role of intending, purposeful agents in explaining why things have come about in a certain way. Stories are about *acts*. Kenneth Burke, whose seminal work is a study of the centrality of the notion of act to narrative (or drama) wrote: "As for 'act,' any verb, no matter how specific or how general, that has connotations of consciousness or purpose falls under this category" [36, p. 14]. Stories are investigations of events as actions; they are, to use Burke's vocabulary, "dramatistic" investigations. Drama stands for the paradigm of action in its full sense as distinct from motion with machine as its paradigm.

Emplotted time, then, is a time of social doings, shaped by the actions of oneself and others. In the therapeutic interaction described above, Donna's first task is to turn the patient into an actor rather than a mere "body" who is acted upon by others. She quite directly asks Steven to do something, to comb his hair, an undramatic habitual action, but an action nonetheless. The interactional play between the two is marked. Donna not only acknowledges but structures her own therapeutic actions in response to his. This gives a dialogic quality to their time together; it also, notably, means that carrying out a completely prescribed treatment plan is antithetical to emplotting a therapeutic narrative. How could one plan, for instance that the patient would ask for a mirror, or, more importantly for a ride? And yet it was the request for a ride which structured the entire session and which allowed a reentry story to unfold.

(c) Time governed by desire

The actions which form the central core, the causal nexus, of the narrative, are not motivated in some trivial sense, as when we are moved to make a cup of coffee or pick up the morning paper; they are driven forward by desire. A story is governed, the folklorist Vladimir Propp [38] tells us, by a "lack" or a need which must be addressed. This lack may be caused by some kind of "insufficiency" [38, p. 34] or created in response to the action of a villain who "disturb[s] the peace" [38, p. 27]. In either case, it is set in motion either by the hero's desire to attain something he does not have, or to right some wrong. The presence of desire brings with it a readiness to suffer. Our desire causes us to take risks (or, pay a price when we fail to take risks) and this in itself causes suffering. Often our object will not be attained, or when attained it will not give us what we hoped for, and these things also cause pain. Our desire for something we do not yet have strongly organizes the meaning of the present and makes us vulnerable to a disjuncture between what we wish for and what actually unfolds.

Desire is even a central feature of our response, as listeners, to the well-told story. The essential place of desire in a narrative mode is particularly striking when we realize not only that the story hero but even the story listener is drawn to desire certain story outcomes and fear others. This point has been well discussed in reader response theory, particularly by the remarkable work of Iser [39]. When a story is told, if that storytelling is successful, it creates in the listener a hope that some endings (generally the endings the hero also cares about) will transpire. When we listen to an engaging story, we wonder what will happen next because we have come to care about what will happen next. In his studies of storytelling among inner city black youths, Labov [40] has pointed out that the most important narrative question which the storyteller's narrative must answer, and in fact must answer so well the question is never explicitly raised, is "So what?" A failed story is one which leaves the audience wondering why anyone bothered to tell it.

A story may be well formed from a purely structural point of view, and may have a clear 'point' but if the audience does not know why the point matters to them, if the events in the story never touch them, the story does not work.

The parallel between the told story and lived time is easily drawn if life in time is characterized, following Heidegger, as a present located between past and future rather than an endless succession of 'nows.' The meaning of the present is always a temporal situatedness between a past and a future which we await. We are not passive in this waiting, however. Desire in the face of an uncertain future plays a central structuring role. We hope for certain endings; others we dread. We act in order to bring certain endings about, to realize certain futures, and to avoid others. While we may not (often are not) successful, we act nonetheless, striving as far as we can to make some stories come true and thwart others. In so acting we may come to decide that endings we thought we desired are not so desirable after all and shift our teleological orientation in favor of a different future. But always we are situated with an eye to the future and that future saturates each present moment with meaning. This is what Heidegger means when he describes us as always in the process of becoming, organized around Care. It is not merely that the agent, somehow, 'pictures' a future state which he then tries to attain. The future belongs to the present because we are, as Heidegger says, "thrown forward" in a stance of commitment, of care, toward a future. We are always, in Heidegger's wonderful phrase, "ahead of ourselves" [41]. M. J. Good's work on the central place of hope in the practice of oncology provides an important perspective on the need for both clinician and patient to find something to hope for [42].

Returning to the case given above, the therapist attempts to shift the patient into narrative time by inviting the patient to be "ahead of himself." They take a tour into the future, both the future of therapeutic encounters and the future which matters, the one which leads out from the hospital back home. The therapy room she takes him to represents a temporary station, a purgatory, which, if endured and

even embraced, offers a path to the outside. Or, at least, that is the narrative the therapist hopes will shape their clinical time together.

In this therapeutic interaction the therapist's concern to generate desire for therapy is evident in many of the actions she takes, including how she interprets the meaning to be made of the patient's own actions. When the therapist asks the patient to comb his hair, he does not at first cooperate. Perhaps her fundamental task in this initial encounter is to create in him a desire to act and, quite specifically, a desire to act in therapy. Since there is no story where there is no desire, much of this initial session with the therapist can be seen as her effort at making therapy a place where there is something to care about. She begins to sketch out possible "endings" which she presumes the patient does, or will, desire – especially becoming free of his role as patient and reconnecting to those he cares about (family, girlfriend), outside the confines of the clinic.

(d) Time of transformation – time dominated by the ending

In a story, time is structured by a movement from one state of affairs (a beginning) to a transformed state of affairs (an ending). In story time, things are different in the end. The structure of beginning-middle-end presumes, of course, that time is marked by anticipation of some end, one which, to make another obvious point, does not exist at the beginning. So narrative time is marked by change, or by the attempt at change. It is time characterized by an effort at transformation. Things may be changed in an outward, public way or there may be an inward difference. People may come to think and feel differently. But it is important that in the time of plot, the agency which most matters in creating change is human agency. Even if other factors are more determinant – physical and even structural conditions – these are background, the setting in which human actors take center stage.

When Donna and Steven take their tour of the hospital, the possibility of transformation is at the heart of the drama they are playing out. At first take, this point is so obvious that it goes without saying. If therapy is not about change, what could it be about? What is powerful in examining the thirty minute interaction between therapist and client is how the topic of transformation figures centrally, and the sort of transformation that is emplotted.

Steven has awakened to a body horrifyingly transformed. Some further bodily transformations will occur as part of a natural healing process, apart from his own actions. And some will occur because of what others do to him. But none of these changes form the core of the plot being sketched by Donna. This is not a narrative of passive awakening; there is no miracle cure and no magician healer. The plot is both more prosaic and more wrenching for it centers on the body transformation which Steven can directly affect through painstaking effort. Perhaps the greatest part of the pain will be Steven's growing acquaintance with his injured body, and his emerging recognition of the limits imposed upon him by that body. Through trying to heal himself, he will discover time and again the limits he must live with and will have to reckon with the loss of possibilities no longer available to him. This reckoning will precipitate inner transformations, changes of personal identity, perhaps even changes of character.

(e) Troubled time

The very drama of narrative is based, in a sense, on the experience of suffering. Even the happy story, the one which ends well, takes us through a drama of plight – a lack or need which sets the story in motion, which propels the protagonist in a quest to obtain his goal through the overcoming of a series of obstacles. The process of overcoming, however fortuitous the result, almost inevitably engenders periods of suffering for the story's heroes. This is such a pervasive feature of the structure of narrative that Propp made it central to his analysis of folktales and later narrativists expanded it to include many other kinds of narratives. And Arendt used it to characterize one moment in a dialectical treatment of the nature of human action.

Narratives are about acting and suffering, Arendt has said. They are about doing something (acting) and what happens as a result

(suffering). Suffering is one name for experience. "Because the actor always moves among and in relation to other acting beings, he is never merely a 'doer,' but always and at the same time a sufferer. To do and to suffer are like opposite sides of the same coin, and the story that an act starts is composed of its consequent deeds and sufferings" [17, p. 190]. The "trouble" that marks narrative time is the necessary counterpoint, a required antithesis, to a causal structure dominated by the concept of human agency. Actions may be the central cause within narrative structure, but their causal efficacy is anything but sure. Nothing is guaranteed in the realm of human action. We do what we can but – in the narrative at least – there are always impediments.

The importance of trouble and suffering in the narrative is due to the sort of actions narratives recount, actions in which desire is strong and in which there is a significant gap between where I now am and where I want to be. If narrative plots turned on the everyday easy-to-accomplish actions which form habitual life (raising my arm to scratch my head, putting up my umbrella in the rain, heating a can of soup for dinner) suffering would not need to enter. The strength of our desire comes in part from the length of the reach required to attain what we want. Most stories we choose to tell feature difficult passages toward precarious destinations, journeys fraught with enemies who may defeat us at any moment. Upon examination, it is surprising how regularly everyday stories carry this plot structure; even tales of victory are set against this implicit backdrop of what might have gone wrong.

In attempting to set a therapeutic story in motion, the occupational therapist need not, of course, invent troubles or obstacles for the patient. These come with chronic disability. Suffering is paramount; adversaries are everywhere. The difficult task for the therapist is locating a space for action at all. Her problem is how to offer sufficient hope to the patient such that the struggle to overcome obstacles becomes meaningful and bearable [41]. Occupational therapists speak often of their need to transform "passive patients" into "active patients." What they mean is that their patients are organized in the hospital to suffer, to wait, to be "done to," as they say. When Donna takes Steven for a tour, she is inviting him into a story in which he will not only suffer passively, as a victim of his injury, but one in which he goes out to battle, so to speak, actively incurring more suffering (certainly more physical pain) in a fight to overcome, where he can, the damage that has been done to his body. Within the therapeutic plot Donna hopes to initiate, the patient becomes an aggressor of a sort, engaging adversaries in an effort to become healed, and treating the therapist as a valued ally and trusted guide in this enterprise. Physicians often see themselves as engaged in a dramatic fight with disease, waging war against cancer cells, for example [42–4]. But in the occupational therapist's emplotment, it is the patient, in alliance with the therapist, who is designated as the narrative hero, the one who must wage the war.

(f)　Suspenseful time: time of the unknown ending

The presence of powerful enemies, and of dangers and obstacles, means that narrative time is a time of uncertainty. Our desire for an ending may be strong, but if our enemies are equally strong, or danger is prevalent, there is no telling what will finally unfold. Hence, the fifth characteristic of narrative time is that it is marked by doubt, by what Bruner [45] speaks of as 'subjunctivity.' This theme is wonderfully developed by Good [4] in his discussion of illness narratives. If lived experience positions us in a fluid space between a past and a future, then what we experience is strongly marked by the possible. Meaning itself, from this perspective, is always in suspense. If the meaning of the present, and even of the past, is contingent on what unfolds in the future, then what is happening and what has happened is not a matter of facts but of interpretive possibilities which are vulnerable to an unknown future.

Life in time is a place of possibility; it is this structure that narrative imitates. For narrative does not tell us that what happened was necessary but that it was possible, displaying a reality in which things might have been otherwise [46]. Endings, in action and in story, are not logically necessary but possible, and seen from the end

and looking backwards, plausible. "To follow a story," Ricoeur writes, "is to move forward in the midst of contingencies and peripeteia under the guidance of an expectation that finds its fulfillment in the 'conclusion' of the story. This conclusion is not logically implied by some previous premises. It gives the story an 'end point,' which, in turn, furnishes the point of view from which the story can be perceived as forming a whole. To understand the story is to understand how and why the successive episodes led to this conclusion, which, far from being foreseeable, must finally be acceptable, as congruent with the episodes brought together by the story" [20, pp. 66–7].

Story time is not, at least in any simple or linear sense, about progress. It is not about building one thing onto another in some steady movement toward a defined goal. Time is characterized by suspense, not only the suspense of not knowing whether a desired ending will come about, but even the suspense of not knowing whether the ending one pictures is the one which will still be desired or possible as the story unfolds.

In the therapeutic plot Donna enacts with Steven, indications of an uncertain future are minimized. If there is one place where therapeutic emplotment in this case diverges from narrative time in the told story, it is over the issue of certainty. For Donna points toward vivid and predictable endings. When they look out toward the Prudential, she speaks confidently of Steven's return home to family and friends. When they look into the door of the therapy room, she speaks of the gains he will make by working through pain. She does not raise doubts about what he will be able to accomplish, or what life he will return to. Her intent appears to be to offer him a hopeful ending, a set of desirable images, to which he might be able to attach himself. And yet, given the despair many patients feel over their ability to transform themselves and their lives upon awakening from a coma or serious operation, her cheerful certainty is set against the bleak, nearly silent uncertainty of a patient who, at the beginning of the session, did not even want to get out of bed. Her brisk assertions can be seen as a kind of whistling in the dark, an attempt to put a brave (or blind) face on a future which is anything but sure, one where things will never be the same.

Conclusion

Clearly, as research in medical anthropology has shown, listening to stories patients tell is essential to understanding their illness experiences. Healer's stories, too, reveal a great deal about both the clinician's experience as healer and the culture(s) of biomedicine. What is added by looking at therapeutic encounters *themselves* as proto-narratives, stories-in-the-making ? Why speak of therapeutic plots? The notion of therapeutic emplotment offers one way to examine the social construction (and reconstruction) of illness and healing as a fluid, shifting process influenced not only by molecular conditions, institutional structures and cultural meanings but also by the exigencies of the concrete situation.

Equally important, narrative analysis of clinical interaction helps to uncover the moral dimensions of clinical practice. As Kleinman and Kleinman [47] argue, therapeutic transactions are fundamentally moral. A central difficulty with the usual clinical depictions of patient sufferings is that in their abstractness, the world of the patient is left out. This world is above all a practical and moral one in which patients have life projects and everyday concerns, things "at stake." Illness, from this point of view, creates a "resistance" that hinders or prevents the sufferer from carrying out plans and projects [46]. The study of a clinical encounter as an unfolding story leads easily to a recognition of its ethical content for "the moral" is integral to the meaning of any story. What was that point of *that* story? we ask when the moral is apparently missing. A narrative analysis offers a way to examine clinical life as a series of existential negotiations between clinicians and patients, ones that concern the meaning of illness, the place of therapy within an unfolding illness story, and the meaning of a life which must be remade in the face of serious illness.

This moral negotiation is easily hidden in the clinical world, disguised in the trappings of a clear-cut technical encounter where, presumably, the task is to get the patient as well as possible in the shortest time possible. Certainly, the work of therapeutic emplotment is not necessarily obvious; treatment can appear as nothing more than a set of procedures. In this paper, I purposely chose a quite ordinary therapy session because there is nothing narratively interesting or of any particular moral import which is immediately evident. While sometimes encounters between occupational therapists and patients are quite dramatic, more often they resemble the interaction between Donna and Steven. Quiet and, at first glance, uneventful. Just a therapist wheeling a patient through the hospital corridors. But an encounter such as this begins to take on significance when recognized as an episode within a larger therapeutic story which is in the process of being constructed. Any therapeutic narrative, in turn, is but a short story in the larger life history of the patient, a life story which is under radical reconstruction while therapy is on-going. Which therapeutic story gets constructed, and what voice the patient has in that story-making, is not inconsequential.

Acknowledgements – I would like to thank Mary-Jo DelVecchio Good, Byron Good, Vincent Crapanzano, Michael Fischer, Linda Hunt, Lindsay French, Arthur Kleinman, Jean Jackson, and Jim Howe for their helpful comments on earlier drafts of this paper.

NOTES

1. Early E. A.
   The logic of well being: Therapeutic narratives in Cairo, Egypt. *Soc. Sci. Med.* **16**, 1491, 1982.
2. Price L.
   Ecuadorian illness stories: cultural knowledge in natural discourse. In *Cultural Models in Language and Thought* (Edited by Holland D. and Quinn N.). Cambridge University Press, Cambridge, 1987.
3. Kleinman A.
   The Illness Narratives: Suffering, Healing and the Human Condition. Basic Books, New York, 1988.
4. Good B.
   The narrative representation of illness. Chap. 6 of *Medicine, Rationality and Experience: An*

Anthropological Perspective. Cambridge: Cambridge University Press, 2004.

5. Schafer R.
   Retelling a Life: Narrations and Dialogue in Psychoanalysis. Basic Books, New York, 1992.

6. Of course, in writing up this case I have created a story, a narrative discourse, from a clinical interaction which I witnessed and described. The interaction I observed has necessarily been transformed into written text through my efforts as ethnographer. However, the claim of this paper is that the narrative I analyze is not simply created by my rendering it in written discourse, but that this narrative structure belongs in a fundamental way to the interaction itself.

7. Holland D. and N. Quinn
   Cultural Models in Language and Thought. Cambridge University Press, Cambridge, 1987.

8. Herrnstein Smith B.
   Narrative versions, narrative theories. In *On Narrative* (Edited by Mitchell W. J. T.). University of Chicago Press, Chicago, 1980.

9. Herrnstein Smith B.
   On the Margins of Discourse. University of Chicago Press, Chicago, 1978.

10. White H.
    The Content of the Form. Johns Hopkins University Press, Baltimore, 1987.

11. White H.
    Metahistory: The Historical Imagination in Nineteenth-century Europe. Johns Hopkins University Press, Baltimore, 1973.

12. Clifford J.
    On ethnographic authority. *Representations* 1, 118, 1983.

13. Clifford J.
    Introduction: Partial truths. In *Writing Culture: The Poetics and Politics of Ethnography* (Edited by Clifford J. and Marcus G.). University of California Press, Berkeley, 1986.

14. Clifford J.
    The Predicament of Culture. Harvard University Press, Cambridge, 1988.

15. MacIntyre A.
    After Virtue: A Study in Moral Theory. University of Notre Dame Press, Notre Dame, 1981.

16. MacIntyre A.
    Three Rival Versions of Moral Enquiry. University of Notre Dame Press, Notre Dame, 1990.

17. Arendt H.
    The Human Condition. University of Chicago Press, Chicago, 1958.

18. Ricoeur P.
    Narrative time. In *On Narrative* (Edited by Mitchell T. J.). University of Chicago Press, Chicago, 1980.

19. Ricoeur P.
    The narrative function. In *Hermeneutics and the Human Sciences* (Edited by Thompson J.). Cambridge University Press, Cambridge, 1981.

20. Ricoeur P.
    Time and Narrative, Vol. 1. University of Chicago Press, Chicago, 1984.

21. Carr D.
    Time, Narrative and History. Indiana University Press, Indianapolis, 1986.

22. Olafson F.
    The Dialectic of Action. University of Chicago Press, Chicago, 1979.

23. Mattingly C.
    Narrative reflections on practical actions. In *The Reflective Turn* (Edited by Schon D.). Teachers College Press, New York, 1991.

24. Mattingly C.
    The narrative nature of clinical reasoning. *Am. J. Occupat. Ther.* 54, 998, 1991.

25. Mattingly C. and N. Gillette
    Anthropology, occupational therapy and action research. *Am. J. Occupat. Ther.* 54, 972, 1991.

26. Forster E. M.
    Aspects of the Novel. Harcourt Brace, New York, 1927.

27. Frye N.
    Anatomy of Criticism. Princeton University Press, Princeton, 1957.

28. White H.
    The value of narrativity in the representation of reality. In *On Narrative* (Edited by Mitchell T. J.). University of Chicago Press, Chicago, 1980.

29. Ricoeur P.
    Time and Narrative, Vol. II. University of Chicago Press, Chicago, 1985.

30. Ricoeur P.
     Time and Narrative, Vol. III. University of
     Chicago Press, Chicago, 1987.
31. Goffman E.
     Frame Analysis. Harvard University Press,
     Cambridge, 1974.
32. Kermode F.
     The Sense of an Ending. Oxford University
     Press, New York, 1966.
33. Fleming M.
     A common sense practice in an uncommon
     world. In *Clinical Reasoning: Forms of In-
     quiry in Therapeutic Practice* (Edited by
     Mattingly C. and Fleming M.). F. A. Davis
     Press, Philadelphia, 1993.
34. Pseudonyms have been used throughout this
     case.
35. Arendt H.
     The Life of the Mind. Harcourt Brace Jova-
     novich, New York, 1971.
36. Burke K.
     A Grammar of Motives. University of
     California Press, Berkeley, 1945.
37. Sacks O.
     The Man who Mistook his Wife for a Hat.
     Perennial Library, New York, 1987.
38. Propp V.
     Morphology of the Folk Tale. University of
     Texas Press, Austin, 1968.
39. Iser W.
     The Act of Reading. Johns Hopkins Univer-
     sity Press. Baltimore, 1978.
40. Labov, W. and J. Waletzky
     Narrative analysis: Oral versions of per-
     sonal experience. In *Essays in the Verbal
     and Visual Arts* (Edited by Helm J.). Univer-
     sity of Washington Press for the American
     Ethnological Society, Seattle, 1967.
41. Heidegger M.
     Being and Time (Translated by Robinson E.
     and Macquarrie J.). Harper and Row,
     New York, 1962.
42. DelVecchio Good M. J., B. Good, C. Schaf-
     fer, S. E. Lind
     American oncology and the discourse on
     hope. *Culture Med. Psychiat.* **14**, 59, 1990.
43. Hunt L.
     Practicing oncology in provincial Mexico:
     A narrative analysis. *Soc. Sci. Med.* **38**,
     843–53, 1994.
44. Good M. J. DelVecchio,   L. Hunt,
     T. Manakato, and Y. Kobayashi
     A comparative analysis of the culture of
     biomedicine: disclosure and consequences
     for treatment in the practice of oncology.
     In *Medical Care in the Developing World*
     (Edited by Conrad P. and Gallagher E.).
     Temple University Press, Philadelphia. In press.
45. Bruner J.
     Actual Minds, Possible Worlds. Harvard
     University Press, Cambridge, 1986.
46. Barthes R.
     Introduction to the structural analysis of
     narrative. In *Image, Music, Text* (Translated
     by Heath S.). Hill & Wang, New York, 1977.
47. Kleinman A. and J. Kleinman
     Suffering and its professional transform-
     ation: Toward an ethnography of interper-
     sonal experience. *Culture, Med. Psychiat.*
     15, 275, 1991.

13

Myths/Histories/Lives

Michael Jackson

No life is sufficient unto itself. A person is singular only in the sense in which astronomers use the term: a relative point in space and time where invisible forces become fleetingly visible (cf. Lévi-Strauss 1990, 625–6). Our lives belong to others as well as to ourselves. Just as the stars at night are set in imperceptible galaxies, so our lives flicker and fail in the dark streams of history, fate, and genealogy. One might say that we are each given three lives. First is our conscious incarnation, occupying most of the space between our birth and death. Second is our existence in the hearts and minds of others – a life that precedes the moment of our birth and extends beyond our death for as long as we are remembered. Finally there is our afterlife as a barely remembered name, a persona, an element in myth. And this existence begins with the death of the last person who knew us in life.

These moments in a person's destiny find expression in different kinds of stories. What begins as a body of raw experience, too humdrum or perhaps too painful to be told, becomes a narrative, and later takes on the lineaments of myth. In this metamorphosis of life into legend, the original figures fade and reform, and often end up carrying the burden of our preoccupations. As Michael Young notes in his brilliant study of the ways myth and life story are interleaved in Kalauna, "myth is reconstructed through lived experience which mediates culture; and culture is reconstructed through lived experience which mediates myth" (1983, 35).

My fieldwork in central Australia brought me to an existential understanding of the way subjectivity inevitably entails intersubjectivity, and vice versa. To come into one's own a person must also feel at home in the world. Paradoxically perhaps, one can only be one's own person to the extent that one belongs to a wider context than the self – family, clan, circle of friends, workplace, or imagined community. Being at home in the world implies, therefore, a dialectics of identity (Jackson 1977, 238). But this perpetual interplay between hermetic and open-ended, enstatic and ecstatic modes of subjective experience implies problems of feedback and control. These cybernetic adjustments between self and other cannot, however, be measured objectively. Rather they are consummated intersubjectively as a sense of balance between one's experience of the world as something alien, external, all-encompassing, and overbearing, and one's experience of having some place in the world, some say over its governance. Every human life drifts between two poles: the entirely egocentric and totalitarian extreme of dominating others, and the masochistic extreme of self-abnegation, inertia, and victimage. For most people, life is a struggle for the middle ground where it is possible to realize one's power to make a difference in the world, to call it one's own, though within the limits of the needs of others, as well as the constraints of history and genealogy.

When in 1993 my wife, Francine, and I went to live with an aboriginal family on an outstation

Michael Jackson, "Myths/Histories/Lives," in *Minima Ethnographica*. Chicago: University of Chicago Press, 1998. Reprinted by permission of the publisher, The University of Chicago Press.

in the rainforests of southeast Cape York, these issues of home and belonging reclaimed my attention. The history of the social world we entered was as tragic and traumatic as any in aboriginal Australia: more than a hundred years of conquest and violent dispossession, of racism and murder, of the brutal breakup of families, of dispersal and deportation, enforced missionization, and the denial of basic civil rights (Loos 1982; Broome 1982; Rosser 1985; Rowley 1972). Successive generations of aboriginal people had been drawn into a wider polity only to find themselves diminished and disadvantaged within it. Their struggle to strike a balance between a sense of their own ethnic solidarity and a sense of place in the national community had been frustrated and often futile.

The traces of this history were everywhere apparent, not in physical relics or ruins but in the lived forms of aboriginal sociality itself, particularly where outsiders were involved. Story after story bore upon the vexed history of black-white relations, though it was clear that this categorical opposition merged with an older and deeper dialectic between self and other, insider and stranger. The family with whom we lived was a case in point. Although the O'Rourkes[1] had endured the mission years stoically, they had been marginalized long before. Traditionally, a retaliatory and retributive killing was demanded if an important man died and sorcery was suspected, and the people living at Banabila – so-called because of the swift tidal current that ran at the mouth of the Bloomfield River – had been the scapegoats. Deemed "the weakest and most friendless" Kuku-Yalanji group, Roth, writing in 1907, noted of them: "one of this tribe is generally, as a last resource, fixed upon as the culprit; the latter is enticed away on some hunting expedition, for a corroboree, etc. and then mercilessly speared from behind" (Roth 1907, 387; cf. 1910, 92).

Like many aboriginal people, the O'Rourkes sought isolation as a survival strategy. But segregationalist and assimilationist government policies left them and others like them no place to hide. Forced into a Lutheran mission in the 1970s, the tactic of physical retreat metamorphosed into social stratagems of withdrawal and subterfuge. Their long history of

marginalization, incorporated as a habitual disposition toward guardedness and reticence, may explain why the O'Rourkes resisted being moved to the mission (they were almost the last to leave their land) and were the first to leave. Of all Kuku-Yalanji "mobs" in the late 1970s, the O'Rourkes were, according to Christopher Anderson, "one of the mission's least powerful and materially worst off" (1984, 385). Yet their isolation implied considerable solidarity. "The O'Rourkes, out in the scrub, sticking together," was the way a local Aboriginal councillor once described them to me.

One cannot begin to understand aboriginal experience of what *we* call history without understanding *their* conception of the past. As I had seen in central Australia, custom and law exist *in potentia* – as the Dreaming – but must be continually brought back into sentient being (*in presentia*) through concerted ritual activity. This perennial recovery of the past is often described metaphorically as a drawing out, waking up, growing up, and giving birth. A person's relation with the past is thus lived as a *social* relation with the forebear whose name he or she carries, as well as with the site with which that forebear is ever-presently associated. In so far as the vital energy of ancestral (past) events is embodied in the land, time is spatialized. In so far as the past is felt to continually reenter the present, time is synchronous. As Veena Das so aptly puts it, the present is constituted as a "spectral present rather than a point present" (1989, 324). Put another way, "there are not two worlds – the world of past happenings and the world of our present knowledge of those past events – there is only one world, and it is a world of present experience" (Oakeshott 1933, 108).

The implication is that we must understand time and space intersubjectively. Many aboriginal people express bafflement and dismay at the ease with which Europeans seem to turn their backs on the past – as if it were *outside* lived experience. As if by implication the injustices and grief that white settlers visited on aboriginal people were now over and done with, dead and buried. For aboriginal people, however, this "history" is reiterated and embodied in the very condition of their contemporary lives, which is why people so readily fuse accounts of their own experience and accounts of their forebears' experiences as if past and present were effectively one.

Although many scholars still tend to separate history and myth – the first supposedly made up of series and successions of events that have actually occurred, the second largely invented, reconstructed, or imagined – it is necessary to set aside or bracket out this kind of distinction if one is to understand aboriginal ways of narrating experience. Phenomenologically, any "cut" between historic and mythopoeic, objective event and interpreted event, is untenable. History is a mode of experience, a world of coexistent facts, in which the past is continually represented (Oakeshott 1933, 108–18).

The key to understanding this phenomenon is memory. As Maurice Halbwachs showed, individual memories, like dreams, are continually being reshaped and reconstructed in the course of a person's *social* engagement with others (Halbwachs 1980). This may occur in the context of dialogue as well as in the course of bodily and ritual interaction (Connerton 1989). In these processes personal memories become collectivized and historicized; they cease to be properties of individual minds and enter into intersubjectivity. As such, the line between immediate and interpreted experience effectively disappears.

Just as aboriginal people tend to gloss over the boundary between biography and myth, so too the line between the historical and the personal is rarely clear-cut. Indeed, there is an onus on the living to actively integrate the past into the present (Rose 1992, 30). As Ronald Berndt observed of Western desert peoples, the existential and moral *actualization* of the received wisdom in myth is something the living must accomplish in the way they choose to live (Berndt 1979, 28). Just as this fusion of Dreamtime and lifetime is achieved through storying, so the past and present are continually collapsed in the stories with which people render accounts of their social and personal reality. One is reminded of the way many young Jewish people speak of *their* suffering during the Holocaust, or African-Americans speak of *their* enslavement, as if they themselves actually experienced events that took place before they were born.

The psychology of separation trauma helps us understand what hastens this fusion of personal and collective memory.

As in any other human society, an aboriginal child's primary orientation is to his or her immediate family and community. These constitute the significant others who mirror and affirm a child's developing sense of who he or she is. In aboriginal Australia this positive identification was often negated by white prejudice and propaganda, which relentlessly emphasized that such modes of belonging were the stigmata of primitiveness and dependency and could only perpetuate a state of aboriginal fallenness, ignorance, ill health, and inferior being. In short, the very loci of people's ontological security – kin, land, language, ancestry – were systematically invalidated. And if the stigma of aboriginal origins were not enough, punishment was meted out in the form of assimilationist policies that permitted children to be taken from their birth parents and licensed police to physically remove aboriginal people from their land and incarcerate them on reserves, missions, and penal settlements.

Existentially, these subversive strategies, punitive measures, and criminalizing and stigmatizing procedures often had the very opposite effects to those that were intended. Rather than make aboriginal people ashamed of themselves and determined to break with tradition, they drove people back to their roots for security and survival. It was in this way that "the stolen generation" came to extol their aboriginality over the so-called golden opportunities they had been given by well-meaning white foster parents for whom traditional aboriginal society offered nothing but illiteracy and alienation. If mythology, land, and language were not available as a matrix in which to place oneself, history was. History became the ontological surrogate of mythology. And the white world was made the dialectical negation of aboriginality. In so far as it had denied blacks any place in it, any rights in it, any choices over its governance, blacks would now define themselves by turning that denial against those who had first used it. Reinventing white history was part of this oppositional process.

In this sense the fusion of biographical and historical horizons is not merely a way of understanding one's situation; it is, more immediately, a strategy of actively coping with it. In translating *my* suffering into the suffering of my people, *I* is transformed into *we*. By the same token, the person who caused my suffering is stripped of his or her particular identity and transformed into an instance of *they*, or further depersonalized as *it*. This transformation of particular subjective experience into a universalized and transsubjective category enables one to grasp and control a situation one experienced first in solitude and powerlessness. It is always easier to bear personal suffering if one can experience it as something shared by many others. Through the sense of kinship born of this identification with fellow sufferers one is able to find common cause against a common foe. The belittling sense of having been singled out and persecuted because of some failing in oneself yields to an empowering sense of being part of a collective tragedy, a shared trauma. No matter what the wound, it is easier to act as one of many who have been victims of a historical wrong than it is to act as the isolated and sole victim of a personal slight.

But another transformation is implicated here. For as long as a traumatized person feels isolated and alone, his or her suffering is experienced and dealt with intrapsychically. This may take the form of repression, self-blaming, self-loathing, self-abuse, and self-destruction. But solidarity with others in whom one recognizes one's own suffering tends to move the locus of these defenses from the intrapsychic to the intersubjective. First, even seemingly self-destructive behavior such as binge drinking and fighting comes to conform to complex rules of sociality (Collmann 1988). Second, one may appropriate the language with which one is vilified and derogated, and use it half-joking against oneself and one's own kind, so tearing it from the oppressor's grasp, asserting control over it, and nullifying its effects (Jackson 1995, 13; Carter 1991). Third, one may rework events that one suffered in impassivity and silence as shared narratives in which one plays the heroic role of trickster. Self-deprecating humor and parody tend to characterize this

transformation from victimage to advantage. Consider, for instance, the following comments by an aboriginal woman on the subject of rape:

> white girls complain if they are raped. Our girls are ashamed of it. They prefer that no one knows because they're afraid to be ridiculed. Others laugh. I've talked to Aboriginal women who've been raped by whites, Greeks, Japanese, Chinese or whatever, and they just toss it off as a joke. A lot of these stories come to us in pidgin English and it does sound funny. It turns out that's one way of covering up their shame, ... by laughing at it. The actual part of a rape, the horrible part, I've never heard that laughed about. But the tricks that lead up to it, the goings on. They talk about it in such a way that it belittles the man who did it. (Gilbert 1978, 20)

In her account of her journey by camel across the Western desert, Robyn Davidson writes of how her Pitjantjatjara traveling companion, Eddie, dealt with an incident in which a white tourist denigrated him by calling him "Jacky-Jacky" and "boy" and ordering him to "come and stand alonga camel" for a photograph. While Davidson was consumed by indignation and anger, Eddie "turned himself into a perfect parody of a ravingly dangerous idiot boong," playing the tourists' stereotypes back at them as burlesque. In this way he turned the tables on the tourists, making them the victims of their own ignorance. Laughing hysterically at the episode later, Davidson saw how bitterness and victimage could be averted through ludic action (1980, 182–4).

Richard Broome has written perceptively of this strategy of the trickster, the ways in which aboriginals mimicked European bosses, assigned them derisive nicknames, or used subterfuge as payback:

> The unhappy peanut farmer in the north saw his best peanuts disappear all day into the mouths of Aboriginal pickers. Aboriginal stockmen on a muster could kill a prime cow, enjoy the good beef and then disguise the carcase to look like a natural death or a dingo killing. Aboriginal boys were expert at spearing vegetables through the cat door of the station store, or at tunnelling under the floor to drain out the flour and sugar from

the bags on the bottom row. Others sabotaged the bosses' equipment. One manager claimed that his "dumb" and "lazy" Aboriginal workers could not be trusted to apply even a few drops of oil periodically to the bore-water rigs and that 25 had blown up in two years at a cost of $5000 each. Strangely, the bore at the Aboriginal camp never broke down. (Broome 1982, 135)

Warlpiri informants described similar strategies to me, detailing how they used all manner of underhand methods – trickery, mimicry, theft, recalcitrance – to counter exploitation and prejudice (Jackson 1995, 96–100). And as many first-contact accounts testify, aboriginal people often told self-disparaging, mimetically inventive, and ludicrous stories about their own initial ignorance of whites as a way of dealing with their traumatic loss of control (Dawson 1981, 105–6).

Another mode of "oppositional practice," sometimes spoken of as a culture of resistance (Cowlishaw 1988), may arise from everyday coping strategies, though it should not be analytically conflated with or reduced to them. Here the ethos of the "oppressor" is openly scorned, political activism appears, and nationalism takes hold. The vilified self is now projected onto a vilified other. Self-hatred becomes a hatred of another, self-blaming is replaced by a search for scapegoats. Instead of withdrawing into oneself, one now withdraws socially from the other, who has become the paradigmatic not-self who once categorized and classified oneself as an abhorred alien.

[. . .]

Here/Now

But the test of anthropological understanding is wordly, not epistemological. Its truth lies in its capacity to help us see that plurality is not inimical but necessary to our integrity, so inspiring us to accept and celebrate the manifold and contradictory character of existence in the knowledge that any one person embodies the potential to be any other. As Terence's famous stoic dictum has it, *humani nil a me alienum puto* – being human, nothing human is alien to me.

The argument is for a view of Being as complex, ambiguous, and indeterminate. It is analogous to the argument ecologists make *against* genetically engineered and global monocultures and *for* indigenous biodiversity as the only effective way of sustaining life on earth. And it echoes the argument Michael Oakeshott makes in his famous essay on conversation. The task of science, he writes, is not to deliver us from the polyphony of Babel but to accommodate disparate voices, disagreeing with being disagreeable, as in conversation (Oakeshott 1991, 488–9).

Put otherwise, the task of ethnography is not to know the Other in any final sense nor even to know the self through the other. Nor is it to change the lives of others, or even to critique one's own culture. Its warrant and worth lie in its power to describe in depth and detail the dynamics of inter-subjective life under a variety of cultural conditions in the hope that one may thereby be led to an understanding of how those rare moments of erasure and effacement occur when self and other are constituted in mutuality and acceptance rather than violence and contempt.

Stopped on a road in order to listen and take notes.

NOTE

1   I use pseudonyms for all the aboriginal families and individuals mentioned in the following pages.

REFERENCES

Anderson, Jon Christopher
    1984   "The Political and Economic Basis of Kuku-Yalanji Social History." Ph.D. diss. University of Queensland, Australia.
Berndt, Ronald M.
    1979   "A Profile of Good and Bad in Australian Aboriginal Religion." Charles Strong Memorial Lecture. *Australian and New Zealand Theological Review* 12:17–31.
Broome, Richard
    1982   *Aboriginal Australians: Black Response to White Dominance.* Sydney: Allen and Unwin.
Carter, Julie D.
    1991   "Am I Too Black to Go with You?" In *Being Black: Aboriginal Cultures in "Settled" Australia.* Ed. Ian Keen. Canberra: Aboriginal Studies Press.

Collmann, Jeff
1988. *Fringe-Dwellers and Welfare: The Aboriginal Response to Bureaucracy.* St. Lucia: University of Queensland Press.

Connerton, Paul
1989 *How Societies Remember.* Cambridge: Cambridge University Press.

Cowlishaw, Gillian
1988 *Black, White or Brindle: Race in Rural Australia.* Cambridge: Cambridge University Press.

Das, Veena
1989 "Subaltern as Perspective." In *Subaltern Studies VI: Writings on South Asian History and Society.* Ed. Ranajit Guha. Delhi: Oxford University Press.

Davidson, Robyn
1980 *Tracks.* London: Jonathan Cape.

Dawson, J.
1981 *Australian Aborigines: The Languages and Customs of Several Tribes in the Western Desert of Victoria, Australia.* Australian Institute of Aboriginal Studies, n. s., no. 26. Canberra.

Gilbert, Kevin
1978 *Living Black: Blacks Talk to Kevin Gilbert.* Ringwood, Victoria, Australia: Penguin Books.

Halbwachs, Maurice
1980 *The Collective Memory.* Trans. Francis J. Ditter Jr. and Vida Yazdi Ditter. New York: Harper and Row.

Jackson, Michael
1977 *The Kuranko: Dimensions of Social Reality in a West African Society.* London: C. Hurst.

Jackson, Michael
1995 *At Home in the World.* Durham: Duke University Press.

Lévi-Strauss, Claude
1990 *The Naked Man.* Vol. 4 of *Mythologiques.* Trans. John and Doreen Weightman. Chicago: University of Chicago Press.

Loos, Noel
1982 *Invasion and Resistance: Aboriginal-European Relations on the North Queensland Frontier 1861–1897.* Canberra: Australian National University Press.

Oakeshott, Michael
1933 *Experience and Its Modes.* Cambridge: Cambridge University Press.

Oakeshott, Michael
1991 *Rationalism in Politics and Other Essays.* New ed. Ed. Timothy Fuller. Indianapolis: Liberty Fund.

Rose, Deborah Bird
1992 *Dingo Makes Us Human: Life and Land in an Aboriginal Australian Culture.* Cambridge: Cambridge University Press.

Rosser, Bill
1985 *Dreamtime Nightmares: Biographies of Aborigines under the Queensland Aborigines Act.* Canberra: Australian Institute of Aboriginal Studies.

Roth, Walter E.
1907 "North Queensland Ethnography: Burial Ceremonies and Disposal the Dead." *Records of the Australian Museum Sydney.* Bulletin no. 9:365–403.

Rowley, C. D.
1972 *Outcasts in White Australia.* Harmondsworth: Penguin.

Young, Michael W.
1983 *Magicians of Manumanua: Living Myth in Kalauna.* Berkeley: University of California Press.

14

The State Construction of Affect

Political Ethos and Mental Health Among Salvadoran Refugees

Janis Hunter Jenkins

You think this mountain is beautiful? I hate it. To me it means war. It's nothing but a theater for this shitty war ... (Response of Comandante Jonas to a foreign journalist's request to take pictures of the mountains, eastern front, El Salvador, 1983. (Quoted from Manlio Argueta's *Cuzcatlan: Where the Southern Sea Beats (1987:1)*.))

One can be a virgin with respect to Horror as one is virgin toward Voluptuousness. (Celine, Journey to the End of the Night. (Quoted in Julia Kristeva's (1982:140) essay on *Powers of Horror: An Essay on Abjection.*))

Introduction

Over the course of the last decade, the intellectual landscape has been marked by an anthropological claim on the study of emotion (Abu-Lughod 1986; Myers 1979; Kleinman and Good 1985; Lutz 1988; Lutz and White 1986; Jenkins 1991; Rosaldo 1980, 1984; Roseman 1990; B. Schieffelin and E. Ochs 1986; E. Schieffelin 1983; Shweder and LeVine 1984; White and Kirkpatrick 1985; Wikan 1990). Joining the existing discourses on emotion in philosophy, psychology, and physiology, anthropological studies of emotion have convincingly established the essential role of culture in constructing emotional experience and expression. The contemporary anthropological interest is rooted in traditions established by psychological anthropology (Bateson 1958; Benedict 1946; Hallowell 1955; Mead 1963; Sapir 1961) and enlivened by more recent interpretive-hermeneutic approaches seeking to collapse classical mind-body dualisms (Csordas 1983, 1990; Frank 1986; Gaines 1982; Good and Good 1982; Kleinman 1982, 1988; Scheper-Hughes and Lock 1987). This intellectual current has led to the anthropological realization that psychobiological theories of emotion have advanced little else than European and North American ethnopsychologies of thought and emotion as somehow separate, mutually exclusive cultural objects. This development has sparked the current fluorescence of theorizing on culture and the self and asserts

Janis Hunter Jenkins, "The State Construction of Affect: Political Ethos and Mental Health among Salvadoran Refugees, *Culture, Medicine and Psychiatry* 15 (1991): 139–65. With kind permission from Springer Science +Business Media: Culture, Medicine and Psychiatry, The State Construction of Affect: Political Ethos and Mental Health Among Salvadoran Refugees, 15, 1991, pp. 139–65.

an inseparability of ideas and sentiments, cognition and affect, thoughts and feelings (Jenkins 1988b; Lutz 1988; Rosaldo 1984).

The present essay seeks to expand the emerging scholarly discourse on the emotions by examining the nexus among the role of the state in constructing a *political ethos*, the personal emotions of those who dwell in that ethos, and the mental health consequences for refugees. By political ethos, I mean the culturally standardized organization of feeling and sentiment pertaining to the social domains of power and interest. Recognition of the essential interrelations between the personal and the political has long been central to feminist scholarship (see Rosaldo and Lamphere 1974) but has yet to be more fully integrated in culture theory in medical and psychological anthropology.

In a recent special issue of this journal concerning discourses on emotion, illness, and healing, Mary-Jo DelVecchio Good and colleagues raise, among other issues, the problem of state control of emotional discourse, defined as "the role of the state and other political, religious, and economic institutions in legitimizing, organizing, and promoting particular discourses on emotions" (DelVecchio Good, B. Good, and Fischer 1988:4). These authors note that examination of politicized passions has been slow in coming. In an ethnographic study of the role of the state in authorizing and sustaining discourses on sadness, they examine how the current Iranian Islamic state has appropriated a traditional religious discourse on grieving, martyrdom and the tragic by redefining it as part of the official state ideology for the Iranian citizenry concerning ideal, morally upstanding affective comportment. In another study of Iranian immigrants to the United States, B. Good, DelVecchio Good, and Moradi (1985) document the interplay of cultural themes, sociopolitical events, and depressive disorder. A similarly convincing case for the social production of affective disorders (in China) has been presented by Kleinman (1986).

The need to make a theoretical move from the state control of emotional discourse to the state construction of affect became particularly evident to me in the course of recent fieldwork with Salvadoran refugees seeking psychological help at an out-patient psychiatric clinic in the northeastern United States. The newly emergent discourses on culture, self, and emotion were not adequate to the task of interpreting the sentiments of persons whose lifeworlds are framed by chronic political violence, extreme poverty, unrelenting trauma and loss. It became apparent that the role of the *state* and other political, religious, and economic institutions must be examined to interpret the dominant ethos of a people. In the context of Salvadoran lifeworlds, I understand the state construction of affect in relation to *a pervasive dysthymic ethos and a culture of terror* (Jenkins 1990a).

In this paper I propose a problematic to advance and refine our understandings of state and politicized sentiments. My argument about the state construction of affect is intended as a bridge between analyses of discourses about affect, on the one hand, and the phenomenology of those affects, on the other. I begin with a brief description of the political ethos in contemporary El Salvador, the process of flight by refugees to the United States, and the reasons for their flight cited by some of those refugees. I then examine mental health consequences of life within the Salvadoran political ethos, with special attention to the underlying ethnopsychology of emotion. I suggest a framework for the analysis of pathogenic trauma that attempts to bridge the collective level of the state construction of affect and the individual level of a phenomenology of affect. I conclude with a discussion of the implications of resilience in the face of the most trying circumstances for a theory of human nature, and several suggestions for further research.

La Vida in El Salvador: La Situacion

In the refugees' narratives of their emigration from El Salvador, they often speak of escape from *la situación. La situación* is the most common way of referring to the intolerable conditions within the country, and condenses a set of symbols and meanings that refer to a nation besieged by both devastating economic problems and violence. Although violence and civil warfare have been common throughout this century, the last eleven years in El Salvador represent the most intensive sustained conflict to plague the country. Since 1979, the new wave of warfare and terror has decimated the population by death and emigration. At least some 75,000 persons have been killed in the past 11 years, with several thousands more "*desaparecidos*" or disappeared, 500,000 displaced within its borders, and an estimated 1,000,000 more who have fled to other countries such as Mexico, Honduras, Panama, the United States, and Canada. In a country that, as of 1979, had a population estimated at 5.2 million persons, one begins to appreciate the horror of the decimation of the Salvadoran people (Fish and Sganga 1988).

El Salvador is a poor country, heavily reliant on agriculture. This most notably includes coffee exports. The other principal economic source is American aid, amounting to $1.4 million per day. Recently, in November 1989, there was a major guerilla offensive, the largest coordinated attack in almost ten years, aimed at dozens of targets throughout the country, including the capital, San Salvador. Counterattacks on the part of the Salvadoran army were swift and pervasive, escalating in intensity to extensive daily bombing and strafing of villages and neighborhoods. I remember all too vividly the month of November 1989 as I watched my Salvadoran friends and research participants, inseparably chained to their telephones, desperately seeking the fate of their parents, children, grandparents, and other family. Not surprisingly, the escalation in the violence at home coincided with a pronounced increase in all kinds of exacerbations of distress and symptomatology.

In November 1989 also we saw the assassinations of six Jesuit Priests (faculty of the National University), their cook and her daughter. The priests, faculty from the University in San Salvador who supported a negotiated peace, were also widely regarded as the leading intellectuals of the country. The late Ignacio Martin-Baró, for example, was the leading social psychologist interested in the mental health consequences of long-term civil war in his country. As a research scholar, Martin-Baró was also particularly interested in the psychological rehabilitation of children who were orphaned by the war, displaced or traumatized by the endless violence. The manner of the Jesuits' assassination, which apparently included torture and

extreme brutality, re-focused attention on the widespread human rights abuses that occur with impunity in El Salvador.

The emotional atmosphere of *la situación* is constructed by a variety of actions and practices. During the offensive, strict enforcement of a curfew from 6:00PM to 6:00AM ensures that no one can be on the streets or in any public place. Failure to adhere to this injunction can, and often does, have mortal consequences. In the private sphere, no socializing of any sort – family gatherings, parties, religious sessions – can be convened. Cross-cutting the public and private domains are "disappearances" and the ever-present evidence of violent death: decapitated heads hanging from trees or on sticks, mutilated dead bodies or body parts on the roadside, or on one's own doorstep. Nearly all of my informants spontaneously narrate their personal experiences of everyday encounters in a landscape of violence. Habituation to *la situación* amounts to a denial of its reality – a bomb going off may be interpreted as a car backfiring. The reality of *la situación* is noteworthy for its profound sense of unreality. Mistrust abounds on all sides, and people commonly say "You can trust no one." A sketch of the situation and habituation to it is only a first step, however, toward inferring a political ethos, which must be fleshed out by considering both preexisting ethnopsychology and the phenomenology of psychopathology in situations where the defense of habituation fails. To my knowledge, no anthropological study has ever been made of the emotional climate of populations under martial law, though analyses are beginning to appear on the specific transmutations of grief and paranoia in countries where "disappearances" have been institutionalized (Scheper-Hughes 1990; Suarez-Orozco 1990).

A repertoire of affective themes and strategies for constructing the emotional atmosphere is more directly evident in the onslaught of media communications that is an important tool in the state programming of sentiment. For a poor people with little formal education (90% non-literate or semi-literate), the principal media sources are radio and television. These sources suggest to a people how they might or ought to feel about *la situación*. Under conditions of civil war and martial law, these state-controlled media convey rigid and dogmatic messages leaving little doubt about which affective sensibilities are being communicated and why a truly moral person should justifiably feel them.

Quite revealing in this respect is a sample of regular programming from an audiotaped radio broadcast on the official Radio Nacional, San Salvador, on November 16, 1989 – the very day during the guerrilla offensive that the Salvadoran military assassinated the Jesuit Priests. Both moral/political and affective rhetorics (explicit and implicit) are operant in the broadcast. In response to the repeated rhetorical question, *Porqué lucha la fuerza armada?* (Why are the armed forces fighting?), several sociocultural, nationalistic, and capitalist values are cited. Most saliently, these include: a right to "keep on believing in God;" the preservation of the "nuclear family as the center of the Salvadoran social life;" "the right to live in liberty and freedom;" "the right to 'equal opportunity' in work, education, health and development;" "the right for citizens to have the right to choose." Appeals are made to the personal and societal value of capitalism and the evident need for a military response to the opposition forces that would overturn the very fabric of society. Subtly distributed among these overt patriotic declarations are messages that allude to the emotional substrate of these values as they exist imperiled by *la situación.* We are informed that the Salvadoran military forces are fighting to put "*friendships without mistrust into practice.*" Repeated again and again are the emotional themes of fear, anxiety, and confusion said to be engendered by guerilla forces. Proper sentiments of hatred and disgust toward the latter and loyalty and love to one's *patria* (mother country) are also salient. A generalized feeling of insecurity is inculcated by constant reiteration that the armed forces are "protecting you, providing for your security, that everything is under control, that the armed forces exercise total control over all the national territory." Such messages would doubtless be unsettling even if there was no immediately perceptible threat, and must be doubly so when they are so immediately contradicted by destruction, aggression, and assassination in all quarters.

The Salvadoran populace is pointedly instructed not to listen to competing counter-discourses – so-called "clandestine" radio broadcasting of the opposition of the Farabundo Marti National Liberation Front or the FMLN – on the grounds that these illicit radio broadcasting stations seek only "to create confusion and uncertainty" in the Salvadoran family. The state construction of the eminently evil "other" (implied or stated as the FMLN and "Marxist" doctrines) is accomplished through reference to "savages" and "mental illness" – indeed, the listening audience is informed that adherence to Marxist doctrine causes mental illness. Religious officials are interviewed summarizing the barbarism and hideous crimes against humanity that the FMLN are accused of committing. They assert that these crimes (alleged, for example, to include placing bombs in hospitals) are worse than anything Christopher Colombus may have committed when he "discovered" America. The Spanish conquistadors, we are informed, would never have gone so far as to place a bomb in a hospital. In announcing the assassination of the Jesuit priests, the murders were attributed to the FMLN and denounced as irrational acts of savagery committed for the purpose of destabilizing the democratic process. (In the foreign press, these attributions of blame to the FMLN were later retracted and ultimately replaced with admissions by the President that the military armed forces had, in fact, committed these atrocities).

Flight from *La Situacion*: Forced Migration and Emotional Distress

Migrants are typically considered in two categories: as immigrants and as refugees. While immigrant implies some degree of choice concerning the decision to leave one's natal country, the designation of refugee is meant to signal that departure from one's native country is involuntary, and repatriation, all but impossible. Although the flight of refugees is not a new phenomenon, the dimensions of this problem have recently intensified. Whether we look to Cambodia, Liberia, Haiti, Argentina, or East Germany, the world's populations are relocating in vast numbers. In a recent report from the U.S. Committee for Refugees (1990a), it is estimated that there are today more than 15 million refugees worldwide. In the last five years alone, the worldwide refugee population has increased by 50%. Many of these refugees leave their homelands under the press of conditions that threaten their personal, familial, and cultural survival. This is true for Salvadorans. The Central American situation of long-term economic conflicts and political violence often compel them not only to leave their natal country but also to live with little or no prospect for safe repatriation.

Refugees from the present study arrive in the United States from El Salvador through a variety of means. One common route is a series of bus trips to the U.S.-Mexico border. Arriving there, refugees make use of a *coyote* or guide who, for a fee, assists groups of people in crossing the border without drawing the attention of immigration officials. These journeys are typically narrated as long, arduous, and dangerous. Sexual violence against solitary women is apparently commonplace. Moreover, *coyotes* are infamous for taking advantage of the persons they claim to serve. Some of the women in the study reported being abandoned or robbed by *coyotes*.

Popular destination points for Salvadoran refugees in the United States include Los Angeles, San Francisco, Washington D.C., New York City, and Boston. Reliable demographic data are currently difficult to acquire since this population is, by necessity, largely underground. Following the immigration law of 1986, legal residence has become particularly difficult to obtain. Under the law, 165,000 Salvadorans sought legal residence in the United States. Aside from the 1986 immigration law, many Salvadorans have sought political asylum from the U.S. government. These court cases are largely unsuccessful: in 1985, for example, only 3% of these applicants won their appeals. This is so because despite the well-documented and widespread human rights violations in El Salvador, the U.S. government does not consider their emigration to be based on a flight from political violence. Rather, such cases are typically considered "economic" in nature; the official view is that refugees have come here merely to enhance their economic future and are not acknowledged to be in personal danger. As Alvarez (1989:61) has eloquently stated, " ... the official stance of the U.S. government and the societal attitudes prevalent in this country are characterized by massive denial, invalidation and indifference towards the collective experiences of violence which the Central American community has endured ... The ever present threat of deportation and their ongoing exploitation leads many refugees to live lives marked by invisibility, frozen grief and despair." Not until late 1990, by act of Congress, were Salvadorans in the United States able for the first time to gain temporary legal status and avoid the threat of deportation.

As part of our ethnographic-clinical study, twenty persons were interviewed at least two times each. Most have been in the United States for at least one year and have family, including young children, who still reside in El Salvador. Most work very long hours – sixty or more – in two jobs, in vigorous efforts to make as much money as possible to send back home to relatives. In spite of these strong economic motives, the reasons given for their flight from El Salvador fall equally under the three categories of escape from political violence, escape from economic conditions, and escape from domestic violence. However, as is clear from the following vignettes, all three reasons for leaving are closely bound up with the overarching political ethos of *la situación*.

Escape from political violence has compelled refugees to leave their homelands in search of safe haven. Nearly all of the women report that they had regularly encountered brutal evidence of the war: mutilated bodies lying on the roadside or in the doorsteps to their homes, family and friends who had disappeared, and the terror of military troops marching through their towns shooting at random and arresting others who would be incarcerated. For many of the women in the study, their narratives of fleeing political violence are suggestive of the relationship between state constructed affects of fear and anxiety, on the one hand, and indigenously defined conditions of *nervios* (nerves), on the other. These narratives also vividly portray everyday encounters with and habituation to truly horrific lifeworlds.

1. From a 36 year old married woman, mother of three:

In my country I had *un susto* (a fright) when a man was dying. Already the man couldn't speak (but) he made signs to me with his eyes. It was during the daytime, and I was going to get some chickens for a Baptism. He could barely move his eyes. He had been shot in the forehead. It was the time of the fair in November. When I came back he was already dead. I returned home with a fever, and it wasn't something I'd ever experienced. Since it was carnival time, strangers came. They kill strangers. They saw *him* throwing away some papers. Yes, I have seen various dead bodies. Since then, I became sick from *nervios*. *Nervios*, upon seeing the dead bodies.

2. From a 38 year old woman, mother of two: This informant survived a series of tortures subsequent to three arrests and imprisonments in the early 1980s. At the time of her first imprisonment, her husband was also taken away by the military, his head covered with a black hood, and assassinated:

When they told me that my husband was dead, for me it was like, like a dream, like something unreal. Yes, there are times he comes into my mind, but I know it's something that will never exist. He's a person that doesn't exist. It's something that I have to try to do, to forget him.

Still, on other occasions she has told me, "I think about him, I dream about him. I hear his voice calling to me." She now resides with their two children in the metropolitan area. She came to the clinic to seek assistance for some intense psychological suffering that has remained with her, in the form of major depression, anxiety, and trauma.

She also reported that her eleven year old daughter has *un problema de nervios*. *Nervios* (nerves) is an indigenous cultural category widely used in Latin America for a variety of forms of distress and disease, including everyday worries, depression, and schizophrenia (Jenkins, 1988a, b) and may refer to a variety of bodily and affective complaints (Low 1985; Guarnaccia and Farias 1988). Although the daughter's doctor told her it was probably nothing and not to worry about it, this has not reassured her. Whenever her daughter gets angry her nose bleeds profusely. This problem began in El Salvador, but now recurs most often when she sees movies or TV about war or violent situations.

Whenever possible, I don't permit her to watch this. Another thing I think is related to her *nervios* is that she laughs uncontrollably for a long time – for an hour or two – laughing to herself. She can't stop laughing. Afterward, she cries.

When I asked her what she thought might have caused this problem, she provided a thoroughly embodied account:

I imagine that it probably happened while I was pregnant (with her). I had a lot of psychological problems. When one is very fearful, a nervous tension that the army is going to come, they're going to come through the streets, you're going to get hit by a passing bullet or the army is beating someone and taking them away – all of this affects a little baby you have inside. I feel that when you're pregnant all the nervous things, all the things that are important to you, all the things you see, the baby feels too. Because it's something inside. I think that everything I went through while I was pregnant is now part of her nervous system. When I was pregnant and we had a strike at the factory. The army would arrive, begin shooting, and throw bombs of tear gas to make us leave. Yes, all this affects you. The tension we had. We had 7 months without working, without receiving a salary, so much worry.

Escape from unrelenting hunger and poverty has impelled refugees to leave their country in search of income-generating work.

1. From a 54 year old woman, mother of four:

In El Salvador it was very hard. I used to wash clothes at the river by the dozens. I would do five dozen. I would get up at 5:00 A.M. and go to the bakery where I got left over bread I used to take the *mercado* to sell until 9:00 A.M. Then I would go to the river. I had no help. I didn't like it because I was hungry and sometimes I wouldn't get paid on time. And I would worry because I wouldn't have enough to feed my children.

I came here because the situation wasn't good, there were strikes by the teachers, there were no classes and then the teachers got together with the students and started to protest. After that, you would find dead bodies without heads and eyes on the roads. In 1980, on my own doorstep, I found many people dead. My son was here (in the metropolitan area), so I came.

2. From a 38 year old mother of two:

As immigrants in this country, the conditions of life are very different. There are so many economic problems, like health care. Employers don't pay MEDICAID, and we can't afford it. We don't have good (enough) jobs to pay for it. The bills add up and add up. It's very difficult, life and health, these days in this country.

(Back home) sometimes we say to ourselves, 'fine, I'm going to the U.S. I am going to earn money, to work.' But it isn't easy. I know persons who come and pass 3–5 months without working. They're new, and especially because of the language they are not able to speak. If you want to work in a restaurant washing dishes or work in cleaning, sure, it's an honest job, but sometimes it's really difficult.

Because it's the *only* thing you can do as an immigrant. To clean, wash dishes, or work in a factory, where they pay minimum wage, $4.25 an hour. And it's little pay for so much work. It's very difficult. In one factory, for example, they don't give benefits, health care, nothing. Sometimes out of necessity you, as an immigrant have to accept it. If you're a parent, it's very difficult.

We come here from our country because of the conditions of living there (in El Salvador), the same situation, always through persecution, bombings, and the rest. For so many things that perhaps someone hasn't seen and at other times for others they have lived it, *en carne propia* (in one's own flesh or lived, bodily experience).

Many of the women in this study also reported that they had fled their homelands to escape family violence. The following vignette also provides a further sense of how both societal and familial representations of violence become part of the embodied experience of women.

1. From a 27 year old married woman, mother of two:

(I have felt *un susto*) when my husband was drinking a lot, already before he would arrive home. Then I would feel my heart, pum, pum, pum. If you are fearful it can make you sick because it can cause you a *crisis de nervios*. I feel that my body isn't me. It can cause a person to go crazy. It makes me have stomach pain, shaking of my body, and it makes me cold.

2. From a 34 year old married woman, mother of two:

I was pregnant at that time (expecting my second baby), when he (my husband) started drinking... (and) he beat me. I was 'very fat' (in a very advanced stage of pregnancy), and he mistreated me. But later, he regretted it because the baby was born unhealthy, with a problem of *nervios*. He mistreated me for no reason when he was drunk. He was treating me like that because his mother told him very bad things about me, but the truth is that his mother never loved him, she was always telling him that I was very bad for him, that she paid his studies so he would marry a 'worthy woman,' not somebody like me because I was *nothing* ... he mistreated me and beat my stomach and then, when the baby was born, he had like a yellow color in his skin, and the doctor told me it was necessary for my baby to remain in the hospital for some time because he was ill. But when my husband found out about the baby's illness he blamed me as well; so you know, I was guilty for everything ... so I began having problems with my *nervios*, since I was pregnant, because his mother as well was treating me as if I was an animal, never like a person ... and then when my baby was born I started to have nightmares ... my daughter was 10 years old by then, and I was suckling my baby and when he arrived home completely drunk then ... she noticed all what was happening and she cried, she became sick from *nervios*, she became very ill. My daughter, sick with *nervios*, was screaming, throwing things around ... it made *me* sick but I couldn't say a word to him because he would beat me, so that I knew that I just had to cry and keep quiet.

During the course of the interview, however, she confided that she was ultimately compelled to flee her native country to escape general conditions of *la situación* and her husband's relentless, violent abuse.

Regular, so-called "domestic" violence and abuse are the bodily experience of many of the Salvadoran women refugees in the study. Indeed, some of them reported that they ran for their very lives from husbands and fathers they feared would kill them if they did not escape their regular physical, and often sexual, abuse. The ways in which societal representations of violence are embodied and reproduced in family settings is a topic of great importance, and something that, at present, we understand very little about. Future studies on this topic should comparatively and historically consider the prevalence of domestic violence (and cultural and sociopolitical values that surround it) both in situations of civil war and its absence. Regrettably, to my knowledge, there currently is little theorizing or systematic data on this subject. The women who spoke about their own personal experiences of domestic violence did so with great shame and apparent reluctance. In this regard, they have much in common with countless other women worldwide who are regularly subjected to acts of violence by male kin within family settings (Campbell 1985; Counts 1990; Levinson 1989).

The importance of analyzing the state construction of affect is evident in the case of El Salvador, *una población asustada* (a frightened population, as Valiente has termed it). Activities of the state, economic conditions, and the domestic environment must be understood not as independent factors but as coordinate dimensions of a single political ethos. As Martin-Baró (1988) wrote, the entire nation can be characterized as one in which state induction of fear, anxiety and terror is elaborated and maintained as a means of social control. Warfare is thus waged through all possible avenues, tanks roll down the streets and bullets fly, minds and hearts are occupied by arresting affects that similarly immobilize. Through long-term exposure to this political ethos the experience of the "lived body" is shot through with anxiety, terror, and despair.

Clinic and Culture

Identifying the mental health concerns of refugee populations poses a substantial challenge for anthropologists and mental health professionals who seek to understand and treat these populations. Clinical literature on refugee mental health often concerns the fundamental question of whether a relationship between refugee experience and mental health status can be demonstrated empirically (e.g., Allodi and Rojas 1983). That these are not necessarily *expected* to be interrelated is so for reasons both scientific and political. First, we must consider the historical context of the current paradigmatic age that privileges biochemistry over contextual features of experience. Second, research that seeks to investigate the health consequences of war-related experience continues to be the subject of political controversy. It was not until 1980, for example, that the Diagnostic and Statistical Manual (or DSM-III) of the American Psychiatric Association included the category of post-traumatic stress disorder, or PTSD. The establishment of PTSD as a psychiatric diagnostic category was intended in large measure to address the cluster of symptoms that has plagued many Viet-Nam war veterans. From the point of view of many of those veterans, the slowness of this acknowledgement generated numerous psychosocial and economic problems for post-war adaptation in the United States.

Symptoms of major depressive disorders and post-traumatic stress disorder (or PTSD) are apparently common among refugees from political violence (Jenkins, Kleinman and Good 1990; Kinzie et al. 1984; Mollica et al. 1987; Westermeyer 1988). Although studies of Southeast Asian refugees have been pursued for a decade or more, studies of psychiatric vulnerability among Central American refugees in North America have barely begun (Alvarez 1990; Farias 1991; Jenkins 1990a,b; Williams 1987). In the research experience of the author and her clinical colleagues, depression, among other psychiatric disorders (e.g., dysthymia, panic disorders and post-traumatic stress syndromes) is very common, and is apparently due to the aftereffects of political violence and inhospitable life conditions in North American urban settings. While forced uprooting and culture conflict are sources of distress, political oppression and turmoil also clearly have an effect independent of migration. In addition, the refugees experience great psychic and bodily suffering in the aftermath of having fled *la situación*. Despite life in what ostensibly one may have hoped for as a "safe haven," *la situación* remains vivid in their dreams (often nightmares), is constitutive of their memories, and is present in the apprehension of everyday life.

According to psychiatric diagnostic and research criteria (DSM-III-R and the SADS), nearly all of the patients in the study had experienced at least one major depressive episode in their lifetime. Most had suffered one or more major depressive episodes within the past two years, and some have struggled with either chronic depression or dysthymia. The women voice a variety of themes of sadness and sorrow in relation to loss and bereavement, helplessness and hopelessness. The language of loss and mourning, however, is often communicated through somatic means, as insomnia, lack of appetite, fatigue, or psychomotor agitation or retardation. As Kleinman (1986, 1988) has demonstrated, somatized expression of depressive disorders is very common for most of the world's population. Many of these women also report symptoms of post-traumatic stress disorder (PTSD), including recurrent nightmares of traumatic violence, a sudden feeling that the traumatic event (or events) are recurring, and irritability or outbursts of anger. Psychiatrists refer to these "active" symptoms as part of the "intrusive" phase of PTSD, whereas symptoms such as restricted range of affect, feeling of estrangement from others, and efforts to avoid feelings associated with the trauma are associated with the so-called "numbing phase." As I argue below in greater detail, the traumatic event in these instances may be construed *broadly* – as the chronic presence of warfare and destruction – and *discretely* – as particular instances of extremely traumatic events such as witnessing an assassination or actually undergoing torture and interrogation.

In Foucault's essay (1973:85) on the relation between "Passion and Delirium," he mused that "(t)he savage danger of madness is related to the danger of the passions and to their fatal concatenation." A contemporary parallel of Foucault's observation is our simultaneous understanding of, for example, depression as an emotion and as a disorder (Kleinman and Good 1985). The problem of understanding the pathogenic consequences of trauma and the character of the resulting disorder is thus compounded by variations in the psychocultural bases of emotional life. In the present context, I can offer only the briefest summary of the Salvadoran ethnopsychology of emotion:

1. In terms of what would be clinically categorized as the "chief complaint" or presenting problem when coming to the clinic, nearly all of the refugees in the study report that they suffer from a variety of problems related to *nervios*. The cultural category *nervios* is deeply embedded within the life contexts of chronic poverty and exposure to violence. *Nervios* refers at once to matters of mind, body, and spirit and does not make good cultural sense in relation to mind-body dualisms.

2. Salvadorans can in general be characterized in terms of a strongly kin-oriented and relatively sociocentric (Shweder and Bourne 1982) or referential (Gaines 1982) sense of self, with the experience and expression of symptoms framed in reference to the family context.

3. Spanish provides a rich lexicon for emotions of sadness and sorrow. Suffering may be reported through language rich in descriptive detail, and with a distinctly existential flavor. In Salvadoran culture, ethnopsychological elaboration of *tristeza* (sadness) or *pena* (sorrow) and an underlying sense of life's tragedy invariably color *la situación*.

4. On a phenomenological level, Salvadorans describe their emotional experiences in terms of bodily sensations. The body sites are often both specific and generalized. It is not uncommon to voice one's suffering as a totalizing bodily experience. Reports of various bodily sensations may be interpreted as signs of malevolent spiritual

influence, and one's suffering could well be related to spirit activity.

5. Also common is the preoccupation with protection from the malevolence of others, as manifest in the ethnopsychologically salient themes of *envidia* (envy) and witchcraft.

6. Salvadorans evidence a great deal of involvement in dream life, and this serves as a means for communicating with distant, missing, or dead loved ones. Sometimes these communications are reported as comforting experiences, as dream memories focus on past family *fiestas* and Salvadoran love of the land and nature. The dysphoric and distressing quality of dream life becomes evident, however, in the alarmingly high incidence of dreams of disembodied and mutilated bodies, knives and other weapons, and a full array of war-related horrors. Especially noteworthy is the fact that most of the dream life situates Salvadoran refugees back home, not in the United States.

7. In Salvadoran ethnopsychology there is the belief that the experience of anger and hostility, whether directed by intimates or in witchcraft, may lead to serious illness or, in extreme cases, death.

Cultural proscriptions of outwardly directed verbalizations of anger and rage may be relevant to a distinct symptom or experience we have observed among some women, something they call *"el calor"* (the heat). *El calor* may be experienced as intense heat rising progressively from the feet and emanating throughout one's whole body. One of my informants told me: "*el calor* is like fire. In your whole body." Another woman described it as the sensation of rolled up newspapers that were set ablaze and she could feel in her chest. The possibility that it is menopause-related does not seem to provide an adequate explanation for this phenomenon, particularly in light of its occurrence even among women from ages 25 to 30. Also, it may occur not only in situations of fear or panic but also under ordinary conditions. We have considered that in some persons the symptom may be related to torture experience, since persons who have been tortured speak of not

only *el calor* but also the sensation of electric shocks throughout their body. Nevertheless, we have also been given these same phenomenological accounts by some persons who have not undergone torture. The clinical relevance of understanding *el calor* was made all to evident recently in a clinical case conference. While waiting for the resident to come into the hospital examining room, a patient was overcome by intense heat throughout her body. To relieve herself she took off her blouse and soaked it in cold water from the sink. When the resident entered the room and saw she was not only distressed but also half-nude, he apparently assumed she was "psychotic" and immediately transferred her to the local state psychiatric hospital, where she remained without the benefit of an interpreter for several days until her family discovered her whereabouts. The fact that *el calor* is a culturally elaborated total body experience leads me to conceive of it not merely as the embodiment of affective distress but also what Csordas (1997) has called a culturally specific "somatic mode of attention."

Meaning, Sense, and Representation: The Traumatized Body

Pierre Janet's work on trauma is undergoing a renaissance because it takes us a step beyond the question of whether trauma bears a causal relationship to illness. With the publication of his work on *Psychological Automatism* in 1889, Janet began to specify the internal dynamics that organize the trauma and the processes that turn trauma into illness. He stated that "traumas produce their disintegrating effects in proportion to their intensity, duration, and repetition" (quoted in van der Kolk and van der Hart 1989:1536). The initial response combines what he termed "vehement emotion" and a cognitive interpretation resulting in dissociation of memory or identity processes and attachment to the trauma such that the person has difficulty proceeding with her life (van der Kolk and van der Hart 1989).

Martin-Baró (1988, 1989) argued that individualized accounts of trauma and illness are insufficient in the context of long-term political violence. Although the trauma and suffering are manifest in individual psychic suffering, it is more appropriate to speak of psychosocial trauma or "the traumatic crystallization in persons and groups of inhuman social relations" (1988:138). The trauma and suffering become manifest in psychic suffering, dysphoric affects, and a variety of forms of psychopathology. Psychosocial trauma is particularly evident in the collective experience of anxiety, fear, paranoia, terror, and above all, denial of reality. Martin-Baró (1990) interpreted the constellation of state-constructed affects, ills, and defenses as a potent means of psychological warfare. His insight is that, through its own peculiar dynamic, war unfolds into a more global phenomenon and is the dominant process that subordinates all other social, economic, political and cultural processes. Moreover, this process affects all members of a society, either directly or indirectly. For example, to a greater or lesser extent, all members of the society may experience the war *en carne propria*. The point is that no one remains untouched, or unchanged, by *la situación*.

Understanding the human meaning of trauma, especially as it affects refugees from political violence, is frequently clouded by failure to distinguish between a relatively enduring traumatic situation and relatively discrete traumatic events. I would suggest that this distinction is relevant in two critical dimensions, namely the state construction of affect and the phenomenology of affect. In the first of these dimensions, the conditions of trauma established by the state and resistance to it come under the distinction between the situation of terror and events of torture. In the second, the modes in which those conditions are taken up into human lives come under the distinction between the situation of distress and events of disease. Torture is different from terror, and disease from distress, by degree and by self-reference. With reference to degree, we might posit that there is a simple continuum between the diffuse effects of the generalized situation and the intensely focused effects of the discrete event. However, torture and disease take on their unique configuration in contrast to terror and distress as a result of what Marx termed the "transformation of quantity into quality," the amplification of a phenomenon

until it takes on a character and consequences quite its own. This understanding parallels that made by biological psychiatrists about the existence of a threshold the crossing of which constitutes a pathogenic alteration of neurological biochemistry. Related to this process is another, more distinctly qualitative threshold associated with the shift in the immediacy of self-reference. The generalized situations of terror or distress bear a relatively diffuse reference to the self, which is precisely the condition for the possibility of denial so characteristic of a political ethos such as that of El Salvador. Stated another way, one may be terrorized by a situation that includes the torture of others, and distressed in a situation that causes mental illness in others, but these can also become immediate events of torture or disease for the self.

Despite the profound differences in degree and self-reference, the essence that terror and torture, disease and distress retain in common is their fundamental dependence on the problem of meaning, sense, and representation. Michael Taussig (1987), in trying to define the culture of terror that existed during the rubber boom in colonial Colombia, discovered that:

> ... terror provided only inexplicable explanations of itself and thrived by so doing ... this problem of interpretation is decisive for terror, not only making effective counterdiscourse so difficult but also making the terribleness of death squads, disappearances, and torture all the more effective in crippling of peoples' capacity to resist (1987:128).

If as Taussig says, terror nourishes itself by destroying sense, Elaine Scarry (1985) shows that this is doubly so in the structure of torture. Interrogation and the infliction of pain, the two basic features of torture, are both language-destroying, and hence destructive of the three principal loci of human meaning: world, self, and voice. Pain creates a "discrepancy between an increasingly palpable body and an increasingly substanceless world" (1985:30), as even familiar objects such as walls, doors, furniture become weapons. Interrogation is not designed to elicit information but to destroy the voice, creating expressive instability in its conflation of interrogatory, declarative, and imperative modes and the exclamatory of each (1985:29), until every question becomes a wounding and every answer regardless of its content becomes a scream. The self's complicity in its own destruction is represented as self-betrayal in that a transformation occurs between the experience that "my body hurts" and "my body hurts *me*," and as betrayal of others in the signing of an unread confession. The effect of the confession is compounded insofar as it is likewise understood as a "betrayal" by the general populace (1985:47).

The same essential dependence on representation is true of distress and disease. Persons in a situation of terror are not necessarily in a situation of distress unless the terror represented as such: distress is a particular stance toward the situation, a consequence of the construal of terror as terror. When the political structure of terror is recognized for what it is, the only self-preserving stance is either to take up arms or to flee. The only other solution is to find collectively acceptable ways not to recognize it. Thus, it is no accident that Salvadorans use precisely the vague word *la situación* to refer to the state of affairs in their country, for it is of necessity rhetorically neutral in its non-acknowledgment of distress. This is especially relevant insofar as the acknowledgement of distress is itself considered a subversive act by the authorities. Jennifer Jean Casolo, the American church worker detained and interrogated by Salvadoran authorities in 1989, reported that when she cried upon hearing the moans of detainees in neighboring rooms, her captors quickly asked if she was "crying for her subversive friends." Her insistence on the human legitimacy of distress was summarized in her response that she would cry for her interrogator if the same was done to him.

Disease too is bodily representation, a constellation of symptoms constituting a clinical entity that may occur in episodes – and with respect to refugees, what counts as disease is a rhetorical and political issue. A recent study of Latin American refugees in Toronto and Mexico City and of families of *desaparecidos* ("disappeared") in Santiago and Buenos Aires found that "victims of torture and refugees from violent political persecution within a period of ten years following the traumatic experience are impaired by psychosomatic and mental symptoms" (Allodi and Rojas 1983:246). Moreover,

families of *desaparecidos* experienced more symptoms than refugees, not only because of the stress of uncertainty but perhaps because they still lived in the mode of terror that stifles resistance and expression of distress. In other words, the authors suggest that families of *desaparecidos* have more symptoms than do refugees because, unlike those who have escaped, they must continue to repress even their distress for fear the authorities will construe its expression as a sign of subversiveness, and possibly kill the *desaparecido*. This study has methodological flaws, and does not arrive at particular diagnoses, but I cite it as an example of a struggle to represent the consequence of political violence as disease in face of the ease of denying that someone in distress is persecuted, or even that persecution is wrong. Someone who is distressed might still deserve that distress, but, as Young (1982) has noted, someone who is sick is relieved of culpability.

The distinction between distress and disease can also be used to delegitimize the relation of suffering to disease, as has been shown by Brown and Harris (1978). They argue against those who – in standard dualistic fashion – would consider depression a disease only if caused biologically and not through stressful life events. They point out that depressive symptoms are prevalent in the general populace as well as among psychiatric patients, and the former may never reach treatment or be cared for by general practitioners precisely because the origin of their illness is understandable as depression originating in stress, or distress. Emphasis on biological causes can misrepresent the impact of distress and trauma by opening the claim that those who develop pathology had a biological predisposition to the disease, or had pre-existing or other compounding pathology. This problem of distress and disease is all the more tenacious because it is not only relevant to the refugee situation, but is inherent in medical thinking. As Kirmayer (1989) argues, "... the definition of discrete disorders remains an artifact of sometimes arbitrary criteria that leave the classification of milder and intermediate forms of distress ambiguous ... both the lay and medical diagnosis and treatment involve selective interpretations that hide some causes and consequences of distress while revealing others" (1989:327, 328).

Suffering and Resilience

It is evident that questions of the parameters of human nature abound in studies of refugees from war-torn countries. What are the limits of human endurance, suffering, and tolerance for conditions and practices (such as torture) that must, by any standards, only be characterized as horrific? How do we come to know and understand the human capacity for extraordinary strength and resilience in the face of human horrors? These basic existential queries have been quite striking to me, a middle class North American female anthropologist, who has imperfectly attempted to know my informants' worlds of phenomenal suffering, on the one hand, and resilience, on the other.

Martin-Baró also concerned himself with the paradox that the suffering inherent in war also offers to some people the opportunity to further develop what we are fond of calling our "humanity" and strength. This process seems to almost completely elude social science concepts of adaptation, or worse yet, adjustment and assimilation. These seem wholly inadequate to the task of understanding how refugees attempt to reconstitute their lives and construct new meanings. For refugees, the kinds of personal, existential, and cultural losses they face virtually guarantee a (potentially unresolvable) grief reaction of profound sorrow and anger. It also seems to me that if, as Obeyesekere (1985) has argued, culture provides for the working through of grief that guards against depression, it would seem that many cultures necessarily fail in the face of circumstances so extreme.

Yet this is not always how it goes. The persistence of strong love of life, family, and native land, in the face of what would seem from a North American point of view overwhelming circumstances, constitutes a puzzle in understanding bodily and spiritual resistance and resilience. Despite a sometimes dizzying array of losses, traumas, somatic symptoms and life crises, Rosa, for example, manages to find the proverbial light at the end of the tunnel. Things were not going well: her apartment building was burned to the ground (there was the strong suspicion by many residents that the match was tossed by the owner of this dilapidated unit for insurance purposes). The new city-owned building she had moved into was populated mostly by *norteamericanos* (Anglo-Americans) whom she perceived as considerably less than enthusiastic about having Latinos in the building. Moreover, she had just learned that her daughter-in-law was again engaged in a "job" (that is, "witchcraft") against her, causing her no end of difficulties. Her therapist, empathetically frustrated and at her own wits end, said, "Ay, Rosa, I just don't know what you can do. I say it's time to get the candles out and light up as many as you can." (Candles are religious objects with spiritual powers that provide protection and good luck.) Rosa responded by saying, "But doctor: don't you know, I've already tried it! I want to, but I can't: If I light the candles, it sets the smoke detector off!" Following this, both patient and therapist reported bursting out in peals of laughter. Thus humor and perseverance in the midst of disaster and misfortune serve as powerful tools for survival. (Also see Argueta 1987 on this point.)

Concluding Remarks

I can suggest the following issues for further theoretical elaboration of the role of the state in constructing affective experience and expression: (1) *covert* (in addition to overt) mechanisms for promoting and legitimating emotion discourses. Analysis of the covert and indirect affective communications (and meta-communications) from the state and other political groups is required since, in many or most instances, such messages go purposefully unacknowledged. Direct knowledge of purposeful intent in communicating a given emotional message would, in many instances, be explicitly disavowed if brought publicly to the foreground; (2) affective communications including symbolic acts and practices that "set" a particular affective tone; (3) the "redundancy" or apparent degree of accord in the nature of affective communications from multiple state and political sources; (4) the presence of competing "counter-discourses" on emotion; (5) institutionally and politically engendered "double binds" as a system of affective interaction, generalized emotional atmosphere, and social control.

My argument has been that state construction of affect and what I have termed the political ethos of a society should be an important dimension of anthropological theorizing about the cultural construction of emotion. This requires that anthropologists be more attuned to political ethos than they have been in the past. Culture, conceived within an interpretive framework of a symbols-and-meanings approach to personal and social worlds cannot fully "hold" the powerful analytic constructions of state and political realities. Likewise trauma, conceived within a framework of individual psychopathology, cannot account for the global affective consequences of terror and distress – the perspective of Janet must be synthesized with that of Martin-Baró. More explicit recognition of the state construction of affect, and research along the lines suggested above, should result in a greatly enhanced dialogue on emotion as psychoculturally and politically constructed.

REFERENCES

Abu-Lughod, Lila
    1986   Veiled Sentiments. Honor and Poetry in a Bedouin Society. Berkeley and Los Angeles: University of California Press.
Allodi, F. and A. Rojas
    1983   The Health and Adaptation of Victims of Political Violence in Latin America. *In* Psychiatry: The State of the Art. P. Pichot, ed. Vol. 6. New York: Plenum Press.
Alvarez, Mauricia
    1990   Central American Refugees. Conference on the "Psychotherapy of Diversity: Cross-Cultural Treatment Issues." Harvard Medical School, Department of Continuing Education.
American Psychiatric Association
    1987   Diagnostic and Statistical Manual of Mental Disorders. Third Edition. Revised. Published by the American Psychiatric Association.

Argueta, Manlio
    1983   One Day of Life. New York: Vintage Books.
    1987   Cuzcatlan: Where the Southern Sea Beats. New York: Vintage Books.
Bateson, Gregory
    1958   Naven. Second Edition. Palo Alto, California: Stanford University Press.
Bateson, Gregory, Don Jackson, Jay Hayley, and John Weakland
    1956   Toward a Theory of Schizophrenia. Behavioral Science 1:251–64.
Benedict, Ruth
    1946 (1934)   Patterns of Culture. New York: Mentor Books.
Brown, George and Tirril Harris
    1978   Social Origins of Depression: A Study of Psychiatric Disorder in Women. London: Tavistock.
Brown, George, J. Birley, and John Wing
    1972   Influence of Family Life on the Course of Schizophrenic Disorders: A Replication. British Journal of Psychiatry: 121:241–58.
Campbell, Jacquelyn
    1985   Beating of Wives: A Cross-Cultural Perspective. Victimology: An International Journal 10(1–4):174–85.
Counts, Dorothy
    1990   Domestic Violence in Oceania: Introduction. Pacific Studies: Special Issue on Domestic Violence in Oceania 13(3):1–5.
Csordas, Thomas J.
    1983   The Rhetoric of Transformation in Ritual Healing. Culture, Medicine, and Psychiatry 7:333–75.
    1990   Embodiment as a Paradigm for Anthropology. Ethos 18:5–47.
    1997   The Sacred Self: Cultural Phenomenology of Charismatic Healing. Berkeley and Los Angeles: University of California Press.
Dunkerley, James
    1988   Power in the Isthmus: A Political History of Modern Central America. London and New York: Verso Press.
Farias, Pablo
    1991   The Socio-political Dimensions of Trauma in Salvadoran Refugees: Analysis of a Clinical Sample. Culture, Medicine, and Psychiatry 15:167–92.
Fish, Joe and Sganga, Cristina
    1988   El Salvador: Testament of Terror. New York: Olive Branch Press.

Foucault, Michel
1973 Madness and Civilization. A History of Insanity in the Age of Reason. New York: Vintage/Random House.

Frank, Gelya
1986 On Embodiment: A Case Study of Congenital Limb Deficiency in American Culture. Culture, Medicine, and Psychiatry 10:189–219.

Gaines, Atwood
1982 Cultural Definitions, Behavior and the Person in American Psychiatry. In Cultural Conceptions of Mental Health and Therapy. A. Marsella and G. White, eds. Dordrecht, Holland: D. Reidel.

Good, Mary-Jo DelVecchio and Byron Good
1982 Toward a Meaning-Centered Analysis of Popular Illness Categories: "Fright Illness" and "Heart Distress" in Iran. In Cultural Conceptions of Mental Health and Therapy. A.J. Marsella and G. White, eds. Pp. 141–66. Boston: D. Reidel.
1988 Ritual, the State and the Transformation of Emotional Discourse in Iranian Society. Culture, Medicine and Psychiatry 12:43–63.

Good, Mary-Jo DelVecchio, Byron Good, and Michael Fischer
1988 Introduction: Discourse and the Study of Emotion, Illness and Healing. Culture, Medicine and Psychiatry 12:1–8.

Good, Byron, Mary-Jo DelVecchio Good, and Robert Moradi
1985 The Interpretation of Iranian Depressive Illness and Dysphoric Affect. In Culture and Depression. A. Kleinman and B. Good, eds. Pp. 369–428. Berkeley: University of California Press.

Guarnaccia, Peter and Pablo Farias
1988 The Social Meanings of Nervios: A Case Study of a Central American Woman. Social Science and Medicine 26:1233–1.

Hallowell, A. Irving
1955 Culture and Experience. Philadelphia: University of Pennsylvania Press.

Ifabumuyi, O.I.
1981 The Dynamics of Central Heat in Depression. Psychopathologie Africaine 17(1–3): 127–33.

Jenkins, Janis H.
1988a Conceptions of Schizophrenia as a Problem of Nerves: A Cross-Cultural Comparison of Mexican-Americans and Anglo-Americans. Social Science and Medicine 26(12):1233–44.
1988b Ethnopsychiatric Interpretations of Schizophrenic Illness: The Problem of Nervios Within Mexican-American Families. Culture, Medicine, and Psychiatry 12(3):303–31.
1990a "Neither Here nor There:" Depression and Trauma Among Salvadoran Refugees in North America. Invited Lecture for 1989–90 (March) Series on "Culturally Sensitive Mental Health Care," Groupe Interuniversitaire de Recherche en Anthropologie Medical et en Ethnopsychiatrie (GIRAME), Montreal, Quebec.
1990b Culture and Depressive Affects: The Embodiment of Fear and Anxiety Among Salvadoran Women Refugees. Working Papers: No. 1/2: (Fall) Center for Twentieth Century Studies. University of Wisconsin, Milwaukee.
1991 Anthropology, Expressed Emotion, and Schizophrenia. 1990 Stirling Award Essay. Ethos vol. 19, No. 4 (Dec.): 387–431.

Jenkins, Janis H., Arthur Kleinman, and Byron Good
1990 Cross-cultural Studies of Depression. In Psychosocial Aspects of Depression. J. Becker and A. Kleinman, eds. New York: Erlbaum Press.

Kinzie, J. David, R. Frederickson, Ben Rath, Jennelle Fleck, and William Karls
1984 Posttraumatic Stress Disorder Among Survivors of Cambodian Concentration Camps. American Journal of Psychiatry 141:645–50.

Kirmayer, Lawrence
1989 Cultural Variations in the Response to Psychiatric Disorders and Emotional Distress. Social Science and Medicine 29:327–39.

Kleinman, Arthur
1986 Social Origins of Distress and Disease. Depression, Neurasthenia, and Pain in Modern China. Yale University Press.
1988 Rethinking Psychiatry. New York: Free Press.
1992 Pain and Resistance: The Delegitimation and Relegitimation of Local Worlds. In Pain and Human Experience. M.J. DelVecchio Good et al., eds. Berkeley: University of California Press.

Kleinman, Arthur and Byron Good, eds.
1985 Culture and Depression: Studies in the Anthropology and Cross-Cultural Psychiatry of Affect and Disorder. Berkeley: University of California Press.

Kristeva, Julia
1982   Powers of Horror: An Essay on Abjection. Translated by Leon S. Roudiez. New York: Columbia University Press.

Levinson, David
1989   Family Violence in Cross-Cultural Perspective. Newbury Park, California: Sage Publications.

Low, Setha
1985   Culturally Interpreted Symptoms of Culture-Bound Syndromes: A Cross-Cultural Review of Nerves. Social Science and Medicine 221(2):187–96.

Lutz, Catherine A.
1988   Unnatural Emotions: Everyday Sentiments on a Micronesian Atoll and Their Challenge to Western Theory. University of Chicago Press.

Lutz, Catherine A. and Lila Abu-Lughod, eds.
1990   Language and the Politics of Emotion. Cambridge University Press.

Lutz, Catherine and Geoffrey White
1986   The Anthropology of Emotions. Annual Review of Anthropology 15:405–36.

Manz, Beatriz
1988   Refugees of a Hidden War: The Aftermath of Counterinsurgency in Guatemala. Albany, New York: State University of New York Press.

Martin-Baró, Ignacio
1988   La violencia politica y la guerra como causas del trauma psicosocial en El Salvador. Revista de Psicologia de El Salvador 7:123–41.
1989   Psicologia politica del trabajo en America Latina. Revista de Psicologia de El Salvador 31:5–25.
1990   De la guerra sucia a la guerra psicologica. Revista de Psicologia de El Salvador 35: 109–22.

Mead, Margaret
1963   (1935) Sex and Temperament in Three Primitive Societies. New York: Apollo. Ministerio de Cultura y Comunicaciones

Ministerio de Cultura y Comunicaciones
1985   Etnografia de El Salvador. Departamento de Etnografia, Dirección de Investigaciones y Direccion de Patrimonio Cultural. Direccion de Publicacion: San Salvador, El Salvador.

Mishler, Elliot and Nancy Waxler
1966   Family Interaction Processes and Schizophrenia: A Review of Current Theories. International Journal of Psychiatry 2:375–413.

Mollica, Richard, G. Wyshak, and J. Lavelle
1987   The Psychosocial Impact of War Trauma and Torture on Southeast Asian Refugees. American Journal of Psychiatry 144(12), 1567–72.

Myers, Fred
1979   Emotions and the Self: A Theory of Personhood and Political Order Among Pintupi Aborigines. Ethos 7:343–70.

Obeyesekere, Gananath
1985   Depression, Budhism, and the Work of Culture in Sri Lanka. In Culture and Depression: Studies in the Anthropology and Cross-Cultural Psychiatry of Affect and Disorder. A. Kleinman and B. Good, eds. Berkeley: University of California Press.

Rosaldo, Michelle
1980   Knowledge and Passion: Ilongot Notions of Self and Social Life. Cambridge: Cambridge University Press.
1984   Toward an Anthropology of Self and Feeling. In Culture Theory: Essays on Mind, Self and Emotion. R.A. Shweder and R.A. LeVine, eds. Cambridge: Cambridge University Press.

Rosaldo, Michelle and Louise Lamphere, eds.
1974   Woman, Culture, and Society. Stanford: Stanford University Press.

Roseman, Marina
1990   Head, Heart, Odor and Shadow: The Structure of the Self, the Emotional World, and Ritual Performance Among Senoi Temiar. Ethos 18:227–50.

Sapir, Edward
1961   Culture, Language, and Personality. In Selected Essays. D. Mandelbaum, ed. Berkeley and Los Angeles: University of California Press.

Scarry, Elaine
1985   The Body in Pain: The Making and Unmaking of the World. New York: Oxford University Press.

Scheper-Hughes, Nancy
1988   The Madness of Hunger: Sickness, Delirium, and Human Needs. Culture, Medicine, and Psychiatry 12:429–58.
1990   Bodies, Death, and the State: Violence and the Taken-for-Granted World. Atlanta, Georgia: Paper presented at the (April) American Ethnological Society Meetings.

Scheper-Hughes, Nancy and Margaret Lock
1987   The Mindful Body: A Prolegomenon to Future Work in Medical Anthropology. Medical Anthropology Quarterly 1:6–41.

Schieffelin, Bambi and Elinor Ochs, eds.
1986 Language Socialization Across Cultures. Cambridge: Cambridge University Press.

Schieffelin, Edward
1983 Anger and Shame in the Tropical Forest: On Affect as a Cultural System in Papua New Guinea. Ethos: 11:181–91.

Shweder, Richard A.
1990 Cultural Psychology: What Is It? *In* Cultural Psychology: Essays on Comparative Human Development. James Stigler, Richard Shweder, and Gilbert Herdt, eds. Cambridge University Press.

Shweder, R.A. and Edmund J. Bourne
1984 Does the Concept of the Person Vary Cross-Culturally? *In* Culture Theory: Essays on Mind, Self, and Emotion. R.A. Shweder and R.A. LeVine, eds. Cambridge University Press.

Shweder, Richard A. and Robert A. LeVine, eds.
1984 Culture Theory: Essays on Mind, Self, and Emotion. Cambridge University Press.

Smith, Carol, ed. (with the assistance of Marilyn M. Moors)
1990 Guatemalan Indians and the State: 1540 to 1988. Austin, Texas: University of Texas Press.

Starn, Orin
1991 Missing the Revolution: Anthropologists and the War in Peru. Cultural Anthropology 6:63–91.

Suarez-Orozco, Marcelo
1989 Central American Refugees and U.S. High Schools: A Psychosocial Study of Motivation and Achievement. Stanford: Stanford University Press.
1990 Speaking of the Unspeakable: Toward Psychosocial Understanding of Responses to Terror. Ethos: 18:353–83.

Taussig, Michael
1987 Shamanism, Colonialism, and the Wild Man: A Study in Terror and Healing. Chicago: University of Chicago Press.

U.S. Committee for Refugees
1990a World Refugee Survey: 1989 in Review. Washington, DC: U.S. Committee for Refugees.
1990b Refugee Reports 9:1–16. Washington, DC: U.S. Committee for Refugees.

Van der Kolk, Bessel A. and Onno van der Hart
1989 Pierre Janet & the Breakdown of Adaptation in Psychological Trauma. American Journal of Psychiatry 146(12):1530–40.

Westermeyer, Joseph
1988 DSM-III Psychiatric Disorders Among Hmong Refugees in the United States: A Point Prevalence Study. American Journal of Psychiatry 145(2):197–202.
1989 Psychiatric Care of Migrants: A Clinical Guide. Washington, DC: American Psychiatric Association Press.

White, Geoffrey and J. Kirkpatrick, eds.
1985 Person, Self, and Experience: Exploring Pacific Ethnopsychologies. Berkeley and Los Angeles: University of California Press.

Wikan, Uni
1990 Managing Turbulent Hearts: A Balinese Formula for Living. University of Chicago Press.

Williams, Carolyn L.
1987 An Annotated Bibliography on Refugee Mental Health. U.S. Department of Health and Human Services. National Institute of Mental Health. U.S. Government Printing Office, Washington, D.C.

Young, Allen
1982 The Anthropologies of Illness and Sickness. Annual Review of Anthropology 11:257.

15

Struggling Along
The Possibilities for Experience among the Homeless Mentally Ill

Robert Desjarlais

Alice is a fortyish native of New England who lives in a shelter of cots and partitions set up on a basketball court in the basement of a large government center in downtown Boston. If she is not staying in the shelter, she is sleeping in a psychiatric hospital or on the city's streets. She considers herself "estranged from society" since the state took her child away ten years ago; she now spends much of her time bumming cigarettes and reading the Bible. She bums cigarettes because she lacks money and does not want to start buying packs of her own lest she pick up an expensive habit. The Bible helps to lessen the noise, worries, and distractions that are part of shelter life. "If I can just read the Bible for 15, 16 hours a day," she says, "and just block out all the rest, then I'm okay." Given the lack of calm in the shelter, and Alice's own troubles, the task is not an easy one. When we cross paths in the building and I ask how she is doing, she often says she is "struggling along." Her response aptly describes what life is like for her and many of the 50 other "homeless mentally ill" who sleep on the basketball court. The nature of the struggle, where people live a routine existence marked by

stress, fear, and distractions, has led me to question one of the basic goals of my ethnographic work there. I set out to understand what Alice and her companions experience every day. But the apparent absence of some of the distinguishing features of "experience" – reflexive interiority, hermeneutical depth, narrative flow – leads me to question the universal relevance of the term.

The concept of experience is one of the most problematic in contemporary anthropology, with the problems relating – at least in part – to the rhetorical and analytic needs it serves. Some use the word *experience* because it appears relatively free of the baggage that concepts such as "self" or "mind" or "affect" carry (Kleinman and Kleinman 1991). Some rely on it to provide the "missing term," as E. P. Thompson found, through which "structure is transmuted into process, and the subject re-enters into history" (1978:170). And some build theories on its turf because they find it gets at something more immediate than "meaning" or "discourse" (Desjarlais 1992; Jackson 1989). The word is of such value that even scholars critical of experiential approaches fear that without it, "cultural analyses seem to float

Robert Desjarlais, "Struggling Along: The Possibilities for Experience among the Homeless Mentally Ill," *American Anthropologist* 96/4 (1994): 886–901. Reproduced by permission of the American Anthropological Association from *American Anthropologist* 96/4 (1994), pp. 886–901. Not for sale or further reproduction several feet above their human ground" (Geertz 1986:374; Scott 1991). Experience, it seems, is a crucial element of contemporary academic thought; to try to write about humans without reference to experience is like trying to think the unthinkable. Yet despite its apparent necessity, as something that can and must be thought, its universality remains in question. We must ask if experience is as essential or as commonplace as many take it to be.

In anthropology the ontology of experience has taken a back seat to its epistemology. Perspectives on the study of experience generally divide anthropologists into two camps. There are those who advocate an anthropology of experience to investigate, through phenomenological means, domains of life – pain, bodies, emotions – that one can only poorly apprehend through cultural analysis. And there are others who find that such an anthropology is epistemologically unfounded, since one can never really know the felt immediacies of another person or society, and irrelevant to more important social and political concerns. In listening to the debates sparked by these different orientations, one gets the sense that everyone knows what is meant by experience. Yet it is rarely defined and, when it is defined, it involves a generic "we." Indeed, the very fact that the category "experience" goes undefined or is couched in universalist terms suggests that it is taken as a fundamental, authentic, and unchanging constant in human life.

The problem with taking experience as a uniquely authentic domain of life is that one risks losing an opportunity to question the social production of that domain and the practices that define its use. Connotations of primacy and authenticity lend legitimacy to the anthropologist's craft, but they can simultaneously limit inquiries to descriptions of the terrain of experience when what we need are critical reflections on how the terrain comes about.[1] Asking about experience can tell you about some things, such as how the everyday comes together, just as asking about labor relations or clan lineages can tell you about other things.

In asking a few questions here, I want to suggest that experience is not an existential given but rather a historical possibility predicated on a certain way of being in the world.

Since this way of being is only one possibility among many, some people live in terms different from experience. This appears to be the case with Alice and many of her companions. Their worlds, to be sure, are marked by interiority and a sensate reflexivity, but the subjective and temporal contours of their lives are distinct from the act of experiencing as it is commonly defined. If we take experience to be simply a sensate awareness of life, or "to be alive when something happens" (which is the traditional meaning of *erleben*, a German word for experience), then the people in the shelter certainly do experience. But today, experience tends to mean something more, and I want to understand what conditions are necessary if people are to experience or, alternatively, to struggle along.

The etymology of *experience* hints at the changing uses of the word. *Experience*, like *experiment* and *expert*, comes from the Latin *experiri*, a compound verb formed from the prefix *ex-* ("out") and a prehistoric base *per- ("attempt, trial") that meant "to try, test" (Ayto 1990). The modern English word *experiment* best preserves the original meaning of experience, though the latter also meant at first "putting to the test." From this came the idea of having "actually observed phenomena in order to gain knowledge of them," which in turn led to the more subjective "condition of having undergone or been affected by a particular event" (Ayto 1990). The subjectivist connotations of experience are only a recent innovation; the idea that to experience is to feel, to suffer, or to undergo was first recorded in 1588 (Barnhart 1988:357). Similar to the trajectory of the Western self, which initially marked an exterior relationship to one's environment but later came to entail a moral, reflexive agent, experience evolved from a verb denoting an external engagement with or testing of one's surroundings to a template marking a person's subjective awareness of that engagement. As Lévy-Bruhl, Hallowell, and others have pointed out, however, human functioning need not depend on such reflective assessments but can assume a wealth of nonintrospective forms. Experience involves only one, rather inward-looking arrangement of human agency among many.[2]

The stress on interiority ties into the affirmation of ordinary life that has earmarked humanist thought and literature and correlates with the Romantic notion that the most authentic truths lie in ourselves (Taylor 1989). A focus on the truths of personal revelations relates closely to modern religious concerns, particularly the Pietist emphasis on religious devotion, with personal experience, as a state of mind or feeling, forming an integral part of the inner religious life. The inner states cultivated through such devotion reveal truths worth talking about. Raymond Williams notes, for instance, that in 19th-century Methodism there were *experience-meetings:* classes "held for the recital of religious experiences" (1983:128). Today, as well, experience is largely rooted in individual agency. A person "has," "learns from," or "discloses" an experience. Privacy, individuality, and reflexive interiority are intrinsic to experience; no one else can experience my toothache, though they might empathize with my suffering. Experience thus readily equates with a person's inner life or consciousness and is often synonymous with subjectivity.[3]

The notion of interiority encourages some to try to understand the essence of experience (Desjarlais 1992) and leads others to suggest that "experience is sensual and affective to the core and exceeds objectification in symbolic forms" (Good 1994:139). The excessiveness of experience points to a second distinguishing feature: experience possesses hermeneutical depth. The sense of depth, like that of interiority, ties into the Western genealogy of the self. While the writings of Augustine, Descartes, and Montaigne brought successively stronger declarations of human inwardness, only with the expressivist yearnings of Wordsworth, Hölderlin, and others to discover and articulate our inner nature does this interiority come to possess significant depth. In modernist times the grounds of experience, rather than those of the self, have possessed the richest depths because experience is often seen as the foundation of human agency (Taylor 1989:465). As Gadamer describes the philosophy of Dilthey and Husserl, "essential to an experience [*erlebnis*] is ... something unforgettable and irreplaceable, something whose meaning cannot be exhausted by conceptual determination" (1975:67). The import of experience is inexhaustible because experience, like a text or a work of art, carries a wealth of meanings that can never be conclusively interpreted (Ricoeur 1970).

The hermeneutical depths of experience distinguish it from the subject matter of traditional cultural analysis. Human experience eludes analysis and resists symbolization. The idea of an excessive, hermeneutically rich plane of being entails the view that the only way to safely study experience is to attend to the perimeter of expressions, stories, and social formations in which it is cloaked.[4] To say that thick description is the best method of analysis here is not to denigrate the available methods but simply to point out the kinds of phenomena in question: experience is too complex, too subtle, and too private to be understood through anything but phenomenological assessments. Even then, "it's all a matter of scratching surfaces," as Clifford Geertz puts it (1986:373). Talk of surfaces and cores suggests a shadow play of interiors and exteriors: we cannot penetrate the containers of experience. The body is often held to be one such container, with the skin serving as an envelope within which, Faulkner writes, "the sum of experience" resides (1986:54).

The sum coheres. Despite the immediacy, richness, and contingency that characterize lived experience, experience works on a principal of unity. Dewey (1926) talks about the "inclusive integrity" of experience, while Oakshott (1985) ponders its "concrete totality." James, Dilthey, Husserl, Merleau-Ponty, and others agree that the sum of experience is greater than its parts. Joyce's Leopold Bloom, Freud's Wolfman, and Proust's remembrances exemplify the integrity of experience; memories, dreams, and sensations snowball into a unified, epiphanic whole. The appeal to wholeness apparently relates, for many, to a modernist desire to develop a concept that might safely absorb the many select features of human agency, such as thought, feeling, and sensation.[5]

Experience builds to something more than a transient, episodic succession of events. The intransience of experience ties into the fact that it effects a lasting and memorable impression on the person who undergoes it. Heidegger suggests that "to undergo an experience with something – be it a thing, a person, or a god – means that this something befalls us, strikes us, comes over us, overwhelms and transforms us" (1971:57). Experience is fundamentally transformative; an experience "does not leave him who has it unchanged," or so says Gadamer in his specification of a "genuine experience" (*erfahrung*) (1975:100). To have an experience, or to learn by experience, suggests an education that can accrue in certain skills, knowledge, or wisdom, though the education hinges on a flux of subjective reflections that other kinds of learning, such as operant conditioning, do not.

To experience, writes Heidegger, "is to go along a way. The way leads through a landscape (1971:67)."[6] The landscape is organized through temporal and spatial lines. Experience, by definition, collects itself through the rhythmic pacings of time. As Carr puts it, "Our experience is directed towards, and itself assumes, temporally extended forms in which future, present, and past mutually determine one another as parts of a whole" (1986:30–1). Narrative typically helps to form the sense of temporal integration. The idea that experience accumulates in time through stories builds chiefly upon the relation between forms of life and narrative orderings of time. From Aristotle to Heidegger to Ricoeur, the interpenetration of narrative and experience has grown stronger in correlation with the predominance of literature in the lives of the educated. The present state of the art is that we can only grasp our lives through narrative, though few question to what degree this inescapable fact applies outside the modern West.[7]

Experience as a whole is subject to similar queries. In much the same way as the truth of sexuality grew out of an economy of discourses that took hold in 17th-century Europe (Foucault 1978), so a set of phrasings of depth, interiority, and authenticity; sensibilities of holism and transcendence; and practices of reading and writing have crafted a mode of being that many in the West would call experience. In taking experience to have a specific meaning and to possess a limited reality, the task is to identify where and when people experience and the conditions that make the process possible. Thinkers such as Taylor and Foucault, who emphasize the priority of language in shaping our lives, tend to speak of incarnations of self or power as generic to an age. Yet these kinds of theories seldom consider the plurality of social, sensorial, and technological forces that occasion diverse ways of being within a society. I find cultural discourses as well as day-to-day contingencies to be evident in the shelter where Alice stays. Experience there is a possibility, not a given, and certain conditions are necessary if people are to experience.

The Shelter

The shelter was set up in the early 1980s by the Massachusetts Department of Mental Health to provide temporary housing for persons troubled by mental illness. To gain a bed, one must be both homeless and mentally ill, which means owning a diagnosis of "schizophrenia," "bipolar disorder," or the like. An individual arrives from a local hospital, another shelter, or the streets to sleep on one of 52 cots set up in the gym of a mental health center that occupies one third of a vast government center. A staff desk guards the entrance to the shelter, which abuts a lobby where many residents spend much of their time talking, sitting, and pacing. Within the shelter, standing partitions separate the men's and women's sleeping areas. Some stay in the shelter for a few weeks, while a handful have been there over five years. They typically leave when they return to the hospital, find a more permanent place to live, hit the street, or get kicked out due to infractions of the shelter's rules concerning drugs or theft.

I frequented the shelter at a time when there was great interest – among psychiatrists, policy-oriented academics, and the general population – in the improvement of services for the chronic and persistent mentally ill, despite severe cuts in health services for the poor and a general push for privatization.[8] Program cuts affected the shelter in two ways: residents lost case managers and treatment programs, and staff worried about losing their jobs.

The staff maintain that the shelter is perceived as the Rolls Royce of shelters. While their guests do not hold the same level of enthusiasm, many do find it to be one of the better shelters in the Boston area. Part of its appeal lies in the safety it provides. The strategy of the staff, however, is to maintain the impermanence of the shelter and make it clear, at meetings and in conversations, that it is "not a home."[9] For the most part, they are successful in getting their point across by balancing safety with a modicum of comfort and a set of rules. Disciplines include throwing a person outside the shelter for an hour (typically for acting up, swearing, or talking too loud for too long) or sending them out for the night (for more egregious acts).

The staff's proclivity to displace people contributes to a distinct political system. In contrast to Foucault's model of "disciplinary" power in the age of reason, which centered on acts of confinement and panoptic visibility, power in the shelter typically involves acts of displacement and obscurity.[10] And whereas the staff, who maintain a proper and durable place, rely on strategies that enable them to keep to themselves in a position of withdrawal, foresight, and self-collection, the residents lack such a place and so have few grounds – spatial, political, economic – on which to stand.[11] To get something done or to effect something in their own interests, they resort to tactical actions that depend less on appropriation of space and concerted technology of knowledge than on diverse opportunities in time, rhetorical phrasings, and other isolated actions.

The strategic orientation of the staff includes a range of rules and protocols that set the tempo of everyday life. A resident must shower every other day, leave the shelter from 9:30 in the morning to 3:30 in the afternoon, perform a rotating set of chores, dine at 5:00, take medications in the evening, and return to the shelter by 9:00 at night. Staff maintain that "the rules are there to provide structure to your lives," as a nurse told several residents one evening. Residents find the multiplicity of restrictions, as well as the way in which they are asserted, unpleasant and infantilizing. Fred, for instance, says that the shelter is "not a home. There are too many rules and regulations." The management's philosophy is that it's a question of choices. As one staff member put it to a group of residents, "Take Freddy, for instance. He has choices. If he wants to stay here instead of in-patient [a locked psychiatric ward on the fifth floor], then when he's feeling nervous and anxious, he can either come up to us and ask for more medication, or he can try to throw a door through a window." Freddy nodded his head and smiled in accommodating agreement.

To understand why people stay in the shelter for months or for years, one needs to know something about "the street," which is where many come from and where they go if they leave without locating an apartment. The shelter residents talk about the street as if it were a single location with a singularly forced sensorium of cold weather, fear, anonymity, transience, and a constant, unsettling tendency to get on one's nerves. Roy, who used to panhandle in front of Dunkin Donuts and who kept mostly to himself for safety reasons, said, "If you're on the street, you get beat up, cheated, robbed, disrespected. You end up sleeping in subways with people stealing money from your pockets, and eating at McDonald's, Burger King, or even out of trash cans if you're desperate." Fred was sleeping in a warehouse before he came to the shelter. "I had all my utensils there, a shelf, a bed, but it was getting cold." When the warehouse burned down, he slept in one of the trains behind North Station. Julie, who lived on the streets for several weeks before I met her, says the isolation snuffs out a person's will to talk and be with others. "People in the street don't talk to anyone." She wore a Red Sox T-shirt, twisted a piece of paper, and paused after each sentence. "A part of you dies on the street. Your spirit dies. You lose the wanting to live inside, the wanting to talk with someone. That part dies too. Once you're outside, you can't come back inside. The street is tough. Homeless people are dying out on the streets. You lose everything but a sense of survival."

The street tends to reduce people to a few material possessions, a couple of friends, and the redundancy of walking, hiding, eating, bumming for cigarettes or change, and sleeping on benches, in the subways, in the woods, or in shelters. For many, the fears and discontinuities of the streets are amplified, on both the mathematical and sensory scales of the word, by concerns commonly associated with mental illness, such as hearing voices, anxiety, or fear of harm. Bruce hears voices, "Young women telling me they're easy to sleep with. That scares me, it scares me." Julie fears that people are planning to kill her on the street. One day she and her daughter escaped from two men in the subway. She fears the voices would get worse if she lived on the streets. "Right at this moment," Martin said one day, "I have this impending sense of doom – that something terrible is going to happen in a few minutes, like this ceiling could fall in on us."

"When you're homeless," Richie says, "you end up with just your body, cause you don't own anything else." With the loss of many possessions, and the public slant to physical movements and functions, the body becomes, at times, the most prominent instrument of engagement, awareness, and retrospection. "Look what I did to my arm," Fred says of a track of scars up his forearm. Some scars are fresher than others. "I did it to prove that I'm sick, the government's sick, the state is sick, and you're sick." Nadia, an aging Polish woman who speaks of concentration camps, says she is losing her voice because of a thyroid problem. One day she lies on the grass with a necklace, an ankle bracelet, and a wrist bracelet made out of interlocking safety pins. "I thought I would adorn my tortured body," she tells me.

Distinct as the residents' concerns are, they suggest that everyday life is marked by a frail sensitivity toward the noises, activities, and potential violence of the streets. The states of feeling common to those who are homeless result less from inherent dispositions than from the constant and tiresome afflictions of the street. A basic orientation, the product of cold nights and fearful sounds, pivots on the sensory range between nervousness and staying calm. People talk of being emotionally tired when they arrive in the building and refer to an inability to deal with distractions. "We're sensitive," Joan says at a group meeting one day. "We can't deal with things. That's why we're here. We're not like the people outside." She says she needs to be familiar with an area before she is comfortable. "It's the adjustment that's the problem. It's okay when you're well.

But when you're sick, it's hard to start off fresh each day."

Given these concerns, many people come to stay in the shelter because there are simply "less worries" there, as one man put it. "I feel safe as long as I'm in the building," Joey once said when I asked how he was doing. Louise, who is "desperate to find an answer to the rambling" of her mind, is looking for a place "to recover from the shock of the elements outside." She says she will stay in the shelter until she feels it is safe for her to move out. Some stay for years for similar reasons.

Within the shelter, much of everyday life orbits around efforts to keep shocks to a minimum and to hold oneself together. "Hypersensory residualness wants to be within equatorial lines," goes the last line of one of Charles's poems. For many, there is a common and pragmatic need to keep the senses within equatorial lines – to seek comfort and safety in the routines of shelter life, and so spend one's days in a way that skirts the fears, worries, and afflictions that impinge. Some try to stay calm by holding onto a thought, a word, a gesture, or a cigarette. Jimmy says he used to pick up a newspaper and hold onto a word and that would calm him down. Chuck works on puzzles for the same reason.

By 3:00 in the afternoon, five to ten tired people are waiting for the shelter doors to open. When they do, many lie in their cots for an hour or so. One of the chief complaints of shelter life is that it is hard to find time and space to oneself. "I suppose you can't ask for much," says Julie. "It's a place for people with problems. And it's a place where everybody's together. You have to be together." But being together has its problems: each resident must sleep with 20 other same-sex fellows on the same half of the basketball court; no partitions separate the beds from one another. During the day, they share six tables, four armchairs, one couch, a TV room, the lobby, and the far reaches of the building. Most confrontations within the shelter involve disputes over these limited resources. One day Matthew, a middle-aged man from Mississippi, sat down at a table where Barbara was seated. "I want to be alone," she said. "Alone?" he asked. "How can you be alone here? Everybody's together.

You could be off somewhere by yourself." A minute later, Matthew walked off.

On the basketball court, much of the tension builds on distracting sights and sounds – the hypersensory residuals of which Charles spoke. "There are 50 tensions here," Sally tells me, one for each person living in the shelter. "It's hard to get a decent sleep here," she added. "Someone is always singing a song." Matthew likes to sit in the plaza on the third floor. "There's too much going on downstairs," he says. "There's two televisions on, radios. I can't see how you can watch TV with all that going on." A similar distraction nags Jimmy. "The building," he says, "keeps you out of your own little world. It's kind of distracting."

"What do you do when the building distracts you?" I asked.

"Play dead."

People pace, play dead, or hold onto a word or the Bible to get through the day. The staff think the routine is self-defeating, but for many who live in the building, it is a question of survival. "It's all right; it's better than nothing," Joey said of a new coat bought at a discount market. "I'm trying to hang in there, you know. Hanging in is good. I'm all right as long as I'm busy. My father says an idle mind is an ill mind."

For most, hanging in there is good enough. People stay busy by talking, smoking cigarettes, and pacing. The goal of many of these activities is to be doing something. Time consists of concrete activities marked by expanses of silence and waiting. "I smoke cigarettes, drink coffee, listen to music, talk with people, you know," Roy says of his daily routine, with the phrase "you know" referring to activities taken for granted. I ask Patty what she did today. "Oh, you know, the usual boring stuff, smoking and eating and talking. In and out, in and out, and I paced a bit today." Pacing helps people to keep busy and calm their nerves. Warren finds that "there's too much pressure sometimes" from staying in the building and spends much of his time walking around the city. One of Joseph's poems, jotted in a notebook, consists of four lines:

> Pacing the floor
> pacing my mind
> walking the floor
> walking my thoughts

For Joseph, pacing up and down is the way to change his luck. His advice for a newcomer is, "Live one day at a time, don't get ahead of yourself, and don't get too worried." Worries for him are the main problem in the shelter; they throw off the equilibrium, the balance. "If you have to get copies for something, or records at the hospital, it can get compressed in here, because of the close quarters and tight spaces." He gets to feeling tight inside, constricted, and pacing helps because it uses up energy, "so much energy from the medication."

Psychotropic drugs are a clear presence in the sensory range of everyday life. Almost everyone who sleeps in the shelter takes medications prescribed by a psychiatrist and given by a nurse. Those who refuse risk a trip to a hospital. The medications help with the voices and lower anxiety, but they can also cause the body to stiffen or to shake. There is no "gray line" with Ralph's medications. Not enough and he gets to hearing voices; too much and he walks around stiffly in a stupor. "I got coffee coming, I got coffee coming. I just took my medication – to smooth out the joints," Joey tells me. Leona takes her medication to make the chemicals connect with one another "like fingers tied together."

Shelter life, despite its many distractions, can be too mundane; it is difficult, at times, to keep from playing dead. Martin says he walks around too much because he has nothing to do with his time. One day he shows me a poem he wrote called "Sheol," the word for the Hebrew netherworld. The poem tells of the Los Angeles street scene, where "people are hanging out, with no thoughts, no feelings." Others refer to similar affinities between mood and setting. "Sometimes I go to my bed area," Leona says, "and it seems so kinda gloomy, dark. It looks moldy, though it isn't really moldy, you know?" Vicki finds that the shelter is like death row and says you sometimes see the same faces in different shelters. "I lost my mind," Lisa said in introducing herself one day. "What does that feel like?" I asked. "I don't feel, I don't feel. I feel numb." Richie says he acts crazy to stop from being bored. He gets the "shelter blues" when he feels depressed and worthless and tries to make himself and others feel more alive by touching and talking to them.

The mundane distractions of shelter life, and the occasional deadening of feeling, turn on caffeine, footsteps, touches, and the constant exchanges between bodies and voices. With these exchanges, abrupt interactions grow tiresome. Matthew was talking one day, partly to me, partly to himself: "Moses was a wise man ..." Nancy walked up and interrupted: "Matthew, can I have a cigarette?" He replied, "I don't want to hear that, Nancy. We're doing the same old song and dance."

Much of everyday life repeats the same old song and dance: the bumming, selling, and sharing of food, cigarettes, and Walkman radios. The staff give out paper tokens to guests if they take showers, make their beds, or water the plants. People use the tokens to pay for snacks, soda, or soap in the evening; they also use them to buy cigarettes from each other. People walk over to a convenience store to buy coffee, cigarettes, or food for others; their cut is 55 cents or so, or a share of the bounty. The going interest on a loan is 100 percent; if Sally loans Chuck five dollars today, he should pay her ten by next week. Cigarettes can be exchanged for conversation, radios for friendship – and sex, at times, for money. "If you have the money," Martin said, "you can get anything you want on the street." Last spring, he bought valium for a dollar a pill and was trying to get a constant supply set up in the building. Drugs, cash, food, and bodies flow in and out of the building in a vast common market.

Language is an integral part of this political economy. A few kind words can set someone up for a free cigarette or a cigarette can be offered in exchange for conversation. The street value of words was brought home to me one October evening when I was talking, in Harvard Square, with someone who frequents the government center. He was selling flowers, which he found in a trash bin behind a florist's shop, for 25 cents each. He said he could offer people bits of his poetry or translations of Chinese characters he wrote on a piece of cardboard, but they might steal his words. "How do I know," he asked, "that if I put my words on this cardboard, or put them into the air, you or someone else won't take my words and sell them somewhere else? No, you gotta be more careful than that these days."

Words are therefore some of the key commodities; they can be bought, sold, shared, or stolen by peddlers, psychiatrists, or ethnographers alike. Words spoken often relate to the exchange of money, and talking to someone can entail an ongoing social and financial contract.

Bruce walks up to Larry one afternoon and says, "Larry, can you talk to me today?"

"Yeah, can I give you 12 [dollars]?"

"That's great, that will make the week easier."

Later, Bruce tells Larry not to be too stern in lending out money. You have to "work in international waters," give "some room in between," and tend to "the give and take." The advice captures well the ethics of a place where money can be tight and debts are not soon forgotten.

One reason for the brevity of conversations in the shelter is that residents find it difficult to follow through on them. As Julie asked me, "Would *you* want to have a conversation with someone who is talking to themselves, who is caught up with their own conversation?" While some hear and respond to voices, others "talk ragtime," which, Peter explains, is talk "about the sky falling down or cows on the roof. It doesn't make any sense. How can you listen to that?" "It's awkward," Joseph said. "People seem rational when they first sit down with you, but then, the next thing you know, they're bouncing off the walls." As it is, conversations frequently involve two planes of discourse, with the distinction leading either to arguments, miscomprehensions, or a complex ambiguity of meaning.

Helen, who sometimes uses a cane, walks slowly through the lobby.

"Where's your cane?" Philippe asks.

"You shut your mouth!" she says to him, and then to me, "He's talking dirty."

Edward was telling Sally and me about the nonfiction novel he intends to write "about making it in the city, today, not yesterday, you know what I mean?" Leona walked by, held a cross at him for several seconds, and flicked her head. "I thought you was a demon," she said, "I thought you was a *demon!* We don't understand one another. We don't *understand* one another!" And then more to me than to

Edward, "We live in the same place, but we don't *know* one another. And that's how most arguments get started around here!"

The risk of conflict caused by "loose tongue fits" (as one woman put it) and the struggle for many "to hang in there" leads to the general consensus that the shelter is "not a place to make friends," as Julie puts it. "Everyone here has problems. Each goes their own individual way. So I have no real friends here." While many lament the lack of friends in the shelter, many also find comfort in the detached but constant companionship that characterizes shelter life. "I like it here," said Sally. "It's good here because I don't feel lonely. There's always people to talk to here. In an apartment by myself, I was going crazy, losing my mind." Another man, who lives alone in a single-room apartment and can be found riding the subway during the day, hangs out in the building at nights for reasons similar to Sally's. "I come here to see Warren and socialize," he told me. "He does his thing and I do mine." His thing is to stand in the stairwell, talk under his breath, and watch Warren pace the lobby. Like others, he likes to be around people but cannot hold onto a conversation for too long.[12] The building provides an arrangement where he can keep to himself in the company of others. Others also tend to share a word here and there but largely go their own ways. Except for a few close ties and love interests, lives are kept separate. Anonymity is more the rule than the exception.

Since social ties are so difficult to maintain, acquaintances are often made out of economic exchanges – loans, payments, negotiations. With these exchanges, companionship, like words, can be for sale. Gary walks over and sits down with Janie. "Do you have an extra cigarette?"

"Only if you sit with me."

"Okay."

Janie slides out a cigarette and hands it to Gary, saying, "You better remember me when I need a cigarette."

"I will."

They smoke in silence.

The economic bases of friendship are evident in the exchanges between Bruce and Larry. The main interactions between these two involve a constant exchange of money, cigarettes, and

lottery tickets, and negotiations on those exchanges. In August, Larry moved into a halfway house while Bruce stayed on in the shelter. Two days after Larry left, Bruce sat down with me and a staff member who asked what he thought about Larry's departure.

"I think a lot about him leaving," Bruce said. "He bummed a lot of cigarettes from me, you know."

"Oh yeah, you also seemed to get a lot in return."

"Yeah, we treated each other right. I don't know, he kind of let it go the last week. I lent him some money the last week, ten dollars one day and some cigarettes the next, but I guess he thought I was setting him up."

"Maybe, you know, he was trying to get some distance from this place."

"Yeah. Maybe so."

As with Bruce and Larry, many ties between shelter residents rest on an ethos of exchange. The most significant consequence of this economics has to do with typical activities in and around the building, which often center on acts of collecting. People bum for cigarettes, panhandle for money, and scavenge back alleys for clothes, food, and empty soda cans. Patty is known to wear up to five hats, even in the summer. Emily walks by a table, spies the Boston Globe, looks at an ad for a department store, reads it, tears it off the page, and carries the clipping to her locker.

The tendencies to collect or to hoard relate, as do many aspects of shelter life, to the economics of homelessness. Joan, for instance, lost her apartment, her library, and her record collection when she fell ill. "It's all gone now." Without a home to keep things, possessions soon fill bags and lockers. "It's not right to take all the things we have," Leona said on hearing that the staff were going to limit the articles guests could keep in their bed areas. "We don't have enough money for a place. That's why we have all our things here, and we can't even keep our own things or our own children." Collecting also arises from marginal shares of Boston's makeshift economies (Hopper et al. 1986). Spending money can be gained by collecting bottles or selling the few quality items found in the trash. A lack of money leads a few to pick through dumpsters in search of food, blankets, or clothing. And food or drink that cannot be immediately consumed tends to be given away or hidden until it can be eaten in privacy.

The principles of accumulation do not end with economics. At a basic level, shelter lives tend to consist of the repetitive collection of the elements of those lives. Memories, for instance, often involve such a collection. Gathered like so much spare change, they are characteristically dreamy and drifting. "One night I was scared of something," Peter says of his nights on the street. "I pulled an alarm because I was scared, and the fire engines came. I told them I was scared and alone and I thought that if I pulled this alarm, they would be able to make me feel good. They threw me in jail for that." Patty recalls, with a similar opacity, an apartment she fixed up in the North End before she got sick. "Oh, it was beautiful," she says. "There were chairs there, and a table, and a tablecloth. I had all my things there. But people were trying to break in, they were trying to kill me." With Patty and Peter, each image shines like a new coin – *this* alarm, *that* tablecloth – but the memory as a whole lacks a dominating narrative fabric. Many other memories have a similarly strong eidetic quality. People remember dates, names, and specific acts and dialogues as if reciting a court docket: "On December 5, 1987, I broke into a real estate office," Phil says one day. But experiential or motivational underpinnings often do not play a role: "I don't know why I did this," he adds. "Maybe cause I wanted money, I can't remember." And then, as if an afterthought: "See, that's why I wonder about these drugs."

The inability to clearly remember an incident or why it occurred relates to several factors: the wear and tear of pharmaceuticals, the affective and cognitive disturbances of mental illness, the tactical focus on single encounters, and, most important, a training distinct from the more mainstream arts of memory. I once asked Phil where he slept the night before he returned to the shelter after a hospital stay. "I forgot." How could he forget? "I can't use my memory all the time," he said. "You see, I never learned how to use my memory like most people do. I have to think about something at least three times before I can remember it."

Like Phil, many residents learn to use their memories in ways distinct from most nonhomeless people. Much of the education relates to the pragmatics of time that comes with living in shelters. The episodic quality of shelter life, where you need to live one day at a time and not get ahead of yourself and where nobody does anything, fixes time as a diffuse and sporadic order. There are eddies when the mundane occurs, and whirlpools when someone is restrained or hospitalized, but much of the day, week, and month consists of a vast ocean of routine, more so than in the street.[13] Chuck says he drinks coffee to keep up with it, but for the most part, it is only a routine: out by 9:00, lunch at noon, back by 3:00, dinner at 5:00, snacks at 7:00, checks in on the first of the month. Because of this event-dependent organization of time, people recall specific dates and events, and everyone talks about the time Walter punched a nurse, but there is little reason to notice the potential links between events and the motivations for actions. The poetics of time are more like those found in Beckett than in Proust; recollections depend on momentary occupations more than any deftly woven remembrances of times past. When the occupations change, the memories take new forms. "You have a child?!" Joan asked a woman she was talking to. "Yeah? Excuse me, I forgot. I've been moving back and forth between hospitals, moving back and forth between the hospital and this place, and I forgot."

As with Julie, who found that the lack of structure in the shelter led her to forget how boring it actually was, a constant migration leads Joan to forget something she once knew, as if a person needs a solid footing to remember. The structure of memory relates to the structure of time. In the shelter, the routines of the clock, the realities of power, the influence of pharmaceuticals, the constant exchanges, and the relative lack of privacy and structure create a sensitivity toward singular moments and exchanges and desires. We cannot speak of a strong narrative line here, for while people tell stories and events tumble along, the episodes rarely add to a narrative wholly dependent on a poetics of coherence, continuity, and climax – as narrative is usually defined.[14]

Barbara and Walter are sitting on the benches in the lobby outside the shelter. She asks him to go to the store to buy her some cigarettes and a soda. He returns to the lobby, hands her a can of Pepsi, a pack of cigarettes, and some coins, and sits down on the far bench with a soda of his own.

"Where's the rest of my change?" she asks.

"What's a few pennies?"

"A few pennies are a few pennies, that's what they are, especially when they're mine."

The two sit and drink their sodas. There is no catharsis to the dispute. They are both angry, but everything seems to diffuse abruptly. The conversation entails a transfer of words that involves less a narrative frame (as I would have anticipated) than a poetics of exchange, confrontation, finite acts, and momentary occupations.

Conclusions

All told, the themes common to many shelter lives are a political agency built out of tactical movements, an acutely tactile engagement with the world, a constant focus on daily concerns, a distanced style of communication, a poetics of pacing and talking centering on unconnected episodes, a makeshift economy of cigarettes and loans and conversations, and a ragtag collection of words, memories, images, and possessions. These basic orientations, in tandem with other cultural, linguistic, and political forces, pattern the conditions of, and the grounds for, what is possible in people's lives. They set up a form of life that we might gloss as struggling along.

The aesthetics of this form of life center on the pragmatics of stasis, expediency, staying calm, and holding oneself together. Given the basic conditions of life on the streets, finding a smooth day where nothing much happens has its value. Since one way to stop thinking about the cold or other distractions is to step out of the flow of time, the acme of this predilection is the pursuit of timelessness. For many, there is a need for days where hanging in there is good enough. To get away from the constant tensions and the fleeting distractions, some suspend the minutes of a day.

Too much calm can get to a person after a while. An idle mind, after all, is an ill mind, and pacing and other activities help to lessen the worries that come with living in the shelter. The trick is to keep the senses within the equatorial lines, to find the grey line between sensory vitality (which can include hearing voices) and walking around in a stupor. A desire for balance is evident in other aspects of shelter life, including the benefits of bargaining with one's colleagues and the perceived need to keep a certain distance from others. In the realm of economics, relations, and the senses alike, the residents of the shelter tend to work toward points of equilibrium, which often come down to a sense of stasis. The stasis, which makes a good deal of sense given how much is impermanent and transient in their lives, tends to grow more fundamental the longer people stay in the shelter.

How does all this compare to the act of experiencing? Although experience and struggling along are not mutually exclusive categories, in which the elements of one would imply the absence or negation of corresponding elements in the other, the two processes do involve distinct aesthetic, temporal, and phenomenal features. Experience entails an aesthetics of integration, coherence, renewal, and transcendent meaning – of tying things together through time. A good day for someone who experiences might be one in which there is a novel integration of personal undertakings, a tale to be told about events bordering on the adventuresome. The features of such a day build on the stuff of novelty, transformation, emplotment, and movement. A good day for someone who struggles along, in contrast, might be a smooth one, where nothing much happens, where a few bucks are earned, where the voices are not too bad, where pressure is relieved through pacing, and where there are enough cigarettes to last the day. The ingredients of such a day draw from the forces of expediency, equilibrium, and stasis.

Sitting in the same place for several hours each day has its consequences. The temporal order of experience, involving as it does a cumulative layering of events that builds to a whole greater than its parts, proceeds along narrative lines of an Aristotelian bent. The gist of experience is that it goes beyond the situation at hand. The temporal order of struggling along, in contrast, involves a succession of engagements, which can include a constant but purely episodic unfolding of events. In the shelter, economic concerns, the press of everyday distractions, and a tactical mode of agency directs the struggles toward temporally finite forms in which future, present, and past need not have much to do with one another.

The phenomenal plane of experience is a thoroughly reflexive one; to experience is to engage in a process of perception, agency, and reflection that is couched in mindful introspection. Struggling along also entails a firm sense of interiority and reflexivity, but the reflections are not as intense as they are with experience. The distracting sights and sounds of the building, which draw or drag a person in different directions, prompt an acutely tactile mode of perception with little room or need to introspect or to contemplate. Day in, day out, things happen much more with the retina, on the skin of the eardrums, and in the tips of the fingers than in any detached haven of mind or body. Experience implies a contained, integrative, and occasionally transcendent adaptation of sensations, images, and lessons; struggling along entails a diffuse and external rain of distractions that prompts a retreat from the world rather than an incorporation or an assimilation of its parts.

What occasions the differences? While the disabling troubles of mental illness surely play a role here, it is a set of specific political, social, cultural, and environmental forces, rather than any inherent will or disposition, that leads people to either experience or struggle along.[15] Both processes are patterned by long-standing cultural orientations, strengthened through a lifetime's interactions, such as a sense of personhood as something unique, interior, and well contained. Yet different formations of time, space, and agency are also at work. Whereas experience derives from environments that offer a lasting sense of privacy, in which a person can dwell within his or her own world for some length of time, acts of struggling along are borne of extensively public spaces, with agency taking shape through constant concerns with one's surroundings. Those concerns can contribute to an episodic

orientation toward time, with each incidence taking precedence over any larger temporal context, as well as to the need, at times, to stop the rush of events and find some point of equilibrium or stasis. Much of the difference rests on the kind of environment in which a person lives: a condition of permanence, detachment, and security gives rise to a process that entails, among other things, a sense of transcendence, of going out into the world and being transformed through those movements. A state of unsettledness, unrest, and constant engagement, in turn, necessitates the act of holding onto a word or a Bible to get through the day.

Each of these ways of being are context-dependent, with the contexts themselves framed by a mix of political and economic forces. In the shelter, struggling along relates directly to a politics of displacement, to a world of acutely public spaces, and to an economics of exchanges and ragtag collectibles. Living in the shelter for any length of time prompts a way of being that enables most people to attend to these concerns.

When the context changes, so do the features of one's life. Henry, for instance, spends a lot of time away from the building. Son of a New Orleans doctor, he prefers smart clothing and "proper" people and long walks through Boston. "Tension builds if you stay in one place all day," he says, "whether you're mentally ill or not." He typically walks about five miles each day, drifting from the park to Newbury Street to the Fenway, and returns around 5:00 p.m. to speak of his adventures. "I kissed a woman on the lips today," he said one evening. "She was sitting on a bench, and she was crying, and so I kissed her. Now she wants to know where I live." As Heidegger might put it, the kiss befalls Henry, strikes him, overwhelms and transforms him. He goes along a way. The way leads through a landscape. The journey through this landscape, with its own landmarks, education, and suspenses, is what we call "experience." Like Henry, a few other residents, principally those who are new to the streets and spend a lot of time away from the building, also carry on in continued reference to a constellation of inwardness, hermeneutical depth, renewal, and narrative orderings of time. A quite different constellation of moving, sensing, and remembering takes form, however, among the majority of those who spend most of their time in the building, making do with day-to-day contingencies.

The presence of two distinct ways of being, with their own defining features, conditions, and constraints, suggests that anthropologists need to rethink their approaches toward the everyday. The ordinary-language notion of experience as the phenomenal, palpable charge of life will probably thrive in anthropology as long as the metaphysic motivating it has its uses – as long, that is, as practice opposes theory and the sensate parries meaning. But for those who figure out what the process of experience might imply, a revaluation of methods and motives is called for. Rather than take experience as an authentic, intensely human, existential given, we need to bracket the category. We need to consider how the word serves certain rhetorical needs that help carve out a way of looking at the world. And we need to consider how the process itself relates to specific social, cultural, political, and material forces.

For the residents of the shelter, a politics of displacement, an episodic sequence of events, and a world of constant public transactions contribute to a certain tack in life. Indeed, some of the most fundamental constellations of time, space, and agency behind this and other struggles appear to be changing in the late-20th century. In the modern industrial era, experience might have seemed an essential part of human nature for some people because its defining features – reflexive depth, temporal integration, and a cumulative transcendence – blended so well with the reigning aesthetics of that age. But the poverty, transience, and contingency that increasingly characterize life on the fringes of postindustrial societies suggests that experience might become, at least in some circles, a relic of the past.

NOTES

1   See Scott 1991 and Williams 1979:164–70.
2   See Crapanzano 1977, Hallowell 1955, Kleinman and Kleinman 1991, Leenhardt 1979, Lévy-Bruhl 1938, and Lienhardt 1961.
3   It is the private aspects of experience that make some wary of experiential approaches in anthropology. Those critical of such approaches tend to question the legitimacy of the research more than the universality and relevance of the concept. Finding that experience denotes a subjective realm that can be only poorly comprehended, they uphold the view that experience is interior, private, and ubiquitous.
4   See Bruner 1986, DelVecchio Good et al. 1992:199, 200, and Jackson 1989.
5   See Williams 1983:127–28, where he notes that the concept of "culture" holds a similar attraction.
6   Heidegger is drawing on the fact that *erfahrung* comes from the Old High German *infaran*, to travel, traverse, pass through, to reach or arrive at (see Needham 1972:171).
7   Becker 1979, Good 1994, and Rosaldo 1986 offer three studies that systematically inquire into the forms of, and conditions for, narrativity in, respectively, Javanese, Turkish, and Ilongot societies.
8   Much of my research involved participant observation in the daily life of the shelter and its surroundings several afternoons and evenings each week. Because I could not and did not want to use a tape recorder, and structured interviews made both residents and staff uncomfortable, I spent much of my time hanging about, listening to and entering into conversations and then immediately finding a place to write down the content of these exchanges. See Aviram 1990, Dennis et al. 1991, Goldfinger 1990, and the special issue on homelessness in the *New England Journal of Public Policy* (1992, Vol. 8, no. 1) for recent assessments of homelessness among persons considered to be mentally ill.
9   Consequently, my research interested the shelter manager in part because he wanted to learn if there was any way he could make shelter life less accommodating to his guests.
10 See Desjarlais n.d.1 and Foucault 1977.
11 The words in quotes and the idea of "strategies" and "tactics" come from de Certeau 1984; see Desjarlais n.d.2.
12 The common desire to be alone in the company of others compares to Corin's (1990) finding that many people with schizophrenia seek out a stance of "positive withdrawal" toward their worlds. Estroff (1981) and Strauss and Carpenter (1981) come to similar conclusions in their phenomenologies of mental illness.

13 Anne Lovell writes of the "permanent temporal dislocation" common to New York City's homeless street people. "I feel dead," one man tells her, "cause that's what dead people do. They never change. ... It's all been like one god damn long humble day." "It's a one-day-at-a-time-Sweet-Jesus kind of thing" says another (Lovell 1992:94, 98). Gounis (1992), in turn, writes insightfully about the institutional routines of several "homeless" shelters in New York City.

14 See Carr 1986 and Ricoeur 1984.

15 I find that acts of struggling along have more to do with environmental and political forces than with the vagaries of mental illness largely because I know of other people who must contend with similar afflictions (including the "de-institutionalized" residents of a halfway house where I worked in the mid-1980s) yet whose lives are organized much more along the lines of "experience." To hear voices, feel paranoid, and think and act differently than others can have a tremendous (and often disabling) effect on a person's life, but the environment in which one lives determines so much more.

REFERENCES

Aviram, Uri
1990 Community Care of the Seriously Mentally Ill: Continuing Problems and Current Issues. Community Mental Health Journal 26:69–88.

Ayto, John
1990 Bloomsbury Dictionary of Word Origins. London: Bloomsbury.

Barnhart, Robert
1988 The Barnhart Dictionary of Etymology. New York: H. W. Wilson Company.

Becker, A. L.
1979 Text-Building, Epistemology, and Aesthetics in Javanese Shadow Theatre. In The Imagination of Reality. A. L. Becker and A. A. Yengoyan, eds. Pp. 211–43. Norword, NJ: ABLEX.

Bruner, Edward
1986 Experience and Its Expressions. In The Anthropology of Experience. V. Turner and E. Bruner, eds. Pp. 3–32. Urbana: University of Illinois Press.

Carr, David
1986 Time, Narrative, and History. Bloomington: Indiana University Press.

Corin, Ellen
1990 Facts and Meaning in Psychiatry: An Anthropological Approach to the Lifeworld of Schizophrenics. Culture, Medicine and Psychiatry 14:153–88.

Crapanzano, Vincent
1977 Introduction. In Case Studies in Spirit Possession. V. Crapanzano and V. Garrison, eds. Pp. 1–40. New York: John Wiley.

de Certeau, Michel
1984 The Practice of Everyday Life. Steven F. Rendall, trans. Berkeley: University of California Press.

DelVecchio Good, Mary-Jo, Paul Brodwin, Byron Good, and Arthur Kleinman
1992 Epilogue. In Pain as Human Experience: An Anthropological Perspective. M-J. DelVecchio Good, P. Brodwin, B. Good, and A. Kleinman, eds. Pp. 198–207. Berkeley: University of California Press.

Dennis, Deborah, John Buckner, Frank Lipton, and Irene Levine
1991 A Decade of Research and Services for the Homeless Mentally Ill Persons: Where Do We Stand? American Psychologist 46:1129–38.

Desjarlais, Robert
1992 Body and Emotion: the Aesthetics of Illness and Healing in the Nepal Himalayas. Philadelphia: University of Pennsylvania Press.
n.d.1 Power and Obscurity. Paper presented at the 93rd Annual Meeting of the American Anthropological Association, Washington, DC, November 1993.
n.d.2 The Office of Reason. Paper presented at the 94th Annual Meeting of the American Anthropological Association, Atlanta, GA, November 1994.

Dewey, John
1926 Experience and Nature. Chicago: Open Court Publishing Company.

Estroff, Sue
1981 Making It Crazy. Berkeley: University of California Press.

Faulkner, William
1986[1936] Absalom, Absalom! New York: Vintage.

Foucault, Michel
1977 Discipline and Punish. New York: Pantheon.
1978 The History of Sexuality, Volume 1: An Introduction. New York: Vintage.

Gadamer, Hans-Georg
    1975   Truth and Method. New York: Crossroad Publishing Corporation.
Geertz, Clifford
    1986   Making Experience, Authoring Selves. *In* The Anthropology of Experience. V. Turner and E. Bruner, eds. Pp. 373–80. Urbana: University of Illinois Press.
Goldfinger, Stephen
    1990   Introduction: Perspectives on the Homeless Mentally Ill. Community Mental Health Journal 26:387–90.
Good, Byron
    1994   Medicine, Rationality, and Experience. Cambridge: Cambridge University Press.
Gounis, Kostas
    1992   Temporality and the Domestication of Homelessness. *In* The Politics of Time. H. Rutz, ed. Pp. 127–49. Washington, DC: American Ethnological Society Monograph Series, Number 4.
Hallowell, A. Irving
    1955   The Self and Its Behavioral Environment. *In* Culture and Experience. Pp. 172–83. Philadelphia: University of Pennsylvania Press.
Heidegger, Martin
    1971   On the Way to Language. New York: Harper and Row.
Hopper, K., E. Susser, and S. Conover
    1986   Economies of Makeshift: Deindustialization and Homelessness in New York City. Urban Anthropology 14:183–236.
Jackson, Michael
    1989   Paths toward a Clearing: Radical Empiricism and Ethnographic Inquiry. Bloomington: Indiana University Press.
Kleinman, Arthur, and Joan Kleinman
    1991   Suffering and Its Professional Transformation: Toward an Ethnography of Interpersonal Experience. Culture, Medicine and Psychiatry 15:275–301.
Leenhardt, Maurice
    1979   Do Kamo: Person and Myth in the Melanesian World. Chicago: University of Chicago Press.
Lévy-Bruhl, Lucien
    1938   L'expérience mystique et les symboles chez les primitifs. Paris: Alcan.
Lienhardt, Godfrey
    1961   Divinity and Experience: The Religion of the Dinka. Oxford: Clarendon.

Lovell, Anne
    1992   Seizing the Moment: Power, Contingency, and Temporality in Street Life. *In* The Politics of Time. H. Rutz, ed. Pp. 86–107. Washington, DC: American Ethnological Society Monograph Series, Number 4.
Needham, Rodney
    1972   Belief, Language, and Experience. Chicago: University of Chicago Press.
New England Journal of Public Policy
    1992   Special issue on Homelessness, Vol. 8, no.1.
Oakshott, Michael
    1985[1933]   Experience and Its Modes. Cambridge: Cambridge University Press.
Ricoeur, Paul
    1970   Freud and Philosophy. New Haven: Yale University Press.
    1984   Time and Narrative, Volume 1. Chicago: University of Chicago Press.
Rosaldo, Renato
    1986   Ilongot Hunting as Story and Experience. *In* The Anthropology of Experience. V. Turner and E. Bruner, eds. Pp. 97–138. University of Illinois Press.
Scott, Joan
    1991   The Evidence of Experience. Critical Inquiry 17:773–95.
Strauss, J.S., and W. T. Carpenter
    1981   Schizophrenia. New York: Plenum Press.
Taylor, Charles
    1989   Sources of the Self: The Making of the Modern Identity. Cambridge: Harvard University Press.
Thompson, E. P.
    1978   The Poverty of Theory or an Orrery of Errors. *In* The Poverty of Theory and Other Essays. New York: Monthly Review Press.
Ware, Norma, Robert Desjarlais, Tara AvRuskin, Joshua Breslau, Byron Good, and Stephen Goldfinger
    1992   Empowerment and the Transition to Housing for the Homeless Mentally Ill: An Anthropological Perspective. The New England Journal of Health Policy 8:297–314.
Williams, Raymond
    1979   Politics and Letters. London: New Left Books.
    1983   Keywords: A Vocabulary of Culture and Society. Oxford: Oxford University Press.

Part III

Governmentalities and Biological Citizenship

Introduction

"To make live or to let die," was Michel Foucault's formula for how populations and individual bodies are the subjects of power, governance, and apparatuses of classification. Who counts as mad and should be in an asylum, and who has post-traumatic stress disorder and should receive reimbursed psychiatric care? Which warlord is (de facto) allowed to access international food aid while allowing his opponents to die? Which diseases receive urgent research funding while others, perhaps more common albeit in populations without the means to pay for drugs, are deemed insufficiently "cost-effective"? In recent decades, such questions of "biopolitics" – the topic of social statisticians and epidemiologists since the eighteenth century – have taken on renewed urgency in the hands of medical anthropologists and medical practitioners, whose ethnographic work provides new windows of insight, new opportunities for ethical debate, and new avenues of possible intervention into spaces of "structural violence" (Farmer 1997, 2003, 2004) and the "biologization of inequality" (Nguyen and Peschard 2003); "social suffering" (Kleinman et al. 1997; Das et al. 2000; Das et al. 2001); "bare life" (Fassin 2001; Biehl 2005; Fassin 2005; Comaroff 2007; Willen 2010); the "violence continuum" (Scheper-Hughes and Bourgois 2004); and "vital technologies" (Lock and Nguyen n.d.).

Ethnography has also generated a panoply of new perspectives on "medical citizenship," or how membership in a state, a society, or even humanity itself is mediated by prevailing regimes of health-related power and knowledge. Following Foucault, unspoken and under-recognized inequalities are often cast as "biopolitics" (Foucault 1990 [1978]); inversely, following Paul Rabinow, subjects who organize around common illness experiences to fight for recognition, therapy, or reparations enact "biosociality" (Rabinow 1996). Such new modalities of engagement with (or subjugation to) state health care systems or other regimes of power include "psychiatric citizenship" (Rhodes this volume), "biological citizenship" (Petryna 2002, this volume), pharmaceutical citizenship (Biehl 2007), "therapeutic citizenship" (Nguyen 2005; Nguyen, Ako, et al. 2007) and even, as medicine is targeted to become ever more individualized or personalized, "anti-citizen"-ship

(Rose 2000). In one sense, we are all "patients-in-waiting" learning to see ourselves through a post-genomics understanding of illness; in this new era, we are all carriers of mutations associated with various risk probabilities, and pharmaceutical and diagnostic regimes are becoming ever more biopolitical (Dumit n.d.).

The five essays in this part take up respectively, a case of "psychiatric citizenship" in a US maximum-security prison; a case of disability-validated "biological citizenship" in the aftermath of the nuclear radiation disaster in Ukraine; a case of social abandonment that is unpacked to reveal not only a series of social exclusions and denials involving a genetic disorder (ataxia) but also, despite all, a vital and expressive "experimental self"; a case of struggle between the state and families over the honor of women in the aftermath of widespread abduction and return after Partition in India; and a case of "medical humanitarianism" illustrating the widespread contemporary dilemmas of triage of asylum seekers and unauthorized migrants in France in which, perhaps counter-intuitively, those who are ill have better claim to refuge than the merely able-bodied.

Building upon her 2004 monograph, *Total Confinement: Madness and Reason in the Maximum Security Prison*, Lorna Rhodes examines the case of a maximum security prison inmate, "Sam," who is the product of multiple disciplining institutions: foster care, juvenile detention, psychiatry, criminal justice, and now super-max. Exploring his subjugation to overlapping, often competing, institutional logics, Rhodes shows how prisoners can become caught between contradictory institutional impulses for punitive discipline or therapeutic healing. Rhodes shows that "even the most disturbed individual" can choose to seek relationships through the medium of "traumatic" or "psychiatric citizenship."

Adriana Petryna's essay, which draws from her 2002 ethnography, *Life Exposed: Biological Citizenship After Chernobyl*, describes the aftermath of the nuclear reactor meltdown at Chernobyl, the resulting spread of radiation disease, and the heightened form of biosociality that emerged as affected Ukrainians claimed medical and financial benefits from the fledgling Ukrainian state on the basis of biological damage they have suffered. Radiation disease and other enduring consequences of this "technogenic catastrophe" are not mere diseases; rather, they extend far beyond the immediacy of individual bodies, across generations, and into complicated local, national, regional, and even global spheres of politics and economics.

In the third essay, João Biehl offers a powerful indictment of how multiple regimes of power, knowledge, and authority – the family, the welfare system, the medical profession, the state – can become so disconnected from an individual's suffering as to produce terrifying forms of "social abandonment," a theme explored in his monographs *Vita* (2005) and *Will to Live* (2007). Biehl's previously unpublished essay interlaces four theoretical threads: (1) the spoken language and written "dictionaries" of Catarina, long-time resident of Vita, a Brazilian facility for the physically and mentally ill and socially abandoned; (2) Giorgio Agamben's powerful but, in the author's view, subjectively vacant notions of "bare life" and homo sacer; (3) Jacques Lacan's notion of the "sinthome," or displaced symptoms; and (4) Gilles Deleuze's contention that we must take desire – not power, à la Foucault – as theoretical point of departure. Biehl's ethnography reveals not only the intimate consequences of structural violence in Catarina's family and in Vita, but also one of medical anthropology's hallmark capacities: to foreground subjectivity and agency, in part by showing how Caterina's struggles to articulate herself and her medical history create "holes in dominant theories and policies" (her misdiagnosis by physicians and her family, and consequently her failure to achieve recognition or help until she found a sensitive and patient listener in Biehl). Subjectivity, in this context, "is neither reducible to a person's sense of herself nor necessarily a confrontation with the powers that be"; rather, it is "the material and means of a continuous process of experimentation."

Veena Das takes up an equally complicated set of subjectivities and subjectivations among women who suffered rape and abduction during the India–Pakistan partition and who were subject by their respective states to retrieval and rehabilitation, often facing rejection and stigma within their families. Here the intimate linkages among political notions of citizenship, patriarchal conceptions of family and authority, and governmental powers show how "sovereignty continues to draw life from the family" and from "the notion of the sexed individual as the basis of the political." Some abducted women faced the "disciplining of sentiment according to the demands of the state" in a manner that violated their will, voided their capacities for subjectivity and agency, and forced them to re-inhabit the forms of embodied trauma that accompanied their kidnapping in the first instance.

Miriam Ticktin's examination of "medical humanism" in the case of *sans papiers*, or unauthorized migrants and refused asylum seekers in France, pivots on the "illness clause," a legal provision that has enabled some *sans papiers* to remain in France temporarily on humanitarian grounds. Despite its purported beneficence, some migrant patients end up "trading in biological integrity for political recognition" either by refusing needed treatment in order to remain sick enough to retain permission stay or, in the most extreme cases, by willingly becoming injured or infected – even with HIV – in order to establish valid grounds for a health-related humanitarian claim. Under these circumstances, damaged biology becomes a "flexible resource" that sick migrants and health care providers can leverage in an effort to stake political claims vis-à-vis the state. Humanitarianism thus emerges as an inherently political form of moral discourse, despite all protestations to the contrary, with potentially "discriminatory, even violent consequences" for its ostensible beneficiaries (see also Pandolfi this volume; Fassin this volume; James this volume; Willen this volume; Fassin 2001, 2005; Fassin and Rechtman 2009). Again medical citizenship is at issue. As Ticktin, following Agamben, writes: "the struggle to define citizenship and the borders of the nation-state is now also a struggle to define the threshold of humanity and life itself."

REFERENCES CITED

Biehl, João
   2005   Vita: Life in a Zone of Social Abandonment. Berkeley: University of California Press.
Biehl, João
   2007   Will to Live: AIDS Therapies and the Politics of Survival. Princeton: Princeton University Press.
Comaroff, Jean
   2007   Beyond Bare Life: AIDS, (Bio)Politics, and the Neoliberal Order. Public Culture 19 (1): 197–219.
Das, Veena, Arthur Kleinman, Margaret Lock, Mamphela Ramphele, and Pamela Reynolds, eds.
   2001   Remaking a World: Violence, Social Suffering, and Recovery. Berkeley: University of California Press.
Das, Veena, Arthur Kleinman, Mamphela Ramphele and Pamela Reynolds, eds.
   2000   Violence and Subjectivity. Berkeley: University of California.

Dumit, Joseph
  n.d.   Drugs for Life. Durham: Duke University Press.
Farmer, Paul
  1997   On Suffering and Structural Violence: A View from Below. In Arthur Kleinman, Veena Das, and Margaret Lock, eds., Social Suffering. Berkeley: University of California Press.
Farmer, Paul
  2003   Pathologies of Power. Berkeley: University of California Press.
Farmer, Paul
  2004   An Anthropology of Structural Violence. Current Anthropology 45(3).
Fassin, Didier
  2001   The Biopolitics of Otherness: Undocumented Foreigners and Racial Discrimination in French Public Debate. Anthropology Today 17(1): 3–7.
Fassin, Didier
  2005   Compassion and Repression: The Moral Economy of Immigration Policies in France. Cultural Anthropology 20(3): 362–87.
Fassin, Didier, Richard Rechtman
  2009   The Empire of Trauma: An Inquiry into the Condition of Victimhood. Princeton: Princeton University Press.
Foucault, Michel
  1990 [1978]   A History of Sexuality, vol. 1. New York: Vintage.
Kleinman, Arthur, Veena Das and Margaret Lock, eds.
  1997   Social Suffering. Berkeley: University of California Press.
Lock, Margaret and Vinh-Kim Nguyen
  n.d.   An Anthropology of Biomedicine. Malden, MA: Blackwell.
Nguyen, Vinh-Kim
  2005   Antiretroviral Globalism, Biopolitics, and Therapeutic Citizenship. In A. Ong and S. J. Collier, eds., Global Assemblages: Technology, Governmentality, Ethics. Oxford: Blackwell Publishers.
Nguyen, Vinh-Kim, Cyriaque Yapo Ako, Pascal Niamba, Aliou Sylla, and Issoufou Tiendrébéogo
  2007   Adherence as Therapeutic Citizenship: Impact of the History of Access to Antiretroviral Drugs on Adherence to Treatment. AIDS 21: S31–S35.
Nguyen, Vinh-Kim and Karine Peschard
  2003   Anthropology, Inequality, and disease: A Review. Annual Review of Anthropology 32: 447–74.
Petryna, Adriana
  2002   Life Exposed: Biological Citizenship after Chernobyl. Princeton: Princeton University press.
Rabinow, Paul
  1996   Essays on the Anthropology of Reason. Princeton: Princeton University Press.
Rhodes, Lorna
  2004   Total Confinement: Madness and Reason in the Maximum Security Prison. Berkeley: University of California Press.
Rose, Nikolas
  2000   The Biology of Culpability: Pathological Identity and Crime Control in a Biological Culture. Theoretical Criminology 4(1): 5–34.
Scheper-Hughes, Nancy and Phillipe Bourgois
  2004   Introduction: Making Sense of Violence. In N. Scheper-Huges and P. Bourgois, eds., Violence in War and Peace: An Anthology. Oxford, Blackwell.
Willen, Sarah S.
  2010   Citizens, "Real" Others, and "Other" Others: The Biopolitics of Otherness and the Deportation of Undocumented Migrant Workers from Tel Aviv, Israel. In N. De Genova and N. Peutz, eds., The Deportation Regime: Sovereignty, Space, and the Freedom of Movement. Durham, NC: Duke University Press.

16

Dreaming of Psychiatric Citizenship
A Case Study of Supermax Confinement

Lorna A. Rhodes

An account of oneself is always given to another. (Judith Butler, Giving an Account of Oneself)

[Supermax] has did me bad. ("Sammy Andrews")

Introduction

In March, 2001, my colleagues and I received a letter from a Washington State prisoner named Samuel Andrews[1] in which he offered himself as a research subject.

> I am writing to ask you guys to consider doing an extensive case study on me ... My situation/history is so unbelievable and complex that any study would not only be revealing but scientifically helpful ... I would like [to be] the person to initiate a campaign in getting funding for a decent prison that houses and treats prisoners very good – like me – who want to be subjected to research tests etc. ... If you talked to me and reviewed my files etc., I'd be a prime candidate for such a prison.

Andrews – who calls himself Sam or Sammy – correctly guessed that we already knew of him, for he was one of the prison system's longest-term and best-known supermax prisoners. At the time of his writing, he had been under intensive solitary confinement for an almost uninterrupted ten years.

When I later interviewed Sam, I explained that I would disguise his identity and scatter quotes in anything I wrote about him. He vigorously rejected this idea, later sending me permission to use "any/all things obtained pertaining to me ... in any/all current and/or future projects."

Until this exchange with Sam Andrews I had refrained from using the case study format in my work on prisons, in part because the circumstances of my research did not lend themselves to long-term engagement with individual inmates' lives. More importantly, I wanted to limit my complicity with the knowledge-producing practices of the prison and the conventional formats that emerge from them. As Dorothy Smith notes, "[C]ase histories and case records have become part of the knowledge basis of the professional discourse ... [and] power relations are necessary to and implicit in [their] structure" (1990: 89, 91). The examinations through which Sammy's case is

Lorna Rhodes, "Dreaming of Psychiatric Citizenship: A Case Study of Supermax Confinement." Written especially for this volume.

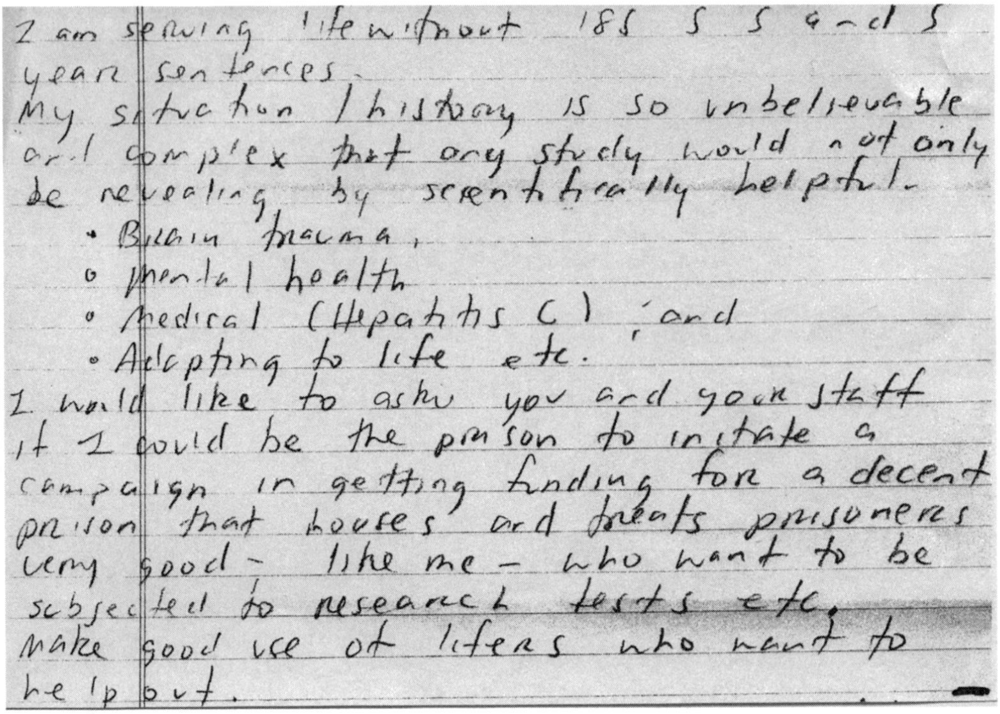

I am serving life without 185 5 5 4 and 5 year sentences.
My situation / history is so unbelievable and complex that any study would not only be revealing by scientifically helpful.
• Brain trauma,
◦ mental health
◦ medical (Hepatitis C) and
◦ Adapting to life etc.
I would like to ask you and your staff if I could be the person to initate a campaign in getting finding for a decent prison that houses and treats prisoners very good – like me – who want to be subjected to research tests etc. make good use of lifers who want to help out.

Figure 16.1   *Sam's Letter Requesting an Interview*

constructed – those "tests" he mentions – cannot be separated from their historical roots in the clinic, the asylum and the prison itself, nor can they be separated from the coercive environment in which he is held (Foucault 1979).[2] But what of the case report when it has become a self-crafting project for its subject? In this article I consider psychiatric case-making as it serves to organize and generate meaning under profoundly isolating and dehumanizing conditions; for Sam, in fact, it is precisely the enmeshment of knowledge with power that affords a small ray of hope.

In 1993 I and a group of colleagues became participants in a collaborative relationship between the University of Washington and the Washington State Department of Corrections. We have worked on initiatives to change the treatment of mentally ill prisoners and conducted research on prisoners and staff in the state's mental health and supermax units.

During the research that forms the background for this paper, I carried out interviews as part of our team and also worked alone as an ethnographer, observing everyday operations, attending meetings, and talking with prisoners and staff in supermax and mental health units in several prisons. The eighty-seven prisoners we interviewed formally were randomly selected, and Sam was not in our sample; he had met me during one of my first visits to a supermax unit, however, and wanted to be included when he heard about our interviews from other prisoners.[3]

Two related contexts frame Sam's situation as a long-term supermax prisoner. The first is the dramatic rise in the incarceration of the mentally ill over the past thirty years, with its accompanying increase in the employment of psychiatrists, psychologists and other mental health professionals in prisons. Our work, as well as recent court cases, demonstrates that mentally ill prisoners are disproportionately

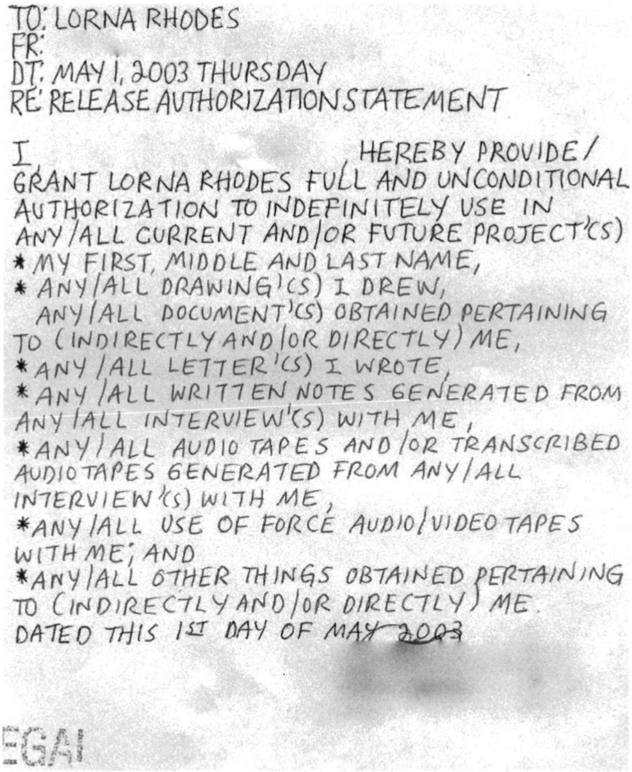

TO: LORNA RHODES
FR:
DT: MAY 1, 2003 THURSDAY
RE: RELEASE AUTHORIZATION STATEMENT

I   HEREBY PROVIDE/
GRANT LORNA RHODES FULL AND UNCONDITIONAL
AUTHORIZATION TO INDEFINITELY USE IN
ANY/ALL CURRENT AND/OR FUTURE PROJECT'(S)
* MY FIRST, MIDDLE AND LAST NAME,
* ANY/ALL DRAWING'(S) I DREW,
   ANY/ALL DOCUMENT'(S) OBTAINED PERTAINING
TO (INDIRECTLY AND/OR DIRECTLY) ME,
* ANY/ALL LETTER'(S) I WROTE,
* ANY/ALL WRITTEN NOTES GENERATED FROM
ANY/ALL INTERVIEW'(S) WITH ME,
* ANY/ALL AUDIO TAPES AND/OR TRANSCRIBED
AUDIO TAPES GENERATED FROM ANY/ALL
INTERVIEW'(S) WITH ME,
* ANY/ALL USE OF FORCE AUDIO/VIDEO TAPES
WITH ME; AND
* ANY/ALL OTHER THINGS OBTAINED PERTAINING
TO (INDIRECTLY AND/OR DIRECTLY) ME.
DATED THIS 1ST DAY OF MAY 2003

Figure 16.2 *Release Form Created by Sam*

confined in supermax prisons (Lovell et al. 2000; Human Rights Watch 2003). Sam, however, is not unambiguously "mentally ill." Rather, he falls into an indistinct zone in which he is neither accepted by psychiatry nor engaged in the various forms of "rational" bad behavior (such as fighting) that send many prisoners into intensive confinement. Prisoners like Sam have been little studied, although they often spend years in solitary as never-resolved "behavior problems." Thus the second context for understanding this case is the discourse on risk that pervades correctional management. "Behavior problems" are regarded as "risky" for the systems in which they are held and rejected by general population units because they have harmed or frightened staff and other prisoners. Though relatively few in number, these prisoners often serve to justify the existence and expansion of intensive confinement (DeMaio 2001).

My goals in this paper are twofold. First, I aim to unpack, through a single detailed example, a specific form of supermax confinement in which psychiatric knowledge figures as a protagonist but not as a solution.[4] My presentation of Sam as a case study depends on the fact that he is already a richly documented "case" within the system, and I draw on the corrections department records, psychiatric case report, and court documents he provided, as well as brief access to his full department case file.[5] Clearly these materials suggest that Sam is disturbed and a danger to others; remedies, if they exist at all, are unclear and contested. However, I do not attempt to diagnose or prescribe. Rather I hope to show the inconclusive role of diagnosis itself and the multiple contradictions that contribute to his situation. My second aim is to consider the way in which Sam is engaged with himself as a "case." Here I use his letters, poems, and drawings, some of which already existed and others created specifically for us, to show how – in an environment almost devoid of materials from which to forge an identity and with his only horizon a solitary cell – Sam finds a way to "give an account of himself to another." His case becomes a form of work, not only for the correctional workers who produce it, but for him as he embraces it and, reaching out for a form of "psychiatric citizenship" that privileges trauma, struggles to frame a coherent narrative out of irretrievable harm.

Anatomy of a Stand-off

Supermaximum prisons are specifically designed to separate prisoners from the general prison population and isolate them from one another. In Washington, seven prisons (that is, complexes of buildings making up more than one security level) include these control or "intensive management" units. Separated by razor wire and other fortifications from the main institutional environments to which they are attached, these "prisons within prisons" operate tightly controlled, technology-intensive regimes.[6] Supermax prisoners are confined for twenty-three or more hours a day in small single cells and removed – cuffed, tethered and under escort – only for brief showers or solitary exercise. Their lives are characterized by lack of physical and mental stimulation, minimal social contact, and extreme dependence on prison staff. Defiant or disturbed prisoners are subjected to forcible removal from their cells ("cell extraction"), the use of pepper spray or electronic controls (tasers, electric shields), confinement in restraint chairs, and the imposition of "isolation time" during which they receive no exercise ("yard") or showers. Surveillance is intense, and food, yard time, showers, toilet paper, and all other items are delivered – sometimes erratically or arbitrarily – based on the schedules and attitudes of staff. The relationship between supermax assignment and prisoners' status and behavior is complex, but in general the seriousness of the crime does not determine supermax placement.

When I interviewed Sam he was living in the control unit of a new prison outside an isolated rural town. Accompanied by a retired prison official, I interviewed him in a visiting booth that had been specially remodeled for the occasion with a new, steel-reinforced ceiling. Staff at the prison considered him exceptionally unpredictable and violent, and Sam had never had a visitor. Cuffed and wearing the white jumpsuit of the control unit prisoner, he was brought by two officers to his side of the booth. As soon as he had signed the consent form and given permission for access to his record, he gazed at us intently through the thick Plexiglas window and said:

> It's too bad I can't sit with you and point out some things in my central file that I think you would find very interesting … you'll see a pattern … They [prison staff] make promises and then they don't hold 'em and instead of making themselves look like a liar they will *poke poke poke poke poke* and then I will *buckle* and then – I'm not saying my behavior is justified – but then I will buckle and then it justifies them not honoring their promise and it puts it all upon me and it's been like that for ten years.

Sammy's central file ran to nine fat volumes, taking up a whole shelf in the records room. It contained the record of his brief incarcerations at the ages of twenty and twenty-two, descriptions of the double murder he committed shortly after his second release, and his steadily worsening relations with prison staff over subsequent years. One item, the computerized record maintained by the corrections department, was eighty pages long. This fragment shows Sam committing infractions – "threatening" staff, "interfering" with staff, "throwing" – every day during mid-December of 2001. Years of identical entries follow one another; as he provokes his keepers they, in turn, bury him in isolation.[7]

The correctional rationale for supermax confinement is that it addresses bad behavior in prison. The reality is that much confusion and obfuscation surrounds this form of incarceration, with some prisoners undergoing long terms of isolation that are unconnected to their behavior. In Sam's case, his chronically unpredictability, violent outbursts, and bad

12/17/01	558	STAFF INTERFER.	N	120	120	APPLIED	DENY GCT ISOLATION 10	CBCC
12/18/01	506	THREATENING	N	30	30	APPLIED	DENY GCT 30 ISOLATION 10	CBCC
12/18/01	506	THREATENING	N	30	30	APPLIED	DENY GCT 30 ISOLATION 10	CBCC
12/19/01	506	THREATENING	N	90	90	APPLIED	DENY GCT 90 ISOLATION 10	CBCC
12/19/01	508	THROWING OBJECTS	N	60	60	APPLIED	DENY GCT 60 ISOLATION 10	CBCC
12/19/01	558	STAFF INTERFER.	N	20	20	APPLIED	DENY GCT 20 ISOLATION 10	CBCC
12/19/01	717	REFUSAL/SAFETY	N	0	0	APPLIED	DENY GCT ISOLATION	CBCC
12/19/01	717	REFUSAL/SAFETY	N	0	0	APPLIED	DENY GCT ISOLATION	CBCC
12/19/01	720	FLOODING	N	0	0	APPLIED	DENY GCT	CBCC

Figure 16.3 *Sam's Department of Corrections Record, December 2001*

reputation throughout the state system meant that risk-averse prison officials would not consider returning him to general population. And in the meantime, everything about supermax has become personal to him. Everything feels like a "poke." He recounts frequent incidents in which "I [felt] I was being messed with," "I got mad," and "I went to war with the guards." As he described these events:

It's after so much pressure they put on me and it's almost like my blood is absolutely boiling and I get so much strength built up in me. I have to get it out of my system. I try to avoid getting gassed [with pepper-spray] and getting gooned ... but mostly I want to fight them people that are hurting me.

The more Sam fights, the more he loses. Yet fighting seems to him the only way to preserve what little autonomy he has, and thus he tightens his isolation and punishment

This stand-off between Sam and the "system" occurs in parallel with a systemic contradiction. In theory the Washington prisons provide psychological services that could redefine his behavior as a sign of illness and enable him to receive treatment in specialized mental health facilities. But these sites are overwhelmed with the seriously mentally ill and their staffs vigorously resist admitting prisoners like Sam, whom they regard as predatory and dangerous to weaker inmates. It was in this context that administrators ordered a psychological assessment for Sam, hoping that it would provide ammunition for a plan to send him to an out-of-state prison.[8] A prison psychologist, Dr. Stratton, interviewed and tested him over a four month period, creating a 45-page, densely written, "Neuropsychological Evaluation." Although the assessment was conducted in an environment of surveillance and constraint, it also constituted one of the few opportunities Sam ever had to talk at length with another person.

My Beautiful Report

When I interviewed him in 2002, Sammy had been in possession of his neuropsychological report for more than five years. In fact, since official papers are one of the few possessions supermax inmates are allowed, he had lived in close proximity to it in an environment almost devoid of other sources of stimulation. Sam said:

> Dr. Stratten wrote probably one of the most fair reports on me, her neuropsychological report. Because of the way I look and talk, people write that there's nothing wrong with this guy. But she said my first problem was post traumatic stress syndrome. I [also] had other diagnoses like depression in remission, I had a characteristic like behavioral problem,

and some other names. Most of the doctors see me under bad terms and they go, this guy he's just a trouble maker, he's no good. They don't never dig under surface.

In her report Dr. Stratton provides results from her extensive psychological testing, including the Hare Psychopathy Checklist (with a score of 30),[9] the MMPI (Minnesota Multiphasic Personality Inventory), and the Personality Assessment Inventory. Of the results of this last test she notes: "Mr. Andrews tended to endorse items that made him look bad and represented extremely bizarre or unlikely symptoms ... it is likely that he was producing a 'cry for help' ... [but] even though his pathology may be overrepresented on this profile, he appeared to be experiencing marked distress and severe impairment in functioning. He is depicted as a person who is angry, resentful, impulsive ... and sensitive in social interactions." Dr. Stratton quotes

Figure 16.4 *Supermax cell with box of official papers (author photo)*

04-27-77 (10) Adjustment Reaction to Childhood

09-19-78 (11) Unsocialized Aggressive Reaction of Childhood

01-14-82 (15) Simple Schizophrenia
Bipolar

03-08-82 (15) Socialized, Nonaggressive Conduct Disorder
Parent-Child Problem

03-09-82 (15) Conduct Disorder, Socialized, Nonaggresive
Adjustment Disorder with Depressed Mood
Parent child Problem
Dysthymic Disorder
Bipolar

07-21-82 (15) Previous diagnosis of Schizophrenia was completely inappropriate

11-01-82 (16) Conduct Disorder Socialized Nonaggressive
Rule out: Major Affective Disorder

09-19-83 (16) Borderline Personality Disorders with features of Narcissism and Aggressivity

10-17-84 (18) Schizophrenic Disorder, Residual Type

03-03-86 (19) Intermittent Explosive Disorder
Bordeline Personality (probable)

08-13-86 (19) Axis I: Bipolar Disorder, Mixed. Intermittent Explosive Disorder.
Axis II: Histrionic Personality Disorder (with Paranoid features)
Axis III: Rule out Organic Brain Syndrome

08-14-86 (19) Axis I: Atypical Psychosis; Rule out Bipolar Disorder.
Axis II: Borderline Traits; Rule out Disorder

08-26-86 (19) Axis II: Mixed Personality Disorder with Antisocial and Histrionic Features

05-28-88 (21) Axis I: Polysubstance Abuse and Intermittent Explosive Disorder
Axis II: Antisocial Disorder, by history

07-01-88 (21) Cocaine Abuse
Mixed Personality Disorder with Antisocial, Histrionic, and
Boederline Features

09-21-89 (22) Axis II: Mixed Personality Disorder with Antisocial and Histrionic Features

09-22-89 (22) Axis I: Alcohol Abuse; Cannabis Abuse; Polysubstance Dependence
Axis II: Antisocial Personality Disorder with Histrionic Features

12-15-92 (26) Borderline Personality Disorder with strong
Passive-Aggressive Features and Antisocial Personality Disorder

09-26-95 (28) Axis I: Intermittent Explosive Disorder
Post Traumatic Stress Disorder, Chronic
Alcohol Abuse, in Full Remission, by History
Cocaine Abuse, in Full Remission, by History
Other Substance Abuse, in Full Remission, by History
R/O   Major Depressive Disorder, Recurrent, in Partial Remission
Axis II: Borderline Personality Disorder with Histrionic, Narcissistic, and
Dependent Features
Axis III: Unknown
Axis IV: Problems with Primary Support System
Problems with Legal System/Crime
Other Psychosocial Problems
Axis V: GAF 51

As these diagnoses are reviewed, some sense of his development is gained. The travesty of these intervening years is that had the earliest professionals known then what is now known (re: working with trauma victims, etc.) Mr. Andrews might have been an entirely different individual.

Figure 16.5 *Diagnostic summary in Sam's neuropsychological report*

extensively from previous evaluations going back to Sam's first hospitalization at the age of ten, producing a palimpsest of the voices and diagnoses of other professionals. I will turn to the portrayal of other aspects of Sam's history in the next section, but first I want to show how the report represents and extends his diagnostic profile.

In the final three pages of Dr. Stratton's report she lists all the diagnoses Sam has ever received, ending with her own. These pages not only reflect complex symptoms but also changes occurring in the diagnostic system itself as the *Diagnostic and Statistical Manual of Mental Disorders (DSM)* is reorganized in the mid-1980s around a system of "axes." On Axis I (major mental disorders), Sam has problems that are considered mental illness – *states* of being that might lend themselves to change with medication or treatment. On Axis II, Sam's behavior is understood in terms of personality disorder – *traits* of character based on the older, more psychoanalytically oriented diagnostic system that the DSM replaced (APA: 2000).[10] These are regarded as intractable, if not impossible to change. Sam's long supermax confinement results from his position between the cracks of these two ways of looking at him. Acknowledged as disturbed but without the potential for any kind of amelioration, he has fallen into an extreme form of what Nikolas Rose calls the "continuous and unending management of permanently problematic persons in the name of ... safety" (Rose 2002).

At the end of her report, Dr. Stratton offers her own view of Sam's diagnostic picture. I will come back to her final conclusion, but in order to understand why this report had no effect on Sam's confinement, we need to consider her recommendations. She does not include antisocial personality disorder in her summation, but this is what she says:

Mr. Andrews is certainly in need of therapy. He needs to resolve both his early sexual trauma and the abuse/neglect at the hands of both of his biological parents. His personality structure/traits that have developed as a result ... are such that they/he would require extensive, frequent and intense individual psychotherapy to resolve ... [But] all the aforementioned

suggestions for treatment are further complicated by the fact that Mr. Andrews is imbued with such a level of psychopathy (Hare, 1985)[11] that he is unlikely to benefit from therapy without first altering his ideas/stance. This certainly presents a double bind for him.

In a note to me and my colleagues, Sam gives his version of this bind:

I believe that IMU is a catch 22, a no-win situation. It breaks inmates it is not meant for and its makes inmates it is meant for. When I say it makes them I mean, it strengthens their resolve. You're damned if you do and damned if you don't.

That is, supermax (or "intensive management") units harm the mentally ill – who do not belong in them – while strengthening the character disordered for whom they are intended.[12]

Writing about the development of the contemporary case study format in the late nineteenth and early twentieth centuries, Elizabeth Lunbeck notes that "The case, in which the facts of psychiatry were embedded, was ... a heuristic fiction that was at the same time real" (Lunbeck 1994, discussing the writings of the psychiatrist E. E. Southard circa 1912). One way this reality manifests for Sam is in the matter of simple attention. The supermax produces an impoverished social economy in which attention is the scarcest of resources. Staff is invested in efficiency and rewarded for withholding themselves from inmates. But as Sam, cuffed to a metal table, sits with Dr. Stratton he undergoes a 30 hour process of interviewing and testing that both "pins him down in his individuality" (Foucault 1979) and expands his world.

This attention also emerges in the report itself, in which we see a layered – both conflicted and complementary – accretion of diagnostic labels as psychiatrists and psychologists work with Sam at various stages in his life. As a child and teenager he inspires a disagreement over whether he is schizophrenic, with a resolution that settles gradually on conduct disorder, borderline personality disorder, and the possibility of organic damage. In its filtering and congealing of these possibilities, the report becomes a "work of abstraction," a heuristic

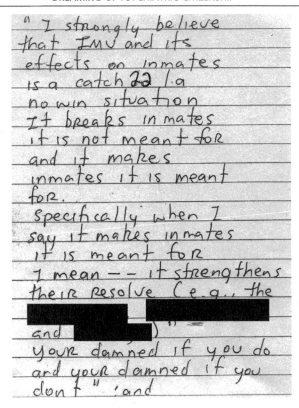

"I strongly believe that IMU and its effects on inmates is a catch 22 I.a no win situation It breaks inmates it is not meant for and it makes inmates it is meant for. Specifically when I say it makes inmates it is meant for I mean —— it strengthens their resolve (e.g., the ▓▓▓▓▓▓▓▓ and ▓▓▓▓)" your damned if you do and your damned if you don't" 'and

Figure 16.6 *Catch 22*

fiction that organizes events around the individual and highlights those elements that confirm certain diagnostic presuppositions (Smith 1990: 92).[13] This relationship of "looping" is what gives the case its weight as both expertise and common-sense.[14]

Dr. Stratton's report makes clear that only one side of Sam's being – the same side that is broken by supermax confinement – might be helped by long-term therapy. The other side, defined by psychopathy and damned by his score on the Hare (a score precisely at the marker for the disorder), is both strengthened by supermax and necessarily suited to it.[15] Thus she is saying to the administrators who are her official readers: do not even think of returning Sam to the general (prison) population, and use the system's scarce resources to help, not him, but the mentally ill.

Why, then, does Sam so cherish his report? He writes in a poem:

I ... [am able to] speak only the words
I've been programmed all my life to speak ...
Chains attached to my limbs everywhere I go
Might as well be attached to my mind
Because it doesn't feel like I have one of my
own

For Sam, the report "speaks," in a way that bypasses, at least in part, his sense of having been programmed, chained, and left with nothing but rage. To understand why, we need first to consider its account of his life and then revisit the diagnostic resolution offered by Dr. Stratton's effort of summation.

Anointed with Bad Karma

Sam lives in an environment governed by a powerful ideology of "personal choice." For the prison workers around him, as well as for

Figure 16.7 *Table with "bullring" where Sam was interviewed by Dr. Stratton (author photo)*

the U.S. press and public, criminals are exemplars of autonomy, individualism, and free will. No matter how seemingly senseless the acts that brought them to prison, these are understood to represent "free" and rational choices. Attending to the circumstances – familial, economic, or political – under which such choices occur is considered by many tantamount to "coddling" or being "soft on crime." It is only in this context that we can understand Sam's attachment to the picture of his life underwritten by Dr. Stratton's assertion that his "complex symptoms/behaviors [are] a result of numerous and diverse influences."

"Influence"

In a poem entitled "Anointed with Bad Karma," Sam speaks of the "unimaginable emotional monsters" that torment him with a "constant reminder that all things are not forgot." Much of his psychological report catalogues this negative karmic territory. He was

first hospitalized before the age of ten, already neglected and abused by his mother, rejected by his father, raped by his father's friends, and possibly suffering head injuries. He has spent all but two or three years since in foster homes, hospitals, youth detention or prison, going to prison initially at age twenty for theft.

These bleak facts recur in the report as Dr. Stratton quotes from the psychiatrists and psychologists who described Sam during his childhood and teenage years. This note was written when he was 11:

Sammy is ... a child who has had virtually no opportunity to develop adequate bonding with a mothering person from infancy onwards. His mother ... can recall little of his early life because, she says, "I was real sick ... " Intense anger and frustration around issues of controls when Sammy was two or three has continued to be a focal point ... Frequent shifts of the caretaker role from mother to natural father and on to hospitalizations, residential care, and home care have certainly played a role in distorting the structuralization of ego and super ego components as the boy has matured.

Here is a later entry, explaining Sam's continuing hospitalizations, consignment to special programs for wayward teens, and extreme violence toward staff and other patients.

At no time in Sammy's life has he experienced a stable environment maintained by reliable parenting figures ... Therefore [he] has not been able to develop any stable internal objects, nor to internalize any limits or standards for behavior. Basic trust does not exist and he consequently has developed a manipulative, ruthlesslessly competitive and opportunistic lifestyle that enables him to survive, but puts him in constant conflict with his environment. It is possible that this sociopathic character has developed around a core of primitive ideation and poor reality testing, which results in severe anxiety and further prevents the conditions that would permit the development of object attachments.

Borrowing from Erving Goffman, we could say that Sam's social identity was spoiled long before he knew he had one (1963). Identity, as Judith Butler points out, always takes shape not only in relation others' influence but also in relation to the requirement – produced by social relations themselves – that one "give an account of oneself" (2005). Most of us do not have in our possession a professional account of our early development. Sam not only has such an account, but one that speaks of him in semi-adult terms as someone with a "ruthless lifestyle" before the age of fifteen. At this point any effort of self-crafting in which he engages must take this report as a resource. But what in it can offer him a sense of value?

The bad mother

Dr. Stratton writes that Sam is unsure of his biological father and was the fourth of six children born to his mother who was, during his childhood, a "bad person, a prostitute." He tells Dr. Stratton, "I stay away from my mother because I can't stand her ... she's wicked." He thinks about "taking her out" because he now believes "that would have solved most of my problems ... I still fantasize about this." He says he "wishes he had not hurt innocent

people but [that he] had hurt somebody who had been guilty of something."

Sam draws an explicit connection between his experience of his mother and his relationship to the Department of Correction.

I've done months in the strip cells because *they've* started something but they want *me* to learn a lesson, [they want to] *make* me learn. That's kind of like what my mom did and I'm real resistant to that now 'cause I wasn't resistant [then] ... She would make me stay on the front porch all night 'cause she didn't want me in the house, she singled me out like that to go sleep on the floor in the back room, she was very violent. I don't understand why she did what she did. I was her convenient punching bag. Just like I don't understand DOC, it's very, very similar. A lot of what she did to me DOC does on a bigger scale now but now I can stand up for myself. I do get mad, my anger is being pulled back from when I was a kid. My current anger it's all mixed so like my blood boils I mean I get it all out. I was certainly put on that assembly line for a manufactured human monster.

The child who was excluded, confined, and tormented by all-powerful adults becomes an adult excluded, confined and tormented by an all-powerful institution. Inserted into circuits of hostility then, he perpetuates them now. He knows it – and has perhaps had enough contact with mental staff to have heard of the compulsion to repeat – yet he cannot extricate himself from the bad mother that is supermax. About his second short incarceration as a young adult he says, "I told them don't let me out of prison because I was so angry and so mentally disturbed. I said please don't let me out because I am going to kill ... If I could go back and do it over I wouldn't have did what I done [but] I just know there were a lot [of] influences."

The crime

Sam has spent almost none of his adult life outside of juvenile facilities or prisons. In the brief interlude after he begged not to be let out, he lived a wildly disorganized life characterized by confused and hostile relations with others, unsuccessful efforts to obtain psychiatric help, and a deep fear that his negative trajectory was unstoppable. He imagines, in fact, that it could have been even worse, and that he might have become the kind of serial killer he had read about. "I used to go out late and night and walk and walk and walk. Deep down inside I feared I could go on a serial murder spree, maybe [of] child molesters to get back at what happened to me as a kid. I thought that maybe I could become something like that that I didn't want to become."

Instead, he went on a less extended killing spree whose motivation still eludes him.

> So suddenly it is as if I am in a dream, watching over myself. I go driving and drinking ... I head out for a crime spree. At first I got it in my head that I am going to make a list of everyone who did me wrong and kill them one by one. [But] in my state of mind I couldn't ... find anyone else to kill ... so I drove to a [convenience store] ... I said give me all the money, which he did – then I shot at him once and missed ... I walked up to where he was laying on the floor and shot him in the head again.

Sam went on to murder a second convenience store clerk, then drove to the sheriff's office and turned himself in.

It is clear from Dr. Stratton's report and from Sam's telling of the crime that although he revisits it compulsively he is confused about responsibility. "I'm not tormented by it," he tells me, "because it's easier for me to blame everybody else. I guess when you do something horrendous like that you don't want to accept it." To Dr. Stratton he says that he knows "someone is guilty" but he is uncertain just who that is. Despite his unusual access to childhood sources, his account breaks up and becomes opaque (Butler 2005: 38) just at the point of its most painful revelation. As Sam describes an unhealed inability to recognize himself in his acts, all he can conclude is that "a lot has been done to me."

The Manufactured Human Monster

In her description of Boston Psychopathic Hospital in the early twentieth century, Lunbeck notes that the "case" emerged simultaneously on three fronts: as a description of a real, living person; as a life story rendered into narrative by social workers and psychiatrists; and as

an "exemplary manifestation" of pathology (1994: 131). Sammy clings to his years-old, "beautiful" evaluation for all these ways in which it allows him to be a person, but especially to his status as an "exemplary manifestation." The idiom of psychology becomes a resource that allows him to project a lost self – a generic, different self – into the dismal expanse of his future. If we return to Dr. Stratton's final summation, we see how her insertion of Post Traumatic Stress Disorder into the list of diagnoses suggests both retrieval and irreversibility.

> As these diagnoses are reviewed some sense of his development is gained. The travesty of the intervening years is that had the earlier professionals known then what is known now, Andrews might have been an entirely different individual.

It is this comment that is the source of Sam's attachment to his report.

> Dr. Stratton says it beautifully: Had they known how to work with trauma victims of sexual and physical abuse when they were treating Andrews as a juvenile and young kid – if they knew back then what they know now, Mr. Andrews would have been an entirely different individual. Alls I can say is when my mom didn't want me she just threw me into the system and the system don't care. I just went through the machineries of the system – what you've got here is what the system has created.

Abandoning the diminutive and becoming "Mr. Andrews" to himself, here Sam finds the one point of redemption in his past. Of all the diagnoses in the DSM, PTSD is the most overtly social. It references a specific rather than a non-specific past, one in which, as Allan Horowitz notes, "environmental causes can lead to dysfunctional psychological mechanisms" (2002:30). PTSD offers Sam a quasi-middle-class deliverance from what he describes as "stress" that might be relieved by the "healing process" of therapy. He is not merely culpable, for he might have been otherwise. Echoing Dr. Stratton, he says, "If I knew [then] what I know now ... I would be out on the streets doing something productive and living a life and married with children. Psychology and all that."

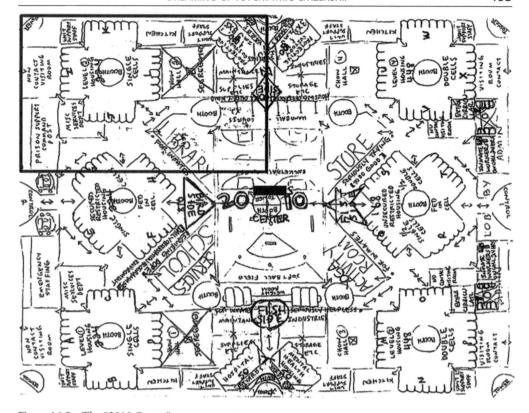

Figure 16.8   *The "2010 Center"*

Nikolas Rose uses the term "anti-citizen" to describe how we represent those whose conduct is "thought to arise from a diminution of self-control, reasonableness, maturity [and] judgment" (2000: 18).[16] Almost everything in Sam's environment points to his position as an anti-citizen – someone both profoundly excluded and, at the same time, made to hold still as an icon of the risk posed by dangerous "others." But by naming him a "trauma victim" and offering PTSD as that which connects him, however tenuously, to something beyond himself, Dr. Stratton offers a narrow opening through which Sam can claim what Lauren Berlant calls "traumatic citizenship" (Berlant 1997).[17] Although psychiatric classification has worked mostly to deny him any kind of coherent treatment, and although he cannot escape the constant reiteration of his culpability, here he finds some possibility for social membership. Provided with an explanation

for his bad "choice," he can offer himself to us as a contribution to the larger world of science.

Complementing the diagnosis of trauma as an antidote to the position of anti-citizen is a drawing Sam sent me shortly before my interview with him. Here he imagines a perfect prison, named for himself, that extends the panoptical interior in which he spends his days. On the back he has written about the "program" such a prison should follow.

This is the "decent prison" of his letter – a huge facility offering both intensified surveillance and opportunities for softball and yoga, the very space and movement Sammy is denied. This fantastical prison represents his request for something better while at the same time suggesting a totalizing identification with the prison's structure and administrative preoccupations, including a replication of its division of the weak from the strong. This is, however, a

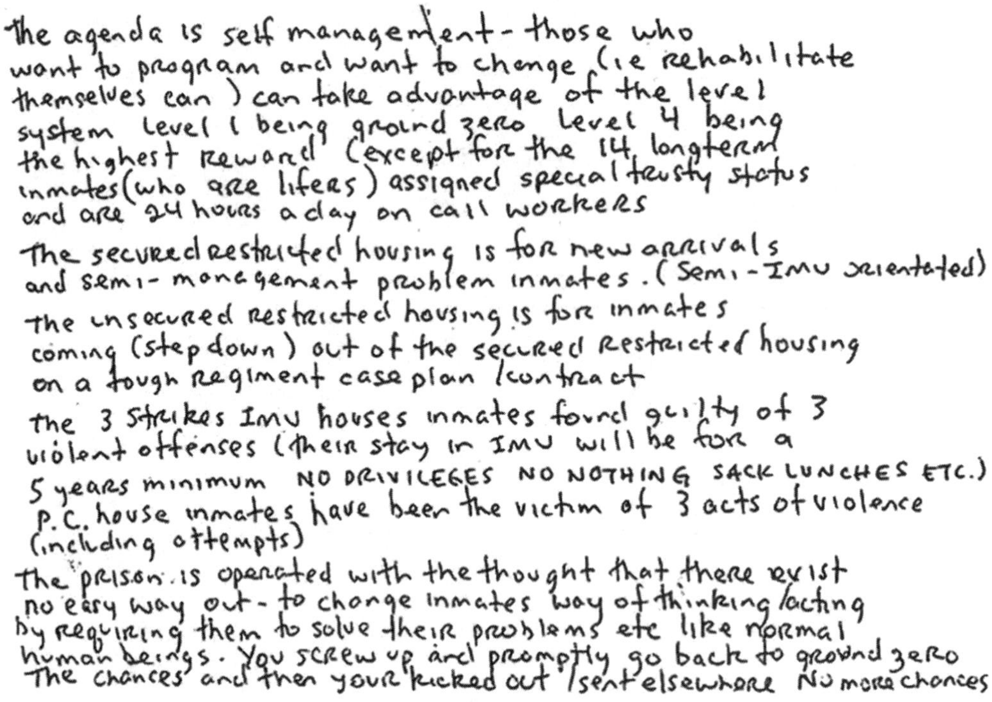

The agenda is self management - those who
wont to program and want to change (ie rehabilitate
themselves can) can take advantage of the level
system level 1 being ground zero level 4 being
the highest reward (except for the 14 longterm
inmates (who are lifers) assigned special trusty status
and are 24 hours a day on call workers

The secured restricted housing is for new arrivals
and semi-management problem inmates. (Semi-IMU orientated)
The unsecured restricted housing is for inmates
coming (step down) out of the secured restricted housing
on a tough regiment case plan /contract

the 3 strikes IMU houses inmates found guilty of 3
violent offenses (their stay in IMU will be for a
5 years minimum NO PRIVILEGES NO NOTHING SACK LUNCHES ETC.)
P.C. house inmates have been the victim of 3 acts of violence
(including attempts)

The prison is operated with the thought that there exist
no easy way out - to change inmates way of thinking/acting
by requiring them to solve their problems etc like normal
human beings. You screw up and promptly go back to ground zero
The chances and then your kicked out /sent elsewhere No more chances

Figure 16.9 *Text describing the 2010 Center's "program"*

Conclusion

In the end, the state of Washington State found a solution of sorts. Sam Andrews was transferred to a federal prison about a year after my interview with him and given a chance to extricate himself from his toxic engagement with a system in which he was all too well known. He wrote that he liked it, and that he hoped eventually to enter a program for personality-disordered prisoners. But this specific, local resolution does not tell us much; there are regime even more punitive than the one he is in. His descriptive note insists, in fact, that here there will be no second chances, only "no more choices" if "you screw up." Sam offers this vision to an imagined audience as a contribution to a meaningful future in which he might be trusted precisely, and only, because he has so thoroughly internalized the terms of his own captivity.

many Sams in the national prison complex – suffering in isolation, hard to classify or place, and living indefinitely between the cracks of psychiatric and correctional management.[18]

Sam's story suggests that we might organize our thinking about such prisoners into three domains.

The institutional stand-off

Sam is in a particularly stark, no-exit bind, the catch-22 of his letter, in which the very things that most trap him are also most "strengthened" by his confinement. The fortified ceiling of the visiting booth is symbolic of the way in which the prison environment has been progressively "hardened" in recent decades, becoming increasingly mechanical, punitive, and technologically driven. At the same time, in a toxic feedback loop, Sam has settled into the chronic reactivity, impulsive violence, and "war" with staff endemic among many who are locked down and institutionalized. We can see in

Sam's case the details of how self-reinforcing this situation can become. On the one hand, in the absence of psychiatric or other intervention, the most available identity is that of the anti-citizen, fully volitional and folded into the larger discourse on rational choice that pervades the prison complex. And on the other, the prison environment itself is internalized as a desired, if dissociated, "other." Whether a prisoner takes up the side of "boiling" rage or of captain in a perfect prison – or, in Sam's case, both at once – everything he does confirms that he belongs where he is. It is not hard to see how a prisoner caught in such predicament becomes ever less able to manage even the most minimal social interaction.

The diagnostic dead end

Much of the literature on the mentally ill in supermax emphasizes psychosis: prolonged isolation either exacerbates or produces hallucinations and other symptoms of severe mental disorder. While there are many issues surrounding the removal of the mentally ill from supermax, the fact of psychosis and the obvious harmfulness of isolation to vulnerable individuals tend to be indisputable. This is perhaps best illustrated by the disturbing examples presented in a recent court case regarding the Wisconsin Supermax at Boscobel and the subsequent ruling that mentally ill prisoners be removed from that facility.[19]

However, while Sam is clearly made worse by isolation, he does not "qualify" as mentally ill. Instead psychiatry – broadly speaking – contributes to the bind he is in by bracketing personality disorder and minimizing the possibility for treatment. The psychological practices of interviewing and testing that document a history of trauma may offer at least a partial explanation for his behavior but, since he is not "truly" mentally ill, they lead only to a dead end. Perhaps the intractability of this convergence of the correctional and clinical should alert us to questions of framing. Is this the only option for thinking about individuals like Sam? Might there be alternative settings and alternative theories that could safely loosen the extremes of his captivity?

Psychiatric citizenship

Writing about violent men, the psychiatrist John Gilligan says that like "a cat on a hot tin roof" they engage in "an endless and futile attempt to find a spot comfortable enough so that [they] can finally come to rest" (1996: 58). Sam – a double murderer abandoned to a conscience he can barely access – appropriates his dossier in hopes that he can find in it a "resting spot" as a victim of trauma and a contributor to science. In doing so he projects an audience for his account of himself – not only me, but the wider world represented by me, my colleagues, and the very fact that we were studying the hidden world in which he lives. His presentation of himself to that imagined audience assumes, not just the existence of an "outside," but the outside as an inherently moral sphere. In that sphere he is a rights-bearing individual fully capable of informed consent. And what he consents to – what he wants us to know – is that his engagement with psychiatric knowledge has given him potential access to a form of social membership, however limited. Using the terms of a psychiatric diagnosis that offers meaning by acknowledging social causation, he addresses us as fellow citizens while implicitly acknowledging our power to withhold our attention.

Is this not also the larger issue represented by the supermax prison? The withholding of meaning and attention, the wholesale abandonment of excluded populations, and the construction of dissociative, madness-inducing environments is premised, in part, on the suppression of any narrative but the one that privileges individual "accountability" and a neo-Darwinian fitness. Sam's story and situation are extreme, but they point to something fundamental: while it is possible to build antisocial environments for which antisocial people are presumably fit, doing so does not address the fact that even the most disturbed individual is ultimately a social being. Sam's "case" suggests that only by taking that into account can we hope to imagine other possibilities.

ACKNOWLEDGEMENTS

I thank "Sam Andrews" for his willingness to tell his story as well as the many staff members and officials of the Washington Department of Corrections who have supported my work. A number of audiences have helped me think about earlier versions of this article; I particularly want to thank those at the Department of Social Medicine at Harvard, the "Psyences" group of the Program for the History of Science, Princeton, and the Department of History and Social Medicine, University of California at San Francisco. I am grateful to the Criminal Justice Roundtable at the University of Chicago, especially Sharon Dolovitch, for their comments, and to David Lovell and Marianne McNabb for generous assistance with this project.

NOTES

1   The names in this chapter are pseudonyms. In order to maintain the confidentiality of others I do not follow "Sam Andrew's" request that I use his real name; the other aspects of his story are not disguised.

2   I do not mean to extend this critical perspective on the case study to every situation, particularly when – unlike in prisons – coercion is not an issue. As Flyvbjerg notes, "a particularly 'thick' and hard-to-summarize narrative … is often a sign [of] a particularly rich problematic" (2006: 237).

3   The University of Washington/Department of Corrections Mental Health Collaboration continued through 2002, directed by David Allen and with David Lovell as full-time investigator. Human subjects approval was given to the research aspects of the project by the University of Washington and the Washington Department of Corrections. Our work was carried out in male-only facilities, with interviews conducted in visiting booths and audio recorded. Several factors made for difficulty gathering in-depth case material on prisoners, including the number of men we interviewed, the constant churning of inmates within the state system, and the difficulties involved in arranging and conducting prison interviews under supermax conditions. See Rhodes 2002, 2004, 2007, and 2009 for more extended discussion of the environment, effects, and implications of supermax prisons.

4   "Psychiatry" as used here stands for the whole of prison mental health treatment. Psychologists do the kind of testing Sam was subjected to; however it is psychiatry that supplies the diagnostic system important to his story as well as the medication that marks him as untreatable.

5   I do not describe here the responses and interpretations of the prison officers, mental health workers (other than those who figure in his own account), and administrators charged with keeping Sam over his long incarceration. Instead I have chosen to tell his story out of the materials he himself offered, both to honor his request and because I hope to protect the confidentiality and safety of those who have had contact with him. See Rhodes 2004, especially chapter 5, for a more complete description of the assumptions underlying the treatment of prisoners like Sam.

6   The contemporary explosion of supermax prisons raises numerous questions beyond the scope of this chapter, including whether and how the technological regime they impose is spreading to lower-security facilities and to other countries, the ways in which they harm those who are not mentally ill, and how assignment to and length of time in supermax is determined. It is not clear how many prisoners are confined to supermax nationwide nor do we know the average length of stay; the difficulty is compounded because supermax facilities are used for short-term as well as long-term stays (in correctional terms, for both "administrative" and "disciplinary" segregation). At the time of my interview with Sam Andrews, Washington State had held about twenty inmates in supermax for more than five years; the average length of stay for Washington prisoners on administrative segregation (not the same as all supermax prisoners) is about two years. At the national level, Herman Wallace and Albert Woodfox – confined for over 30 years at the Louisiana State Penitentiary – have spent the longest time in solitary confinement. See, e.g., Rhodes, 2004, 2009; DeMaio, 2001; Kurki and Morris 2001.

7   On Sam's record, "GCT" refers to good conduct time; the numbers refer to time added to his prison term, which are recorded even if an

inmate is serving a life sentence. Sam was an "intensive management" prisoner assigned to the state's various supermax (or, in Washington, "intensive management") units; in theory this status is administrative, not punitive, and "isolation" was being added as punishment. "Isolation" means that a prisoner continues to be held in his supermax cell but is denied his daily out-of-cell time for yard and showers; prolonged isolation involves periodic suspension to allow for occasional showers and limited exercise.

8 Such transfers, though difficult to arrange, are not uncommon for those prisoners who become "problems" – for a variety of reasons – within a particular system. In Sam's case, he had filed a lawsuit against Washington State that resulted in a strong recommendation from the court to seek out of state placement.

9 Robert Hare is a Canadian psychologist who has written extensively about psychopathy (an unofficial and extreme variant of antisocial personality disorder). His theories about the disorder are behind many popular representations of "psychopathic killers" and his diagnostic "checklist" is widely used in corrections. See http://www.hare.org/ Accessed July 14, 2009.

10 For a fuller picture of the use of the *DSM* in prisons see Rhodes 2004. For an anthropologist's interpretation of the *DSM* classification of the personality disorders, see Nuckolls 1992.

11 Probably Hare 1985.

12 Sammy participates here in a distinction – and set of assumptions about what is and is not "mental illness" – that is pervasive in prison systems and criminal justice more generally. These diagnostic categories are enacted not only through assessments such as Dr. Stratton but also in spatial and labor arrangements that reinforce their seeming inevitability. See Rhodes 2004, Kurki and Morris 2001.

13 Both Smith (1990) and Lunbeck (1994) note that the case study format took its contemporary shape in institutional contexts in which auxiliary professionals (social workers and psychologists, especially) reported to physicians.

14 For discussion of looping effects see Ian Hacking (1986) and Erving Goffman (1961).

15 More on the meaning of psychopathy in the prison context can be found in Rhodes (2002) and Toch (1998).

16 In variations on this theme, Jonathan Simon writes of the "waste management prison" (2007) and Ruth Wilson Gilmore describes the racialized policies of the US incarceration complex as exposure to premature death (2007).

17 Berlant's definition of citizenship is helpful for understanding Sam's interest in diagnosis as a form of relationship: "By citizenship I refer ... both to the legal sense in which persons are juridically subject to the law's privileges and protections by virtue of national identity status but also the experiential, vernacular context in which people customarily understand their relation to state power and social membership" (Berlant 2002:108).

18 For accounts of prisoners similar to Sam see Butterfield (1995) and Porter (1998).

19 Jones 'El v. Berg (164 F. Supp. 2d1096, 1098 [W.D. Wis. 2001].

REFERENCES

American Psychiatric Association
2000 Diagnostic and Statistical Manual of Mental Disorders: DSM-IV-TR. Washington, DC: American Psychiatric Association.

Berlant, Lauren
1997 The Queen of America Goes to Washington City. Raleigh: Duke University Press.

Berlant, Lauren
2002 The Subject of True Feeling: Pain, Privacy, and Politics. *In* Wendy Brown and Janet Halley, eds., Left Legalism, Left Critique. Durham, NC: Duke University Press, pp. 105–33.

Butler, Judith
2005 Giving an Account of Oneself. New York: Fordham University Press.

Butterfield, Fox
1995 All God's Children: The Bosket Family and the American Tradition of Violence. New York: Avon.

DeMaio, J. R.
2001 If You Build It, They Will Come: The Threat of Overclassification in Wisconsin's Supermax Prison. Wisconsin Law Review: 207–47.

Flyvbjerg, Bent
2006 Five Misunderstandings About Case-Study Research, Qualitative Inquiry 12(2): 219–24.

Foucault, Michel
1979 Discipline and Punish: The Birth of the Prison. New York: Vintage.
Gilligan, John
1996 Violence: Our Deadly Epidemic and its Causes. New York: Putnam.
Gilmore, Ruth Wilson
2007 Golden Gulag: Prisons, Surplus, Crisis, and Opposition in Globalizing California. Berkeley: University of California Press.
Goffman, Erving
1961 Asylums: Essays on the Social Situation of Mental Patients and Other Inmates. New York: Doubleday
Goffman, Erving,
1963 Stigma: Notes on the Management of Spoiled Identity. New York: Prentice-Hall.
Hacking, Ian
1986 Making Up People. In Thomas C. Heller, Morton Sosna, Christine Brooke-Rose, and David E. Wellbery Heller, eds., Reconstructing Individualism: Autonomy, Individuality, and the Self in Western Thought. Stanford: Stanford University Press.
Hare, Robert
1985 Checklist for the Assessment of Psychopathy in Criminal Populations. In M. H. Ben-Aron, S. J. Hucker, and C. D. Webster, eds., Clinical Criminology. Toronto: Toronto Institute of Psychiatry, pp. 157–67.
Horowitz, Allan
2002 Creating Mental Illness. Chicago: University of Chicago Press.
Human Rights Watch
2003 Ill-Equipped: US Prisons and Offenders with Mental Illness (October 21), www.hrw.org/en/reports/2003/10/21/ill-equipped-0 (accessed Sept. 7, 2009)
Kurki, Leena and Norval Morris
2001 The Purposes, Practices and Problems of Supermax Prisons. In Michael Tonry, ed., Crime and Justice: A Review of Research. Chicago: University of Chicago Press.
Lovell, David, Kristin Cloyes, David G. Allen, and Lorna A. Rhodes
2000 Who Lives in Supermaximum Custody? A Washington State Study. Federal Probation 61(3): 40–5.
Lunbeck, Elizabeth
1994 The Psychiatric Persuasion: Knowledge, Gender and Power in Modern America. Princeton University Press.

Nuckolls, Charles
1992 Toward a Cultural History of the Personality Disorders. Social Science and Medicine 35(1): 37–47.
Porter, Bruce
1998 Is Solitary Confinement Driving Charlie Chase Crazy? New York Times Magazine, Nov. 8: 52–7.
Rhodes, Lorna A.
2002 Psychopathy and the Supermaximum Prison. Ethnography 3(4): 442–66.
Rhodes, Lorna A.
2004 Total Confinement: Madness and Reason in the Maximum Security Prison. Berkeley: University of California Press.
Rhodes, Lorna A.
2005 Changing the Subject: Conversation in Supermax. Cultural Anthropology 3(20): 388–411.
Rhodes, Lorna A.
2007 Supermax as a Technology Of Punishment. Social Research 74(2): 547–56.
Rhodes, Lorna A.
2009 Supermax and the Trajectory of Exception. Studies in Law, Politics, and Society 47: 193–218.
Rose, Nikolas
2000 The Biology of Culpability: Pathological Identity and Crime Control in a Biological Culture. Theoretical Criminology 4(1): 5–34.
Rose, Nikolas
2002 At Risk of Madness. In T. Baker, and J. Simon, eds., Embracing Risk: The Changing Culture of Insurance and Responsibility. Chicago: University of Chicago Press.
Simon, Jonathan
2007 Governing Through Crime: How the War on Crime Transformed American Democracy and Created a Culture of Fear. New York: Oxford University Press.
Smith, Dorothy
1990 The Conceptual Practices of Power: A Feminist Sociology of Knowledge. Boston: Northeastern University Press.
Toch, Hans
1998 Psychopathy and Antisocial Personality in Forensic Settings. In Theodore Millon, Eric Simonsen, Morten Birket-Smith, and Roger D. Davis, eds., Psychopathy: Antisocial, Violent, and Criminal Behavior. New York: Guilford Press.

17

Biological Citizenship
The Science and Politics
of Chernobyl-Exposed Populations

Adriana Petryna

"Common sense is what is left over when all the more articulated sorts of symbol systems have exhausted their tasks." (Clifford Geertz, Local Knowledge[1])

Introduction

This essay explores the forms of scientific cooperation and political management that emerged after the Chernobyl nuclear disaster of 1986. It is about how such managements are interconnected with global flows of technology and their integration into state-building processes, new market strategies, and governance and citizenship in post-Soviet Ukraine. Together with such dynamics, the essay considers, through ethnographic example, how local claims of disease and health are refracted through such institutions, how the sociopolitical contexts in which scientific knowledge is made can influence particular courses of health and disease and outcomes of these conditions. The aim here is to articulate the circumstances through which communities of "at-risk" populations come into being; to show how norms of citizenship are related to such circumstances; and to show how such norms propagate through everyday scientific understandings and practices related to institutions of medicine and law in Ukraine. A set of working relations informs or is at stake in

the propagation of individual claims of being at risk. They involve the sciences of global institutions and experts, national sciences and laws, local bureaucratic contingencies, and familial dynamics of suffering. These relations are indeed "working" in the sense that they affect perceptions of the seriousness and scale of the disaster, claims to its continuing harm, and the scientific, economic, and political modes through which such harm is addressed. How do different systems of modeling risk from Chernobyl affect people's capacities to reason politically? How might the choice of illness, rather than health, become a form of "common sense" expressive of these models? These questions are explored in a context in which science is inextricably connected to state-building processes, and market developments are quite productively intertwined, generating new institutions and social arrangements through which citizenship, experience, and ethics are being altered.

My book, *Life Exposed: Biological Citizens after Chernobyl*, elucidates how scientific knowledge and Chernobyl-related suffering were tooled to access social equity in a harsh

Adriana Petryna, "Biological Citizenship: The Science and Politics of Chernobyl-Exposed Populations," *Osiris* 19 (2004): 250–65. Reprinted by permission of the publisher, The University of Chicago Press.

market transition. More generally, it showed that in this new state, science and politics were engaged in a constant process of exchange and mutual stabilization.[2] This essay builds on that material by showing how contested attempts to intervene and to quantify radiation risk shaped the nature of the postdamage legal and political regime. Viewed longitudinally, the Chernobyl aftermath exemplifies a process wherein scientific knowability collapses and new categories of entitlement emerge. Ambiguities related to categorizing suffering create a political field in which a state, forms of citizenship, and informal economies of health care and entitlement are remade. This appropriation of suffering at all levels is one aspect of how images of suffering are becoming increasingly objectified in their legal, economic, and political dimensions.[3] This essay is specifically concerned with how these objectifications become a form of common sense and are enacted by sufferers in ways that can intensify the political stakes of suffering and promote protection, as well as new kinds of vulnerability, in domestic, scientific, and bureaucratic arenas.

The Event

The Chernobyl nuclear reactor's Unit Four exploded in Ukraine on April 26, 1986. The damages from this disaster have been manifold, including immediate injury in the form of radiation burns and death to plant workers, damaged human immunities and high rates of thyroid cancer among resettled populations, and substantial soil and waterway contamination. Soviet reports attributed the cause of the disaster to a failed experiment. According to one official report, "The purpose of the experiment was to test the possibility of using the mechanical energy of the rotor in a turbo-generator cut off from steam supply to sustain the amounts of power requirements during a power failure."[4] Many of the reactor's safety systems were shut off for the duration of the experiment. A huge power surge occurred as technicians decreased power and shut off the steam. The unit exploded once at 1:23 A.M. and then again. Due to particular wind-pressure gradients that day and in the following

weeks, the radioactive plume moved to an estimated height of eight kilometers. Subsequent attempts to extinguish the flames of the burning graphite core proved only partly successful. By most accounts, they even exacerbated the danger of the situation. For example, an attempt was made to suffocate the flames with tons of boron carbide, dolomite, sand, clay, and lead dropped from helicopters. As a result, the core's temperature increased. The cloud of radiation rose dramatically and moved across Belarus, Ukraine, Russia, Western Europe, and other areas of the Northern Hemisphere.[5]

An official announcement of the disaster came almost three weeks after the event. In that time, roughly 13,000 children in contaminated areas took in a dose of radiation to the thyroid that was more than two times the highest allowable dose for nuclear workers for a year.[6] A massive onset of thyroid cancers in adults and children began appearing four years later. Had nonradioactive iodine pills been made available within the first week of the disaster, the onset of this disease could have been significantly reduced. Soviet administrators contradicted assessments of the scale of the plume made by English and American meteorological groups. The Soviets claimed the biomedical aspects of Chernobyl were under control. Dr. Angelina Guskova of the Institute of Biophysics in Moscow initially selected 237 victims to be airlifted to her institute's acute radiation sickness ward. Acute radiation syndrome (ARS) was diagnosed among 134 of them. The official death toll was set at 31 persons, most of them fire fighters or plant workers.

The disaster continued, especially among the groups of workers who were recruited or went voluntarily to work at the disaster site. Among the hundreds of thousands of paid and unpaid laborers,[7] work ranged from bulldozing polluted soil and dumping it in so-called radiation dumpsites (mohyl'nyky), to raking and shoveling pieces of the reactor core – radioactive graphite – that had dispersed over a vast area, to constructing fences around the reactor, to cutting down highly contaminated surrounding forests. By far the most dangerous work involved the adjacent reactor's roof. In one-minute intervals, workers (mainly military recruits) ran onto the roof, hurled radioactive debris over parapets into containers below with their shovels, and then left. Many of these volunteers called themselves "bio-robots"; their biologies were exploited "and then thrown out." Based on extensive interviews, some laborers felt trapped and unable to leave the disaster area; this sentiment was particularly felt by unpaid military recruits and local collective farmworkers recruited to do the most menial and dangerous of tasks. Some said they went gladly, believing their tripled salary more than compensated for their risk. However, it cannot be definitively said that money truly compensated them for the suffering that was to come.

Five months after the disaster, a so-called sarcophagus (now simply called the Shelter) was built to contain the 216 tons of uranium and plutonium in the ruined reactor. At present, the power plant is decommissioned. Some fifteen thousand people conduct maintenance work or service the Zone of Exclusion. Most of the exclusion zone is located in Ukraine. The zone circumscribes the disaster site and covers thirty kilometers in diameter. Zone entry is limited to the plant's workers.

Ukraine inherited the power plant and most of the Zone of Exclusion when independence was declared in 1991. The government announced new and ambitious standards of safety. It focused its resources on stabilizing the crumbling Shelter, implementing norms of worker safety, decreasing the possibility of future fallout risk, and decommissioning all units of the Chernobyl plant. These acts were important from a foreign policy standpoint. Showing that it could adhere to strict safety standards, Ukraine became the recipient of European and American technical assistance, loans, and trading partnerships. The legacy of Chernobyl has been used as a means of signaling Ukraine's domestic and international legitimacy and staking territorial claims; and as a venue of governance and state building, social welfare, and corruption.

Some maintenance workers lived in government-constructed housing units in Kyiv, the country's capital, sixty miles south of the disaster area. They work in the zone for two weeks and then return home for two weeks. I met one such worker in 1992, the first time I traveled to the country. He identified himself as a "sufferer," a legal classification instituted in 1991 for Chernobyl-affected individuals. He complained about how little his compensation (about five U.S. dollars a month) was in relation to rising food prices.[8] The man was in absolute despair, trapped because he had nowhere else to work. He said he had attempted to find employment elsewhere, but nobody would hire him on account of his bad health and work history. The man linked his suffering to first a precarious and dangerous Soviet management of the aftermath, and then a complex medical and legal apparatus he felt unable to navigate. He then showed me a work injury, a flap of skin that had puckered and formed a kind of ring just above his ankle. Direct contact with a source of ionizing radiation had apparently caused it. His sense of violation and loss were clear when he referred to himself as a "living dead," whose memory of who he was in a former life "is gone."

In 2000, I interviewed the director of the Shelter complex. What I learned was that almost a decade after independence, worker protections, in spite of some improvements, were still deficient. The director told me that norms of radiation safety were inoperative. In a place of tremendous economic desperation, people *competed* for work in the Zone of Exclusion, where salaries were relatively high and steadily paid. Prospective workers engaged in a troubling cost-benefit assessment that went something like this: if I work in the Zone, I lose my health. But I can send my son to law school. "Taking this risk is their individual problem. No one else is responsible for it," the director told me. He compared Ukraine's mode of enforcing safety standards with European modes and told me that the "value" of a dose exposure remained untallied in Ukraine. In Europe, such values are calculated on the basis of the rem-expenditures workers incur; international safety standards limit the amounts. Despite the existence of these international limitations, the director's comment suggests that norms of worker exposures are in fact being decided locally and within the constraints of a national economy. In effect, he was revealing to me the extent to which workers' lives are undervalued by being overexposed (for much less pay). Yet however undervalued his workers' lives may be, they are still driven to work by a situation in which economic forces are overwhelming. In such an environment, physical risks escalate and risky work is seen as acceptable and even normal.

"As a result of all the compounding uncertainties in the factors involved," wrote Frank von Hippel, "our estimates of the long-term health consequences of the Chernobyl accident are uncertain even as to the order of magnitude."[9] Indeed, available models of assessment could not account for the scope of the disaster. As the short history of the disaster indicates, rational-technical responses and political administrations (both in the Soviet and Ukrainian periods) have been compounding factors in the medical and welfare tragedy that now affects more than 3.5 million people in Ukraine alone. Contested scientific assessments of the disaster's extent and medical impact, the decision to postpone public communication, and the economic impetus to work in the exclusion zone have made Chernobyl a *tekhnohenna katastrofa* (a technogenic catastrophe). This is a term that was used among my informants, including people fighting for disability status, local physicians, and scientists. It suggests that not only radiation exposure but also political managements have produced new biological uncertainties.

Ulrich Beck noted that Chernobyl was an "anthropological shock" in Western Europe. The shock came from the fact that everyday knowledge proved useless in the face of this catastrophe, as did expert knowledge.[10] This "collapse" of knowledge also occurred, but in another way, in the other Europe. Chernobyl was associated with the collapse of Soviet life in general. Knowledge about risk, how to deliver it, how to value it, became something of a political resource. In this disaster's wake a state, a society, and knowledge and experience of health have been reconfigured.

In exploring this aftermath, I use a methodological approach that involves moving back and forth between vulnerable persons and the everyday bureaucracies and procedures by which they express their desires, claims, and needs for protection and security. Such an ethnographic mode of engagement is in itself meant to question the possibility of a linear account or an all-or-none moral or political solution to this complex reality. Instead, its dynamics are approached from a prismatic point of view to gain a broader perspective on the interests and values involved in particular claims and sites.

Experimental Models and Ethnographic Methods

Between 1992 and 1997, I conducted archival and field research in Ukraine, Russia, and the United States. In Ukraine, I worked with resettled families and radiation-exposed workers. I also carried out archival research in the country's new Chernobyl Ministry, the Health Ministry, and Parliamentary Commissions on Human Rights. I conducted interviews with key scientific and political actors in Kyiv and Moscow, comparing scientific standards informing concepts of biological risk and safety in the Soviet and post-Soviet administrations of the aftermath. The very nature of the problem, that is, understanding the everyday lived aspects of the Chernobyl aftermath, led me to a number of different sites and challenges. One of those challenges involved understanding how scientific knowledge about radiation risk was being circulated, assimilated, or rejected at the various levels (international, national, and local) in which interventions were being made.

I examined claims about the scale of the disaster made by scientific experts affiliated with the International Atomic Energy Agency. I compared expert knowledge with that of basic scientists in U.S. radiation laboratories and learned about how radiobiologists went about evaluating radiobiological effects at the cellular and subcellular levels.

As a consequence, I could better situate expert claims and their measures in the context of their laboratory production and testing. I soon discovered that there was a "black box" separating knowledge about the effects of low-dose radiation at the animal (laboratory) level and human (field) level. The dose-effect curves for high doses of radiation were one to one and fairly straightforward. The same could not be said for ongoing exposures at low doses (a typical condition after Chernobyl). On the one hand, experts promoted their authority, based in part on their mastery of what composed appropriate evidence of Chernobyl-related injury. On the other hand, there was considerable disagreement at the laboratory level over what the terms for interpreting radiation-induced biological risk in human populations are. International experts' projections about the health effects of Chernobyl often contradicted people's lived sense of those effects. For Ukrainian scientists, the lack of consensus at the basic science level meant that the criteria of evaluation of injury were, in essence, contestable.

Ukraine became a most compelling place to examine the relations between risk, rational-technical power, and the emergence of new populations. Indeed, a new political, economic, and moral arena had been thrown open owing to the absence of consistent evaluative criteria. During the period of my field research, the country saw the growth of a population claiming radiation exposure qualified them for some form of social protection. Social protections included cash subsidies, family allowances, free medical care and education, and pension benefits for sufferers and the disabled. This new population, named *poterpili* (sufferers), numbered 3.5 million and constituted 7 percent of the population. A political economy of Chernobyl-related illnesses with new kinds of social categories and hierarchies of entitlement was emerging. An individual classified as "disabled" received the best entitlement package as compared with a mere "sufferer." Nonsufferers, that is, people outside the Chernobyl compensation system, had even less or no chance of receiving state social benefits. Scientific know-how became essential to the negotiation of everyday life and the maintenance of one's status in the Chernobyl system. One had to know one's dose and be able to relate it to one's symptoms and work experiences in the Zone of Exclusion. The effectiveness of this knowledge determined the place one could occupy and how long one could occupy it in the system of management of Chernobyl populations.

Today, approximately 8.9 percent of Ukraine is considered contaminated. On average, 5 percent of its state budget is spent on Chernobyl-related expenses. This includes costs related to the environmental cleanup and technical support of the destroyed reactor. The majority of funds (65 percent), however, are spent on social compensations and financial maintenance of the Chernobyl public health and scientific apparatus. Belarus was much more heavily affected than Ukraine. Nearly 23 percent of its territory is contaminated. Contrastively, Belarus expends much less than its southern neighbor does on affected populations; it has curbed its sum of Chernobyl claimants – as has Russia.[11] Dr. Guskova, who oversees the Russian compensation system for workers of nuclear installations, including Chernobyl, is a well-known critic of Ukraine's compensation system. She told me that Ukrainians were inflating their numbers of exposed persons, that their so-called invalids "didn't want to recover." She saw the illnesses of this group as a "struggle for power and material resources related to the disaster."

In response to her former colleague's indictment, Dr. Angelina Ceanu, a neuro-physiologist and physician to Chernobyl victims in Kyiv, told me, "It is inconceivable that an organism of any kind is passive to its own destruction." Her response was based on evidence from experiments conducted by the Soviet radiobiologist V. L. Komarov. In one experiment conducted in the late 1950s, he observed that sleeping rats, without provocation, woke up when exposed to small amounts of ionizing radiation. From these examples one can begin to appreciate how competing scientific models (animal vs. human; psychometric vs. biological; laboratory vs. field-based), financial agendas, and distinct moral attitudes regarding the need for scientific work in this arena were not simply at odds with each other. Their confrontation opened up a novel social arena consisting of contested claims around radiation illness. Indeed, a number of civic organizations lobbying for the right to compensation for such illnesses evolved with the biomedical and political institutions promoting "safe living" in Ukraine. These so-called *fondy* (funds) were conduits of international charity and represented the concerns of exclusion zone workers and resettled persons living in Ukraine. These funds enjoyed tax-exempt status and with their numbers (more than 500 in 1996) established an informal economy of a variety of imported goods, including vehicles, drugs, and frozen and dry food-stuffs. In short, the Chernobyl aftermath became a prism of the troubled political-economic and social circumstances that typified the Ukrainian transition to a market economy. The production of scientific know-how, markets, and state formations were mutually embedded, generating new inequalities and opportunities in the redefinition of citizenship and ethics.

This work is based on multiple lengthy research visits to various state, scientific, and domestic contexts during 1992–1995, fieldwork conducted during 1996–1997, and a follow-up visit in 2000. The Radiation Research Center, also known as Klinika, became a primary focus of the field research. The center was established in 1986 to monitor the health of zone laborers; shortly afterward it began providing similar services for resettled persons. Its national-level Medical-Labor Committee (Ekspertiza) comprises scientists, physicians, and administrators who have the authority to diagnose illnesses as Chernobyl-related (there are twelve regional committees). Patients with illnesses diagnosed as such receive a document, the so-called Chernobyl tie, which qualifies bearers to receive compensation privileges as a result of their Chernobyl-related illnesses. By 1996, the center had become the site of intense scientific and legal disputes. I observed physicians, nurses, and patients as they negotiated over who should receive the tie. I looked into current research, particularly in the center's neurological division. I also carried out interviews with sixty middle-age male and female patients and reviewed their medical histories, their illness progressions, and their experiences in attempting to qualify for disability status. A significant aspect of my research focused on the daily lives of the clinic's male patients and their families. I was concerned with how their belonging to a political economy of illness displaced their self-perceptions and roles as breadwinners and paternal figures. I traced changing experiences of *lichnost'*, a Russian-Soviet model of personhood evidenced

in a person's work ethics and level of commitment to a collective of laborers,[12] the effects such changes had on domestic life, and the techniques household members used to have their illnesses count in the rational-technical domain in which their futures came to be addressed.

These anthropological concerns illustrate the extent to which definitions of health and illness are embedded within spheres of politics and economics and are almost always connected with dimensions that go beyond the immediate body, such as interpersonal and domestic relationships. Arthur Kleinman has elucidated the "social course" of illness.[13] Other anthropologists, such as Veena Das and Nancy Scheper-Hughes, have been concerned with constructions of health as they indicate discrepancies in power, social position, and inequality, particularly as lived by marginal groups and individuals. Recent ethnographies of science have portrayed how, more and more, biomedical technologies play a key role in that constructedness. PET scans, genetically based diagnostics, and sonograms image biological facts and are therefore inseparable from the objects they recognize and remake as disease.[14] Social problems, health problems, and the technologies that image them are also linked. Anthropologist Paul Farmer has shown how patterns of "structural violence" affect the construction and expansion of populations at risk for diseases. Deteriorating health care, limited treatments, and inequalities are worsened by structural adjustment programs and have led to epidemics of preventable infectious diseases such as multidrug-resistant tuberculosis. Indeed, "social forces and processes come to be embodied as biological events."[15] In Ukraine, efforts to remediate the health effects of Chernobyl have themselves contributed to social and biological indeterminacy and novel formations of power. Radiation exposures and their unaccountability, bureaucratic interventions by the state and failures to intervene, the growth of clinical regimes, and harsh market changes intensified the course of illness and suffering. Thus in the Chernobyl aftermath, illness and health are engendered and made sense of within the technical and political domain in which they come to be addressed.

Constructed Unknowns

In what follows, I address some of the scientific elements that played a key role in measuring and delineating the scope of the disaster and defining remediation and compensation strategies. In this context, matters such as atmospheric dispersion maps, international scientific cooperations, and local scientific responses, as well as people's involvement in bureaucratic and testing procedures, led up to what can be called a "technical and political course of illness." Examples of people's engagement with, and influence on, such courses will then be discussed.

Most scientists today would agree that given the state of technology at the time of the disaster, specialists "did not know how to make an objective assessment of what had happened."[16] Tom Sullivan, who until recently directed the Atmospheric Release Advisory Capability (ARAC) group at Lawrence Livermore Laboratory in Livermore, California, agrees with this general appraisal.[17] Prior to the Chernobyl disaster, Sullivan's ARAC team had generated atmospheric dispersion models of the size and movement of nuclear plumes resulting from American and Chinese aboveground nuclear weapons tests and the Three Mile Island accident. "A 200 by 200 kilometer area had been sufficient to model prior radiation releases," he told me. "We did the imaging near the Chernobyl plant using this 200 kilometer square grid, but the grid was so saturated, I mean, you couldn't even make sense of it because every place had these enormously high radiation values. ... *Our codes were not prepared for an event of this magnitude.*"[18]

Soviet scientists, too, were unprepared, but they did not admit their ignorance. In an August 1986 meeting with the International Atomic Energy Agency (IAEA), they presented a crude analysis of the distribution of radiation in the Zone of Exclusion and in the Soviet Union: "assessments were made of the actual and future radiation doses received by the populations of towns, villages, and other inhabited places. As a result of these and other measures, *it proved possible to keep exposures within the established limits.*"[19]

The issue at stake is the state's capacity to produce and use scientific knowledge and nonknowledge to maintain political order. Historian Loren Graham, for example, has written about how "false" sciences such as Lysenkoism, which denied the existence of the gene and advocated labor-intensive methods of accelerating crop yields, have been instrumental in shaping work psychology and social life in the socialist project.[20] The fact is that limited Soviet maps of Chernobyl helped to justify limited forms of dosimetric surveillance and resettlement actions. Nonknowledge became essential to the deployment of authoritative knowledge. High doses absorbed by at least 200,000 workers during 1986–1987 were insufficiently documented. According to one biochemist, many of the cleanup workers "received 6–8 times the lethal dose of radiation."[21] "They are alive," he told me. "They know that they didn't die. *But they don't know how they survived.*" His statement speaks to the extent to which not only knowledge but also ignorance were constructed and used as state tools for maintaining public order. As science historian Robert Proctor tells us in his informative book on how politics shapes cancer science, ignorance "is not just a natural consequence of the ever shifting boundary between the known and the unknown." It is a "political consequence" of decisions concerning how to approach what could and should be done to mitigate danger or disease.[22]

Chernobyl also became a venue for unprecedented international scientific cooperation and human research. President Mikhail Gorbachev personally invited a team of American oncologists led by leukemia specialist Robert Gale (UCLA) to conduct experimental bone marrow transplantations upon individuals whose exposures were beyond the lethal limit and for whom these transplantations were deemed appropriate. Additionally, 400 workers selected by Dr. Guskova and others received a genetically-engineered hematopoietic growth factor molecule (rhGM-CSF), thought to regenerate stem cell growth. Though the results of the transplantations and trial proved unsuccessful, the medical work on this cohort (and the objective indices created around them) helped consolidate an image of a biomedical crisis that was being successfully controlled by cutting-edge scientific applications. In an effort to alleviate the public's fear, Dr. Gale appeared on television and walked barefoot in the zone with one of his children.

As this internationalization of science ensued, however, the physical management of contamination at the accident site was internalized – to the sphere of Soviet state control. One policy statement released by the Soviet Health Ministry at the height of these cooperations, for example, directed medical examiners in the Zone of Exclusion to "classify workers who have received a maximum dose as having "vegetovascular dystonia," that is, a kind of panic disorder, and a novel psychosocial disorder called "radiophobia" (or the fear of the biological influence of radiation). These categories were used to filter out the majority of disability claims.[23] Substantial challenges to this Soviet management came from certain labor sectors in subsequent years. At the end of 1989 only 130 additional persons were granted disability; by 1990, 2,753 more cases had been considered, of which 50 percent were authorized on a neurological basis. Levels of political influence of specific labor sectors are reflected in the order they received disability: coal miners, then Ministry of Internal Affairs workers (the police), and then Transport Ministry workers. These various labor groups would soon realize that in the Ukrainian management of Chernobyl, forms of political leveraging had to be coupled with medical-scientific know-how.

Arguably, the new Ukrainian accounting of the Chernobyl unknown was part and parcel of the government's strategies for "knowledge-based" governance and social mobilization. In 1991 and in its first set of laws, the new parliament denounced the Soviet management of Chernobyl as "an act of genocide." The new nation-state viewed the disaster as (among other things) a key means for instituting domestic and international authority. Legislators assailed the Soviet standard for determining biological risk to populations. The Soviets had established a high of 35 rem (a unit of absorbed dose), spread over an individual's lifetime (understood as a standard seventy-year span), as the threshold of allowable radiation dose intakes. This threshold limited the scale of resettlement actions. Ukrainian law lowered the Soviet threshold dose to 7 rem, comparable to what an average American would be exposed to in his or her lifetime. In effect these lowered measures for safe living increased the size of the labor forces going to the exclusion zone (since workers had to work shorter amounts of time if they were to avoid exceeding the stricter dose standards). The measures also expanded territories considered contaminated. A significant new sector of the population would want to claim itself as part of a state-protected post-Soviet polity. A biophysicist responsible for conducting retrospective dose assays on resettlers told me: "Long lines of resettlers extended from our laboratory doors. It wasn't enough that they were evacuated to 'clean' areas. People got entangled in the category of victim, by law. They had unpredictable futures, and *each of them wanted to know their dose*."

Statistics from the Ukrainian Ministry of Health gave evidence of the sharp increase in 1991 of zone workers, resettled persons and inhabitants of contaminated territories registering their disability, and the annual patterns of enrollment of this new population for which the state committed itself to care. The statistics also show that the sharpest increase in the clinical registration of illnesses occurred under the category "symptoms and other inadequately known states," Class 16 in the International Classification of Disease, ICD 10 (see Figure 17.1). These states typically include afflictions such as personality changes, premature senility, and psychosis.

Figure 17.1 *Symptoms and other inadequately known states (per 10,000)*

1982	1983	1984	1985	1986	1987	1988	1989	1990	1991	1992
1.3	1.7	1.7	1.9	2.3	2.7	5.9	34.7	108.3	127.4	141.3

SOURCE: Ministry of Statistics, Kyiv, Ukraine.

Ukrainian claims to a sudden expansion of Chernobyl health effects became a target of international skepticism. Ukrainian scientists were often rebuked for their "failure to use modern epidemiological methods and criteria of causality and a reliable data system." As a World Bank consultant noted, "Right now virtually any disease is attributed to Chernobyl, and no effort is being made either to prove or disprove these claims that would satisfy standard epidemiological criteria of causality."[24] For the government, however, one can argue that these new statistics became a kind of "moral science,"[25] a resolute display of its intention to make visible the effects of the Soviet mismanagement of the disaster and to guarantee its own social legitimacy while keeping world attention on the Chernobyl risk.

In this daily bureaucratic instantiation of Chernobyl, tensions among zone workers, resettled individuals and families, scientists, physicians, legislators, and civil servants intensified. Together, these groups became invested in a new social and moral contract between state and civil society, a contract guaranteeing them the right to know their levels of risk and to use legal means to obtain medical care and monitoring. The sufferers and their administrators were also supported by the nonsuffering citizens, who paid a 12 percent tax on their salaries to support compensations. The hybrid quality of this postsocialist state and social contract comes into view. On the one hand, the Ukrainian government rejected Western neoliberal prescriptions to *downsize* its social welfare domain; on the other hand, it presented itself as informed by the principles of a modern risk society. On the one hand, these Chernobyl laws allowed for unprecedented civic organizing; on the other hand, they became distinct venues of corruption through which informal practices of providing or selling access to state privileges and protections (*blat*) expanded.[26]

Ethnographic accounts have illustrated that postsocialism's future cannot be based in predictive models or treated as unproblematic flows toward free markets. Michael Burawoy and Katherine Verdery point to the links between the socialist and post-socialist worlds as well as growing dependencies between postsocialist state formations and global economics.

Such dependencies "have radically shifted the rules of the game, the parameters of action within which actors pursue their daily routines and practices."[27] Ethnographic methods are critical for elucidating such interrelated processes at local levels. This is particularly true with regard to assessing the decisions people make based on limited choices available to them and the informal aspects of power that inform those decisions.

Shifts in aggregate human conditions and the circumstances of citizenship are also at stake in these changing political and economic worlds. The principles of a "classical citizenship" endow citizens with natural and legal rights protected as matters of birthright.[28] Regardless of nationality, such protections were granted to all Ukrainian inhabitants when the country declared independence. Yet birthright remains an insufficient guarantor of protection as the lives of inhabitants of some Ukrainian areas cannot be fully, or even partly, protected owing to long-term environmental challenges. For these inhabitants, the very concept of citizenship is charged with the superadded burden of survival. The acquisition and mastery of certain democratic forms related to openness, freedom of expression, and the right to information are primary goals to be sure. Yet populations are also negotiating for the even more basic goal of protection (i.e., economic and social inclusion) using the constituent matters of life. Such negotiations expose certain patterns that are traceable elsewhere: the role of science in legitimating democratic institutions, increasingly limited access to health care and welfare as the capitalist trends take over, and the uneasy correlation of human rights with biological self-preservation.

Biological Citizenship

In Ukraine, where democratization is linked to a harsh market transition, the injured biology of a population has become the basis for social membership and for staking claims to citizenship. Government-operated radiation research clinics and nongovernmental organizations mediate an informal economy of illness and claims to a "biological citizenship" – a demand for, but limited access to, a form of social welfare based on medical, scientific, and legal criteria that recognize injury and compensate for it. These demands are being expressed in the context of losses of primary resources such as' employment and state protections against inflation and a deterioration in legal-political categories. Struggles over limited medical resources and the factors that constitute a legitimate claim to citizenship are part of postsocialism's uncharted terrain. Against a stark and overwhelming order of insecurity, there are questions to be asked about how the value of another's life is being judged in this new political economy, about the ability of scientific knowledge to politically empower those seeking to set that value relatively high, and about the kinds of rationalities and biomedical practices emerging with respect to novel social, economic, and somatic indeterminacies. The indeterminacy of scientific knowledge about the afflictions people face and about the nature of nuclear catastrophe materializes here as both a curse and a source of leverage. Ambiguities related to the interpretation of radiation-related injury, together with their inextricable relations to the social and political uncertainties generated by Soviet interventions and current political-economic vulnerability, make the scope of the afflicted population in Ukraine and its claims to injury at once plausible, ironic, and catastrophic.

One instance of how these scientific and political dynamics operated in the everyday: the country's eminent expert on matters related to the disaster, Symon Lavrov, was well-regarded internationally for having developed computerized fallout models and calculating population-wide doses in the post-Soviet period. He told me, however, that "when a crying mother comes to my laboratory and asks me, Professor Lavrov, 'tell me what's wrong with my child?' I assign her a dose and say nothing more. I double it, as much as I can." The offer of a higher dose increased the likelihood that the mother would be able to secure social protection on account of her potentially sick child. Lavrov and the grieving mother were two of the many figures whose efforts I documented. The point is the following: the mother could offer her child a dose, a protective tie with the state, which is founded on a probability of sickness, a biological tie. What she could offer, perhaps the most precious thing she could offer her child in that context, is a specific knowledge, history, and category. The child's "exposure" and the knowledge that would make that exposure an empirical fact were not things to be repressed or denied (as had been tried in the Soviet model) but rather things to be made into a resource and then distributed through informal means.

Specific cases illustrate how these economic and state processes, combined with the technical dynamics already described, have laid the groundwork for such "counter-politics."[29] Citizens have come to depend on obtainable technologies and legal procedures to gain political recognition and admission to some form of welfare inclusion. Aware that they had fewer chances for finding employment and health in the new market economy, these citizens accounted for elements in their lives (measures, numbers, symptoms) that could be linked to a state, scientific, and bureaucratic history of mismanagement and risk. The tighter the connection that could be drawn, the greater the chance of securing economic and social entitlement. This dimension of illness as counterpolitics suggests that sufferers are aware of the way politics shapes what they know and do not know about their illnesses and that they are put in a role of having to use these politics to curb further deteriorations of their health, which they see as resulting, in part, from a collapsing state health system and loss of adequate legal protections.

Probability in relation to radiation-related disease became a central resource for local scientific research. This play with probability was being projected back into nature, so to speak, through an intricate local science. Young neuropsychiatrists made the best of the inescapability of their political circumstances (they could not get visas to leave the country) as they integrated international medical taxonomies into Soviet ones and developed classifications of mental and nervous disorders that in expert literatures were considered far too low to make any significant biological contribution. For example, neuropsychiatrists were involved in a project designed to find and assess cases of mental retardation in children exposed in utero in the first year after the disaster. In the case of one such child, a limping nine-year-old boy, researchers and parents pooled their knowledge to reconstruct the child's disorder as having a radiation origin. Even though the boy's radiation dose was low, he was given the status of sufferer because of his mother's occupation-related exposure (she was an emergency doctor who elected to work in the zone until late in her pregnancy) and also because a PET scan did reveal a cerebral lesion that was never hypothesized as being related to anything other than radiation. (It could have been birth trauma.) As researchers constructed a human research cohort, they were also constructing a destiny for the newly designated human research subjects. It was precisely the destiny the parents were intent on offering to this child – a biological citizenship.

These radiation-related claims and practices constituted a form of work in this market transition. A clinical administrator concurred that claims to radiation illness among the Ukrainian population amounted to a form of "market compensation." He told me, "If people could improve their family budgets, there would be a lot less illness. People are now oriented towards one thing. They believe that only through the constitution of illnesses, and particularly difficult illnesses, incurable ones, can they improve their family budgets." Administrators such as he informed me that they should not to be "blamed too much" for fueling an informal economy of diagnoses and entitlements. Complicities could be found at every level, and the moral conflicts they entailed were publicly discussed. Another administrator who authenticated compensation claims told me illnesses had become a form of currency. "There are a lot of people out of work," he said. "People don't have enough money to eat. The state doesn't give medicines for free anymore. Drug stores are commercialized." He likened his work to that of a bank. "The diagnosis we write is money."

The story of Anton and Halia (age forty-two in 1997) shows the ways such complicity functioned in the most personal arenas. The new institutions, procedures, and actors that were at work at the state level, at the research clinic, and at the level of civic organizations were making their way into the couple's *kvartyra* (apartment). Anton's identity as a worker, his sense of masculinity, and his role as a father and breadwinner were being violently dislocated and altered in the process. In 1986, the state recruited Anton to work for six months in the Zone of Exclusion, transporting bags of lead oxide, sand, and gravel to the reactor site. The bags were airlifted and deposited using helicopters. He had no idea how much radiation he absorbed during those six months. From 1991 on, Anton routinely passed through the clinical system, monitored like any "prospective" invalid. His symptoms mounted over time. He had chronic headaches, lost his short-term memory, exhibited antisocial behavior, developed a speech disorder, and experienced seizures and impotence, as well as many other problems. Despite the growing number and intensity of his symptoms, his diagnosis did not "progress" from an initial listing as a "psycho-social" case.

When I met Anton and his wife, Halia, they were trying to manage on a small pension he received as a sufferer. Anton saw himself as bankrupt, morally as well as economically: "The state took my life away. Ripped me off, gone. What is there to be happy about? An honorable man cannot survive now. For what? For what? We had a life. We had butter. We had milk. I can't buy an iron. Before I could buy fifty irons. The money was there. My wife's salary is less than the cost of one iron." He told me that he did not know "how to trade goods" or to sell petty goods on the market. His meager pension left Anton with few options. He found himself confronting the shameful option of breadwinning with his illness in the Chernobyl compensation system or facing poverty. Over time, and in a concerted effort to remove Anton's psycho-social label, the couple befriended a leader of a disabled workers' activist group in a clinic. Through him they met a neurologist who knew the director of the local medical-labor committee. The couple hoped this individual would provide official support for Anton's claim of Chernobyl-related disability.

The economic motives for these actions were clear. Yet it was difficult for me to see this man giving up everything he knew or thought about himself to prove that his diffused symptoms had an organic basis. Neurology was a key gateway to disability; neurological disorders were most ambiguous but most possible to prove using diagnostic technologies, self-inducements, and bodily display. At each step, Anton was mentally breaking down; he fell into a pattern of abusive behavior. His legal-medical gamble – this gaining of life in the new market economy through illness – reflected the practices of an entire citizenry lacking money or the means of generating it. This approach has become common sense, in Clifford Geertz's words, or that which is "left over when all [the] more articulated sorts of symbol systems have exhausted their tasks."[30]

When I returned in 2000 to Kyiv to conduct further research, I discovered that current democratic politicians, many of whom drafted the original compensation laws as sovereignty-minded nationalists, now saw the Chernobyl compensation system as a dire mistake that has "accidentally" reproduced a socialist-like population. Funds and activist groups were now supported by socialist and communist leaderships, who lobbied for continued aid in an increasingly divided parliament. Meanwhile, international agencies such as the World Bank cited the Chernobyl social apparatus as a "dead weight" to Ukraine's less-than-ideal transition to a market economy. Bank officials were so ill-disposed toward the system that they made its quick extinction a condition of future loan contracting. The disappearance of this exposed population from the state's radar seems ever more likely. Once "protected" by a safety-conscious state, this exposed population is being left alone to their symptoms and social disarray.

Opinions about how the state should address the fate of these Chernobyl victims also serve as a kind of barometer of the country's changing moral fabric. Rural inhabitants who normally received the least in terms of socialist redistribution tended to be sympathetic to the victims' struggles. Among inhabitants of Kyiv and other urban centers, there is a growing consensus that the invalids are "parasites of the state, damaging the economy, not paying taxes." Many youths who had been evacuated

from the zone do not want to be associated with groups of sufferers as this association makes it more difficult for them to find employment.

Chernobyl was a key political event, generating many effects, some of which have yet to be known; its truths have been made only partly known through estimates derived from experimental science. The immediate postindependence discourse in Ukraine centered on the "truth" of Chernobyl. Ukrainians tried to put their suffering in perspective vis-à-vis the repressive model of science and state: the number of people who died, how the government deceived citizens about the scale of the disaster, how the maps of contamination were misrepresentative, and so on. As harsh market realities entered everyday life, this model of organizing suffering quickly gave way to a different kind of scientific and political negotiation, one which had directly to do with the maintenance, and indeed the remaking, of a postsocialist state and population.

If, at the level of the modern state, spheres of scientific production and politics are in a constant process of exchange and mutual stabilization, then what I have suggested here is that stabilization proves to be a much more difficult task. At stake in the Chernobyl aftermath is a distinctive postsocialist field of power-in-the-making that is using science and scientific categories to establish the state's reach. Scientists and victims are also establishing their own modes of knowledge related to injury as a means of negotiating public accountability, political power, and further state protections in the form of financial compensation and medical care. Biology becomes a resource in a multidimensional sense – versatile material through which the state and new populations can be made to appear. This postsocialist field of power has specific physical, experiential, political, economic, and spatial aspects. It is about knowledge and constructed ignorance, visibility and invisibility, inclusion and exclusion, probabilities and facts, and the parceling out of protection and welfare that do not fit predictive models. It is also about how individuals and populations become part of new cooperative regimes in scientific research and in local state-sponsored forms of human subjects protection. In this context, suffering is wholly appropriated and objectified in its legal, economic, and political dimensions. At the same time, these objectifications constitute a common sense that is enacted by sufferers themselves in ways that can promote protection as well as intensify new kinds of vulnerability in domestic, scientific, and bureaucratic spheres.

NOTES

1 Clifford Geertz, *Local Knowledge: Further Essays in Interpretive Anthropology* (New York, 1983), 92.

2 Adriana Petryna, *Life Exposed: Biological Citizens After Chernobyl* (Princeton, 2002).

3 Arthur Kleinman and Joan Kleinman, "The Appeal of Experience; The Dismay of Images: Cultural Appropriations of Suffering in Our Times," *Daedalus* 125 (1999): 1–24. See also Veena Das, *Critical Events: An Anthropological Perspective on Contemporary India* (Oxford, 1995). I use pseudonyms for the majority of people interviewed for this essay. Names that appear in scientific and legal print are in some cases actual.

4 See Soviet State Committee on the Utilization of Atomic Energy, *Report to the IAEA* (Vienna, 1986), 16.

5 See Alexander Sich, "The Denial Syndrome (Efforts to Smother the Burning Nuclear Core at the Chernobyl Power Plant in 1986 Were Insufficient)," *Bulletin of Atomic Scientists* 52 (1996): 38–40.

6 See Yurii Shcherbak, "Ten Years of the Chernobyl Era," *Scientific American*, April 1996, 46.

7 Estimates vary from 600,000 to 800,000. These workers came from all over the Soviet Union. The labor pool, however, drew heavily from the Russian and Ukrainian populations.

8 The karbovanets (Krb) was Ukraine's legal tender from 1992 to 1996. Exchange rates per US$1.00 plunged between 1992 and 1993. In March 1992, the exchange rate was Krb640:$1. By March 1993, that rate had fallen to Krb12,610:$1. Subsequent rates were as follows: 1994 – Krb104,200:US$1; 1995 – 179,900:$1; 1996 – 188,700:$1. The hryvnia (Hrn) replaced the karbovanets at Hrn1: Krb100,000 in September 1996. The exchange rates were as follows: 1997 – Hrn1.84:US$1; 1998 – 2.04:$1; 1999 – 4.13:$1; 2000 – 5.44:$1.

9 Frank von Hippel, *Citizen Scientist* (New York, 1991), 235.

10 Ulrich Beck, "The Anthropological Shock: Chernobyl and the Contours of a Risk Society," *Berkeley Journal of Sociology* 32 (1987): 153–65.

11 In Russia, the number of people considered affected and compensable has been kept to a minimum and remains fairly stable (about 350,000, including 300,000, Zone of Exclusion laborers and 50,000 resettled).

12 Oleg Kharkhordin, *The Collective and the Individual in Russia: A Study of Practices* (Berkeley, Calif., 1999).

13 Arthur Kleinman, *Social Origins of Distress and Disease* (New Haven, Conn., 1986).

14 Emily Martin, *Flexible Bodies: Tracking Immunity in American Culture from the Days of Polio to the Age of AIDS* (Boston, 1994); Rayna Rapp, *Testing Women, Testing the Fetus: The Social Impact of Amniocentesis on America* (New York, 1999); Joseph Dumit, *Picturing Personhood: Brain Scans and Biomedical Identity* (Princeton, N.J., 2004).

15 Paul Farmer, *Infections and Inequalities: The Modern Plagues* (Berkeley, Calif., 1999), 5.

16 *One Decade After Chernobyl* (Vienna, 1996).

17 ARAC is a national emergency response service for real-time assessment of incidents involving nuclear, chemical, biological, or natural hazardous material.

18 Sullivan's team offered technical assistance through a Swedish intermediary, but the offer was refused by Soviet administrators.

19 Soviet State Committee on the Utilization of Atomic Energy, *The Accident at Chernobyl Nuclear Power Plant and Its Consequences.* Information complied for the IAEA Expert's Meeting. Aug. 25–29, 1986, Vienna; Zhores Medvedev, *The Legacy of Chernobyl* (New York, 1990).

20 Loren Graham, *What Have We Learned about Science and Technology from the Russian Experience?* (Stanford, Calif., 1998).

21 Symptoms of acute radiation sickness begin at 200 rem. At 400 rem, bone marrow failure sets in. Lethal dose (LD100) is a dose exposure that causes 100 percent of the death of cells or the human. LD50/30 is a

dose exposure that causes 50 percent of the
death of cells or the human within thirty
days.

22   Robert Proctor, *Cancer Wars: How Politics
Shapes What We Know and Don't Know
about Cancer* (New York, 1995), 7.

23   In my interviews, I heard instances of workers
mimicking symptoms of ARS (vomiting, for
example). This shows the level of desperation
on the part of some of them to receive permission to leave the zone.

24   World Bank, *Managing the Legacy of Chernobyl* (Washington, D.C., 1994), 7:6.

25   Ian Hacking, *Taming of Chance* (Cambridge, 1990).

26   For an elaboration of the concept of *blat*, see
Alena Ledeneva, *Russia's Economy of
Favours: Blat, Networking, and Informal
Exchange* (Cambridge, 1998).

27   Michael Burawoy and Katherine Verdery,
*Uncertain Transition: Ethnographies of
Change in the Postsocialist World* (Lanham,
Md., 1999), 2.

28   Dominique Schnapper, "The European Debate
on Citizenship," *Daedalus* 126 (1997): 201.

29   Colin Gordon, "Government Rationality:
An Introduction," in *The Foucault Effect:
Studies in Governmentality*, ed. G. Burchell,
C. Gordon, and P. Miller (Chicago, 1991), 5.

30   Geertz, *Local Knowledge* (cit. n. 1).

18

Human Pharmakon
Symptoms, Technologies, Subjectivities

João Biehl

Science is Our Consciousness

Dictionary
Diagnostics
Marriage for free
Paid marriage
Operation
Reality
To give an injection
To get a spasm
In the body
A cerebral spasm

Without a known origin and increasingly paralyzed, a young woman named Catarina spent her days in Vita, an asylum in southern Brazil, assembling words in what she called "my dictionary." Her handwriting was uneven and conveyed minimal literacy. "I write so that I don't forget the words," she told me in January 2000, three years after I first met her in this institution of last resort. "I write all the illness I have now and the illnesses I had as a child."

Vita was initially conceived as a Pentecostal treatment center for drug addicts, but since the mid-1990s it was run by a philanthropic association headed by a local politician and a police chief (Biehl 2005). Over time, Vita became a "dumpsite" for people who, like Catarina, had been cut off from social life and formal institutions. Caregivers referred to Catarina as "mad" and haphazardly treated her – and the more than one hundred surplus bodies who were also *waiting with death* in Vita – with all kinds of psychiatric drugs (donations that were by and large expired).

The dictionary was a sea of words. Blended with allusions to spasm, menstruation, paralysis, rheumatism, paranoia, and the listing of all possible diseases from measles to ulcers to AIDS were names such as Ademir, Nilson, Armando, Anderson, Alessandra, Ana. "Dictionary, social study. Chronic spasm, encroached rheumatism, generational rheumatism. I leave the question in the air. Is it worthwhile to make my life a misfortune? Human body?" She writes to remain alive, I told myself. These are the words that form her from within. She is fighting for connections.

Why, I asked Catarina, do you think families, neighbors, and hospitals send people to Vita?

João Biehl, "Human Pharmakon: Symptoms, Technologies, Subjectivities." Written especially for this volume.

"They say that it is better to place us here so that we don't have to be left alone at home, in solitude ... that there are more people like us here. And all of us together, we form a society, *a society of bodies*." And she added: "Maybe my family still remembers me, but they don't miss me."

Catarina had condensed the social reasoning of which she was the human leftover. I wondered about her chronology and about how she had been cut off from family life and placed into Vita. How had she become the object of a logic and sociality in which people were no longer worthy of affection and accountability, though they were remembered? And how was I to make sense of these intimate dynamics if not by trusting her and working through her language and experience?

Philosopher Giorgio Agamben (1998) has significantly informed contemporary biopolitical debates with his evocation of the *homo sacer* and the assertion that "life exposed to death" is the original element of Western democracies (p. 4). This "bare life" appears in Agamben as a kind of historical-ontological destiny – "something presupposed as nonrelational" and "desubjectified" (1999). A number of anthropologists have critiqued Agamben's apocalyptic take on the contemporary human condition and the dehumanization that accompanies such melancholic, if poignant, ways of thinking (Das and Poole 2004; Rabinow and Rose 2006).

Whether in social abandonment, addiction, or homelessness, life that no longer has any value for society is hardly synonymous with a life that no longer has any value for the person living it (Biehl 2007; Bourgois and Schonberg 2009; Garcia 2008). Language and desire meaningfully continue even in circumstances of profound abjection. Such difficult and multifaceted realities and the fundamentally ambiguous nature of people living them give anthropologists the opportunity to develop a human, not abstractly philosophical, critique of the non-exceptional machines of social death and (self) consumption in which people are caught. Against all odds, Catarina and many others keep searching for contact and for ways to endure, at times reworking and sublimating symptoms in their search for

social ties. People's practices of survival and inquiry, their search for symbolic authority, challenge the analytic forms we bring to the field, forcing us to articulate more experience-near and immediately relevant conceptual work.

I picked up the dictionary and read aloud some of her free-associative inscriptions: "*Documents, reality, truth, voracious, consumer, saving, economics, Catarina, pills, marriage, cancer, Catholic church, separation of bodies, division of the estate, the couple's children.*" The words indexed the ground of Catarina's existence; her body had been separated from those exchanges and made part of a new society.

What do you mean by the "separation of bodies"?

"My ex-husband kept the children."

When did you separate?

"Many years ago."

What happened?

"He had another woman."

She shifted back to her pain: "I have these spasms, and my legs feel so heavy."

When did you begin feeling this?

"After I had Alessandra, my second child, I already had difficult walking ... My ex-husband sent me to the psychiatric hospital. They gave me so many injections. I don't want to go back to his house, he rules the city of Novo Hamburgo."

Did the doctors ever tell you what you had?

"No, they said nothing." She suggested that something physiological had preceded or was related to her exclusion as mentally ill, and that her condition worsened in medical exchanges. "I am allergic to doctors. Doctors want to be knowledgeable, but they don't know what suffering is. They only medicate." Catarina knew what had made her an abject figure in family life, in medicine, in Brazil – "I know because I passed through it."

"When my thoughts agreed with my ex-husband and his family, everything was fine," Catarina recalled, as we continued the conversation later that day. "But when I disagreed with them, I was mad. It was like a side of me had to be forgotten. The side of wisdom. They wouldn't dialogue, and the science of the illness was forgotten. My legs weren't working well ... My sister-in-law went to the health post to get the medication for me."

According to Catarina, her physiological deterioration and expulsion from reality had been mediated by a shift in the meaning of words, in the light of novel family dynamics, economic pressures, and her own pharmaceutical treatment. "For some time I lived with my brothers ... But I didn't want to take medication when I was there. I asked: why is it only me who has to be medicated? My brothers want to see production, progress. They said that I would feel better in the midst of other people like me."

You seem to be suggesting that your family, the doctors, and the drugs played an active role in making you "mad," I said.

!"I behaved like a woman. Since I was a housewife, I did all my duties, like any other woman ... My ex-husband and his family got suspicious of me because sometimes I left the house to attend to other callings. He thought that I had a nightmare in my head. He wanted to take that out of me, to make a normal person. I escaped so as not to go to the hospital. I hid myself; I went far. But the police and my ex-husband found me. They took my children. I felt suffocated. I also felt my legs burning, a pain, a pain in the knees, and under the feet." Catarina added that "He first placed me in the Caridade Hospital, then in the São Paulo – seven times in all. When I returned home, he was amazed that I recalled what a plate was. He thought that I would be unconscious to plates, plans, and things and conscious only of medications. But I knew how to use the objects."

Through her increasing disability, all the social roles Catarina had forcefully learned to play – sister, wife, mother, worker, patient – were being annulled, along with the precarious stability they had afforded her. To some degree, these cultural practices remained with her as the values that motivated her memory and her sharp critique of the marriage and the extended family who had amputated her as if she had only a pharmaceutical consciousness. But she resisted this closure, and in ways that I could not fully grasp at first, Catarina voiced an intricate ontology in which inner and outer state where laced together, along with the wish

to untie it all: "Science is our consciousness, heavy at times, burdened by a knot that you cannot untie. If we don't study it, the illness in the body worsens. ... Science ... If you have a guilty conscience, you will not be able to discern things."

"After my ex-husband left me," she continued, "he came back to the house and told me he needed me. He threw me onto the bed saying, 'I will eat you now.' I told him that that was the last time... I did not feel pleasure though. I only felt desire. Desire to be talked to, to be gently talked to."

In abandonment, Catarina recalled sex. There was no love, simply a male body enjoying itself. No more social links, no more speaking beings. Out of the world of the living, her desire was for language, *the desire to be talked to.*

Contemporary Symptoms

In this essay, I explore Catarina's ties to pharmakons and chart the interpersonal and medical crossroads in which her life chances took form. As she wrote: "*Not slave, but housewife. Wife of the bed. Wife of the room. Wife of the bank. Of the pharmacy. Of the laboratory ... The abandoned is part of life.*" Her "ex-family," she claims, thinks of her as a failed drug regimen. The family is dependent on this explanation as it excuses itself from her abandonment. In her words: "*To want my body as a medication, my body.*" Catarina fights the disconnections that psychiatric drugs introduced in her life – between body and spirit, between her and the people she knew, in common sense – and works through the many layers of (mis)treatment that now compose her existence. While integrating drug experience into a new self-perception (the drug AKINETON which is used to control the side effects of anti-psychotics is literally part of the new name Catarina gives herself in her notebooks: CATKINE) she keeps seeking camaraderie and another chance at life.

I find Jacques Lacan's theoretical investigation of "Le Sinthome" (an ancient way of writing what would later be called symptom – 2005) especially helpful for this inquiry into the relationship between symptoms, medical technologies, and subjectivities. In his 1975–76 Seminar, Lacan elaborated on the concept of the sinthome as the enigmatic fourth element that tied the imaginary, the symbolic and the real together (p.21). With a nature of their own, symptoms convey the inextricably knotted processes of identity. They are the support of subjects trying to organize the complex relationship between body and language; in Lacan's words, "We recognize ourselves only in what we have. We never recognize ourselves in what we are" (p. 120).

In classic psychoanalysis, symptoms are addressed to the analyst and might be dissolved through interpretation and analytic work – but the sinthome, Lacan argues, testifies to the persistence of the traumatic Real. Trauma is an event that remains without the possibility of symbolization. Or as Žižek (1989) puts it, the sinthome is "an inert stain resisting communication and interpretation, a stain which cannot be included in the circuit of discourse, of social bond network, but is at the same time a positive condition of it" (p.75). Lacan said he learned from Joyce ("he was the sinthome") that it is only through art and "these little pieces of writing" that we can "historically enter the Real" (2005, p.68), undo supposed truths, and reinvent and give substance to the sinthome. As Lacan states, "it is the knot that gives writing its autonomy" (p.140).

This attention to the vision and work of sublimation can also inspire ethnographers: Listening as readers and writers, rather than clinicians or theoreticians, our own sensibility and openness become instrumental in spurring social recognition of the ways ordinary people think through their conditions. While Lacan builds on Joyce, anthropologists bring back the everyday stories and writings of characters that might otherwise remain forgotten, with attention to the ways their own struggles and visions of themselves create holes in dominant theories and policies. Ethnographic details reveal nuanced fabrics of singularities and the worldliness, rather than exceptionality, of people's afflictions and struggles; they make explicit the concreteness of processes and failed or foreclosed anticipations. Perhaps

the creativity of ethnography arises from this effort to give form to people's own painstaking arts of living and the unexpected potentials they create, and from the descriptive work of giving these observed tensions an equally powerful force in our own accounting.

Catarina's "little pieces of writing" evince pain and an ordinary life force seeking to break through forms and foreclosures and define a kind of subjectivity that is as much about swerves and escapes as about determinations. By working with Catarina I came to see that subjectivity is neither reducible to a person's sense of herself nor necessarily a confrontation with the powers that be. It is rather the material and means of a continuous process of experimentation – inner, familial, medical, and political. Always social, subjectivity encompasses all the identifications that can be formed by, discovered in, or attributed to the person. Although identity-making mechanisms are quite difficult to detect, this process of subjective experimentation is the very fabric of moral economies and personal trajectories that are all too often doomed not to be analyzed. I am thinking here of a diffused form of control that occurs through the remaking of moral landscapes as well as the inner transformations of the human subject (Biehl et al. 2007; Jenkins and Barrett 2003).

Subjectivities have quickly become "raucous terrae incognitae" for anthropological inquiry, writes Michael M. J. Fischer: "landscapes of explosions, noise, alienating silences, disconnects and dissociations, fears, terror machineries, pleasure principles, illusions, fantasies, displacements, and secondary revisions, mixed with reason, rationalizations, and paralogics – all of which have powerful sociopolitical dimensions and effects" (2007: 442). As Catarina conveys, subjectivity does not merely speak as resistance, nor is it simply spoken (or silenced) by power. It continually forms and returns in the complex play of bodily, linguistic, political, and psychological dimensions of human experience, within and against new infrastructures and the afflictions and injustices of the present (see Corin 2007; M. Good et al. 2008; Kleinman 2006; Petryna 2009; Tsing 2004). To grasp the wider impact of how medical technologies are becoming interwoven in the very fabric of symptoms and notions of well-being, we must account comparatively for the ways such life forms are fundamentally altering interpersonal relations, domestic economies, and identity-making processes in both affluent and resource-poor contexts (Fassin and Rechtman 2009; Pinto 2008; Reynolds Whyte 2009). The study of individual subjectivity as both a strategy of existence and a material and means of sociality and governance helps to recast totalizing assumptions of the workings of collectivities and institutions (Scheper-Hughes 2008). It also holds the potential to disturb and enlarge presumed understandings of what is socially possible and desirable.

In many ways, Catarina was caught in a period of political economic and cultural transition. Since the mid-1990s, Brazilian politicians have deftly reformed the state, combining a respect for financial markets and innovative and targeted social programs. Many individuals and families have benefited from pharmaceutical assistance and income distribution programs, for example. An actual redistribution of resources, powers, and responsibility is taking place locally of these large-scale changes and for larger segments of the population, one could argue, citizenship is increasingly articulated in the sphere of consumer culture (Caldeira 2000; Edmonds 2007). Yet, without adequate investments in infrastructural reforms, many families and individuals are newly overburdened as they are suffused with the materials, patterns and paradoxes of these various processes and programs, which they are, by and large, left to negotiate alone.

As institutional care becomes increasingly outsourced to entrepreneurs and local communities, and as powerful pharmaceutical drugs circulate without even a doctor visit, human relationships to medical technology are increasingly constituted outside the clinical encounter. New populations and forms of intimacy are now emerging around technology at community and domestic levels, as in the case of large-scale AIDS treatment and the massive and often unregulated dissemination of psychiatric drugs. Amid the "pharmaceuticalization of public health" (Biehl 2007) and in the daily rituals of medication and adherence, new

conceptions of political belonging and ideas of what life is for begin to take shape. As interrelations such as kinship become mediated by technology in new ways, we need to account for novel social realities as pharmaceuticals and other health technologies open up and relimit family complexes and human values – as well as for the agency that solitary and chemically submerged subjects such as Catarina/CATKINE express and live by.

In a 1972 lecture, Lacan said that capitalism was now the new discourse of the master and as such it overdetermined social bonds (see Declercq 2006; Žižek 2006). He spoke of the effects of an absolutization of the market: Subjects do not necessarily address each other to be recognized but experience themselves in the market's truths and commodities (increasingly a bioscientific market – Petryna 2009, Rajan 2006). Although people might have access to the products of science, those countless objects are made to never completely satiate their desires or the desires of those who mediate the access to technologies (Biehl et al. 2001). A few years earlier, Lacan stated, "The consumer society has meaning when the 'element' that we qualify as human is given the homogenous equivalent of any other surplus enjoyment that is a product of our industry, a fake surplus enjoyment" (1991, p. 92). Or, as Catarina suggests, these days one can conveniently become a medico-scientific thing and ex-human for others. In the contemporary version of the astute capitalistic discourse we seem to be all proletariat patient-consumers, hyperindividualized psycho-biologies doomed to consume diagnostics and treatments (for ourselves and surrounding others) and to experience fast success or self-consumption and lack of empathy. Or, can we fall for science and technology in different and more lively and caring ways?

By staying as close as I could, for as long as I could, to Catarina's struggles to articulate desire, pain, and knowledge, I also came to see the specificity and pathos of subjectivity and the possibilities it carries. While her sense of herself and of the world was perceived as lacking reality, Catarina found in thinking and writing a way of living with what would otherwise be unendurable. Thus, subjectivity also contains creativity, the possibility of the subject adopting a distinctive symbolic relation to the world to understand lived experience. By way of speech, the unconscious, and the many knowledges and powers whose histories she embodies, there is a subjective *plasticity* at the heart of Catarina's existence.

In sum, the currents of medical isolation and technological self-care that shape Catarina's existence actually represent global trends (Ecks 2005; Good et al. 2007; Lakoff 2006; Luhrman 2000; Martin 2007; Petryna et al. 2006). Technoscience enables novel types of experiments and interventions and allows people to imagine and articulate different desires and possibilities for themselves and others (Boellstorff 2008; Dumit 2004; Farmer 2008; Inhorn 2003; Rapp 1999; Whitmarsh 2008). Science and medicine are more than tools of control or even personified inanimate objects, but rather represent one actor in a process that always involves at least two sides acting on each other (Biehl and Moran-Thomas 2009; Fischer 2009).

"*I need to change my blood with a tonic. Medication from the pharmacy costs money. To live is expensive.*" Catarina embodies a condition that is more than her own. People are increasingly grappling with the healing and destructive potentials of technology at the level of their very self-conceptions. While painfully wrestling with symptoms and drug side-effects, kinship ties are recast, patterns of consumption redefined, and possibilities for alternate futures are opened from within sick roles. Technology thus becomes a complex intersubjective actor, with transformative potential that must be negotiated with and even cared for in order to actualize its fragile chance for a new beginning. As medical technology becomes a potential way to explore the new people we might be or the relationships we might imagine, Sherry Turkle notes (2008: 29): "Inner history shows technology to be as much an architect of our intimacies as our solitudes."

Vital/Deadly Experimentation

"Clearly no one knows what to do with drugs, not even the users. But no one knows how to talk about them either," Gilles Deleuze wrote in a 1978 article entitled "Two Questions on Drugs" (2006:151). The use of illegal substances was then on the rise and, according to Deleuze, those who knew of the problem, users and doctors alike, had given up a deeper understanding of the phenomenon. Some spoke of the "pleasure" of drug use, something quite difficult to describe and which actually presupposes the chemical. Others evoked extrinsic factors (sociological considerations such as communication and incommunicability and the overall situation of the youth). For Deleuze, such drug-talk was of little help and addiction therapeutics remained *terrae incognitae*. The philosopher posed two questions:

1   Do drugs have a specific causality and how can we explore this track?
2   How do we account for a turning point in drugs, when all control is lost and dependence begins?

Deleuze's answers were tentative. Yet, he sketched a few ideas and concepts that I find useful for my own inquiry into the widespread and largely unregulated use of legal substances – psychiatric drugs – among the urban poor in Brazil today. Data from the government's database for health resource use between the years 1995 and 2005 show that the country's psychiatric reform was accompanied by a significant fall in the percentage of resources dedicated to psychiatric care (Andreoli et al. 2007). In 1995, for example, psychiatric hospital admissions accounted for 95.5 percent of the mental health budget, down to 49.3 percent in 2005. Meanwhile, there has been a dramatic increase in resource allocation for community services and for pharmaceutical drugs. Drug provision rose from 0.1 percent in 1995 to 15.5 percent in 2005 – a 155-fold increase in the national budget. Second-generation antipsychotic drugs were responsible for 75 percent of the expenses with drugs in this period. Interestingly, the rise in drug allocation was followed by a relative decrease in the number of psychiatrists hired – psychologists and social workers have been hired at three times and twice the rates of psychiatrists from 1995 to 2005. Catarina's travails are entry points into the anthropological communities and ways of being that have emerged in the wake of this pharmaceuticalization of mental health in the service of a diffused form of governance and of market expansion.

Back to Deleuze, for a moment, to the time when psychiatric markets had not yet further confounded the drug scene. For him, the question about whether drugs do have a "specific causality" does not imply exclusively a scientific (i.e., chemical) cause on which everything else would depend. Likewise, Deleuze makes clear that he was not after a metaphysical causality or identifying transcendental organizational planes that would determine popular drug use. After all, Deleuze did not share Michel Foucault's confidence concerning power arrangements. In a 1976 article called "Desire and Pleasure," Deleuze reviewed Foucault's then recently published *The History of Sexuality* (1976). In that book, Foucault took a new step with regard to his earlier work in *Discipline and Punish* (1975): now power arrangements were no longer simply normalizing; they were constituents of sexuality. But "I emphasize the primacy of desire over power," wrote Deleuze. "Desire comes first and seems to be the element of a micro-analysis ... Desire is one with a determined assemblage, a co-function" (2006:126).

Attentive to historical preconditions *and* singular efforts of becoming, Deleuze said that he pursued "lines of flight." For him "all organizations, all the systems Michel calls biopower, in effect reterritorialize the body" (2006:131; see Foucault 2007). But a social field, first and foremost, "leaks out on all sides" (ibid.: 127). In an interview with Paul Rabinow in the mid-1980s, Deleuze once again emphasized that he and Foucault did not have the same conception of society. "For me," he said, "society is something that is constantly escaping in every direction.... It flows monetarily, it flows ideologically. It is really made of lines of flight. So much so that the problem for a society is how to stop it from flowing. For me, the powers come later" (2006:280).

The analytics of biopolitics and of normalization cannot fully account for the drug phenomenon, nor can the Freudian unconscious. The failure of psychoanalysis in the face of drug phenomena, Deleuze argues, "is enough

to show that drugs have an entirely different causality" than sexuality or the oedipal theory. The libido follows world-historical trajectories, be they customary or exceptional. And real and imaginary voyages compose an interstitching of routes that must be read like a map. These internalized trajectories are inseparable from becomings (Deleuze 1997:61–67). Deleuze thus distinguishes his cartographic conception of the unconscious from the archaeological conception of psychoanalysis. "From one map to the next, it is not a matter of searching for an origin, but of evaluating displacements" (1997:63). Every map is a redistribution of impasses, of breakthroughs, thresholds and enclosures on the ground. "It is no longer an unconscious of commemoration but one of mobilization" (idem). Unconscious materials, lapses and symptoms are not just to be interpreted, but rather it is a question of identifying their trajectories to see if they can serve as indicators of a new universe of reference, "capable of acquiring consistency sufficient for turning a situation around." Maps should not only be understood in terms of extension, of spaces constituted by trajectories, adds Deleuze: "There are also maps of intensity, of density, that are concerned with what fills the space, what subtends the trajectory" (64).

Thus, when it comes to studying the domain of drugs, Deleuze brings desire into view as part and parcel of drug assemblages. He speaks of specific "drug-sets" engendered by the flows of drugs and people and of the need to map their territory or contours. "On the one hand, this set would have an internal relationship to various types of drugs and, on the other to more general causalities" (2006:151). Deleuze is particularly concerned with "how desire directly invests the system of perception" of both drug users and non-users (families and experts, for example) and how systems of perception (especially space–time perception) are connected to more general external causalities (contemporary social systems, chemical research, and therapeutics). This project would require, it seems, a distinctive ethnographic sensibility and new analytical tools. This sensibility and tools would address the ways drug consumption/dependence are at once a chemical, intimate, social, and economic matter, and how historical changes and techno-political apparatuses coalesce around drugs and in the emergence of new kinds of subjectivities and social pathways as well as new kinds of expertise and authority.

Deleuze is also concerned with the extent to which "microperceptions are covered in advance" and whether there is variation in dependence built into drugs (2006:153). "The drug user creates active lines of flight. But these lines roll up, start to turn into black holes, with each drug user in a hole, as a group or individually, like a periwinkle. Dug in instead of spaced out" (idem). For Deleuze, two things must be distinguished: the domain of *vital experimentation* and the domain of *deadly experimentation*. "Vital experimentation begins when any trial grabs you, takes control of you, establishing more and more connections, and opens you to connections" (idem). This kind of experimentation can blend with other flows, drugs, and dangers. "The suicidal occurs when everything is reduced to this flow alone: 'my' hit, 'my' trip 'my' glass. It is the contrary of connection; it is organized disconnection" (idem).

In what follows, I revisit my ethnographic data and Catarina's writing. I further explore 1) the treatment constellation (or "drug-set" in Deleuze's words) in which Catarina became the woman who no longer exists – "My ex did everything to get medication;" "*I am a sedative*" – and the knowledge she produced as an abandoned psychopharmaceutical subject; 2) How Catarina redirected her clinical and familial abandonment and invented a new name and an alternative existential stage for herself with whatever means she had available, particularly writing – "*The pen between my fingers is my work. I am convicted to death.*" Writing as a therapeutic means, as a possibility of life: "*To be well with all, but mainly with the pen.*"

The Body as Medication

People's everyday struggles and interpersonal dynamics exceed experimental and statistical approaches and demand in-depth listening and long-term engagement. From 2000 to 2003, I took numerous trips to southern Brazil to work with Catarina, sometimes for weeks, sometimes for months. Catarina's puzzling language required intense listening. And I have chosen to listen to her on a literary rather than on a clinical register. Since the beginning, I have thought of her not in terms of mental illness but as an abandoned person who, against all odds, was claiming experience on her own terms. She knew what had made her a void in the social sphere – "*I am like this because of life*" – and she organized this knowledge for herself and for her anthropologist, thus bringing the public into Vita. "I learned the truth and I try to divulge what reality is."

Catarina's free and elusive verse slowly began to shape the terms of my own inquiry and cognition. "*João Biehl, Reality, CATKINE.*" I studied all the twenty-one volumes of the dictionary Catarina was composing and discussed the words and associations with her. Her knowledge revealed complicated realities. In her recollections and writing, I found clues to the people, sites, and interactions that constituted her life. As an anthropologist, I was challenged to reconstruct the worldliness, the literality of her words. With Catarina's consent, I retrieved her records from psychiatric hospitals and local branches of the universal health care system. I was also able to locate her "ex-family" members in the nearby city of Novo Hamburgo. On a detective-like journey, I discovered the threads of her life. Everything she had told me about the familial and medical pathways that led her into Vita matched with the information I found in the archives and in the field. As I juxtaposed her words with medical records, family versions and considerations, I was able to identify those noninstitutionalized operations that ensured Catarina's exclusion and that are, in my view, the missing contexts and verbs to her disconnected words. The verb to kill was being conjugated and she knew it: "*Dead alive, dead outside, alive inside.*"

Catarina was born in 1966, and grew up in a very poor place, in the western region of the state of Rio Grande do Sul. After finishing fourth grade, she was taken out of school and became the housekeeper as her youngest siblings aided their mother in agricultural work.

The father had abandoned the family. In the mid-1980s, two of her brothers migrated and found jobs in the booming shoe industry in Novo Hamburgo. At the age of eighteen, Catarina married Nilson Moraes, and a year later she gave birth to her first child. Shady deals, persistent bad harvests and indebtedness to local vendors forced Nilson and Catarina to sell the land they inherited to take care of Catarina's ailing mother, and in the mid-1980s, the young couple decided to migrate and join her brothers in the shoe industry. In the coming years, she had two more children. As her illness progressed and her marriage disintegrated, her eldest two children went to her husband's family, and her youngest daughter was given up for adoption.

Catarina was first hospitalized at Porto Alegre's Caridade Hospital in April 27, 1988. The psychiatrist who admitted her recalled what he heard from the neighbor who brought her in: "Patient experienced behavioral changes in the past weeks, and they worsened two weeks ago. Patient doesn't sleep well, speaks of mystical/religious matters, and doesn't take care of herself and the house. She says that God gives signs to her when people mock or doubt her, and that she has received a gift of transmitting her thoughts to people." The doctor reported that she "had no clinical ailments and no psychiatric history." Catarina was placed in a unit for chronic schizophrenic patients. The doctor prescribed: Haldol, Neozine, Mogadon, and Akineton. At discharge, her diagnosis was "Acute paranoid reaction."

In multiple admissions at the Caridade and São Paulo Hospitals between 1988 and 1995, the diagnosis given to Catarina varied from "schizophrenia" to "post-partum psychosis" to "unspecified psychosis" to "mood disorder" to "anorexia and anemia." In tracing Catarina's passage through these psychiatric institutions, I saw her not as an exception but as a patterned entity. Caught in struggles for deinstitutionalization, lack of public funding, and the proliferation of new classifications and treatments, the local psychiatry didn't account for her particularity or social condition. Thus, she was subjected to the typically uncertain and dangerous mental health treatment reserved for the urban working poor. Clinicians applied medical technologies blindly, with little calibration to her distinct condition. Like many patients, Catarina was assumed to be aggressive and thus was overly sedated so that the institution could continue to function without providing adequate care.

Although Catarina's diagnosis has softened over the years (mimicking psychiatric trends), she continued to be overmedicated with powerful antipsychotics and all kinds of drugs to treat neurological side effects (such as Akineton). On several occasions, nurses reported hypotension, a clear indicator of drug overdose. Consider this entry from March 9, 1992: "Patient is feeling better, dizzy at time. She keeps saying that she needs to sign her divorce. She says that she is no longer hearing God talking to her. As patient walks, she stumbles and leans against the walls. Patient complains of strong pains in her legs." For Catarina, as for others, treatment began with a drug surplus and was then scaled down, or not, through trial and error. As I read her medical records, I could not separate the symptoms of the psychiatric illness from the effects of the medication, and I was struck that doctors actually did not bother to differentiate between the two in Catarina.

To say that this is "just malpractice," as a local psychiatrist puts it, misses the productive quality of this unregulated medical automatism and experimentalism: Pharmaceuticals are literally the body that is being treated. And the process of overmedicating Catarina caused many of the symptoms that she called "rheumatism." As doctors remained fixated on her "hallucinations," the etiology of her walking difficulties, which nurses actually reported, remained medically unaddressed. The medical records also showed that her husband and family were difficult to contact, that they left wrong telephone numbers and addresses, and that, on several occasions, they left Catarina in the hospital beyond her designated stay.

I visited the Novo Hamburgo psychosocial service where Catarina was serviced in between hospitalizations. I found the following record by a nurse, written in December 12, 1994: "I drove Catarina home. But as she now lives alone, I left her at the house of her mother-in-law, called Ondina. Catarina was badly received. The mother-in-law said that Catarina should die, because she was stubborn and aggressive, didn't obey anyone, and didn't take her medication."

"We have at least five hundred Catarinas in here right now," told me Simone Laux, the coordinator of the service, after I told her about Catarina and my work with her. By "five hundred Catarinas," she meant most of the female clientele of the service which was treating around fifteen hundred people a month. About half of the clients got free psychiatric drugs at the city's community pharmacy.

"When the service began in the late 1980s, it was meant to deal mainly with schizophrenia and psychosis," reported psychologist Wildson Souza, "but this has changed a lot, both diagnostically and numerically. There is an immense growth of mood disorders." Souza cited "unemployment, harsh struggle to survive, no opportunities for social mobility, urban violence" as contributing to this "epidemic of mental suffering." And suggested that the service had become the vanishing social world, the welfare state, and the social medicine that was no more: "Many factories are closed, people don't have jobs or health plans or family support ... They need some form of recognition and help, and they demand it from SUS [the universal healthcare system]. Nothing is isolated."

"We have three women's groups here," continued Laux: "Most of them are not psychotic. But at some points in their lives, they had a crisis or were at risk of committing suicide. All of them have a story that resembles Catarina's." Daniela Justus, the service's psychiatrist, replied: "Catarina is not searching for a diagnostics, but for life." Catarina's story shows that the patterning of the mass patient and her dying at the crux between abandonment and overmedication are both public and domestic affairs, I noted. "Indeed," replied psychologist Luisa Ruckert, "families organize themselves so that they are no longer part of the treatment and care." The major exception is when cash is involved, stated Andreia Miranda, the service's occupational therapist. "Families keep their mentally ill relatives as long as they can manage their disability income."

Dr. Justus then expanded on the family's role in fostering illness: "When patients improved – and we saw this quite often at the Caridade – families discontinued treatment, and the person had to be hospitalized again." Crisis situations were constantly induced. The relation between the family and mental illness, I was told, is made explicit in the culture of psychopharmaceuticals: "In our group sessions, we can see that the fragility of a minimal social integration is revealed in everyone's relation to the medication, the fight over its discontinuation, the lack of money to buy it, or the problems with forgetting to take it." Families, in fact, come into the service demanding medicines: "When I ask them to tell their story," said Ruckert, "many times they say, 'No, I came here to get a medication for her.' They want to leave with a prescription."

In sum, the family crystallizes its way of being in the ways it deals with psychiatric drugs. "Bottom line," Ruckert continued, "the type of ethics the family installs serves to guarantee its own physical existence." The decision to make persons and things work or to let them die is at the center of family life. And science, in the form of medication, brings a certain neutrality to this decision-making process. "In the meetings," added Ruckert, "the patient quite often realizes that, given the continuing process of exclusion, she has already structured her own perception and codification of reality." Rather than psychosis, out of all these processes a para-ontology comes into view – a Being beside itself and standing for the destiny of others. The "irreversible" condition of the mentally afflicted gives consistency to an altered common sense (Geertz 2000). "She died socially," said Laux pushing the conversation back to Catarina. "That is the pain that aches in us ... when we realize this: she cannot opt to live."

Biological Complex

In August 2002, I was able to get the genetics service of the Hospital das Clínicas, one of the ten best in the country, to see Catarina. Fourteen years after entering the maddening psychiatric world, molecular testing revealed that she suffered from a genetic disorder called Machado-Joseph disease, which causes degeneration of the central nervous system (Jardim et al. 2001). Her brothers had the same diagnostics. I was happy to hear the geneticists who saw Catarina say that "she knew of her condition, past and present, and presented no pathology." Dr. Laura Jardim was adamant that "there is no mental illness, psychosis or dementia linked to this genetic disorder. In Machado-Joseph your intelligence will be preserved, clean, and crystalline." Of course, biopsychiatrists could argue that Catarina may have been affected by two concomitant biological processes, but for me the discovery of Machado-Joseph was a landmark in the overwhelming disqualification of her as mad and shed light on how her condition had evolved over time.

While reviewing the records of the one hundred families that are cared for by Dr. Jardim's team, I found that spousal abandonment and an early onset of the disease were quite common among women, just like it had happened with Catarina, her mother, her younger aunt and a cousin. Affective, relational and economic arrangements are plotted and realized around the visible carriers of the disease, and these gendered practices ultimately impact the course of dying. I also learned that after the onset, Machado-Joseph patients survive on average from 15 to 20 years, most dying from pneumonia in wheelchairs or bedridden. Scientists have firmly established that the graver the gene mutation, the more it anticipates disease. And while the gravity of the gene mutation can account for 60 percent of the probability of earlier onset, the unknown 40 percent remains. Among siblings, Dr. Jardim told me "the age of onset is almost always the same." How then to explain Catarina's early onset, in the late teens, and her brothers' onset in their mid to late 20s?

The various socio-cultural and medical processes in which Catarina's biology was embedded, I thought, pointed to the materiality and morality of this "unknown 40 percent" – in other words: the social science of the biological mutation. To this Dr. Jardim responded: "At the peak of her suffering, they were dismembering her... this dying flesh is all that remained." Rather than being the residue of obscure and undeveloped times, Catarina's condition was part of a regularity, forged in all those public spaces and hazy interactions where a rapidly changing country, family, and medicine met.

In ancient Greece, every year two men – "true scum and refuse" – were chosen to be cast out of cities, as part of the festival of the Thargelia (Harrison 1921: 97). Initially, they were seen as the remedy for a city suffering from famine or pestilence; later, they became the means through which cities prevented mischief (Girard 1996). These men were called *pharmakoi*, and, for them, there was no return to the city. Historians disagree over the ways in which they were chosen for this scapegoat role and whether they were actively killed or simply allowed to die (Harrison 1921: 104, 105; Derrida 1981: 132).

Catarina is, in a literal sense, a modern day *pharmakos*. The handling of her defective body was at the heart of the various scenarios people empirically forged and in which they saw themselves with her through institutions such as medicine, city government, and law. Consider the words of her ex-husband: "After we married, they told me the problems the family had. My mother's cousin said 'Poor Nilson, he doesn't know what he has got his hands in.' I didn't believe it until I saw it. *Deus me livre* [May God free me from this]... I got to know her relatives. An aunt of hers died of this problem, and so did some of her cousins ... I told myself, 'Ah, that's how it is ... they will see.' "

These were revenge-laden words – as if through Catarina the man had taught them all a lesson. In retrospect, Catarina has meaning not as a person but as a representative of a collective and its pathology. Her growing social irrelevance took form around this medical unknown and its physical expressions, allowing Nilson now to read family ties as a retaliatory exchange.

And what are your plans? I asked Nilson.

"To make my life. To progress. I am content with my family now. This woman doesn't give me the problems I had before. A person must help herself. As I said, the doctor gave Catarina treatment so the illness would not come back. It was just a matter of taking the medication, but she didn't help herself ... What has passed is over. One must put a stone over it."

Catarina is physically cast out, a stone set over her in life. As her naturalized destiny reveals, medical science has become a tool of common sense, foreclosing various possibilities of empathy and experience. Pharmaceutical commerce and politics have become intimate to lifeworlds and it is the drug – the embodiment of these processes – that mediates Catarina's exclusion as a *pharmakos*. Both the empirical reality through which living became practically impossible for Catarina and the possibility of critique have been sealed up. As Catarina repeatedly told me: "They all wouldn't dialog and the science of the illness was forgotten. I didn't want to take the medication ... Science is our conscience, heavy at times, burdened by a knot that you cannot untie. If we don't study it, the illness in the body worsens."

In *Plato's Pharmacy*, Jacques Derrida follows the term *pharmakon* as it stands for writing in Platonic philosophy. Acting like a *pharmakon*, both as remedy and as poison, writing is the artificial counterpart to the truth of things that speech allegedly can apprehend directly. According to Plato, argues Derrida, writing is considered "a consolation, a compensation, a remedy for sickly speech" – "writing is the miserable son" (1981: 115, 143). While living speech is conformity with the law, writing is a force wandering outside the domain of life, incapable of engendering anything or of regenerating itself: "a living-dead, a weakened speech, a deferred life, a semblance of breath ... It is like all ghosts, errant" (143). For Derrida, however, writing qua *pharmakon* is an independent order of signification. Operating as *differance* – "the disappearance of any originary presence" – writing is at once "the condition of possibility and the condition of impossibility of truth" (168).

The term *pharmakon* that Plato used has been overdetermined by Greek culture, Derrida points out: "All these significations nonetheless appear ... Only the chain is concealed, and to an inappreciable extent, concealed from the author himself, if any such thing exists" (1981:129). The contemporary philosopher sees as a concealed connection between *pharmakon* as writing and *pharmakos*, the human

figure excluded from the political body. Derrida thus brings to light the scapegoat figure of the *pharmakos*, which, interestingly, is absent from Platonic philosophical reflection. "The city body proper thus reconstitutes its unity, closes around the security of its inner courts, gives back to itself the word that links it with itself within the confines of the *agora*, by violently excluding from its territory the representative of an external threat or aggression. That representative represents the otherness of the evil that comes to affect or infect the inside by unpredictably breaking into it" (Derrida 1981:133).

The figure of the *pharmakos* in philosophical thought is quite pertinent, but the place kept by the death of the Other in city governance also remains a key problem to be addressed. In speaking of Catarina as a modern day *human pharmakon*, I argue that her life and story is paradigmatic of a contemporary familial/medical/political structure that operates like the law and that is close to home. Pharmaceutically addressed, she was now the evil cast out, both subjectively and biologically. In the end, Catarina was a failed medication that, paradoxically, allowed the life, sentiments, and values of some to continue in other terms.

The ethnography of Vita and Catarina also makes it painfully clear that there are places today, even in a state founded on the premise of guaranteeing human rights, where these rights no longer exist, where the living subjects of marginal institutions are constituted as something other, between life and death. Such places demonstrate how notions of universal human rights are socially and materially conditioned by medical and economic imperatives. Vita also confirms that public death remains at the center of various social structures, animating and legitimating charity, political actors, and economic strategies.

The being of the people in Vita is fundamentally ambiguous. This ambiguity gives the anthropologist the opportunity to develop a human, not philosophical, critique of the machine of social death in which these people are caught (see Rancière 2004). This entails: (1) Making explicit that Vita and zones of social abandonment elsewhere, in both poor and rich contexts, are not spheres of exceptionality but rather extensions of what is becoming of family, state, medicine – they are the negative nature, so to speak, of common sense in this moment of capitalism; (2) Illuminating the paradoxes and dynamism involved in letting the other die; (3) Repopulating the political stage with ex-humans; (4) Bringing into view the insights, ambiguities, and desires (alternative human capacities) they also embody and inquire into how they can be part and parcel of the much needed efforts to redirect care.

Literature and Health

Catarina's vision was to be absolutely real. But while trying to speak she was overwhelmed by the chemical alterations of drugs, layers and layers of chemical compounds that other people used to work on her and drug side-effects that were her body and identity now. To speak the unspeakable, she resorted to metaphors and to writing. In the following dictionary entry, for example, she tries to break open the reader's blindness and brings a Greek tragic figure and her three brothers and three children together with her renamed self and the always lacking clinical register:

"*Look at Catarina without blindness, pray, prayer, Jocastka, there is no tonic for CAT-KINE, there is no doctor for any one, Altamir, Ademar, Armando, Anderson, Alessandra, Ana.*"

Medical science is part and parcel of Catarina's existence – the truths, half-truths, and misunderstandings that brought her to die in Vita and upon which she subsisted. "*Pharmacy, laboratory, marriage, identity, army, rheumatism, complication of labor, loss of physical equilibrium, total loss of control, govern, goalkeeper, evil eye, spasm, nerves.*" "*In the United States, not here in Brazil, there is a cure, for half of the disease.*"

Catarina's dictionary is filled with references to deficient movement, to pain in the arms and legs, to muscular contractions. In writing, as in speech, she refers to her condition, by and large, as "rheumatism." I followed the word rheumatism as it appeared throughout the dictionary,

paying close attention to the words and expressions clustered around it.

At times, Catarina's writings relate her growing paralysis to a kind of biological and familial marker, alluding to a certain "*blood type becoming a physical deficiency,*" "*a cerebral forgetfulness,*" and an "*expired brain and aged cranium*" that "*impede change.*" Most of the time, however, Catarina conveys the manmade character of her bodily affections. In the following inscription, for example, she depicts rheumatism as a mangling of the threads people tinker with:

"*People think that they have the right to put their hands in the mangled threads and to mess with it. Rheumatism. They use my name for good and for evil. They use it because of the rheumatism.*"

Her rheumatism ties various life-threads together. It is an untidy knot, a real matter that makes social exchange possible. It gives the body its stature and it is the conduit of a morality. Catarina's bodily affection, not her name, is exchanged in that world: "*What I was in the past does not matter.*" Catarina disappears and a religious image stands in her place: "*Rheumatism, Spasm, Crucified Jesus.*" In another fragment, she writes: "*Acute spasm, secret spasm. Rheumatic woman. The word of the rheumatic is of no value.*"

Catarina knows that there is a rationality and a bureaucracy to symptom management: "*Chronic spasm, rheumatism, must be stamped, registered.*" All of this happens in a democratic context, "*vote by vote.*" We must consider side by side the acute pain Catarina described and the authoritative story she became in medicine and in common sense – as being mad and ultimately of no value. The antipsychotic drugs Haldol and Neozine are also words in Catarina's dictionary. In a fragment, she defiantly writes that her pain reveals the experimental ways science is embodied: "*The dance of science. Pain broadcasts sick science, the sick study. Brain, illness. Buscopan, Haldol, Neozine. Invoked spirit.*"

An individual history of science is being written here. Catarina's lived experience and ailments are the *pathos* of a certain science, a science that is itself sick. There has been a breakdown in the pursuit of wisdom, and there is commerce. The goods of psychiatric science, such as Haldol and Neozine, have become as ordinary as Buscopan (hyoscine, an over-the-counter antispasmodic drug) and have become a part of familial practices. As Catarina's experience shows, the use of such drugs produces mental and physical effects apart from those related to her illness. These pharmaceutical goods – working, at times, like rituals – realize an imaginary spirit rather than the material truth they supposedly stand for: medical commodities are then supposed subjects. There is a science to Catarina's affects, a money-making science. As transmitters of this science, her signs and symptoms are of a typical kind.

In Catarina's thinking and writing, global pharmaceuticals are not simply taken as new material for old patterns of self-fashioning. These universally disseminated goods are entangled in and act as vectors for new mechanisms of sociomedical and subjective control that have a deadly force. Seen from the perspective of Vita, the illnesses Catarina experienced were the outcome of events and practices that altered the person she had learned to become. Words such as "Haldol" and "Neozine" are literally her. As I mentioned earlier, the drug name Akineton (biperiden) is reflected in the new name Catarina gave herself: "*I am not the daughter of Adam and Even. I am. the Little Doctor. CATKINE.*"

Abandoned in Vita to die, Catarina has ties to pharmakons. Her desire, she writes, is now a pharmaceutical thing with no human exchange value:

"*Catarina cries and wants to leave. Desire, watered, prayed, wept. Tearful feeling, fearful, diabolic, betrayed. My desire is of no value. Desire is pharmaceutical. It is not good for the circus.*"

I find Deleuze's insights on literature and health (1997) quite helpful in reflecting on Catarina's work of sublimation and the values it creates in Vita. Deleuze says that writing is "a question of becoming, always incomplete, always in the midst of being formed, and goes beyond the matter of any livable or lived experience. It is a process, that is, a passage of Life that traverses both the livable and the

lived" (p.1). He thinks of language as a system that can be disturbed, attacked, and reconstructed – the very gate through which limits of all kinds are crossed and the energy of the "delirium" unleashed.

The "delirium" suggests alternative visions of existence and of a future that clinical definitions tend to foreclose. Language in its clinical state has already attained a form, says Deleuze: "We don't write with our neuroses. Neuroses or psychoses are not passages of life, but states into which we fall when the process is interrupted, blocked, or plugged up. Illness is not a process but a stopping of the process" (p.3). The radical work of literature, however, moves away from "truths" and "forms" (since truth is a form in itself) and towards intermediate, processual stages that could even be virtual. Writing is inseparable from becoming, repeats Deleuze, and becoming "always has an element of flight that escapes its own formalization" (p.1). To become is not to attain a form through imitation, identification, or mimesis, but rather to find a zone of proximity where one can no longer be distinguished from a man, a woman, or an animal – "neither imprecise, nor general, but unforeseen and nonpreexistent, singularised out of a population rather than determined in a form" (ibid.). In Deleuze's words: one can institute such a zone of indifferentiation with anything "on the condition that one creates the literary means for doing so" (p.2).

While I tried to restore context and meaning to her lived experience of abandonment, Catarina was herself producing, in her dictionary, a theory of the abandoned subject and her subjectivity that was ethnographically grounded. Consider this stanza:

"*Catarina is subjected
To be a nation in poverty
Porto Alegre
Without an heir
Enough
I end*"

In her verse, Catarina places the individual and the collective in the same space of analysis, just as the country and the city also collide in Vita. Subjection has to do with having no money and with being part of a nation gone awry. The subject is a body left in Vita without ties to the life she generated with the man who, as she states, now "rules the city" from which she is banished. With nothing to leave behind and no one to leave it to, there remains Catarina's subjectivity – the medium through which a collectivity is ordered in terms of lack and in which she finds a way to disentangle herself from all the mess the world has become. In her writing, she faces the concrete limits of what a human being can bear, and she makes polysemy out of those limits – "*I, who am where I go, am who am so.*"

One of the guiding principles of Deleuze's philosophy is the link between the real and the imaginary as always co-existing, always complementary. They are like two juxtapositional or superimposable parts of a single trajectory, two faces that ceaselessly interchange with one another, "a mobile mirror"... "bearing witness until the end to a new vision whose passage it remained open to" (1997: 63). In Catarina's words, real and imaginary voyages compose a set of intertwined routes. "*I am a free woman, to fly, bionic woman, separated.*" "*When men throw me into the air, I am already far away.*" These trajectories are inseparable from her efforts of becoming. "*I will leave the door of the cage open. You can fly wherever you want to.*"

Actualized by literature, this mobile mirror reveals beneath apparent persons the power of an impersonal, says Deleuze, "which is not a generality but singularity at the highest point: a man, a woman, a beast, a child ... It is not the first two persons that function as the condition for literary enunciation; literature begins only when a third person is born in us that strips us of the power to say 'I' " (1997:3). The shift to the indefinite – from "I" to "a" – leads to the ultimate existential stage where life is simply "immanent," a transcendental field where man and woman and other men and women/animals/landscapes can achieve the web of variable relations and situated connectedness called "camaraderie."

"There, in Novo Hamburgo it is Catarina. Here it is CATKINE," she told me when I asked her why she invented this name.

"I will be called this now. For I don't want to be a tool for men to use, for men to cut.

A tool is innocent. You dig, you cut, you do whatever you want with it.... It doesn't know if it hurts or doesn't. But the man who uses it to cut the other knows what he is doing."

She continued with the most forceful words: "I don't want to be a tool. Because Catarina is not the name of a person ... truly not. It is the name of a tool, of an object. A person is an Other."

Psychopharmaceuticals had mediated Catarina's expulsion from the world of exchanges (as if she were ignorant of the language she spoke) and were now the thing through which she recounted bodily fragmentation and withering. This was what she was left with: "enjoyment enjoying itself" (*se goza gozo*), as she wrote in the dictionary. "*Pleasure and desire are not sold, cannot be bought. But have choice.*" The opportunity to "restart" and a human choice were all she wanted. This was what Catarina affirmed in her love stories in Vita. "I dated a man who volunteered as a security guard here," she told me. "He bought me a ring and a bracelet, shampoo, many things. We met at night and had sex in the bathroom. But people were trying to separate us. Vera began to say that he was her boyfriend, too. So I gave him the ring back. He refused to take it back. I said, 'I will not throw this into the garbage,' so I put it in my suitcase. After we split, he had other women here ... But as far as I am concerned, I was not his prey. I didn't fall to him. I wanted it. I have desire, I have desire. I am with Clóvis now."

Catarina refused to depict herself as a victim. Her body experienced, along with hunger, spasms, and pain, uncontrollable desires, an overflow unthinkable in terms of common sense. While exposing Vita as a place of total annihilation, she also spoke of the vitality of sexuality and affirmed agency. She spoke openly of having sex "in the bathroom and in the pharmacy" with Clóvis, a man who after passing through the rehabilitation areas became the infirmary's "nurse." For her, desire and pleasure were gratifying, "a gift that one feels." During sex, she said, "I don't lose my head, and I don't let my partner lose his head. If it is good for me, I want to make it good for him, too." She was, in her own words, "a true woman" (*mulher de verdade*): "Female reproducer, reproduces, lubrification, anonymous reproducer, to fondle the aggressive lust, and manias."

"Scientific decadence, kiss, electricity, wet, mouth kiss, dry kiss, kiss in the neck, to start from zero, it is always time, to begin again, for me it is time to convert, this is salvation day, Clóvis Gama, CATKINE, Catakina Gama, Ikeni Gama, Alessandra Gomes, Ana G., to restart a home, a family, the spirit of love, the spirit of God, the spirit becomes flesh inside."

Coda

As fieldwork came to a close, Oscar, one of Vita's volunteers on whom I depended for insights and care, particularly in regard to Catarina, told me that things like this research happen "so that the pieces of the machine finally get put together." Catarina did not simply fall through the cracks of various domestic and public systems. Her abandonment was dramatized and realized in the novel interactions and juxtapositions of several contexts. Scientific assessments of reality (in the form of biological knowledge and psychiatric diagnostics and treatments) were deeply embedded in changing households and institutions, informing colloquial thoughts and actions that led to her terminal exclusion. The subjects in Vita are literally composed by morbid scientific – commercial – political changes. Following Catarina's words and plot was a way to delineate this powerful, noninstitutionalized ethnographic space – the crossroads – in which the family gets rid of its undesirable members. The social production of deaths such as Catarina's cannot ultimately be assigned to any single intention. As ambiguous as its causes are, her dying in Vita is nonetheless traceable to specific constellations of forces and human values.

Once caught in this space, one is part of a machine, suggested Oscar. But the elements of this machine connect only if one goes the extra step, I told him. "For if one doesn't," he replied, "the pieces stay lost for the rest of life. They then rust, and the rust terminates with them." Neither free from nor totally determined by this machinery, Catarina dwelt in the luminous lost edges of human imagination that she expanded through writing.

Catarina remarked that other people might be curious about her words, but she added that their meaning was ultimately part of her living: "There is so much that comes with time ... the words ... and the signification, you will not find in the book. It is only in my memory that I have the signification ... And this is for me to untie." Catarina refused to be an object of understanding for others. "Nobody will decipher the words for me. With the pen, only I can do it ... in the ink, I decipher."

We might face Catarina's writing in the same way we face poetry. She introduces us to a world that is other than our own, yet close to home; and with it, we have the chance to read social life and the human condition via pharmakons differently. To engage with her life and writing is also to work upon oneself. "I am writing for myself to understand, but, of course, if you all understand I will be very content."

Catarina refused to be consigned to the impossible, and she anticipated an exit from Vita. It was as difficult as it was important to sustain this anticipation: to find ways to support Catarina's search for ties to people and the world and her demand for continuity, or at least its possibility. With an eye to the possibilities and noninevitability of people's lives, we must also continually address the concrete powers that bury anticipation and that turn flows into systematic disconnection rather than new circuits of recognition and care. Out of this intricate ethnographic tension emerges a sense of the present as embattled and unfinished, on both sides of the conversation and of the text.

ACKNOWLEDGMENTS

Excerpts of this essay appeared in my book *Vita: Life in a Zone of Social Abandonment* (University of California Press, 2005) and in articles published in *Annual Review of Anthropology* (2009) and *Current Anthropology* (2010) – I am very thankful to Amy Moran-Thomas and Peter Locke for their help in writing these articles. I also want to thank Robson de Freitas Pereira for his helpful comments and insights. I acknowledge the support of the Center for Theological Inquiry and of Princeton University's Program in Latin American Studies and of the Grand Challenges Initiative in Global Health and Infectious disease.

REFERENCES

Agamben, Giorgio
1998 Homo Sacer: Sovereign Power and Bare Life. Stanford, CA: Stanford University Press.

Agamben, Giorgio
1999 Remnants of Auschwitz: The Witness and the Archive. New York: Zone Books.

Andreoli S. B., N. Almeida-Filho, D. Martin, M. D. Mateus, and J. de J. Mari
2007 Is Psychiatric Reform a Strategy for Reducing the Mental Health Budget? The Case of Brazil. Rev. Bras. Psiquiatr. 29(1): 43–6.

Biehl, João
2005 Vita: Life in a Zone of Social Abandonment. Berkeley: University of California Press.

Biehl, João
2007 Will to Live: AIDS Therapies and the Politics of Survival. Princeton: Princeton University Press.

Biehl, João and Amy Moran-Thomas
2009 Symptom: Technologies, Social Ills, Subjectivities. Annual Review of Anthropology 38(1).

Biehl, João and Peter Locke
2010 Deleuze and the Anthropology of Becoming. Current Anthropology, in press.

Biehl, João with Denise Coutinho and Ana L. Outeiro
2001 Technology and Affect: HIV/AIDS Testing in Brazil. Culture, Medicine and Psychiatry 25(1): 87–129.

Biehl, João, Byron Good, and Arthur Kleinman, eds.
2007 Subjectivity: Ethnographic Investigations. Berkeley: University of California Press.

Boellstorff, Tom
2008 Coming of Age in Second Life: An Anthropologist Explores the Virtually Human. Princeton: Princeton University Press.

Bourgois, Philippe and Jeff Schonberg
2009 Righteous Dopefiend. University of California Press.

Caldeira, Teresa
2000 City of Walls: Crime, Segregation, and Citizenship in São Paulo. Berkeley: University of California Press.

Corin, Ellen
2007 The "Other" of Culture in Psychosis: The Ex-centricity of the Subject. *In* João Biehl, Byron Good and Arthur Kleinman, eds., Subjectivity: Ethnographic Investigations. Berkeley: University of California Press, pp. 273–314.

Das, Veena and Deborah Poole, eds.
2004 Anthropology in the Margins of the State. James Curry.

Declercq, Frédéric
2006 Lacan on the Capitalist Discourse: Its Consequences for Libidinal Enjoyment and Social Bonds. Psychoanalysis, Culture & Society 11(1): 74–83.

Deleuze, Gilles
1997 Essays: Critical and Clinical. Minneapolis: University of Minnesota Press.

Deleuze, Gilles
2006 Two Regimes of Madness: Texts and Interviews 1975–1995. New York: Semiotext(e).

Derrida, Jacques
1981 Plato's Pharmacy. *In* Dissemination. Chicago: University of Chicago Press, pp. 61–171.

Dumit, Jospeh
2004 Picturing Personhood: Brain Scans and Biomedical Identity. Princeton: Princeton University Press

Ecks, Stefan
2005 Pharmaceutical Citizenship: Antidepressant Marketing and the Promise of Demarginalization in India. Anthropology & Medicine 12 (3): 239–54.

Edmonds, Alexander
2007 The Poor Have the Right to be Beautiful : Cosmetic Surgery in Neoliberal Brazil. Journal of the Royal Anthropological Institute 13(2): 363–81.

Farmer, Paul
2008 Challenging Orthodoxies: The Road Ahead for Health and Human Rights. Health and Human Rights 10(1): 5–19.

Fassin Didier and R. Rechtman
2009   The Empire of Trauma: An Inquiry into the Condition of Victimhood. Princeton: Princeton University Press.

Fischer, Michael M. J.
2009   Anthropological Futures. Durham: Duke University Press.

Fischer, Michael M. J.
2007   To Live with What Would Otherwise Be Unendurable: Return(s) to Subjectivities. In João Biehl, Byron Good, and Arthur Kleinman, eds., Subjectivity: Ethnographic Investigations. Berkeley: University of California Press, pp. 423–46.

Foucault, Michel
1979   Discipline and Punish: The Birth of the Prison. New York: Vintage Books.

Foucault, Michel
1980   The History of Sexuality. Volume I: An Introduction. New York: Vintage Books.

Foucault, Michel
2007   Security, Territory, Population – Lectures at the College de France 1977–1978. New York: Palgrave Macmillan.

Garcia, Angela
2008   The Elegiac Addict: History, Chronicity and the Melancholic Subject. Cultural Anthropology 23(4): 718–46.

Geertz, Clifford
2000   Common Sense as a Cultural System. In Local Knowledge: Further Essays in Interpretive Anthropology. New York: Basic Books.

Girard, René
1996   The Girard Reader. New York: Crossroad.

Good, Byron, Subandi, and Mary-Jo DelVecchio Good
2007   The Subject of Mental Illness: Madness, Mad Violence, and Subjectivity in Contemporary Indonesia. In João Biehl, Byron Good and Arthur Kleinman, eds., Subjectivity: Ethnographic Investigations. Berkeley: University of California Press, pp. 243–72.

Good, M. DelVecchio, S. T. Hyde., S. Pinto, and B. Good, eds.
2008   Postcolonial Disorders: Ethnographic Studies in Subjectivity. Berkeley: University of California Press.

Harrison, J. E.
1921   Epilegomena to the Study of Greek Religion. Cambridge: Cambridge University Press.

Inhorn, Marcia
2003   Local Babies, Global Science: Gender, Religion, and In Vitro Fertilization in Egypt. New York: Routledge.

Jardim L. B., M. L. Pereira, I. Silveira, A. Ferro, J. Sequeiros, and R. Giugliani
2001   Machado-Joseph Disease in South Brazil: Clinical and Molecular Characterizations of Kindreds. Acta Neurologica Scandinavica 104: 224–31.

Jenkins, H. Janis, and Robert J. Barrett, eds.
2003   Schizophrenia, Culture, and Subjectivity: The Edge of Experience. Cambridge: Cambridge University Press.

Kleinman, Arthur
2006   What Really Matters: Living a Moral Life Amidst Uncertainty and Danger. New York: Oxford University Press.

Lacan, Jacques
1972   Del Discurso Psicanalitico (Milan). Unpublished translation.

Lacan, Jacques
1989   Science and Truth. Newsletter of the Freudian Field 3: 4–29.

Lacan, Jacques
1991   Le Seminarie Livre XVII: L'Envers de la psychanalyse. Paris: Seuil.

Lacan, Jacques
2005   O Seminário, Livro 23: O Sinthoma, 1975–1976. Rio de Janeiro: Jorge Zahar Editor.

Lakoff, Andrew
2006   Pharmaceutical Reason: Knowledge and Value in Global Psychiatry. Cambridge: Cambridge University Press.

Luhrman, Tania
2000   Of Two Minds: The Growing Disorder in American Psychiatry. New York: Alfred A. Knopf.

Martin, Emily
2007   Bipolar Expeditions: Mania and Depression in American Culture. Princeton, NJ: Princeton University Press.

Petryna, Adriana
2009   When Experiments Travel: Clinical Trials and the Global Search for Human Subjects. Princeton, NJ: Princeton University Press.

Petryna, Adriana, Andrew Lakoff, and Arthur Kleinman
2006   Global Pharmaceuticals: Ethics, Markets, Practices. Durham: Duke University Press.

Pinto, Sarah
2008 Where There is No Midwife: Birth and Loss in Rural India. Oxford/New York: Berghahn Books.

Rabinow, Paul and Nikolas Rose
2006 Biopower today. Biosocieties 1(2): 195–217.

Rajan, Kaushik S.
2006 Biocapital: The Constitution of Postgenomic Life. Durham, NC: Duke University Press.

Rancière, Jacques
2004 Who Is the Subject of the Rights of Man? The South Atlantic Quarterly 102(2/3): 297–310.

Rapp, Rayna
1999 Testing Women, Testing the Fetus: The Social Impact of Amniocentesis in America. New York: Routledge.

Reynolds Whyte, Susan
2009 Health Identities and Subjectivities: The Ethnographic Challenge. Medical Anthropology Quarterly 23(1): 6–15.

Scheper-Hughes, Nancy
2008 A Talent for Life: Reflections on Human Vulnerability and Resistance. Ethnos 73(1): 25–56.

Tsing, Anna
2004 Friction: An Ethnography of Global Connection. Princeton, NJ: Princeton University Press.

Turkle, Sherry (ed.)
2008 The Inner History of Devices. Cambridge: MIT Press.

Whitmarsh, Ian
2008 Biomedical Ambiguity: Race, Asthma, and the Contested Meaning of Genetic Research in the Caribbean. Ithaca, NY: Cornell University Press.

Žižek, Slavoj
1989 The Sublime Object of Ideology. New York: Verso.

Žižek, Slavoj
2006 Jacques Lacan's Four Discourses. In www.lacan.com/zizfour.htm (accessed August 3, 2008).

19

The Figure of the Abducted Woman
The Citizen as Sexed

Veena Das

Writing in 1994, the well-known historian of the subaltern Gyanendra Pandey took the neglect of the Partition in the social sciences and in Indian public culture as a symptom of a deep malaise. Historical writing in India, he argued, was singularly uninterested in the popular construction of the Partition, the trauma it produced, and the sharp division between Hindus, Muslims, and Sikhs it left behind. He attributed this blindness to the fact that the historian's craft has never been particularly comfortable with such matters as "the horror of the Partition, the anguish and sorrow, pain and brutality of the 'riots' of 1946–47." The analytical move in Indian historiography, Pandey further argued, was to assimilate the Partition as an event in the intersecting histories of the British Empire and Indian nation, which left little place for recounting the experience of the event for ordinary people.[1]

In recent years, many writers, including Pandey, have produced impressive testimonial literature on the Partition in an attempt to bring ordinary people's experiences into the story of this event. Corresponding to this development is the scholarly effort to show how anxiety about Hindu-Muslim relations, especially about sexuality and purity of women, circulated in the public domain in the late nineteenth and early twentieth centuries in the popular forms of cartoons, comic strips, posters, and vernacular tracts. Part of the burden of this chapter is to try to understand how public anxieties around sexuality and purity might have created the grounds on which the figure of the violated woman became an important mobilizing point for reinstating the nation as a "pure" and masculine space.[2] At stake, then, is not simply the question of "silence" but also that of the genres that enabled speech and gave it the forms it took. It is instructive that there has been no attempt to memorialize the Partition in the form of national monuments or museums. No attempt was made, for that matter, to use the legal instruments of trials or public hearings to allow stories of mass rape and murder to be made public or to offer a promise of justice to the violated persons. There was no dramatic enactment of "putting history on trial" that Shoshana Felman sees as the particular feature of twentieth-century collective traumas.[3] In

Veena Das, "The Figure of the Abducted Woman: The Citizen as Sexed," in *Life and Words: Violence and the Descent into the Ordinary*. Berkeley: University of California Press, 2007. © 2007 by the University of California Press – Books. Reproduced with permission of the University of California Press – Books in the format Textbook via Copyright Clearance Center.

fact, the trope of horror was deployed to open up the space for speech in the formal setting of the Constituent Assembly debates and in popular culture, and it gave the recounting of the event a tonality of rumor.

Consider first the numbers and magnitudes as these are cited in official reports. As Pandey argues, numbers are not offered here in the sober register of a judicial tribunal or a bureaucratic report based upon careful collection of data – rather, these function as gestures toward the enormity of the violence. I might add that this mode of reporting was not peculiar to the Partition. It was part of a wider bureaucratic genre that used numbers and magnitudes to attribute all kinds of "passions" such as panic, incredulity, or barbarity to the populace when faced with a crisis such as an epidemic or a riot – thus constructing the state as a rational guarantor of order. We shall see how the figure of the abducted woman allowed the state to construct "order" as essentially an attribute of the masculine nation so that the counterpart of the social contract becomes the sexual contract in which women as sexual and reproductive beings are placed within the domestic sphere under the control of the "right" kinds of men.

The Abducted Woman in the Imaginary of the Masculine Nation

How did the gendering of suffering allow a discourse of the nation to emerge at the time of the Partition? What precise work does the figure of the abducted woman and her recovery do in instituting the relation between the social contract and the sexual contract at the advent of the nation? While I am sympathetic to the question of repression of women's voices in the accounts of the Partition that has animated the work of many feminist historians, I would like to frame this in a different model than that of trauma. Instead of deploying the notion of trauma, I ask what kind of protocols for telling their story might have been imported into the task of making visible (or audible) the suffering of women in the nationalist discourse? I take the figure of the abducted woman as it

circulated in the political debates soon after the Partition of the country and ask how this was anchored to the earlier figures that were available through myth, story, and forms of print culture in the early-twentieth-century discourse on this figure. How was the figure of the abducted woman transfigured to institute a social contract that created the nation as a masculine nation?

One of the earliest accounts of the violence of the Partition rendered the story in the following terms:

> The great upheaval that shook India from one end to the other during a period of about fifteen months commencing with August 16, 1946 was an event of unprecedented magnitude and horror. History has not known a fratricidal war of such dimensions in which human hatred and bestial passions were degraded to the levels witnessed during the dark epoch when religious frenzy, taking the shape of a hideous monster, stalked through the cities, towns and countryside, taking a toll of half a million innocent lives. Decrepit old men, defenseless women, helpless young children, infants in arms, by the thousand were brutally done to death by Muslim, Hindu and Sikh fanatics. Destruction and looting of property, kidnapping and ravishing of women, unspeakable atrocities, and indescribable inhumanities, were perpetrated in the name of religion and patriotism.[4]

The government of India set up a Fact Finding Organization on the communal violence. Although the files containing these reports were never made public, G.D. Khosla, who was a justice of the Punjab High Court and was in charge of producing this report, interviewed liaison officers of the Military Evacuation Organization in charge of the large-scale evacuation of the minorities from one dominion to another. Based on this information, Khosla put the figure of loss of life in both warring communities between 200,000 and 250,000 and the number of women who were raped and abducted on both sides as close to 100,000. Some support for this is provided in information given to the House in the context of legislative debates of the Constituent Assembly, where it was stated on December 15, 1949, that 33,000 Hindu or Sikh women had been abducted by

Muslims and that the Pakistan government had claimed that 50,000 Muslim women had been abducted by Hindu or Sikh men.

Joint efforts made by the governments of India and Pakistan to recover abducted women and restore them to their relatives led to the recovery of a large number of women from both territories. It was stated on behalf of the government in the Constituent Assembly on December 15, 1949, that 12,000 women had been recovered in India and 6,000 in Pakistan. The figures given by Khosla on the basis of the Fact Finding Organization were that 12,000 Hindu or Sikh women were "recovered" from the Punjab and the frontier regions in Pakistan and 8,000 Muslim women from the provinces of Indian Punjab.

As I said earlier, Pandey makes the subtle point that numbers function here not as forms of reporting in which we can read bureaucratic logic but rather as elements of rumor in which the very magnitudes serve to signal both excess and specificity. He argues that in the official reports as well as in reports by prominent political leaders, the circulation of such stories served to transform hearsay into "truth." What Pandey misses in his analysis, it seems to me, is that the magnitudes established that violence was taking place in a state of exception, which, in turn, opened the way to authorize the state to undertake extraordinary measures by appeals to the state of exception. I argue that the circulation of the figure of the abducted woman, with its associated imagery of social disorder as sexual disorder, created the conditions of possibility in which the state could be instituted as essentially a social contract between *men* charged with keeping male violence against women in abeyance. Thus, the story about abduction and recovery acts as a foundational story that authorizes a particular relation between social contract and sexual contract – the former being a contract between men to institute the political and the latter the agreement to place women within the home under the authority of the husband/father figure.[5] The "foundational" event of inaugurating the nation then is itself anchored to the already circulating imaginary of abduction of women that signaled a state of disorder since it dismantled the orderly exchange of women.

The state of war, akin to the Hobbesian state of nature, comes to be defined as one in which Hindus and Muslims are engaged in mutual warfare over the control of sexually and reproductively active women. The origin of the state is then located in the rightful reinstating of proper kinship by recovering women from the other side. If one prefers to put it in the terminology of Lévi-Strauss, one could say that the state reinstates the correct matrimonial dialogue of men. The foundational event of the inauguration of the state brings something new into existence, but the event does not come from nowhere – it is anchored to imageries that already haunt Hindu-Muslim relations.

The Discourse of the State

A conscious policy with regard to abducted women and children born of sexual and reproductive violence was first initiated in the session of the Indian National Congress on November 23 and 24, 1946, when delegates expressed grave concern about the fate of women who were violated during the communal riots. Dr. Rajendra Prasad, who was later to become the first president of independent India, moved a resolution that received wide support from prominent leaders of the Congress Party, including Jawaharlal Nehru:

The Congress views with pain, horror and anxiety the tragedies of Calcutta, in East Bengal, in Bihar and in some parts of Meerut district. The acts of brutality committed on men, women and children fill every decent person with shame and humiliation. These new developments on communal strife are different from any previous disturbances and have involved murders on a mass scale as also mass conversions enforced at the point of a dagger, abduction and violation of women and forcible marriage.

The operative part of the resolution then stated the obligation of the Congress Party toward such women:

The immediate problem is to produce a sense of security and rehabilitate homes and villages, which have been broken up and destroyed.

Women, who have been abducted and forcibly married, must be restored to their homes. Mass conversions, which have taken place forcibly, have no significance or validity and the people affected by them should be given every opportunity to return to their homes and the life of their choice.[6]

This resolution was adopted in November 1946. The situation, however, worsened from March 1947, so that three weeks after India and Pakistan achieved their independence as separate states, the representatives of both dominions met on September 3, 1947, and agreed that steps should be taken to recover and restore abducted persons. Both sides pronounced themselves against recognition of forced marriages.

The All India Congress Committee met in the middle of November and reiterated that "during these disorders large numbers of women have been abducted on either side and there have been forcible conversions on a large scale. No civilized people can recognize such conversions and there is nothing more heinous than abduction of women. Every effort, therefore, must be made to restore women to their original homes, with the co-operation of the Governments concerned."[7]

An interdominion conference followed the Congress session, at which the two dominions agreed to the steps to be taken to recover abducted women and children. The implementation of these decisions led to a recovery of large number of women from both sides – between December 1947 and July 1948, 9,362 women were reported to have been recovered in India and 5,510 in Pakistan. At this time both governments worked toward the creation of a legal instrument for the work of recovery. As a result, appropriate ordinances were issued in India on January 31, 1948, and in Pakistan in May 1948. The ordinance in India was renewed in June 1949. In December 1949 the Constituent Assembly passed the Abducted Persons (Recovery and Restoration) Act of 1949, which remained in force until October 31, 1951.

The events outlined above point to the manner in which the state took cognizance of the sexual and reproductive violence directed against women. To some extent this obligation was generated by the expectations of the affected population. The devastated refugees who had lost their homes, their families, and their possessions in the bloody riots and were housed in refugee camps in Delhi thought it appropriate to address the leaders of independent India as appropriate recipients of their laments. In this manner, they were not only creating a framework for the state to legitimately take up the task of recovery of abducted women but also learning that claiming entitlements over women of one's own community could be seen as a legitimate affair of the state.

Khosla reported that refugees in distress made loud and frantic appeals to all departments of government. Pandit Nehru received letters in the months of August, September, and October seeking his personal intervention to save a relative left behind or to recover a piece of property or a precious possession abandoned in Pakistan. People wrote to him, accusing him of enjoying a victory that had been won at the expense of the Hindus of the west Punjab. Khosla quoted a letter by a retired schoolmaster addressed to Pandit Nehru: "What has compelled me to write this to you is the fact that in casting about my eyes I fail to find anyone in the world except you who can help me in my calamity."[8] How was the nation to respond to such investment of both despair and hope in its leaders?

The Question of National Honor

For the new nation state of India, the question of the recovery of abducted women and children then became a matter of national honor. There was a repeated demand, publicly enunciated, that the state must take the responsibility of the recovery of women and children upon itself. The new government in India tried to reassure the people of its intention in this regard through several press releases. For instance, Rajashree Ghosh cites a press release published in *The Statesman* of November 4, 1947, that "forced conversions and forced marriages will not be recognized and that women and girls who have been abducted must be restored to their families."[9] Various administrative mechanisms for the recovery of women were operative in the early stages of the recovery operations including the Office of the Deputy High Commissioner, the Military Evacuation Organization, the Chief Liaison Officer, and the Organization for Recovering Abducted Women, consisting of social workers and other officials. All these efforts culminated in an interdominion agreement signed on September 3, 1947, and finally the Abducted Persons (Recovery and Restoration) Act of 1949. Through these legal instruments, each country provided facilities to the other for conducting search and rescue operations. Both agreed that the exchange of women should be equal in number. Wide powers were given to the police to conduct the work of recovery, and arrangements were made for housing the recovered women in transitory camps. Disputed cases were to be referred to a joint tribunal for final settlement.

In terms of procedure, the Indian government set up Search and Service Bureaus in different cities in the Punjab where missing women were reported. This information was then passed on to the relevant authorities, and a search for these women and children was mounted. The Indian government accepted the help of several women volunteers, especially those with a Gandhian background, to help in the recovery process. Prominent among these women were Mridula Sarabhai, Rameshwari Nehru, and Kamlabehn Patel. In her memoirs of this period Kamlabehn Patel reports that "in those days it wasn't prudent to trust any male, not even policemen as far as the safety of women was concerned."[10] Several transit camps were set up, such as the Gangaram Hospital Camp in Lahore and Gandhi Vanita Ashram in Amritsar. Kamlabehn herself was in charge of the transit camp in Lahore to which recovered women and children were brought. They were then transferred to India or Pakistan, as the case might be, under police escort. A woman or child who was claimed by a close relative in the case of an Indian citizen could be handed over to the relative only at Jullundher in the presence of a magistrate.

Taken at face value it would appear that the norms of honor in the order of the family and the order of the state were mutually supportive.

The families with whom I worked related stories of a generalized nature in which the heroic sacrifices made by women were lauded, but to speak in the first person on the facts of abduction and rape was not easy. [. . .] Elsewhere I explore the specific ways in which stories were framed in the first person, and especially the place of silence in the "telling."[11] Here I am interested in the logic of the state of exception with regard to the way that law was instituted to shape the nation as a *masculine* nation, so that the social contract became a contract between men conceived as heads of households. As so many statements that I have quoted show, normality was seen as restoration of women "to their families." Men appear here as heads of households rather than as individuals sprung from the earth, as in the famous mushroom analogy favored by Hobbes in conceptualizing the makers of the social contract.

It is my contention that once the problem of abducted women moved from the order of the family to the order of the state (as in the demand for legislation), it sanctified a sexual contract as the counterpart of the social contract by creating a new legal category of "abducted person" (applicable, however, only to women and children) who came within the regulatory power of the state. There was an alliance between social work as a profession and the state as *parens patriae,* which made the official kinship norms of purity and honor much more rigid by transforming them into the law of the state.

The discussion on the Abducted Persons (Recovery and Restoration) Act of 1949 in the Constituent Assembly focused on three issues.[12] The first was the definition of a civilized government and especially the responsibility of the state to women on whom violence had been unleashed. The second was the definition of an abducted person, and the rights of women abducted by men. The third issue was the rights of children born of "wrong" sexual unions and the obligations of the state toward them. The connecting thread between these three issues is the notion of national honor and preservation of purity of the population through which the sexual contract is made the grounds for a social contract that institutes the nation as a masculine nation.

In introducing the bill, Shri N. Gopalaswami Ayyangar, the then Minister of Transport and a distinguished lawyer, stated that there were experiences associated with the partition of the country in regard to which "most of us will have to hang our heads down in shame." He went on to say that "among the many brutalities and outrages which vitiated the atmosphere ... none touched so low a depth of moral depravity as these mass abductions of women on both sides. ... Those of us who think of civilized government and want to conduct the government on civilized lines should feel ashamed."

As is clear from this statement, the state distanced itself from the "depths of moral depravity" that the population had shown and took upon itself the task of establishing a civilized government. Part of the definition of this civilized government was to not only recover women defined by the new nation as "our" women but also to restore to the opposite side "their" women. The interest in women, however, was not premised upon their definition as citizens but as sexual and reproductive beings. As far as recovery of women held by the "other" side was concerned, what was at stake was the honor of the nation because women as sexual and reproductive beings were being forcibly held. This was explicit in the demands made by several members that not only should the recovery of women on both sides be more or less equal but also that women in their reproductive years should be "recovered." Shri Gopalaswami Ayyangar especially referred to this criticism, saying that several critics alleged that "while in India we have recovered women of all ages and so forth, in Pakistan they had recovered for us only old women or little children." He went on to counter this criticism by citing figures to show that the distribution by age of recovered women from both dominions was, in fact, roughly equal. Of the total women recovered, he said, girls below the age of twelve from Pakistan and India were 45 and 35 percent, respectively. In the age group 12 to 35 years old, the recovery was 49 percent in Pakistan and 59 percent in India, while the percentage dropped to about 10 percent for women older than 35. This discussion clearly shows that national honor was tied to the regaining of control over the sexual and reproductive functions of women. The social contract that would legitimate both nations was seen as one instituted by men in which they were capable of recovering their own place as heads of households by placing the sexuality and reproductive powers of women firmly within the family.

Thus the figure of the abducted woman signals the impossibility of the social contract because the sexual contract that would place men as heads of households (not as a matter of kinship but as matter *for the state*) was in jeopardy. Pandit Thakur Das Bhargava explicitly drew on this figure when he stated during the debates, "You will remember, Sir, how when one Ellis was kidnapped by some Pathans the whole of Britain shook with anger and indignation and until she was returned Englishmen did not come to their senses. And we all know our own history, of what happened at the time of Shri Ram when Sita was abducted. Here, where thousands of girls are concerned, we cannot forget this. We can forget all the properties, we can forget every other thing but this cannot be forgotten."[13]

Then there was the question of whether Muslim women needed to be returned to their own families. It is interesting to note the particular tonality that crept into Pandit Thakur Das Bhargava's statement that "I don't suggest for a moment that the abducted Muslim girls should be kept here because I believe that not only would it be good for them to be sent away but it is equally good for us to be rid of them. I don't want immorality to prosper in my country."

It is important to note here that to be a citizen as a head of the household demands that men's own sexuality be disciplined, oriented to the women who have been placed "correctly" within the family, and that children who would claim citizenship are born of the right kind of union of men and women. Elsewhere I have analyzed courtroom talk in the cases of rape in Indian courts of law to argue that "male desire" is construed as a natural need in the judicial discourse on rape, so that whenever the cultural and social constraints are removed, men are seen as falling into a state of nature in which they cannot control their appetite for sex. I quote here from an earlier paper, where I argued that

> it is male desire which is considered as "natural," hence "normal," and the female body as the natural site on which this desire is to be enacted. Women are not seen as desiring subjects in the rape law – as wives they do not have the right to withhold consent from their husbands, although the state invests its resources in protecting them from the desires of other men. Paradoxically, women defined in opposition to the wife or the chaste daughter, i.e. women of easy virtue, as the courts put it, also turn out to have no right to withhold consent. ... A reading of female desire as interpreted by the courts demonstrates, that while men are seen to be acting out their "natural" urges when engaging in "illicit" sex, women who show any kind of desire outside the confines of marriage are immediately considered "loose." By escaping the confines of male-centered discourses of sexuality and alliance, these women are then castigated by becoming the objects of any kind of male desire. Rape is not a crime but is reduced to an act that she herself deserves or seeks.[14]

Clearly, the deeply rooted assumptions about the husband/father figure continue in the juridical unconscious even when the figure of the abducted or raped woman appears in the singular in post-Independence India.

Let us consider the next question – Who is an abducted person? According to the bill, "An 'abducted person' means a male child under the age of sixteen years or a female of whatever age, who is, or immediately before the 1st day of March 1947 was, a Muslim and who, on or after that day, has become separated from his or her family and is found to be living with or under the control of a non-Muslim individual or family, and in the latter case includes a child born to any such female after the said date."[15]

We shall take up the question of children defined as "abducted" under the provisions of the bill later. As for the women, it was clear that the bill failed to make any provision for ascertaining whether a woman wished to return to her original family or not. This question was raised by several members. The sharpest criticism came from Thakur Das Bhargava, who stated, "You want to take away the rights of a major woman who has remained here after the partition. ... My submission is that the law of nations is clear, the law of humanity is clear, the Indian Penal Code is clear, the Constitution we have passed is clear, that you cannot force a woman who is above 18 to go back to Pakistan. This Bill offends against such a rule."

In addition to the manner in which the rights of a woman to decide her future course of action were taken away by the state to protect the honor and purity of the nation, there was also the question that the bill gave wide powers to the police to remove a woman forcibly if she came under the definition of an abducted woman under its clauses. This, as Shri Bhargava pointed out, took away the rights of habeas corpus from a person who was treated as an abducted person even if she were mistakenly so labeled.

When several members of the House pointed to the increasing evidence that many women were refusing to go back to their original families and were practically coerced by social workers to return, Shrimati G. Durgabai, speaking on behalf of both the social workers and the women's movement, defended the social workers on the grounds that they knew best what the women's true preferences were. Durgabai's statement is worth quoting in detail:

> Questions are also asked: Since these women are married and settled here and have adjusted themselves to the new environment and to their new relatives here, is it desirable that we should force them to go back? It is also argued: These women who have been able to adjust themselves to their new surroundings are refusing to go back, and when they are settled, is it desirable that we should force them to go back? ... These are the questions we have to answer. May I ask: Are they really happy? Is the reconciliation true? Can there be a permanent reconciliation in such cases? Is it not out of helplessness, there being no alternative that the woman consents or is forced to enter into that sort of alliance with a person who is no more than the person who is a murderer of her very husband, her very father, or her very brother? Can she be really happy with that man? Even if there is reconciliation, is it permanent? Is this woman welcomed in the family of the abductor?

Paradoxically the authority of the woman social worker was used to silence the voice of the woman as subject and to put upon her an obligation to *remember* that the abductor to whom she was now married was the murderer of her husband or her father. The disciplining of sentiment according to the demands of the state collapsed the duty to the family with duty to the state. The women themselves seem to have been caught in the impossible situation where the obligation to maintain a narrative continuity with the past contradicted the ability to live in the present. Durgabai herself testified to the apprehensions of the women at the prospects of returning to their original homes: "Sir, we the social workers who are closely associated with the work are confronted with many questions when we approach a woman. The women say, 'You have come to save us; you say you have come to take us back to our relatives. You tell us that our relatives are eagerly waiting to receive us. You do not know our society. It is hell. They will kill us. Therefore, do not send us back.' "

Yet at the same moment that these apprehensions were expressed, the authority of the social worker was established by the statement that "the social workers associated with this work know the psychology of these abducted recovered women fully well. They can testify to it that such a woman only welcomes an opportunity to get back to her own house." The refusal of many women to go back and the resistance that the social workers were encountering in the field was explained away by an attribution of false consciousness or a kind of misrecognition to the women. The appropriate sentiment in all such cases was coercively established as a desire for the original home that allowed men on both sides of the border to be instituting the social contract as *heads of households* in which women were "in their proper place."

Children and Reproductive Futures

We come now to the category of children defined as abducted. As stated earlier, the bill defined any child born to a woman after March 1, 1947, as an abducted person if its mother came under the definition of an abducted person. These, in short, were children born through "wrong" sexual unions. The discussion in the Constituent Assembly focused on several issues. First, how were rights over a child to be distributed between the male and the female in terms of their relative contributions to the process of procreation? Second, what legal recognition was to be given to children whose parents were not considered to be legally married since the bill held all forcible marriages to be null and void? Third, was there a contradiction between the legality established by the state and the customary norms of a community regarding the whole question of determining the legitimacy of a child? Finally, if only one parent was entitled in these cases to transmit filiation as a basis for establishing citizenship, was it the relationship with the mother or the father that was to be considered relevant for creating the necessary credentials for citizenship?

Although there was no explicit enunciation of a theory of procreation and the relative contributions of the male and the female to the procreative process, analogies drawn from nature were sometimes used. For instance, Pandit Thakur Das Bhargava stated at one point in the discussion that he did not understand how a general rule could be formulated by which the child was to be handed over to the mother rather than the father: "It takes only nine to ten months gestation during which the child has to remain in the mother's womb. ... It should not be made a rule that in every case the child is to be given over as a matter of rule. It is something like the rule that when you plant a tree it grows on the ground; therefore the tree goes with the land and the fruit of the tree goes with the tree. A child is the fruit of the labour of two persons. There is no reason why the father should be deprived in each case. Why should we make this rule?"

Analogies from nature, especially from the activities of agriculture or horticulture to conceptualize procreation, are part of the repertoire of ideas contained in Hindu texts and in the popular ideas regarding procreation.[16] What is important here is that a theory about the "labor" of reproduction enters into the state's repertoire of ideas even as it is articulated in opposition to the provisions of the bill. Although Durgabai did not pose the question in these terms, she questioned the rights of the male on the grounds that he was an abductor. Men who had forcibly abducted women, sold them, and used them for commercial purposes, she argued, could not claim rights over the children born to these women. In contrast to the earlier argument, Durgabai's interpretation would be that it was not the joint labor of a man and a woman that had created such a child but the plunder by men of women's bodies. Hence, "What right has the abductor to keep the child? The child has to go with the mother."

Another member, Shri Brajeshwar Prasad, also evoked the notion that in nature there was no question of illegitimacy or legitimacy of a child, and that it was only the conventions of society that made children legitimate or illegitimate. In his words, "Sir, I do not know how a child born of a man and a woman can ever become illegitimate. This is a notion I have not been able to grasp, but still knowing full well the attitude of the present Government, knowing full well the attitude of the Hindu society, we have to take the facts as they are and the illegitimate children if they are to live in India, they will remain as dogs, as beasts."

In the above discussion it was clear that the question of the legitimacy or illegitimacy of the children was related to the fact that it was the provisions of the bill that had made all unions that may have started with abduction and ended with marriage illegal and thus the children born to such unions illegitimate. As one member, Shri Brajeshwar Prasad, put it, even if a natural attachment had developed between the abductor and the abducted woman, the law did not recognize such marriages. Therefore, a woman could continue to stay with her abductor "only as a prostitute and a concubine," while her children could only remain in the country as illegitimate children who would be a "standing blot on Hindu society."

A contradiction between state-defined legality and community-based legality was pointed out by Chaudhari Ranbir Singh, at least as he saw the matter, for he thought it would be a mockery to the country if children born to Muslim women were sent away on the grounds that they would be mistreated as illegitimate children here. "There is a general custom in our Punjab," he stated, "particularly in the community to which I and Sardar Bhupinder Singh Man belong, that, regardless of religion or community of the woman one marries, the offspring is not regarded as illegitimate, and we give him an equal share." Clearly a wide variety of customary norms regarding children born to women through proscribed sexual unions existed that were now standardized into one single law by which illegitimacy was defined.

How are we to understand this moment as foundational in terms of the relation between the social contract and the sexual contract in defining the nation-state? I suggested earlier that the figure of the abducted woman had circulated in the late nineteenth and early twentieth centuries as the site of anxiety for defining the place of men as heads of households.[17] It is important to note that the question of a father's rights over his children after his conversion to another religion was not a new question – it had legal precedents. For instance, whether a man who had converted to Christianity could continue to claim conjugal rights over his wife had been debated before the colonial courts as well as the issue of whether a man's "natural" rights over his child overrode the dissolution of marriage after conversion. I have argued elsewhere that although the courts were reluctant to apply English common law to these cases, arguing that the legal imagination must contend with people of one faith living under a political sovereign who owes allegiance to another faith, the general consensus was that the father's right could not be denied.[18] It now became possible to set aside the legal precedents on these questions and to take away custody from the father in the case of children born to women who had been forcibly possessed, precisely because the foundational event was located within an imagination of a state of emergency when normal rules were set aside. In the next section I discuss these issues briefly and then conclude with the question: Why is the state interested in women as sexual and reproductive beings?

Anchoring the Figure of the Abducted Woman

Recent work on the nexus between ideas of sexuality, obscenity, and purity shows that the images of lustful Muslim males and innocent Hindu women proliferated in the propaganda literature generated by reform Hindu movements such as the Arya Samaj and political organizations such as the Hindu Mahasabha and the Rashtriya Sevak Sangh.[19] Charu Gupta has recently marshaled impressive material from the vernacular tracts published in Uttar Pradesh in the late nineteenth and early twentieth centuries to show that mobilization of the Hindu community, especially by new forms of religio-political organizations such as the Arya Samaj and the Hindu Mahasabha, drew upon the image of the lustful Muslim as a threat to Hindu domesticity. Consider the following passage from a speech delivered by Madan Mohan Malviya in 1923 on the subject of kidnapping, cited by Gupta:

> Hardly a day passes without our noticing a case or two of kidnapping of Hindu women and children by not only Muslim *badmashes* and *goondas,* but also by men of standing and means, who are supposed to be very highly connected. The worst feature of this evil is that Hindus do not stir themselves over the daylight robbery of national stock. ... We are convinced that a regular propaganda is being carried on by the interested party for kidnapping Hindu women and children at different centers throughout the country. It is an open secret that Juma Masjids at Delhi and Lahore are being used as headquarters of these propagandists. ... We must do away with this mischievous Muslim propaganda of kidnapping women and children.[20]

References to the lustful Muslim and appeals to the innocence of Hindu women who could be easily deceived by Muslim men were plentiful. In some cases, harshness of Hindu customs against widows was evoked to explain why Hindu women fell into the traps of seduction laid by wily Muslims. Gupta is surely correct in concluding that evocation of these fears provided an emotive basis for arguments in favor of Hindu "homogeneity and patriarchy."[21] I think we can go further – for the story of abduction has implications for the very staging of sovereignty, such that when this story appears magnified at the time of the Partition, it becomes the foundational story of how the state is instituted and its relation to patriarchy. It invites us to think the story of the imaginary institution of the state in Western theory from this perspective rather than the other way around.

It should be obvious that the line of argument proposed here does not see the family simply as the institution located in the domain of the private but proposes that sovereignty continues to draw life from the family. The involvement of the state in the process of recovery of women shows that if men were to become ineffective in the control they exercise as heads of families, thus producing children from "wrong" sexual unions, then the state itself would come to be deprived of life. The figure of the abducted woman acquires salience because it posits the origin of the state not in the mythic state of nature, but in the "correct" relations between communities. Indeed, the mise-en-scène of nature itself is that of heads of households at war with other heads of households over the control of the sexual and reproductive powers of women rather than unattached "natural" men at war with each other. There is an uncanny address here to Lévi-Strauss's notion of the original state as one in which men are posited as relational beings and exchange of women is the medium through which this relational state is achieved.[22] The disturbance of proper exchange then comes to be construed as a disturbance in the life of the state, robbing it of the sources from which it can draw life. Does this story located at the particular juncture of the inauguration of the nation-state in India tell us something about the nature of sovereignty itself?

In an acute analysis of the relation between fatherly authority and the possibility of a woman citizen, Mary Laura Severance argues that in Hobbes we have a predication of fatherly authority based on consent rather than something that is natural or originary, as claimed by Sir Robert Filmer.[23] But, as she notes, the consent of the family to be ruled by the father is, in effect, a neutralization of his power to kill. By grounding the power of the father in the consent of the family, Hobbes is able to draw a distinction between fatherly and sovereign authority as two distinct but artificial spheres. However, this is done within the framework of the seventeenth-century doctrine that women are unfit for civil business and must be represented (or concluded) by their husbands. The sexual contract and the social contract are then two separate realms. As Severance notes, however, the idea of the state of nature as that in which every man is in a state of war with every other man should be modified to read that every *father*, as the head of the family, is at war against every other *father*. In her words, "the members of each individual family 'consent' not to the sovereign's but to the father's absolute rule; they are not parties to the 'contract' that brings the commonwealth into existence."[24] I would claim that this war of "fathers" is what we witness in the acts of abduction and rape. The state's commitment to the recovery of women is the acknowledgment of the authority of the father as the necessary foundation for the authority of the state. I find it useful to think of Rousseau's analysis of the figure of the woman in the discussion on sovereignty in *Émile* to show that the notion of the sexed individual as the basis of the political has a deep linkage with the idea of the life of the sovereign.[25]

As I have argued elsewhere,[26] the figure of the woman in Rousseau is introduced not so much as the symmetrical opposite of the man but rather as the obligatory passage through whom the man moves along the road of marriage, paternity, and citizenship. While the scene of seduction is necessary for the pupil in *Émile* to be inserted into the social, his capability to be a citizen is proved by learning how to renounce the very lure of the woman who was his passage into sociality. The parable of Sophie, whom Émile must both learn to love and through whom he must learn to overcome his fear of death, points to the close relation for a man between learning how to inhabit society through the engagement with sex and how to become a good citizen by overcoming the fear of separation and death. It is worth pausing here to reflect on this.

It is from Émile's journey into citizenship that we learn the multiple chains of signification in which the figure of Sophie is inserted. She is the chimera who is inserted into the text – figure of seduction, the future mother of a family, and one through whom Émile learns that to be a good citizen is to overcome his fear of death by giving a law to the desires of his heart. Hence, she is the seductress in the present, the maternal in the future, and the teacher of duty and code of conduct. Without her, he can overcome physical ills, but with her and then despite her, he will become a virtuous citizen: "When you become the head of a family, you are going to become a member of the state, and do you know what it is to be a member of the state? Do you know what government, laws, and fatherland are? *Do you know what the price is of your being permitted to live and for whom you ought to die?*"[27]

There are two thoughts here. The first is that to be a citizen of the state, you must be the head of a household; the second is that you must know for whom you ought to die. For the woman, the duty as a citizen is confounded with her duty to her husband. A woman's comportment must be such that not only her husband but also his neighbors and friends must believe in her fidelity. When she gives her husband children who are not his own, we are told, she is false both to him and to them and her crime is "not infidelity but treason."[28] Thus, woman as seductress holds danger for the man, because she may use her powers of seduction to make the man too attached to life and thus unable to decipher who and what it is worth dying for. In her role as mother, she may deprive him of being a proper head of the household by giving him counterfeit children. That this is treason and not infidelity shows how the mother, who was completely excluded as a figure of thought in Hobbes, comes to be incorporated into the duties of citizenship. For Rousseau the individual on whose consent political community is built is, no doubt, a sexed individual, but the woman has the special role of not only introducing the man to forms of sociality but also teaching him how to renounce his attachment to her in order to give life to the political community.

Within this scheme, women's allegiance to the state is proved by their role as mothers who bear legitimate children (recall the remark about the crime of bringing illegitimate children into the world being not about infidelity but about treason); and men learn to be good citizens by being prepared to die to give life to the sovereign. Once the individual is recognized as social because he is sexed, he is also recognized as mortal. In Rousseau, we saw that man is said to receive life from the sovereign. Political community as population is dependent on reproduction: thus, the citizen's investment of affect in the political community is attested by his desire to reproduce and to give the political community legitimate "natural" children. A corollary is that a woman's infidelity is an offense not only against the family but also against the sovereignty of the state.

We can see now that the *mise-en scène* of abduction and recovery places the state as the medium for reestablishing the authority of the husband/father. It is only under conditions of ordered family life and legitimate reproduction that the sovereign can draw life from the family. Gupta's work allows us to see that the earlier imagination of the Hindu woman as seduced or duped by the Muslim man is complemented by the idea that her attraction to Muslim practices is an offence against the patriarchal authority of the Hindu man, imagined within the scene of colonialism. Thus, for instance, Gupta gives examples from many vernacular tracts in which the practice of Hindu women praying to the Muslim *pirs* (holy men given the status of saints, especially among Shi'a Muslims), a common religious practice of Hindus and Muslims alike, is construed as a betrayal of the Hindu man – a mocking of his potency – that to my ears sounds remarkably akin to the act of treason that Rousseau attributes to women who bring "wrong" children into the world. The following quotation from a vernacular tract offers a particularly telling example:

God believes in the worship of only one husband for women, but they pay service to Ghazi Mian for many years. ... Where before Hindu women worshipped their husband for a lot of

love and produced a child, today they leave their husband and go to the dead Ghazi Mian and at his defunct grave ask for a child. It is not women but men who are to be blamed for this hateful act. Even when they are alive, instead of asking their wife to become a true *pativrata* [a woman devoted exclusively to her husband, regarding him as a god], they allow her to go to the dead grave of a Turk to ask for a child and become an infidel.[29]

In the introduction to this chapter, I juxtaposed the problem of the silence on the Partition with the excess of speech in the mode of rumor – encountered not only in popular imagination but also at the heart of the official documentation of the event. The analysis offered here takes the legal and administrative discourse on the abducted woman as an important site for understanding how the social contract was grounded in a particular kind of sexual contract. The trope of horror through which this space of (excess) enunciation and action was opened up under the sign of the state not only drowned out the voices of women but also recognized their suffering as relevant only for the inauguration of sovereignty. [...]

NOTES

1 Gyanendra Pandey, "The Prose of Otherness," in *Subaltern Studies,* ed. David Arnold and David Hardiman (Delhi: Oxford University Press, 1994), vol. 8, 188–221, quotation from 205.

2 Rada Ivekovic, *Le sexe de la nation* (Paris: Non & Non, Éditions Léo Scheer, 2003).

3 Shoshana Felman, *The Juridical Unconscious: Trials and Traumas in the Twentieth Century* (Cambridge, MA: Harvard University Press, 2002), 7.

4 G.D. Khosla, *Stern Reckoning: A Survey of the Events Leading Up to and Following the Partition of India* (Delhi: Oxford University Press, 1989; first published in 1949).

5 See Veena Das, "Narrativizing the Male and the Female in Tulasidas's Ramacharitamanasa," in *Social Structure and Change: Ritual and Kinship,* vol. v, ed. A.M. Shah, B.S. Baviskar, and E. Ramaswamy (Delhi: Sage Publications, 1998), 67–93.

6   *Proceedings of the Indian National Congress 1946–1947* (New Delhi: Government of India, 1947).

7   Ibid.

8   Khosla, *Stern Reckoning*, 234.

9   Rajashree Ghosh, "The Constitution of Refugee Identity," unpublished M. Phil. dissertation, University of Delhi, 1991.

10 Kamlabehn Patel, *Mula Suta Ukhledan* (Bombay: R. R. Seth, 1985).

11 Veena Das, *Life and Words* (Berkeley: University of California Press, 2007).

12 The following quotations from these discussions are taken from *Constituent Assembly of India (Legislative) Debates* (New Delhi: Government of India, 1949).

13 The mythic motif of the abduction of the innocent Sita by Ravana and her subsequent banishment by Rama was evoked as a metaphor in popular literature as well as popular Hindi films.

14 Veena Das, "Sexual Violation and the Making of the Gendered Subject," in *Discrimination and Toleration,* ed. K. Hastrup and G. Urlich (London: Kluwer Law International, 2002), 257–73, quotation from 271.

15 The text of the Abducted Persons (Recovery and Restoration) Act, 1949 (Act No. LXV of 1949), is reproduced as Appendix 1 in Menon and Bhasin, *Borders and Boundaries,* 261.

16 On the relative weight given to men and women in the procreative process in Punjabi kinship, see Das, "Masks and Faces."

17 I owe this insight to the important work of P. K. Dutta and Charu Gupta.

18 See Veena Das, "Paternity, Sovereignty and the Argument from Nature," in *Powers of the Secular Modern: Talal Asad and His Interlocutors,* ed. David Scott and Charles Hirschkind (Stanford: Stanford University Press, 2006, 93–113).

19 See Paola Bachetta, *La construction des identités dans les discours nationalists hindous (1939–1992): le Rahstriya Swayamsevak Sangh et la Rashtriya Sevika Samiti* (Lille: ANRT, Université de Lille III, 1996), and Charu Gupta, *Sexuality, Obscenity, Community: Women, Muslims, and the Hindu Public in Colonial India* (New York: Palgrave, 2002; first published, Delhi: Permanent Black, 2001). Page references are to the Palgrave edition.

20 Gupta, *Sexuality, Obscenity, Community,* 248.

21 Gupta, *Sexuality, Obscenity, Community,* 267.

22 Claude Lévi-Strauss, *The Elementary Structures of Kinship,* rev. ed. trans. J. H. Bill and J. R. von Sturmore, ed. Rodney Needham (London: George Allen & Unwin, 1969).

23 Mary Laura Severance, "Sex and the Social Contract," *Journal of English Literary History,* 67, no. 2 (2000): 453–513. I remind the reader that in Filmer's theory fatherly power is the basis for kingly power – hence, the father had the right to kill the son without incurring any legal penalty. See Sir Robert Filmer, *Patriarcha and Other Writings* (Cambridge: Cambridge University Press, 1991; first published in 1680). I discuss this in some detail in my essay "Paternity, Sovereignty and the Argument from Nature."

24 Severance, "Sex and the Social Contract," 456.

25 Jean-Jacques Rousseau, *Émile* (New York: Everyman's Library, 1974; first published in 1911). Page numbers are from the 1974 Everyman's Library edition.

26 Das, "Paternity, Sovereignty and the Argument from Nature."

27 Rousseau, *Émile,* 448, emphasis added.

28 Rousseau, *Émile,* 325.

29 Cited in Gupta, *Sexuality, Obscenity, Community,* 292 (translation by Gupta).

20

Where Ethics and Politics Meet
The Violence of Humanitarianism in France

Miriam Ticktin

While I was conducting fieldwork in Paris, the former president of the gay-rights activist group Act-Up Paris told me that he had received phone calls from undocumented immigrants inquiring how they could infect themselves with HIV and thereby obtain legal status in France. Although this particular account of HIV self-infection is anecdotal, the rhetoric of willed self-infection can be located in the larger reality I observed during the course of my research between 1999 and 2001: I increasingly saw undocumented immigrants, or *sans papiers* (literally those without papers), turn to physical injury or infection to claim the basic rights supposedly granted to all "human beings."[1] This tendency to turn to illness for papers occurred in the wake of the limited success of the social movement by and for undocumented immigrants in France to secure basic human rights. It also coincided with the introduction of a humanitarian clause in French law – what I call the "illness clause" – that gives people with serious illnesses the right to stay in France and receive treatment.[2]

In this article, I examine the role of humanitarianism and compassion in the development of an ethical configuration that has made illness a primary means by which to obtain papers in France. I open with the HIV anecdote to introduce the notion of the often-unintended consequences of ethical discourses such as humanitarianism or practices that claim to further social justice. More broadly, I use this example as an entryway into what I see as an incipient or emergent ethical configuration in which people end up trading in biological integrity for political recognition.

The sacred place of biological integrity in this emergent ethics became apparent to me over the course of my fieldwork with undocumented immigrants. I initially went to Paris to examine the promises and failures of human-rights discourse in the sans papiers movement and, more broadly, to understand transnational ethical and legal regimes. Thus, in addition to working with sans papiers organizations and nongovernmental organizations (NGOs), I conducted research at various hospitals, state medical offices, and clinics both within and just outside of Paris that focused on marginalized populations (those *en situation de précarité*). In the clinics, social workers and doctors worked hand in hand, driven by the conviction

Miriam Ticktin, "Where Ethics and Politics Meet: The Violence of Humanitarianism in France," *American Ethnologist* 33/1 (2006): 33–49. Reproduced by permission of the American Anthropological Association from *American Ethnologist* 33/1 (2006), pp. 33–49.

that social and medical issues are intertwined, particularly for those designated "les exclus" by the French – society's excluded. Early on in my observations, however, I noted that the first question many social workers asked their undocumented clients was, "Are you sick?" and if an individual answered yes, they would ask almost too eagerly, "How sick?" I gradually understood that the answer they hoped for was "Very sick," because it provided clients with the one clear means by which to apply for papers. A woman from an immigrant-rights association confirmed this conclusion at a workshop on sans papiers and HIV/AIDS, stating, "Isn't it terrible? We almost wish for illness when we talk to sans papiers." This wish for illness, of course, was not born of malice but of a desire to better help the undocumented.

The illness clause is a provision of the 1998 amendment to the Ordonnance of 2nd November 1945 no. 45–2658 on Conditions of Entry and Residence of Foreigners that grants legal residency permits to those in France with pathologies of life-threatening consequence if they are declared unable to receive proper treatment in their home countries. The logic behind this provision was humanitarian and exceptional; indeed, legal permits for illness are officially given for "humanitarian reasons." The French state felt it could not deport people if their deportation had consequences of exceptional gravity, such as their deaths.

Despite the goal to keep it exceptional, the illness clause – instituted as a humanitarian provision – has come to play an important role in the politics of immigration. In this article, therefore, I explore the consequences of a politics of immigration largely grounded in a humanitarian logic. How does humanitarianism function as politics – how does it address inequality and injustice? My main contention is that, when humanitarianism, often enacted through a moral imperative of compassion, fills in for the failure of political-rights discourses and practices, the exclusionary effects can be brutal; indeed, I argue that, rather than furthering human dignity, the result is a limited version of what it means to be human. By drawing on ethnographic

examples of how humanitarianism works on the ground, in "a space of concrete problems, dangers, and hopes that are actual, emergent, and virtual" (Rabinow 2002:145), I trace its contours and its often-counterintuitive consequences.

My argument has two main theoretical points. First, I suggest that humanitarianism, although driven by the moral and ethical imperative to relieve suffering, can have discriminatory and even violent consequences in the absence of guiding political principles and practices. These consequences are all the more striking because they are unexpectedly found at the very heart of the compassion that grounds humanitarian action. Here, I engage in a debate about the contemporary resurgence of discourses of moralism and how they blur boundaries between legal, political, and ethical – moral orders. I am particularly interested in the growing emphasis on the role of compassion, sympathy, and benevolence in political life – sentiments that play a crucial part in the discourses of what some call "global civil society." NGOs fighting in the name of human rights, environmentalism, and cultural preservation, among many other causes, intervene on behalf of a moral order, each fighting for a role in "the global meritocracy of suffering" (Bob 2002).

One of the most prominent of these movements is humanitarianism, which grew in global importance and visibility over the course of the 1990s. The massive proliferation of humanitarian organizations, the awarding of the 1999 Nobel Peace Prize to Médecins Sans Frontières (MSF, or Doctors Without Borders), and the entry of humanitarianism into common political discourse – illustrated by British Prime Minister Tony Blair's government calling the bombing of Kosovo a "humanitarian bombing" – are just a few examples of its growing presence." There has been a concomitant focus on suffering, in the name of which humanitarianism intervenes.[3] As just one example, the diagnosis of posttraumatic stress disorder (PTSD) has increased exponentially in recent years, giving public prominence to the suffering and trauma endured in a variety of contexts, from military interventions to domestic disputes. Yet how does the recognition of suffering result in a political program for change? Although the question of how moral demands translate into politics has a history as long as political philosophy itself, I am interested in its current manifestation precisely because moral demands have increasingly filled the space of political action.

[. . .] My second point is that this moralism has created another type of politics, even while being labeled *apolitical*. I engage here in the contemporary debate about biopolitics and humanitarianism, which relies heavily on work done by philosopher Giorgio Agamben. Agamben, in turn, builds on the intersection of works by Michel Foucault and Hannah Arendt. Agamben (1998:133) suggests that humanitarian organizations can only function by grasping human life as "bare life," the Greek *zoe*, the fact of living common to all beings – life unqualified by the political and social communities that distinguish humanity from other types of life. Bare life is life excluded from the polis, and insofar as human beings are political or social beings, the polis marks the boundary between human and nonhuman. In fact, my research suggests that humanitarianism does not simply produce or reproduce bare life as separate from political life, even if the protection of bare or biological life is its goal; rather, it allows for the recombination of bare life and political life in new ways, such that the political dimension of human life is never lost. Political subjects can be found in the most "apolitical" of spaces. The political aspect of life, however, is radically transformed – often in undesirable ways. In other words, the political choices allotted to sans papiers, although still choices, are composed of undesirable options: poverty, exploitation, exclusion, or illness.

In this article, I first discuss how humanitarianism has been transformed into a form of politics, functioning as a transnational system of governance tied to capital and labor even while purporting to be apolitical. To this end, I examine the distinction between human rights and humanitarianism, or between a juridical and a humanitarian logic, grounding my argument in the context of French immigration policies. I then examine the illness clause as a

practical example of the turn to a humanitarian politics.

I focus in the second half of the article on the consequences of humanitarianism as politics. I fill out my argument that the joining of ethics and politics actually limits rather than expands notions of humanity. Thus, I describe new biopolitical practices and the unexpected diseased and disabled citizens that are produced by humanitarianism as a system of governance, and I end by discussing how a limited humanity is produced on the ground by a politics of compassion. I show that the humanity protected is one of suffering bodies and biological life devoid of social and political content; yet this is a notion of humanity that, even in its minimalism, keeps intact racial and gender hierarchies. Indeed, the struggle to define citizenship and the borders of the nation-state is now also a struggle to define the threshold of humanity and of life itself.

My intention in this article is not to call into question people's illnesses or disabilities as somehow inauthentic but, rather, to understand the effects of a new "biosocial" space, and here I draw on Paul Rabinow's (1996) concept not only to refer to a social community created by shared illness but also to indicate the way that biology is used as a flexible social resource. For instance, once an undocumented immigrant is given papers for illness, he or she might choose to escape this biological community in favor of another political or cultural identity. Biosociality here becomes the socially framed choice to draw on one's biology.[4]

I write, finally, with the recognition that in exposing the violence at the heart of this humanitarian practice, I may be helping to further undermine a key opening to legality that sans papiers have benefited from. Yet I do so because the underlying regime of which it is a part is, ultimately, inherently destructive, not only reproducing a racially stratified society built on the colonial legacy but also maintaining certain people as less than human. Moreover, the violence inherent in this particular French ethical configuration has larger global echoes. Ultimately, my underlying question concerns the notion of humanity promoted by a politics based on humanitarianism – what is the image of the human that this politics projects?

The Shift from Human Rights to Humanitarianism

The issue of illegal immigration erupted into the French public imagination in 1996, when a powerful social movement calling for basic human rights for illegal immigrants gained world media attention through the occupation by 300 African immigrants of the Saint Bernard church in Paris. The ensuing violent eviction by French police of the immigrants, many of whom were women and children, caused an uproar. The movement organized by and for these immigrants changed their labeling from *illegal immigrants* to *sans papiers*. This was a self-conscious move away from the image of criminality and suspicion associated with clandestinity to one of people deprived of basic human rights. [. . .]

To understand the terms chosen by the sans papiers, the place of both human rights and humanitarianism in the French imaginary and in French public debate is crucial to note. France is the originator of both the NGO MSF (now nearly synonymous with humanitarianism in the contemporary world) and the 1789 Declaration of the Rights of Man and Citizen, on which the 1948 UN Declaration of Human Rights is largely based. The French, therefore, have much invested in their identity as global moral leaders, especially in today's climate in which geopolitics and moral codes are intimately intertwined. Perhaps even more important for my purposes is the distinction between human rights and humanitarianism – a distinction that is not always evident in the U.S. context but is more clear in the French one. My focus here is on what happens when humanitarianism is forced to take on a primary role in government, largely subsuming a system based on rights. Without advocating for a regime of human rights at the expense of humanitarianism, I am interested in the consequences of a humanitarian logic filling in for the failure of rights discourses and practices.

Although both human rights and humanitarianism are complexly constituted transnational institutions, practices, and discursive regimes, in a broad sense, human-rights institutions are largely grounded in law, constructed to further legal claims, responsibility, and accountability, whereas humanitarianism is more about the ethical and moral imperative to bring relief to those suffering and to save lives; here, the appeal to law remains opportunistic. Although both are clearly universalist discourses, they are based on different forms of action and, hence, often institute and protect different ideas of humanity. The political discourse of human rights has its origins in the French Revolution and the Enlightenment movement away from religion and toward a secular vision of humanity, whereas humanitarianism was initially a form of religiously inflected charity. Even the "new" humanitarianism – which can be dated to the 1970s and the founding of MSF, followed by the development of an industry of NGOs – often perceived reason to be an "enemy of humanity" because this medical humanitarianism advocated action on the basis of emotion; founders such as Bernard Kouchner and Xavier Emmanuelli both identify the Catholic Church as a forerunner and inspiration (Taithe 2004).[5]

Human rights and humanitarianism do, of course, overlap, and humanitarianism cannot be defined accurately just in terms of religion, or emotion, or as outside the political or legal realms it necessarily engages with: Indeed, humanitarianism is legally instituted through the laws of war. [. . .] Such a separation, however, is seldom possible in practice.

The French situation reveals such a shift in emphasis from rights to the practices of humanitarianism in regulating immigration. The issue of "les sans papiers" was one of the major platforms on which the Socialists entered into power in 1997; Prime Minister Lionel Jospin's government promised to deal with sans papiers more generously, respecting their basic human rights. Despite this rhetoric, the promised reexamination of cases of undocumented immigrants in 1997 and the new law in 1998 on entry and residence of foreigners were both much less generous than promised. [. . .] Despite the proliferation of human-rights NGOs, and regardless of the protests that take place at a rate and level rarely attained elsewhere, very little ground has been gained. These cries for human rights fall on now-deaf state ears.

Indeed, the social movement seems to have come to an impasse with its appeals to human-rights principles. The larger context is one in which refugees have been increasingly viewed with suspicion by both the French state and the French public and conflated with economic migrants. This conflation has been made explicit in recent policies of restricting asylum to control migration flows, joining two processes that should be entirely independent. As Hubert Védrine, the minister of foreign affairs stated, "The practice [of asylum] followed must maintain a just balance with our desire to control migration flows" (1997; cf. Delouvin 2000:70). More broadly, asylum policies must be seen as part of prohibitionist, restrictive immigration policies, in which the state seeks to close all doors. In this climate of closure, many examples can be cited of human-rights violations by the state itself, not to mention by nonstate actors; for instance, immigrants are imprisoned in detention centers without trial, despite condemnations of the inhumane and insalubrious conditions in the centers.[6] Similarly, immigration officials are known to be utterly arbitrary in their dealings. My interviews with both sans papiers and immigration officials, combined with my experience in accompanying sans papiers to state offices, revealed that how one is treated depends on which immigration office one goes to, the official one meets at the desk, how many that official decides to admit that day, the "look" of the immigrant, and so on. Undocumented immigrants are subject to entry on a case-by-case basis and have to prove their merit without knowing the rules being applied.

Paradoxically, this arbitrariness was exaggerated by the new law that went into effect in 1998, which added Article 12bis, the right to "private and family life," to the two previously existing conditions for legal immigration – family reunification and asylum. [. . .] In the absence of a spouse or children in France that would allow one to enter under the family reunification clause, Article 12bis 3 gives those who have lived in France for ten consecutive years the right to papers. Residency, however, must be proven, not simply declared. [. . .] For people who have been trying to erase any trace of their presence so as not to be deported, providing official proof of each month of residence for over ten years is a nearly impossible task – practically a contradiction in terms.

The inscription of this article in the law, thus, in many ways simply legitimized the arbitrariness practiced by the préfectures (local governments), working along the lines of what immigrant-rights lawyer Danielle Lochak (2001) calls a "humanitarian" logic rather than a juridical one. Law always involves interpretation, and it is always enacted in specific contexts that help determine its meaning; the difference here is that, because the law is so open-ended, those asking for the protection it affords are entirely dependent on eliciting the compassion or pity of those enacting it. Indeed, this open-endedness takes on even more significance in the French context, in which the civil-law tradition involves applying the law, not interpreting or building on it.

The new clause is not alone in being subject to arbitrary application; family reunification and asylum have been equally compromised. [. . .] The creation of a new type of asylum – "subsidiary asylum" – which comes with fewer attendant rights, is another example of the increasing attempt to limit people's ability to claim rights. This is the consequence of a politics of immigration based on closure (Lochak 2001:41).

To understand the nature of this politics of closure, which has resulted in an increasingly important role for humanitarianism, it helps to take a step back [. . .]. At an event to support sans papiers, Ahmad, an ex-sans papiers, said to me incredulously, "It was so much easier to find work on the black market! I never had trouble. Now that I have papers, I can't find work." In France, as elsewhere in the industrialized world, a significant tension has emerged: As increasingly restrictive legislation has forced borders closed, transforming the so-called open European space into Fortress Europe, the black market and informal economies have grown, and labor conditions are otherwise changing to favor temporary, insecure forms of labor with no legal protection. In this sense, the increased demand for workers in the agricultural, garment, and construction industries in France is met by closed juridical doors: Undocumented immigrants are desired precisely because they can be denied all rights (Fassin 2001b). Ahmad exemplifies this tension between industry wanting and needing labor and the nation-state refusing to let people legally onto its territory. The French state is complicit in this process, having passed laws that produce a category of persons who are neither legalizable nor deportable. On another register, this liminal status is part of an increasing tension between regimes of circulation for capital and people – capital circulates freely, whereas people cannot – a consequence of the changed relationship between states and capital (cf. Sassen 1996).

How does this political economy relate to the shift to humanitarianism? Both the discourse and practice of medical humanitarianism have followed this flow of exploitable labor from the South into the urban centers of the industrialized North; just as MSF started by intervening in crises of governance and economy in the South, so, too, it now intervenes in industrialized centers like Paris – cities in which it has established offices for local concerns. Just as it protects a particular vision of life in war-torn zones, working to ease the immediacy of suffering, so, too, it now intervenes to ease suffering when the larger societal and political structures of the North fail to do their job – when they let increasingly large portions of their population fall through the cracks. Here, medical humanitarianism governs the less desirable portions of the population when the state abandons them (cf. Ong 1999). In this sense, ethical systems in the form of medical humanitarianism are part of the transnational circulation of capital and labor, linking the political economy of immigration to the political economy of health and illness.[7]

The Illness Clause

The illness clause emerged as an alternative to human-rights discourse and discourses of social injury for those whose appeals to rights did not easily coincide with state interests or whose positioning has not allowed their claims to be heard.[8] To reiterate, the 1998 amendment grants legal residency permits to those already living in France who have pathologies that entail life-threatening consequences if they are declared unable to receive proper treatment in their home countries; the goal is to permit them to receive treatment in France. Indeed, it was the lobbying of medical humanitarian groups such as MSF and Médecins du Monde (Doctors of the World) that helped turn the illness clause into law in France in response to what was perceived as arbitrary treatment of those who were sick – sometimes helping them, sometimes deporting them.

The "illness permit" was instituted formally in 1998. That is, only in 1998 did the Ministry of Health officially become involved in the immigration process, which normally falls under the rubric of the Ministry of Interior. Nevertheless, the *banlieue* (suburb) outside Paris that receives the highest number of claims for legal status began the practice of taking illness into account in claims for papers in 1990. I conducted my fieldwork primarily in this suburb and in Paris. I followed sans papiers through the different steps of the trajectory to papers: To access the illness clause, the sans papiers are referred by their own doctors to immigration authorities and then by the immigration officers at the préfectures to state health officials.[9] It is ultimately the job of these officials to ascertain if people's conditions are of sufficient gravity to merit granting papers for treatment in France, although the permits are actually issued by the préfectures, with the understanding that they rely upon the state health officials' opinions. The state office in which I did a large part of my research is one of the few in which nurses receive the sans papiers in person. Other offices receive sans papiers' files by mail; the files are initially sorted through either by nurses or administrators and then passed to doctors. The state medical doctor can recommend that a medical certificate be granted for varying lengths of time, from a period of three months to an indeterminate (long-term) period, depending on the illness and the doctor's interpretation of the length of treatment needed. People can claim citizenship after a period of five years on the basis of their residency on French soil; thus, continual renewal of illness permits may eventually lead undocumented immigrants to citizenship.

Very little about the process is systematic. The law states that people should receive papers if they suffer from a pathology that has life-threatening consequences and they do not have access to treatment in their own country. Yet there are no lists of life-threatening pathologies and no easily accessible information on whether people can receive treatment in their home countries. The doctors are urged to contact the Direction de la Population et des Migrations (Office of Population and Migrations) for information. But no source takes into account people's substantive ability to access medical treatment: Do they live far away from city centers? Do they have the means of transport to hospitals or doctors? Do they have the money to get treatment or to continue treatment if it involves subsequent trips to medical facilities? These questions are not addressed in the guidelines. They are asked at the discretion of the medical officials receiving the case or at the préfecture beforehand. Already, one sees the discretionary power of the nurses, doctors, and immigration officials and the advantages and disadvantages that sans papiers derive from being able to interact face to face with state officials. Ultimately, the immigration officers at the préfecture make the decision about who will receive an illness permit and for what duration, and although, in theory, they should follow the advice of state doctors, they do not necessarily do so. Thus, although legalizing the process was an attempt to systematize the arbitrary treatment of the sans papiers, in practice, the illness clause has made

little difference to the nature of the process. Instead, a different logic has been instituted, one based on benevolence and compassion.

With the possibility of obtaining papers effectively shut off to new immigrants and refugees – who, as I have mentioned, are seen as either criminal or economically burdensome – those already in France without papers have turned to the illness clause as a means to ease the exploitation that is a regular part of being undocumented, believing – rightly or wrongly – that papers will solve all their problems. Statistics back up my ethnographic work, demonstrating the increasing importance of the illness clause. The local statistics from [. . .] the state medical office in which I did my research show that applications for the illness residency permit increased seven times over the course of the 1990s and that three-quarters of applications were given positive responses. More recent statistics are even more striking. [. . .] Table 20.1 shows that the number of positive responses increased by 44 percent just in that particular *département*, from 889 in 1999 to 1,287 in 2000. Table 20.2 shows the types of illnesses admitted and their frequencies and the type of permit granted – top among the illnesses is HIV, but cardiovascular illnesses, cancer, diabetes, and tuberculosis are all included.

How does the French state reconcile the denial of papers to immigrants who are perceived to be economically burdensome with the decision to give papers and social services to immigrants who are sick? Stated otherwise, why is it that illness is allowed to travel across borders, whereas poverty cannot? The framing

Table 20.1 *Distribution of recommendations for illness permits given by the state medical doctor (MISP) in the region where I observed: 1998, 1999, and 2000*

Recommendation	1998	%	1999	%	2000	%
Negative	233	23	97	10	325	20.0
3 months	71	7	145	15	266	16.5
6 months	102	10	158	16	314	19.5
1 year	127	13	174	18	265	16.5
Long term	422	42	412	42	442	27.5
No opinion (lack of information)	52	5	0	0	0	0.0
Total	1,007	100	986	100	1,612	100
			889		1,287	
			accepted		accepted	

Table 20.2 *Most frequently encountered pathologies in the state medical office where I observed: 1998, 1999, and 2000*

Pathologies	1998	%	1999	%	2000	%
HIV	113	15	124	16	156	12.6
Cardiovascular	74	10	88	11	139	11.3
Rheumatology, trauma, orthopedic	67	9	81	10	144	11.6
Cancer	49	7	50	7	57	4.6
Diabetes	44	6	41	5	89	7.2
Psychiatry	42	6	44	6	87	7
Urinary-nephrology	26	4	39	5	61	5
Otorhinolaryngology, ophthalmology	54	7	53	7	89	7.2
Tuberculosis	36	5	40	5	67	5.4
Gastroenterology	24	3	26	3	47	3.8
Pneumonic	32	4	22	3	44	3.6
Hepatitis	25	3	48	6	45	3.7
Gynecology	25	3	15	2	44	3.6
Neurology	29	4	22	3	42	3.4
Endocrine	36	5	27	4	25	2
Hematology					17	1.4
Sterility					26	2.1
Diverse (multiple pathologies)	62	8	52	7	56	4.5
Subtotal	738	100	772	100	1,235	100
In process	53		82		89	
Accompanying adults	46		85		211	
Undiagnosed					29	
Absence of pathology					48	

of the illness clause helps to explain this. Although the French state instituted the illness clause out of "respect for human dignity," it was only ratified because it was perceived as outside the political realm. That is, it was instituted in May 1998 under the right to "private and family life." Placing this clause under the aegis of the "private" exempts it from debates about the politics of immigration, citizenship, and notions of the French nation and ignores the structural problems and economic demand that may have caused the immigration in the first place. Instead, the clause focuses attention on what is construed as an apolitical, suffering body. This clause is based on the notion of the universality of biological life – what I have already mentioned as Agamben's "bare life."

State officials and doctors confirmed to me that the space of pure life honored in the illness clause is conceived of in opposition to political community. [...] Despite increasingly restrictive legislation that has managed to alter and limit the right to health care, that right remains the most extensive of all those granted to immigrants, whatever their legal status – more comprehensive than any civil, political, or social rights (Fassin 2001a).[10]

As proof that this clause is humanitarian and apolitical in nature and that it remains in the realm of the private, the French state does not automatically include a work permit with the illness visa – initial attempts to do so rendered the clause too politically contentious. [...] The visa given for illness is thereby isolated from all other aspects of life – it is narrowly focused on the healing of suffering, injured, or disabled bodies, disqualifying its recipients from taking any economic, social, or political role in French society. Consequently, those who gain entry on the basis of chronic illness, such as those who are HIV + and who are fully capable of sustaining a full-time job, are for the most part not given the right to work. Although their papers formally allow them to rent apartments, open bank accounts, and travel on the metro without the risk of being arrested and deported, they do not have the substantive means to rent apartments, and they have nothing to put in bank accounts and no money to buy metro tickets. Ironically, in the name of human dignity, the French state indirectly sanctions work on the black market. In this sense, a doctor named Isabelle who worked at one of the clinics for undocumented immigrants where I observed suggested that, in her experience, the illness clause was "a curse." It was worse than nothing because it gave people hope, and yet, because work permits were not granted with the papers, it paved the way for greater exploitation of their misery, making them work in situations of virtual slavery and prostitution. She suggested that politicians got rich on the backs of those working on the black market – "Why else are they not deported?" she asked. "It must mean that it is profitable for the state to keep them."

Economic profitability of undocumented immigrants aside, the illness clause is also productive of a particular moral economy, in which a new hierarchy of morals takes shape and certain ethical configurations gain credence. Here, humanitarianism functions as politics and has inevitably unanticipated consequences. The threatened body associated with political asylum has been recast as suspect, conflated with that of the economic immigrant – or, in the words of former Socialist minister Michel Rocard (1996), "the misery of the earth," which, he claimed, France cannot absorb. With humanitarianism as the driving logic, only the suffering or sick body is seen as a legitimate manifestation of a common humanity, worthy of recognition in the form of rights; this view is based on a belief in the legitimacy, fixity, and universality of biology. As just one example of this new moral economy, Didier Fassin (2001a, 2001b) has documented that, as the number of permits for medical reasons has increased, the number granted under the title of refugee has significantly diminished. What are considered basic human rights are themselves now circumscribed to fit the limited understanding of human life. It is in this sense that I speak of the space of the apolitical suffering body as the very center and grounding of the new politics of citizenship in France, a humanitarian space at the intersection of biopolitical modernity and global capital, in which contradictory and unexpected diseased and disabled citizens emerge.

Diseased and Disabled Subjects

I turn in the second half of this article to a discussion of the consequences of humanitarian governance, beginning with the counterintuitive subject positions produced by this shift to humanitarianism in the politics of immigration. Here, political subjects can be found in the most "apolitical" of spaces.

I have been arguing that this shift to seeing the suffering body as more legitimate than the threatened or deprived person reveals the desire to recognize the universality of biological life above all else: that is, to find common humanity in apolitical suffering, a universal humanity that exists beyond the specificities of political and social life. Indeed, according to Agamben, humanitarianism as a practice cannot help but grasp human life in the figure of "bare life," thereby reproducing the very idea of a form of life distinct from political life. Liisa Malkki has ethnographically confirmed this tendency, demonstrating how humanitarian practices make refugees into "universal man" – how they set up a "bare, naked or minimal humanity" (1996:390). Of course, humanitarianism does work to reduce people to "pure victims" (Malkki 1996), making it easier for them to be configured as objects of charity rather than of law. Yet, when one looks closely at this process, one sees that bare life and political life actually combine in new ways as a result of humanitarian practices, particularly when humanitarianism takes over the space of political action and responsibility. In other words, people elide victimhood and reduction to bare life in interesting, albeit troublesome, ways; political action is constituted as a series of biological compromises. More to the point, however, is whether this type of political action can be considered desirable or acceptable.

Part of the reason for recognizing the universality of life involves controlling, managing, and cultivating it; this is the biopolitics that Foucault (1978) speaks of, making the individual body and population part of the problem of sovereign power, in which the power/knowledge of life allows for its transformation. In other words, neither humanitarianism nor the state's support of humanitarianism can be understood outside the context of disciplinary power – the state does not act "altruistically" in recognizing a common humanity. If life is not only the object of political struggle but also the very grounding of sovereignty, as Agamben suggests – building on Foucault – then the power to define bare life, that is, the power to draw the line and decide who and what is included and excluded from the juridical and political realms is what actually constitutes sovereign power. Paradoxically, the state's focus on the universality of biological life is turned on its head. [...] Sans papiers demonstrate how biology is not the domain of the incontestable – biological norms are created.

Contradictory subject positions emerge from a politics based on this belief in the universality of life, but only as biological life. On one end of the spectrum is the person who infects her- or himself with HIV in an effort to be treated like a human being, to be granted legal recognition and, hence, acknowledged as part of humanity, willfully disabling her- or himself to live more fully. [...] On the other end is the person who refuses the possibility of treatment – purposefully giving up bodily integrity to maintain human dignity in the face of the stigma of HIV/AIDS. Here, bodily integrity and human dignity are decoupled and differently reconfigured. For instance, one day as I sat with the state nurses while they attended to undocumented patients requesting papers to stay and receive treatment in France, I watched as a woman named Amina refused to even speak the name of her illness. The nurses questioned her many times: "What do you have?" they asked. "What are your symptoms?" She shook her head and said nothing. Originally from Mali, Amina had come with her baby strapped onto her back in a colorful wrap, and she spent her time unraveling herself and the baby to change his diapers, responding distractedly to the nurses' questions. She handed over a slew of documents, both medical and legal – the telltale pile of papers that all those who are "paperless" must carry wherever they go – a cruel irony, indeed; after the nurses had thumbed through the majority of her documents, their attitude suddenly changed from mild annoyance to care and concern. And one nurse asked her again, "Do you really not know what you have?" This time, Amina responded that, yes, yes, of course, she did. She left it at that – the illness remained unnamed. The nurses promised her papers and told her to take care of herself and the baby. When she left, I was told that both Amina and her baby were HIV +.

This phenomenon was explained to the nurses and me by another woman named Fatoumata, who also opened up exceedingly hesitantly when questioned. Fatoumata had recently been released from prison. She had been arrested on drug-related charges and infected with HIV through needle use. She told us about the many infected African women in Paris who simply reject the opportunity to obtain a visa that would not only grant them basic rights, such as the right to housing, but would also permit and pay for their regimen of triple therapy – a visa that would literally provide them with both the right to live and life itself. The stigma of HIV/AIDS is so great in their communities that they would rather compromise their bodily integrity and pay with their lives than live ostracized and without dignity. Fatoumata had a tough exterior, but when she mentioned her inability to trust her closest family or friends with the news that she was HIV+, she began to cry softly.

In talking to Fatoumata, I became aware of the gendered nature of the stigma of HIV/AIDS among African communities in France. All pregnant women in France must, by law, be tested for HIV, whereas men are never forced to get tested. Thus, more women find out about their illness than do men, leading to an unequal gender dynamic and a particularly gendered stigma in African communities. Indeed, this dynamic has the consequence of increasing the numbers of women granted papers through the illness clause; it also results in more women than men having to lead double lives, hiding their diagnosis from their loved ones, or leading lives that define them solely in terms of their illness, existing outside all community affiliation except for the patient groups they may belong to. In other words, this stigma creates a subject position for women, in particular, in which their reason for living becomes their illness – it becomes their only source of social recognition – yet it is also their death sentence.

[...] The nurses told me about other cases of people purposefully not treating their illnesses, prolonging them to keep their legal status. [...] Even something as simple as a cataract can serve the purpose of prolonging one's stay. Of course, it means that the advantages of legality are exchanged for the difficulties of living one's life partially blind. I say this with an added caveat, in that those who do not treat themselves often have good structural reasons for not doing so, such as not having sufficient money to cover the costs, or the time, or the means to get to and from the hospital. The nurses themselves agreed that a patient's reasons for not pursuing treatment were not always clear. The point here is still valid, however; one must remain diseased to remain in France and to eventually claim citizenship. Both the medical officials and sans papiers realize this.

Each of the cases mentioned plays on different configurations of bodily integrity and human dignity. Along this spectrum are other unanticipated subject positions. For instance, one of the doctors I worked with treated a patient who took on the identity of a person who had AIDS, including taking the person's medication – in fact, he literally stole the identity of a friend of his who died of AIDS. He did this to get French papers – to obtain legal recognition that enabled both a life free from daily violence and a modicum of human dignity. Paradoxically, his dignity was not recognized, in the sense of his unique, individual self; he preferred to give up that identity to get legal recognition as someone else, again complicating theories of the liberal individual that ground notions of French citizenship.

Finally, the case of a Senegalese woman named Aicha illustrates the results of a politics of humanitarianism that creates political subjects, albeit with limited political choices. Aicha had a thyroid tumor and a serious skin condition aggravated by heat. She left her family in Senegal, including her five children, to live in France and treat her condition. Aicha had lived in France during her first marriage

and, thus, had some knowledge of the medical system. Her illnesses were chronic, however; she needed both the thyroid medication and the skin creams on a constant basis, and neither medication was readily available in Senegal. She left her life and family, ironically, to protect what the French law calls her right to "private and family life"; not only was she not legally permitted to bring her children to France, but she was also not given papers to work, transforming her life into a monotony of shelters in which she slept at night – shelters force people out at 8 a.m. – and cafés and parks in which she sat during the day to pass the time.

The nurses and doctors at the hospital clinic for the disenfranchised where Aicha received treatment were her main source of community – and even their friendship and support were contingent. As she stood outside, they complained to me that they did not need to see her anymore and wished she would leave space for other patients. In their understandable desire to give others a chance at health and bodily integrity, the larger structural reality of which they are a part dictates that they deprive Aicha of her only source of humanity that goes beyond biological life. Occasionally, she wondered aloud to me whether her life was worth living – what kind of life was it, she asked, with no family, no work, no money, no fulfillment, and nothing to wake up to each morning except one's illnesses, the simultaneously driving and disabling force of her life? She cannot escape her state of injury, which is not only named as such but also embodied. She is just one of the new subjects produced by the French nation-state – given life by the consequences of ethical regimes such as humanitarianism that are both created and circumscribed by global capitalism.

In the face of what can be called a new space of "biosociality," in which biology is remodeled not only on culture but also on structural need – in which biological compromises are made as a primary form of political action – the subjects that I have just described are not easily explained by liberal notions of the self, of the good life, or of human flourishing (cf. Petryna 2002:4). In this emergent ethics, those with cancer, HIV, polio, or tuberculosis – and even occasionally those with more explicitly socially and politically grounded injuries such as rape or disfigurement – become the most mobile, the most able to travel without hiding themselves in the cold-storage containers of trucks or making mad dashes through the English Channel tunnel or across the straits of Gibraltar. [. . .] The emergence of the disabled as the modal subject of political economy [. . .] thus exposes the standard of able-bodiedness [. . .] as fictional, constructed and normativized for a certain type of economic and civic functionality. Indeed, the assumption that the normative human is able-bodied begs redefinition of who is included in the category of "human."

How can one make sense of these subject positions? In what sense are they the result of a form of politics based on humanitarianism? Although the ill and disabled are not entirely stripped of their political or social qualities, they exemplify the dangers of humanitarian government insofar as it limits one's political and social choices and capacities – it forces one to conceal one's political self, all the while drawing on that self. In fact, the paradox of willed infection or disability suggests that sans papiers can act in one of two ways: They can choose to suffer from exploitation, exclusion, and poverty, or they can suffer from illness. But what kind of choice is this, and what kind of humanity does it sustain? The question becomes, how have these two options come to be interchangeable, how can they be bartered against one another – how is it that self-inflicted violence has come to have the same value as the violence of being undocumented? How is a compromised biological life equated with a compromised political life? And how can one characterize or explain this type of ethics and its related politics? I turn now to the way the politics of humanitarianism actually works on the ground, helping to answer these questions and, ultimately, to contribute to understanding what kind of humanity a politics of humanitarianism reproduces.

The New Politics of Compassion: A Limited Humanity

Dr. Amara, who worked at the clinic for undocumented immigrants that I had been observing, suggested to me that I might be interested in a paradox he had witnessed. He explained to me that several of his HIV+ patients had stopped taking their medication once they had received their papers, despite having received papers to gain access to the medication. This seemingly incomprehensible act reveals the violence at the heart of this story: Without political recognition, undocumented immigrants exist as a form of "living dead" (Mbembe 2003; Petryna 2002:3), in a state that, in the immediacy and intensity of their struggle for survival, is indistinguishable from the threat of physical death.[11] The difference between the type of future each remedy guarantees – papers or medication – is elided. In this sense, it is unclear to both doctors and patients which is the more virulent form of suffering: no papers or no medication. The conflation of the two reveals a new territory in which the politics of immigration and citizenship is at once a politics of life and death. In this scene, biological life and political life have taken on equal significance – life as someone sick is interchangeable with life as a politically recognized subject. Indeed, being sick is what is required to be a political subject (cf. Petryna, 2002).

How did this happen? [. . .] What I have been articulating so far is the result of the simultaneous institution of a humanitarian illness clause and the closing of borders to immigrants and refugees. [. . .] Although one might have imagined that this concept of humanity based on the universality of biological life would come closer to equality, [. . .] in fact, this concept has been put into play through a politics of compassion that emphasizes benevolence over justice, standards of charity over those of obligation – one that ultimately protects and encourages a limited and limiting notion of humanity.

In shifting the politics of immigration to a politics of humanitarianism, those who enact the humanitarian clauses suddenly wield great power – they become the gatekeepers. In this case, they include the state nurses and doctors as well as the medical establishment more broadly. In the state office where I observed, the medical officials [. . .] explicitly joined social and medical, knowing that [. . .] they are inextricably intertwined. Yet the medical officials also admitted to being constrained by their relationship with the préfecture; despite acting out of a desire to further a notion of social justice, they could not simply let everyone in, because they were being monitored. [. . .] To be kept in the decision-making circles, they had to maintain legitimacy – and their legitimacy depended on only letting in people who suffer from pathologies that have life-threatening consequences.

Yet what qualifies as "life threatening" when life itself remains undefined? [. . .] Life is ultimately defined quite pragmatically, by the particular context in which requests for papers are received and by those applying the clause. As noted, this is a relatively arbitrary process. [. . .]

What this means, of course, is that different understandings of "life" are being played out and that the structure of the particular state medical office is a major factor in outcome. The face-to-face interaction between the nurses and sans papiers largely determined how "life threatening" was interpreted in the particular state office where I observed and, thus, who was granted permits for illness. The personal interaction allowed for compassion to be evoked – it allowed the sans papiers to appear as people, not simply as files or pathologies. It allowed for their social realities to be included in the judgment. Yet a face-to-face encounter allows for performances on both sides, and if one does not perform in the desired manner, one may be penalized and excluded.

The dilemmas and the evocation of compassion came for nurses and doctors with the more complicated cases [. . .]. In the late 1990s, for instance, a young Algerian woman named Fatima came to Paris after having been raped and disfigured by her uncle. [. . .] Both her uncle and aunt blamed her for the rape. Fatima was therefore sent to France, where her mother was living. The nurses said that she looked horrible. They decided to give her temporary papers to receive medical care. When the treatment was finished and her permit about to expire, Fatima returned to the state medical office to ask for a renewal of her papers. As they later explained to me, the nurses understood that she would return to a "pitiful" life in Algeria; she would be forever shamed because of her rape and, hence, unmarriageable. According to them, her life would be one of ostracization and loneliness. They decided that, in the face of this reality, they would rather grant her authorization to stay in France for treatment for an indeterminate period – which means, effectively, forever, if she so chooses, renewing her illness permit until she can apply for citizenship. The treatment they prescribed was psychological – she was considered to be suffering from trauma. They were very clear when talking to me that this decision crossed over into the realm of social justice; but they saw themselves inevitably implicated in moral decision making, which they believe is required at a fundamental level in caring for people's health and well-being.

I deeply respect the medical officials for allowing their view of health to include the social and for allowing the disenfranchised to remain when all other doors were and are increasingly closed. Clearly, however, the health officials' decisions are not based on laws, or rules, or rights. Ultimately, they are within the discretion of the person who receives the case. The state medical officials' decisions are, thus, based at least in part on a notion of humanitarianism and compassion or, as it may happen, the lack thereof. I found that the result depended on the way the sans papiers' story was told and on the emotions evoked. Indeed – perhaps unsurprisingly – I found that compassion is elicited differently according to race and gender. Some people's stories of suffering do not strike a chord in the nurses or doctors.

Thus, for instance, I sat with the nurses as a 25-year-old Algerian man came in one day. Not long after he entered the office, he started crying. He claimed that he had had a heart attack a few days earlier, which the nurse, Felicia, pointed out was not true. He had a heart murmur, she said, looking down at his file. He said that he could not go on. If he was sent to Algeria, who would take care of his wife and his mother? "Last week I was going to commit suicide," he said. "I've never done anything to anyone, I haven't committed a crime and still they do this to us, they break up couples!" I could tell Felicia was getting impatient. Her tone of voice changed. The man told a long story about his mother, who was a healer, and his wife, who was sick, and he kept saying how unfair it was to have a heart attack at his age! He was worked up and kept repeating himself. When he left, Felicia said "son nez est grand comme un bec" [his nose is as large as a beak], gesturing toward her own nose, pretending it was growing, insinuating that the man was lying. She claimed his marriage was one of convenience because the wife was 39 and he was only 25. Why Felicia was immediately so suspicious is hard to say. The man certainly exaggerated, and his story did not make complete sense. But, then, he was distraught and crying. At the time, I was surprised by Felicia's reaction because she rarely lost patience, and I concluded that the man must have elicited a negative feeling in her – nothing concrete, because to me, the message he conveyed largely rang true.

As Arendt (1990) notes, compassion is most effective in face-to-face interactions, when those who do not suffer come face to face with those who do. In the state medical offices, however, the suffering is not always immediately apparent – the immigrant has to make a case for it, either in person or in his or her file, and the emotional commitment involved in compassion is dependent on [. . .] circulating narratives, images, and histories and often on maintaining an unequal power relation between nurse and patient and citizen and foreigner – distinctions that are already heavily gendered and racialized. To be accepted as a French subject on the basis of compassion, one must be accepted as plausible; and images of the Other inform the legitimacy of one's performance. Whereas compassion in Fatima's case was clearly based on a familiar Orientalist narrative about pitiful Muslim women, Algerian men are depicted in the French public imaginary as violent and deceitful and as oppressive to women. These images are the colonial legacy and in some ways have become all the more intense since the bitter war of Algerian independence from French colonial rule.

The man described above might have had a better chance in an office in which simply his file was presented, in which he did not need to appear in person; in other words, face-to-face interactions are not the answer for everyone. As critics of the humanitarian movement have noted, for help to be extended, humanitarianism often requires the suffering person to be represented in the passivity of his or her suffering, not in the action he or she takes to confront and escape it (Boltanski 1999:190; Malkki 1996). Whether the Algerian man who claimed to have had a heart attack was indeed lying or not, his performance was not convincing because it was too active, he demonstrated too much agency — he was perceived as strategic and not as a suffering, passive body. His personality took up too much room in the narrative.

Conclusion: An Anti-Enlightenment Universality?

My ethnographic research demonstrates the difference between bare life as conceived and practiced: Although, in theory, bare life may be the grounding of humanitarian action and the sovereign exception, the concept is enacted differently in differing places, both creating and requiring new realms of biosociality. The politics of humanitarianism, thus, show how conceptions of bare life blend with politics and the near impossibility of getting beyond socially embedded and mediated interpretations of life. In this particular instance, humanitarianism leads to a politics of life and death, quite literally, in which one's death warrant in the form of AIDS can secure life in France, and citizenship is only given to those who remain diseased. In this sense, one must see the medical realm as an important new site of sovereign power, in which doctors, nurses, and state officials become gatekeepers not only to the nation-state but also, more importantly, to the very concept of "humanity," in the sense that humanitarianism protects individuals by virtue of their membership in humanity.

[. . .] In this emergent regime of humanitarianism, one must inquire into the consequences of its (often) arbitrary nature, asking what conditions evoke compassion and why and what hierarchies are reproduced by it. The ability of such a system to further a more just world must be seriously interrogated when humanitarianism acts as a form of policing, choosing exceptional individuals and excluding the rest. For instance, although compassion may abolish the distance between people, opening the hearts of sufferers to the suffering of others, thereby creating an affective public space by its very definition, compassion is unable to generalize. In joining people in the immediacy and intensity of suffering, compassion abolishes the space between people in which political matters are located, shunning the processes of persuasion, negotiation, and compromise, which are the methods of law and politics (Arendt 1990:86–7).

The citizens produced by the joining of humanitarian ethics and politics have inequality literally inscribed on their bodies. They are forever marked and interpellated as sick, as already handicapped – they can never realize equality. This politics of humanitarianism shows itself to be a politics of universality, but an anti-Enlightenment universality – one that sets biological life against explicitly rational, political beings.[12] Immigrants are stripped of their legal personas when identified solely as suffering bodies, and, as such, they cannot be protected by law; they are rendered politically irrelevant. And although they may be liberated from suffering, they are not liberated into full citizenship.

To understand the nature of their particular status, Arendt's ideas are once again instructive. She argues that being thrown out of one's national community means being thrown out of humanity altogether – being stateless deprives one of the essence of humanity – its political character (Arendt 1951). Conversely, she suggests that citizenship, as membership in a polity, conveys full belonging in the category "humanity." In what I have described, government by humanitarian discourses and practices actually does not allow undocumented immigrants to be expelled from humanity altogether, as Arendt believes, because it is now instituted and enacted in a supranational political framework (i.e., through NGOs, among other institutions); but it does create and sustain a humanity that is very limited and forced to make new forms of biological compromise. Ultimately, it sustains a more powerful distinction between citizen and human while impoverishing the idea of the human: One can be either a citizen or human but not both – once one is affirmed as part of humanity and protected by humanitarian clauses, one loses one's political and social rights. Here, for instance, the people entering France through the humanitarian clause come from already marginalized backgrounds, primarily from former colonies; this process, thus, reinforces racial hierarchies while casting France as benevolent. Indeed, the postcolonial space created through this politics of humanitarianism continues in the manner of its colonial predecessors, reconfigured for ever-greater forms of exclusion.

I want to be clear here: I am not arguing that the discourse of human rights is in the past [...] but, rather, that an incipient or emergent discourse overlaps and coexists with it and is becoming increasingly powerful. Ethical regimes must be understood as always contextualized, now as part of larger, transnational regimes of labor, capital, and governance. [...] It is not accidental that medical humanitarianism is playing an increasingly important role in both the North and South, intervening in the name of basic human life in ways that neither human-rights organizations nor development projects are allowed to do. Rights entail a concept of justice, which includes standards of obligation and implies equality between individuals. Humanitarianism is about the exception rather than the rule, about generosity rather than entitlement. The regime of humanitarianism [...] is an ethics that, when taken to the extreme, entails selling one's suffering, bartering for membership with one's life and body. As the political body loses legitimacy in an increasingly globalized world in which national sovereignty is at stake and borders of all kinds are zealously guarded, the supposedly apolitical suffering body is becoming the most legitimate political vehicle in the fight for a broader concept of social justice; our task is not only to understand the consequences of this shift but also to form a response to it.

NOTES

1 I am not suggesting that huge numbers of people, if any, are trying to infect themselves. And although I cannot offer statistics, I can say that the very inclusion of this phenomenon as part of the rhetoric of the politics of immigration is indicative of a certain larger qualitative political shift.

2 I am deeply indebted to Didier Fassin, both medical doctor and anthropologist, for alerting me to the existence of the illness clause and for helping me to establish contacts in state medical offices and hospital clinics.

3 The focus on suffering in public and political life has been mirrored in the discipline of anthropology. For instance, *Social Suffering*, edited by Arthur Kleinman, Veena Das, and Margaret Lock, came out in 1997 and was followed by two more volumes on the same theme (Das et al. 2000; Das et al. 2001). These volumes group together many types of hitherto differently named experiences, such as the pain and trauma of atrocity, poverty, substance abuse, street violence, domestic violence, HIV/AIDS, and so on, with the goal of drawing attention to the multiple forms of suffering in the current global political economy. That said, they also point to a tension between those suggesting that this suffering is the result of the current climate and those suggesting that suffering unifies people as human beings across time – that it is the tie that binds humanity.

4 Although I use the term *biosociality* somewhat differently than Rabinow does, I still focus on practices of life as important sites of new knowledges and powers and employ the term to indicate the ways that nature is known and remade through technique. Instead of the techniques of scientists, however, I refer to the techniques of "ordinary" lay people – such as undocumented immigrants – who manipulate their biology to the extent that they overcome the nature–culture split. In this way, what I describe is on a continuum with Adriana Petryna's (2002) work on what she calls "biological citizenship" in Ukraine, in which the damaged biology of a post-Chernobyl population has become the grounds for social membership and the basis of staking citizenship claims. As Petryna states, in such contexts, pain and suffering are made into social instruments, which does not mean that they are any less authentic but that new values are being attached to them. I thank an anonymous reviewer for insight into the ways the situation I am describing differs from Rabinow's original notion of "biosociality."

5 I want to be clear that I am concerned primarily with humanitarianism less in its legal form – under the rubric of the laws of war – than in its shape as a form of urgent ethical action driven by sentiment and need, albeit broadly sanctioned by law.

6 Although detention centers fall under the rubric of the administrative system, not the judiciary, the treatment of people in these centers still constitutes violations of basic human rights. Indeed, the phenomenon of detention centers demonstrates how the move from the juridical sphere to an administrative one (which encompasses humanitarianism) allows for new forms of injustice.

7 For a wonderful analysis of the relationship between capitalism and human rights, drawing on Emile Durkheim, see Collier 2002.

8 For a discussion of the limits of human rights in this context, see Ticktin 2002.

9 To get to a doctor can, in itself, be a trial for the undocumented; a whole new set of challenges are posed for those trying to find a doctor who will refer patients to the immigration office (see Ticktin 2002).

10 I refer here to the Sarkozy laws of 2003.

11 Judith Butler provides another way of thinking about this phenomenon: Those excluded from legitimate social and political community are kept "on the far side of being" (2000:81), not given the type of recognition that allows the notion of human to come into being.

12 I would like to thank Nadia Abu El-Haj for helping me see this.

REFERENCES

Agamben, Giorgio
    1998 Homo Sacer: Sovereign Power and Bare Life. Daniel Heller-Roazen, trans. Stanford: Stanford University Press.

Arendt, Hannah
  1951 Origins of Totalitarianism. New York: Meridian Books.
  1990 On Revolution. Harmondsworth, UK: Penguin Books.
Bob, Clifford
  2002 Merchants of Morality. Foreign Policy, March–April:36–45.
Boltanski, Luc
  1999 Distant Suffering: Morality, Media and Politics. Graham Burchell, trans. Cambridge: Cambridge University Press.
Brown, Wendy
  1995 States of Injury: Power and Freedom in Late Modernity. Princeton: Princeton University Press.
Butler, Judith
  2000 Antigone's Claim: Kinship between Life and Death. New York: Columbia University Press.
Collier, Jane
  2002 Durkheim Revisited: Human Rights as the Moral Discourse for the Postcolonial, Post-Cold War World. In Human Rights: Concepts, Contests, Contingencies. Austin Sarat and Thomas R. Kearns, eds. Pp. 63–88. Ann Arbor: University of Michigan Press.
Das, Veena, Arthur Kleinman, Margaret Lock, Mamphela Ramphele, and Pamela Reynolds, eds.
  2001 Remarking a World: Violence, Social Suffering, and Recovery. Berkeley: University of California Press.
Das, Veena, Arthur Kleinman, Mamphela Ramphele, and Pamela Reynolds, eds.
  2000 Violence and Subjectivity. Berkeley: University of California Press.
Delouvin, Patrick
  2000 The Evolution of Asylum in France. Journal of Refugee Studies 13(1):61–73.
Fassin, Didier
  2001a The Biopolitics of Otherness: Undocumented Foreigners and Racial Discrimination in French Public Debate. Anthropology Today 17(1):3–7.
  2001b Quand le corps fait loi. La raison humanitaire dans les procédures de régularisation des étrangers. Sciences Sociales et Santé 9(4):5–34.
Fassin, Didier, and Alain Morice
  2000 Les épreuves de l'irrégularité: Les sans-papiers, entre déni d'existence et reconquête d'un statut. In Exlusions au coeur de la cité.

Dominique Schnapper, ed. Pp. 260–309. Paris: Anthropos.
Foucault, Michel
  1978 The History of Sexuality, vol. 1: An Introduction. New York: Vintage Books.
Fox, Renée
  1995 Medical Humanitarianism and Human Rights: Reflections on Doctors Without Borders and Doctors of the World. Social Science and Medicine 41(12):1607–16.
Kleinman, Arthur, Veena Das, and Margaret Lock, eds.
  1997 Social Suffering. Berkeley: University of California Press.
Lochak, Danièle
  2001 L'humanitaire perversion de l'etat de droit. Sciences Sociales et Santé 19(4):35–42.
Malkki, Liisa
  1996 Speechless Emissaries: Refugees, Humanitarianism, and Dehistoricization. Cultural Anthropology 11(3):377–404.
Mbembe, Achille
  2003 Necropolitics. Public Culture 15(1):11–40.
Mouffe, Chantal
  2000 Which Ethics for Democracy? In The Turn to Ethics. Marjorie Garber, Beatrice Hanssen, and Rebecca L. Walkowitze, eds. Pp. 85–94. New York: Routledge.
Nattrass, Nicoli
  2005 [Cases of people infecting themselves with HIV in South Africa]. National Public Radio, April 6.
Ong, Aihwa
  1999 Flexible Citizenship: The Cultural Logics of Transnationality. Durham, NC: Duke University Press.
Petryna, Adriana
  2002 Life Exposed: Biological Citizens after Chernobyl. Princeton: Princeton University Press.
Rabinow, Paul
  1996 Essays on the Anthropology of Reason. Princeton: Princeton University Press.
  2002 Midst Anthropology's Problems. Cultural Anthropology 17(2):135–49.
Rocard, Michel
  1996 La parte de la France. Le Monde, August 24: Point du Vue.
Rorty, Richard
  1993 Human Rights, Rationality, and Sentimentality. Yale Review 81(4):1–20.

Sassen, Saskia
    1996   Losing Control? Sovereignty in an Age of Globalization. New York: Columbia University Press.
Taithe, Bertrand
    2004   Reinventing (French) Universalism: Religion, Humanitarianism and the "French Doctors." Modern and Contemporary France 12(2):147–58.
Terry, Fiona
    2002   Condemned to Repeat? The Paradox of Humanitarian Action. Ithaca, NY: Cornell University Press.
Ticktin, Miriam
    2002   Between Justice and Compassion: "Les Sans Papiers" and the Political Economy of Health, Human Rights, and Humanitarianism in France. Ph.D. dissertation, Department of Cultural and Social Anthropology, Stanford University.
    2005   Policing and Humanitarianism in France: Immigration and the Turn to Law as State of Exception. Interventions: International Journal of Postcolonial Studies 7(3):347–68.
Védrine, Hubert
    1997   Address to the Law Commission. Paris, November 6.
Young, Allan
    1995   The Harmony of Illusions. Princeton: Princeton University Press.
    2001   Our Traumatic Neurosis and Its Brain. Science in Context 14(4):661–83.

Part IV
The Biotechnical Embrace

Introduction

The "biotechnical embrace" and the "medical imaginary," phrases which organize this set of readings on biomedicines, were introduced by Mary-Jo Good (1995b, 1996, 2001, this volume) to draw analytic attention to the power of contemporary high technology medicine in the public imagination. Physicians and patients are often deeply moved by the medical imaginary, energized and embraced intellectually, emotionally, and physically by medicine's future possibilities and innovative technologies. The readings in this section demonstrate various ways the wedding of biotechnology and biomedicine is taken up in the affective domains of illness, therapeutics and health policies, and the ways it engages the public imagination. Each reading explores medicine's biotechnical innovations and successes but also the ironic and dark sides of the marketing of high technology medicine, so widely desired, sought after, yet restricted.

Beginning in the 1970s, medical anthropologists launched ethnographic investigations of Western or "cosmopolitan" medicine in the societies in which they worked. In *Asian Medical Systems*, Charles Leslie and Fredrick Dunn (1976) introduced the term "cosmopolitan" to acknowledge that biomedicine is not merely a "Western" phenomenon, but that as with Ayurveda or Greek or Chinese medicine, contemporary biomedicine circulates globally and is adapted to local social and cultural settings. Anthropologists also turned their ethnographic attention to medical systems in the diverse societies of North America and Europe. *Physicians of Western Medicine* (Hahn and Gaines 1985) heralded this new focus in anthropology and was soon followed by other collections (Lock and Gordon 1988; Pfleiderer and Bibeau 1991; Lindenbaum and Lock 1993; Berg and Mol 1998).

This new anthropology of biomedicine had several characteristics. First, anthropologists investigated biomedicine as one among many forms of healing and knowledge. Ethnographies of "the inner life of medicine" (Good and Good, ms) explored "how medicine constructs its objects" (B. Good 1994), its specialty knowledge and diagnostic categories (Barrett 1988; Gifford 1988; Young 1994; Martin 2007), and its reproduction of the profession through performative and narrative actions (M. Good 1995a). Second, anthropologists focused on the internal worlds of laboratories and clinics, and the social, legal and ethical structures that constitute medicine as a complex institutional and ideological phenomenon (Lock et al. 2000). Research paralleled innovations in bioscience, such as studies of the new genetics related to reproductive health (Becker 2000; Inhorn 1994; Rapp 2000), breast cancer (Koenig 1998), and genomic endeavors (Heath and Rabinow 1993; Taussig 2004); and ethical dilemmas arising from futile use of technology at the end of life (Good et al. 2004; Ruopp et al. 2005; Kaufman and Morgan 2005). Third, anthropologists implicitly or explicitly compared biomedical cultures through studies of specialty knowledge and practice and varied patient experience. Examples include oncology in the United States, Italy, Japan and Mexico (Good et al. 1990; Good et al. 1994; Good et al. 1995c; Gordon 1993; Gordon and Paci 1997); pediatric oncology and dying children (Bluebond-Langner 1978); and gynecology and obstetrics in Japan and the North America (Lock 1993; Kaufert 1992; Martin 1987).

During the 1990s, anthropologists were particularly drawn to studies of organ transplantation and brain death, bringing new political, comparative and global perspectives to a field previously occupied by sociologists and medical ethicists (Ikels 1997; Hogel 1996). Lock followed changing definitions of brain death and transplantation practices in Japan (2002) for over a decade. Scheper-Hughes (2006) supported young scholars on quests to uncover the dark side of the organ transplant world through the Berkeley Organwatch project; essays by Cohen and Sanal in this volume benefitted from that collaboration. Anthropological fascination with the social meanings of organs and transplantation, "the gift" and kinship donors, continues the flow of publications (Sharp 2006; Wailoo et al. 2006).

When HIV/AIDS emerged, stunning the newly afflicted and the bioscientists of NIH and the academy, medical anthropologists swiftly took up research linked to advocacy. Many critiqued global health policies and postcolonial power relations that dehumanized and marginalized the afflicted poor (Farmer et al. 1993; Farmer 1995; Schoepf 1993). Anthropologists recounted physician colleagues' conversations of being "overwhelmed by disease entity" and fearing AIDS threatened medicine's "intellectual and therapeutic enterprise" (Good et al. 1999; Raviola and Good et al. 2002; Eaton 2008). A sea change in advocacy, intervention, and global policy occurred when anti-retrovirals became "technically sweet" – imaginable, feasible to manufacture, effective, and with a soft market price (Kim and Farmer 2006, this volume).

The five essays in this part illustrate diverse ways biomedicine and its technological interventions live in different social worlds. The first essay, by Mary-Jo DelVecchio Good, emerged from collaborative research with clinical investigators – oncologists and internists – and their patients. Observations of clinical interactions, interviews, and cyberspace communications generated four epistemic terms – the medical imaginary, the political economy of hope, the biotechnical embrace, and the clinical narrative. Good analyses experiences of doctors and patients with oncology's experimental and mundane technologies, the specialty's aesthetics of statistics and language of odds and chances, and its offering of "choices", manifesting the dominant American thematic of "freedom of choice" even when only momentarily deflecting death (Patterson 2000). Her studies showed that medical technologies are caught up in affective domains of illness and healing, that caring is conveyed through technical acts, and that fantasies of biomedicine's power to explain and treat even intractable diseases often lead to aggressive use of medical technologies, even at the end of life, but also to societal investments and commitments, such as "the war on cancer" driven by a robust "political economy of hope" (M. Good 1995a, 1995b).

Lawrence Cohen's essay sets the standard theoretically, empirically, and ethnographically for documentation and analysis of the international "organ trade." Cohen tells a story of gender, poverty and persistent indebtedness which comes to be inscribed on the bodies of the poor, mostly on women's bodies, through the sale and taking of a kidney. The unintended consequences of foreign trained transplant surgeons returning to India to establish state of the art clinics has led to seeking patients and donors/sellers, and to a rise of regional black markets, kidney zones, and sellers' parks, where money can be exchanged for a kidney. The bioethics language of shortages of organs in India, Cohen argues, creates a "purgatorial anxiety over organs" which masks the limited access to basic medical care, the realities of the transplant market, and the family debt cycles of its discarded exploited kidney donors.

Aslihan Sanal's essay opens with an observation of a television crew secretly filming one of Turkey's most esteemed transplant surgeons. Sanal introduces us to a media imaginary of Turkey's medical transplant world and its "organ mafia." She explores internalized fantasies, anxieties and psychological displacements carried by new technologies for physicians as well as patients. Transplant surgery is as prestigious for Turkey as it is for Turkey's leading transplant surgeons, whose cultural and professional power allow them to set rules, ethics, and medical standards for their transplant communities. Yet these surgeons also experience fears of unpredictable media anger and their own unease in declaring and determining brain death. Sanal exposes the emotional and psychological consequences of cultural double-binds for doctors and patients, who carry out their work amidst changing legal rules, competing organ-sharing philosophies (privatized versus socialist) and media panics over organ mafias.

Marcia Inhorn's essay explores reproductive technologies in conservative spaces, in late twentieth century Egypt. Inhorn finds that Egyptian physicians recently trained in assisted reproductive technologies, their innovative clinics, and television soap operas about infertility and "Babies of the Tubes" feed the public's imagination about IVF. The Arabic "Babies of the Tubes" confuses some women. Are "tubes" the blocked fallopian tubes, the causal diagnosis that leads many women to seek IVF treatments? Or are "tubes" the popularly imagined "glass tubes" in which egg and sperm are mixed to create "a test tube baby"? Inhorn's story of Sakina, a poor woman who sells her gold and seeks alms to pursue IVF, highlights a dark side of the medical imaginary, when efficacy is questionable, cost almost always daunting, and patients are emotionally and financially vulnerable, as infertile women and couples often are in Egypt as elsewhere in the world. IVF statistics are positively spinned (as elsewhere) and newly trained IVF physicians, energized by biotechnical possibilities, disregard potential harm to patients who cannot truly afford IVF. Religious interpretations delineating permissible uses of IVF technologies for Muslims as discussed by Inhorn (2004) in this and later essays, may be read in comparison with Kahn's (2000) *Reproducing Jews* on IVF in Israel.

The final essay, by Jim Yong Kim and Paul Farmer, physicians-anthropologists and founders of the NGO Partners-in-Health, is a call for action marking critical historical developments between 1996 and 2006. It follows Kim's tenure as special assistant to the director of the World Health Organization (2003–2005). Documented efficacy of antiretroviral medications, the feasibility of manufacturing dramatically less expensive generics, and the biotechnical commitments to vaccine development energized Kim and Farmer's challenge to commonly held views among public health communities that the poor could not be trusted with the latest HIV anti-retrovirals (due to fear of promoting drug resistance with erratic compliance and once exorbitant costs). Kim's WHO project, known as "3 by 5" – 3 million AIDS patients on antiretroviral medications by 2005 – established a widely accepted global policy goal; and with the vast increase in global health funding and the availability of technically sweet ARTs at low cost, Kim and Farmer led the moral fight to make treatment of the poor with the best innovative antiretrovirals the global norm for public HIV programs. Through the model programs of Partners in Health and the global policy influences of WHO, Kim and Farmer brought the fruits of the bench, new biotechnologies, to communities of poor patients. Research and practice, anthropology and medicine, are wed in the work of these scholar advocates.

REFERENCES

Barrett, Robert
  1988   Clinical Writing and the Documentary Construction of Schizophrenia. Culture, Medicine and Psychiatry 12(3): 265–99.
Becker, Gaylene
  2000   The Elusive Embryo: How Women and Men Approach New Reproductive Technology. Berkeley and Los Angeles: University of California Press.
Berg, Marc and Annmarie Mol, eds.
  1998   Differences in Medicine: Unraveling Practices, Techniques, and Bodies. Durham, NC: Duke University Press.
Bluebond-Langner, Myra
  1978   The Private Worlds of Dying Children. Princeton, NJ: Princeton University Press.
Dunn, Fred
  1976   Traditional Asian Medicine and Cosmopolitan Medicine as Adaptive Systems. In Charles Leslie, ed., Asian Medical Systems. Berkeley: University of California Press.
Eaton, David
  2008   Ambivalent Inquiry: Dilemmas of AIDS in the Republic of Congo. In Mary-Jo DelVecchio Good et al., eds., Postcolonial Disorders. University of California Press.
Farmer, Paul
  1995   AIDS and Accusation: Haiti and the Geography of Blame. Berkeley: University of California Press.
Farmer, Paul, Shirley Lindenbaum and Mary-Jo DelVecchio Good, eds.
  1993   Women, Poverty and AIDS: An Introduction. Culture, Medicine and Psychiatry 17: 387–97.
Gifford, S.M.
  1986   The Meaning of Lumps: A Case Study in the Ambiguities of Risk. In C. R. Janes, R. Stall, and S. M. Gifford, eds., Anthropology and Epidemiology. Dordrecht: Reidel.

Good, Byron
    1994   Medicine, Rationality, and Experience: An Anthropological Perspective. Cambridge:
    Cambridge University Press.
Good, Mary-Jo DelVecchio
    1985   Discourses on Physician Competence. *In* Robert Hahn and Atwood Gaines, eds.,
    Physicians of Western Medicine. Dordrecht: Reidel.
Good, Mary-Jo DelVecchio
    1995a   American Medicine: The Quest for Competence. Berkeley: University of California
    Press.
Good, Mary-Jo DelVecchio
    1995b   Cultural Studies of Biomedicine: An Agenda for Research. Social Science & Medi-
    cine 41: 461–73.
Good, Mary-Jo DelVecchio
    1996   L'Abbraccio Biotecnico: Un Invito al trattamento sperimentalein. *In* Pino Donghi,
    ed., Il sapere della guarigione. Spoleto, Italy: Laterza, pp. 25–62.
Good, Mary-Jo DelVecchio
    2001   The Biotechnical Embrace. Culture, Medicine and Psychiatry 25: 395–410.
Good, Mary-Jo DelVecchio and Byron Good
    n.d.   The Inner Life of Medicine. Ms.
Good, Mary-Jo DelVecchio, Byron Good, Cynthia Schaffer, and Stuart E. Lind
    1990   American Oncology and the Discourse on Hope. Culture, Medicine and Psychiatry
    14: 59–79.
Good, Mary-Jo DelVecchio, L. Hunt, T. Munakata, and Y. Kobayashi
    1993   A Comparative Analysis of the Culture of Biomedicine: Disclosure and Conse-
    quences for Treatment in the Practice of Oncology. *In* Peter Conrad and E. Gallagher, eds.,
    Health and Health Care in Developing Countries: Sociological Perspectives. Philadelphia:
    Temple University Press, pp 180–210.
Good, Mary-Jo DelVecchio, with Esther Mwaikambo, Erastus Amayo, and James M'Imunya
    Machoki
    1999   Clinical Realities and Moral Dilemmas: Contrasting Perspectives from Academic
    Medicine in Kenya, Tanzania, and America. Daedalus 128(4): 167–96.
Good, Mary-Jo DelVecchio, T. Munakata, Y. Kobayashi, Cheryl Mattingly, and Byron Good
    1994   Oncology and Narrative Time. Social Science and Medicine 38(6): 855–62.
Good, Mary-Jo DelVecchio, Nina Gadmer, Patricia Ruopp, Matthew Lakoma, Amy Sullivan,
    Ellen Redinbaugh, Robert Arnold, and Susan Block
    2004   Narrative Nuances on Good and Bad Deaths: Internists' Tales from High-technology
    Work Places. Social Science and Medicine 58: 939–53.
Gordon, Deborah
    1990   Embodying Illness, Embodying Cancer. Culture, Medicine and Psychiatry 14: 275–
    97.
Gordon, Deborah and Eugenio Paci
    1997   Disclosure Practices and Cultural Narratives: Understanding Concealment and Si-
    lence around Cancer in Tuscany, Italy. Social Science & Medicine 44: 1433–52.
Hahn, Robert and Atwood Gaines
    1985   Physicians of Western Medicine. Dordrecht: Reidel.
Heath, Deborah and Paul Rabinow, eds.
    1993   Bio-Politics: The Anthropology of the New Genetics and Immunology. Culture,
    Medicine and Psychiatry 17(1), Special Issue.
Hogle, Linda
    1996   Transforming "Body Parts" into Therapeutic Tools: A Report from Germany. Med-
    ical Anthropology Quarterly 10: 675–82.

Ikels, Charlotte
1997   Kidney Failure and Transplantation in China. Social Science & Medicine 44: 1271–83.

Inhorn, Marcia C.
1994   Quest for Conception: Gender, Infertility, and Egyptian Medical Traditions. Philadelphia: University of Pennsylvania Press.

Inhorn, Marcia C.
2006   He Won't Be My Son: Middle Eastern Muslim Men's Discourses of Adoption and Gamete Donation. Medical Anthropology Quarterly 20: 94–120.

Kahn, Susan
2000   Reproducing Jews: A Cultural Account of Assisted Conception in Israel. Durham, NC: Duke University Press.

Kaufert, Patricia and Margaret Lock
1992   What are Women for? Cultural constructions of Menopausal Women in Japan and Canada. *In* V. Kerns and J. K. Brown, eds., In Her Prime. Urbana: University of Illinois Press.

Kaufman, Sharon and Lynn M. Morgan
2005   The Anthropology of the Beginnings and the Ends of Life. Annual Review of Anthropology 34: 317–41.

Koenig, Barbarah, H. T Greely, L. M. McConnell, H. L. Silverberg, and T. A. Raffin
1998   Genetic Testing for BRCA1 and BRCA2: recommendations of the Stanford Program in Genomics, Ethics, and Society. Breast Cancer Working Group. Journal of Women's Health 7: 531–45.

Leslie, Charles, ed.
1976   Asian Medical Systems: A Comparative Study. Berkeley: University of California Press.

Lindenbaum, Shirley and Margaret Lock, eds.
1993   Knowledge, Power and Practice: The Anthropology of Medicine and Everyday Life. Berkeley: University of California Press.

Lock, Margaret
1993   Encounters with Aging: Mythologies of Menopause in Japan and North America. Berkeley: University of California Press.

Lock, Margaret and Deborah Gordon, eds.
1988   Biomedicine Examined. Kluwer Academic Publishers.

Lock, Margaret, Allan Young, and Alberto Combrosio, eds.
2000   Living and Working with the New Medical Technologies: Intersections of Inquiry. New York: Cambridge University Press.

Martin, Emily
1987   The Woman in the Body: A Cultural Analysis of Reproduction. Boston, MA: Beacon Press.

Martin, Emily
2007   Bipolar Expeditions: Mania and Depression in American Culture. Princeton, NJ: Princeton University Press.

Patterson, Orlando
2000   Ordinary Liberties: Americans' Views and Experiences of Freedom (in ms).

Pfleiderer, Beatrix and Gilles Bibeau, eds.
1991   Anthropologies of Medicine. Heidelberg, Germany: Vieweg.

Rapp, Rayna
2000   Testing Women, Testing the Fetus: The Social Impact of Amniocentesis in America. New York: Routledge.

Raviola, Guiseppe, M'Imunya Machoki, Esther Mwaikambo, and Mary-Jo Good
2002 HIV, disease Plague, Demoralization and "Burnout" of the Medical Profession in Nairobi, Kenya. Culture, Medicine and Psychiatry 26: 55–86.

Ruopp, Patricia, Mary-Jo D. Good, Matthew Lakoma, Nina M. Gadmer, Robert M. Arnold, and Susan D. Block
2005 Questioning Care at the End of Life (Physicians' Reflections on Errors and Mistakes). Journal of Palliative Care 8(3): 510–20.

Sanal, Aslahan
2005 Flesh Yours, Bones Mine: The Making of the Biomedical Subject in Turkey. PhD dissertation, Massachusetts Institute of Technology.

Scheper-Hughes, Nancy
2006 Community Differences: Post-Human Ethics, Global (In)justice, and the Transplant Trade in Organs. In Keith Wailoo, Julie Livingston, and Peter Guarnaccia, eds., A Death Retold. Chapel Hill, NC: University of North Carolina Press.

Sharp, Lesley
2006 Strange Harvest: Organ Transplants, Denatured Bodies, and the Transformed Self. Berkeley, CA: University of California Press.

Schoepf, Brooke
1993 AIDS action-research with women in Kinshasa, Zaire. Social Science & Medicine 3: 1401–3.

Taussig, Karen-Sue
2004 Bovine abominations: genetic culture and politics in the Netherlands. Cultural Anthropology 19: 305–36.

Wailoo, Keith, Julie Livingston, and Peter Guarnaccia, eds.
2006 A Death Retold: Jesica Santillan, the Bungled Transplant, and the Paradoxes of Medical Citizenship. Chapel Hill: University of North Carolina Press.

Young, Allan
1995 The Harmony of Illusions. Princeton: Princeton University Press.

21

The Medical Imaginary and the Biotechnical Embrace

Subjective Experiences of Clinical Scientists and Patients

Mary-Jo DelVecchio Good

Subjective experiences of clinical scientists who produce and deliver high-technology medicine and of patients who receive treatment via this technology are fundamental to understanding the political economy and culture of hope that underlie bioscience and biomedicine. In this essay, I examine interpretive concepts linking bioscience and biotechnology and their societal institutions to subjective experience. These concepts are the medical imaginary, the biotechnical embrace, the political economy of hope, and the clinical narrative. Drawing on research and observations of the culture and political economy of biomedicine in the United States and internationally, I illustrate these interpretive concepts with examples from studies of clinical scientists, oncologists and their patients, and venture capitalists, as well as observations of public actions and discourses.

Cultural and social studies of biomedicine and biotechnology lend themselves to examining a concept that anthropologists Fischer (1991) and Marcus (1998) call "multiple regimes of truth" through multisited and comparative ethnographic research in science and technology. Although acknowledging the importance of "cultural pasts" and "cultural differences," Fischer argues that "it is increasingly artificial to speak of local perspectives in isolation from the global system ... the world historical political economy" and "transnational cultural processes" (1991:526). This formulation echoes recent trends in anthropological studies of biomedicine and biotechnology and of scientific research and clinical culture. Such studies highlight the dynamic relationship, tensions, and exchanges between local worlds in which medicine is taught, practiced, organized, and consumed and global worlds in which knowledge, technologies, markets, and clinical standards are produced. Although we may speak about a plurality of biomedicines that are socially and culturally situated rather than about a single unified body of knowledge and practice, such local worlds

Mary-Jo DelVecchio Good, "The Medical Imaginary and the Biotechnical Embrace: Subjective Experiences of Clinical Scientists and Patients," in J. Biehl, B. Good, and A. Kleinman, eds., *Subjectivity: Ethnographic Investigations*. Berkeley: University of California Press, 2007. © 2007 by University of California Press – Books. Reproduced with permission of University of California Press – Books in the format textbook via Copyright Clearance Center.

are nevertheless "transnational" in character: they are neither cultural isolates nor biomedical versions of indigenous healing traditions. Rather, global standards and technologies overlie local meanings and social arrangements in nearly all aspects of local biomedicine.

Comparative Queries

This perspective encourages comparative questions: How do local and international political economies of medical research and biotechnology shape medicine's scientific imaginary; its cultural, moral, and ethical worlds; and inequalities of use, access, and distribution of medicine's cultural and material "goods"? How do local and international ideologies, politics, and policies influence professional and institutional responses to specific needs of particular societies – from the disease plague of HIV to scarcity and poverty, trauma and civil strife, and public health and profit-driven health-service markets? What form does the "political economy of hope" take? How do the culture of medicine and the production of bioscience and biotechnology "live" in respective societies?

J. Rouse, an American philosopher of science and society, speaks about American science, about the "openness" of science, arguing for acknowledgment that "the traffic across the boundaries erected between science and society is always two-way." Rouse discusses the idea of destabilizing "distinctions between what is inside and outside of science or between what is scientific and what is social" (1992:13). Bruno Latour, the prominent French scholar of the biosciences, also contends that "scientific work continually draws upon and is influenced by the culture 'outside' science." (Rouse 1992:13). Although these comments are part of a long-lived internal debate among scholars of science studies, the concept they propose of two-way traffic across science and society is perhaps even more striking in biomedicine. The flow of knowledge, scientific and medical cultural power, market wealth, products, and ideas is thus not only between local cultures and institutions that create medical knowledge and organize practice, ethics, and the medical market but also between the culture and market of international and cosmopolitan biomedicine and its local variants.

The dynamics of the global-local exchange challenge our notions of "universalism" in clinical science and "local" knowledge in clinical practice, stimulating a rethinking of the boundaries not only between science and society but also between the local and the global. With this sense of the transnational fluidity of knowledge and practices, appropriated locally and regionally and integrated into local culture, I wish to turn to the interpretive concepts that link bioscience and biotechnology to society and that have grown out of comparative cross-cultural analyses and conversations with colleagues from Europe, Africa, and Asia, as well as emerged from my own research in the United States and Indonesia. These concepts are "the medical imaginary," "the political economy of hope," "the biotechnical embrace," and "the clinical narrative."

The Medical Imaginary and the Political Economy of Hope

An ethnographic slice through "multiple regimes of truth," narratives of patient experience and of clinical science, and documents on medicine's political economy suggests ways in which the affective and imaginative dimensions of biomedicine and biotechnology envelop physicians, patients, and the public in a "biotechnical embrace." The medical imaginary, that which energizes medicine and makes it a fun and intriguing enterprise, circulates through professional and popular culture. Clinicians and their patients are subject to "constantly emerging regimes of truth in medical science" (Cooke 2001; Marcus 1995:3), and those who suffer serious illness become particularly susceptible to hope engendered by the cultural power of the medical imagination. The connection between medical science and patient populations and the cultural and financial flow thus becomes deeply woven; we can measure the intensity of such connections in part through the flourishing of disease-specific philanthropies, through nongovernmental organizations (NGOs) and political health-action groups, and through the financial health of the National Institutes of Health ($20.5 billion in the 2001 budget, $23.3 billion in 2002, $27.1 billion in 2003, and $27.9 billion in 2004), even under a political regime that promotes tax cuts and small government.

Americans invest in the medical imaginary – the many-possibility enterprise – culturally and emotionally as well as financially (Freudeheim 2002). Enthusiasm for medicine's possibilities arises not necessarily from material products with therapeutic efficacy but through the production of ideas with potential but as-yet-unproven therapeutic efficacy. An officer of one of the most successful biotechnology firms in America has indicated that biotechnology enterprises are in the business of producing ideas about potential therapeutics, from designer anticancer therapies to the manipulation of damaged genes.

> Think about a biotechnology company as a pharmaceutical company. ... If you start with an idea and you are by definition working on something in the pharmaceutical industry that is likely to fail 90% of the time. ... one of the myths of biotech. ... you are proposing to start a company in which there is a 90% chance of failure, the cost of product development is $500–$900 million, and from idea to the time when you have a revenue stream from product development is twelve to fifteen years. So your question is really, against that fundamental absurdity, how do you build a business, right?
>
> If you start at that purely abstract level, what do you have to sell? You don't have your product yet, so what do you have to sell to feed the beast that you are about to build? Well, there are only two things that you have to sell: ... you can sell things that are or look or smell like equity. ... What's the problem with that? At the end of the day, the pie is so split up, nobody makes any money on their equity, the dilution is intolerable. So what else do I have to sell? Well, instead of selling pieces of the company, an interest in the home, I can sell pieces of pieces, which I call rights – for example, in certain of my discoveries or products – and this is where the pharmaceutical companies come in ... They say we will pay for you to do some research on our behalf; we will take the product that results from it; we, the pharmaceutical company, will commer-

cialize it and pay you a royalty. So I withstand the dilution, I start generating revenues from collaboration, ... and then I hand off the more expensive parts of forward integration of manufacturing and sales, I don't have to take on those burdens.

> ... So call those your children. Keep the family alive by selling your children. The question is "is the nature of your platform prolific enough that in having sold off some of your children, you haven't sold off all of your future?" Because if ... at the end of the day, [you are only] getting some royalties, from the 10% of your efforts that didn't fail, you are never going to be a big company. (Holtzman 2001)

Such firms seek to make public the scientific imaginary; until very recently, they have been the darlings of venture capital and continue to attract considerable investment. (See the business sections of the *New York Times* and the *Wall Street Journal* for analyses of recent market trends and for documentation of volatility in the financial side of the medical imaginary.) However, companies whose fortunes appear bright because of the remarkable scientific promise of potential and authorized new pharmaceutical products may find that the questionable long-term efficacy of once-promising drugs, such as VIOXX or hormone-replacement therapy (HRT), can threaten financial futures and disrupt evolving clinical practices. One such example is Johnson and Johnson's Eprex, an innovative platelet enhancer for treating anemia in cancer patients. Red-cell aplasia, the inability to produce red blood cells, has been associated with this formerly billion-dollar product (Pollack 2002; also Tagliabue 2002; Varmus 2002; and on HRT, Kolata 2002).

At more mundane levels, Americans live in a world in which the medical imaginary has star billing in medical journalism, television advertisements, and globally popular television productions such as *ER*. (*ER* is among the most popular television programs in Indonesia and China; the medical imaginary is a global phenomenon.) The imminent discovery of cancer cure, effective genetic therapy, the manufacturing of new and better mechanical hearts, the engineering of tissue and the genetic alteration of pig cells to offset organ shortages, the latest results of clinical trials on AIDS therapies and reports of their effectiveness, cost, and contested patents – all become part of the daily global circulation of popular, business, and medical knowledge. Our vast interests, financial and certainly emotional, in the political economy of hope are evident in daily market reports and public discourses. Recent stories on the Abiomed mechanical heart illustrate the more extreme version of the link between product development and the political economy of hope. (See Stolberg 2002 about a patient who lived for nine months with the heart.)

The circulation of knowledge and of the ethereal products of the medical imaginary is of course uneven. The robustness of local scientific and medical communities, NGOs, and political health activists influence how people share, access, and use this global knowledge. (See these recent studies: on Brazil, Bastos 1999; on American research oncology, Cooke 2001; on French science, Rabinow 1999; and on medical missions for high-technology treatment of multidrug-resistant tuberculosis [MDRTB] and HIV for the poor, Farmer 1999, 2004.) Alternative stories, misuses, and failures of medicine's cultural power and possibilities are also part of the traffic in the medical imaginary: failures (in genetic therapy leading to patient death); fraud (in clinical trials in oncology); discouragement (upon learning that promising therapeutics are ineffective); greed (physicians trafficking in organs or brokering transfers from the poor to the rich; Cohen 1999; Sanal 2004). Yet these tales are set in the larger optimistic story of the hope and the many-possibility science of medicine.

The Biotechnical Embrace

The image of the biotechnical embrace emerged serendipitously out of studies of the culture of oncology during the past decade and conversations with my colleagues in medicine, ethics, and social science in the United States, Europe, Asia, and Africa. The concept of "embrace" conjured the subjective experiences and affective responses of many clinicians and their patients when using new biotechnologies,

high-technology experimental treatments, and even salvage therapies. Among my American medical colleagues are those who acknowledge the phenomenon, are energized by enthusiasm albeit tempered with irony, and recognize when patients are embraced. (One pediatrician and ethicist has incorporated the term into lectures on the latest transplant therapeutics.) The specifics of popular and professional enthusiasm for biomedicine and nascent technologies may be characteristically American, as some of my European colleagues suggest, but "embracing and being embraced" fundamentally link contemporary high-technology medicine and bioscience to the wider society.

Whether this enthusiasm is for new reproductive technologies, effective therapies to treat HIV or MDRTB, innovative organ-transplantation procedures, progress in therapeutic gene manipulation, or efficacious treatments for common life-threatening diseases such as cancer and heart disease, it sparks the medical imagination and drives the political economy of hope, as well as our society's investment in medical adventures and misadventures.

Clinical Narratives and Ethnographic Frames

The two worlds of American academic clinical oncology – the therapeutic and the scientific – provide vivid examples of how patients and their clinicians embrace, even as they are embraced by, biotechnology and how American medical culture generates enthusiasm for experimental clinical science and "medicine on the edge." (The success of Jerome Groopman's [2000] essays on cancer patients and experimental treatments is evidence of strong interest among certain groups of Americans.) In my studies of the culture of clinical oncology, I developed the concept of the "clinical narrative" to capture the dynamics of clinical interactions between oncologists and their patients that evolve over time through arduous and often lengthy therapeutic journeys. (See our work on clinical narratives and oncology studies in the reference list; of particular relevance are M. Good 1995a, 1995b, and M. Good et al. 1990, 1994; see Mattingly 1994 and

1998 for her creative work on therapeutic emplotment and Mattingly and Garro 2000 for elaboration.)

Narrative Analysis

When literary concepts such as narrative are introduced into observations of everyday clinical life, new aspects of medical work and therapeutic processes become evident. Concepts drawn from narrative analysis – plot, emplotment, and narrative time – illuminate how affect and desire play out in clinical narratives, seducing patients and clinicians and enveloping both in a world of the medical imagination, with a many-possibility regime of truth and with fantastic but apparently purposeful technical acts. This analytic approach highlights not only how clinical stories arises and how oncologists develop narrative strategies, but it also identifies antinarrative clinical talk, in which events have no meaning, strategies of communication fail, and clinical plots fragment or fail to emerge. This type of talk is common to medicine globally. (See B. Good 1994, B. Good and M. Good 1994, 2000; M. Good and B. Good 2000; Mattingly and Garro 2000; Ricoeur 1981a, 1981b; Brooks 1984; Iser 1978; and Eco 1994 for references on narrative analysis.)

Narrative analysis enables disaggregation of specialty power and its economic underpinnings; it leads us to ask how the cultural power and scientific robustness of clinical medicine at the academic medical center where our projects took place come into play – in "plotting" a coherent therapeutic course, structuring clinical time, installing desire for treatment, giving hope, and in the case of diseases resistant to standard treatment, inviting patients to open their bodies to experimental treatments that are often of questionable efficacy. In the American case, oncologists use clinical narratives to incorporate evidence-based medicine into clinical culture and to introduce therapeutic meaning through reliance on the findings of clinical trials and relevant research in the biosciences. And through the clinical narrative, the aesthetics of statistics – how one conveys the odds and

chances of particular treatments to patients – emerge as culturally shaped and institutionally sanctioned, taking on a centrality in the narrative discourse, even as the narrative skirts ultimate questions of death, and addressing the immediacy of therapeutic activities.

Patients' ironic engagement with their clinicians, as they negotiate the meanings of these clinical narratives, the odds and statistics, and the fantastic and questionable, affords a glimpse into how the medical imaginary engenders a certain bravado, an experience with many possibilities, that supports and sustains the emotional, financial, and cultural investment in experimental procedures and treatments (Gould 1996).

Worlds of Oncology

Case examples from our oncology studies illustrate how clinical narratives connect the public, in particular patients, to high-technology medical science and how patients experience and discuss invitations into a biotechnical embrace. Complementing these clinical examples are illustrations from a forum created and dominated by patients, BMT-Talk, a cyberspace network connecting bone-marrow-transplant (BMT) patients, friends, kin, researchers, and curious clinicians, some of whom dispense second opinions from as far away as Brazil. The global connection is evident. In addition, public documents from insurance hearings open additional perspectives on oncology's multiple "regimes of truth."

In the American culture of high-technology medicine, oncologists are expected to invite patients to enter the world of experimental therapeutics when cancer is resistant to standard treatments. Through this invitation to "salvage therapy" (a clinician's term), a clinical narrative that weds the experimental to the therapeutic begins to unfold. Clinical narratives direct action and technological interventions. They inscribe treatment experiences on a patient's psyche and soma, under the guise of multiple plots and subplots that the professional subspecialties envision for patient and clinicians.

"Rules Change": ABMT and High-Dose Chemotherapies

The current controversy about autologous bone-marrow transplants (ABMTs) for metastatic breast cancer poses an ethical dilemma about societal and individual costs, both financial and personal. As a medical oncologist noted in conversation in 1993, this expensive "salvage therapy" had dubious therapeutic credentials; and in clinical trials to that date, patients who initially responded positively to transplants "were all relapsing at six or eight months after the transplant." Yet, in 1994, some patients sued their insurers who refused coverage for these treatments, and many more medical oncologists encouraged their use. (A now-infamous suit brought by a California Kaiser patient who was refused coverage in 1994 helped establish this "experimental treatment" as a standard of care by 1995–96. "No HMO [health maintenance organization] would be able to refuse coverage now because of that suit," claimed the chief of surgery at the Harvard teaching hospitals in 1996.)

By 1995, clinical studies indicated that mortality from the procedure decreased from 30 percent to 3 percent, as innovative posttreatment care was introduced and healthier patients were recruited. Although the cost of providing autologous stem-cell/bone-marrow transplants declined quickly and dramatically (from approximately $150,000 in 1993 to $60,000–$75,000 today), as the technological fix became "technically sweet," increasingly efficient and standardized, and as treatment locales shifted from lengthy hospitalizations to outpatient services, questions continued about long-term therapeutic efficacy. As the bioscience of the field alters and decisions to choose competing therapeutic options (such as platelet treatments with new pharmaceuticals) become ever more complicated, especially given the uncertain efficacy of many treatments and the potential for serious clinical errors, careful orchestration of the medical imaginary is necessary. Yet, even with questionable efficacy, we see patients and physicians captured by the biotechnical embrace, with enthusiasm about the possibilities of the experimental.

ABMT for metastatic breast cancer is a prime example of enthusiasm based on questionable clinical science.

Normalizing the Experimental

Clinician-scientists such as Dr. William Peters of Duke University Medical School were among the early public promoters of experimental therapeutics, normalizing the technologies and the apparent high-tech oddities, turning the unusual into an event no more odd than a coffee break and adopting the housekeeping metaphors of daily life. In his persuasive presentation at federal government hearings on whether Medicare/Medicaid would support coverage of ABMT for metastatic disease, Dr. Peters characterized the procedure as follows:

As our famous philosopher once said: "the future just ain't what it used to be" – this is what most people think of bone marrow transplants as being – a high-technology facility with isolation procedures, use of high-tech equipment, multiple supportive care efforts and so on. What is really, happening is that, in the last few years, this is occurring more frequently. Two women from our institution (post transplant day two and day six) – are waiting for coffee to be delivered to the hotel where they are staying during their bone marrow transplant. We now essentially do all our bone marrow transplants as outpatient procedures. If one looks at the 100-day mortality in patients undergoing transplants, you can see that, back in the mid-1980's, the therapy-related mortality in the first hundred days was at over 30%. Now, it is in the range of about 3%. In fact, if you look at the 30-day mortality [it has dropped] from 15% down to the 3% to 4% realm. This represents massive change in therapy-related mortality. (Peters 1994)

Ironic Humor: The Twilight Zone and the Medical Imagination

Patients, like clinicians, play the numbers. Ironic humor and an edge of cynicism (hope against hope?) mix with the medical imagination and the slightly bizarre imaginary of what the future might hold. The following comments by patients about the clinical narrative created for them are illustrative.

Mrs. R, a witty fifty-four-year-old educator, suffers from metastatic disease and is a candidate for autologous bone-marrow transplant and high-dose chemotherapy (Cytoxan). She discusses therapeutic choices with her medical oncologist and the transplant surgeon. The excerpts I include here cover several meetings over a period of nine months. When we first met Mrs. R, she was with the medical oncologist, who had just informed her that she had metastatic disease secondary to breast cancer.

The first excerpt is from her third visit with the medical oncologist, with whom she discusses "choices" and recommendations from the transplant surgeons, in August. The patient's sense of humor is dry; her comments nevertheless capture the strangeness and uncertainties of experimental treatments and medicine on the edge.

Patient (Mrs. R) comments to the interviewer about ABMT: I guess if I had a concern, my concern is – is it going to damage my immune system so that it's going to make things worse? It seems like a very archaic sort of technique. [Speaks about postponing a vacation]. I don't want to jeopardize this great 15 percent to 20 percent chance. I really don't have a choice, do I?

Medical oncologist: Yes, you do have a choice. You don't have a choice if you're only focusing on the big picture and ten years down the road. Then you don't have a choice because these choices can give you a chance. But if you focus on the next five years—

Mrs. R: Five years is nothing.

Medical oncologist: So you don't have a choice. It's your choice.

Mrs. R: He [the transplant specialist] said it is not a choice.

The second encounter, which took place the following February, begins with an interview between the patient and the researcher; it then focuses on the clinical encounter as the physician removes the stem cells.

Mrs. R: This is supposed to stimulate the stem cells to grow ... and then they harvest them in ten days. It's kind of like gardening.

Interviewer: It's just a very short growing period. Like radishes.

Mrs. R: That's right. Like radishes. That's right. These little radishes. That's right.

...

Interviewer: So, I have my usual question, how does all this feel at this point?

Mrs. R: Like a giant mistake. The truth? Like I made a mistake. I shouldn't be doing this. ... I wasn't feeling sick. And, you know, right now it's getting toward the big time, and I don't want to do it. I don't want to be here. I want to be on with my life. This is inconveniencing my life, and I don't like that. Does that sound adequate enough? So I am saying why the hell did I decide to do this? This is stupid. Besides, the whole thing is Twilight Zone.

...

Transplanter: Good, good, good. Okay. So the fun part starts.

Mrs. R (to interviewer): He's got this sadistic humor.

Interviewer: You know you're in trouble when he starts rubbing his hands.

Mrs. R: Oh, that's a sign? Okay. He's kind of got that Frankenstein look. What are we going to make today?

...

(After that day's procedures)

Mrs. R: You know what the hardest part – not even the hardest part, but – I guess the irony of the whole thing is to go through all this and have absolutely not only no guarantee at the end, but not even an indication. ... No way to have any idea whether it worked or didn't work. When you think about it, it seems like at the end they should be able to say, "it looks good," or "it doesn't look good."

Interviewer: What did they say about that?

Mrs. R: If I'm alive and well in five years they'll call it a success, and I'll follow the 20 percent success rate. It's a hindsight thing. And it's funny, one of the things that we did do initially that we've gotten off that we have to get back on, I think, was to go on a diet and become vegetarian [referring to tamoxifen and the idea that soy is a natural tamoxifen]. ... You listen to the medical profession but you must do your own thing. So I'll keep eating tofu. So, I'll keep eating tofu. So, I don't know. It's all so interesting. The teachers gave me a huge party. Very nice, a surprise party. And they sent out invitations and they called it a shower. They had a shower for me, a shower of friendship, they called it.

Five weeks after this interview, the patient returned for a follow-up treatment just after news articles revealed that a competing institution, the esteemed Dana Farber Cancer Center, had inadvertently overdosed two women during high-dose chemotherapy, leading to one patient's death (*Boston Globe*, March 22, 23, 24, 1995). The Joint Commission on Accreditation of Hospitals placed the center on probation.

In April, Mrs. R evaluated for her oncology nurse her physicians' skill at extracting bone marrow (not only for therapeutic purposes but for a clinical observation study). She scored each of them: "a five, a seven, a three!"

Nurse: Not a ten?
Mrs. R: Ten does not exist, nobody can get a ten.
[Just as no ABMT patient can be assured of a cure.]
Mrs. R: I decided that [cancer] can be a chronic disease. It doesn't have to be a – I always believed it was a death sentence. ... Now my next big decision is, they did the second bone marrow for their research ... to see if there's any breast cancer cells in the bone marrow. So do I want to know the answer to that?
Nurse: I don't think they can tell you the answer to that.
Mrs. R: Yeah, he said he could.
Nurse: Right ... and you don't know what to do with the information ... he shouldn't have even told you there was an option.
Mrs. R: I'll have to think about that.

The oncology nurse and patient conclude with additional talk about the 15 percent to 20 percent cure rate and about the uncertainty and ambiguity of what the future holds.

Narrative strategies in this type of clinical encounter draw heavily on humor, and many patients in our study responded in kind. Humor lends irony to ambiguity. Nevertheless, the clinicians and patient fully experienced the experimental nature of the procedure. Notably, in May 1999, the American Society for Clinical Oncology released data from five clinical trials comparing ABMT with high-dose chemotherapy to standard treatment protocols. Four of the five studies detected no difference in longevity, although one study indicated a small difference in quality of life (www. ASCO). The single trial that reported greater effectiveness was discovered to be flawed by fraudulent research and science. The clinician investigator responsible, Dr. Werner Bezwoda, chair of the oncology and hematology department of the University of Witwatersrand Medical School in Johannesburg, South Africa, acknowledged he adjusted his data in order to gain fame (Waldholz 2000). Clinical narratives may inadvertently introduce fraudulent science and treatment of questionable efficacy and high toxicity, even as they offer the power of scientific discovery and biotechnical innovation.

Wile E. Coyote: BMT-Talk in Cyberspace

BMT-Talk is filled with the fantastic – with images of the archaic, the Frankenstein, the cyborg, and the bizarre aspects of treatment. Below, a young patient writing about a bone-marrow transplant for his/her multiple myeloma also draws on American metaphors of the flexible cartoonlike and regenerating body (the coyote appears in many forms and, like a cat, has multiple lives).

The thing that is weird to me is that the transplant, unlike a liver or kidney or other organ transplant, isn't what's supposed to help against the disease [multiple myeloma]. What's supposed to do the damage to the cancer/tumor cells is the chemotherapy. The transplant is a rescue technique because without it the chemo would be fatal. Wow. It's a really bizarre idea – like if the water in your aquarium were tainted somehow, you'd put a ton of salt or other medicines in it, then pump it ALL out (leaving the fish inside the aquarium), waiting for it to dry out, and then pumping the water back in and hoping the fish could still swim (and not just float upside down!). Hmmm ... well I just thought up that analogy, and it's not quite right, but it's kind of how I feel about it. We'll drop a 16-ton weight on you. That'll kill all the cancer. Then, you'll walk along like an accordion, as though you were Wile E. Coyote in a Road Runner cartoon, until you pump the air back into yourself. In fact, we'll pump it in for you! ... I know it's the best chance I have, but I can't help feeling that it's going to seem awfully primitive in (hopefully) not many years. It feels like with all the technological and medical advances we've made, we're not that far removed from bloodletting!

Patients' subjective experiences with BMT procedures – from enthusiasm to disappointment and struggle – contrast with those of physicians who have cared for BMT patients for whom the procedure has failed.[1] In our recent study of internists' emotional responses to patient deaths (M. Good et al. 2004), we found an alternate and chilling version of the bizarre "BMT-Talk," as illustrated in the following interview excerpts, which I present by clinician rank – faculty physicians (attendings), second-to fourth-year residents, and interns.[2]

Attendings commenting on training in bone-marrow stem-cell transplant:

> The big hope – there are incredible highs and lows – the high is when you get the disease to go away with the transplant and you have done good.

> Sometimes transplant units are like a morgue; the transplant people don't see it that way; house staff rotate through and comment about it all the time.

> It's a big risk, an up-front risk, a 20 percent mortality rate from the procedure.

> Intellectually, bone-marrow transplantation is a numbers game – I firmly believe in the ability to cure the other 60 percent.

> We threw everything we could at her and she died anyway, which is unfortunate, but that was the standard of care with transplant.

> It was the standard transplant story: go in, get chemotherapy, radiotherapy, get the transplant, get sick a couple of weeks later, get sicker, get sicker, get sicker, wind up in the ICU, died a week later.

> I don't expect transplants to work.

> Although you haven't killed them theoretically, you have at least contributed to their death prematurely.

Some comments from residents:

> I finished off my responsibility, but the next year I did not want to go back to the bone-marrow–transplant unit

> Bone-marrow transplant is such an odd realm of the medical world, and frankly other programs don't even see any of it.

> And this 35-year-old woman, like all people who enter transplant, looked good, then died of it.

> Being given high doses of chemotherapy and a bone-marrow transplant is not a natural event. Sometimes oncology in general kind of bugs me, in that it seems – especially for bone-marrow–transplant patients ... I was feeling, Why are we doing this?

And, finally, interns:

> They come to the ICU and we have to tell them, to tell their families. It's just so frustrating that the people don't know [the high rate of failure of BMT procedures].

> I'm on a bone-marrow–transplant team, so this is like the worst of ... I don't know.

These excerpts exemplify physicians' internal critique of practices they regard as clinical irrationalities. Their experiences with patients' deaths rather than recovery convey the negative side of the medical imaginary and the biotechnical embrace.

Metaphors of Entering the Bizarre

Patients in our studies also used metaphors of the bizarre. Even standard chemotherapy feels like one is "off to see the wizard." A primary-school teacher, fifty-three years of age, sang us a little ditty to the tune of "I'm off to see the Wizard, the wonderful Wizard of Oz," a song she sings with her daughters as they drive to chemotherapy treatment: "I'm off to see the wizard, I'm off to chemotherapy."

Other patients, especially those who seek every possible treatment, articulate their ambivalence in succumbing to the embrace of oncology's power:

> It makes me wonder what people are willing to accept when they think of something, some institution or doctor as being the best. Is it how bad you feel? [laughs] Is it how absolutely

miserable and sick you are made as a result of a treatment they are willing to invite you to have? Is that what being a good patient is all about? Not complaining ... I wonder, when will it be enough?

Metaphors of living are, of course, equally central to the way patients address the medical imaginary and the seduction of the biotechnical embrace, the desire for hope. The aesthetics of science are wed to art in the poignant reconfiguration of Botticelli's *The Birth of Venus* in *Art.Rage.Us* (Tasch 1998). Venus is refigured with a subtle, surgically elegant mastectomy, still beautiful. Thus, as life continues, beauty too may endure despite the inscriptions on the body of consequences of clinical narratives, medicine's technically sweet fixes, and life's illness traumas.

Concluding Reflections

As we deconstruct American clinical culture, particularly the worlds of oncology, we find a persistent rhetoric of humanism contrasted with that of technology. Such public and professional dichotomies may lead us astray, endorsing professional power over lay knowledge. And yet the metaphoric language of many patients is profoundly affective, expressing hope and interest in the possibilities of biotechnical innovations and therapeutics, whether in consultation with their clinicians or in the less structured interviews with researchers. In BMT-Talk, cyberspace connections often appear to heighten the emotionality of discourses and graphic debates with other patients about the limits of therapeutic options. The affective dimensions of high-technology medicine are clearly soteriological (B. Good 1994), reflecting a salvation ethos that is fundamental to bioscience and biomedicine and to the political economy and culture of hope. The biotechnical embrace creates a popular culture that is enamored with the biology of hope, attracting venture capital that continues even in the face of contemporary constraints to generate new treatment modalities.

I began this essay by considering the relationship between science and society and its connection to the relationship between the global and the local in biomedicine,

particularly high-technology medicine. A global moral dilemma arises when the cultural traffic from the biosciences and its attendant marketing of biomedical products influence the practice of clinical medicine in societies of scarcity. Whereas the world's dominant economies invest private and public monies in the production of biotechnology and aggressively seek to integrate these advances into clinical practice – thereby reaping financial as well as scientific returns on capital investments – all societies confront difficult questions about rationing biomedical interventions that are assumed to be central to competent clinical medicine. Local clinicians are thus subject to constantly shifting and competing claims and regimes of truth from the worlds of scientific power and transnational biomedicine. (See Bastos 1999 for a discussion of similar issues in AIDS science.) As metaphors of science and society merge, ethical questions arise about how best to serve all patients. Integrating cultural, ethical, and political-economy analyses of contemporary popular and professional biomedical cultures is critical to unmasking links between interests, be they economic or cultural, and policies on "best medical practices" for the global medical commons. How medicine serves humanity in the third millennium may be at least marginally affected by the way in which anthropology tackles this interdisciplinary analytic project.

NOTES

1   To illustrate, the following describes a bone-marrow transplant for acute lymphocytic leukemia: "Treatment begins with chemotherapy designed to kill as many cancer cells as possible. If the cells have spread to the brain, the patient will also undergo radiation therapy and chemotherapy injected directly into the spinal fluid. Generally, 70 to 80 percent of the patients achieve remission after chemotherapy. To reduce the risk of relapse, the patient is given maintenance chemotherapy treatments. Sixty-five percent of the patients relapse after remission, and begin aggressive chemotherapy again. Bone Marrow Transplants are usually performed during the second remission. Studies have found 60 percent long term survival rates (survival

beyond three years) for those patients who receive BMT in the first remission, and 40 percent long term survival rates for those who receive them in the second. (Many doctors prefer to wait to see if a patient relapses after the first round of chemotherapy before deciding to perform BMT)." (www.peds.umn.edu/centers/BMT/all.html).

2 The study, Physicians' Emotional Reactions to Their Patients' Deaths, was funded by the Nathan Cummings Foundation. The primary investigators are Susan D. Block, M.D., Dana Farber Cancer Institute and Department of Psychiatry, Brigham and Women's Hospital; and Robert M. Arnold, M.D., University of Pittsburgh Medical Center. Research took place between 1999 and 2001. In addition to myself, the Boston research team included Patricia Ruopp, EdD, Nina Gadmer, Matt Lakoma, and Amy Sullivan, PhD. (See Good et al. 2004, for a project description.)

REFERENCES

Bastos, Cristiana
  1999 *Global Responses to AIDS: Science in Emergency.* Bloomington: Indiana University Press.
Brooks, Peter
  1984 *Reading for the Plot: Design and Intention in Narrative.* New York: Vintage Books.
Cohen, Lawrence
  1999 "Where It Hurts: Indian Material for an Ethics of Organ Transplantation." Special issue, "Bioethics and Beyond." *Daedalus* 128(4): 135–65.
Cooke, Robert
  2001 *Dr. Folkman's War: Angiogenesis and the Struggle to Defeat Cancer.* New York: Random House.
Eco, Umberto
  1994 *Six Walks in the Fictional Woods.* Cambridge, MA: Harvard University Press.
Fairview-University Medical Center
  2000 "Acute Lymphocytic Leukemia." Blood and Marrow Transplant Program, Fairview-University Medical Center, University of Minnesota. www.peds.umn.edu/centers/BMT/all.html.
Farmer, Paul
  1999 *Infections and Inequalities: The Modern Plagues.* Berkeley: University of California Press.

Farmer, Paul
  2004 *Pathologies of Power: Health, Human Rights, and the New War on the Poor.* Berkeley: University of California Press.
Fischer, Michael M. J.
  1991 "Anthropology as Cultural Critique: Inserts for the 1990s Cultural Studies of Science, Visual-Virtual Realities, and Post-Trauma Polities." *Cultural Anthropology* 6:525–37.
Freudeheim, Milt
  2002 "The Healthier Side of Health Care." *New York Times*, October 23.
Good, Byron
  1994 *Medicine, Rationality, and Experience.* Cambridge: Cambridge University Press.
Good, Byron, and Mary-Jo DelVecchio Good.
  1994 "In the Subjunctive Mode: Epilepsy Narratives in Turkey." Social Science and Medicine 38(6):835–42.
Good, Byron, and Mary-Jo DelVecchio Good.
  2000 " 'Fiction' and 'Historicity' in Doctors' Stories: Social and Narrative Dimensions of Learning Medicine." In *Narrative and the Cultural Construction of Illness and Healing*, ed. Cheryl Mattingly and Linda Garro (Berkeley: University of California Press).
Good, Mary-Jo DelVecchio
  1995a "Cultural Studies of Biomedicine: An Agenda for Research." *Social Science and Medicine* 41(4):461–73.
Good, Mary-Jo DelVecchio
  1995b *American Medicine: The Quest for Competence.* Berkeley: University of California Press.
Good, Mary-Jo DelVecchio
  2001 "The Biotechnical Embrace." *Culture, Medicine, and Psychiatry* 25:395–410.
Good, Mary-Jo DelVecchio, Nina M. Gadmer, Patricia Ruopp, Matthew Lakoma, Amy M. Sullivan, Robert M. Arnold, Susan D. Block.
  2004 "Narrative Nuances on Good and Bad Deaths: Internists' Tales from High-technology Work Places." *Social Science and Medicine* 58 (March): 939–53.
Good, Mary-Jo DelVecchio, and Byron Good
  2000 "Clinical Narratives and the Study of Contemporary Doctor-Patient Relationships." In *The Handbook of Social Studies in Health and Medicine*, ed. Gary L. Albrecht, Ray Fitzpatrick, and Susan C. Scrimshaw (London: Sage Publications Ltd.).

Good, Mary-Jo DelVecchio, Byron J. Good, Cynthia Schaffer, and Stuart E. Lind
1990 "American Oncology and the Discourse on Hope." *Culture, Medicine and Psychiatry* 14:59–79.

Good, Mary-Jo DelVecchio, Tsuenetsu Munakata, Yasuki Kobayashi, Cheryl Mattingly, Byron Good
1994 "Oncology and Narrative Time." *Social Science and Medicine* 38(6): 855–62.

Gould, Stephen Jay
1996 *Full House: The Spread of Excellence from Plato to Darwin*. New York: Harmony Books.

Groopman, Jerome
2000 *Second Opinions: Stories of Intuition and Choice in the Changing World of Medicine*. New York: Viking.

Holtzman, Steven
2001 Interview with Michael M. J. Fischer, Byron Good, and Mary-Jo DelVecchio Good. January 16.

Iser, Wolfgang
1978 *The Act of Reading: A Theory of Aesthetic Response*. Baltimore: Johns Hopkins University Press.

Kolata, Gina
2002 "Scientists Debating Future of Hormone Replacement." *New York Times*, October 23.

Marcus, George, ed.
1995 *Technoscientific Imaginaries: Conversations, Profiles and Memoirs*. Chicago: University of Chicago Press.

Marcus, George, ed.
1998 "Ethnography in/of the World System: The Emergence of Multi-sited Ethnography." In *Ethnography through Thick and Thin* (Princeton, NJ: Princeton University Press).

Mattingly, Cheryl
1994 "The Concept of Therapeutic 'Emplotment.'" *Social Science and Medicine* 38 (6):811–22.

Mattingly, Cheryl
1998 *Healing Dramas and Clinical Plots*. Cambridge: Cambridge University Press.

Mattingly, Cheryl, and Linda Garro, eds.
2000 *Narrative and the Cultural Construction of Illness and Healing*. Berkeley: University of California Press.

Peters, William
1994 Presentation to federal government hearings on Medicare/Medicaid coverage of bone-marrow transplant.

Pollack, Andrew
2002 "U.S. Inquiry and Lawsuit Draw Reaction of Drug Maker." *New York Times*, July 20.

Rabinow, Paul
1999 *French DNA: Trouble in Purgatory*. Chicago: University of Chicago Press.

Ricoeur, Paul
1981a *Hermeneutics and the Human Sciences*. Ed. and trans. John B. Thompson. Cambridge: Cambridge University Press.

Ricoeur, Paul
1981b "Narrative Time." In *On Narrative*, ed. W. J. T. Mitchell (Chicago: University of Chicago Press), 165–86.

Rouse, Joseph
1992 "What Are Cultural Studies of Scientific Knowledge?" *Configurations* 1(1):1–22.

Sanal, Aslihan
2004 " 'Robin Hood' of Techno-Turkey or Organ Trafficking in the State of Ethical Beings," *Culture, Medicine and Psychiatry* 28(3):281–309.

Stolberg, Sheryl Gay
2002 "On Medicine's Frontier: The Last Journey of James Quinn." *New York Times*, October 8.

Tagliabue, John
2002 "Mystery Effect in Biotech Drug Puts Its Maker on Defensive." *New York Times* Business section, October 2.

Tasch, Jacqueline A., ed.
1998 *Art.Rage.Us: Art and Writing by Women with Breast Cancer*. San Francisco: Chronicle Books.

Varmus, Harold
2002 "The DNA of a New Industry." *New York Times* Opinion page, September 24.

Waldholz, Michael
2000 "South African Doctor Admits Falsifying Data on Treatments for Breast Cancer." *Wall Street Journal*, February 7.

22

Where It Hurts
Indian Material for an Ethics of Organ Transplantation

Lawrence Cohen

Prologue: The Scar

We are sitting in a one-room municipal housing-project flat in a Chennai slum, in a room filled with photographs of the man of the house posing with Tamil political leaders. His wife, one of the persons I am interviewing this June 1998 morning, all of whom had sold a kidney several years earlier for 32,500 rupees (roughly $1,200 at the time of sale), is speaking about why poor people get into debt. Chennai used to be called Madras, and it has become the place where people come in search of a "selling-their-kidneys-to-survive" story. This woman has invited us – myself, the hospital orderly Felix Coutinho who hooked me up with her, and the four other sellers we have found – to use her place for interviews. All of the sellers are women, and all but one have gone through Dr. K. C. Reddy's clinic to have the operation. "Operation" is one of the few words I recognize in the Tamil conversation that Mr. Coutinho is translating. I am used to working in north India and the United States, but neither English nor Hindi is of particular use at this moment. As they are cut out from the flesh, organs

reconstitute the spaces of bodily analysis, and to delineate these spaces I have found myself continually moving about and ever more reliant, uncomfortably, on translation.[1]

Dr. Reddy has been India's most outspoken advocate of a person's right to sell a kidney. His practice – until 1994, while it was arguably still legal to remove someone's kidney without a medical reason – was apparently exemplary: education for potential sellers on the implications of the operation, two years free follow-up health care, and procedures to avoid kidney brokers and their commission. My anthropological colleague Patricia Marshall, on her own and with the Omani transplant surgeon Abdullah Daar, studied the practice of Reddy and his colleagues.[2] She did not find evidence of the often-reported practices of cheating, stealing from, or misinforming sellers. Marshall introduced me to Reddy and to the general practitioner who had run his follow-up clinic for local sellers.

When I first visited the follow-up clinic, an estate with an abandoned air set back from the Poonamalai High Road, I met Coutinho sitting on the verandah with several other orderlies. He

Lawrence Cohen, "Where It Hurts: Indian Material for an Ethics of Organ Transplantation," *Daedalus* 128/4 (1999): 135–66. © 1999 by the American Academy of Arts and Sciences.

had previously been the go-between hooking up sellers with the clinic and knew where to find them. We talked for a while: there were not many patients. The follow-up clinic had closed when Reddy shut down his program in the wake of India's 1994 Transplantation of Human Organs Act, which made the selling of solid organs unambiguously illegal, authorized the harvesting of organs from the bodies of persons diagnosed as brain dead, and forbade the gift of an organ from a live donor other than a parent, child, sibling, or spouse. There were exceptions, approved by Authorization Committees set up in each state that implemented the Act to ensure that the donor was some kind of relation or close friend. *Frontline*, a Chennai-based newsweekly, had published an article the year before documenting how easily these committees were circumvented.[3] As long as the paperwork was in order, the investigative team argued, it was virtually impossible for committee members to differentiate an altruistic donation from a sale masquerading as such.

Coutinho and I sat on the verandah and talked about my project. He was interested in helping out, he said, because he, too, was a social worker. Later he told me about his project, the LOVE Foundation, a home for the destitute elderly that he and some friends from his church had set up. Would I consider visiting the LOVE home and helping it out? We agreed to meet the next morning to visit Ayanavaram and Ottery slums, and when I had had enough of kidneys for me to talk to the Secretary of LOVE.

Many investigators had taken this route before, into the Chennai slum: the abject stories, the repeated and identical image of a man or a woman turning his or her flank to the camera and tracing the line of the scar. The slum of choice was Villivakkam, nicknamed "Kidneyvakkam" because so many of its residents had undergone the operation. Raj Chengappa, senior deputy editor at the newsmagazine *India Today*, told me that after breaking the Villivakkam story in the early 1990s with an article called "The Great Organs Bazaar," he was deluged with calls from American and European based media.[4] Villivakkam gothic became routinized, as in its wake of scandal and shock did a counter-narrative in which sellers were informed agents making rational choices under unenviable but real conditions. Information brokers joined organ brokers in leading filmmakers and reporters – and, following them, anthropologists, ethicists, and medical factfinding teams – along well-rutted paths to predictable stories. Depending upon the need, terrains of violence or of agency and reason materialized. There was material in the slum for all manner of social workers.

***

Few of the growing number of Villivakkam experts have commented on what is to the outsider a pronounced feature of the slum's topography: it is saturated with pawnshops where moneylenders buy and sell gold and other precious items. Outside many shops in the slum's central shopping area are boards noting the day's buying and selling prices. Women in particular examine jewelry they are considering buying to consolidate their earnings or bargain over the money and credit earned by pawning their gold. There are few banks.

I worried that Villivakkam might not be the place to begin, given the neighborhood's media glut and my sense of the emergence of information brokers offering investigators whichever version of the trade they seem to want to find. I asked Coutinho whether there were other neighborhoods, where one might learn something new. We ended up in the Ayanavaram municipal projects, in the room with the political pictures, listening to one woman after another recount her story. Similar stories, but different in quality from the various public accounts, *neither* tales of graphic exploitation nor heroic agency. There were obvious biases: Coutinho was identified with Reddy, and his presence might have dampened any accounts of malpractice or exploitation. Conversely, I was signifiably well-off – dressed like the middle class, foreign, and white – and the possibility of future patronage might have heightened accounts of poverty and disappointment. We came in the late morning, when many of the women were back from domestic service but the men were still out working or looking for day jobs; we may have overestimated the proportion of women to men sellers. But the one man we interviewed as well as all of the women said that few men in this neighborhood had undergone the operation. In each neighborhood, the stories we heard varied in the details of a body and its particular situation, but shared several common threads.

What was common: I sold my kidney for 32,500 rupees. I had to; we had run out of credit and could not live. My friend had had the operation and told me what to do. I did not know what a kidney was; the doctors showed me a video. It passes water; it cleans the blood. You have two. You can live with one, but you may get sick or die from the operation or from something later. You have to have the family planning operation because without a kidney childbirth is very dangerous. I had already had *that* operation.

This, too: What choices did I have? Yes, I was weak afterwards, sometimes I still am. But generally I am as I was before. Yes, I would do it again if I had another to give. I would have to. That money is gone, and we are in debt. My husband needs his strength for work, and could not work if he had the operation. Yes, I also work.

* * *

Around us are several pictures of the husband meeting with the beloved late chief minister of Tamil Nadu, known by his initials: MGR. The husband organizes for the All India Anna Dravida Munnetra Kazhagam party in the housing project. The wife says he had been better connected with leaders in the days when MGR was alive. She nods toward MGR in the photo: "He needed a kidney, too," she says. "He was dying, and received one from his niece; they did the operation in America. At that time, I did not know about kidneys. If I had, I would have given him *both* of mine."

Why Chennai? Deeper poverty and debt are found elsewhere, but the urban south was the first fertile ground for organ harvesting. Part of the answer is not surprising. Both primary health care and tertiary medical innovation are more developed in south India, leading not only to some of the earliest transplantations in India but also to greater access to medical institutions for persons across class lines. For the question of contemporary kidney sales in Chennai, additionally relevant is the fact that the relation of medicine to what we might term the constitution of the citizen's body is gendered.

What might such a link between gender, citizenship, and the possibility of transplantation entail? Cecilia Van Hollen has studied the high usage of reproductive medicine and family planning by poor women in Chennai and other cities in the state of Tamil Nadu.[5] The situation differs significantly from much of north India, where women have been less likely to utilize state biomedical interventions like tubal ligations.[6] Many poor women in Chennai incorporate surgery and other obstetric and family-planning procedures into their lives, frequently electing extensive medical intervention. Van Hollen's findings suggest the ubiquity and intensive character of this medicalization as central to any account of agency in women's encounters with the state. *What they said* in Ayanavaram: I already had that operation. They told me I needed to have it before I could have the kidney operation, *but I already had it.*

Thus, most women have chosen to undergo tubal ligation before the decision to sell a kidney is imagined. The emergence of Chennai's various "Kidneyvakkams" must be located in the *prior operability* of these bodies. The operation here is a central modality of citizenship, by which I mean the performance of agency in relation to the state. It is not just an example of agency; it is agency's critical ground. In other words, having an operation for these women has become a dominant and pervasive means of attempting to secure a certain kind of future, to the extent that means and ends collapse: to be someone with choices is to be operated upon, to be operated upon is to be someone with choices. "Operation" is not just a procedure with certain risks, benefits, and cultural values; it confers the sort of agency I am calling citizenship.

Intriguingly, in these interviews the operation was said to weaken men more than women. A prior moment of contest over operability was, of course, the nationwide "Emergency" more than two decades earlier with its legacy of coercive family-planning operations, and particularly vasectomies.[7] Current accounts of the operation's greater danger to men draw upon memories of that earlier time, as well as upon a more generalizable phenomenology of male anxiety in the face of imagined female regeneration.[8] In these wo-men's accounts of their husbands' concerns, an operable citizenship came at far higher risk to men: it literally "unmanned" them. Regions like the "kidney belts" of rural Tamil Nadu feeding the Bangalore industry, where more sellers were men than in Chennai, often com-prised settlements of mostly male migrant workers paying off large debts in the wake of the collapse of the booming power-loom indus-try. Women were back in the village, and were less likely than urban women to have been hospitalized in childbirth or to have had pro-cedures like tubal ligations.[9]

I would have given him both of mine: if the gendered terms of citizenship in Chennai are set in part by one's operability, and if women here are the primary sites of the operation, then this woman's proposed gift of both of her kidneys to MGR can be rethought. Her gesture momentarily seems to redeem the operative losses of citizenship by framing them as a crit-ical gift that might have saved the famous leader. Our hostess transforms her second op-eration from an abject transaction to an act that reconstitutes Tamil Nadu's beloved late chief minister. A young man, the son of another woman who sold her kidney, complained to us later that day that other boys call him names: "Your mother is a kidney seller!" The current order of the commoditization of everything, in which the operation transforms this mother into a prostitute, is countered here by resusci-tating MGR as the politician-father and the idealized order he has come to represent. In invoking MGR's need for a kidney, this seller rescripts her sale into a gift to the Tamil leader that revives the idealized social relations of that time and renders all such sales unnecessary.

* * *

Within the terms of such an imaginable gift, what language would pain take? One of the women in the room offers the beginning of an answer. Her operation, she says, caused her body to hurt. "It still hurts." She points to her flank, to the scar. "It hurts there." I ask her, through Coutinho, to describe the pain. There is no data in India on the effects of nephrec-tomy for these very poor sellers, most of whom lack long-term primary care. I begin to ask her

more and more specific questions, sensing a symptom.

She looks at me, then at Coutinho. She had been talking, before my asking her about this pain, about her husband: a story of sporadic work, frustration, and drinking. Were we listening? She looks toward her scar again, and she says: "*That's* where he hits me. There. When I don't have any more money."

Arthur Kleinman has written of ethno-graphy as the study of what is at stake, an elegant and deceptively transparent formula-tion.[10] The stakes in the postoperative scar differ for the women in the room, for the doctors in Bangalore, for the husband who hits, and for me. For the women, the scar has two moments: a recent past when it marked their successful efforts to get out of extreme debt and support their households, and an in-debted present when it has come to mark the limits of that success. A sign of the embodiment of the loans one seeks to supplement wages and give life to one's family, the scar reveals both the inevitability of one's own body serving as collateral and the limits to this "collateraliza-tion." One has only one kidney to give, but the conditions of indebtedness remain. At some point the money runs out and one needs credit again, and then the scar covers over the wound not of a gift but of a debt.

For the doctors, the scar is the sign that nephrectomy can and does heal, given their knowledge of the operation, skills, and com-mitment to what they are doing. Life for life, another physician had said: the real wound is poverty and the operation provided the money to heal it. And yet there is the persistent fear, the counter-knowledge that things can and do go wrong, not only in the healing of the flesh but in the healing of the impoverishment the flesh stands for. Doctors know that sellers have little to no access to hospital care, that they often have to work at strenuous labor, that they are undernourished, and that they live in neigh-borhoods where infectious disease and alcohol are endemic. They know that much of the money passes quickly through the hands of sellers and goes to moneylenders and that many sellers lack bank accounts. In a different register, doctors also know the public is con-cerned about rumors of organ-thieving gangs, and rival hospitals might foment an accusation against one or another of them: both public anxiety and the strategies of rivals can bring the police in at any moment. No matter how good the surgery, the scar could still betray them, and sellers have to be kept out of sight. Like de Sade's libertines, the doctors try to erase all evidence of the cut.

For me, there was the search for traces of a more accountable medical narrative. Also, and less credibly, there were the thrill of the chase, the elite pleasures of building theory, and perhaps the premature anxiety over new biosocial arrangements that Paul Rabinow has called "purgatorial" driving my attack on medical practice from a putatively higher ground.[11]

And for the husband? I never met him, and for all my easy if persistent repugnance I do not know how to imagine the pain of the wound he felt on another's body and the absence behind the arc of his blows.[12] One is left with an inadequate sense of the deformation of the operation's promise, and with it the scar's slow slide from a mark of positive exchange to one of persistent debt.

Life for Life

Contemporary debate on the ethics of the sale of organs surgically removed from the bodies of the poor is shifting. Increasingly, philosophers, physicians, and social scientists are willing to suspend concern and to consider the case for a market in human organs. In India – the most well known of what is now a large number of countries supporting an emerging market in kidneys – several prominent opponents of sales have reversed their position. One of the most vocal of these is R. R. Kishore, formerly a high-ranking medical bureaucrat and currently an active player in the multilateral conferences and task forces constituting the global expansion of the field of bioethics. An architect in the development of the 1994 Transplantation of Human Organs Act, Kishore, in a 1998 interview in Delhi with my colleague Malkeet Gupta and me, concluded that he had made a terrible mistake.

Kishore went through his reasoning carefully. Cadaveric donation will not work in our country, he said, repeating a frequently heard claim. The infrastructure is not adequate; the mentality will not support it. And even though in a few years "we will be able to grow fetuses like popcorn" – a tantalizing phrase – the use of clone technology may have its ethical limits. For the needs of our population, Kishore suggested, we have to reconsider our stance. He turned to a bit of role-playing: "Look, I'm a man dying of hunger. I ask this one for help, he does nothing. That one, nothing. Now I ask you. You say: I'm also dying. I need an organ. I'll help you if you help me." Allowing for an exchange of one man's surplus money for another man's surplus kidney is not really traffic, Kishore concluded, but "life for life." Everybody wins.

A more sophisticated version of this case for the sale of organs has been made by the British philosopher Janet Radcliffe-Richards and endorsed by her fellow members of the WHO-supported International Forum for Transplant Ethics in a 1998 article in *The Lancet*.[13] In brief, the group has made four points:

1 The standard arguments against the sale of kidneys rely less on logic than emotion, and require more to justify paternalist refusals to allow people to do as they wish with their bodies.

2 Such arguments make an exceptionalist case for the exploitation, coercion, and risk of selling organs while ignoring the myriad other exploitative, coercive, and risky things poor people do to survive *and will have to do more of* if organ sales are disallowed.

3 The particular forms of exploitation involved in the organ trade are in large measure due to its informality and illegality, and the best response to them may be to centralize, formalize, and legalize the trade.

4 The fact that few people with chronic renal failure are able to avail themselves of this expensive option is no indictment of the kidney trade in itself but of the nature of private medicine and, more generally, of the political economy, and responses should focus there.

The authors go on to challenge many of the communitarian, slippery-slope, and denial-of-agency arguments made by opponents of a regulated market. In a nutshell, the traffic in kidneys, if properly regulated by the state, is a win–win situation. You get a kidney, I get money, and we both therefore survive against all hope.

I wish to provide suggestions from field materials for why neither Kishore's nor the International Forum's theoretical formulations may be adequate on the ground. These formulations are not necessarily the dominant ones, either in India or in the global world of bioethical debate, but they are important because they challenge an easy paternalism. I take seriously Radcliffe-Richards's call to go beyond any a priori malfeasance of organ sales, reading her concern in line with Rabinow's criticism of an ethics of suspicion in his work on genomic debate.[14] She asks us at the least to consider the case for organ sales rather than to jump into the sort of purgatorial ethics of alarm and remorse depicted by Rabinow. Fair enough. But just as the paternalist ethicist depicted by Radcliffe-Richards presumes "nefarious goings on" *prematurely*, before the fact, so she (along with her colleagues in the *Lancet* piece) appears to make several premature counter-presumptions of recognizable terrains of agency, risk, exchange, and bureaucratic rationality.

Thus, our purgatorial paternalist is content to read the wretchedness of selling an organ in formalist terms without asking about relative risks and benefits for persons whose wretchedness will not disappear with the banning of such transactions. But in parallel fashion, Radcliffe-Richards's thoughtful rationalist is content to presume from scattered news clippings and equally wretched stories (for example, of a Turkish man whose sick daughter dies because he cannot sell his kidney to save her) that we can speak with some authority about risks and benefits in the emerging Kidneyvakkams of the world without sustained inquiry.

The question of authority is critical. Both the straw-man paternalist and the rationalist operate through a particular logic of deferral, what I have framed as a persistent writing before the fact. This persistence is not incidental, I would suggest, but constitutive of our writing to the extent we occupy what I will term the space of *ethical publicity*. To get at

what I mean by this phrase, my argument will have three parts, which will address "ethics" as a practice more or less central to all social and human scientists of medicine under the exigencies of globalization. As such, "ethics" is an ideal type. If my argument – which in its understanding of ethics as a central feature of globalization comes out of conversation with the recent work of Rabinow – is reduced only to a disciplinary attack, then I will have failed.[15]

First, I will suggest that practices of deferral allow for the reduction of ethical analysis to a transactional frame in which all considerations outside of dyads like buyer-seller, donor-recipient, or doctor-patient are reduced to secondary processes. Alan Wertheimer's thoughtful book *Exploitation* offers an example of the value and limits of such a reduction more generally.[16] For the International Forum as for Kishore, the goal seems to be to get to a win-win scenario, achievable as a matter of life for life. Policy is to be built on an understanding of social analysis as an aggregation of individual transactions.

Second, the transactional frames – describable once questions of particular institutional forms and processes are reduced to secondary phenomena – are flexible and exportable. There is a global audience for *The Lancet*; but even before the report was published almost every Indian transplant surgeon I interviewed in Bangalore and Chennai was conversant with the particulars of Radcliffe-Richards's writing. Ethics must be able to travel light. Neither the purgatorial visions of religiously based ethics, nor social-scientific specificity, nor modes of critical or post-structural analysis serve the contemporary moment well: they are not ecumenical, not economical, and fail to valorize the emergent subject of globalization. Radcliffe-Richards's ethics are sensibly concerned with the small minority of Indians who can afford the cost of dialysis or transplantation. For the rest, there is no point in worrying too much about organ sales, as nothing short of massive social change would have an impact on health care anyway. As medical care and expensive biotechnology become increasingly synonymous, less eschatological options for the health care of the poor become unimaginable. Several Bangalore surgeons whose procedures, unlike those of K. C. Reddy, provided inadequate to no follow-up care to poor sellers were among the most vocal popularizers of Radcliffe-Richards's writings and of the subsequent *Lancet* report. Arguments will always be productively misread, but the point is that certain ethics travel well precisely because of the flexibility of their reductive transactional frame.[17]

Third, not only flexible but also purgatorial ethics can be mobilized to serve the exigencies of the moment. Kidney scandals have erupted in Bangalore, Delhi, and many other Indian cities on a regular basis, with doctors arrested on the grounds of tricking the poor and gullible into an unnecessary operation during which a kidney was removed. Though such events certainly may have occurred on occasion, the scandals I have studied appear to be based on trumped-up charges. Accusations are used by hospital owners and politicians in league with the police to challenge rival combines of medicine and politics: given widespread public concern across class about organ theft, kidney scandals are devastating for politics and business and therefore are an increasingly useful regulative mechanism.

What is the relation between the flexible ethics of life for life and the purgatorial ethics of nefarious goings-on? My sense is that despite their substantive opposition, these modes of engagement share at least some things, things I group under the heading of publicity. Ethics has become the dominant mode of public conversation about emergent biosocial situations.[18] I mean "public" conversations in the double sense that has emerged via Kant and Habermas, and their critics from Horkheimer and Adorno to Michael Warner: a conversation that not only is located *in* the public sphere but more fundamentally is constitutive *of* it.[19] I will term as "ethical publicity" the rationalization of emergent biosociality through flexible logics of win-win, logics that posit an identity ("life for life") between the life of the comparatively wealthy person in organ failure and that of the debtor pressed to sell one of her organs. As Nancy Scheper-Hughes has noted, this public is divided into bodies that can be designated patients and bodies that can be designated sellers: one is either a client of the new

biosociality or a vendor to it.[20] Unlike ethical publicity and its realism, scandalous publicity – by which I include the mobilization of purgatorial ethics into public scandal – demands a single public united in opposition to a piracy that yokes together imaginary and real tissue flows.

***

The position of philosophical consideration – the abstract perusal of the case for organ sales – is a poor defense against one's misapplication to the extent one occupies such a position of ethical publicity. The challenges that medical anthropologists have offered to ethical publicity, though partaking (as does this essay) of the same purgatorial much that blurs reasoned apperception, remain critical maneuvers as long as the fiction of distanced ethical consideration substitutes flexible transactions for institutional and local specificity. In particular, Arthur Kleinman's critical engagement with bioethics and Nancy Scheper-Hughes's refusal to allow us any remove from the bodies and lives of poor donors and sellers map out localized responses by ethnographers that must complement critical distance.[21]

The first problem is the dyad. Take, for example, the very real claims of sellers to be able to do as they wish with this unexpected resource. Sellers are presented within flexible ethics as having a need (for money) and a desire (to sell an organ for that money). "Yes, I would do it again." But listen further in Chennai: " . . . if I had another to give." And further: "I would have to." Radcliffe-Richards would question paternalist denials to the poor of their agency, an understandable move against a vanguard logic that invokes false consciousness whenever "the poor" do not tell ethnographers what they want to hear. But the question is not whether the statement "I would do it again" is coerced or alienated speech but rather what happens if one keeps listening: "I would have to." Does the opposition of agency and coercion sufficiently account for this "would have to"?

The problem with an ethical argument of this sort is the unrelenting presumption that ethics can be reduced to a primary transaction.[22] This reduction frames most relevant considerations as second-order phenomena and generates a utopian formula: *if* second-order phenomena can be controlled for, *then* an ethics is possible. But in fact the primary transaction is constituted out of the very second-order phenomena that the analyst would defer: everyday indebtedness and extraordinary debt bondage in which money passes from the patient through the donor and to the moneylender and other creditors. If one keeps listening, beyond the desire that sets the market in motion, one regains the temporal specificity lost in these transactional analyses: "I would have to. That money is gone and we are in debt." In the Tamil countryside with its kidney belts, debt is primary. But it is not only debt that constitutes the frame of the primary transaction and troubles its claim of life for life. In Chennai city, debt intersects with operability and the contingent logic of biopolitical regulation. Operable women are vehicles for debt collateral – and bear the scar. "My husband needs his strength for work, and could not work if he had the operation." "Yes, I work too."

Against what is heard, the two kinds of publicity constitute alternate public terrains. For ethical publicity, gender and debt become second-order phenomena, and ethics is restored to rational actors *pace* Adam Smith. What happens several months down the line is elided. Rational consideration appears not only removed from the purgatorial but also removed from outcomes distant *in time* from the primary transaction.

In scandalous publicity, as manifest in Indian and international media, images of male victims showing the scar from an involuntary nephrectomy are ubiquitous. These are not the bodies of rumor: an operation has occurred, perhaps involving some measure of coercion. But the point here is that the public scar is almost always male: men offer the paradigmatic surfaces bearing scars that in urban areas cover operations on female bodies. Scandalous publicity reconstitutes the "Emergency."

* * *

How do we steer between a flexible ethics that reduces reality to dyadic transactions and a purgatorial ethics that collapses real and imaginary exploitation in the service of complex interests? I am in the midst of a four-year study in Chennai, Bangalore, Delhi, and Mumbai (Bombay), and in lieu of a full answer I offer six points as part of a work in progress.

1. *No data exists on the long-term effects of nephrectomy to sellers or families.*

Many surgeons in these four cities reported an absence of long-term effects and then went on to insist that follow-up research was impossible since they have no way of knowing where the itinerant or illiterate sellers have gone. Yet the ability of activist physicians, fact-finding teams of ethicists, and journalists to locate sellers suggests that epidemiological research on such long-term effects is eminently possible and would seem to predicate any future calculations of risk-benefit ratios.

After Reddy, two of the most internationally prominent physicians who are advocates for organ sales are Drs. S. Sundar and A. K. Huilgol of the Karnataka Nephrology and Transplantation Institute (KANTI), housed in Bangalore's Lakeside Hospital. All physicians in Bangalore and Chennai acknowledged the high standard of care KANTI offers: medically, it is an exemplary site. Like Reddy, Sundar and Huilgol make no secret of their commitment to organ sales as a win–win scenario in the context of local conditions. Like Reddy, they are carefully acquainted with Radcliffe-Richards's work and cite it to challenge opposing positions as both intellectually unsustainable and naïve. Unlike Reddy, however, Sundar, in several 1998 interviews, deflected my question each time I asked about meeting his former sellers. When pressed, he pleaded the impossibility of finding these people or learning much from them.

Many of the Bangalore sellers have come from the Salem–Erode kidney belt. According to social workers and small-town reporters working in that region, these sellers are primarily men who left unirrigated "dry" farming districts for the promise of steady work as the power-loom industry dispersed from cities like Chennai to cheaper production sites. Unlike the Ayanavaram and Villivakkam sellers, these men are more likely to be recent migrants who are indeed harder to follow. This difficulty has been used to forestall attempts to generate data.

Part of Sundar's cautiousness may arise from the possibility of KANTI's knowing or unknowing involvement in the trade. Sundar denies awareness of any illegalities: if his patients say the donor is a relative or family friend, and if the state authorization committee has concurred when necessary, it would be wrong, he argues, not to go ahead. Sundar is open about patients who seek out the committee. KANTI in fact makes a public display of its transparency. The waiting room is lined with large wall charts listing the numbers of every procedure carried out by KANTI and its sister clinics in the state. News clippings attesting to KANTI's popularity in Bangladesh are hung along with a computer-generated sign from Bangladeshi patients thanking the clinic.

Despite this transparent design, three members of the Karnataka State authorization committee who were interviewed acknowledged that few of the donors they were asked to consider were relations or friends, from KANTI or most other Bangalore clinics. Why do committee members approve these donors, then? The state secretary who runs the committee said in an interview with me that patients and physicians have political allies who pressure the committee to grant approvals. Reddy is but the most prominent of several transplant doctors who specifically accused Sundar and Huilgol of "going too far" in turning transplants into big business. Reddy claimed that KANTI has advertised in Sri Lanka and Bangladesh for patients and that Sundar and Huilgol had come to the Kidneyvakkams of Chennai in search of sellers. Part of Reddy's concern might have been territorial: the urban Kidneyvakkams had for several years supplied Chennai clinics, while the rural kidney belts to the west had supplied Bangalore. "They have become greedy," he said – suggesting that, far from being unable to determine the provenance of kidneys, Sundar and Huilgol themselves served as procurers.

Sundar and Huilgol may well be the victims of false accusations by competitors. But their resistance to follow-up research is striking. The only things missing from the prodigious display of data shown by KANTI on its walls, in its publications, on its web site, and through its dealings with the press are the bodies and

statistics of donors. The second time I tried to get Dr. Sundar to talk about a possible follow-up study of donors he took out a copy of a Radcliffe-Richards article from his desk and asked me if I had read her. He read choice phrases of the article to me, dismissing my concerns over sellers as paternalist. But where were the donors? If the market structure of transplantation deflects attention from the actual bodies of sellers onto ideologically constituted proxies, how complicit are flexible ethics in maintaining postoperative inattention to sellers?

2. *Decisions to sell a kidney appear to have less to do with raising cash toward some current or future goal than with paying off a high-interest debt to local moneylenders. Sellers are frequently back in debt within several years.*

The Ayanavaram slum dwellers who sold their kidneys described their reasons for selling and their desire to sell again if biologically possible in terms of a transaction not with the present or future – an operation to pay for, a house to but, a shop to set up, a wedding to finance – but with the past. They were in debt, and could no longer manage their indebtedness and still feed and shelter a household. This finding is tentative, for as most of these borrowing and lending transactions are through private moneylenders and small shopkeepers as opposed to state or private banks or credit associations, data to confirm sellers' and nonsellers' patterns of indebtedness are difficult to generate. But the testaments of sellers do correlate with the work of investigative journalists in Chennai. Furthermore, they make sense within the topography of credit in poor Chennai neighborhoods, in which moneylenders and pawnbrokers are ubiquitous.

None of the Chennai sellers interviewed claimed to have a bank account, and they offered the usual reasons: they were illiterate or poorly literate and of low status, and therefore could not negotiate the language and status practices of the bank bureaucracy with any certainty. Stories of money lost to bankers were common. Jewelry offered a seemingly more practical locus for saving, though stories of gold stolen or appropriated were not uncommon. Most of the kidney money went to pay off debt, and the expenses of husbands and children – education, marriage, medical costs, legal fees – took the rest. Several of the women interviewed mentioned men who drank up the savings.

Persons sell a kidney to get out of debt, but the conditions of indebtedness do not disappear. All of the thirty Chennai sellers with whom Coutinho and I spoke were back in debt again. Organs and blood, from the perspective of the debt broker, are but two of the multiple sites of the collateralization of the poor, ranging from patterns of debt peonage with lengthy pedigrees to expanding new markets in children for adoption, labor, and sex work. Technological transformation like that mediated by the emergence of cyclosporine offers new biosocial strategies for debt markets seeking under the logic of capital to expand.

The argument here is that the decision to sell may be set for debtors by their lenders, who advance money through an embodied calculus of collateral value. In other words, the aggressiveness with which moneylenders call in debts may correlate with whether a debtor lives in an area that has become a kidney zone. If so, the decision whether or not to sell is a response not simply to some naturalized state of poverty but to a debt crisis that might not have happened if the option to sell were not present. Based upon these interviews and discussions with historians, social workers, and journalists in Chennai, my hypothesis is that kidney zone – the vakkams and belts of Tamil Nadu – emerge through interactions between surgical entrepreneurs, persons facing extraordinary debt, and medical brokers. As a region becomes known to brokers as a kidney zone, their search for new sellers intensifies. Persons in debt are approached. In urban areas, more women than men respond. Creditors, who must advance and call in loans with an eye to interest, collateral, and reproduction – that is, to how much of the debtors' resources to take while keeping them alive and healthy enough to be able to make future payments and take out more debt – also respond to these shifting circumstances.

Debtors' recounting of the process of debt supports such a process, as does my informal observation of moneylenders and discussions with Chennai and rural Tamil Nadu journalists and social workers who cover questions of credit and debt. More analysis of local credit practices is needed.

3. *Few persons in India can afford the cost of transplantation or dialysis, so whether or not organ sales are legalized the majority of persons with end-stage renal disease will die. Programs to prevent end-stage renal disease are few, and prevention is not part of the dominant European or American conversations on organ sales, whether pro or con.*

The first part of this finding is a commonplace. Radcliffe-Richards and her colleagues accept it but argue that the question of the poor's access to medical care is irreducible to their access to transplant surgery. Purgatorial anxiety over organs is a self-serving substitute for concern over universal health care.

Again, at an imagined distance this logical maneuver makes sense. But reformulated in terms of ethical publicity, it deforms in a predictable fashion. At KANTI, when I asked Sundar how he could support a market in kidneys given no data on the risks to Indian sellers, he, like Reddy and most other transplant physicians interviewed, responded that when a person dying from poverty comes to your door and asks why you will not help him, the situation requires action. The scenario of a request from a dying person is disconcerting and problematic, for the vast majority of persons living with and dying from renal disease could not and would not be attended to, as they lack the funds for dialysis or transplantation. Yet the sellers fulfill the terms of the ethical scenario as set by these doctors: a dying person asks you for help – what do you do? Somehow, such a scenario does not trouble these physicians in the way the suffering of the more well-to-do appears to.

When I asked the KANTI team about this apparent inconsistency, they smiled indulgently. We are a poor country, Sundar reminded me, and as much as it would improve my business to have the government pay for transplantation for the majority of Indians,

I do not think it can be a priority for us. Government money needs to go to primary care.

The move is impressive, and dizzying. Sundar, and the majority of transplant doctors who concur with him, are masters of ethical publicity. There is no need to worry about health risks to the poor seller, because a physician must always worry about the individual patient: his or her ethical compact is with the individual sufferer. Yet there is no need to worry about the majority of individual sufferers, because an Indian physician must always think on the societal level, where the money would be better spent on inoculations. What is alarming is the sleight of hand by which individualist and communitarian rationales for a medical ethics replace each other in turn to justify business as usual.

In this context, the inattention to questions of prevention, to renal medicine that in the long term might be both affordable and effective for "a poor country," is particularly significant. Communitarian logic serves only to justify inattention and to slough off poor patients to public hospitals. Transplant physicians, despite their immersion in bioethics and communitarian appeals, are with notable exceptions not involved in campaigns of public education or the development of low-cost alternatives to current dialysis. Their persistent resistance to cadaveric donation, which would provide an alternative to the use of the organs of the poor, is troubling. Most surgeons interviewed cited India's "infrastructure" or "mentality" as problems, but several pioneering cadaveric programs in the country are emerging, and their founders argue that the single most significant impediment to success is the unwillingness of most private transplant clinics to participate. Reliance on cadavers cuts down on a ready supply of organs and diminishes profits. In Bangalore, John and Rebecca Thomas – trained in Pittsburgh, the Mecca of transplant surgery – launched an effort to build an equivalent to the United Network for Organ Sharing (UNOS), a distribution and information network linking brain-dead cadavers to persons on a waiting list. Their efforts, though publicly applauded, have been met with significant resistance. No hospital wants to give away its own cadavers to a pooled list. Both brain-

death transplantation and lists are far from perfect alternatives to sales, as the work of Margaret Lock on the former and Scheper-Hughes on the latter have shown.[23] But debate on cadavers has not focused on the medical and ethical limits of brain death as a viable concept. Rather, lip service under a rhetoric of development is paid to ever-deferred infrastructural and institutional possibilities.

4. *Buyers of kidneys often underestimate the risks and long-term costs of immunosuppressive therapy, leading to dose tapering and organ rejection after catastrophic expenditure.*

Buyers no less than sellers are at risk. Scheper-Hughes has documented the predicament of poor organ recipients in Brazil who cannot afford to maintain cyclosporine immunosuppressant therapy and so taper or pool doses. Members of the Bangalore Kidney Patients' Welfare Association, which meets once a month in a city park to distribute low-cost immunosuppressant therapy (but not the most expensive and most necessary drug, cyclosporine), offer similar stories of middle- and working-class persons who utilize networks – relatives, job benefits, insurance, and statewide "governor's funds" set up for medical emergencies – to raise the cash for the operation, for the organ in the case of sales, and for the medication. These organ recipients anticipated one to three years of diminishing immunosuppressant therapy, and thus either were not anticipating the long-term costs adequately or simply did not realize that therapy might last for many more years. A monthly dose of cyclosporine costs more money than many of these families bring in each month as income. Further ethnographic work is needed to study the preoperative interactions between patients and doctors to understand what message about long-term costs patients are receiving and how they interpret it over time.

Part of the problem is that younger nephrologists are less aggressive in how many tissue factor "matches" there need to be between donor and recipient kidneys in order to go ahead with the operation. Cyclosporine, in combination with other drugs, makes a transplantation with fewer matches medically viable in certain patients. With the predominance of transplants of kidneys from nonrelatives (now disguised under the terms of the 1994 act), requiring fewer matches means one is more likely to find available sellers and conduct more procedures. I have witnessed debates between older and younger physicians over the appropriate number of matches. As the number of matches comes to be seen as less important, the length of time patients will remain on cyclosporine increases. Patients and physicians reported one to three years as a ballpark figure to me, but the figure may be based on data from a different climate of tissue typing and matching.

Novartis, the maker of cyclosporine, is ubiquitous in the global transplant world and in India. It funds many conferences, not only on organs but on medical ethics more generally, and its representatives attend public gatherings like those of the Welfare Association. At one such meeting, one recipient's father literally begged the drug representative for a free month's supply of the drug as he had no credit left. The drug was provided, and apparently this exchange was a repeated scene. Novartis becomes the great benefactor for this organization of recipients, and no actions to lower the price are proposed.

5. *In major urban centers, the growing number of transplant programs led to intensified competition in the mid-1990s for recipients who could afford the cost: the ethics of transplantation in India are driven less by a shortage of donors than by market demands given a shortage of recipients.*

KANTI is one of eight transplant centers that was established in Bangalore within a decade, in a state where dialysis is almost nonexistent. This rapid expansion was in part a function of demand, though the supply of persons who could afford the triple cost of operation, organ, and drugs was quickly exhausted. Beyond demand, a transplantation ward advertises a new or competitive private hospital as modern and well-equipped: this reputation may be profitable beyond the income generated by the ward itself. Transplantation signifies (marketable) modernity.

As the supply of persons who could afford the operation diminished, competition between these many programs intensified, and directors began looking for new markets. With the passage of the 1994 act, the number of foreign recipients – typically from the Persian Gulf region, Europe, and Asia – went down sharply. Hospitals were worried about scandals, and it was harder to pass off a local donor as a friend or relation of a foreigner. Clinics like KANTI looked to both Sri Lanka and Bangladesh, where recipients without relatives could bring their own donors or sellers. With the number of applicants for kidneys in decline, it is possible that middle- and working-class households who could afford the operation but not the immuno-suppression were more aggressively approached. This impression is the one offered by Welfare Association members, but further study is needed.

If clinics face less a shortage in organs than a shortage in persons wealthy enough to take them, they need to organize their practice around a manageable and relatively low-cost source of human material. Recipients can go elsewhere, and one must have potential kidneys ready. The business of these clinics depends on the market, and would be made far more risky with a turn to cadaveric donation.

The point here runs against the continual language of *shortage* that some ethicists take for granted. Putting aside the vexed issue of whether one can even speak of a shortage of people's organs – an issue drawing on a philosophical analysis of property extending from Locke to Marx and seldom engaged within the ethical literature under consideration here – one must ask whether the critical shortage is not of donors but of *recipients*. The practices and the ethics we need to consider are rooted in the economics of this latter shortage.

6. *The rapid growth of transplant medicine in the 1990s was part of a larger period of medical institution-building in India in which high-end, privatized medical care became a major site of investment and foreign monetary exchange, and new public-private assemblages emerged linking medical institutions and political influence to various sources of capital –*

liquor, armaments, pharmaceuticals, and "black money."

Transplant medicine, as a continual goad to public and foreign anxiety, became a strategic site for intervention within and between competing assemblages. The frequent manufacture of scandals in which doctors are accused and jailed as kidney thieves appears to be one such intervention.

One must differentiate kidney panics from kidney scandals. In panics, stories of missing or murdered children circulate and become tied to fears over kidney thieves and to the legitimation of state and international involvement. The stories are often based on real disappearances and child loss in the contexts of malnutrition and hunger, of debt bondage and child labor. State agencies are challenged or attacked, and state responses focus upon denying the stories and providing the materials for renarrativization.[24]

Scandals are not threats to state order but forms of publicity collaboratively produced by a mix of state and nongovernmental agencies. The police arrest a group of doctors and the media are notified. Emerging accounts are framed not as positings of hidden gangs and state conspiracies but as stories of greed and corruption. Brokers and doctors collude in tricking people into having medical tests with the promise of a job; people wake up with a scar. Such scandals have taken place in Bombay (not yet Mumbai) in 1993, Bangalore in 1994, Jaipur in 1996, and the Delhi suburb of Noida in 1998. Most of these trials are still pending.

It is, of course, possible that the physicians accused are guilty of all charges. Scheper-Hughes has carefully documented organ theft worldwide, even though she began her research to show the opposite: that these stories were symptoms of histories of poverty and state violence but not necessarily "real" thefts. Certainly worse examples of medical malfeasance occur daily. Yet one must exercise caution. With a large and growing number of persons in debt crises there would seem to be no immediate shortage of sellers, and it is not clear why clinics would take the high risk of cheating someone. Then again, police can be easily bought off, and the victims in most of the

scandals (but not all) were socially marginal and unlikely to be heard. At present, one must defer final judgment.

Why, though, in each of these cases do the police act with such speed on the claims of poor and socially marginal accusers? In Noida, a senior superintendent of the police with a medical background was specifically transferred in to monitor the case. The accused physicians have mobilized their political connections in an effort to be released, but according to several state medical officials who spoke with me on the grounds of anonymity, the word has come down from the chief minister's office that the case is not to be touched.

The earlier Bangalore scandal was similarly surrounded by hearsay. The Yellamma Dasappa Hospital, where the scandal was centered, is owned by an industrial group that was competing with another industrial group for a lucrative state contract to supply cheap liquor. (Most of the city's hospitals are owned by large industrial concerns, several by liquor companies.) Several hospital administrators, social workers, and journalists suggested that the contract negotiations lay behind the manufactured scandal. The police denied this.

"Manufactured" is deceptive here. If most transplant clinics have violated the letter and spirit of the Indian Penal Code and the later 1994 act in using sellers or passing them off as family or friends, and if sellers are provided minimal care and shunted back to the villages or slums, most clinics are therefore vulnerable to accusation – thus KANTI's strategy of performative transparency. But why police involvement? Most new clinics and hospitals have had to rely upon extensive political patronage to wade through regulations designed to promote a public health sector and limit private growth. Available urban land often has squatter colonies, and significant political capital is needed to move a potential "vote bank." Conversely, the new hospitals offer a variety of services to politicians and industrialists, ranging from a source of political patronage to a literal tax shelter where industrialists and others under trial for foreign exchange and tax violations can be admitted to defer a court date in perpetuity. Journalists and other cosmopolitans in each of the aforementioned cities where kidney scandals continue offered dozens of accounts of the nexus between the new medicine, politics, and industry – some substantiated, many not.

Transplantation, both because it is a critical site of publicity around which periodic panics emerge and because it often involves a nested series of illegalities and produces a class of potentially exploited persons, seems to have become a key node around which competition for control of medical, industrial, and political resources is negotiated. The paradox is therefore created of a politics that tries to quell kidney panics while abetting the periodic negotiation of scandals.

What is the relevance of these scandals to the sociology and ethics of the market in organs? First, they push us to take seriously the need for an ethnography of the state. Radcliffe-Richards and her colleagues make a classic transparency argument, parallel to those used to defeat prohibition or decriminalize prostitution and drugs: if there is exploitation, then legalizing and regulating the market cleans it up while allowing sellers their autonomy. But this argument presumes a state structure, one in which increased regulation has a specified effect and the organization of the state can address the organization of the market. But what if the organization of the trade *mirrors* the organization of the Indian state in its need for brokers? The presumption of the ethicists seems to be that once India is developed into a certain assemblage of rational bureaucratic forms, the current abuses will disappear. This presumption imposes a narrative of the development of the state with little empirical grounding. In consideration of the recent work of Akhil Gupta on the ethnography of the Indian state as well as the writing of Veena Das, Ravi Rajan, and others on the bureaucratic management of treatment for the Bhopal gas disaster victims, what seems more likely is that any new central bioauthority will generate a new class of agents demanding payments from sellers.[25] Such "bioethical brokers" may supplement, rather than eradicate, currently existing tissue brokers and debt brokers in the lives of the poor. At any rate, these are empirical questions that require ongoing ethnography before distanced consideration can be achieved.

Coda: Other Ethics

Neither Kishore, Reddy, and Sundar nor the agents of public scandal currently hold the field in India, although things change fast. Medical activist organizations like the Voluntary Health Association of India (VHAI) still attract multilateral fiscal support and steer a course between acknowledging some nefarious goings-on and passing over transplantation to arrive at more urgent questions of infections, environmental degradation, and access to primary health and hospital care. The dominant formation in Indian bioethics is purgatorial, but with a somewhat different lineage from the ethics challenged by Rabinow. Missionary discourse and aesthetics predominate, and the message of a new science stressing care against commerce and love against paternalist medicine offers the reclamation of society against a sense of loss experienced and inscribed as colonial. Such missionary ethics form another public space, one that travels well along certain routes. At the Fourth World Congress of Bioethics in Tokyo, Japan, in 1998, one of the dominant presences was Darryl R. J. Macer, the author of *Bioethics is Love of Life: An Alternative Textbook*.[26] Macer challenged most professional ethical stances, but in his repeated "All you need is love" theme what really fell out of the equation was politics. Against flexible ethics, Macer and his followers downplayed any VHAI-type response and set up a global mission, a secretariat of love.

But if the only alternatives to a world split between clients and vendors are reconstitutions of Christian love, the result seems to be that vendors are authorized to define themselves through the gift, with clients remaining the beneficiaries. In Bangalore and Delhi I was told stories of persons possessed by a kind of donation madness: a man desperate to give away any organ he could; a couple who insisted all their wedding guests sign up to donate something. But in conversations with recipients, I continue to hear love in a different sense: *Why should I put a family member I care about at risk by asking him or her to donate an organ when I can just buy one?*

* * *

The production of scandal, through sociologically complex linkages of state and market agencies and old and new media, maintains the image of a distinctive state apparatus that can intervene to regulate medical abuses against the poor. This image is central to ethical publicity, justifying its presumption of a universal and liberal state structure allowing the invisible hands of utility and reason to guide an individualist ethics of radical autonomy. The public productions of such an ethics are consumed and elaborated by transplant professionals and more generally by the corporate/political hybrid of contemporary health care.

To what world do such ethics speak? Midway through this research, we are left with scattered signs: a woman offering both of her kidneys to MGR; a man in a park begging to a Novartis representative; a postoperative complication of a painful scar that began to hurt when the money ran out.

NOTES

1 George Marcus has written several well-known essays on the risks and benefits of anthropology spreading itself thin, collected in *Ethnography through Thick and Thin* (Princeton: Princeton University Press, 1998).

2 Patricia A. Marshall, "Organ Transplantation: Defining the Boundaries of Personhood, Equity and Community," *Theoretical Medicine* 17 (1) (1996): R5-R8; Patricia A. Marshall and Abdullah S. Daar, "Cultural and Psychological Dimensions of Human Organ Transplantation," *Annals of Transplantation* 3 (2) (1998): 7–11.

3 "Kidneys Still for Sale," *Frontline* 14 (25) (23–26 December 1997); "Options before Kidney Patients," ibid.; "For a Cadaveric Transplant Programme," ibid.

4 Raj Chengappa, "The Great Organs Bazaar," *India Today*, 31 July 1990, 60–7.

5 Cecilia Coale Van Hollen, "Birthing on the Threshold: Childbirth and Modernity among Lower Class Women in Tamil Nadu, South India," Ph.D. dissertation, Department of Anthropology, University of California at Berkeley, 1998; and "Moving Targets: Routine IUD Insertion in Maternity Wards in Tamil Nadu, India," *Reproductive Health Matters* 6 (11) (1998): 98–106.

6 Patricia Jeffery, Roger Jeffery, and Andrew Lyon, *Labour Pains and Labour Power: Women and Childbearing in India* (London: Zed Books, 1989); Van Hollen, "Birthing on the Threshold."

7 Van Hollen, "Birthing on the Threshold."

8 See Gilbert H. Herdt, *Guardians of the Flutes: Idioms of Masculinity* (New York: McGraw-Hill, 1981) and Klaus Theweleit, *Male Fantasies* (Minneapolis: University of Minnesota Press, 1987–9).

9 Van Hollen, "Birthing on the Threshold."

10 Arthur Kleinman, *Writing at the Margin: Discourse between Anthropology and Medicine* (Berkeley: University of California Press, 1995), 98–9.

11 Paul Rabinow, *French DNA: Trouble in Purgatory* (Chicago: University of Chicago Press, 1999).

12 See Veena Das, "Wittgenstein and Anthropology," *Annual Review of Anthropology* (1998). Das offers Wittgenstein's figure of feeling pain in another's body to frame the possibilities and consequences of an anthropology of suffering. Here this figure is extended and inverted.

13 Janet Radcliffe-Richards, "Nepharious Goings On: Kidney Sales and Moral Arguments," *Journal of Medicine and Philosophy* 21 (4) (August 1996): 375–416. Janet Radcliffe-Richards et al., "The Case for Allowing Kidney Sales," *Lancet* 351 (9120) (27 June 1998): 1950–2.

14 Radcliffe-Richards, "Nepharious Goings On"; Rabinow, *French DNA*.

15 See Gísli Pálsson and Paul Rabinow, "Iceland: The Case of a National Human Genome Project," *Anthropology Today* 15 (5) (October 1999): 14–18.

16 Alan Wertheimer, *Exploitation* (Princeton: Princeton University Press, 1996).

17 I use "flexibility" mindful of Emily Martin's adaptation of the social and economic uses of the term to the study of bodily experience, politics, and research first done by David Harvey. See Emily Martin, *Flexible Bodies: Tracking Immunity in American Culture from the Days of Polio to the Age of AIDS*

(Boston: Beacon Press, 1994); and David Harvey, *The Condition of Postmodernity: An Enquiry into the Origins of Cultural Change* (Oxford: Blackwell, 1989).

18 The concept of the "biosocial" was developed by Rabinow through the Foucauldian concept of biopolitics as a way to address critical linkages between biology and society other than the adaptationist reduction of sociobiology. See Paul Rabinow, *Essays on the Anthropology of Reason* (Princeton: Princeton University Press, 1996).

19 On Kant, see James Schmidt, ed., *What is Enlightenment?: Eighteenth-Century Answers and Twentieth-Century Questions* (Berkeley: University of California Press, 1996). On the Frankfort School, see Craig Calhoun, ed., *Habermas and the Public Sphere* (Cambridge, Mass.: MIT Press, 1992).

20 Nancy Scheper-Hughes, "Theft of Life: The Globalization of Organ Stealing Rumours," *Anthropology Today* 12 (3) (1996): 3–11.

21 Kleinman, *Writing at the Margin*; Scheper-Hughes, "Theft of Life."

22 Nancy Scheper-Hughes has been making a similar point in her current work on organ transactions in Brazil and South Africa.

23 Margaret Lock, *Twice Dead: Circulation of Body Parts and Remembrance of Persons* (Berkeley: University of California Press, forthcoming); Nancy Scheper-Hughes, personal communication.

24 I have written about one such panic, in the city of Varanasi and its hinterland in 1996. Lawrence Cohen, *No Aging in India: Alzheimer's, The Bad Family, and Other Modern Things* (Berkeley: University of California Press, 1998).

25 Akhil Gupta, "Blurred Boundaries: The Discourse of Corruption, the Culture of Politics, and the Imagined State," *American Ethnologist* 22 (2) (1995): 375–402; Veena Das, *Critical Events: An Anthropological Perspective on Contemporary India* (Delhi: Oxford University Press, 1995); S. Ravi Rajan, personal communication.

26 Darryl R. J. Macer, *Bioethics is Love of Life: An Alternative Textbook* (Christchurch, New Zealand: Eubios Ethics Institute, 1998).

23

"Robin Hood" of Techno-Turkey or Organ Trafficking in the State of Ethical Beings

Aslihan Sanal

Prologue

"Can I have a part of the money now?" asks the man. "I want to buy dresses for my two daughters before the holidays." The camera zooms in on the other man, Dr. S., a surgeon in green surgical dress.

"Yes, I will give you three hundred dollars before the operation, and three thousand dollars after."

"Will I recover quickly?" asks the man in a low tone.

"Yes, in a few days you should be fine. And then you can spend some time with your family. Do not worry about your health my friend," he reassures him. "I am here, and I will take care of you. You just have to show up a day before the operation. Promise? I trust you. Look, everyone benefits from this; you can pay your debts and get your children back from your wife's parents, while saving the life of a poor Israeli who has traveled all the way to Istanbul to find a kidney. She survives and you get your family back." (Cut.)

Three days later, late in the afternoon. Uğur Dündar, the TV host, walks with a two-man camera team into a private hospital in Istanbul. Hurrying, he walks down the white corridors. The camera follows him. (Cut.)

Zooming, the camera shows Dr. S., who has just come out of the hygiene room, holding his arms upward. (Slow motion.) He looks back and then turns around. Voices melt away. (Back to normal motion.) "Dr. S.!" Dündar yells at him. "Aren't you Dr. S. ?" He continues, "Stop him! What are you getting prepared for? Who will you operate on? Hold him!" Dr. S. walks away and disappears in a crowd of nurses and staff. The camera cannot catch him. (Cut.)

The image starts shaking. We are in front of the hospital. Dr. S. is walking away with his lawyer. Dündar is running after him with the cameraman. "Confess it Dr. S.!" shouts Dündar, "You were about to transplant a poor man's kidney into an Israeli patient. We talked to the patients. We set up a hidden camera

Aslihan Sanal, "'RobinHood' of Techno-Turkey or Organ Trafficking in the State of Ethical Beings," *Culture, Medicine and Psychiatry* 28/3 (2004): 281–309.

already a few days ago. We filmed the whole story. We got you Dr. S. How much did you get this time? How much does the Organ Mafia charge for such operations?" Dr. S. does not say a word and walks away. (Cut.)

We are back in the TV studio. "Aaaand . . . " says a loud and determined voice, "Dündar has performed a public service again, and he caught the Organ Mafia as they were about to start a new illegal kidney transplantation. Dündar will always serve the welfare of the Turkish people and enlighten you. He will serve justice, no matter what!"

(from *The Arena Show*, Winter 1999, Channel D, Turkey)

The illegal organ trade is a public issue in Turkey. In 1997 and 1999, the Arena Team, the producers of a TV show on Turkey's Channel D, broadcast two cases documenting a Turkish transplant surgeon, Dr S.,[1] conducting illegal kidney transplantations between Turkish kidney sellers and Israeli purchasers.

The show labeled Dr S. the "Organ Mafia doctor" and helped create the imaginary of a medical underground community in Turkey and in international trade networks. The narrative was a Faustian one in which the actors – patients, doctors, dealers, and donors – bargained with evil, dividing this kind-of-medical and kind-of-personal practice into categories of the criminal and the innocent. The patient who went to a Mafia doctor was still considered innocent, as he or she only wanted to survive. The donor who sold his organ was closer to the evil than the buyer, because he had a pact with the dealer and had violated the integrity of his soul by violating the integrity of his body. The dealers and "Mafia doctors" were shown as the actual criminals. Dr S., with his very short haircut, tiny figure, dark, tanned skin, and frameless eyeglasses, looked more like a scientist figure from an apocalyptic 1930s movie than a transplant surgeon. The crime setting and the criminals seemed as if they were marginal to the Turkish transplantation community, as if illegal international kidney transplantation was conducted by people who had no relationship to legitimate transplant practices in Turkey. The scandal revealed by *The Arena Show* was intensified

because catching an "Organ Mafia doctor" "illegally" at work in a prominent private hospital threatened the widespread trust in good, upscale private medicine. Dr S. transformed the image of high-tech medicine in Turkey, where there is not much public awareness of scientific malpractice or experimentation on human subjects.

In the Field

In this paper I argue that ethical issues of organ trafficking are not limited to marginal private clinics and doctors such as Dr S. All living-related organ transplantations in Turkey involve similar ethical dilemmas: according to transplant surgeons, most organ recipients pay their donors and the demand for living-related transplantations is increasing every year because of the lack of cadavers from which to harvest kidneys, and most doctors in Turkey argue that organ trafficking is due to this lack. They believe there are many religious and cultural reasons, but the main problem lies in the lack of respirators in intensive care units and the unwillingness of the young doctors to make the brain death diagnosis required by law to declare a person dead and available as a potential organ source. Like in Japan, where brain death diagnosis was impossible because of the belief that the soul remained in the body as long as the heart was beating (see Lock 2002), Turkish doctors have had a hard time believing in the new human invention, made possible by respirators, of death while the heart still beats. Although the transplantation law in Turkey dates back to 1979 (National Newsletter 1979, as cited in Haberal 1993), I have been told that doctors avoided making brain-death diagnoses; they are not obligated to do so. The law enables them to make the diagnosis if they act with a clear conscience. Torn between a law inspired by Western models of medicine and traditional practices and beliefs, Turkish doctors are engaged in ethical struggle at every step, balancing "ethics" as defined by law, "ethics" as defined by their values of saving life, and the "ethics" of their personal conscience.

I am interested in understanding where judicial, cultural, and social categories of "human rights" and "crime" are constructed, so I have chosen to write on transplantation practices in state and university hospitals and the ethical dilemmas doctors encounter. Furthermore, I am concerned that critical medical anthropology displaces widespread ethical dilemmas faced by medicine in general onto the criminal, marginal characters of media imagery. For this reason, in this paper I draw on Agamben's (1988) usage of the threefold corpus (body, state, law) to question medical practice. Only with a better understanding of the corpus will we be able to have a better understanding of what kind of politics creates *bios* today. Here I am speaking of the biological corpus on which experiments are done, the legal corpus that expands for its own sake and through its own logic, and the sovereign corpus that is viewed as free of crime because it incorporates the ideals of the state. The Organ Mafia is symbolically "cast out" from this tripartite corpus. And its creation, in this context, is a diagnostic symptom of the transition "Turkish medicine as corpus" is experiencing as transplantation technology turns the human body into a means to an end and not just an end in itself. Today, this corpus regenerates and expands through biomedical technologies and introduces us to a new medicalized idea of the human created by doctors who feel they practice in the midst of a criminal environment. Here I interpret the corpus much like Cassirer (1962) sees the "spirit" in the age of the Enlightenment, but in reverse – the corpus is antithetical to the consciousness active throughout the Enlightenment. Cassirer's vision of the spirit was a soul slowly blossoming through its engagement with life, through the experiences of the scientists and the visions of interpreters. Enlightenment was carried in the spirit of a consciousness that grew with an engaging contribution to human mind, not necessarily to morality. The corpus, on the contrary, is a materialized form: rigid, nontransparent, and imposed through bureaucracy.

While the sale of organs is illegal in Turkey, the definition of *crime* within the transplantation community is disputable. For example, any patient who is diagnosed with kidney failure gets to know at a very early stage of diagnosis, right in the hemodialysis centers, the "possibilities" that exist for finding or buying a kidney. Doctors operate on patients who they suspect might have paid their donors. Sometimes doctors also refuse to care for patients who do not use the dialysis fluids produced by the doctor's own facilities. Some doctors in Turkey advise their wealthy patients to go to India or Russia to have a transplantation, and some take bribes under the name of "charitable donations." In short, if commodification of body parts is illegal, then the path to crime begins in the hospitals and throughout the medical community (see Friedläender 2002). Many doctors feel the very act of saving lives through transplantation is a gray area of criminality, and that criminality itself is part of the state corpus within which they must work. As such, the Organ Mafia is a symptom of ethical disputes within the corpus.

Besides doctors' narratives, I looked into patients' lives. Patients' narratives illuminate the experiences of those who, in one way or the other, have become a part of illegal kidney transplantation. With their voices, I question a human condition in which scientific statements, political experimentation (in the form of Turkey's two different politics of organ sharing), and the media shape patients' experiences in Turkey. These conditions are such that patients' and donors' feelings and emotions are expressed only through the political and economic conditions they feel a part of. Their speech, which unites their experience and makes it meaningful, is politicized and mediatized, but at the same time it is distanced from the realm of crime. People expressed love and hate, pain and suffering in low tones when they narrated the experience of their operations. *Crime* was not something they felt they were engaged in, even if they purchased a kidney. They felt they were engaged in something else – some kind of *business of life*, of their own lives, and the lives of those who give them life.

Crime and healing, two notions heavily loaded with emotions, are suppressed in the "rationality" of medical statements in the hospitals. There, "money," "statistics," "organ-share databases," "kinship," "ethnicity," "West versus Orient," and "corpses versus living bodies" are the main categories physicians use to talk about the conditions of organ transplant-ation. In physicians' narratives, science, technol-ogy, politics, and economy shape the human condition of kidney transplantation. As such, instability in Turkish political life, an authority struggle within the medical system, a transplant-ation law which promotes living donors and does not improve the conditions for donations from cadavers, and the privatization of Turkish hospitals in the 1990s seem to contribute to the reasons Turkish people donate, transplant, and receive organs illegally, and why Turkey has become a market for organs in the Middle East. In this business of life, emotions, feelings, guilt, and anxiety are left unspoken, while tech-niques on survival create a discourse on life strategies.

To illuminate the facets of my argument, I first describe the politics of organ share in Turkey, which is divided between two organ transplantation centers, one in Istanbul and the other in Ankara. Then, I explore the privatiza-tion of Turkish medicine in recent years. After this brief topography on organ transplantation practices and institutional structures, I show how media steps in to create the criminal. Finally, I give diverse accounts of patients who had kidney transplants under various different conditions. From a patient's point of view, the set of tyrannical relations in the exchange of organs is shaped by a chain of events the patient goes through, from the first moment of kidney failure diagnosis to the end of the kidney trans-plantation. In their book *Spare Parts*, Fox and Swazey (1992) argue that living-related dona-tions have a tyrannical aspect in their effects on both recipients' and donors' posttransplanta-tion lives. Fox and Swazey adapt Marcel Mauss' concept of gift exchange of the exchange of body parts, arguing that organs are viewed as spare parts by physicians, and when tissue typing matches, members of a family feel obliged to donate. Both recipient and donor experience ongoing relations, desires, and obligations, and the recipient in particular feels she or he must give something in exchange, although nothing is equivalent to the gift of life. The nexus of felt obligations Fox and Swazey call "the tyranny of the gift." Organ trafficking, in principle, operates around this idea of gift exchange. The choice of the donor becomes a link in this chain of events, as do the choice of the hospital, the country of transplantation, and the doctor. In the mean-time, a set of underground players becomes agents of this, by now, *crime*. The final section of the article covers how patients talk about their conditional experience of a life of crime.

Methods

I began doing this fieldwork with the assump-tion that public, state, and medical institutions had created a regulated community around formal and informal norms, and thus also created the "criminal," the Organ Mafia. Though the phrase "Organ Mafia" requires clarification here. When I say Organ Mafia, I do not necessarily mean just Dr S., but a busi-ness that is structured on trading illegal migrant labor, prostitution, and opium, as well as organs, throughout eastern Europe and the Middle East. In narrating this story of crime and medicine, I use Dr S.'s case as the doctors were using it: for them, Dr S. was a *modality* they talked about in regards to what had to be done to improve the conditions of organ trans-plantation and prevent the spread of the image of an Organ Mafia. Unlike the public, the med-ical community totally rejected claims about the Organ Mafia. They believed that Dr S. was an unfortunate case and that there was no such thing as the Organ Mafia in Turkey. I use Dr S.'s unfolding character in each narra-tive as a way of exploring the changing and diverse understanding of crime in Turkey today. The way the term "mafia" is used in public rhetoric refers to a kind of business which is not legal, but which in some cases is more people-friendly than state law and administration. The semantics and pragmatics of the term "mafia" will become more trans-parent the more the social structures involved in organ trade are delineated.

This delineation can only be done with in-depth qualitative research methods. Most interviews were audio- or video tape-recorded. In general I interviewed the physicians first, and then with their permission and introduc-tions, I spoke to patients at their bedsides. In this article, people's names – except for those of the heads of the transplantation units – have been changed to pseudonyms.

Aside from my work in the hospitals, I spent time with the camera crew who filmed Dr S. doing illegal operations. I was allowed to use their archives and interview them about the programs on organ trafficking they produced from 1997 to 2000. I also collected other material from the media and interviewed journalists. I was lucky to have a snowball effect, a continuum of interviews by storytellers who directed me to the people they felt I should interview next. This gave rise to a coherent and unfolding story that engaged most of the people who were part of this business of life. I interviewed doctors and patients at the Organ Transplantation Unit at Istanbul University Hospital, the Dialysis and Organ Transplantation Unit at Haydarpaşa Numune Hospital in Istanbul, and the Transplantation Unit at Başkent University Hospital in Ankara. The following ethnography attempts to map the complex set of relations within the Turkish transplantation community, with its doctors, experts, donors, and patients, in an attempt to illuminate the conditions of the making of life, crime, and the exchange of body parts.

Transplantation in Turkey

The organ transplantation community in Turkey is large; it operates in 28 centers in 14 cities. Yet one striking thing about organ transplantation in Turkey is the very low rate of cadaver kidney transplantation (15–20 percent of all kidney transplantation in Turkey). In the last decade, most transplantations have been made from living-related donors and were regulated by the Organ Transplantation Act of 1979 and 1982. In the past 25 years of transplantation history in Turkey around 1,200 patients have had cadaver organ transplantations (Haberal 1993).

There are two distinct politics of organ sharing in Turkey which manifest as two medical authorities over the geographical and informational distribution of organ sharing. There are two separate organ-sharing databases, one in Ankara and one in Istanbul, which do not collaborate with each other. The database in

Istanbul was established by Dr Uluğ Eldegez in 1990. He is the founder of the Organ Coordination Center in Istanbul and the head of the Transplantation Unit at Istanbul University. Ankara's database was founded by Professor Mehmet Haberal, the Rector of Başkent University, the director of the Başkent University Hospital, the head of the Transplantation Center at Başkent University, and the founder of the Turkish Transplantation Society. Both directors are transplant surgeons, but they have different politics of organizing their transplantation centers. Eldegez collaborates with international organ-sharing groups Eurotrans and United Network for Organ Sharing (UNOS), whereas Haberal has closer contacts with the Middle Eastern Society for Organ Transplantation, although he also works with UNOS and Eurotrans. These centers challenge and compete with one another: according to both directors, the criterion for success for a transplantation center is the number of operations performed per year. However, the number of patients waiting for a transplant is outrageous, physicians suggest, pointing to the total number of dialysis patients in the country, which they estimate is around 30 thousand. Obviously, patients and doctors look for bodies that will contribute to the success of the transplantation center. They need donations. On the one hand, they have to increase the number of donations from cadavers; on the other, doctors need to find ways to increase the number of transplantations. Hence the divided nature of the database, the totally different transplantation politics between Ankara and Istanbul, and the lack of donations from cadavers become a burden on a transplantation patient's life. The struggle between Istanbul and Ankara over identifying patients and donors, occupying hospitals, and controlling Turkey topographically causes two different politics of sharing bodies and also opens up a space for organ trafficking.

Launching Kidney Transplantation

Dr Haberal, the director of Başkent University in Ankara, was the first transplantation surgeon in Turkey. In 1975, he performed the first kidney transplantation on a 12-year-old patient with a kidney from his mother. Three years later, in 1978, he received a kidney from Eurotrans and transplanted it into a Turkish patient. The same year, he proposed a law to the parliament on brain death and organ transplantation, which was passed in 1979 (Haberal 1993). With the legalization of the brain death diagnosis, Haberal had the chance to transplant the first kidney from a cadaver in Turkey in 1979, from a patient who had been killed in a traffic accident. In those years, he was working as a surgeon at Hacettepe University Hospital in Ankara. From 1975 to 1992, in transplant centers across Turkey coordinated from Ankara, 931 kidney transplantations were conducted with kidneys from both living donors and cadavers. After the political transitions of the 1990s, Haberal founded the Turkish Organ Transplantation Society in 1991, and in 1993 he became the President of Başkent University.

During this time, especially in the late 1970s and early 1980s, Haberal noticed that the rate of organ donations from cadavers was very low in Turkey. To sustain the improvements in Turkish transplantation surgery, he initiated two measures. The first one was the creation of three categories of kinship for living-related donations, and the second was developing a medical technique which kept a kidney from cadaver viable for many hours (111) before it was to be transplanted (Haberal et al. 1987). The law which defined this kinship was inspired by regulations in the United States. The *first degree of kinship* was defined as the parents and children of a patient. The *second degree of kinship* covered the distant relatives, such as uncles and cousins. The *third degree of kinship* defined a group of potential donors who were emotionally attached to the patient but not necessarily biologically related, such as partners, stepchildren, and friends. This new group of donors defined through social kinship actually became the core group who later on started selling their organs to patients. Today, when I speak of donors as sellers, we are still in the realm of legality, not crime, as long as these donors have signed papers for their voluntary act.

These new categories of kinship were passed into law in 1982, creating a way for kidney patients to bring their donors with them when they went to arrange transplant surgery. According to a doctor at Başkent University, the unrelated donors were a big issue:

The whole thing is out of control because patients bring their donors introducing them as their relatives or they claim the third degree of kinship, the emotional tie … It is difficult to tell who is who. Poverty is the main problem we are facing in Turkey and under these circumstances transplantation regulations are not ethical enough.

Eighty percent of the donations in Başkent University hospital were living related, signifying the nature of transplantation practices in central Turkey. According to this same doctor,

It would be impossible to control and prove the kinship and the kind of voluntary act on behalf of the donor. We do not reject a patient who brings his or her own donor. Actually, in this hospital there is no other way: either you find a donor or we put your name on the list for cadavers. Dr. Haberal does not take care of patients who go to Russia or India to have a transplant and then come back and want to be taken care of. Due to the low donation rates from cadavers, most patients have to bring their own donors unless they want to be listed in the organ-sharing database.

In the early 1980s, Haberal noticed the problem of the low donation rate from cadavers and developed a technique that kept a kidney fresh for 111 hours. This way, the transplant center could take the kidneys Eurotrans did not want to transplant. They started using kidneys from old people, or kidneys which were thought to be no longer viable. However, Haberal's technique has been highly criticized, and not without reason, by his European colleagues. Dr İki, a transplant surgeon working for a private hospital in Istanbul, remembered the debate on the 111-hour kidney during one of the Eurotrans conferences in Norway. At that conference, Haberal was blamed for conducting many operations which risked his patients' lives according to EU criteria. "Most of his patients die," İki told me. "They call his list *Schindler's List*! The number of operations a doctor makes should not be the criteria of success," he concluded.

Statistics and numbers overwhelm the value of life in the race toward technological leadership in medicine. The measure of medical service in transplantation surgery was represented to me in the statistics about the number of transplantations a center conducts per year. In the narratives I collected from both Istanbul University and Başkent University, the number of operations is represented as the measure of achievement. Since Turkey's rates of transplantation are far behind those of Europe and the United States, techniques of organ donation, such as new definitions of kinship and the 111-hour kidney, became important elements in meeting the West's level of surgery. Turkish modernity is the cornerstone of the corpus, which manifests the power of Western morality against the "irrational" ghost of the Ottomans. This is a moral struggle measured in numbers. Biopolitics (Foucault 1980) becomes the ideal of the Turkish surgeon, who fights not just for the lives of his or her patients, but also for the modernity of the state and society. The ideals of the modern medical corpus mutually reinforce the Turkish state and society's claim to participate in what Ataturk once called "the level of Civilizations."

According to Dr Eldegez, in the last 20 years there have been over one thousand kidney transplantations from cadavers in Turkey in total, whereas in Europe the average transplantation rate is 3,500 per year, over 95 percent of which are transplantations from cadavers. In some years the donation rate from cadavers even dropped down to three percent in Eldegez's unit. Under these circumstances, the 30 thousand dialysis patients and patients listed in organ-sharing databases in Ankara and Istanbul were urged to find donors.

Istanbul and Transplantations from Cadavers

Since 1991, the main task of Dr Eldegez's Organ Transplantation Coordination Center has been to organize organ sharing mainly in Istanbul and western Turkey. Politically, Eldegez is situated in opposition to Ankara, to

the state, to Haberal, and to the privatization of medicine. Instead of developing techniques and regulations for pursuing living-related organ donations, he believes in promoting donations from cadavers, reforming the Turkish medical system, and improving the conditions of intensive care units (ICUs). Eldegez's main concern is the attitude of ICU doctors towards organ transplantations. Besides, he believes, ICUs do not even have enough respirators, which forces doctors to decide which patients have the right to live, so it is very difficult to keep track of brain deaths. A 1991 survey of how many patients had brain death in Istanbul that year found that the Organ Transplantation Coordination Center had been informed about less than ten percent of these. The low rate of donation from cadavers and the image the media created of illegal transplant operations exacerbated the problem. "All of this news together with conflicts in the medical community discourages the donation from cadavers. People are scared of doctors today. In regard to brain death, they [patients' family members] believe their patient will be harvested by doctors and delivered into the hands of Mafia dealers," Eldegez told me.

According to Eldegez, the organ-sharing network in Turkey should be controlled by a civic organization coordinated by doctors. Political parties and state interventions should be separated from this system. The first measure to be taken is the reformation of the insurance system, which is currently distributed among different ministries and controlled by different political parties. Once all transplantation patients are insured by a common insurance system (as with Germany's Allgemeine Krankenversicherung, for example), patients will be able to get the hospitalization they need anywhere in Turkey regardless of their connections with different political interest groups. This would eliminate the gap between the transplant choices of the rich and the poor, bring equality to all citizens, and reform the health care system overall. With his socialist ideals, Eldegez hopes not only for better health care overall, but for improved conditions for organ transplantations as a modality of exchange that creates a new social bond between persons and groups, patients and donors. "Gift exchange" (Mauss 1990) applies here to the kind of exchange dominating organ donations. Mauss says that a gift carries the personality of the giver, and this enables social solidarity. This form of exchange is enhanced by the literal donation of a part of the self through kidney donation (Sharp 1995). To Mauss, gift exchange is not based on a voluntary act of giving, even though it seems to be. To Eldegez, the tyrannical psychology behind giving a part of one's self *should* only be practiced in a socialist health care system, to prevent the commodification of the self through the commodification of the body. To prevent any sales of body parts and exchange between living bodies – or in other words what Marx (1990) called commodity fetishism, whereby a commodity is decontextualized from the social means of its production – Eldegez's unit is dedicated to harvesting organs only from cadavers, not living bodies.

Eldegez believes that privatization is another burden on the medical community. Many doctors choose to work for private hospitals, and patients who can afford to go to these hospitals believe that they get the right treatment. This creates a negative image of public hospitals, and patients think doctors perform better in their private office hours or in private hospitals because they get paid right away.

> Most of our patients are poor. We have patients who come to us with money and they want to have a private operation. I send them to Russia, or they might go wherever they want to. We do not do such kind of business here. But of course in most living related donation cases I have the feeling that they pay for the kidney; or, for example, the father is ill, then one of the sons gets an apartment from his brothers in exchange for his kidney. Or they promise to take care of him financially. Such internal deals are very common. This is actually against the organ transplantation law. However, we just do what we are required, we operate under the law Haberal made.

Eldegez encourages patients to go to other countries for transplantation and when they come back, he takes care of them at the transplantation unit at Çapa Medical School. Although he is not very supportive of this intermediary system, to him what counts is a patient's life. "Saving a patient's life" and "strategies of finding a donor" – two key points in Eldegez's organ transplantation policies – are opposite to Haberal's politics. According to Eldegez, when a patient brings a donor who legally declares his kinship tie to the patient, then there is nothing the doctors can do except operate on the patient. As long as a doctor is not involved in arranging the donor-recipient tie and does not get money for the operation, he should not be held responsible for whether the donor was selling his organ or not.

This was the main cause of controversy about Dr S., Eldegez believes. "He was our friend and he worked here. The only thing I can tell is that he does not respect the norms and ethics of being a transplant surgeon too much." In this discourse, when Eldegez speaks of norms and ethics, he refers to the responsibility of a doctor to transplant a kidney in accordance with the law. However, as long as the doctor is not informed of the patient–donor deal, he can technically do the operation without violating the law. In Eldegez's discourse of conscience, ethics refer to the formal norms inspired by medical oaths, thus they are total, they are law. It is the law which has constructed an untenable definition of *ethical behavior*, so that it is difficult for those transplant surgeons who do transplants from living donors to avoid being complicit in illegal criminal pacts between patients and donors. Besides, knowledge of donors' and patients' private lives can influence a doctor's conscience, which can eventually affect the doctor's consciousness of agency. For this reason, Eldegez's unit at Çapa is dedicated to operating only with organs harvested from cadavers.

Eldegez blames Haberal for making a law that opens the way for the commodification of body parts. Haberal, on the other hand, seeks social techniques such as the kinship definition and medical techniques such as the 111-hour kidney to be able to integrate more patients and donors into the system. He pursues this goal by using the means available in Turkey's transforming economy and political life.

The circumstances under which organ transplantations are pursued at Eldegez's unit at Istanbul University are much different than at Haberal's unit at Başkent University. Istanbul University is a state university hospital which gets its financial support from the Ministry of Educational Affairs, whereas Başkent University is *avakif*, or foundation, university, controlled by the Ministry of Health. Dr Haberal, whose name circulated in the 2000 presidential elections in Turkey, oversees and directs Başkent University's funds. Most of the medical appliances and hemodialysis fluids used at Başkent are produced in Haberal's own factories and sold to his own hospital. The consumption of his own goods has thus become a source of income for Haberal. Yet he also profits from state subventions, because the foundation hospitals "seem" to be established for charity reasons, and so are exempt from particular taxes. When I visited Haberal, the medals and honors he had received from many Turkish business societies caught my attention. He was chosen as Businessman of the Year by the Turkish Industrialists' and Businessmen's Association (TÜSIAD), which is the highest award a businessman can get in Turkey.

Conditions in the two university hospitals are very different. The transplantation unit at Istanbul University is financed by state support and the charity of the patients. Availability of medical appliances depends on the Ministry of Educational Affairs. The university hospital does not have the means to experiment, order new drugs or medical devices, extend its bed capacity, or hire more experts, although it has the reputation of being the oldest and most respected medical school in Turkey, and it organizes the organ transplantation community in most parts of the country. Nevertheless, Eldegez is primarily a surgeon; he follows the rules.

The Ministry and the Politics of Organ Sharing

During the years of his administration at the Ministry of Health, Naci Uz prepared a new organ transplantation regulation which was brought into force in June 2000, just as I was starting my research. The regulation is intended to redefine and rearrange the institutions active in the organ-sharing network in an attempt to unite them under one database. According to Uz, the Ministry of Health's model for this new regulation was Spain, which has the most efficient organ-sharing network.

Organ and tissue sale and purchase are strictly forbidden in Turkey (National Newsletter 1979 as cited in Haberal 1993). The fourth paragraph of the Organ Transplantation Act prohibits the advertising of organ donation for other than scientific, statistical, and news-related purposes. Paragraph 10 says that organ and tissue transplantation has to be pursued by medical institutions which have the staff and equipment necessary to pursue such an operation (National Newsletter 1979 as cited in Haberal 1993). The mention of medical institutions in the tenth paragraph defines the institutions which are licensed by the Ministry of Health to work in the health sector in general. Naci Uz is attempting to redefine this institutional space. The new regulation of June 2000 aims to establish a National Organ and Tissue Coordination Center with which all of the organ transplantation units are supposed to be affiliated. It also aims to increase the number of private clinics and hospitals involved in organ sharing and transplantation in the future.

The new regulation suggests that organ and tissue transplantation centers can be established in both private and public hospitals under the license of the Ministry of Health. The only parts which would remain public were the cornea banks. With the new change, university hospitals will also be able to open their own organ and tissue banks.

The new regulation is intended to open a new path leading to the privatization of organ transplantation practices while centralizing the whole system under the control of the Ministry of Health.

[…]

The Ministry of Health is represented by MHP (the Nationalist Action Party) and headed by Minister Osman Durmuş. One of Dr Durmuş's most alarming public actions was his decision to reject humanitarian aid offered by Greece and the United States following an earthquake in August of 1999 (see Sabah Online 1999). Although this order was canceled by Prime Minister Bulent Ecevit of DSP (the Democratic Left Party), Durmuş's nationalist politics were a topic of debate for a long time. During the period of the earthquake emergency, Durmuş ordered all of the private hospitals in Istanbul to care for the earthquake victims for free. Even though there was a brief reaction to this order, the hospitals opened their ER services and cooperated with Durmuş (Milliyet Newspaper 1999). It was during this time that newspapers alarmed the public with headlines about the Organ Mafia. As the tension increased during the hundreds of aftershocks, these headlines caused more panic than the actual physical threat of the earthquake. While experts and politicians were trying to calm people down by denying the existence of an Organ Mafia, the earthquake victims were already arming themselves to protect their families against the Organ Mafia and the looters. This was the most extreme moment of Organ Mafia imagery for Turkish people. However, that fear of the Organ Mafia would accompany the fear of potential violence from looters at a time of national mourning is not surprising. There were a great number of nameless bodies carried to private hospitals, and with a death toll of 14 thousand, thousands of missing people could have been targets of the Organ Mafia.

Dr S. remembers those days very well.

My 13-year-old daughter called me. She was on vacation with her mother in the south. She asked me if it was true that the Organ Mafia was kidnapping injured children for their organs. Can you imagine how I felt like? My daughter was asking me if I was killing small children for their kidneys. But what can she think? When they say Organ Mafia, the first person that comes to mind is me. I told her that if I am the Organ Mafia – that is how people call me – if I am the Organ Mafia, then my child, I am telling you, I promise, no children and no human beings are being kidnapped or killed for a piece of kidney.

Dr S. was very touched as he remembered those days of accusations.

Moreover, it is impossible to do any operations under such panic. Let us leave all the psychological pressure over the doctor aside, it is still impossible to do the tissue typing, to find the recipient, to find a crew, to find a place. Also, one has to be inhuman to think that a doctor is actually capable of pursuing such a difficult operation with the corpses of innocent people, just for money. I believe that the looters were mainly interested in kidnapping children. They are a big problem in Turkey, but it is always covered. This time they put the blame on me.

Dr Eldegez also believes that the Mafia could not be responsible for such a large number of missing people whose families insist that they have been rescued and sent to hospitals to be taken care of. Whatever the cause, literally hundreds of families lost their rescued relatives, children, and parents, and believe they must have disappeared in the hospitals. The peak of the tragedy was thought to be that masses of kidnapping and loss meant nothing to a group of people who traded bodies underground. The public was horrified with these headlines, but somehow, it was also not a surprise. It was not impossible to think that those who had the power to organize underground crime would create an economy of poor people's bodies in times of political and social chaos and state emergency.

Privatizing Medicine

While the state invented new ways of expanding its organ transplantation politics, a new form of health care conquered patients' and doctors' dreams: privatization. With new investors in the health care sector, Turkey began receiving its "medical diaspora" back to work in private hospitals. This 1990s phenomenon altered the ways in which an ideal health care system, with Western-educated doctors and high-tech hospitalization, offered the best care for patients.

When I met with Dr Ali, one of the first professional hospital managers in Turkey, he was just back from the United States. He had participated in seminars on hospital management during his internship at Columbia University in New York, and then was offered a job to help establish a big private hospital in Istanbul. Privatization of medicine is a growing business in Turkey. For Dr Ali the job offer was worth moving back to Turkey, like many Turkish doctors have decided to do in recent years. He recruited most of his medical staff from this new community of Turkish doctors.

Dr Ali considers himself a businessman. As we spoke of medicine and business, Ali mentioned Dr Yüksel Şen, who owns more than 50 medical institutions in Turkey, more than 20 of which are in Istanbul. According to Dr Ali, Dr Şen is a conservative traditional businessman. "He does not know how to do management, he does not like sharing [patients], and he does business like in the old days. He is old fashioned. He is the biggest mafia in medicine. He closes some deals through people he knows best and buys hospitals."

Dr Ali told me about the profits of investing in medicine. His hospital, he said, received 30 percent of a surgeon's fee for each operation that the surgeon did there. The hospital also charges patients for accommodation expenses and gets a share of the coverage from the insurance company they have an agreement with – in the end, the hospital has three sources of income from each operation. "Organ transplantations are not pursued in private hospitals yet, and state insurance covers all transplantation operation costs, but we will try to change this," Dr Ali told me.

> What we want is to be able to open private organ and tissue banks and do organ transplantation in private hospitals like ours. There are illegal operations in Turkey, because of the gap between the poor and the rich. The wealthy will pay for it by all their means. So why does the state still insist on such centralized regulations? When we make it private, we will be able to control the legal status of the operations at least. There will be no criminal activity. They put an end to Dr. S.'s medical career. It is the most unfortunate thing. He is the best transplant surgeon in this country, and of course he will do transplantation. This is his job.

Dr İki, the head surgeon of the private hospital Dr Ali works for, also agreed that Dr S. had been treated unfairly throughout his career, and that was why he was now pursuing private operations.

> He has become the scapegoat of the whole medical community. They exiled him to SSK Hospital at Kartal. If you are a doctor in Istanbul and they appoint you to Kartal SSK, this means they are exiling you, and that they want to get rid of you. He contradicted the other doctors a lot. He was aggressive. But if I were him, I would be doing the same – I would also be operating in private—. Dr. S. is the best transplant surgeon in Turkey, and he should not stop practicing his job just because of the medical community.

Dr S.'s favorite hospital owner is Dr Şen, and Dr S. also views Şen as a successful businessman. "He knows many people, and that is how he makes his money," Dr. S. told me. This "knowing many people" also means Dr S. trusts the power of the people he is good friends with. "Business is business," and "medicine as business," Dr S. suggested, requires the same skills as any other newly opening enterprise in Turkey. Two of the hospitals where Dr S. was caught performing operations belonged to Şen. The first time, Dr. S. was kicked out of Kartal SSK because he was caught by Arena Team preparing for a transplantation from a seller to a buyer that was taking place in one of Şen's hospitals. After this incident, Dr S. was kicked out of his civil service post for good and banned from practicing medicine for six months. By the end of his ban, he had started working in another hospital owned by Şen. He could never work for a state hospital again, nor could he teach at a medical school. Since a medical degree can never be rescinded by the state, he could still operate in private hospitals. So he could not reject Şen's offer. In the last four years, he told me, he operated on 360 patients, and only 2 of them had died.

Before Dr S. started working as a "criminal" doctor, he lived in France, where he learned transplantation surgery. The Turkish government sent him to Paris's Paul Brousse Hospital. During his years in France and then in Italy, he met many transplantation surgeons from all over Europe and the Middle East. Eurotrans and Middle Eastern Society for Organ Transplantation conferences served as platforms for information exchange and meeting sports where friendships were made. One of the friends Dr S. made this way, an Israeli physician, still sends him many patients from Israel in Turkey. In the meantime, Dr S. also travels abroad to conduct operations. "I operated in France, Italy, Germany, Ukraine, and Israel," he told me.

> Once in Ukraine, I was invited to make a couple of transplantations. I arrived there at night, and I went to the hospital to meet the doctors and nurses. I had a great team working there for me. Anyway, then I went to my hotel. In the morning I was driving to the hospital, I turned on the radio. Of course I did not understand the language; but I heard two words, "Organ Mafia," which were repeated over and over again. First I thought I was dreaming or mishearing. But then they repeated it so many times, I thought there might be a trouble in the hospital. I called them from my cell phone. They told me that the police were somehow informed about the operations and they were looking for me everywhere. I had to go back directly to the airport and fly back home.

Dr S. was very enthusiastic about this story. He was amazed by the fact that they could not catch him. Even though this was the only story he told me about his international operations, a friend of Dr S. told me that wealthy patients from all over Europe would send their jet planes to Dr S. for organ transplantations. He remembered the last time he received a bottle of vodka from Dr S.:

> It must have been last January [2000], soon after he was caught treating Israeli patients. He went to Moscow and did ten operations in a row there. He is so talented that they invite him everywhere. By the increase in his reputation, he also started becoming more professional. Now, he does not find the donors for the patients. He used to do that before. Now, he is asking patients to find their own donors.

This physician was put in jail with Dr S. after Arena Team caught Dr S. in December 1999. He did not approve of these operations, but he had

no choice but to accept when Dr S. told him that he was going to operate on some patients from Israel. Moreover, Dr S. had an agreement with the owner of the hospital.

> But Dr. S. felt very guilty, as I was also taken to interrogation with him. He knew I do not like this kind of business. He apologized many times. He is a good guy, and I like the way he resists the medical community and its established old-fashioned, elitist attitude.

The relationship between this physician, Dr S., and Dr. Şen adds a new level to the complexity of the politics of the transplantation community in Turkey. On one side Haberal and Eldegez disagree on the politics and techniques of organ share, and on the other side the Ministry of Health's intervention in this situation with a new privatization policy gets intertwined with private investors' desires to make a profitable business of body parts, creating a complex set of relations in the definition of *crime in medicine*.

In the 1980s Turkey was a land of unlimited possibilities for private investors. Prime minister and former president Turgut Özal, from ANAP (the Motherland Party), had taken measures to open the Turkish market to foreign investments. He encouraged Turkish businessmen to invest in all kinds of ventures by exempting them from state taxes. It was in those years that Haberal started his first hemodialysis fluid production factory. In the early 1990s private hospitals were founded in the spirit of Özal's privatization policies. Today, there are 137 licensed hospitals in Istanbul, and 111 of them are private. Şen alone owns more hospitals than the number of all the public hospitals in Istanbul. The 26 state, social security, and university hospitals take care of those who cannot afford private insurance. Most of their patients are clergy, workers, farmers, and small tradesmen.

"Private practice is a good source of income," one doctor who just left a state hospital in Ankara and moved to Istanbul to work in a private clinic told me.

> But the main money in medicine goes to hospital owners. Most of the public insurance and all of the private insurance covers the private

treatments. The price range of these operations has been controlled by the Turkish Medical Association since 1998, because the private insurance companies have found out that many doctors have been writing false prescriptions for patients – things like declaring an operation due to a traffic accident which actually was a cosmetic nose surgery – became normal. Fraud had become a part of the routine in the medical community and the Ministry of Health could not control it. So private insurance companies actually have forced the Turkish Medical Association to set up a price range in U.S. dollars to control fraud because they could not make profits any longer. One could imagine that the increasing number of private hospitals would be an even better damper for the fraud, but it happened just the opposite way. The private hospital owners have turned medicine into a business and they do not want to share with doctors; nor do they want to be accused of fraud by the insurance companies. So as they become stronger, they are changing the rules of the game.

Where to Find a Kidney

The hemodialysis center is the first place kidney patients meet after they are diagnosed with renal failure. In this period of time the patient's daily routines become dependent on the schedule of the hemodialysis center, where a machine takes control of the body's "cleansing needs" for four hours three to four times a week. At the hemodialysis center, the patient meets other patients, learns about the course of kidney failure from other patients' experiences, shares his or her suffering every day, and gets to know patients who are waiting for kidneys.

It is also at this stage of the treatment when the patient starts to understand that he or she cannot live forever by going to the dialysis center. The blood-cleansing machine becomes a symbol for the beginning of the end of a patient's life with renal failure; as a result, the patient starts considering having a kidney transplantation. The economic status of a patient has an enormous influence on the kind of transplantation being considered – from a living-related donor or a cadaver. Other patients' opinions, experiences, and advice also contribute to this decision-making. Moreover, the choice of the hemodialysis center – which is not optional, but which depends strictly on the kind of public insurance the patient has – becomes central to the creation of the setting in which the patient seeks possibilities for a kidney transplantation.

The main organ transplantation units and hemodialysis centers are located in public hospitals which receive patients who have the required state insurance covered by any of the three main types of public insurance. But not everyone is insured by one of these big institutions. In general, the poor, especially selfemployed farmers and peasants in Eastern and Northern Turkey and those who have never been employed or who cannot pay their own insurance taxes, are left out of this system. A public health expert told me that the "green card" regulation launched in the early 1980s was meant to solve this problem. According to this plan, those who could prove their poverty would be given a green card which they could use to receive treatment in any state hospital. "Though," she said,

> just like everything in the Turkish medical system, this got out of control. People who knew people in the bureaucracy received the cards, and people who were really in need of them could not get any. According to statistics, every town was supposed to distribute a number of green cards. Who knows who took advantage of this distribution.

Ayşe, a patient at Haydarpaşa Numune Hospital who had had a kidney transplantation a week earlier, was a green card patient. She was very happy with the transplantation from cadaver she had, which, in her words, "gave an end to [my] suffering at the machine in the dialysis center." The hemodialysis center she was consigned to from Haydarpaşa Numune Hospital was two hours away from the Sultanbeyli slums, the part of the city where she lived with her husband and two children. Ayşe was a farmer. She was from a small village in Trabzon, where all of her brothers and sisters still lived by farming. After she got ill and could get treatment in Istanbul with her green card, she and her husband and children decided to move to Istanbul. Today, her

husband works in a factory. Both of her children go to school, but her eldest daughter (13
years old) also had to take care of the household
over the last five years, as Ayşe was going to
the dialysis center three times a week. Ayşe used
to take the bus to the dialysis center at
7:00 A.M., change three buses, and finally, after
a two-hour bus ride, wait standing in line in
front of the hemodialysis center for at least
three hours.

> Finally at noon I could go inside to have the
> transfusion. Even though I was already very
> tired of a six-hour adventure of getting there,
> I was always happy about meeting my other
> family there. We shared the same life, and I
> would not have recovered and kept my own
> family strong if they had not been there for me.
> The blood transfusion is such a nightmare ex-
> perience that no one who has not been through
> it can understand. We always talked about
> how it would be if one of us gets an organ.
> You know we are all in the same listing [Istan-
> bul University's database]. I will go back to
> them as soon as I get out of this hospital. They
> need me as well. And my nightmares are over.
> Every night I dreamt of my gall bladder and of
> my kidney. I dreamed that I could pee just like
> anyone. I dreamed that I was drinking water,
> gallons of water. Now, it is over, I am fine.

Even though Ayşe had eight brothers and
sisters, she did not want to ask them if they
could donate a kidney to her. If anything
happened to any one of them, they could not
take care of their families, as they were all even
poorer than her. The physical work on the farm
was overwhelming, and her family members
had not been as lucky as her in getting green
cards. "So if anything happened because of the
kidney they donated, no one, no hospital, no
doctor would take care of them," she told me.
Ayşe was one of the lucky ones among the poor,
getting a kidney from a cadaver after waiting
five years.

Those who can afford to buy a kidney or
have relatives who donate one to them feel
even more "fortunate" than Ayşe. Sinan was
one of these more "fortunate" patients. "In
my time," he told me,

> it was not hard to find the dealers. The
> doctors knew them in the hemodialysis

centers. They would advise you to go there,
and make your connections with them, if you
were willing to have an operation in India or
Russia. There were two important criterions:
hygiene conditions as well as the reputation
of the doctors, and the amount of money you
had to pay for the best service. My boss
helped me out with the money. He was very
generous.

Sinan is a 42-year-old IT manager in a travel
agency in Istanbul. He underwent transplantation in Moscow five years ago.

> In the early nineties, I started having kidney
> problems. One day in 1995 my kidney stopped
> functioning. My boss flew me to Florida to
> West Palm Beach the next day and I went to
> the JFK Hospital for treatment. They did tests
> and still could not find out why my kidney did
> not function from one day to the other. There,
> they advised me to do peritoneal dialysis
> instead of hemodialysis. Then I came back to
> Turkey. Meanwhile, I started looking for a
> kidney. I have no relatives; my parents have
> passed away, and I have no siblings. So the
> only solution was to *find* one.
>   That was the time when I heard that Dr. S.
> was doing private operations. I met him for
> the first time when I was diagnosed in 1995.
> He told me that he could do the operation for
> me. He told me that he could bring a kidney
> for me from India and do the operation in
> Istanbul. It would cost around $25,000. I did
> not want such a thing. But in that one meet-
> ing, he told me the most valuable advice ever,
> that I should mentally prepare myself for the
> new kidney. Then I went to Haberal, and he
> told me to leave Istanbul and go to Başkent
> University in Ankara where they would put
> me on their list and take care of me there. He
> did not give me any hope or possible dates
> for the operation, so I was not interested in
> his offer. I had visited Dr. S. in his private
> practice. He was not a public figure back
> then. I guess he was working for Kartal SSK
> Hospital. My meeting with Haberal was very
> brief. But I was trying to find a solution, so I
> tried everything.

So going to Russia, where "dead Russian
bodies," as Sinan said, "belong to the Russian
state," was his only chance. Sinan thought the

Russian state "did whatever it wanted" with the corpses.

In the end, I decided on the Russian solution because I also talked to three or four patients who went through this company to Moscow and they recovered very well. When I went to Moscow, I already knew a lot about their system, such as the food, or life in Moscow. They were very helpful and informative. ... At the time, India was very popular, but I was told that hygiene there was very bad. One of my colleagues in the company also had a transplant a few years ago in Russia. He encouraged me to think about going there. I looked into the contact he gave me. It was a small private company in Istanbul which no longer exists because they had problems with some of the patients. It was simple, I called them, and talked to them; and they sent me to Moscow. They did all the tests at the hospital there as well. I was at a state hospital in downtown Moscow and there was a large team of doctors, who were perfectly equipped. I had the operation a month later. The kidney started to work immediately, but I had a small problem. I had to have another operation, so I stayed in Moscow for two months. During this time, I was required to reside at the hospital in case there was an organ available, they could operate on me immediately. I could not use peritoneal dialysis there because their system was unsuitable for this. I switched back to hemodialysis again. However, I could leave the hospital and go sightseeing. One day a friend who also was waiting for a kidney and I went to dine at a Turkish restaurant in Moscow. When we came back, the hospital staff were looking for me everywhere in panic. They had a kidney for me. They asked if I had eaten anything. They had to take all the Turkish food out of my stomach, and then I had the operation.

Sinan thought that the transplantation conditions in Russia might have changed in the last five years, just as life in general is changing so rapidly there.

I do not know the conditions of transplantation in Russia now, but back then I stayed at a state hospital. The Russians in Moscow organized my stay there as well as my operation. So I paid them, and I imagine they paid for the operation and hospital expenses. It was a private organization I was sent to by this Turkish company. The year I had the operation, twelve Turkish patients were sent there by the same company. There were also German patients, many of them! And of course Russians from former Soviet republics were there. I did not see people of any other nationality.

[...]

Another patient I met at Istanbul University's transplantation unit was Osman Gez. He had had a kidney transplantation ten years ago, and he had to be taken care of by the transplantation unit all his life. He received the 13th kidney transplant from a cadaver to be conducted at the Istanbul University. However, initially he had not been planning on having a kidney from a cadaver.

I was at home visiting my village. One day, while farming in the fields, I had an attack [renal failure]. I came to Istanbul, and went to Cerrahpaşa Hospital. They told me I should go to a dialysis center. Then at the dialysis center, I was told to go to Istanbul University's transplantation center to put my name on the organ waiting list. In the meantime, a friend from our neighborhood here in Istanbul told me that he could sell his kidney to me. He was in need of money. His daughter had a heart problem and he needed money to operate on her. So I asked him to come with me to Istanbul University to do the blood tests and tissue typing. He came with me, had the blood tests, but then disappeared. The tissues did not match, but we wanted to find him and give him the money he needed for his daughter's operation. My sons went to the address he gave us, but it was the wrong address. We could not find him anywhere. In the meantime, I started waiting at the transplantation center with my wife, and then Eldegez asked me what I was waiting for. I told him I was waiting for a cadaver. He was mad at me. He said there were no cadavers, and that I should go home. I kept waiting. He saw me again, and yelled at me again. He said, "You idiot, how can I find you an organ? There are no organs here, go home!" But I still waited. At 7:00 P.M. that night a cadaver came in. So I had my operation. It is God's gift to me. If I had not kept waiting, I would not have had the operation.

Since then, Mr Gez has had good fortune. He has not been ill, and his family has taken good care of him. Next to his room at Istanbul University's transplantation unit, I met a 38-year-old woman, Leyla, with another story. This time it was a kidney operation in India.

In April 1992, I went to India. A friend of mine had a transplantation there, and she advised me to do the same. It all happened pretty soon. I was actually planning on having a cadaver kidney transplantation in London. But then, as I heard that the organ in India would be from a living donor, I preferred that. I arranged all the organizational things by myself. I bought my flight ticket and I got my visa. When I got to the airport, the only thing I knew was the name of the doctor and the name of the hospital in Bombay. Luckily the plane was full of Turkish people who were going there for the same reason. I was very happy to see this, you know, because I was all by myself. My husband did not want to accompany me. My brothers did not want to go with me either. My mother had to take care of my son. So I had no one. Anyway, then, we landed in Bombay. There was a Turkish guy who met us there; and before going to the hotel, we went directly to the hospital to make the tissue-typing test. They then listed us in their database, to match us with donors. Usually in ten days, one gets a kidney in India.

After I settled down in the hotel, I started going to the dialysis. It took them fifteen days to find me a suitable donor. In the meantime I traveled in India, and did some sightseeing. Then they called me. They had found a donor who was a 20-year-old man. I somehow did not want to meet him, but I am grateful to him. Two weeks after the operation, I came directly back to Istanbul University's transplantation unit where they took care of me for 15 days. Everything went smoothly until now. I have some blood pressure problems recently, and that is why I am here.

While Leyla was in Bombay, there were 15 patients from Antep, Mardin, Van, Ankara, and Istanbul there with her, all waiting for kidney transplantations. She was surprised to see so many people from so many different places, as it had taken her a long time to find out about it in Istanbul. "But I guess," she said, "once one is in need of a kidney, then one makes a lot of inquiries about it, and finds the people who are involved in this business."

Wherever patients come from, and whatever they can afford, they find the way and the means to have a transplantation. There is no single pattern or route among the four examples above, except that these individuals were all as mobile as they could afford in their search for a kidney. Almost all of the patients whose names are listed in Istanbul University's database are very poor. They can neither afford to pay for a kidney, nor can they ask their family or relatives for a favor, since they are just as poor. The rest of the patient group finds ways – what they call companies – to go abroad to have a transplantation.

The transplantations Dr S. performs are very expensive. Only very rich people can afford to be his patients. According to his friend, Dr S. must be receiving around $100,000 per operation. Şahin, the editor of the *Arena Show* program, believed that the money is much more than that. The price of a kidney was around $40,000 on the illegal market before the Arena Team documentary was shown on television. The show had a negative effect, driving prices higher. One of the cameramen – who filmed Dr S. with a hidden camera while they arranged the setup to catch him – told me that there were Israeli patients ready to pay up to $1 million for a kidney and a transplant by Dr S., whereas Sinan had paid $25,000 for his operation in Russia in 1995, and it cost Leyla $15,000 to have a kidney transplantation in India in 1992. The price range for a kidney varies depending on the wealth of the patient and the risks doctors take operating on the patient. According to Şahin, the most recent market is Bulgaria, which is closer to Turkey than India or Russia and has enough technology and educated staff to conduct transplantations. Iraq has come into play very recently as well – Iraqi soldiers sell kidneys to Turkish recipients in Adana, near Turkey's border with Syria and Iraq, the Arena Team believes.

The organ trade in the Middle East seems to follow paths similar to trade routes for opium, prostitution, and illegal migrant labor, according to the Arena Team. One of the cameraman thought that the dealers engaged in this business were hired by the Mafia, which has its own companies or works for doctors like Dr S. This cameraman thought that Dr S. must have solid contacts with the dealers, since he finds the organs for his own patients (as also indicated by Sinan, to whom Dr S. promised to bring an organ from India). Another physician was more careful about accusing Dr S. of underground criminal activity. He believed that there was a connection between the European Mafia and Turkish Mafia, but that Dr S. did not belong to either one because he was not engaged in any criminal activity per se. There was no theft of organs, only the sale of organs by the poor to the rich. Dr S. was merely doing operations on patients who would otherwise die.

[...]

Conclusion

[...]

In this paper, I have tried to illustrate the nature of kidney transplant patient groups in Turkey with a few examples. While affordability is the major motivation influencing the decision a patient makes to purchase a kidney from a poor seller, a patient's family structure, place of birth, education, sex, income level, profession, and age play a significant role in this decision, and all of these things create complex reasons why a patient considers buying an organ.

Among doctors, the discourse of ethics and legitimacy in Turkey (as elsewhere) must at least appear to be consistent with the standards required by the international community. But the "spirit" that undermines faith in brain death or oversees the selling of organs provides a window onto a world where patients' (and the public's) wishes and legitimate medical worlds pass completely by one another with regards to categories of "the right to stay alive," "remaining human," and "human rights." Fischer (2003) describes this condition in terms of the unstable "ethical plateaus" of contemporary medical worlds. Ethical plateaus are strategic terrains on which multiple technologies interact, creating a complex topology of perception and decision-making (Fischer 2003). In this paper, I have tried to show how changes in political economy, technology, legal definitions and regulations, and transnational exchange networks, all affect modalities of ethics. It is in these strategic terrains that what counts as human rights and innocence and criminality are constructed in an unemotional language.

In an age when medicine has created a worldview which finds its truth in biology (Agamben 1998), Dr S., in a timely fashion, has become the "Robin Hood" of Turkey. Patients I have talked to, with a few exceptions, believe that Dr S. is a great surgeon who saves patients' lives, regardless of his portrayal in the media. Patients' health care is always dependent on the mercy of the doctor, in spite of state-governed institutions, and yet in the negotiations between doctor and patient, "morals of the street" – or as one doctor put it, "the Ottoman morality" – do not correlate with the modern ethics doctors learn during internships and fellowships abroad or that they are bound by international standards to observe. When healthcare becomes privately funded, patients often think they are back in the realm of traditional ethics, where exchange is negotiated as part of mutual trust within a network of obligations, and where monetary and other means are part of that nexus of exchange. For doctors the conflict of moralities is no less difficult: "Ottoman ghosts" or "a feeling for the right thing" inhibits many doctors from declaring a person brain dead. Conversely, privatization is a way not just to evade rigid bureaucratic ethics, but to pioneer a new modality of ethical calculation for saving lives in an emerging technoscientific world, one that is merged with symbols of modernity and national self-esteem and that operates within a state which uses 'privatization' as a means of justifying what used to be 'criminal.'

To some anthropologists (Lock 2002; Scheper-Hughes 2002), what is of greater concern in organ transplantations is the human desire to survive at any cost. Dr S. provides a case study in which such accounting discourses are forged and tested. "A patient would *pay* with all his or her means not to die," said Omer, who had a kidney transplant from his father a few years ago. At Omer's dialysis center, Dr S. was a folk hero. Omer even thought that Dr S. was in prison next to such mafia chiefs as Dündar Kilic and Alaaddin Cakici. For Omer and many other patients, Dr S. was the Robin Hood of Turkey. Patients' narratives on Dr S.'s heroism resembled traditional stories such as the Koroglu, an epic cycle from the Bolu region of Anatolia that tells of a hero fighting the injustices of the Ottoman regime. Dr S. is believed to fight the injustices of how state institutions select and treat their patients. These institutions place patients on death watch on waiting lists, whereas Dr S. will "help" anyone who mobilizes their resources to buy care. That these people might more often be the wealthy than the poor does not undo the principle of responding to need against bureaucratic inertia and hopelessness.

I find a striking set of experiential implications: given the complexity of issues involved in organ donation and trafficking, patients live in a world in which they narrate their experiences using partly the rhetoric of physicians, partly references to the mafia disseminated by rumor and the media, partly the language of social kinship ties, and partly personal assumptions. But only in few cases do they express their experiences in relation to suffering, pain, or guilt – in short, with their feelings. In this new ethical terrain of a second life through the donation of a body part from another person, what seems more artificial and needs explanation are the conditions of living in a strange new corpus (law, state, body) which creates an incoherent understanding of the "human," the "person," and "human rights." The media and the politics of organ sharing shape patients' narratives and help create the demand for the economy of the business of life. This economy has already established a legitimate space for itself in hospitals, taking organs from the poor to give to the rich and at the same time ambiguously making the mafia into heroes. Human rights become an invalid category as patients try to survive their illness.

This new worldview, based on belief in the truth of biology and served for public consumption through the popularization of science in the media, seems to have become the principle of the corpus, which now teaches us to become the right human for its purposes. All personal emotions are suppressed in this worldview except for collective fear, which becomes the measure of heroism and of oppression. The corpus thus expands, using privatization in some cases to legitimize the criminal.

NOTE

1 A patient – who had never met him – told me that Dr S. was the "Robin Hood" of kidney transplantations: a hero who takes from one body to give to another. However, in noir techno-Turkey, it is an inversion of the mythic Robin Hood of Sherwood Forest, who takes from the rich and gives to the poor. This inversion is part of the naturalization of a form of biosociality in which the poor must struggle against the legalized structures of power that would preclude them from the economic and biological means of life. On biosociality, inverting E. O. Wilson's sociobiology, and extending Foucault's biopower, see Rabinow 1996; see also Cohen 2003, Dumit 2000, Biehl 1999, Fischer 2003, Foucault 1980, and Petryna 2002. The biosociality of this "Robin Hood" is a world in which patients can feel that a surgeon doing transplants using purchased body parts is engaging in heroic acts in a state medical system whose tyrannical definition of *morality* prevents doctors from saving patients' lives. Figures such as Dr S. are born not through their evil intentions, but because of a demand for "life." In such moments, biosocial relations shape a *Weltanschauung* in which the lives of the poor come to be taken for granted as resources to prolong the lives of the ill.

REFERENCES

Agamben, Giorgio
  1998   Homo Sacer: Sovereign Power and Bare Life. Stanford: Stanford University Press.
Biehl, Joao
  1999   Other Life: AIDS, Biopolitics and Subjectivity in Brazil's Zones of Social Abandonment. Unpublished PhD dissertation, University of California, Berkeley.
Cassirer, Ernst
  1962   The Philosophy of Enlightenment. Boston: Beacon Press.
Cohen, Lawrence
  1999   "Where It Hurts": Bioethics and Beyond. Daedalus 128(4): 143–9.
  2003   Operability, Bioavailability and Exception. Medical Anthropology and Cultural Psychiatry Seminar Series, May 2003. Department of Anthropology, Harvard University, Cambridge, MA.
Dumit, Joe
  2000   When Explanations Rest: 'Good Enough' Brain Science and the New Biomental Disorders. In Living and Working With the New Medical Technologies: Intersection of Inquiry. Margaret Lock, Alan Young, and Alberto Cambrosio, eds., pp. 209–32. Cambridge, UK: Cambridge University Press.
Fischer, Michael
  2003   Emergent Forms of Life and the Anthropological Voice. Durham: Duke University Press.
Foucault, Michel
  1980   Power/Knowledge. New York: Pantheon.
Fox, R., and J. Swazey
  1992   Spare Parts: Organ Replacement in American Society. New York: Oxford University Press.
Friedläender, Michael
  2002   The Right to Sell or Buy a Kidney: Are We Failing Our Patients? The Lancet 359 (9310): 971–3.
Haberal, Mehmet
  1993   Doku ve Organ Transplantasyonlari [Tissue and Organ Transplantations]. Ankara: Haberal Egitim Vakfi.

Haberal, M., S. Sert, N. Aybasti., H. Gulay, G. Arslan, Y. Gurgen, T. Kucukali, and N. Bilgin
  1987   Cadaver Kidney Transplantation Cases With a Cold Ischemia Time of Over 100 Hours. Transplantation Proceedings 19(5):4184–8.
Lock, Margaret
  2002   Twice Dead: Organ Transplants and the Reinvention of Death. Berkeley: University of California Press.
Marx, Karl
  1990   Capital, Vol. 1 London: Penguin.
Mauss, Marcel
  1990   The Gift: The Form and Reason for Exchange in Archaic Societies. New York: Norton.
Milliyet Newspaper
  1999   Sasirtan Zihniyet [Surprising Mentality]. Milliyet Newspaper, June 23. Available from http://www.milliyet.com.tr/1999/08/23/index.html.
Petryna, Adriana
  2002   Life Exposed: Biological Citizens After Chernobyl. Princeton, NJ: Princeton University Press.
Rabinow, Paul
  1996   Artificiality and Enlightenment: From Sociobiology to Biosociality. In Essays on the Anthropology of Reason. Princeton, NJ: Princeton University Press.
Sabah Online
  1999   Yardimi kibarca reddettik [We Refused Aid Politely]. Sabah Online, August 22. Available from http://garildi.sabah.com.tr/cgi-bin/sayfa.cgi?w + 30 + /.
Scheper-Hughes, Nancy
  2000   The Global Traffic in Human Organs. Current Anthropology 41(2): 191–224.
  2002   Rotten Trade: Millennial Capitalism, Human Values and Global Justice in Organs Trafficking. The Journal of Human Rights.
Sharp, Lesley
  1995   Organ Transplantation as a Transformative Experience: Anthropological Insights Into the Restructuring of the Self. Medical Anthropology Quarterly 9(3): 357–89.

24

Quest for Conception
Gender, Infertility, and Egyptian Medical Traditions

Marcia C. Inhorn

Sakina's Story

On a rainy day in late November 1988, Sakina sat weeping on a bench in a corridor of Shatby Hospital. Just told that both of her fallopian tubes were blocked and that the only way for her to achieve pregnancy was through in vitro fertilization (IVF), Sakina was inconsolable. Her worries were many. First, she feared the reaction of her husband, Hany, who was tired of spending his hard-earned money on her infertility therapies and who had told her three times over the past year that he planned to divorce her and remarry "for children" if she did not become pregnant soon. Second, she was concerned about the cost of IVF, given that her first instruction was to purchase two packets of medicine costing £E 350 ($140) each. Having only £E 100 ($40) left after selling her last gold bracelet for £E 300 ($120), Sakina knew that she was definitely unable to afford IVF on her own and that Hany, with his small salary as a laborer in a textile factory, was probably unwilling and unable to finance this expensive therapy. Third, she was worried about the effect of IVF on her body. Although

as the daughter of a dāya, or traditional healer, she had already tried many painful ethnogynecological and biogynecological therapies, Sakina heard from other women in the hospital that the IVF doctors "took things from the tubes and put them back" and, frankly, she had no idea which "tubes" they were talking about or whether these tubes were the same ones that the doctor had said were "blocked" in her body. Fourth, as a Muslim woman, Sakina was uncertain about the acceptability of IVF in her religion. Although she suspected that IVF was not forbidden as long as "it's from the husband," she was uninformed about the opinions of religious experts on this subject and feared Hany's interpretation of the religious permissibility of the procedure. Finally, Sakina was extremely concerned about the reaction of her family and neighbors to her bringing home a "tubes baby" – a baby that might face perpetual ostracism if the nature of its creation was made known to the community. Thus, she realized that if she were to undertake IVF, she would have to keep this fact secret from everyone – except, of course, from her sympathetic mother.

Marcia C. Inhorn, "'He Won't Be My Son': Middle Eastern Muslim Men's Discourses of Adoption and Gamete Donation," *Medical Anthropology Quarterly* 20/1 (2006): 94–120. Reproduced by permission of the American Anthropological Association from *Medical Anthropology Quarterly* 20/1 (2006), pp. 94–120. Not for sale or further reproduction

However, of all of these concerns, Sakina's financial worries were the most immediate and were the ones that had made her burst into tears in the doctor's office. When the doctor told her to purchase the two packets of expensive medicine, she told him that she could not afford even one packet and would therefore be unable to undertake IVF therapy. He offered to provide one packet of the drug for free if she would agree to participate as a subject in his clinical study of IVF patients. Furthermore, he told her of a government pharmacy in midtown Alexandria where the drug could be purchased for only £E 220 ($88). However, with only £E 100 ($40) to her name, Sakina was still £E 120 ($48) short.

A week after her despairing episode in the hospital, Sakina returned to Shatby, smiling, with a packet of the expensive IVF medication in hand. During the ensuing week, she had received *zakawāt*, or alms, from some upperclass Egyptians to whom she had told her sad story and who, taking pity on her, gave her the remaining £E 120 as a charitable donation. However, this did not solve all of Sakina's problems. For one, she had no refrigerator in which to store the sensitive drugs, and when she told the doctor that she had kept the packet of drugs at room temperature for several days, he admonished her for failing to follow his instructions. Second, she was told that the drugs she had purchased would be good for only "one trial" of IVF and that subsequent attempts to make a "tubes baby" would require additional medication.

Sakina's most serious problem, however, involved delays. Although she and other women with blocked tubes were told that the IVF procedure would begin at the hospital imminently, a month of waiting turned into two months, and then into three, and, eventually, a year. During this interval, Sakina and other women like her were advised by their physicians to resell their expensive medications, lest the drugs lose their therapeutic efficacy and the women lose their money.

Thus, more than a year after that fateful day in November 1988 when Sakina was told about her need for IVF, her dreams for a *ṭifl l-anābīb*, or a "baby of the tubes," were still not realized. For Sakina – and many other poor infertile Egyptian women like her – a test-tube baby was, in fact, not in the making by the end of the 1980s.

Test-Tube Babies on TV

By the end of 1988, when Sakina ventured to Shatby Hospital to earn of her need for IVF, the subject of IVF was familiar to many urban Egyptians, who recognized this assisted reproductive technology by the name *tifl l-anābīb*, literally, "baby of the tubes." Following an announcement in *Al-Ahram* newspaper in July 1987 of the first Egyptian "test-tube baby," the Egyptian media began to capitalize on Egypt's newest reproductive technology, in the form of factual discussions of the technique, debates over the religious permissibility of the procedure, and melodramatic television dramas about infertile women undergoing IVF. In fact, in a popular televised *tamsīlīya*, a dramatic, fictional soap opera that aired in 1989, the story was told of a woman who spent thousands of Egyptian pounds undergoing IVF following years of hopeless infertility. Unfortunately, the protagonist was forced to remain in bed throughout her pregnancy – a false representation – and, at four months, she miscarried her "baby of the tubes" in a dramatic twist of fate.

This television show served as the primary means by which the Egyptian public learned about IVF, although the information conveyed about this new reproductive technology was flawed and viewers' understandings were thus extremely incomplete. Suddenly, women who had never before heard of "test-tube babies" were instant experts on the subject, having watched the soap opera and drawn rudimentary information from it. As one woman described it, "They take the *nutfa* from him, his back, and another from her, and they put it in a jar. And they put chemicals in to revive the dead worms, and the worms start to grow in a jar, and it becomes a child – not a jar like pickles, [but] like an aquarium where the child grows for seven to nine months, and they put it in a nursery. The woman has to stay on her back all the time."

Thus, following the airing of the *tamsīlīya*, "*ṭifl l-anābīb*" became a household word in

Egypt, although, as apparent in this woman's description, few Egyptians understood much about how "babies of the tubes" were actually created or how many had been born in Egypt. The misleading rumor that many test-tube babies had in fact been born in the country was perpetuated by publicity surrounding the eventual birth in Cairo of IVF quadruplets to a woman who had been infertile for seventeen years.

Although most of the national publicity about IVF in Egypt emanated from Cairo, where the first private IVF center was established in 1986 (Serour, El Ghar, and Mansour 1990), Alexandria, too, became the site of major IVF activity, with the emergence of both a private IVF clinic and a public program at the government's military hospital. However, both of these IVF pilot programs failed to produce any "babies of the tubes" and were discontinued almost immediately.

Nevertheless, having begun a successful AIH (artificial insemination by husband) program, administrators at Shatby Hospital decided to continue with plans to expand their assisted reproductive technology program to include IVF. Laboratory supplies necessary for IVF were ordered from abroad; extra laboratory personnel were hired; research projects involving IVF were designed; and IVF candidates such as Sakina were selected from the patient population and enlisted in the IVF program. Furthermore, as noted previously, a widely read national newsmagazine called *October* – equivalent to *Time* or *Newsweek* in the United States – announced in a lengthy article that Shatby Hospital had begun its own "baby of the tubes" program. This article alone brought hundreds of women to the hospital hoping to undergo IVF. Some were women who had undergone unsuccessful IVF trials in Cairo or Alexandria; some were women who had discovered that they could not afford the costs associated with IVF in a private center; and some were simply infertile women who thought that a "baby of the tubes" might provide the long-awaited solution to their infertility problems.

Of the hundreds of infertile women who came to Shatby seeking IVF, only a small number (including 15 percent of the infertile women in this study), actually entered the IVF program as

candidates. Most of these women were those with confirmed bilateral tubal obstruction, for whom AIH was not possible and IVF was their only real hope for achieving pregnancy.

Women's Concerns

Yet, for these women, most of whom were poor, their eagerness to undergo IVF was tempered by numerous practical and moral concerns, similar to those described for AIH, but of a slightly different order. Their questions about IVF, as we shall see, revolved not only around its expense and religious permissibility, but around the complicated "mechanics" of a new reproductive technology in which the technological imperative of biomedicine is perhaps quintessentially embodied.

What kind of "tube"?

Many Egyptians, both men and women alike, were troubled by IVF because of the difficult question of "tubes." As we have seen, many Egyptian women had heard about women's "tubes" (that is, fallopian tubes) and realized that their blockage constituted a major infertility problem. Yet, the structure and function of these tubes and their location in relation to other female reproductive organs were subjects only partially understood by most women, who viewed the uterus and ovaries as the major female reproductive parts. As IVF became popularized in Egypt, however, many women came to realize that "babies of the tubes" were for infertile women with blocked tubes. But were these "tubes" of the same kind?

After seeing the soap opera, many Egyptians came to surmise that the term "baby of the tubes" actually referred to babies conceived and even interned in glass tubes during the course of gestation. Naturally, the thought of babies "artificially produced" in glass test tubes was one most disturbing to Egyptian men and women, whose convictions about the necessity of natural, God-given conception, childbirth, and parent-child ties were extremely strong. As a result, many Egyptians suspected that IVF was most certainly *harām*, or forbidden, as reflected in women's discourse on the subject. As women explained:

> They've just invented test tubes and everything two years ago. I consider a child brought this way not to be my own child. It's not the same as when you carry a child in your body. These artificial ways don't feel the same – the tenderness and love.

> It's not the same as when you carry the child inside you and suffer with it. It's as if you're taking it from someone else. It grows outside the womb of the mother, so it's like going and getting it "ready-made."

> They say they put a tube into the woman and after nine months, she delivers normally. But what would the father feel? If the father does have a child, will he still love the one of the test tube? This is *ḥarām*, of course, because God stopped your pregnancy, so you come and put in tubes? It's as if you're saying, "God didn't give me, so we'll get her pregnant."

A number of important themes emerge from these and other women's statements. First, women were extremely concerned about the "artificial versus natural" creation of fetuses "outside versus inside" women's bodies. In a Muslim country where adoption is prohibited by Islamic law, parenthood is synonymous with "natural" (that is, biological) parenthood, which, for most Muslims, is tantamount to the gestation *inside a woman's body* of her own husband's fetus. Fetuses that are viewed as being gestated outside the woman's body – even if produced through the conceptive substance(s) of husband and wife – are not only deemed unnatural, but, like orphans, would be viewed as strangers by a husband and wife, who will therefore lack appropriate parental sentiments. In addition, many women feared the unknown aspects of IVF, including the dubious origin of the products of conception used in the procedure (which, unlike AIH, could come from both male, and female donors); the excessive experimentation on women's bodies, and the tampering with natural processes best left to God. Indeed, women's ultimate fears were of God himself, whose will would be defied if human beings were to attempt to "play God" through the production of man-made babies.

In addition, as reflected in women's statements, considerable confusion existed over the mechanics of IVF, fueling women's concerns about the artificiality of the process, especially the perplexing aspect of prolonged extracorporeal gestation. Given the lack of disclosure on the part of physicians, even women who were being considered or prepared for the procedure could only speculate as to the technical aspects of IVF, based on what they could deduce from the news media, from the infamous soap opera, or from physicians' veiled comments. Because these sources provided only cursory explanations, most women's understandings about the nature of IVF were superficial at best.

Women who were better informed about the mechanical aspects of IVF understood that the procedure involved the initial creation of the embryo outside of the woman's womb through a process that involved extraction of the woman's reproductive component (although few were sure of what this was) and mixture of this component with the husband's component (either "worms," "fluid," or "spermatic animals") in a glass container, or tube. After some period of time, ranging in women's minds from twenty-four hours to three months, the fetus, kept in a "machine" or "incubator" during this period "outside," was returned to the woman's uterus through a process of "injection," as in AIH.[1]

Yet, even women who understood the basic aspects of the procedure were often misinformed about important details. As one such woman explained, "The first thing, they get the sperm. They take one of the eggs out. They mix it in something that looks like a uterus, a glass or a tube. Then they ask her if she wants a boy or a girl. They choose the right worm, and they put it in the thing that looks like the uterus of the woman, and they leave it for three months. After that, they do a very small operation with two stitches and put it back in her uterus. Then she is pregnant."

Women who had some idea about the technical aspects of IVF were usually less likely to view the procedure as morally or religiously forbidden, as an act "going against God." In fact, these women, most of whom were infertile, were more likely to laud IVF as the best exemplar of medical progress. As one such advocate of high-tech reproductive medicine explained, "Now medicine is very advanced. In the old days, lots of people couldn't have kids. But now we have 'tubes babies.'" Another commented, "We see that infertility was there ever since the Prophet's time, only then they didn't have test tubes and things that they have now. So now a woman can go and plant a child in a test tube and have her own baby, but she couldn't do that long ago. This is because science has become very advanced."

Accepted by Islam?

Because of their superior knowledge of the technical aspects of the IVF procedure – including the use of a husband's sperm and wife's ova – infertile women were also more likely than others to accept IVF as religiously permitted. Although a *fatwā*, or formal Islamic legal opinion, on the permissibility of IVF was issued by the grand *shaikh* of Al-Azhar Mosque, Shaikh Gad El Hak Ali Gad El Hak, as early as March 23, 1980 (El Hak 1981), few Egyptians were aware of the *shaikh*'s pronouncement even by the end of the decade. In his opinion, the *shaikh* clearly specified that IVF was an acceptable line of treatment as long as it was carried out by expert scientists with sperm from a husband and eggs from a wife with "no mixing with other cells from other couples or other species, and ... the conceptus is implanted in the uterus of the same wife from whom the ova were taken" (Aboulghar, Serour, and Mansour 1990).

Infertile women who were being considered for IVF tended to be best informed about this theological opinion, having sought advice from religious clerics in some cases. Yet, many women, both infertile and fertile, continued to doubt that Islam would permit such a "strange and unnatural" act as the creation by physicians of a "ready-made child" from "outside the womb." As with AIH, women's husbands tended to be even more doubtful, creating problems for women who were thus thrust into the position of convincing their husbands of IVF's religious permissibility.

However, many Egyptians' anxieties about the religious permissibility of IVF were relieved

when the popular televised Muslim cleric, Shaikh Muhammad Mitwali al-Shaarawi, condoned the use of IVF (with husbands' sperm and wives' ova) as a last resort for infertile couples. Yet, many Egyptians – and especially the fertile, who were less attuned to such matters – were not aware of Shaarawi's statements, as reflected in the high percentages of those who believed IVF to be *ḥarām* or were unsure of its religious permissibility.

How successful is IVF?

In addition to these moral-religious concerns, another major question in the minds of infertile women was whether or not IVF was successful in most cases. For poor women, such information was crucial, given the expense of the procedure. As with AIH, women were usually shocked to learn that IVF was not free, even in a public hospital, and that the major expense revolved around purchasing ovulation-inducing agents that could cost anywhere from five hundred to one thousand Egyptian pounds (two hundred to four hundred dollars) per treatment cycle. This problem of expense was coupled with the problem of availability; ... "new-age" ovulation-inducing agents necessary for IVF were often obtained from abroad and were not widely available in most Egyptian pharmacies.

When women being prepared for IVF learned that one thousand pounds might purchase them only one trial of IVF – and that up to six trials might be necessary without any guarantee of reproductive success – their enthusiasm for the procedure naturally waned. For this reason, success rates were rarely conveyed by physicians, although women were obviously curious to know whether amounts exceeding one thousand pounds would "buy" them a baby. Women often noted that they would spend all the money they could muster on IVF if only it would guarantee them a pregnancy outcome. What they were rarely told, however, was that pregnancy rates in the world's best IVF centers were often less than 30 percent (Jones 1988), and that success rates in start-up programs, such as the one at this hospital, could be expected to be much less. In essence, then, Egyptian women being prepared for IVF had minimal guarantees of success, although most of them did not realize this.

How soon, if ever?

Given that many women with bilateral fallopian tubal blockage came to view IVF as their last resort – their "only hope" in their quest for conception – the realization that the highly touted IVF program had yet to become a reality at the hospital more than a year after its promised inception was also a source of frustration and fear for many women, especially those like Sakina who had promptly purchased expensive IVF drugs in preparation for the procedure. When women who had purchased these drugs were told to "sell them back" to pharmacies before their expiration dates, IVF candidates began to panic, criticizing the hospital for false advertising of its program. Questions that had once been framed by IVF candidates as "how soon?" came to be posed as "will there ever be?" Unfortunately, by the end of the 1980s, IVF had yet to become a reality at Shatby Hospital, because of numerous political, economic, and logistical problems beyond the control of those who had hoped to make the IVF program a success.

Epilogue

After many delays, the long-awaited inception of the IVF program at Shatby Hospital occurred in the early months of 1991, almost two and a half years after the announcement of the program in *October* magazine. The equipment necessary to run an IVF laboratory was slow in coming to Alexandria, but by early 1991, it had arrived, and soon thereafter the IVF laboratory and an accompanying andrology laboratory for high-tech semen analysis were in place. A team of young physicians, several of whom were trained in IVF in the United States and Great Britain, was assembled to run the assisted reproduction program (both AIH and IVF) in the hospital.

The first delivery of an Alexandrian "baby of the tubes" occurred in early 1992, only ten months after the IVF program's inception. The baby was delivered by cesarean by the gynecology professor who had referred the case, and members of the Egyptian media, including those from the television, radio, newspapers, and magazines, were received during the delivery by the head of the IVF program, who was also the chairman of the University of Alexandria Department of Obstetrics and Gynaecology.

In addition, at the time of this writing, there are five or six ongoing IVF pregnancies at Shatby Hospital, other than those that have ended in spontaneous abortion. However, there have been some problems in following the IVF pregnancies, because many of the infertile women in the program consider it shameful to have become pregnant through IVF and therefore do not return to the hospital when they discover that they are pregnant with a "baby of the tubes."

It is important to point out in closing that, even as IVF has successfully unfolded in Alexandria, many daunting questions about the implementation and future of IVF in Egypt – similar to those raised by concerned feminists in the West – remain. For example, will the focus on IVF divert attention away from the primary prevention of infertility in Egypt, especially among the poor, who are at greatest risk for infertility but who can least afford the new reproduction technologies? Will the commercialization of IVF in Egypt lead to the proliferation of for-profit clinics run by unscrupulous physicians, whose *raison d'être* is financial gain rather than the reproductive success of women? Will success rates be inflated and massaged in Egypt as they are elsewhere to boost the spirits of physicians and to encourage persistence among patients? Will the choice to undergo IVF turn into pressure for Egyptian women, who will be "compelled to try" IVF over and over again and hence become trapped in endless infertility careers? Will IVF lead to the commodification of life in Egypt, with perfect babies being manufactured and purchased for a significant price only by the affluent? Will IVF reinforce existing patriarchal, pronatalist biases in Egypt, leading to the continuing disenfranchisement of infertile women who have failed in their mandate to reproduce? Will IVF lead to further untoward manipulation of and experimentation on Egyptian women's bodies, such that embryos become the "leading actors" and women mere "living laboratories" for the products of man-made conception? And, finally, will the effectiveness and safety of IVF be monitored in Egypt, given the current absence of professional or consumer bodies concerned with technology assessment and biomedical ethics?

Although the future of IVF in Egypt is quite uncertain, perhaps it is heartening to realize that ethical debates about research in human reproduction have begun to emerge in Egypt and elsewhere in the Muslim world (Anees 1989; Serour 1992), leading to the development of incipient guidelines and standards for the practice of IVF in both research and clinical settings (Serour and Omran 1992). Currently, Egypt leads the way in these efforts to forge a safe path for IVF and the other NRTs in the Muslim world and may very well serve as a model for other Muslim countries attempting to implement these technologies (Serour, El Ghar, and Mansour 1991). As Serour and his Egyptian colleagues note, the total Muslim population in the world is 1.14 billion (1988 estimate), mostly located in developing countries and particularly in Africa and Asia. If one considers that 24 percent of the population of developing countries consists of women of reproductive age and that 10 percent (on average) of all married women of reproductive age experience infertility, then approximately 27 million Muslim women may be currently infertile and may either accept or reject IVF treatment services as they become available (Serour, El Ghar, and Mansour 1991).

Thus, the experiences of poor infertile Egyptian women such as Sakina, as they attempt to grapple with the complex practical and moral dilemmas posed by IVF, may well serve as a guide for the therapeutic journeys of other Muslim women, whose voices and stories have yet to be heard.

NOTE

1   The standard IVF protocol involves nine steps, occurring over four weeks (Harkness 1992), as follows: (1) a woman's current menstrual cycle is halted with gonadotropin-releasing hormone (GnRH) agonists; (2) ovulation is then induced through the administration of fertility drugs for eight to twelve days; (3) ultrasounds and blood tests are performed to monitor the development of ovarian follicles over a six- to twelve-day period; (4) serum progesterone levels are measured to assess the growth of the uterine lining; (5) mature eggs (usually at least four) are retrieved from the woman vaginally through ultrasound-guided aspiration of the follicles; (6) ova and sperm (obtained through the male partner's masturbation) are prepared in the laboratory and then combined for fertilization and cell division over a period of about forty-eight hours; (7) embryos emerging through the fertilization process are transferred (injected by a catheter) into the woman's uterus through the cervix within two days of egg retrieval; (8) the woman receives hormonal support, usually progesterone, for the first eight to ten weeks of pregnancy or until menstruation occurs; and (9) a pregnancy test is usually performed ten to twelve days after an IVF transfer.

REFERENCES

Aboulghar, M. A., G. I. Serour, and R. Mansour
    1990   "Some Ethical and Legal Aspects of Medically Assisted Reproduction in Egypt." *International Journal of Bioethics* 1:265–8.
Anees, Munawar Ahmad
    1989   *Islam and Biological Futures: Ethics, Gender and Technology.* London: Mansell.
dos Reis, Ana Regina Gomez
    1987   "IVF in Brazil: The Story Told by the Newspapers." In *Made to Order: The Myth of Reproductive and Genetic Progress,* ed. Patricia Spallone and Deborah Lynn Steinberg, 120–31. Oxford: Pergamon.
El Hak, Gad El Hak Ali Gad
    1981   *Medically Assisted Reproduction. Fatwii.* Cairo: Al-Azhar University.
Harkness, Carla
    1992   *The Infertility Book: A Comprehensive Medical & Emotional Guide.* Berkeley, CA: Calactial Arts.
Jones, Howard W., Jr.
    1988   "Recent Advances in In Vitro Fertilization (IVF)." In *Human Reproduction: Current Status/Future Prospect,* ed. R. Iizuka and K. Semm, 65–79. Amsterdam: Elsevier.

Serour, Gamal I., ed.
   1992   *Proceedings of the First International Conference on "Bioethics in Human Reproduction Research in the Muslim World."* Cairo: International Islamic Center for Population Studies & Research, Al-Azhar University.
Serour, Gamal I., and A. R. Omran
   1992   *Ethical Guidelines for Human Reproduction Research in the Muslim World.* Cairo: International Islamic Center for Population Studies & Research, Al Azhar University.
Serour, G. I., M. El Ghar, and R. T. Mansour
   1990   "In Vitro Fertilization and Embryo Transfer, Ethical Aspects in Techniques in the Muslim World." *Population Sciences* 9:45–54.
   1991   "Infertility: A Health Problem in Muslim World." *Population Sciences* 10:41–58.

25

AIDS in 2006
Moving toward One World, One Hope?

Jim Yong Kim and Paul Farmer

For the past two decades, AIDS experts – clinicians, epidemiologists, policymakers, activists, and scientists – have gathered every two years to confer about what is now the world's leading infectious cause of death among young adults. This year, the International AIDS Society is hosting the meeting in Toronto from August 13 through 18. The last time the conference was held in Canada, in 1996, its theme was "One World, One Hope." But it was evident to conferees from the poorer reaches of the world that the price tag of the era's great hope – combination antiretroviral therapy – rendered it out of their reach. Indeed, some African participants that year made a banner reading "One World, No Hope."

Today, the global picture is quite different. The claims that have been made for the efficacy of antiretroviral therapy have proved to be well founded: in the United States, such therapy has prolonged life by an estimated 13 years[1] – a success rate that would compare favorably with that of almost any treatment for cancer or complications of coronary artery disease. In addition, a number of lessons, with implications for policy and action, have emerged from efforts that are well under way in the developing world. During the past decade, we have gleaned these lessons from our work in setting global AIDS policies at the World Health Organization in Geneva and in implementing integrated programs for AIDS prevention and care in places such as rural Haiti and Rwanda. As vastly different as these places may be, they are part of one world, and we believe that ambitious policy goals, adequate funding, and knowledge about implementation can move us toward the elusive goal of shared hope.

The first lesson is that charging for AIDS prevention and care will pose insurmountable problems for people living in poverty, since there will always be those unable to pay even modest amounts for services or medications, whether generic or branded. Like efforts to battle airborne tuberculosis, such services should be seen as a public good for public health. Policymakers and public health officials, especially in heavily burdened regions, should adopt universal-access plans and waive fees for HIV care. Initially, this approach will require sustained donor contributions, but many African countries have recently set

Jim Yong Kim and Paul Farmer, Kim, "AIDS in 2006: Moving toward One World, One Hope?" *New England Journal of Medicine* 355/7 (2006): 645–7.

targets for increased national investments in health, a pledge that could render ambitious programs sustainable in the long run.

As local investments increase, the price of AIDS care is decreasing. The development of generic medications means that antiretroviral therapy can now cost less than 50 cents per day, and costs continue to decrease to affordable levels for public health officials in developing countries. All antiretroviral medications – first-line, second-line, and third-line – must be made available at such prices. Manufacturers of generic drugs in China, India, and other developing countries stand ready to provide the full range of drugs. Whether through negotiated agreements or use of the full flexibilities of the Agreement on Trade-Related Aspects of Intellectual Property Rights, full access to all available antiretroviral drugs must quickly become the standard in all countries.

Second, the effective scale-up of pilot projects will require the strengthening and even rebuilding of health care systems, including those charged with delivering primary care. In the past, the lack of a health care infrastructure has been a barrier to antiretroviral therapy; we must now marshal AIDS resources, which are at last considerable, to rebuild public health systems in sub-Saharan Africa and other HIV-burdened regions. These efforts will not weaken efforts to address other problems – malaria and other diseases of poverty, maternal mortality, and insufficient vacination coverage – if they are planned deliberately with the public sector in mind.[2] Only the public sector, not nongovernmental organizations, can offer health care as a right.

Third, a lack of trained health care personnel, most notably doctors, is invoked as a reason for the failure to treat AIDS in poor countries. The lack is real, and the brain drain continues. But one reason doctors flee Africa is that they lack the tools of their trade. AIDS funding offers us a chance not only to recruit physicians and nurses to underserved regions, but also to train community health care workers to supervise care, for AIDS and many other diseases, within their home villages and neighborhoods. Such training should be undertaken even in places where physicians are abundant, since community-based, closely supervised care represents the highest standard of care for chronic disease,[3] whether in the First World or the Third. And community health care workers must be compensated for their labor if these programs are to be sustainable.

Fourth, extreme poverty makes it difficult for many patients to comply with antiretroviral therapy. Indeed, poverty is far and away the greatest barrier to the scale-up of treatment and prevention programs. Our experience in Haiti and Rwanda has shown us that it is possible to remove many of the social and economic barriers to adherence but only with what are sometimes termed "wrap-around services": food supplements for the hungry, help with transportation to clinics, child care, and housing. In many rural regions of Africa, hunger is the major coexisting condition in patients with AIDS or tuberculosis, and these consumptive diseases cannot be treated effectively without food supplementation.[4] Coordination among initiatives such as the President's Emergency Plan for AIDS Relief, the Global Fund to Fight AIDS, Tuberculosis, and Malaria, and the World Food Program of the United Nations can help in the short term; fair-trade agreements and support of African farmers will help in the long run.

Fifth, investments in efforts to combat the global epidemics of AIDS and tuberculosis are much more generous than they were five years ago, but funding must be increased and sustained if we are to slow these increasingly complex epidemics. One of the most ominous recent developments is the advent of highly drug-resistant strains of both causative pathogens. "Extensively drug-resistant tuberculosis" has been reported in the United States, Eastern Europe, Asia, South Africa, and elsewhere; in each of these settings, the copresence of HIV has amplified local epidemics of these almost untreatable strains. Drug-resistant malaria is now common world-wide, extensively drug-resistant HIV disease will surely follow, and massive efforts to diagnose and treat these diseases ethically and effectively will be needed. We have already learned a great deal about how best to expand access to second-line antituberculous drugs while increasing control over their use[5]; these lessons must be applied in the struggles against AIDS, malaria, and other infectious pathogens.

Finally, there is a need for a renewed basic-science commitment to vaccine development, more reliable diagnostics (the 100-year-old tests widely used to diagnose tuberculosis are neither specific nor sensitive), and new classes of therapeutics. The research-based pharmaceutical industry has a critical role to play in drug development, even if the overall goal is a segmented market, with higher prices in developed countries and generic production with affordable prices in developing countries.

There has been a heartening increase in basic-science investments for tuberculosis and malaria; funding for HIV research at the National Institutes of Health remains robust. Yet the fruits of such research will not arrive in time for those now living with, and dying from, AIDS and tuberculosis. New tools to prevent, diagnose, and treat the diseases of poverty will be added to the stockpile of other potentially lifesaving products that do not reach the poorest people, unless we develop an equity plan to provide them. Right now, our focus must be on improving access to the therapies that are available in high-income countries. The past few years have shown us that we can make these services available to millions, even in the poorest reaches of the world.

The unglamorous and difficult process of increasing access to prevention and care needs to be our primary focus if we are to move toward the lofty goal of equitably distributed medical services in a world riven by inequality. Without such goals, the slogan "One World, One Hope" will remain nothing more than a dream.

NOTES

1. Walensky RP, Paltiel AD, Losina E, et al. The survival benefits of AIDS treatment in the United States. J Infect Dis 2006;194:11–9.

2. Walton DA, Farmer PE, Lambert W, Léandre F, Koening SP, Mukherjee JS. Integrated HIV prevention and care strengthens primary health care: lessons from rural Haiti. J Public Health Policy 2004;25:137–58.

3. Behforouz HL, Farmer PE, Mukherjee JS. From directly observed therapy to *accompagnateurs*: enhancing AIDS treatment outcomes in Haiti and in Boston. Clin Infect Dis 2004; 38:Suppl 5:S429–S436.

4. Paton NI, Sangeetha S, Earnest A, Bellamy R. The impact of malnutrition on survival and the CD4 count response in HIV-infected patients starting antiretroviral therapy. HIV Med 2006;7:323–30.

5. Gupta R, Kim JY, Espinal MA, et al. Responding to market failures in tuberculosis control. Science 2001;293:1049–51.

Part V
Biosciences, Biotechnologies

Introduction

Anthropologists and ethnographers have paid attention to laboratory life and the demarcations of science and practical knowledge since the early decades of the twentieth century when Fleck's monograph on moral accounts of syphilis and the scientific Wasserman test (1935), Malinowski's observations on practical knowledge and mythic charters of social knowledge (1948), Evans-Pritchard's work on how the needs of moral as well as practical explanations for illness and death can involve also protection of explanatory systems from falsification (1937), and Levi-Strauss's speculative essay on the homological interactions between neurological, physiological, performative, and cognitive-cultural systems in hysterical conversion reactions and difficult childbirth (1949) provided the beginnings of what today is known as science studies. Laboratory studies proper got their start with Latour and Woolgar's ethnography of a neuroendocrinology lab at the Salk Institute (1979), Latour's historical examination of Pasteur's bacteriology lab (1984), and Sharon Traweek's work in the high energy physics labs at the Stanford linear accelerator and Japan's KEK lab in Tskuba science city (1988). In the last two decades, anthropologists have had a powerful hand in creating new kinds of science studies by challenging and reshaping the canon of science, technology, and society (STS) that was dominated in the 1980s by social studies of knowledge (SSK), social construction of technology (SCOT), philosophy of science, and history of (scientific) ideas (Fischer 2003, 2009). In the past decade, this work has become more deeply linked with medical anthropology.

This part explores five intersections between medical anthropology and the emergent field of science, technology, and society involving the critical roles of (1) the physician-scientist; (2) epistemic things and experimental systems; (3) living tissue as tools for research and therapy; (4) instruments that displace and mediate perception; and (5) heterogeneous distributed organizational models.

The opening essay by Michael M. J. Fischer provides a map of the bioscience and biotechnology terrain in the wake of the transformations of the Bayh-Dole Act of

1980, which encouraged universities with federal funding to transfer technologies to the market for development and therapeutic use, and the Chakrabarty vs. Diamond Supreme Court decision, also in 1980, which opened the flood gates to patenting of human-made micro-organisms as a manufacture or composition of matter. It does this through an account of (1) a physician-scientist, Dr. Judah Folkman, (2) a program of research (angiogenesis inhibitors as a way to cut off blood supply to cancer tumors), and (3) a series of ten hurdles and obstacles in the path of getting basic science through the development pipeline into therapeutic use.

The second essay, by molecular biologist and historian Hans-Jörg Rheinberger, provides a historical transect through biotechnologies that have transformed the way we think of our biological nature and now are troubling our policy debates. We no longer are merely discovering biology, but now writing with biology and creating things that never before existed. Traditional distinctions (discovery/invention, nature/culture, structure/freedom, ethics/ontology, soteriology/phenomenology) collapse, upsetting policy debates, and opening up new questions. Is genetic engineering or stem cell research "unnatural"? What would that even mean? If they are just cultural choices, then what are their social or ecological implications?

Hannah Landecker's essay (Landecker 2000) is one of her investigations into tissue technologies as part of the biomedical effort to learn how to tap into the regenerative repair systems of the body (Landecker 2007). Her topics of investigation span early efforts to keep organs alive outside the body, to transfuse blood, to make organ transplantation work, and to immortalize cell lines as tools for research. The first immortalized cell line, HeLa, named after an African American woman, Henrietta Lacks, provides a wonderful case for exploring social and cultural entanglements. Initially HeLa was a neutral tool disseminated freely among researchers. However, in the 1960s it became racialized and politicized as non-HeLa lines seemed to be contaminated by HeLa ones, and in the 1990s it was reframed as a commodity with monetary value. In the first decade of the twenty-first century, the lack of understanding of how mouse or hamster cells and fragments of human cells interact in the making and passaging of immortalized lines would bedevil debates over human embryonic stem cell line research. When President George W. Bush (2001–2009) limited the spending of federal research funds to already established embryonic stem cell lines, many were found unusable for exploring human stem cells because they were passaged on mouse cell matrices.

Contests over patenting, ownership, informed consent, who controls the use of tissue for research, and even the directions of research became increasingly layered in the 1990s. Landecker has written about the suit by John Moore against the University of California over appropriation of his hairy leukemia cells to make an immortalized line for research without his knowledge, claiming that he should have the right to give the cells to researchers of his own choosing (Landecker 1998).

More recently patient groups have pioneered not just fundraising to get researchers to work on their "orphan diseases" (diseases with too few patients to draw investment interest from pharmaceutical or biotech companies), nor just provision of tissues and willing medical subjects, but also new legal agreements to share patenting and licensing that give patients some voice in how to direct research (e.g. PXE [pseudoxanthoma elasticum] International, the LAM [lymphoangioleiomytosis] Treatment Alliance).

The next essay by Joe Dumit explores how knowledge circulates and how it is transformed as it moves along feedback loops from lab to clinic to media to lay-people; and also how instruments, visuals, advertisements, and drugs are used as technologies of what Dumit dubs "objective self fashioning," that is, the use of objects as templates for stabilizing the self. These core themes frame Joe Dumit's *Picturing Personhood* (2005) and *Drugs for Life* (2010 forthcoming) as well as Nathan Greenslit's work (2007) on direct to consumer marketing of pharmaceuticals and Emily Martin's research on the medicalization of women's bodies, immunology, and bipolar disorders (1987, 1994, 2008). Dumit's essay on the creation of the PET (positron emission tomography) scan machine provides an exemplar of how differently its images are interpreted by its designers, radiologists, brain researchers, the media, families of schizophrenics, and courtroom judges. Images for scientific publications are selected for the sharpest contrasts, and media tend to mislabel scans as "pictures" of ill versus normal brains, a mislabeling reinforced by courtroom lawyers arguing insurance or insanity cases and preferred by families of schizophrenics who want it to be a biological disease not one of family dynamics, and who in turn were sources of funding for developing one of the first PET machines. The superimposition today of CT scans and PET makes slippages between the flow of blood, oxygen use, and glucose metabolism on the one hand, and anatomical pictures of ill brains on the other, a little less compelling.

Similar slippages occur when the pharmaceutical industry adjusts the statistics of genetic predispositions, the thresholds at which drugs are indicated, and the segmentation of markets through advertising, especially in emotionally targeted, intellectually playful, and inclusively "knowing" infomercials that recruit consumers by having them take self-diagnostic surveys. We are all "patients in waiting" in a postgenomic world where we each carry mutations with their profiles of predispositions, under unknowable conditions, for risk of illness. "Patients in waiting" are resources for "surplus health" extraction, analogous to political economy "surplus value" extraction (Dumit 2010 forthcoming; Petryna 2002, 2005, 2009; Sunder Rajan 2010 forthcoming).

Increasingly we are dependent upon instruments that see beyond the human eye, aggregate or package information in non-transparent ways, or deal with massive amounts of information beyond the processing capacities of the individual human brain. How databanks are made to interact with one another to generate new hypotheses about toxicogenomics or other fields of complex interactions and accumulations of effect is a rich arena where epistemic things, modeling, and reality checks are challenging puzzles for both scientists and ethnographers of scientific production (Fortun and Fortun 2007; K. Fortun 2001).

Kaushik Sunder Rajan's *Biocapital: The Constitution of Postgenomic Life* (2006) and forthcoming edited volume *Lively Capital* consolidate work in the political economy of biotechnology (Cooper 2008; Rabinow 1996; Petryna 2005, 2009; K. Fortun 2004; M. Fortun 2008; Fortun and Fortun 2007, Hayden, 2003; Peterson 2004). Sunder Rajan places these political economy analyses on a global stage, where populations are being re-stratified in not just biopolitical (national government) or biosocial (patient groups) ways, but also as global experimental subjects and patients in waiting, resources for extraction of surplus health.

REFERENCES

Cooper, Melinda
>2008   *Life as Surplus: Biotechnology and Capitalism in the Neoliberal Era*. Seattle: Washington University Press.

Dumit, Joseph
>1997   "A Digital Image of the Category of the Person." In G. Downey and J. Dumit, eds., *Cyborgs and Citadels: Anthropological Interventions in Emerging Sciences and Technologies*. Santa Fe, NM: School of American Research Press.

Dumit, Joseph
>2005   *Picturing Personhood*. Princeton University Press.

Dumit, Joseph
>2010   *Drugs for Life*. Durham: Duke University Press.

Evans-Pritchard, E. E.
>1937   *Witchcraft, Oracles and Magic among the Azande*. Oxford: Clarendon Press.

Fischer, M. M. J.
>2003   *Emergent Forms of Life and the Anthropological Voice*. Durham: Duke University Press.

Fischer, M. M. J.
>2009   *Anthropological Futures*. Durham: Duke University Press.

Fischer, M. M. J.
>2010   "Lively Biotech and Translational Research." In K. Sunder Rajan, ed., *Lively Capital*. Durham: Duke University Press.

Fleck, Ludwik
>1935   *Entstehung und Entwicklung einer wissenschaftlichen Tatsache. Einführung in die Lehre vom Denkstil und Denkkollektiv*. Schwabe und Co., Verlagsbuchhandlung, Basel. (E. T. 1979. *The Genesis and Development of a Scientific Fact*. Chicago: University of Chicago Press.)

Fortun, Kim
>2001   *Advocacy after Bhopal*. Chicago: University of Chicago Press.

Fortun, Kim
>2004   "From Bhopal to the Informating of Environmental Health: Risk Communication in Historical Perspective, Special Issue." In Gregg Mitman, Michelle Murphy, and Christopher Sellers, eds., *Landscapes of Exposure: Knowledge and Illness in Modern Environments*, OSIRIS 19.

Fortun, Kim and Michael Fortun
>2007   "Experimenting with the Asthma Files." Paper presented at Lively Capital III, University of California, Irvine, April 13–14.
>2007   (Forthcoming in Sunder Rajan, ed., 2010.)

Fortun, Michael
>2008   *Promising Genomics*. Berkeley: University of California.

Greenslit, Nathan
>2007   "Pharmaceutical Relations: Intersections of Illness, Fantasy, and Capital in the Age of Direct-To-Consumer Marketing." PhD dissertation, MIT, HASTS.

Hayden, Cori
>2003   *When Nature Goes Public: The Making and Unmaking of Bioprospecting in Mexico*. Princeton: Princeton University Press.

Landecker, Hannah
>1998   "Between Beneficence and Chattel: The Human Biological in Law and Science." *Science in Context* 12(1):203–25.

Landecker, Hannah
  2000   "Immortality in Vitro: A History of the HeLa Cell Line." In Paul Brodwin, ed., *Biotechnology and Culture*. Bloomington: Indiana University Press.
Landecker, Hannah
  2007   *Culturing Life: How Cells Became Technologies*. Cambridge, MA: Harvard University Press.
Latour, Bruno
  1984   *Microbes: Guerre et Paix*. Paris: Métailié. (E.T., 1993, *The Pasteurization of France*. Cambridge, MA: Harvard University Press.)
Latour, Bruno and Steve Woolgar
  1979   *Laboratory Life: The Construction of Scientific Facts*. Princeton: Princeton University Press.
Lévi-Strauss, Claude
  1949   *The Effectiveness of Symbols*. English Translation, *Structural Anthropology*. New York: Basic Books (1973).
Malinowski, Bronislaw
  1948   *Magic, Science and Religion, and Other Essays*. New York: Free Press.
Martin, Emily
  1987   *The Woman in the Body*. Boston: Beacon Press.
Martin, Emily
  1994   *Flexible Bodies: Tracking Immunity in American Culture from the Days of Polio to the Age of AIDS*. Boston: Beacon Press.
Martin, Emily
  2008   *Bipolar Expeditions: Mania and Depression in American Culture*. Princeton: Princeton University Press.
Peterson, Kris
  2004   "HIV/AIDS and Democracy in Nigeria: Policies, Rights, and Therapeutic Economies." PhD dissertation, Rice University.
Petryna, Adriana
  2002   *Life Exposed: Biological Citizens after Chernobyl*. Princeton: Princeton University Press.
Petryna, Adriana
  2005   "Ethical Variability: Drug Development and Globalizing Clinical Trials." *American Ethnologist*, 32(2).
Petryna, Adriana
  2009   *When Experiments Travel: Clinical Trials and the Global Search for Human Subjects*. Princeton: Princeton University Press.
Petryna, A., Lakoff, and A. Kleinman, A., eds.
  2006   *Global Pharmaceuticals: Ethics, Markets, Practices*. Durham: Duke University Press.
Rabinow, Paul
  1996   *Making PCR*. Chicago: University of Chicago Press.
Rheinberger, Hans Jörg
  1997   *Toward a History of Epistemic Things: Synthesizing Proteins in the Test Tube*. Stanford: Stanford University Press.
Rheinberger, Hans Jörg
  2000a   "Beyond Nature and Culture: Modes of Reasoning in the Age of Molecular Biology and Medicine." In M. Lock, A. Young, and A. Cambrosio, eds., *Living and Working with the New Medical Technologies*. New York, Cambridge: Cambridge University Press.

Rheinberger, Hans Jörg
    2000b "Cytoplasmic Particles: The Trajectory of a Scientific Object." In L. Daston, ed., *Biographies of Scientific Objects*. Chicago: University of Chicago Press.

Rheinberger, Hans Jörg
    2000c "Gene Concepts: Fragments from the Perspective of Molecular Biology." In P. J. Beurton, R. Falk, H.-J. Rheinberger, eds., *The Concept of the Gene in Development and Evolution*. Cambridge: Cambridge University Press, pp. 219–39.

Sunder Rajan, Kaushik
    2006   *Biocapital: The Constitution of Postgenomic Life*. Durham: Duke University Press.

Sunder Rajan, Kaushik
    2007 "Experimental Values: Indian Clinical Trials and Surplus Health." *New Left Review*. 45:67–88.

Sunder Rajan, Kaushik, ed.
    2010   *Lively Capital*. Durham, NC: Duke University Press.

Traweek, Sharon
    1988   *Beamtimes and Lifetimes*. Cambridge, MA: Harvard University Press.

26

Dr. Judah Folkman's Decalogue and Network Analysis

Michael M. J. Fischer[1]

Translation to the clinic proceeds along a pathway strewn with obstacles, and it's actually harder than making the discovery because it involves other people, and involves all their different views. (Judah Folkman, 21 September 1999)

In a wonderfully comic but serious account of the changing sites of medical discovery, Judah Folkman lays out ten reasons, a decalogue, that it is nearly impossible to get discoveries from the lab into the clinic. He begins with a quick survey of the shift from discoveries made by physicians at the bedside in the nineteenth and early twentieth century, to the need for laboratories and the rise of the physician-scientist often fostered by training at NIH in the mid twentieth century, to today the increasing difficulties of maintaining the dual career of physician-scientist, and the disjunctures caused by new discoveries coming increasingly from basic scientists without much clinical experience and unaware of many important clinical clues. It is no accident, he suggests, that angiogenesis research began in a surgical laboratory (his), not in a molecular laboratory. In a molecular laboratory, like that of his good friend Robert Weinberg, he joked, one thinks of the life of cells that are flat, while surgeons like himself think that cells are crowded like they are in cancer tumors. It is for that reason that programs like the Health, Science, and Technology Program, the joint MIT-Harvard MD/PhD program, were founded to bring the two cultures of basic science and clinical practice together, to solve the problem of the disappearing physician-scientist, and to not leave things to the pharmaceutical companies without using clinical clues.

Folkman describes a series of different career paths among his colleagues who maintain both labs and clinical practice, and the difficulties they face. Chief among the difficulties is "translation." Indeed, he estimates, some forty percent of the medical school faculty would say their obligation is only to do basic work in the laboratory and publish. "They say you have no obligation to get into the problems of translating to the clinic because it is a political morass ... the other half of the faculty feels that if you find something that could improve the care of patients, it would be unethical not to help in some way guiding it into the clinic." He uses his own experience with a new protein that has anti-cancer activity that his lab published in *Science* in 1999, a potent

Michael M. J. Fischer, "Lively Biotech and Translational Research." Written especially for this volume.

angiogenesis inhibitor, with no toxicity, many animal tests, known genetics, and made as recombinant in large quantities. Cancer patients are dying at a rate of 1500 a day in the US, one an hour of melanoma, or half a million deaths a year. So what are the obstacles to actually getting this protein into the clinic?

The decalogue of obstacles includes: (1) patenting, (2) the break up of collaborations, (3) "their culture has to fit your proteins," (4) internal company rejection ("it's always in the cafeteria"), (5) transferring skills (the Stradivarius problem), (6) Fridays are cancellation days, (7) clinical trials, (8) "for your little protein, change a million dollar manufacturing process?," (9) physician resistance, (10) stock manipulations.

1 Patenting

Idealistic students like to think that patents are unnecessary, everything should be in the public domain. We have ten micrograms, the gene, the cDNA, all the assays, and we want to go to a company to make ten kilos, enough to treat a hundred patients for one year. No patent, they will not even talk. That's not the only problem, and it is not merely that an ethical shift had to occur institutionally and professionally. Before 1974 the Harvard Medical School and its hospitals did not have a patent policy: the policy was to publish, to put all research in the public domain. (MIT has had a patent policy since 1900.) The view was that it was not ethical to patent because you should not be making money based on patients' illnesses. Folkman, deadpans, "Then they found out that was actually okay, because most of the patents do not make any money. In fact, nobody makes much money on these kinds of patents. And the reason is ... by the time the FDA has approved it, eight years, by the time it has gone into the market and has been allowed to be used, it is fifteen years, the patents have run out."

2 The Break Up of Collaborations

The second problem comes with the assignment by the lawyers of one of the co-authors of a scientific paper with the status of inventor. It is a classic transition from gift economies of affluence to capitalized economies of scarcity, the accent being on the ethical transitions. The attorneys are thinking about challenges to the patents: a patent will always be challenged if it is worth anything. It will be infringed upon and the infringers will say "sue us." In court tests, patents show their weaknesses and can be invalidated. The more people are named as inventors the easier to show that some of them had nothing to do with the idea, even though they may have helped with the chemistry, or done other things. "If you had collegiality, it goes away in one day." Say you had four authors and the lawyers say the first author is not the inventor. The first author gets upset because although the inventor did the sequencing, the first author thought of it, but the attorneys determine that it was the sequencing that was the first demonstration of principle. The inventor could get all the benefits, even though at this stage no one knows what they are: someone licenses the patent and the licensing fee goes to the inventor; the drug gets into the clinic, and milestone fees have to be paid – to the inventor. Folkman tries to solve the problems ahead of time with written agreements that such fees will be divided between co-authors. But he recalls a ten-year merit award shared with a colleague in San Francisco, talking on the phone, sending things back and forth, publishing together. "And then they sent us some of their cells from which we found a totally unexpected new protein. Harvard patented it, and we said co-inventors. The attorney said 'nothing doing'; just because they sent you the cells does not mean they are inventors. So it made a lot of hard feelings, and we wrote out that we just would equally distribute [whatever proceeds]." It is neither that Harvard is playing hardball, nor that the attorneys are being unmindful of their clients' egalitarian feelings. Rather if a patent is really worth anything, it will be infringed upon and tested in court. For a research group leader, these facts of life mean the need always to repair relationships. Folkman wryly comments, "I just tell you the end result is you lose colleagues. You have to get them back. So a lot of my colleagues ... refuse to patent anything."

3 "Their culture has to fit your protein."

Academic scientists need companies to manufacture larger quantities than they can produce in university laboratories, and to bring it through the regulatory process. But, says Folkman, "It turns out that big companies prefer to make small molecules and small companies prefer to make big proteins." In 1991 Michael Roddey in Folkman's lab discovered angiostatin, one of the first angiogenesis inhibitors that could regress a tumor.

> Here's what happens when you have a new discovery ... and you are funded by National Cancer Institute grants: you go into debt right away because it is unscheduled. Suddenly you have to have ... different equipment ... new mice ... and you have to hire somebody who does protein chemistry. So what you do is, you take money from all the other grants, and immediately you write a grant and hope that in nine months it will be funded and you will pay back. So we did that, but the study section said 'you will never be able to purify this' ... So they turned the grant down. No, now nine months down the road we had a $250,000 deficit in a big lab, and the hospitals will not cover that ... what they do is start turning off your heat, light, salaries. So what do you do next? ... So I wrote to a whole series of companies, all of whose CEOs had been my students: ... president of Merck ... Upjohn ... Lilly, all Harvard Medical School. And I got appointments right away ... However (this is 1991), what would we do with an angiogenesis inhibitor? Nobody understood it, only the scientists understood it.

So he went to biotech start up companies. There were, he said, 129 biotech companies "hanging on for their life in Boston. They have no income. They have three more years of funding. The burn rate is going to close them in two years." But they understood it right away. "They have the most advanced, youngest scientists, they are not yet so conservative because they have not made any money. So they said,

'terrific idea, but we are broke.' They are all in debt. They fear it will take resources away from their idea. So a company is a zero-sum game." In the case of angiostatin there was finally one small company in Maryland, EntreMed, "a tiny company, about eight people, and they had just become capitalized, nothing to do yet. So they took on this project ... and in the bargain we got endostatin and a couple of other things that were discovered because [EntreMed] gave a grant to Children's Hospital."

In the case of anti-angiogenic anti-thrombin, the discovery reported in *Science*, September 17, 1999, the match with Genzyme came about differently. Genzyme was a tiny company at the time, but was one of two that made antithrombin which would be an easier source for the fragment of antithrombin than purifying it from blood (which was how it was discovered). They made antithrombin-3 for people with who get blood clots due to a deficiency of the protein. They made it in transgenic goats. They could get 500 milligrams per liter from goat milk, much more than the best fermenter (75 milligrams, if the E. coli work properly). They had all the patents for the process, and after pasteurizing the milk they had 75% active, and threw out the 25% inactive. Heating it a little longer and adding citrate and from that 25% they could produce the anti-angiogenic anti-thrombin protein. The president and founder of the company was enthusiastic.

4 Company Cultures ("it's always in the cafeteria")

Getting the leadership of a company to adopt the project is not a guarantee that the rest of the company will go along. Companies are zero-sum games, and if the president says we are going to work on this new protein, "it is as if he brought home a second wife ... In his presence everybody is gung ho. But then comes the undermining. It's extremely subtle. It's always in the company cafeteria. I hear it's not working. That's the rumor. Then they talk to the press and they say, well it's from a lab, you can't reproduce the results. It's incredible. You have tremendous, tremendous rumors.

They are afraid that resources will be siphoned off." Folkman had such an experience with Bristol-Meyers. Some companies have strategies for dealing with this: they spin off a new company under a young vice-president, and tell him if he succeeds he will be established in the parent company.

5 The Stradivarius Problem: Transferring Skills

Next is the classic problem of teaching another lab or a company. These are classic problems in science joked over in corridor talk and in such terms as having "good hands," and analyzed more fully by the chemist Michael Polanyi's lectures on *Tacit Knowledge* (1966), the sociologist of science, Harry Collins' account of physics labs (1974), and the historians of science Steven Shapin and Simon Shafer's account of Boyle and the Royal Society's experiments in the seventeenth century (1985). It is a standard problem in the scaling up from experimental systems to industrial production, from systems that are still returning knowledge through their instability and need for skill to reliable high quality-controlled processes.

"If you are a basic scientist, Ph.D., and you get a call, 'we cannot reproduce your results,' it is a chilling sleep-losing experience. It implies you have manipulated the data." Folkman alludes to his headline problems when the NIH claimed they couldn't reproduce his results. When you see someone who has received such a call,

> they are pale white the next morning ... drained; they cannot do any work, they are worried that their theory is over. Now, to a surgeon it is a source of pride ... Surgeons in the locker room refer to this as the Stradivarius problem. Too bad about surgeon Jones that his mortality is twice as high as mine ... They see it as a skill problem, and most of the time that is what it is.

In the National Cancer Institute case, the problems were leaked to the press "because nobody wants to be at fault." It didn't work at NIH, but when the NIH team came up to Boston with their mice, it worked. One of the problems turned out to be room temperature. Mice cannot sweat or shiver. Experiments at MIT had shown that mice are most comfortable at 26° Celsius. Folkman's rooms were thus set at 26°. "One of the [NIH] rooms we went to was at 20°, and we said we could tell this is not right, because in our rooms we sweat when we are in there for hours." So they did an experiment and found at 20° tumors did not grow on the mice. To keep their core temperature at 37°, the only thing the mice could do to conserve heat was to close off blood vessels, vasoconstrict. This was another proof of the anti-angiogenic concept: by vasoconstricting the tumors are starved of blood and cannot grow.

6 Fridays are Cancellation Days: Time-investment Gambles

In big companies, with many competing drug candidates, they cannot have more than eight in the pipeline at a time, so if they suddenly have a new candidate doing well in the clinic and closer to market, they shift resources there. "And suddenly your little project, which is so fantastic, is stopped for two or three years, and there is nothing you can do about it." You have to try to write contracts and licensing agreements that include every foreseeable possibility. "Suppose they decide to sit on it to keep competitors out. It is a business decision, not a moral or any other kind of decision. Then we get the right to take it back and there is a penalty."

In the case of EntreMed and angiostatin, licensing was in 1991 with only a few micrograms; it took until 1994 to publish it in *Cell*; until 1996 to learn how to make the recombinant; and another year to establish what to make it in (yeast, E. coli) in terms of stability, cost, and scale-up. By then, endostatin, which had been discovered later (*Cell* 1997) proved to be easier to be produced and was out by 1999. Folkman says,

> People forget. Proscar, Merck's prostate drug, took twenty-one years from the time it was discovered in the laboratory to the time they could figure out how to make a structure that was stable in a bottle ... The AIDS drugs, which were done at warp speed, were eight

years, and they had everybody working on two shifts at Merck. They paid exorbitant fees for overtime. And still there is a shortage that is massive ... Herceptin, the same way: there's a lottery, a breast cancer lottery, so you can get this good drug or not. Genetech is trying to build a factory, but they cannot make it fast enough.

7 Clinical Trials

Clinical trials present a series of complicated ethical and practical problems: placebos, dose escalation, deployment of hope, selecting who gets into trials, patient migration to higher dose trials (so earlier trials cannot be completed) protocol violations, protecting physicians who decide who gets into the trials, shortages, and difficulties of timely scaling up as soon as good results are assured.

8 "For your little protein, change a multimillion dollar manufacturing process?"

Take the case of a drug that has been proven to work, tumors regress in animals and people, "and you put it in a patient's intravenous and it does not work." It takes awhile to trouble shoot: the problem is that this protein sticks to the polyvinyl plastic in the tubing. Change the tubing? "Try that: there are only three tubing manufacturers in the country. Abbott is the biggest. Change our tubing? Are you out of your mind? For your little protein, we are going to change a multimillion dollar manufacturing process ... it is FDA approved and we have not had any problems? We are not changing our tubing. Make your own tubing." So then change the protein so that it does not stick? If you change the icing, the FDA will say it is a new protein and you will have to start all over. The details of manufacturing, packaging and transporting can have unexpected consequences. Monsanto learned an expensive lesson that stainless steel pipes for fermenters could not be sterilized with steam if they had angles: viruses could harbor in the bends, and

the pipes had to be curved. Similarly, one of Folkman's problems when NIH could not replicate his results eventually turned out to be the dry ice on which all proteins and drugs were shipped in plastic containers. Carbon dioxide gas goes through plastic and within three hours can agglutinate, unfold, denature, or otherwise damage proteins. So new packaging needed to be invented.

9 Physician Resistance

When there is something really new, it is often hard to educate physicians. They are threatened because it takes so long to learn how to do things really well in the clinic. Key examples: Semmelweiss trying to teach people in Prague to wash their hands before delivering a baby to prevent the transmission of streptococcus (childbed mortality was 30%), and being kicked out of the hospital for his efforts; Flory in 1941 unsuccessfully trying to persuade military physicians in England to use penicillin for soldiers dying of streptococcal septima, and having to come to the U.S. before people would listen; resistance to using Tagamet for bleeding ulcers at MGH in the 1960s (when Folkman was chief resident) instead of gastric surgery (a procedure that no one does or knows how to do any more); and Proscar, the prostrate drug, made by Merck that did the same for prostatectomies, but only because Merck mounted an ad campaign directly to older men who insisted they would go to other doctors if their physician continued to refuse prescribing it for them.

A minor problem here is also the insurance companies who can keep saying it is experimental, and as long as they say that, they do not pay for it. More insidious is another element of the market.

10 Stock Manipulations

If a small company like EntreMed begins to have some success, there are short sellers. Someone puts a rumor on the Internet, or a mischievous question: "have you heard that they are having trouble manufacturing, scaling up, or whatever. It is not a statement, just a question. The Securities and Exchange Commission cannot fault you. Others chime in, 'is that true?' Suddenly the stock is down and the company has to be sold. And then another rumor and the stock rises. 'Have you heard about this new publication that says it is okay?' " "It is amazing," Folkman concludes, "this goes on all the time. There are a lot of greedy people."

NOTE

1 While the terms "decalogue" and "network" are mine, in this piece I have tried to capture Folkman's voice. Those, like myself, interested in the actual "music" of science, the expressiveness of how scientists talk, can turn to the longer essay from which this one is condensed, paraphrased and excerpted. Where I have have used quotation marks, these come from my transcriptions of his lectures which he gave permission to tape. Elsewhere I have used his turns of phrase, but it would be tedious and pointless to mark out each fragment with single and double quotation marks. Those interested can turn to the fuller transcriptions. In the longer essay, I place Folkman in a larger global network of "Lively Biotech and Translational Medicine" (in Sunder Rajan, ed., 2010).

REFERENCES

Bielenberg, Diane and Patricia A. D'Amore
2008 "Judah Folkman's Contribution to the Inhibition of Angiogenesis." *Lymphatic Research and Biology* 6(3-4):203–7.
Collins, Harry M.
1974 "The TEA Set: Tacit Knowledge and Scientific Networks." *Science Studies* 4:165–86.
Fischer, Michael M. J.
2010 "Lively Biotech and Translational Medicine." In K. Sunder Rajan, ed., *Lively Capital*. Durham, NC: Duke
O'Reilly M. S., T. Boehm, Y. Shing, N. Fukai, G. Vasios, W. S. Lane, E. Flynn, J. R. Birkhead, B. R. Olsen, and J. Folkman
1997 "Endostatin: An Endogenous Inhibitor of Angiogenesis and Tumor Growth." *Cell* 88:277–85.
Polanyi, Michael
1966 *The Tacit Dimension*. Garden City, NY: Doubleday.
Ribatti, Domenico
2008 "Judah Folkman: A Pioneer in the Study of Angiogensis." *Angiogenesis* (Mar.), 11(1):3–10.
Shapin, Steven and Simon Schaffer
1985 *Leviathan and the Air-Pump: Hobbes, Boyle, and the Experimental Life*. Princeton: Princeton University Press.

27

Beyond Nature and Culture
Modes of Reasoning in the Age of Molecular Biology and Medicine

Hans-Jörg Rheinberger

Introduction

Is there one culture, are there several different cultures of biomedicine? [...] In the context of attempting an anthropology of knowledge, Yehuda Elkana stated almost two decades ago: "There is no general theory of culture or of a cultural system" (1981: 8). This is an apodictic statement, indeed; but it leaves room for crossing boundaries between scientific disciplines, systems of practices, and social contexts, just as molecular biology has overturned the boundaries of the traditional biological disciplines and their academic containment over the past decades. It allows me to follow the "molecularization" of biology with respect to some aspects of medicine, of medical care, and to the concept of health.

In his marvellous book. The *Pasteurization of France* (1988[1984]), Bruno Latour describes the rise of microbiology, its articulation with, and its takeover in the realm of medical practice, of urban sanitation, and of a first wave of biotechnology in *fin-de-siècle* France that quickly swept over Europe as a whole.

The movement became tightly connected with the name of Louis Pasteur (and Robert Koch in Germany). Latour describes the process as an extended chain of translations: "At one end, France; at the other, those who in their laboratories make the microbes visible; in the middle, the hygienists who translate the data from the laboratories into the precepts of hygiene" (1988[1984]: 56). The possibility of the Pasteurian takeover of medicine was grounded in a "shared misunderstanding" (Latour 1988 [1984]: 120). Applied microbiology promised the *prevention* of illness, not just cure, for the whole population. Once successfully disseminated, shared convictions, with their inherent simplicity, turn into misunderstandings. However, it is precisely such misunderstandings that constitute the vehicles for historically effective cultural movements.

Latour's structural description of the Pasteurian revolution comes surprisingly close to the translation chain which characterizes the current project of sequencing the human genome: at one end, the tens of thousands of fragments of the human chromosomes

Hans-Jörg Rheinberger, "Beyond Nature and Culture: Modes of Reasoning in the Age of Molecular Biology and Medicine," in M. Lock, A. Young, and A. Cambrosio, eds., *Living and Working with the New Medical Technologies: Intersections of Inquiry.* New York: Cambridge University Press, 2000. Reprinted by permission of the publisher, The University of Chicago Press chopped up in pieces and kept in the refrigerators of the research laboratories; on the other, the competition of the biotechnology companies for leadership in molecular engineering; and in between, the hospitals, the health agencies, and the criminologists who convert the data of the laboratories into the precepts of a molecular medicine and a DNA-based recognition of health and treatment of illness. The possibility of the molecular takeover of medicine is grounded in another shared misunderstanding: healthy genes, not just cure, for the whole population. Whether this emerging new misunderstanding delivers a realistic picture of the causes and the distribution of diseases in contemporary Western societies is not a matter of discussion in this chapter. It is clear, however, that the prospect of "molecularizing" diseases and their possible cure will have a profound impact on what patients expect from medical help, and on a new generation of doctors' perception of illness. Its effects will by far transcend such major transformations in medical practice as the "Pasteurization" of Europe in the late nineteenth century, or the "antibiotization" of anti-microbial therapy beginning with the Second World War. At any rate, the identification of a mutated gene such as that thought to be responsible for Huntington's disease, on the upper arm of chromosome 4, and other comparable genes, have a good chance these years of covering the front pages of major newspapers. The Huntington disease gene took ten years to be identified. Although the search for such a gene started long before the genome project took shape, it was quickly perceived as one of the achievements of the project. This is the result of the recursive powers of such an endeavour.

Molecular Biology, Gene Technology, and Molecular Medicine

In 1949, the already world-famous, somewhat eccentric protein chemist and Nobel laureate Linus Pauling published an article in *Science*. In this article, he and his colleagues Itano,

Singer and Wells from the California Institute of Technology in Pasadena traced back to an electrostatic charge difference in the oxygen-transporting molecule haemoglobin, what physicians had long since known under the phenomenological term of sickle cell anemia. Pauling accompanied this publication with the publicity-demanding, triumphant accouncement that sickle cell anemia was a "molecular disease" (Pauling et al. 1949). The publication date of this article is often quoted as the birth date of "molecular medicine." Biomedicine promised to open its own, genuine atomic age.

A little less than fifty years later, at the time of this conference, the encompassing project of sequencing the whole human genome is well under way. Conceived around 1985 in the United States, this daunting, molecular genetic piece of big science has meanwhile been capillarized, has grown into a worldwide network, and has spawned additional genome sequencing projects. The whole effort has been budgeted to amount to no less than $3 billion. In view of the diversification of projects, and sources accordingly, that has already taken place, no one will any longer be able to count how much it will have cost in the end. The project itself has set in place a mechanism for dissemination and changing its own boundaries. To paraphrase Latour's characterization of the Pasteurian program, a century earlier, for fighting against microbial diseases: "It is not a question of ideas, theories, opinions. It is a question of ways and means" (Latour 1988 [1984]: 47). Like the Pasteurians, the molecular biologists and the project managers of the National Institutes of Health and the Department of Energy, who initiated the program of molecularizing human medicine, "placed [their] weak forces in ... places where immense social movements showed passionate interest ... [They] followed the demand that those forces were making, but imposed on them a way of formulating that demand to which only [they] possessed the answer, since it required [men] of the laboratory to understand its terms" (Latour 1988[1984]: 71). Those molecular biologists engaged in human genetics attempt to precisely localize all human genes and to sequence the three billion or so building blocks of our genetic heritage in their entirety. One of the most outspoken advocates of the project(s), Nobel prize winner and co-discoverer of the DNA double helix, James Watson, justifies the venture with the following argument: "For the genetic dice will continue to inffict cruel fates on all too many individuals and their families who do not deserve this damnation. Decency demands that someone must rescue them from genetic hells." And he asks: "If we don't play God, who will?" (Watson 1995: 197). Who is "we"?

Between roughly 1940 and 1970, a new paradigm had been established in biology: molecular biology. In 1948, one of the founders of cybernetics, Norbert Wiener, in a truly visionary gesture, drew a résumé of the history of biology in modern times. The organism of the seventeenth and early eighteenth centuries, he said, was a mechanical automaton. The organism of the nineteenth century was a steam engine. The organism of the twentieth century, however, according to Wiener, had become a medium of communication and control, pervaded by the crucial concepts of message, noise, information and coding (1961[1948]: 62–9).

So far, historians of biology disagree whether the development of information theory and cybernetics in the 1940s had a direct influence on the take-off of the "New Biology" as advocated by Warren Weaver (Judson 1979; Kay 2000; Keller 1995). They agree, however, on the basic argument that with molecular biology, a paradigm shift has occurred that involves the notion of information. Indeed, this would be hard to deny, although there have been arguments to the contrary (Sarkar 1996). I find it safe to state that biologists and physicians engaged in basic medical research have started to view the organism under a new perspective. They have come to envision the fundamental processes of life as based on the storage, transmission, change, accumulation and expression of genetic information. According to this view, there is a genetic program entrenched in the punctuated sequence of the DNA building blocks of the chromosomes. The development of the organism as well as its overall metabolism is regulated by means of a differential retrieval of this genetically enshrined instruction, that is, its

transposition into biological function. As a result of this process, the proteins (and some RNAs) govern, either as structural elements or as biocatalysts, that is, enzymes, the life phenomena of the cell and of whole organisms. The "central dogma" of molecular biology, explicitly formulated in 1958 by Francis Crick (1958), has pervaded all of contemporary biophysics, biochemistry, cell biology and genetics, and has provided it with a new super-slogan: DNA makes RNA, RNA makes protein. The material basis of the genes is DNA which duplicates with every cell division, a process called replication. RNA carries the genetic message gene from the nucleus to the cytoplasm in a process called transcription. A very sophisticated molecular machinery with the ribosomes in its center is said to translate the sequential information of messenger RNA into molecular prescriptions that are realized through the three-dimensionally folded proteins in metabolism.

The basic insights into these molecular processes were gained in the years between 1953 and 1965. The work of Maurice Wilkins, Rosalind Franklin, Francis Crick and James Watson exposed the double-helical structure of DNA and immediately suggested a possible mechanism of gene duplication. Paul Zamecnik and Mahlon Hoagland, and Jacques Monod and François Jacob identified the two RNA-molecules that mediate between the genes (DNA) and the gene products (proteins), transfer RNA and messenger RNA, respectively. Monod and Jacob also provided a first model for gene regulation. Heinrich Matthaei and Marshall Nirenberg as well as Severo Ochoa and his co-workers clarified the relation between these two basic categories of biological macromolecules: the genetic code. (For detailed overviews see Judson 1979; Morange 1994.)

It is extremely compressed but probably fair to say that the essential epistemic achievements of this first phase in the history of molecular biology basically rested on two conditions which at the same time constituted its early drive. First, the transition of a small group of researchers to simple, biophysical, biochemical and genetic, model systems; and second, the development – by far not all of them in the context of molecular biology! – of a series of biophysical, biochemical and genetic technologies. Examples of the former are bacteria, viruses and finally macromolecules. Examples of the latter are, just to mention a very few of them, X-ray crystallography, analytical and preparative ultracentrifugation, electron microscopy, radioactive tracing, more and more sophisticated sorts of chromatography and electrophoresis, as well as the experimental tools of phage and bacterial genetics. It goes without saying that these two series of events interacted and evolved in interplay by becoming combined.

Indeed, these techniques and their results were crucial for the coming into being of molecular biology. But despite much public praise and hope, they were of quite limited immediate influence on medicine and its practices. In many cases, the results, in the form of molecular representation they took on, simply did not lend themselves to therapeutical application (as in the case of sickle cell anemia). In other cases, they basically sanctioned a practice that was well under way and had developed without the direct impact of molecular biology, as in the case of antibiotics, which revolutionized antibacterial therapy in the late 1940's and early 1950's. In still other cases, molecular techniques expanded diagnostic potentials, but did not qualitatively change, much less revolutionize the possibilities of metabolic correction. Examples are nuclear medical screening and enzyme tests.

The advent of gene technology, genetic engineering or, as some prefer to say, applied molecular genetics, since the beginning of the 1970s has effected a decisive prospective change in the relation between molecular biology and medicine. Gene technology developed in three waves. The first was marked by the identification of restriction enzymes and the construction of recombinant plasmids at the beginning of the decade. The second was characterized through the development of novel DNA sequencing techniques towards the end of the 1970s. The third set the stage for the big genome projects around the middle of the 1980s and included pulsed-field electrophoresis, artificial chromosomes, partially automated DNA sequence analysis with fluorescent probes, automated DNA and RNA synthesis, and the polymerase chain reaction (PCR). Within a timespan of less than twenty years, molecular geneticists have learned not only to understand the language of the genes in principle, but to spell it. In other words, they have learned to read, to write, to copy and to edit that language in a goal-directed manner. These are, of course, metaphors. But today, there exist precise and powerful functional equivalents to each of these analogies of language and of writing, and they have neatly been installed in the form of special and more and more easily manipulable techniques. Those are the procedures of DNA sequencing (reading) and of DNA synthesis (writing), both automatized in recent years; DNA multiplication in the form, for example, of the polymerase chain reaction (copying); and the arsenal of operations resulting in changes in the molecular structure of the genes such as site-directed mutagenesis and refined restriction and ligation, deletion and inversion of bits and pieces of DNA (editing).

The emergence of these so-called "recombinant DNA technologies" has created a new situation, and with that, has led back to higher organisms. The central tools of recombinant DNA work – such as restricting, transcribing, replicating and ligating enzymes; plasmids, cosmids, artificial chromosomes, and other molecular transport systems – are not sophisticated analytical and electronic machinery. They are themselves macromolecules that work and perform in the wet environment of the cell. With gene technology, the central technical devices of molecular biological intervention have themselves become parts and indeed constituents of the metabolic activities with which, at the same time, they interfere. The scissors and needles by which the genetic information gets tailored and spliced are enzymes. The carriers by which it is transported into the cells are nucleic acid macromolecules. This kit of purified enzymes and molecules constitutes a "soft" technology that life itself has been evolving over a period of some three billion or even more years, according to the recent estimations of paleobiology. It is able to function and is adapted to operating within the proper confines and in the milieu of the intact living cell. With gene technology, informational molecules are constructed according to an extracellular project and are subsequently implanted into the intracellular environment. The organism itself transposes them, reproduces them, and "tests" their characteristics. With that, the organism as a whole advances to the status of a locus technicus – that is, to the status of a space of representation in which new genotypic and phenotypic patterns are becoming probed and articulated. This technique is of potentially unlimited medical impact. For the first time, it is on the level of *instruction* that metabolic processes are becoming susceptible to manipulation. Until that point was reached, medical intervention, even in its most intrusive physical, chemical and pharmacological forms, was restricted to the level of metabolic *performance*.

With the possibility of manipulating the genetic production program of an organism by its own, unmodified and modified components, the molecular biologist, as a molecular engineer, abandons the working paradigm of the classical biophysicist, biochemist or geneticist. He no longer constructs test tube conditions under which the molecules and reactions occurring in the organism are analyzed. Just the other way round: he constructs objects, that is, basically, instruction-carrying molecules which no longer need to pre-exist within the organism. In reproducing them, expressing them, and screening their effects, he uses the milieu of the cell as their proper technical embedding. The intact organism itself is turned into a laboratory. It is no longer the extracellular representation of intracellular processes, i.e., the "understanding" of life that matters, but rather the intracellular representation of an extracellular project, i.e., the deliberate "rewriting" of life. From an epistemic perspective, this procedure makes the practice of molecular biology, *qua* molecular engineering, substantially different from traditional intervention in the life sciences and in medicine. This intervention aims at *re-programming* metabolic actions, not just interfering with them. As Leroy Hood, one of the leading biotechnologists at Caltech, has put it: from now on biologists will work on models whose appropriateness will be *"tested in biological systems or living organisms"* themselves (1992: 162).

If we are to believe Donald Chambers from the University of Illinois (Chicago), the editor of a recently published *Festschrift* on the occasion of the fortieth anniversary of the DNA double helix, the new biology that resulted from this crucial transformation has effected "dramatic advances in the biomedical sciences. Molecular medicine is not a vision for the future, but is at hand as our intrepid gene hunters identify genetic lesions of disease, develop new diagnostics, and achieve mechanistic understandings that will yield new, rational, molecular therapies" (1995: 413). In the same volume, Sir Walter Bodmer of the Imperial Cancer Research Fund in London prophesies that essentially all human genes, estimated to be in the order of 100,000, will be found, sequenced and localized on their respective chromosomes within the next forty, if not the next ten years. This knowledge, he conjectures, will be summarized in a "book of man" (1995: 423). Others, such as Walter Gilbert, Nobel laureate and Harvard professor, speak of a "vision of the grail" (1992: 83).

Let me just mention a few of Bodmer's examples that, not to count diagnostic procedures such as restriction fragment length polymorphism (RFLP), will be the outcome of "molecular medicine" within the next four decades: "corrective measures" for the carriers of the Huntington gene, Alzheimer's disease, and some 5,000 clinically diagnosed diseases with a genetic component; drugs and diets for the large risk group of people prone to suffer from heart diseases; preventive measures for populations with an elevated risk of genetically induced cancer; specific forms of immune suppression for patients suffering from genetically determined allergies, including hay fever and asthma; cures for specific deficiencies in behaviour or performance such as dyslexia for which a genetic basis is assumed; an effective vaccination against HIV; DNA-based cancer therapies as well as vaccines against certain forms of cancer. The list could be prolonged. In any case, Bodmer leaves no doubt that the practical medical benefit of the genome analysis projects for efficiently fighting diseases, for which there has been no cure so far, will be enormous and indeed unprecedented.

Moreover, Sir Walter Bodmer is of the opinion that this overall information on the human genome "will enable genetic analysis of essentially any human difference" (1995: 414). In view of this easy and gliding linguistic transition to a new genetic determinism, one might ask what at all, in the long run, might remain outside the realm of "molecular medicine." We are not hearing here the voices of isolated propagandists of a new eugenics, we are hearing the virtually unified voice of an international elite of the biomedical complex. None of these experts, to be sure, is supposed to plead for eugenically motivated measures on the level of the population. Since the end of the Second World War, medical genetics in the Western countries has increasingly become oriented towards the sick person, the individual that carries a potential genetic burden. It is oriented towards individual counselling and bound to respect personal decisions. But precisely here, the dilemma is located. Not only diseases are genetically inherited. Essentially normal, as well as very trivial, characteristics are also genetically inherited. What will then count as normal? Consequently, Bodmer asks himself: "Will alterations ever be offered? Will germline therapy ever be accepted?" (1995: 424). Just to take a very simple example: shall parents, in the future, have the right to decide what kind of eye colour their child will have? Bodmer is quite outspoken about the fact that the decision as to whether to allow such interventions "will become entirely a social and a political ... rather than a scientific decision" (1995: 425). But if so, then we urgently need a serious discussion about the social and ethical dimensions of a molecular or, as Thomas Caskey from the National Institutes of Health puts it, "DNA-based medicine" (1992: 112). To leave such discussion about the scope and limit of genetic intervention and action to the biomedical experts alone will then be plainly counterindicated.

Today already, we are witnessing a global, irreversible transformation of living beings, animals and plants, towards deliberately engineered beings. Future natural evolution will appear as insignificant in this perspective. The usual objection at this point, especially from scientists, is that the adoption of the viewpoint of such a radical break produced by molecular genetics is not justified. After all, it is said, evolution itself has invented and practiced the means of horizontal gene transfer, and the cultivation and breeding of plants and animals by the enhancement of mechanisms of genetic change goes back to the Neolithic civilizations. I disagree with this view of smooth transition. To this argument, I would like to oppose a quotation of David Jackson, a former student of James Watson at Harvard and Paul Berg at Stanford, who chose a career in industry and became an investigator of the American Pharma Trust DuPont Merck:

I would argue that the ability to read, to write, and edit DNA is functionally unprecedented in human history. All we have ever been able to do before is to select among the various combinations of genes that the mechanisms of genetics have presented to us. And, while we have developed very powerful and very sophisticated selection procedures, selecting from among a set of alternatives over which one has almost no control is fundamentally different from being able to write and edit one's own text. (Jackson 1995: 364)

That is, from the point of view of the practitioner, what molecular biology and medicine enables us to do. Who is "us"?

Writing and reading, as forms of calculation, instruction and legislation, have profoundly shaped the social body and political power structure of Western societies from their pre-Greek inception in Mesopotamia through the Gutenberg galaxy of the Renaissance and the expansion of printing during the Industrial Revolution to the microchip industry of today, with DNA-chips on the horizon. What is new about molecular biological writing is that we now gain access to the texture, and hence the calculation, instruction and legislation of the human individual's organic existence, that is to a script which until now it has been the privilege of evolution to write, to rewrite and to alter. What Darwin called "methodical", or "artificial selection" has barely scratched the surface of this script within the last 10,000 years of human evolution. For artificial selection, in a way, itself still was nothing more than a specific human mode of natural evolution. This has now gone and with it, natural evolution will become marginal. Molecular biology will arrive at inventing the biological future. Once more Jackson: "The ability to write and edit DNA is the basis for a synthetic and a creative capability in biology that has not previously existed" (1995: 364). Toward the end of this millennium, it has moved a big step towards the vision of Robert Sinsheimer some twenty years ago, at the dawn of recombinant DNA technology. "For the first time in all time, a living creature understands its origin and can undertake to design its future" (Sinsheimer 1969).

Conclusion: Beyond Nature and Culture

The more molecular biology has blurred the contours of what genes might be on a molecular level (Fischer 1995), "genes for such-and-such," as public icons, have become more abundant than ever. What is at stake in the current public discourse of molecular biology, as Evelyn Fox Keller rightly observed, is a profound "transfiguration" of the longstanding question of "genetic determinism" (Keller 1992: 288). An optimistic version of this observation would be that the quest after a "genetic analysis of essentially any human difference" will finally result in an inflation of the argument from genetics. In view of what has been said above, it can at least be stated that the traditional dichotomy between "nature" and "nurture," between "biology" and "culture," is about to collapse. One of the leading narratives of Enlightenment philosophy in general and of the modern sciences in particular has been to conceive of the development of human society as liberating (wo)mankind from the constraints of nature. It has been trying to draw a clear distinction between natural history on the one hand, and social history as superseding and replacing the former, on the other hand. It is intriguing to argue that molecular biology, as one of the results of this process, definitely subverts the perception of history from which it originated. It makes us realize that the result of its scientific conquest is not to supersede, but to change our natural history, that the very essence of our being social

is not to supersede, but to alter our natural, that is, in the present context, our genetic condition. We come to realize that the *natural* condition of our genetic makeup might turn into a *social* construct, with the result that the distinction between the "natural" and the "social" no longer makes good sense. We could say as well that the future *social* conditions of man will become based on *natural* constructs. The "nature" and the "social" can no longer be perceived as ontologically different. They are no longer useful concepts to describe what is going on at the frontiers of the present "culture of biomedicine." We become aware that we live in a world of hybrids for the characterization of which we run short of categories. As Latour says, in claiming that we have never been modern – at least not in the sense of successfully separating culture from nature: "Instead of always being explained by a mixture of the two "pure" transcendences, the activity of nature/society making becomes the *source* from which societies and natures originate" (Latour 1992: 282).

NOTE

This paper makes use of two earlier articles:
Rheinberger, Hans-Jörg 1995 "Beyond Nature and Culture: A Note on Medicine in the Age of Molecular Biology." *Science in Context* 8(1): 249–63.
    1996 "Molekulare Medizin als Paradigma? Gentechnologie im Blick von Wissenschaftstheorie und medizinischer Ethik." In Heinz Schott (ed.), *Meilensteine der Medisin*. Dortmund: Harenberg Verlag, pp. 555–61.

REFERENCES

Bodmer, Walter
    1995 "Where will Genome Analysis Lead Us Forty Years On?" In Donald A. Chambers (ed.), *DNA: The Double Helix, Perspective and Prospective at Forty Years*. New York: New York Academy of Sciences, pp. 414–26.
Caskey, Thomas C.
    1992 "DNA-Based Medicine: Prevention and Therapy." In Daniel J. Kevles and Leroy Hood (eds.), *The Code of Codes*. Cambridge, MA: Harvard University Press, pp. 112–35.

Chambers, Donald A.
1995 "The Double Helix: Prospective. Introduction." In Donald A. Chambers (ed.), *DNA: The Double Helix, Perspective and Prospective at Forty Years*. New York: New York Academy of Sciences, p. 43.

Crick, Francis H. C.
1958 "On Protein Synthesis." *Symposia of the Society for Experimental Biology* (London) 12: 138–63.

Elkana, Yehuda
1981 "A Programmatic Attempt at an Anthropology of Knowledge." In Everett Mendelsohn and Yehuda Elkana (eds.), *Sciences and Cultures: Anthropological and Historical Studies of the Sciences*. Dordrecht and Boston: Reidel, pp. 1–76.

Fischer, Ernst Peter
1995 " 'How Many Genes has a Human Being?' The Analytical Limits of a Complex Concept." In Ernst Fischer and Sigmar Klose (eds.), *The Human Genome*. München: Piper, pp. 223–56.

Gilbert, Walter
1992 "A Vision of the Grail." In Daniel J. Kevles and Leroy Hood (eds.), *The Code of Codes*. Cambridge, MA: Harvard University Press, pp 83–97.

Hood, Leroy
1992 "Biology and Medicine in the Twenty-First Century." In Daniel J. Kevles and Leroy Hood (eds.), *The Code of Codes*. Cambridge, MA: Harvard University Press, pp. 136–63.

Jackson, David A.
1995 "DNA: Template for an Economic Revolution". In Donald A. Chambers (eds.), *DNA: The Double Helix, Perspective and Prospective at Forty Years*. New York: New York Academy of Sciences, pp. 356–65.

Judson, Horace F.
1979 *The Eighth Day of Creation: Makers of the Revolution in Biology*. New York: Simon and Schuster.

Kay, Lily E.
2000 *Who Wrote the Book of Life?* Stanford: Stanford University Press.

Keller, Evelyn Fox
1992 "Nature, Nurture, and the Human Genome Project." In Daniel J. Kevles and Leroy Hood (eds.), *The Code of Codes*. Cambridge, MA: Harvard University Press, pp. 281–99.

Keller, Evelyn Fox
1995 *Refiguring Life. Metaphors of Twentieth-Century Biology*. New York: Columbia University Press.

Latour, Bruno
1988[1984] *The Pasteurization of France*. Trans. Alan Sheridan and John Law Cambridge, MA: Harvard University Press.

Latour, Bruno
1992 "One More Turn After the Social Turn." In Ernan McMullin (ed.), *The Social Dimensions of Science*. Notre Dame: University of Notre Dame Press, pp. 272–92.

Morange, Michel
1994 *Histoire de la biologie moléculaire*. Paris: Editions Is Découverte.

Pauling, Linus C., A. Harvey Itano, S. J. Singer and Ibert C. Wells
1949 "Sickle-Cell Anaemia, A Molecular Disease." *Science* 110: 543–8.

Sarkar, Sahotra
1996 "Biological Information: A Sceptical Look at Some Central Dogmas of Molecular Biology." In Sahotra Sarkar (ed.), *The Philosophy and History of Molecular Biology: New Perspectives*. Dordrecht: Kluwer Academic Publishers, pp. 187–231.

Sinsheimer, Robert
1969 "The Prospect of Genetic Change." *Engineering and Science* 32: 8–13.

Watson, James
1995 "Values from a Chicago Upbringing." In Donald A. Chambers (ed.), *DNA: The Double Helix, Perspective and Prospective at Forty Years*. New York: New York Academy of Sciences, pp. 194–7.

Wiener, Norbert
1961[1948] *Cybernetics, or Control and Communication in the Animal and the Machine*. New York: M.I.T. Press and John Wiley & Sons.

28

Immortality, In Vitro
A History of the HeLa Cell Line

Hannah Landecker

A tissue is evidently an enduring thing. Its functional and structural conditions become modified from moment to moment. Time is really the fourth dimension of living organisms. It enters as a part into the constitution of a tissue. Cell colonies, or organs, are events which progressively unfold themselves. They must be studied like history. (Alexis Carrel, "The New Cytology")

The double is neither living nor dead: designed to supplement the living, to perfect it, to make it immortal like the Creator, it is always "the harbinger of death," It disguises, by its perfection, the presence of death. By creating what he hopes are immortal doubles, man tries to conceal the fact that death is always already present in life. The feeling of uncanniness that arises from the double stems from the fact that it cannot but evoke what man tries in vain to forget. (Sarah Kofman, Freud and Fiction*)*

In 1951, a piece of cancerous cervical tissue was cut from a woman named Henrietta Lacks, Lacks died eight months later of cancer. Live cells from the biopsy were grown in test tubes, supplied with nutrient medium, and kept at body temperature in an incubator. Named HeLa, from the first two letters of Lacks's first and last names, and called an immortal cell line, descendants of these original cells continue to grow and divide in laboratories around the world. Proliferating with these glass-bound populations of cells are narratives of their life and origin.

The cells live and the woman does not. They somehow stand for her and she for them; otherwise, this pair of circumstances would not present itself as a paradox, much less one that has generated such fascinated attention from 1951 to today. That one party in this relation should be alive and the other dead creates a dramatic tension which continues to generate scientific papers, newspaper and magazine articles, and television documentaries. The resolution of the paradox in these narratives is always the same: the woman and the cells are immortal, the woman through the cells' life and the cells through the woman's death. It is a personification of the woman who died that gains immortality, while the woman's death is necessary to elevate the cells from unremarkable life – maintained in laboratories for over forty-six years – to immortal life.

It is not surprising in itself that HeLa should be personified. Cell lines are made to stand in

Hannah Landecker, "Immortality, In Vitro: A History of the HeLa Cell Line," in P. E. Brodwin, ed., *Biotechnology and Culture: Bodies, Anxieties, Ethics.* Bloomington: Indiana University Press, 2000. Reprinted by permission of Hannah Landecker.

for persons in the first place; they function in the laboratory as proxy theaters of experimentation for intact living bodies. The visualization of cellular processes by placing living cells under glass, where they are accessible to microscope and camera, has become part of what we understand to be the "life" of the body. As sites of manufacturing – of viruses or proteins or antibodies – cell lines are the tools of the industry whose product is human health. Their identification as "living" and "human" entities cannot fall from them, because it is this origin that gives them commercial and scientific value as producers of biological substances for use by humans and their validity as research sites of human biology.

Given that these living technologies are thus necessarily understood to be human, I wish to ask more specifically how the material existence of the cell line redefines the designations used to describe that existence. To this end, I trace the history of the cell line and its personifications. Lacks's story is simultaneously what happened to a person and her body and a narrative vehicle through which journalists and scientists have imagined and witnessed the possibilities for lives and bodies constantly being changed by the rapid development of these "technologies of living substance" made from human tissues. Lacks's photograph graces many of the accounts; the cell line bears fragments of her name; the cells bear various proportions of the genetic material of which her body was composed when it was alive, the body that was the source of cells whose varied descendants continue to live and reproduce in laboratories all over the world. However, the meaning of this material lineage is repeatedly being renegotiated in the changing personifications of the cell line.

More than an exercise in cataloguing variations on a theme, this history demonstrates how the personifications of the cell line shift alongside the development of differing experimental roles in biology, medicine, and biotechnology, The physical matter, technical practice, and economic significance of growing cells in vitro – tissue culture – generated new knowledge about and fresh meanings for the concepts of human, alive, and immortal. These are both shaped by and interact with wider cultural narratives, from modern medicine's triumph over polio in the 1950s to anxieties over race and purity in the 1960s and 1970s to, most recently, a recasting of the story in economic terms.

In a sense, I mimic the narratives I am analyzing, by structuring the following history of the HeLa cells around the changing definitions of in vitro immortality over the course of the twentieth century. This is meant, in the end, to serve as a critique rather than a retelling; the final point of this essay is to highlight that the death of the person who was Henrietta Lacks has been obscured by the personification of her cells as an immortal entity.

Immortality in the History of Tissue Culture

HeLa cells were called immortal within a year of their cultivation in vitro. The only way to understand what seems a rather rapid jump to conclusions is to place the establishment of this line in the context of the history of tissue culture. This essay is not the place to recount the history of tissue culture; instead, I choose to take up a single strand of its development in the United States. The work of Alexis Carrel at Rockefeller Institute in New York City from 1910 to 1938 is important in the context of this essay, because it was Carrel who first proposed the concept and the supporting technology of indefinite life of tissues in vitro. He drew his initial inspiration from Ross G. Harrison, an embryologist, who had shown in 1907 that he could keep a piece of embryonic frog neural tissue alive long enough to watch a single nerve fiber growing out from it, Harrison thus demonstrated how valuable information could be gleaned from the isolation and maintenance of a living system in which the "behavior of certain cells could be observed when removed from the bewildering conditions ... within the embryonic body" (6).

However, it was Carrel who first tried to grow human cells in vitro. He did not aim to keep tissues alive long enough to observe some aspect of their behavior; rather, his goal was their "indefinite" or "permanent" life. Drawing on the philosophy of Henri Bergson, Carrel developed a theory of corporeal life in which physiological processes were the "substratum of duration." Time was recorded only when the metabolic products of these processes were allowed to remain around the tissues being grown in vitro:

> If these metabolites are removed at short intervals and the composition of the medium is kept constant, the cell colonies remain indefinitely in the same state of activity. They do not record time qualitatively. In fact, they are immortal. (Carrel, "Physiological Time" 620)

This theory translated into meticulous technical practices such as washing ("rejuvenating") the cells every few days, the design of special glassware for these procedures, and strict protocols to ensure asepsis. By 1912, Carrel declared the "permanent life of tissues outside of the organism" an issue only of more perfect technique, and he claimed to have established a culture of embryonic chicken heart fibroblasts. These cells would live in vitro for thirty-four years, when they were discarded two years after Carrel's death (Carrel, "Permanent Life"; Ebeling).

From its beginnings, the living cell in culture – in particular the human cell – has been an uncanny object. Tissue culture was developed using living matter cut from fetal cadavers and tumors. The living qualities of these cells, acted out in isolation from the organism and visible to the observer – contracting, beating, forming synaptic nets, proliferating, migrating – are what make them useful for biology. Their isolation gives them the character of autonomous life – which is especially evident in the early fascination of Carrel and other tissue culturists with applying new techniques of timelapse cinematography to the study of cells in culture. These silent films of cells enlarged to screen size made visible the movement and division of entities previously seen only in the fixed, stained state of classical histology, and they enhanced the perception of an autonomous sphere of life. "Tissue and blood cells are always in the process of becoming," wrote Carrel. "They do not show their true physiognomy ... under the microscope. ... [C]ells appear on the film as mobile as a flame" ("New Cytology" 337).

From this early history comes not only the sense of a kind of life extracted from the confines of the animal or human body but an enduring connection with magic and sorcery. One textbook of cell biology states that "until the early 1970s, tissue culture was something of a blend of science and witchcraft," which refers both to the understanding of successful tissue culture as an "art" that had to be learned in a hands-on apprenticeship and the aesthetic setting of the early tissue culture laboratories (Alberts et al. 161). Carrel and those he trained staffed their laboratories with technicians dressed in black robes and hoods, ostensibly to minimize reflections which might interfere with the delicate operations, while the air was kept moist with "witches' cauldrons" of steam (Witowski 281). Although contemporaries and historians have blamed Carrel for making tissue culture out to be more difficult – and more occult – than it really was, thus scaring off potential practitioners, to my mind there is no doubt that his sense of the possible was extremely important to the establishment of in vitro immortality as a desired scientific object.

Getting tissue or cells to live in glass has also been the venture to get them to live indefinitely outside of the animal body. What good, after all, is a technology that only lives for a matter of days or months? Much better is one that will – if fed and maintained – reproduce itself and serve as a constant medium for repeatable experiments. However, the permanent life of cells outside of the body did not turn out to be an easily achievable goal, and HeLa was established only after years of effort with other cells, animal and human.

The Establishment of the Hela Cell Line

In the laboratory of George Gey and Margaret Gey, at Johns Hopkins University Hospital, the ongoing attempt to establish cell lines from human tissues intersected with another research program to determine the relationship between two types of cervical cancer. The first was a non-invasive form of cancer involving only the epithelial surface of the cervix. The second was invasive carcinoma involving the deeper basal layers and leading to metastasis. Although it is now understood that the former is a precursor of the latter, this was still unresolved in 1951. George Gey had been recruited to the project to grow cervical cancer cells in the hope that their life under glass would reveal something about their action in the body. It was into this context that Henrietta Lacks entered when she sought treatment for intermenstrual bleeding. After initial uncertainty on the part of the Johns Hopkins' treating physicians as to the nature of the lesion they saw on her cervix, they took a biopsy of the lesion and made the diagnosis of cervical cancer. Without her knowledge or permission, Lacks became part of the cervical cancer research project when a piece of the biopsy material was sent to the Gey laboratory.

In 1951, when it became clear that HeLa cells were going to continue growing and dividing unperturbed by their artificial environment, it did not take long before the label of "immortality" was applied to them and their role as a cell line quickly overshadowed any part in the cervical cancer study. George Gey distributed samples of HeLa to his colleagues around the world. Because – as one tissue culturist put it – "HeLa cells can be grown by almost anyone capable of trypsinizing cells and transferring them from one tube to another," their cultivation quickly became a widespread practice (Bang 534).

Gey never attempted to patent or otherwise limit the distribution of HeLa cells, clearly not anticipating the chain letter effect of sending out cultures which were then grown up, split into parts, and sent on to others. Almost immediately, a company called Microbial Associates, Inc., began growing HeLa cells for commercial sale. In 1954, Gey expressed dismay over the number of laboratories working on HeLa in a letter to a colleague. Gey's correspondent, Charles Pomerat, reacted to this statement with some amusement:

With regard to your statement ... of disapproval for a wide exploration of the HeLa strain, I don't see how you can hope to inhibit progress in this direction since you released the strain so widely that it now can be purchased commercially. This is a little bit like requesting people not to work on the golden hamster[1]

Indeed, by this time, HeLa cells were being mass-produced as part of a push for the rapid evaluation of the polio vaccine, which Jonas Salk developed in 1952. HeLa cells were chosen as the "host" cell for measuring the amounts of antibodies the poliovirus antigen produced. The Tuskegee Institute, a historically black college in Alabama, was appointed by the National Foundation for Infantile Paralysis to be the locus of production. A laboratory was committed to the sole purpose of producing as many as twenty thousand tube cultures of HeLa per week (Brown and Henderson).

George Gey had as little control over the story that he released into the public domain as he had over the cells. Because of intense national interest in the subject of polio, the HeLa cell line came quickly to the attention of journalists. Gey did not want to release Lacks's name, and so he informed an interested writer from the National Foundation for Infantile Paralysis that he could not see fit to reveal the name of the cells' donor. However, it was clear in the reply to this refusal that the writer had asked Gey's permission only as a formality; he had already learned Lacks's name.

An intrinsic part of this story would be to describe how these cells, originally obtained from Henrietta Lakes [sic], are being grown and used for the benefit of mankind. Here is a situation where cancer cells – potential destroyers of human life – have been channeled by medical science to a new, beneficent course. ...

"Incidentally," the writer smugly concluded, "the identity of the patient is already a matter of public record inasmuch as newspaper reports have completely identified the individual,"[2] Another journalist writing for *Colliers* in 1954 was more discreet, referring to "an unsung heroine of medicine named Helen L." (Davidson 79). Helen L. was characterized in this piece as a young Baltimore housewife whose unfortunate early death turned her into an "unsung heroine" because of the HeLa cells' research role. Her death and her immortality were uttered in the same sentence: "Mrs. L. has attained a degree of immortality she never dreamed of when she was alive, and her living tissue may yet play a role in conquering many diseases in addition to the cancer which killed her" (Davidson 80).

In this version of immortality, the cells were understood to be a piece of Henrietta Lacks that went on growing and living, encased in a test tube instead of a body. The cells were seen as universal human cells. They served as a substrate in the design of a polio vaccine that was to be applied to millions of people. They were used to produce standardized nutrient media for use in culturing all kinds of cells. They were utilized to figure out methods for growing other cells and how to produce large numbers of them. They were referred to as the "golden hamster" of cell biologists, and their concomitant personification was in the form of an angelic figure, an immortalized young Baltimore housewife, thrust into a kind of eternal life of which such a woman would never dream.

To understand how death becomes a footnote to immortality in this narrative, I will do a close reading of one of the retellings of HeLa's origin story. When George Gey died (of cancer) in 1970, his colleagues wrote a peculiar memorial tribute to him in the journal *Obstetrics and Gynecology*, entitled "After Office Hours: The HeLa Cell and a Reappraisal of its Origin." They wrote that the original biopsy

> secured for the patient, Henrietta Lacks (fig. 2) as HeLa, an immortality which has now reached 20 years. Will she live forever if nurtured by the hands of future workers? Even now, Henrietta Lacks, first as Henrietta and then as HeLa, has a combined age of 51 years. (H. W. Jones et al. 945)

Beside this statement is figure 2 – a photograph of a young woman, smiling into the camera, hands on hips. Underneath the photograph, the caption reads "Henrietta Lacks (HeLa)," as if the photograph of the woman held the image of the incipient cell line, as if the woman *was* the cell line, that according to these gynecologists, "if allowed to grow uninhibited under optimal cultural conditions, would have taken over the world by this time."

The reappraisal promised by the tribute's title was another look at the original biopsy slides of Henrietta Lacks. Upon reexamining

the slides, Gey's colleagues wrote that what had been originally diagnosed as epidermoid carcinoma of the cervix in its early stages was actually an adenocarcinoma, a rarer, more aggressive form of cancer involving a different kind of cell. While some readers might expect this admission to cause reconsideration of the treatment of the patient, who died within eight months of diagnosis – in particular, as one of the authors was a physician responsible for this patient's diagnosis and treatment – this is not the case. They wrote:

> while it is necessary to record that the first continuous cell strain is not of epidermoid carcinoma of the cervix ... the exact histopathologic nature of HeLa is but a footnote to the abiding genius of George Gey. (946)

Thus the woman is paradoxically made immortal by the engine of her death, in the form of a biopsy used to diagnose her ailment (inaccurately) that becomes research material without her permission, to end up as a footnote to the abiding genius of the scientist.

The question of whose immortality is involved in the establishment of cell lines is further accentuated by the predilection some scientists showed for trying to establish immortal cell lines from pieces of their own bodies or the bodies of close relatives. In 1961, Leonard Hayflick of Wistar Institute established a cell line from his newborn daughter's amniotic sac. The amnion, which grows from the fetal tissues, was of the same genetic makeup as Leonard Hayflick's daughter, and because it carried his genes, it was literally his "daughter cell" (Hayflick, "Establishment" 608). He named the cell line WISH, an acronym which stood for Wistar Institute and Susan Hayflick, his daughter.

In 1966, Monroe Vincent was diagnosed as having a benign tumor of the prostate. He promptly attempted to grow some of the cells taken from his prostate, and he established the cell line MA 160, named not after himself but after the biomedical supply company Microbial Associates, Inc., in which he was a partner. HeLa was itself scientific progeny – letters to George Gey referring to HeLa called the cell line "your precious baby."[3] Gey is fondly remembered for hand-delivering the cultures personally to other scientists: " 'He would put his glass tubes containing the cells in his shirt pocket, use his body heat to keep them warm, and then fly to another city and hand them to a fellow scientist.' "

From Beneficence to Notoriety

This benign version of immortality came to an abrupt end in the 1960s. First, new scientific work that studied aging through cell culture revealed that only cancerous cells had the ability to keep dividing indefinitely. This drew a sharper line of definition between normal and cancerous cells. Carrel's famous immortal chicken heart cell culture had supposedly been composed of normal cells, in which "permanent life" had been induced by removing them from the body and manipulating their environment, but in 1961 this was shown to have been something of a fraud, when Hayflick demonstrated that normal somatic cells in culture consistently divide for a set number of generations and then all die at once. Cells reproduce by replicating their DNA and dividing into two daughter cells. When a whole population of cells goes through division, it is said to double. Hayflick showed that cells taken from human fetal tissue will always undergo about fifty doublings before dying. Even if the culture is frozen, and no matter how long it stays frozen, when thawed it will pick up where it left off and in total complete approximately fifty doublings. Cells taken from adults consistently go through about thirty doublings (Hayflick, "Biology") What is more, the finite number of doublings is species-specific. Chicken cell culture will go through thirty-five doublings at the most, not thirty-five years worth of doublings. Thus it seemed impossible that Carrel's culture could have been composed of normal chicken cells.

Hayflick concluded that the chick embryo extract preparation used as nutrient medium for Carrel's cultures provided new viable embryonic cells at each feeding. Others have hypothesized that Carrel's proximity to Peyton Rous at Rockefeller Institute led to the normal somatic chicken cells being infected with Rous sarcoma virus and thus rendered capable of the same kind of unlimited division seen in cancerous

cells (for example, see Harris 45). The cause for the famous culture's immortality could not be investigated as it was thrown away in 1946.

More important was the stark distinction drawn between normal body cells and cancer cells with this work. Intrinsic to this distinction was the finite life span of populations of normal cells, a limit only cancer cells could break. Normal somatic cells were euploid, that is, contained a normal number of chromosomes. Cancer cells were aneuploid, showing abnormal chromosome numbers. Immortality was not available to normal, euploid cells except through freezing. They could be "transformed" with a virus or mutagen, but then they became aneuploid and behaved like cancer cells. Immortality was thus a characteristic solely of cancerous, aneuploid cells, and it was one of the traits that made cancer a menacing and mortal disease of the body.

Malignancy and cancer were already associated with uncontrolled cell proliferation and metasticization, but it was not until after 1966 that HeLa cells were understood or described in these terms. Certainly it was recognized that HeLa cells came from the cancerous tissue that caused Henrietta Lacks's death, but the emphasis had been on their control by scientists, their harnessing as producers of knowledge in the victorious battles against polio, and the less successful but still hopeful attempt to understand and contain cancer. This sense of control came to an abrupt end with the second and more profound disruption of a benign image of in vitro immortality.

This disturbance was the announcement that HeLa cells had contaminated and overgrown many of the other immortal human cell cultures established in the 1950s and 1960s. Because one human cell looks much like another, only cross-species contamination – which could be seen by counting chromosomes – had up to this time been identified in cell culture. This changed with the introduction of techniques of genetic identification. At the Second Decennial Review Conference on Cell Tissue and Organ Culture in September 1967, geneticist Stanley Gartier announced that he had profiled eighteen different human cell lines and judged them all to have been contaminated and overtaken by HeLa cells.

Gartler had tested the eighteen lines electrophoretically for a set of enzymes known to be genetically polymorphic, that is, to differ slightly among different people. All eighteen cell lines contained exactly the same enzyme profiles, indicating that they were all the same rather than eighteen distinct human cell types. All eighteen had the same profiles as the HeLa cell. The key piece of evidence in this study was the profile for a particular enzyme called G6PD (glucose-6-phosphate dehydrogenase), which is a factor in red blood cell metabolism. Gartler stood up in front of an audience of tissue culturists and said:

> The G6PD variants that concern us are the A (fast) and B (slow) types. The A type has been found only in Negroes. ... The results of our G6PD analyses of these supposedly 18 independently derived human cell lines are that all have the A band. ... I have not been able to ascertain the supposed racial origin of all 18 lines; it is known, however, that at least some of these are from Caucasians, and that at least one, HeLa, is from a Negro. (Gartler, "Genetic" 173)

The terminology of cell culture was already dense with the connotations of lineage, culture, proliferation, population, contamination, and, most recently, malignancy. With the delivery of this paper, Gartler used these terms in a scientific explanation which marked the contaminating cell line as black and the contaminated lines as white.

At this moment, the narratives surrounding the HeLa cell changed dramatically. Prior to Gartler's work in 1966, race had not entered into the discussions of either HeLa cells or their donor, Henrietta Lacks. In fact, Gartler had to write to George Gey early in 1966 to ask about Lacks's race.

> I am interested in the racial origin of the person from whom your HeLa cell line was initiated. I have checked a number of the early papers describing the development of the HeLa cell line but *have not been able to find any information pertaining to the race of the donor*.[4] (Emphasis added)

After 1966, the race of the donor was central to the scientific evidence of cell culture contamination, and metaphors and stereotypes of race framed scientific and journalistic accounts of the cell line.

The following analysis traces this transformation of scientific and popular rhetoric in detail. It is not sufficient to assert that one discourse of contamination merged with one of miscegenation, as if this were the inevitable course of events. It was by no means inevitable; I argue that Gartler emphasized the least sound piece of his repertoire of evidence of contamination, an error which was then promulgated by those who tested, extended, and reported on Gartler's work. This particular course of events reveals much about the functioning of concepts of biological race in American biology in the late 1960s and 1970s.

First, it is necessary to support my assertion that Gartler emphasized the weakest part of his evidence of HeLa contamination of other cell lines, keeping empirically stronger arguments in the background as supporting evidence. Gartler did not have to explain his results in the manner he did, highlighting the G6PD typing. When he tested each of the cell lines for particular enzymes, he was looking for variations in structure between the same genes in different humans. The resulting enzymes differ slightly in amino acid sequence, a difference which can then be visualized as lines on a gel. In addition to G6PD, Gartler also used three other sets of polymorphic electrophoretic variants. Each of these three variants occurs in differing proportions across the world's population, much like blood types, and could not be categorized as being specific to any one population. In Gartler's own words, the statistical likelihood of all eighteen cell lines carrying the same profiles for these systems of polymorphisms was statistically "absurdly low," regardless of the purported race of the various donors of the cells (Gartler, "Apparent" 750). In other words, Gartler's evidence of contamination would have been conclusive even without any reference to racial difference.

Any eighteen people, in particular eighteen unrelated people from the diverse population of the United States, would show different enough enzyme profiles to be distinct from each other. The same enzyme profile for all eighteen would be strong evidence of contamination of all of them by the same cell line.

Thus an explanation based on human genetic variation, which lurked in the background of Gartler's paper as supporting evidence, was empirically more sound than that which he chose to highlight, the G6PD types and their supposed racial correlations.

The presence of G6PD type A or B in a cell culture was correlated in his account with the racial categorization of the patient donor as black or white, a categorization presumably noted by the physician-scientist on the basis of the patient's self-designation or the physician's visual assessment. The correlation implied an equivalence of the two kinds of racial categorizations – by G6PD variation and visual judgment. Gartler suggested that an apparently white donor could not have been the origin of a cell line expressing G6PD type A, which is not true at all. This weakness was noticed by the founder of one of the cell lines said to be contaminated by HeLa. As this was a commercially marketed cell line, contamination was a threat to its economic value. Almost immediately, Monroe Vincent – whose cell line was made from his prostate – published a denial that MA160 was HeLa-contaminated. He hypothesized that the G6PD type A in MA160 could be inherited from potential remote "Negro ancestry" in his lineage (Fraley et al. 541).

Even with this weakness, G6PD continued to be the main marker in testing for HeLa contamination of cell lines. The consequence of this emphasis was the essentialization of cells as "black" or "white" – an error possible only in the prevailing confusion about concepts of biological race. An essential black/white difference was simpler for Gartler to explain and easier for his audience to understand as "proof" than would an explanation based on human genetic variation. This fact indicates that the concept of population had not yet managed to displace the concept of race for these biologists. Gartler had been working since the early 1960s with a cell culture that carried a mutation at the G6PD locus, and as a geneticist he was well acquainted with the voluminous literature concerning the incidence of G6PD variation in populations around the world. However, his audience of cell biologists was not trained in population genetics, nor were these cell biologists familiar with its

methods. Their responses gave G6PD type A a simplified, essentialized status as a "black gene," as if the register of race went from skin to cell to enzyme to gene. This marker, taken from the context of population genetics and used as an identifying test for contamination in cell culture, lost all the subtleties and complications of a gene frequency within a population and became, instead, an absolute indicator of difference.

Once the lines between cell types were demarcated in this fashion, the crossing of these boundaries meant that the scientific community experienced two simultaneous disruptions. First was the disruption of a complacent sense of control. If Gartler was right, these scientists had mistakenly been doing experiments on cells that they thought were breast cancer or colon cancer or amnion cells but were in fact all HeLa cells. This was a threat to the integrity and value of past work, an imputation of carelessness in their technical practice, and the sudden switch from HeLa as a founding success to HeLa as the source of catastrophe. Second, it was the disturbance of a previously unarticulated presumption of race. There had been no "information pertaining to the race of the donor" to this point, and in its role as a breakthrough, a standard, a universal, HeLa and its concomitant personification as an angelic and immortal Henrietta Lacks were unmarked and assumed to be white.

At the same time, the synecdoche between cell and person functioned to make the cell populations of petri dishes analogous to populations of people. The scientists moved readily between the language of cells in culture to that of people in culture. One respondent to Gartler's paper stood up to remind the audience that cross-species contamination occurred easily in tissue culture, a statement which exemplifies the facile slide from "human cell" to "human":

We all remember clearly a number of years ago – maybe 5 – when this contamination business began and everybody was very defensive: the L cells contaminating the rabbits, the HeLa cells contaminating the mouse. ... Now, here comes the HeLa: human contaminating human. (Hsu 191)

Human contaminating human, explained in terms of racial difference, meant an immediate introduction of the metaphors of miscegenation. The immediacy of this response is better understood within the larger context of American history.

The late 1960s saw the arguing of the landmark United States Supreme Court case of *Loving v. Virginia*, ruling in 1967 that the Virginia miscegenation law was unconstitutional. As in science, the validity and utility of racial categories were being challenged. This ruling was followed by a general move on the part of most American states to repeal statutes that defined racial categories, usually by blood proportion (Pascoe 67–8). This included the "one drop of blood" rule which defined a person as black if they had so much as a single drop of black blood. Miscegenation laws, present from the 1660s to the 1960s, asserted an absolute interdiction of sexual or marital crossing of the racial border. However, the existence of the one drop rule, and its aim to demarcate black from white absolutely, admitting no middle ground, indicated that this border was crossed all the time. Originating in American slavery, when the master's rape of the female slave was an "open secret," the one drop of black blood criterion and miscegenation laws worked to deny any kinship across racial boundaries (Jan Mohammed).

That these boundaries were still anxiously regarded – and that kinship across them was still being denied – is evident in the audience discussion after Gartler delivered his paper. There was a great deal of defensive rejection of his conclusion of widespread HeLa contamination from these members of the tissue culture community, some of whom had founded the cell lines Gartler was identifying as contaminated. Leonard Hayflick's WISH – the cell line made from his daughter's amniotic sac – was one of the cell lines Gartler identified as carrying the genetic marker he said was "found only in Negroes" ("Genetic" 173). Hayflick, apparently a white man, is reported to have stood up during the discussion following Gartler's paper and said " 'I have just telephoned my wife, who assured me that my worst fears are unfounded' " (qtd. in Gold 30). Themes of miscegenation and pollution, the fear of impregnation of the white

woman by the black man, and doubt in the genealogy of the scientists thus came to the fore within minutes of Gartler's conclusions.

After Gartler made his argument about HeLa contamination, the description of what happened to cells in culture was structured by these metaphors of miscegenation. Scientists passed on this explanation to journalists, who used this narrative to tell the HeLa story to a larger audience. The scientists also read the journalists' accounts, footnoting them in their scientific papers. The warnings about the danger of HeLa contamination, for example, played up a "one drop of HeLa" theme: "If a non-HeLa culture is contaminated by even a single HeLa cell, that cell culture is doomed. In no time at all, usually unnoticed, HeLa cells will proliferate and take over the culture" (Culliton 1059). One drop was enough.

The racial metaphors altered but did not completely change the way tissue culture had been understood up to this point. Even with the earlier famous chicken heart cell culture, there was a consistent obsession with hypothetical calculations of the total volume of cells the immortal culture produced; with HeLa, these were calculations of a swamping of a white population by a black one. Ross Harrison had mused in 1927 that had it been possible to allow all of the cells in Alexis Carrel's chicken heart culture to multiply, it would "now greatly outweigh the terrestrial globe," while in 1937 P. Lecomte De Noüy envisioned the same set of cells reaching a volume "more than thirteen quatrillion times bigger then the sun" (Harrison 18; De Noüy 104). This "mathematical calculation" abruptly became a threat, a literal "fear of a black planet" in the case of HeLa. The calculation was of a fleshliness that not only outweighed the globe but threatened to take it over: "HeLa, with a generation time of about 24 hours, if allowed to grow under optimal cultural conditions, would have taken over the world by this time" (H. W. Jones et al.947). The calculation of the putative volume of the culture when "allowed" to multiply freely was not just of a cell culture but of how much Henrietta Lacks would weigh now, if all her cells were to be put back together – an "incredible amount" (Curtis).

Gartler's findings and methodology were taken up by Walter Nelson-Rees, director of a cell culture laboratory at the University of California, Berkeley, who was charged by the National Cancer Institute with keeping stocks of standard reference cells. Starting in 1974, Nelson-Rees began publishing lists of cell lines he judged to be HeLa-contaminated – an alarmingly high number. Contamination proved to be widespread. It is impossible to estimate how much research was invalidated by the findings that the researchers were mistakenly working on the wrong type of cell. Contaminated cell lines included a set of six cell cultures given to American scientists by Russian scientists under a biomedical information exchange that Nixon and Brezhnev negotiated in 1972 (Nelson-Rees et al. 751).

High profile incidents such as these, the emphasis on the "provenance" of cell lines (one of Nelson-Rees's favorite terms), the consistent use of the G6PD marker system, and Nelson-Rees's penchant for personifying HeLa cells all contributed to a revived interest in the figure of Henrietta Lacks in the 1970s and into the 1980s. The inability of scientists to explain why HeLa contaminated other cultures, but rarely the other way around, fed into a characterization of the cells as voracious, aggressive, and malicious.

A large number of articles about HeLa and Henrietta Lacks appeared in magazines and newspapers from *Science* to *Rolling Stone* between 1974 and 1977. Unlike the writers in the 1950s, these authors were not interested in the figure of the self-sacrificing housewife. Although cell cultures were being identified by this time by karyological studies – the appearance of their chromosomes – and a number of other systems of genetic polymorphism not characterized as specific to black or white populations, cell identity was still being explained primarily through the G6PD system. HeLa cells were depicted as having a distinct, identifiable biological race due to their particular genetic structure. Michael Rogers, reporting in the *Detroit Free Press*, explained this to his readers by writing, "In life, the HeLa source had been black and female. Even as a single layer of cells in a tissue culture laboratory, she remains so" (D4).

This identity as black and female was combined with a character described variously as "vigorous," "aggressive," "surreptitious," "a

monster among the Pyrex," "indefatigable," "undeflatable," "renegade," "catastrophic," and "luxuriant," The narrative of reproduction out of control was linked with promiscuity through references to the cell's wild proliferative tendencies and its "colorful" laboratory life. Rogers reported that he first heard about Henrietta Lacks through graffiti on the wall of the "men's room of a San Francisco medical school library" (D1). Nelson-Rees, the self-appointed watchdog of HeLa contamination for the cell culture community, was fond of talking about the appearances of "our lady friend." When describing the letters Nelson-Rees wrote to his fellow biologists when he suspected they were working with HeLa-contaminated cell lines, another journalist wrote, "It was like a note from the school nurse informing the parents that little Darlene had VD," Problems of contamination of cell lines were described as the scientific community's "dirty little family secret" (Gold 63, 64, 78).

In the personification of Henrietta Lacks as promiscuous and lascivious, in the characterization of HeLa cells as akin to venereal disease, in the facile linking of race and contamination, and in what I call the "one drop of HeLa" narratives of miscegenation and hybridity, I see the long reach of what Hortense Spillers has called the "American grammar" of race, that "the ruling episteme that releases the dynamics of naming and valuation remains grounded in the originating metaphors of captivity and mutilation" (68). The distressing literality of the excision, cultivation, exchange, mutation, and sale of a living, reproducing fragment of a black woman's cervix – without her or her family's knowledge or permission – evokes Spillers's theorization of the "captive body," as that which has been severed from its motive will and active desire. The captive body is "culturally unmade" by becoming "a thing for" the captor, removed and renamed (67).

I would argue further, that the racialized rhetoric of contamination is not something apart from the immortality narratives that I discussed earlier. With Gartler's 1967 bombshell to the tissue culture community, the desired scientific progen – the immortal cell line – the "precious baby," exhibited more autonomy than was expected or wanted of it and the promise turned to menace. The baby transformed into a monster, supplanting and destroying more legitimate scientific progeny, such as the tokens of political good will on the part of Russian scientists, the WISH line, and Monroe Vincent's prostate cells. Because this transformation was detected and narrated in terms of racial difference, the already menacing aspect of malignant immortality became inextricably wound with a threat to scientific order and a set of racial and sexual metaphors of contamination and miscegenation.

These anxieties provoked by the HeLa cells' repetitive appearances are underpinned by the more general transgressions of the object of the immortal cell line across understandings of the life and death of intact bodies. Tissue culture was designed as a microcosm of the human body; it is the double, made for the visualization of disease processes and as the stuff of experimental practice. In some cases, it is made from the bodies of the experimenters. This double, as Sarah Kofman observes, is "neither living nor dead"; it is "designed to supplement the living, to perfect it, to make it immortal" (148)—but faced with this double, there is a shock, a lack of recognition.

Conclusion

The two forms of immortality that I have gone through here – the beneficent immortal chicken heart, wonder fathered by modern science, cells in a test-tube body form of immortality, and the racialized, malignant, out-of-control immortality have both functioned to deflect attention from what mobilized them in the first place – Henrietta Lacks's death. This is evident in the treatment of her apparent misdiagnosis as a footnote to scientific genius. It is also manifest in the volatile, threatening personification arising from the contamination narrative.

This effacement of death has not dropped away with the 1990s version of the HeLa story. Rather, the immortalized Henrietta Lacks has taken on a distinctly economic cast. In media accounts, she has become a figure of economic exploitation, with a contemporary right to sue for compensation. Lacks has become

personified as the holder of an investment account, where the original capital was those first biopsy cells (for example, see Stepney). These should have had a dollar value from the beginning, because look what they would be worth today, after all these years in the investment account that is the burgeoning biotechnology industry. Lacks's family is cast into the role of the rightful heirs to the proceeds of this "investment" who cannot collect, because nobody ever patented the cells and thus it is difficult to pin down either past or present profit, or any one party who could benefit from the commercial exchange of HeLa cells and all their products and permutations.

Race reenters the story here as demarcating lines of economic power and privilege. As one of George Gey's colleagues commented to him in 1954, it was "out of the goodness" of Gey's heart that HeLa cells, only three years after their establishment, had become "general scientific property."[5] As a black woman from a black family, Henrietta Lacks walked into a clinic at Johns Hopkins University Hospital, where there was no institutional, ethical, or legal framework to ensure that she or her family was in a position to execute any kind of decision – out of the goodness of their hearts or otherwise – as to the fate of the cells.

Her family and friends, long left out of the story, are now being interviewed as key players in a drama where Henrietta Lacks's cells became important tools of modern medicine without her or her family's permission. With contemporary awareness that significant tools of modern medicine are also valuable commodities, endless reproduction and worldwide distribution remain part of a story of Lacks's immortality, but the metaphors have become those of the growth of capital and those of miscegenation and contamination have retreated into the background of the story.

An analysis of the significance of this story to contemporary discussions of the body as property, the implications of laws which allow for patenting of living organisms and materials, and other cases of immortal cell lines made from human tissues remains to be written. In anticipation of these concerns, this essay has attempted yet one more return to the origin of the HeLa cell line. What this return had indicated is that at the establishment of this cell line exists a moment of irredeemable silence. Lacks's illness and treatment in 1951 at Johns Hopkins took place in an institutional, cultural, and scientific setting that had no room in it for heroic agency or any other expression of personal will on her part, even the simple act of donation. Recognition of this absence places the establishment of the first immortal human cell line and the science of tissue culture within the long and troubled history of human experimentation (see Lederer).

The relationship between immortal cell lines and human experimentation has been obscured by a "false and misleading plenitude" of personification. This functions to animate the cells with an autonomous will, as though they were beneficent or malevolent independent of the scientific apparatus and constant tending that maintains their "life" in the laboratory. The narrative of immortality – beneficent, malignant, or monetary – masks the death at its origin. Although it is difficult to say whether an accurate diagnosis of adenocarcinoma would have helped in Lacks's treatment, the total absence of questioning of the circumstances and adequacy of her medical treatment – even with the clearly stated admission of diagnostic error published in 1971 – indicates the power of the concepts of immortality produced by the life of these cells.

The HeLa cell line, even though referred to as an individual entity with a clear physical relation to an individual named Henrietta Lacks, does not exist in a single place, is not a tiny vial containing an ever-living cell. The cells grow and divide, are split up to make new cultures, and are distributed to live and divide further in laboratories around the world. Various generations of them remain in stasis, stored in the freezers of cell culture banks. The original biopsy was a piece of tissue, not a single cell, and there exist many subtypes of the HeLa cell line. HeLa cells have been used for years as one part in hybridization procedures which merge two kinds of cells to make a new and distinct cell line. To speak of the HeLa cell line is to speak of a distributed, heterogenous thing which is always growing, multiplying, and changing.

HeLa thus serves as its own metaphor. It is not a story to which there is a single conclusion.

Immortality, the uncanny double, and the cultural, scientific, and individual effects of ideas of biological race have existed in an intricate reciprocity with the matter and practice of the science of tissue culture in this history. The resulting personification of HeLa simultaneously captures and erases human experience of this twentieth-century biomedical reach toward the technical alleviation of aging and death.

NOTES

1 Charles Pomerat, letter to George Gey, 5 March 1954, George Gey Papers, Alan Mason Chesney Medical Archives, Baltimore. All letters cited are quoted with permission from the George Gey Papers.
2 Ronald H. Berg, letter to George Gey, 24 November 1953. Berg was referring to a story that had appeared in the *Minneapolis Star* in 1954 and gave Lacks's name, although it is unclear who released the name.
3 C. M. Pomerat, letter to George Gey, 19 February 1954. Dr. George Gey, Jr. (qtd. in Kelly A_1).
4 Stanley Gartler, letter to George Gey, 16 March 1966.
5 Charles Pomerat, letter to George Gey, 5 March 1954.

REFERENCES

Alberts, Bruce, et al.
   Molecular Biology of the Cell, and ed. New York: Garland, 1989.
Bang, Frederick
   "History of Tissue Culture at Johns Hopkins." *Bulletin of the History of Medicine* 51 (1977): 516–37.
Brown, Russell, and James Henderson
   "The Mass Production and Distribution of HeLa Cells at Tuskegee Institute, 1953–1955." *Journal of the History of Medicine* 38 (1983): 415–31.
Carrel, Alexis
   "The New Cytology." *Science* 73 (1931): 331–45.
Carrel, Alexis
   "On the Permanent Life of Tissues outside of the Organism." *Journal of Experimental Medicine* 15 (1912): 516–28.

Carrel, Alexis
"Physiological Time." *Science* 74 (1929): 618–21.

Culliton, Barbara J.
"HeLa Cells: Contaminating Cultures around the World." *Science* 184 (1974): 1058–59.

Curtis, Adam
Interview. BBC Radio. 14 Apr. 1997.

Davidson, Bill
"Probing the Secret of Life." *Colliers* 14 May 1954: 78–83.

De Noüy, P. Lecomte
Biological Time. New York: Macmillan, 1937.

Doyle, Richard
On Beyond Living: Rhetorical Transformations of the Life Sciences. Stanford: Stanford University Press, 1997.

Ebeling, Albert H.
"Dr. Carrel's Immortal Chicken Heart." *Scientific American* Jan. 1942: 22–24.

Fee, Elizabeth
"Venereal Disease: The Wages of Sin?" *Passion and Power: Sexuality in History.* Ed. Kathy Peiss and Christina Simmons. Philadelphia: Temple University Press, 1989. 178–98.

Foucault, Michel
"What Is an Author?" *Language, Counter-Memory, Practice.* Ed. Donald Bouchard. Trans. Donald Bouchard and Sherry Simon. Ithaca: Cornell University Press, 1977. 113–38.

Fraley, Elwin E., et al.
"Spontaneous *in vitro* Neoplastic Transformation of Adult Human Prostatic Epithelium." *Science* 170 (1970): 540–2.

Gartler, Stanley
"Apparent HeLa Cell Contamination of Human Heteroploid Cell Lines." *Nature* 217 (1968): 750–1.

Gartler, Stanley
"Genetic Markers as Tracers in Cell Culture." *Second Decennial Review Conference on Cell Tissue and Organ Culture, September 1967.* National Cancer Institute Monograph 26: 167–90.

Gold, Michael
A Conspiracy of Cells: One Woman's Immorial Legacy and the Medical Scandal It Caused. Albany: State University of New York Press, 1985.

Haraway, Donna J.
"Universal Donors in a Vampire Culture: It's All in the Family: Biological Kinship Categories in the Twentieth-Century United States." *Un-*

common Ground: Toward Reinventing Nature. Ed. William Cronon. New York: Norton, 1995. 321–66.

Harris, Henry
The Cells of the Body: A History of Somatic Cell Genetics. Cold Spring Harbor: Cold Spring Harbor Laboratory Press, 1995.

Harrison, Ross G.
"On the Status and Significance of Tissue Culture." *Arch. exp. Zellforsch* 6 (1927): 4–27.

Hayflick, Leonard
"Biology of Human Aging." *American Journal of the Medical Sciences* 265 (1973): 433–45.

Hayflick, Leonard
"Establishment of a Line (WISH) of Human Amnion Cells in Continuous Cultivation." *Experimental Cell Research* 28 (1962): 14–20.

Hsu, T. C.
"Discussion of Genetic Markers in Cell Culture." *Second Decennial Review Conference on Cell Tissue and Organ Culture, September 1967.* National Cancer Institute Monograph 26: 191–5.

JanMohammed, Abdul R
"Sexuality on/of the Racial Border: Foucault, Wright, and the Articulation of 'Racialized Sexuality.' " *Discourses of Sexuality: From Aristotle to Aids.* Ed. Donna Stanton. Ann Arbor: University of Michigan Press, 1992. 94–116.

Jones, Howard W., et al.
"After Office Hours: The HeLa Cell and a Reappraisal of Its Origin." *Obstetrics and Gynecology* 38 (1977): 945–9.

Jones, James H.
Bad Blood: The Tuskegee Syphilis Experiment. 2nd ed. New York: Free, 1993.

Kelly, Jacques
"Her Cells Made Her Immortal." *Baltimore Sun* 18 Mar. 1997: A1 + .

Kofman, Sarah
Freud and Fiction. Trans. Sarah Wykes. Oxford: Polity, 1991.

Lederer, Susan
Subjected to Science: Human Experimentation in America before the Second World War. Baltimore: Johns Hopkins University Press, 1995.

Nelson-Rees, Walter, et al.
"HeLa-like Marker Chromosomes and Type-A Variant Glucose-6-Phosphate Dehydrogenase Isoenzyme in Human Cell Cultures Producing Mason-Pfizer Monkey Virus-like Particles." *Journal of the National Cancer Institute* 53 (1974): 751–7.

Pascoe, Peggy
    "Miscegenation Law, Court Cases, and Ideologies of Race in Twentieth-Century America." *The Journal of American History* 53 (1996): 44–69.

Pauly, Phillip
    Controlling Life: Jacques Loeb and the Engineering Ideal in Biology. Berkeley: University of California Press, 1990.

Rabinow, Paul
    "Severing the Ties: Fragmentation and Dignity in Late Modernity." *Essays on the Anthropology of Reason.* Princeton: Princeton University Press, 1996. 129–61.

Rogers, Michael
    "The HeLa Strain." *Detroit Free Press* 21 Mar. 1976: D1 + .

Spillers, Hortense
    "Mama's Baby, Papa's Maybe: An American Grammar Book." *Diacritics* 17.2 (1987): 65–81.

Stepney, Rob
    "Immortal, Divisible: Henrietta Lacks Died 40 Years Ago but Her Cells Live On and Multiply." *Independent* 13 Mar. 1994: 50.

Witowski, J. A.
    "Alexis Carrel and the Mysticism of Tissue Culture." *Medical History* 23 (1979): 279–96.

29

A Digital Image of the Category of the Person

Joseph Dumit

Given the explosive rate at which the fields of molecular genetics and neurobiology are expanding, it is inevitable that the perception of our own nature, in the field of sex as in all attributes of our physical and mental lives, will be increasingly dominated by concepts derived from the biological sciences. (S. A. LeVay)

[...]

Objective Self-Fashioning

Within [a] broad sketch of three symbiotic actors – experts, laypersons, and mediators – each drawing upon and reconfiguring the presuppositions of the others, I am going to concentrate my attention on the aspect I call objective self-fashioning. The objective self is an active category of the person that is developed through references to expert knowledge and invoked through facts. The objective self is also an embodied theory of human nature, both scientific and popular. Objective self-fashioning calls attention to the equivocal site of this production of new objective knowledge of the self. From one perspective, science produces facts that define who our selves are objectively, which we then accept. From another perspective, our selves are fashioned by us out of the facts available to us through the media, and these categories of persons are in turn the cultural basis from which new theories of human nature are constructed.

Kramer provides an excellent illustration of this by relating how both he and his patients incorporate the fact that Prozac makes some people "better." Out of this fact Sam fashions a new objectively true self and a new history (of a self that was defective until Prozac), while Kramer goes on to experiment with Prozac and draw upon other human and animal facts to propose a new set of theories of human nature, packaged for a popular audience and read by psychiatrists and other neuroscientists.

Objective self-fashioning is thus an acknowledgment of local mutations in categories of persons highlighting the active and continual process of self-definition and self-participation in that process. Objective self-fashioning is how we take facts about ourselves – about our bodies, minds, capacities, traits, states, limitations, propensities, etc. – that we have read, heard, or otherwise encountered in the world, and *incorporate* them into our lives. As anthropologists and other scholars we are [...] most often in the mediator role, casting theories of objective selves out of our own categories of the person.

These cases point to two interrelated meanings of objective self-fashioning: (1) How we

Joseph Dumit, "A Digital Image of the Category of the Person," in G. L. Downey and J. Dumit, eds., *Cyborgs and Citadels: Anthropological Interventions in Emerging Sciences and Technologies.* Santa Fe, NM: SAR Press, 1997. Reprinted by permission. © 1997 by the School for Advanced Research, Santa Fe, New Mexico.

come to understand ourselves as subject to the scientific, medical, and technical discourses of objectivity, and (2) How these discourses choose "us" as their object of study. The difference between the two meanings is a matter of point of view. On the one hand these cases point to the ways in which we fashion our selves – person, body, brain, and mind – out of ready-made objective types, and therefore subject ourselves to the disciplines of science and technology, expertise and machines. This kind of self encounters objectivity in the form of resistance; who we are is a product of discourse networks and technologies over which we have little control (Kittler 1985). On the other hand the practices of science, technology, and medicine fashion selves as objective facts through scientific experimentation, subject selection, and medical taxonomic exercises. This latter case emphasizes social and disciplinary production of selves, while the former emphasizes cultural presuppositions built into concepts and practices.

Attending to the categories of the person built into facts and attending to facts-in-the-world as facts enables us to see more clearly how medical and scientific claims, along with our own, are as much about dividing persons as they are about describing them. Here, along with Emily Martin, I believe we should also "acknowledge the varieties of ways in which experience resists science and medicine" (Martin 1987). More specifically, the question of objective self-fashioning raises the issue of creativity with regard to facts. Rayna Rapp, for instance, has followed the different ways in which people incorporate the possibilities and results of amniocentesis into their lives – for one mother, the fact of a genetic defect means a decision to abort, while for another it means preparing to take proper care of a challenging baby (Rapp 1990, 1993). Martin and Rapp are both calling for a reader-response analysis of our relation to science, medicine, and other facts of life.

PET Scanning in Courts and at the Movies

With PET imaging, we can begin to explore the degree to which biological and social factors affect brain chemistry.

Perhaps one day we will speak of an individual's brain chemotype as well as his or her genotype and phenotype. (Henry N. Wagner, Jr., and Linda E. Ketchum)

I am concerned with objective self-fashioning as a result of my work in the field of positron emission tomography (PET) scanning, a brain-imaging technique that promises to provide images of the living brain in action as it thinks, worries, adds, gets sad, and goes mad. I have been examining what might be called, following Stone (1992), the "virtual community" of PET scans – the heterogeneous community of people who interact with these scans and each other. In addition to fieldwork among those who work with the injection and imaging of radiopharmaceuticals, I have interviewed graduate students, imaging technologists, and PET researchers. I have also followed how PET scans have appeared on TV, in newspapers, and in Hollywood movies. In particular, my attention has been drawn to the use of PET scans as authoritative facts in claims about how the world and people objectively are – that is, what attributes and properties our objective bodies have, and what this means for the rest of our persons: our lived bodies, subjective souls, and/or our selves (see, for example, Begley 1991).

The PET scan, produced in university research laboratories, is one of the iconic centerpieces of the 1990s' "Decade of the Brain." This recent technology produces images of living brain and body functions through the use of radioactive tracers. Unlike CT (computed tomography) and MR (magnetic resonance), which provide images of the tissue and structure of the brain, PET produces high-resolution, functional images of blood flow and glucose consumption within the brain. Producing PET images is an extremely capital- and expertlabor-intensive process. PET requires an infrastructure – including interdisciplinary personnel, a cyclotron, a nuclear chemistry lab, high-speed computers, and a scanner – that costs upwards of six million dollars to install and one to two million dollars a year to operate. Government fears of high-cost medicine have contributed to the fact that PET did not enter regular clinical medicine as CT and MRI did, but has remained an experimental science into the 1990s (Dumit 1995).

After an experiment is designed and representative subjects selected, a small cyclotron is used to produce radioactive isotopes. These isotopes are short-lived, with half-lives that range from two minutes to two hours. They are immediately "tagged" or attached onto other chemicals to form radio-labeled substances, or radiopharmaceuticals. Fluorine-18, for instance, can be tagged onto glucose, and Oxygen-15 can be tagged onto water. The radiopharmaceuticals thus formed either mimic or are analogs of substances regularly circulating through the brain.

The next step is to set up the experiment, inject the human subject with the radiopharmaceutical, and place him or her in the scanner. While the subject carries out some task (such as looking at words) or attempts to maintain some state (such as rest or anxiety), his or her brain is assumed to be using energy differentially in those regions involved in that activity or state. Scans can be taken quickly for a "picture" of blood flow during a thirty-second period, or they are taken after forty minutes for a "picture" of the glucose utilization up to the scan.

The scanner depends on the physics and biophysics of positron emission. As the radiopharmaceutical decays in the brain, it emits positrons that travel a short distance, run into an electron, and burst into two photons or gamma rays that fly off at almost 180 degrees. The scanner consists of a ring of detectors connected to a computing system that reacts when two detectors are hit by gamma rays at about the same time. The computer then assumes that there was a positron along the line between the two detectors.

After collecting hundreds of thousands of data points, the computer attempts mathematically to reconstruct the approximate spatial density of the radiopharmaceutical, a process involving many assumptions about brain biochemistry and metabolism. The result is a simultaneously simple (in the sense of transparent) and complex image of a human brain at work. In addition to appearing in popular magazines and newspapers, these images are increasingly being used in court cases to argue for

incompetency and insanity as well as neurotoxic damage and head trauma (see, for example, Stipp 1992).

To begin considering the role these images can play in our own lives, I would like to present an example of PET as depicted in a popular film about schizophrenia, violence, and insanity. The following is my own transcription of part of the final four minutes of a 1989 movie, *Rampage*, directed by William Friedkin. I believe it represents the first use of PET in a Hollywood movie. At this point in the script, Charles Reese has committed six grisly murders and is about to be found guilty of them by a jury.

In a courtroom.
Defense attorney: [*whispering to his client, Charles Reese*] We still have a shot to save your life. We can still show the jury that you weren't responsible.

Cut to the Judge's chamber.
Defense attorney: Your honor, I'm going to request that a PET scan be performed as part of a defense to show the jury that he is mentally ill, during the penalty phase.
Prosecutor: A PET scan purports to show only a patient's brain chemistry at a certain moment of time. In this case it is after the crime is committed.
Judge: A PET scan is a form of medical imaging which is used in the diagnosis of epilepsy, some Alzheimer's, as well as mental deficiency. Depriving Mr. Reese of putting this in front of the jury...
Prosecutor: [*interrupting*] It's only another gadget to hide Mr. Reese's responsibility.
Judge: [*pausing, contemplating*] Well, we're going to err on the side of caution. I'm going to order the test. We'll let the jury evaluate it. Nobody knows what it will show.

Cut to medical laboratory, Charles Reese is put in the PET scanner. A computer-generated rotating skull is shown, peeled back to reveal a rotating brain in red, then green.
Two scans come up side by side. One is labeled "Normal Control," the other "Reese, John." The scans look significantly different.
Medical Doctor: [*pointing to Reese's scan*] These are abnormal patterns, without a doubt.
Defense Attorney: What does that tell you?

Medical Doctor: Well, this yellow-green area here is consistent with schizophrenia. What you are seeing is a computer-enhanced image of the chemistry of the brain. And what it shows is a picture of madness.

Cut to the courtroom again.Jury Foreman: Your honor, based on the new scientific evidence, We, the jury, find that the defendant should go to a state mental hospital.
At the end of the movie, text: "Charles Reese has served four years in a state mental facility. He has had one hearing to determine his eligibility for release. His next hearing is in four months."

In the microcosm of this movie, a convicted brutal murderer is not put into prison but is treated as a mentally diseased subject who may be released in the near future. The sole element presented to account for the jury's decision is a PET scan. The words of the doctor – "This is his brain ... These areas are definitely abnormal ... consistent with schizophrenia ... a picture of madness" – concatenate a history of struggle and controversy within the medical and legal communities regarding a host of relationships: PET scan to brain, brain to schizophrenia, schizophrenia to insanity. In the movie, the PET scan stands as *the fact*, the linchpin referent, which holds the chain of connections together, convincing a jury that an abnormal brain scan is an abnormal brain is an abnormal person who does not bear responsibility for murder.

Not one of these connections, however, is settled in the scientific and medical community, in the legal community, or in my own mind. Medical anthropologist Horacio Fabrega discusses the reluctance of Anglo-American society to accept a theory of illness-caused deviance. He suggests that this is primarily due to a need to have the will be socially or rationally motivated: "In essence, mental illness as a defense of homicide requires a suspension of our attribution of personhood if the latter is equated with willful symbolic behavior" (Fabrega 1989:592). Although I think that this argument makes sense in general when comparing societies, I am interested in the ways in which the attributes of personhood in the US are continually contested using batteries

of facts. *Rampage* is an intervention into the facts of PET and the facts of life, presenting as it does a definition of PET, a set of presumptions about imaging and mental illness, and a possible scenario of PET's use in a court. Watching the movie, one confronts these facts of PET and is drawn into the virtual community of its images

What is the status of these "facts" proclaimed via Hollywood? Are they true? These questions trip me up as I watch a world of biotechnopower where technology judges who is responsible/sane/rational and who is not. This is a "view of the world that might be different from my current one" (Martin 1985:195). Like Emily Martin, I often find myself stumbling "over accepting [these] scientific medical statements as truth" (1985:10). But Hollywood reframes the question of truth, calling for an examination of the ways in which new facts, worlds, and persons are produced, distributed, and incorporated. For example, *Rampage* mediates between experts who presumably provided the details of PET, brains, and schizophrenia, and us lay viewers.

Though some might want to claim that there is a set of accepted medical truths, the purpose of this paper is to work with a notion of uneven flows of knowledge and contradictory versions of acceptability and legitimacy. We don't know how much we don't know about medical truths. Hollywood movies, along with best-selling novels written by physicians and our own doctors' advice, help to shape our notions of "accepted medical knowledge" and thus help shape our categories of the person. As part of my ethnography I follow this shaping process, examining how facts travel in the world, but also how they never travel alone. Instead they are packaged in the form of stories, explanations, and experiences, as authorized or unauthorized accounts, and they necessarily include definitions of human nature. Faced with novel facts, we may indeed stumble over accepting them.

When I have shown the movie clip from *Rampage* and pictures of PET scans during talks, some people with social constructionist tendencies and some with strong feelings about the social or psychodynamic nature of schizophrenia have been upset over the biosocial totalitarian implications of this apparently seamless presentation of clear difference between "them" and "us." I want first to note that despite constant work on PET and schizophrenia over the last twenty years, there is still much disagreement over whether PET is ready yet for clinical work with mental illness. In addition, over 90 percent of the PET community furiously opposes the use of PET for the insanity defense (Mayberg 1992; Rojas-Burke 1993). In spite of this unreliability for regular clinical work, in some places PET has nevertheless been heavily supported, including financially, by mental illness activists, that is, organized families of people with mental illness. Here another set of contests emerges. Should researchers look for biological correlates of schizophrenia, and how should such correlates be interpreted? What do the facts mean? Surprisingly, the meaning of these facts does not emerge solely from the research community; the whole virtual community must be examined.

In order to examine this story I have to back up forty years to the beginning of the "biological revolution" in psychiatry. During the 1950s and through the early 1960s, new pharmacological agents – drugs such as thorazine (chlorpromazine), lithium, and valium, which helped reduce symptoms in mental patients – were discovered and allowed many patients to live at home for the first time (e.g., Andreassen 1984, 1989). In the 1960s and 1970s, however, mental illness treatment critics organized to reform institutionalization practices. These critics created an uneasy alliance with psychotherapeutic psychiatrists who were invested in talking cures, and together they campaigned heavily for the notion that schizophrenia and the affective disorders were psychogenic. These "antipsychiatrists" argued that mental illness was socially constructed and therefore in need of social cures, not drugs (Laing 1967; Szasz 1970). Their argument drew in part on the fact that there were no known biological mechanisms for mental illness. Perhaps, the antipsychiatric camp argued, drugs only affected the symptoms, not the cause.

In the late 1970s and 1980s the increasing availability of new diagnostic techniques such as computed tomography (CT) scanning and PET scanning changed this perspective. These techniques offered different ways of examining

living brains (Pardes and Pincus 1985). The medical imaging advantage was measured in two ways. First, it allowed correlation between brains and diagnosis among living humans, thus permitting anew the equation of "brain = illness." Second, medical imaging promised to provide early warnings of the onset of mental illness, one of the largest problems in its treatment and prevention.

PET in particular was hailed as significant because it promised to provide functional images of the brain in action. Early on, it was realized that many head injuries, strokes, and epilepsies leave the structure of the brain relatively unchanged but show up with different degrees of clarity on PET scans. In biological psychiatry, such proof of pathology was talked about as a Holy Grail. One biological psychiatrist, for instance, began a review of PET with the statement, "In the 1970s, the antipsychiatry movement almost had us (Szasz 1970), but now we have proof" (Kuhar 1989). For this subdiscipline, eager to demonstrate the physiology of mental illness, images of brain differences between mentally ill patients and non-mentally ill controls were facts that implied that a full biological explanation of mental disease was only a matter of time. This technique thus functioned as a promise that mental illness was not "in the head" but in the brain.

Patients, Victims: On Seeing Oneself in a Brain Mirror

I find a tremendous interest in PET scanning everywhere I go. I do a lot of public speaking, and I find that people are very interested in this. And they are always appreciative of the first ten minutes where I go through how positrons decay into gamma rays and the coincidence detections. They follow this, they understand it, they have a concept of how they whole thing works, and they are terribly fascinated with the whole idea. People are tremendously interested in the brain. You know, almost everybody thinks they are going to get Aizheimer's disease. If for no other reason, they want to know what is going on. (Richard Haier)

To illustrate the ongoing negotiation of personhood and illness and call attention to the wider virtual community of objective self-fashioning around PET, I turn now to one site of my fieldwork, the Brain Imaging Center at the University of California at Irvine (UCI). This center was unlike most PET centers in two important respects. First, it was located in a psychiatry department, not in a chemistry, nuclear medicine, or radiology department. Second, for a PET center, it was extremely underfunded. Other major PET centers have received either Department of Energy or National Institutes of Health program grants to support the multimillion-dollar costs of laboratories in nuclear medicine or radiology. UCI's program was started in a psychiatry department and purchased its scanner and then its cyclotron with bank loans. Monthly payments were dependent upon an external fee schedule that dampened free operation. In the words of one researcher.

> YY: We were sort of a shoestring operation. I think we were sort of an upstart in some sense, because other places that have PET centers are much better endowed than we were. We were sort of the scrappy, come-from-behind, shoestring budget kind of guys. And we did things on a budget that is probably one-tenth of the budget that Hopkins or UCLA has for their PET centers. They are very well endowed and they support their PET centers in a maximum way. I think that we have a much more sort of guerrilla-type operation. We are unconventional in that we did so many things on our own, but I think we were fairly productive. We've done a fair amount of work even though we are on a shoestring budget, relative to a lot of other facilities.

This PET center operated from such a precarious financial position that its researchers spent much time doing local community outreach. They found a ready alliance with the mental illness community in Orange County, especially with families who had schizophrenia among their children. As Haier details below, the psychodynamic approach, while supporting the social nature of schizophrenia, often localized this causation into the family and specifically in the mother.

> RH: The Lockhardts contributed $250,000 to help pay for our scanner ... By that time, the scanner had arrived and we were making pictures, they had schizophrenia in their family, and they were very interested in it. And they knew our emphasis was going to be on schizophrenia. We always approach it that in the long run, the main help will come through research. Probably not for people who currently have it, but because there is a genetic component, there are still the grandchildren to worry about. And families find this compelling. Remember, even in the late '80s, the public was just coming out of the idea of the schizogenic mother, that schizophrenia was somehow induced because the mother was doing something wrong. Virtually every set of parents that we talk to now, when schizophrenics are now in their twenties and their thirties, almost every parent has had the experience of going to a psychologist early on and getting the idea that somehow they were at fault. So it is all in their memory. And the idea that it is biological has caught on real fast over the last five or eight years. Family groups have organized around this to support biological research, and imaging is obviously at the heart of that. So it is kind of a natural sequence of events.

Supporting PET research became a means for these families to empower their participation within science, stay informed, and come to understand their role as accountable to, but not responsible for, the fact of familial schizophrenia. Along with the National Alliance for the Mentally Ill (NAMI), these families advocated a biological redefinition of mental illness and actively helped to produce facts about the nature of personhood and mental illness (OTA 1992). Objective self-fashioning is here a strategy without which such research might not get done.

Within the daily practice of clinical psychiatry, these brain-imaging techniques have also helped sufferers deal with the fact of mental illness symptoms. The following excerpt is from an interview with Dr. Joseph Wu, a psychiatrist at UCI.

JD: Do you show the patients their PET scans?

JW: Oh yes. We try and show them the PET scans, and then some of these patients will refer them out to people. I have a part-time private practice with some of them, and they may like to continue with me.

JD: Does it help them overcome part of the stigma of mental illness?

JW: I think so. I think that definitely. One of the intrinsic messages is that the depression isn't something to be ashamed of; it is an illness which needs to be understood. And it is not something that is their fault.

I think that there is a destigmatization that occurs with the biological emphasis. It is a fine line, because there are some arenas of personal responsibility that people can and should assume for their feelings. But I think it is a very narrow and tricky balance. It is important not to think that it is all biology; that can lead to a certain eschewing of what is appropriate for one's own role in understanding one's emotions. On the other hand, I think that people can go overboard, and say, "Gee, I'm entirely at fault for how I feel." [It is important] to try and understand one's role in helping to monitor one's emotions without being unnecessarily harshly judgmental of oneself.

The reconfiguration of mental illness as biological through the use of PET scans becomes part of a personal reconfiguration of one's own category of person. A strict division between the biological self and the personal self is not at issue here. Rather, the relations between the two selves are redistributed so that, although the patient must continue to experience the illness and live with it, she or he no longer has to identify with it. The diseased brain, in this case, becomes a part of a biological body that is experienced phenomenologically but is not the bearer of personhood. Rather, the patient who looks at his or her PET brain scan is an innocent sufferer rationally seeking help.

Other researchers who have also shown patients their scans have agreed that, especially in cases of neurological and mental diseases, which are often accompanied with self-disgust or a sense of failure, both the scan and the process help legitimate the problem. They make it something that can at least be explored. These patients (and their families) want schizophrenia and depression to be medicalized, to have a single cause or explanation, even if there is no solution or cure for them.

Anthropologists of medicine have long explored this kind of effect as a crucial aspect of every health care system. Jean Jackson discusses the failure of culture to come to grips with chronic pain (Jackson 1994; see also Good et al. 1992). The tension Jackson describes involves mental versus physical pain. Chronic pain sufferers seek out, even hope for, positive test results, even cancer, because then there would be something to point to and work on to solve the problem. Regarding depression, Dr. Wu concurred with this interpretation when I asked him about the history of psychiatry.

JD: Dr. Wu, Nancy Andreasen has written about the biological revolution in psychiatry. You were in medical school during this time. Did you also get the other side of psychiatry?

JW: Oh, very much so. I would say that most of the psychiatrists in this department are still analytically, dynamically, focused. I would say that biologically oriented psychiatrists still make up a minority of the faculty. Maybe 30 to 40 percent, as opposed to the psychodynamically oriented people [who] are 50 to 60 percent.

JD: Do both of these sides come into play in your work?

JW: Somewhat. For me, when I do a study of depression, there is a part of me, a whole human dimension, that really tugs at my heart. Part of me feels moved by the pain of the patient that we work with. I am also moved by the courage and the willingness that many of these people have to participate in this study, even with the depth of their emotional pain and anguish. I think we try to offer to them the gratification that comes with knowing that they are contributing to the fund of knowledge that will eventually help to, we hope, eliminate depression or mitigate it. And that is something that many of these people find appealing, because there may be some greater purpose to their suffering. It is a way of reconnecting in some sense with the broader community. It is a way of making a personal meaning out of the emotional pain that they suffer from. For me, I see the whole biological aspect as not being contradictory or mutually exclusive from the psychodynamic aspect. I really see it as complementary and synergistic with the dynamic aspect. There are some people that see it as either/or. I see it more as a both/and type of proposition.

PET research into mental illness has thus become an area of study worthy of community support and patient contribution. The both/and approach to psychiatry, popularized by writers like Peter Kramer (1993), involves realizing that the brain can be altered by the social environment *and* by genetic development and drugs. The kindling theory, for instance, suggests that repeated abuse during childhood can build up depressed reactions until the depression is neurologically self-sustaining (Post and Ballenger 1984, cited in Kramer 1993:110–18, 334). The brain becomes "rewired" as if the person had been born that way. In the same vein, both psychodynamic talk therapy and psychopharmaceutical drug treatment can change brain chemistry and rewire the brain toward freedom from depression. Note that the brain remains the bearer of mental illness, but has now become an intersection for social and biological influences.

Dr. Wu's "both/and" approach to psychodynamic and biological explanations of mental illness arises, I suspect, from taking patients' perspectives into his account. Patients are able to participate in social and medical reform by participating in research that might produce facts implying a category of person who suffers from a physiological rather than a psychological disturbance.

If we see that responsibility and causations are part of our categories of persons, this example demonstrates the flexibility and contestibility of these categories. Patients and activists are actively getting together to support and promote research on the shared biological nature of mental illness because of their desire to see the results and their hope for cures. Paul Rabinow has called this grouping on the basis of biological commonality "biosociality" (Rabinow 1992). A key point to remember here is that the facts of biology around which these groups are organizing are not necessarily fully decided within the scientific community. Yet they provide the means for social action, justifications for support of certain kinds of research, and arguments for a biological understanding of mental illness. The facts enable the groups to further promote a category of the objective person that does not, in their view, prejudge them and condemn them to blame and guilt. This involves understanding the many very different ways facts (science, technology, nature) and experience (subjectivity, personality, culture) are constantly shaping and tripping over each other. These people are working creatively to refigure responsibility for mental illness, in this case to biology, in an attempt to gain control over this part of their world.

The challenge here isn't just to the social construction of mental illness. This is not a simple story of the gradual emergence of the right view of depression, schizophrenia, and PET scanning. Biological psychiatry, for instance, often leads to deinstitutionalization, which burdens lower-income communities more than upper-income ones. But this story is not one of victims and blame. By tracing facts-in-the-world throughout the virtual community of PET images, I hope that responsibility for these situations might be multiplied – that accountability might adhere to experts, mediators, and laypersons alike for their participation in objective self-fashioning.

Cyborg: Machines My Eyes and Ears

My present research with PET scanning is concerned with investigating chemical reactions constantly taking place inside the human brain, and how these reactions affect how we think, feel and act ... how they affect whether we are afraid, violent or destructive ... Perhaps we will be able to learn enough about the brain chemistry of fear, violence and destructiveness to save ourselves from the problems of interpersonal violence and war. (Henry N. Wagner)

When PET researcher Henry Wagner (1986: 253) says that "In PET, we now have a new set of eyes that permits us to examine the chemistry of the human mind," he is pointing to a particular kind of humanoid: a cyborg whose experience of vision includes the physiology of the brain as witnessed through PET scanning. Kramer and Sam listen to Prozac to hear Sam's true self speak. Some of us may shudder at the alienation implied in selves mediated by radiotracers, new pharmaceuticals, and multimillion-dollar bioscience. Others may breathe a sigh of relief at not being blamed for personally constructing schizophrenic children, at finally being respected as having wonderful children who happen to have a visible and therefore real brain dysfunction. Still others may wonder when and how they will be classed as normal or abnormal, or if the binary categorization will finally prevail.

In conclusion, I have tried to point out some of the ways in which contemporary biomedical and scientific practices are culturally situated. These practices are participating in ongoing negotiations not just of specific brain-behavior-mind links but also of the nature of human nature and the significance of human differences. I have tried to show both the complexity of the process of producing contemporary neuroscientific facts and images as well as the numerous ways in which practical considerations often build in assumptions about human nature with undesirable and socially unequal consequences. My purpose is not to point a finger at any particular sets of people or techniques. I think it is necessary to recognize the social and cognitive benefits of these practices for many, many people. Rather, I am seeking to find a language to talk about multiple accountabilities between the diverse communities engaged with PET.

The challenges of how to understand the continuing and increasing presence of biotechnopower require close attention not only to the multiple uses and arenas of facts-in-the-world but also to their deployment within discourses of objectivity and to the ways that they have built-in, presupposed notions of human nature. The point is that science and medicine turn out to be our business on a daily basis. We are involved in them, they involve us, and they draw upon the ways in which we configure the person. My hunch is that this process will reveal much about the multiple circuits of theory transfer from laypersons to experts and back again to laypersons via all kinds of mediators—movies, magazines, personal physicians, and anthropologists. These circuits of fact distribution and presupposition are worth understanding if we want to play a critical role in our own understanding of our selves.

REFERENCES

Andreassen, Nancy.
1989 *Brain Imaging: Applications in Pychiatry.* Washington, DC: American Psychiatric Press.
Andreassen, Nancy.
1992 "Neuroradiology and Neuropsychiatry: A New Alliance." *American Journal of Neuroradiology* 13:841–3.
Begley, Sharon.
1991 "Thinking Looks Like This: PET Scans Show the Brain Recalling and Cogitating." *Newsweek* 118 (22):67(1).
Dumit, Joseph.
1995 "Mindful Images: PET Scans and Personhood in Biomedical America." Ph.D. diss., History of Consciousness, University of California-Santa Cruz.
Fabrega, Horacio
1989 "An Ethnomedical Perspective of Anglo-American Psychiatry." *American Journal of Psychiatry* 146:588–96.
Good, Mary-Jo, P. Brodwin, Byron J. Good, and Arthur Kleinman, eds.
1992 *Pain as Human Experience: An Anthropological Perspective.* Berkeley: University of California Press.
Jackson, Jean.
1994 "Chronic Pain and the Tension between the Body as Subject and Object. In Thomas J. Csordas, ed., *Embodiment and Experience: The Existential Ground of Culture and Self.* Cambridge: Cambridge University Press.

Kramer, Peter.
   1993   *Listening to Prozac; A Psychiatrist Explores Antidepressant Drugs and the Remaking of the Self.* New York: Viking
Kuhar, Michael J.
   1989   "Perspectives." In N.A. Sharif and M.E. Lewis, eds., *Brain Imaging: Techniques and Applications.* New York: Halstead Press.
Laing, R.D.
   1967   *The Politics of Experience and the Bird of Paradise.* Harmondsworth, UK: Penguin.
Martin, Emily.
   1987   *The Woman in the Body: A Cultural Analysis of Reproduction.* Boston: Beacon Press.
Mayburg, Helen S.
   1992   "Function Brain Scans as Evidence in Criminal Court: An Argument for Caution." *The Journal of Nuclear Medicine* 33 (6):18N–19N, 25N.
OTA (Office of Technology Assessment)
   1992   *The Biology of Mental Disorders.* New Developments in Neuroscience Series. Washington, DC: US Congress.
Pardes, Herbert and Harold Alan Pincus,
   1985   "Neuroscience and Psychiatry: An Overview." In H. Pardes and H. Pincus, eds., *The Integration of Neuroscience and Psychiatry.* Washington DC: American Psychiatric Press.
Post, Robert M. and James C. Ballinger, eds.
   1984   *Neurobiology of Mood Disorders.* Baltimore: Williams and Wilkins.

Rabinow, Paul.
   1992   "Artifiality and Enlightenment: From Sociobiology to Bioscciality." In Jonathan Crary and Sanford Kwinter, eds., *Incorporations.* New York: Zone Books (distributed by MIT Press).
Rapp, Rayna.
   1990   "Constructing Amniocentesis: Maternal and Medical Discourses." In Faye Ginsburg and Anna Lowenhaupt, eds., *Uncertain Terms: Negotiating Gender in American Culture.* Boston: Beacon.
Rapp, Rayna.
   1993   "Accounting for Amniocentesis." In Shirley Lindenbaum and Margaret Lock, eds., *Knowledge, Power, and Practice: The Anthropology of Medicine and Everyday Life.* Berkeley: University of California Press.
Rojas-Burke, J.
   1993   "PET Scans Advance as Tool in Insanity Defense." *Journal of Nuclear Medicine.* 34(1): N13–14.
Stipp, David.
   1992   "The Insanity Defense in Violent-Crime Cases Gets High-Tech Help." *Wall Street Journal* 4 March: A11.
Stone, Allucquere Roseanne.
   1992   "Virtual Systems." In Jonathan Crary and Sanford Kwinter, eds., *Incorporations.* New York: Zone.
Szasz, Thomas.
   1970   *The Manufacture of Madness: A Comparative Study of the Inquisition and the Mental Health Movement.* New York: Harper and Row.

30

Experimental Values
Indian Clinical Trials and Surplus Health

Kaushik Sunder Rajan

Two prominent Indian physicians recently described the clinical trials of new drugs in India as a 'new colonialism'. [...] But a moral critique of this kind, however legitimate in its own terms, does not adequately grasp the network of economic and social relations that the international health industry has established on a global scale. Even if all clinical trials conducted in India or other Third World countries adhered to the letter of the law and the spirit of ethical codes, the very structure of this network would remain one of exploitation. I shall outline here the dynamics of clinical trials in India, focusing especially on the huge capacity currently being built up in anticipation of the transfer of global trials to the subcontinent. This will provide a basis for interpreting the phenomenon in terms of concepts developed by myself and others currently researching this field, particularly those of *biocapital* and *surplus health*.

I. The Landscape of Clinical Trials

[...] The clinical-trials procedure is an elaborate one, conducted in a number of stages and contributing to the immense time, risk and expense of the drug development process:

a pre-clinical toxicological testing, [...] dosage studies, and a three-phase trial in humans. Phase I trials are conducted on a small number of healthy volunteers [...] Phase 2, [...] involves a few hundred subjects, who may be either patients or healthy individuals. Phase 3 involves large-scale randomized trials on several thousand people, usually patients suffering from the ailment for which the therapy has been developed. These trials are frequently coordinated across multiple centres, increasingly on a global scale.

The sponsors for trials are generally biotechnology or pharmaceutical companies [...]. Universities and publicly funded laboratories play a major role in the early stages of discovery – the identification of potential lead molecules and the conduct of pre-clinical tests – but the institutional structure of drug development is such that they increasingly license promising molecules to corporations that take them through clinical trials. This means that the biomedical and experimental rationales for clinical trials are completely entwined with the market value these companies see in the drugs [...] According to the Healthcare Financial Management Association's newsletter, twenty years ago, 80 per cent of clinical research trials

Kaushik Sunder Rajan, "Experimental Values: Indian Clinical Trials and Surplus Health," *New Left Review* 45 (2007): 67–88.

were conducted through academic medical centres. In 1998, estimates indicated the number of [these] centres as investigator sites had dropped to less than half. Health research and production is thus progressively captured by capital, and now needs to be seen as a semi-autonomous branch of it. The organizational complexity of clinical trials does however mean that it has been hard for pharmaceutical companies to manage them, leading to the emergence of an entirely new sector devoted to the management and administration of clinical trials. These companies, known as clinical research organizations (CROs), are now an integral part of the overall biomedical economy.

A plurality of actors

The movement of clinical trials to international – non-US – locations started in earnest in the mid-1990s. Adriana Petryna (2005) cites figures that point to a dramatic growth in the number of human subjects recruited into these trials, from 4,000 in 1995 to 400,000 in 1999. A 2006 study by the consulting firm A. T. Kearney shows that roughly half of the 1,200 US clinical trials in 2005 made use of an international site. In the 1990s, as Petryna notes, most of this growth occurred in countries that had agreed to harmonize standards in commercial drug testing with the guidelines set by the International Conference on Harmonization of Technical Requirements for Registration of Pharmaceuticals for Human Use. These primarily included Latin American and Eastern European countries, but not yet India. Over the past two years, however, India has become one of the most dynamic sites for the establishment and growth of clinical research.

In India, a range of local actors currently see the country as providing an extremely attractive destination for outsourced clinical trials from the West. [. . .]

The most central, perhaps, are members of the burgeoning CRO industry. These are the most immediate beneficiaries of trials coming to India, and are therefore keen to create conditions for these trials to grow in a sustained and streamlined fashion. CROs are the major drivers of the build-up of clinical-research

infrastructure, and particularly influential in building a regulatory framework for the conduct of trials. It is estimated that there are approximately a hundred CROs of reasonable size operating in the country at the moment. [. . .]

The Indian pharmaceutical industry is another interested party. It is in the process of retooling its business model in the wake of India's signing of the patent regime imposed by the WRO. Indian patent laws formerly allowed only process and not product patents on therapeutic molecules. This meant that one could not patent a drug itself, only the specific manufacturing process that produced it – allowing Indian pharmaceutical companies to reverse-engineer generic versions of drugs that had product patent protection in the West. The WRO regime now rules out such reverse engineering for the twenty-year duration of the patent. This has forced a number of leading Indian drug companies into an R&D-driven business model, whereby they, like their Western counterparts, engage in the much riskier process of new drug discovery and development. Clinical trials become a constitutive part of this business model, because new drugs cannot be developed without subjecting them to an elaborate regime of safety and efficacy testing. In other words, the Indian pharmaceutical industry has itself served as a spur to the CRO sector. WTO entry may also have made India a more attractive research destination from the perspective of Western trial sponsors seeking to outsource, since their intellectual property is better protected under such a regime.

A third set of actors consists of the regulatory agents of the state. The immediately responsible body in India is the Drug Controller-General of India, roughly equivalent to the US Food and Drug Administration. This body, a fairly peripheral presence on the Indian regulatory landscape until a few years ago, is now in the process of recreating itself as a serious agenda-setting organization. The Ministry of Science and Technology is also actively involved through its Department of Biotechnology, which sees clinical research as part of a wider initiative to make India a global biotechnology power. It has pumped money into biotechnology and clinical-research initiatives, especially to open institutes that can perform or facilitate such research around the country. The Department is currently funding several new clinical research training centres around India, [...] Building the human-resource capability to conduct and monitor trials in India is a key challenge, and a number of entrepreneurial ventures are fully engaged in training the labour force required. Finally, there are the physicians who actually conduct the trials, though in the Indian context they have a relatively marginal presence compared to the CROs in setting the infrastructural and regulatory agenda for research.

There is a strong common interest among these actors – though this applies somewhat less to physicians – not just in building up a research infrastructure in India, but also in promoting the country as a global destination for clinical trials. The experimental potential of Indian populations as trial subjects melds seamlessly with the market potential that Indian CROs perceive from an influx of these trials, and this convergence is facilitated by a larger historical moment that sees the Indian state branding and marketing itself to investors at global forums.

Economics and ethics

Some of the enthusiasm around clinical trials within India is mirrored in the West by agents who might outsource clinical trials to the country. For the most part, however, the anticipated surge in trial contracts to India remains speculative. The infrastructure-building occurring in India is very real; but it is a bet on future outcomes that, like any other speculation, may or may not pay off. To understand the clinical-trial situation in India, we must consider both the enthusiasms and the reservations of Western agents.

The anticipation of global clinical trials coming to India is based on the expectation that it would serve the interests of Western trial sponsors – especially US biotech and pharmaceutical companies – to outsource these trials to the subcontinent. [...]

The various perceived advantages in taking clinical trials to India include, among others,

that of cost; estimates suggest that overall clinical-trial expenses for a multinational company could be reduced by 30 to 50 per cent, thanks to lower labour and infrastructure costs. There is also a perceived recruitment advantage – the assumption being that it is easier to obtain Indians for such trials, especially 'treatment-nave' subjects. A major problem for drug companies conducting trials in the US is that Americans are therapeutically saturated, already taking so many drugs that it is hard to determine the efficacy of the molecule being tested without having to confront a whole range of interactions that muddy the data considerably.

Other factors come into play when assessing the attractiveness of a country as a clinical-trial location. The recent report by A. T. Kearney (2006), which provided an 'attractiveness index' for countries as trial destinations, considered – in addition to cost efficiency and patient pool – 'regulatory conditions', 'relevant expertise' and 'infrastructure and environment'. Indian actors are focusing on these three key areas as part of their capacity-building efforts; and indeed, Kearney already ranks India as the second most attractive destination, after China, for clinical trials outside the US. India scored much higher than the US in terms of patient pool and cost efficiency, but lower on the other three counts.

However, the scenario is more complicated than one in which Western multinationals are tearing down the door to exploit cheap Indian populations. For early-stage trials in particular, it is uncertain how strong the pressure is for Western companies to outsource to India. There are obvious advantages in terms of cost and the ease of volunteer recruitment; but there is also a downside in terms of the relative difficulty of monitoring trials – very important if the data generated is to pass muster with the FDA – and the potential public-relations disaster that could attend an early-stage trial that went disastrously wrong in a Third World context. Indeed, the Kearney report points out that in August 2005, the top twelve pharmaceutical companies were running 175 ongoing trials in Germany – attractiveness index 4.69 – and 161 in the UK – attractiveness index 5.0 – compared to 26 in India, which had an attractiveness index of 5.58. In 2004, Pfizer invested roughly $13 million in clinical trials in India, but this is put in perspective by the fact that its total global R&D expenditure was $8 billion. Perhaps more than pharmaceutical companies themselves, it is Western CROs who see real value in finding new destinations for some of their already outsourced activity. Therefore, while there are convincing market rationales for taking trials to India, and an already strong flow of trials there through the multinational CRO industry, much of the capacity building in clinical research in India is still a bet on potential value from trials that could be outsourced in future.

Capacity building in this context means something far more extensive than the experimental infrastructure for conducting clinical trials, which is perhaps the easiest component in a country like India where material and financial resources are no longer so limited. [...] A more elaborate challenge is building an adequate regulatory infrastructure, which needs to be far stronger if India is to host global trials. This is especially so for trials outsourced from a US-based sponsor, which needs to meet the FDA's stringent criteria. Adriana Petryna has argued for a state of 'ethical variability', suggesting that ethical practices for clinical trials vary between First and Third World locales (2005a, 2005b). While in practice it is quite possible that the implementation of ethical guidelines is ultimately stricter in the First World, it is important to note the very serious attention now given to ethics by both the Indian regulatory agencies and the CRO industry there. Of equal importance is what such ethics comprise, and what is left out.

An ethical-trial protocol is primarily concerned with the question of informed consent. This includes the entire apparatus surrounding the consent process, especially an institutional review board infrastructure. Ethical practices in India are enshrined in guidelines that the government published in 2001. In 2005, these guidelines were converted into laws, known as Schedule Y. Interestingly, India is the only country in the world where the violation of good clinical practice is a criminal rather than a civil offence. At the same time, global trials that are valid in the eyes of the FDA need to be

harmonized with what are known as International Conference on Harmonization protocols. Indian regulators are thus currently involved in a massive standardization process, driven by the Indian CRO industry. As legally embodied, then, Indian ethical guidelines are likely to be at least as stringent as those for the conduct of clinical research in the US, and in some ways more so.

Members of India's CRO industry bristle at the suggestion that clinical trials will move to India because it is possible to cut ethical corners there. This idea has been part of the debate around Indian clinical trials, [...] CRO leaders are acutely aware of the need to build a positive media image for their industry, and place great emphasis on the ways in which Schedule Y exceeds the demands of the International Conference on Harmonization. Specifically, Schedule Y is concerned with ensuring extra care in gathering informed consent from illiterate subjects and in considering what might constitute 'ethical' compensation for poor subjects recruited into early-stage trials – the logic here being that lucrative remuneration can actually act as a coercive incentive. [...]

Outside the enforcement potential of Schedule Y, however, a larger regulatory body with the scope of the FDA is still absent. As mentioned earlier, the Drug Controller-General of India is the nominal equivalent, but its remit is still basically limited to approving drugs for the market or for import into the country. Part of the regulatory effort currently under way in India consists in building a more substantial regulatory body with oversight powers that parallel those of the FDA, and whose conduct can be harmonized with that of its US counterpart. This was a central recommendation of the Mashelkar Committee Report of October 2005, which proposed a National Biotechnology Regulatory Authority that would regulate not just pharmaceuticals, but also agricultural products, transgenic crops, food and feed, and transgenic animals and aquaculture.

Ethics, legally enshrined and contractually enforced, are integral to the capacity-building effort around clinical research in India. Members of the CRO industry are the most active drivers in building an ethical regulatory infrastructure. Nonetheless, the form this ethic takes – quite literally, the 'informed consent' form that the volunteers sign – does not mitigate the fundamental structural violence of clinical trials conducted in the Third World. I will elaborate on this below, developing a critique of the movement of clinical trials to India in the context of the global logics of biocapital and surplus health. The clinical-research landscape in India cannot be reduced to the neo-colonial exploitation of the local population as 'guinea pigs' by rapacious multinational interests, where cutting corners is the norm and ethics easily sacrificed. A more nuanced analysis would take account of the desire on the part of the Indian state and corporate actors for the country to become a global experimental site, while noting that a comprehensive attention to ethics is quite compatible with the structural violence of global biocapital.

2. 'Good Clinical Practice': A Case Study

[…]

Consider, for instance, the case of Vimta Laboratories, based in Hyderabad. Vimta can claim in many ways to be the gold-standard Indian CRO. Founded in 1991, it is one of India's oldest; it is the only CRO that is publicly traded on the Bombay Stock Exchange, and the only one in the country that has been audited twice by the FDA – passing both times with flying colours. […]

Vimta's concern with informed consent, and its processes for securing it, exemplify the insistence on good clinical practice in India. On a visit to Vimta as part of my fieldwork, the first room I was shown was the waiting and screening room. This looks like the waiting room of a railway station; subjects come in and are given their consent forms, along with a basic questionnaire to determine whether they are qualified to participate, in this case in a Phase I trial. The walls of the waiting room are empty, except for a single bulletin board. This outlines all the risks that could accrue to participants in a clinical trial, but it is written only in English. I was told that in order to

participate, subjects have to be literate – though not necessarily in English – and male; Vimta only enrols females if the trial sponsor specifies a need for female subjects.

Beyond the waiting room is a long corridor, off which are a number of rooms where different types of medical examination are conducted on trial volunteers. First, their height and weight are recorded. If the subject weighs less than 55 kilos he is not accepted, as the risk of complications is too high. There is then a general physical exam, after which the tests become progressively more invasive; an ECG is conducted in a third room, blood drawn in a fourth – and sent to the pathology lab for analysis – and an X-ray taken in a fifth. I learned while being walked through this corridor that the consent forms the subjects sign in the waiting room are only for the medical screening procedures – if they are selected to participate in the trial, they sign a separate form, specific to the trial in which they are enrolled.

A number of the trials conducted at Vimta are Phase I trials on healthy volunteers. Recruiting subjects for these trials, as I mentioned earlier, has become increasingly difficult in the United States. I was told that volunteer retention is much better in India than in the US, because 'people trust doctors here'. Interestingly, while it is in principle a challenge to recruit healthy people to have risky molecules administered to them, the entire set-up here seems to emphasize 'selection' – almost as if being accepted for a trial were a test that only those who are fit enough can pass. Moreover, the subjects are only ever referred to as 'volunteers', suggesting no doubt their autonomous rational agency, the same agency that is contractually codified through the consent form.

No access to drugs

Such deep and, I believe, sincere concern with informed consent and good clinical practice, reflected both in national laws and in the practices of companies such as Vimta, does not, however, even touch on the major question of access to drugs. In the US, clinical trials at least implicitly suggest a social contract in which a small number of people are put on potentially risky medication for the sake of a larger social good – the development of new therapies. Those recruited into Phase I trials tend to be less well-off in the US as well, so that the social contract can never be a pure liberal one between rational individuals. [...] Nonetheless, there is an animating liberal sentiment which absolutely presumes that the therapy, if developed, will eventually be accessible. And even if this is access via the market, for a price, thus raising issues of affordability and distributive justice, these issues can in principle be addressed through liberal welfare-state mechanisms. In the Indian context, by contrast, there is no guarantee that an experimental drug tested on a local population will necessarily be marketed there after approval – let alone be made available at an affordable cost. The Indian state has made no moves to ensure this, for example through such mechanisms as compulsory licensing regulations. The likely outcome is therefore a situation where Indian populations are used purely as experimental subjects without the implicit social contract of eventual therapeutic access.

The question of access to drugs is certainly a live one in the Indian medical community. [...] A leading Delhi-based psychiatrist in a prominent private hospital – who preferred to remain anonymous – told me that 'while we understand the need for conducting trials, there is need for more uniform regulatory control'. This is not someone outside the circuit of clinical research; he is himself engaged in testing a number of psychiatric drugs. Most of the trials such prominent physicians conduct, however, are categorized as Phase 3, and involve patients they are treating, which puts their practice under a different ethical calculus – having to do with pastoral care – from that of CROs looking to increase Phase I trials on healthy volunteers, where the issue is simply one of experimental subjectivity. The relationship of such trials to drug access is an acute question for this physician, especially as regards subjects who may need to continue taking the experimental medication that is tested upon them if it is shown to have positive effects. The only mechanisms that exist to provide such access, however, arise from the policies of the companies sponsoring the trials, or the concerns of the centre conducting the trial. The same

physician told me: 'In the last two trials, the companies said they'll try and make the drugs available. We have yet to see if that will happen. If it doesn't happen, then we will only participate with companies that give an absolute commitment.'

While this physician and the hospitals where he works might be willing to take such an uncompromising stand on linking clinical experimentation with therapeutic access and pastoral care, such a linkage is less likely to figure in the calculations of the CROs, especially those focused on early-stage trials, since their source of values lies directly in increasing the number of trials they can conduct, rather than in providing tangible therapeutic benefits to patients. As suggested earlier, it is the CRO industry rather than physicians that is currently driving the establishment of regulatory infrastructure in India. The Delhi-based psychiatrist told me that while there is intense debate within the psychiatric community in India over the relationship of clinical trials to drug access, physician investigators are involved only to a very limited extent in efforts to streamline the regulatory process.

This subjection of patients to experimental regimes without an insistence on concomitant therapeutic access does not seem to arise primarily from any reluctance of Western pharmaceutical companies to market drugs in India. It is true that 85 per cent of all global drug sales are currently accounted for by US, European and Japanese markets, though the burgeoning middle class in India may be a factor in the companies' future planning. At the present time, however, the only real avenue for any sort of therapeutic access to experimental drugs is through the 'compassionate use' programmes of a number of pharmaceutical companies, which make the drugs tested in Phase 3 trials available to the sick volunteers for a fixed period of time after completion of the trial. No one in the Indian CRO industry whom I talked to, and no one who is actively involved in developing clinical-practice guidelines, felt it was necessary to insist that drugs tested in India should be marketed there, in contrast to the vigorous discussion among physicians of the relationship between clinical trials and access to drugs. 'Ethics', therefore, are provisional and partial, bearing primarily at this point on concerns about informed consent.

The uncoupling of experimental subjectivity from therapeutic access, which – through acts of omission – occurs at a legal and regulatory level, enrols Indian experimental subjects in the cause of health, but locates them outside a regime of pastoral care. In other words, these experimental subjects contribute in some nebulous sense to health by making themselves available as experimental subjects, but this is in no way necessarily linked to their own healthiness, or that of other Indians who might obtain access to new medication as a consequence of the risks to which the volunteers are exposed. The nature of these risks was brought home to me during my tour of Vimta, when I was shown a room, at the time dark and secluded, with just four beds in it. This, I was told, is the intensive care unit where trial subjects are admitted and ministered to in case of adverse effects. It looked like a medical emergency room of the kind used to attend to accidents on the factory floor. It re-emphasized not just the high-risk nature of experimental subjectivity, but that being a trial subject is, specifically, high-risk *labour*.

3. Expropriation, Exploitation, Violence

A theoretical critique of the global biomedical economy, situating the latter in relation to the logics of expropriation and exploitation, requires the introduction of the key concepts of *biocapital* and *surplus health*. By biocapital, I refer to the simultaneous systemic and emergent production of the life sciences, especially biomedicine, alongside the frameworks of capital and the market within which such technoscience increasingly operates. There are three layers of specificity to biocapital: institutional, epistemic and structural/epochal.

First, the biomedical industry, like any other, has its specific institutional terrain. In the US, this terrain is seen as partitioned into 'upstream' and 'downstream'. Downstream lie big multinational pharmaceutical companies, with the human and capital resources to bring drugs to market. These are supplemented by a few biotech companies that have managed to grow sufficiently to join the marketing effort. Upstream companies conduct more basic research, focusing on informatics, the development of diagnostic kits or the provision of research tools to other companies. Clinical-research organizations fit into this model as downstream facilitators to large pharmaceutical companies. There are particular risks in this marketplace, in view of the enormous time spent on drug development (roughly fifteen years), the cost ($800 million per drug, according to the industry, though that is most certainly inflated) and the risk (only one in five drugs makes it through clinical trials). And there are particular power hierarchies within it, such as the hugely powerful position of big pharmaceutical companies in the value chain relative to smaller biotech companies.

The second layer of specificity is epistemic. For instance, emergent life sciences such as genomics have the potential to radically reconfigure our understanding of life in ways that parallel the fashion in which neo-liberal logics of capital are reconfiguring our understanding of value. While I do not elaborate on this point here, I believe that to describe the institutional arrangements of the life sciences is not a sufficient basis for comprehending biocapital in all its complexity; emergent epistemologies are also crucial.

These first two layers of specificity are internal to biocapital. The third has to do with the larger epochal transformations in capitalism as a whole, which preface some of biocapital's structural logics. The transformation that is pertinent to understanding biocapital is what Joseph Dumit (2005a, 2005b, 2006) identifies as the change in the logic of the biomedical industry, shifting away from being 'an arm of capital' to becoming 'an industry in itself'. At an earlier stage of capitalist development, medicine was integral to reproducing the conditions under which industrial production was made possible. Capital needed healthy workers. But just as the logic of commodity production became self-perpetuating and self-sustaining, to the point where commercial activity became an end in itself, so too has the logic of the production of health for work become self-perpetuating and self-sustaining, turning into an industry that produces health not for work's sake, but for health's sake. In biocapital, health operates directly as an index of value, unmediated through the labour-power of the worker. In Foucauldian terms, it is not labour but life itself which becomes the locus of value in biocapital, with health becoming the index of life, rather than the facilitator of labour.

Crucial to this transformation is the emergence of the value-form of surplus health. Dumit defines surplus health as 'the *capacity* to add medications to our life through lowering the level of risk required to be "at risk" . This occurs by setting biomedical risk thresholds. Clinical trials become a part of the apparatus through which such a lowering of the risk level takes place. An analogy might be made with the way in which machinery, in Marx's analysis in Volume One of *Capital*, operates not to reduce work, but to increase surplus labour by widening the gap between waged work and the potential productivity of the worker.

Surplus health refers to the market value that pharmaceutical companies gain from the potential for future illness of those who might one day consume their drugs – which includes anyone with the buying power to constitute a market for therapeutics. As with surplus-value in the Marxian sense, surplus health is an animating abstraction, in this case of the logic of pharmaceutical risk. Just as the setting of wage rates is the material calculus for the unfolding of surplus-value, so the setting of biomedical risk thresholds is the material calculus upon which surplus health unfolds. And as machinery serves to increase surplus-value by increasing the potential for labour over and above that remunerated by wages – through an increase in the *efficiency* of labour – so too can clinical trials serve to increase surplus health by demonstrating therapeutic efficacy.

Similarly, just as machinery requires labour to operate it – which, during the era of industrial capital, was high-risk work – so clinical trials require experimental subjects as their high-risk labour. Dumit suggests that biomedical markets in advanced liberal societies – especially the United States – depend on the generation of surplus health, which in turn operates through the setting of risk thresholds. The knowledge of disease risk provided by diagnostic-testing capabilities, and calibrated through these thresholds, enables the marketing of drugs for diseases that are increasingly reframed as 'chronic'. Just as much of the manufacturing labour previously performed by the working class in the First World was later exported to Third World peripheries, so much of the Phase I experimentation, initially performed on marginal populations in the US, is now being exported to Third World sites such as India. The experimental subjects there, outside the circuits of pastoral care and therapeutic consumption, come to be *merely risked*. But these very circuits rely for their constitution on the existence of such 'merely risked' subjects. These experimental subjects provide the conditions of possibility for the neo-liberal consumer subjects for whom surplus health is generated.

The context of consent

The 'merely risked' volunteer is subjected to a logic of expropriation integral to the structural logic of biocapital that I am trying to trace. Bodies are made available to the global machinery of experimentation, machinery driven by the value logic of pharmaceutical capital. Indeed, the global scale of these circuits is precisely a function of capital's value considerations. Without the cost rationales for outsourcing clinical trials to the Third World, their globalization would not have become such a dynamic imperative – such trials had, after all, been an important part of the American drug development landscape for nearly half a century before moves to take them abroad began in the mid 1990s. And without the property mechanisms, harmonized and enforced globally through the WTO, that provide patent protection to multinational pharmaceutical interests, globalizing capital would not have had the security to realize its aspirations. Similarly, capital considerations drive the Indian CRO industry to a vigorous build-up of infrastructure to attract clinical trials, increase trial recruitment, and uncouple these considerations from any serious concern with therapeutic access.

In this situation, the partial ethic enshrined in 'good clinical practice', far from mitigating the structural violence of capital, serves instead to facilitate it. The instrument through which this takes place is the liberal contract embodied in the informed consent form. Just as the wage is the materialized contractual form through which individuals are 'freed' from serfdom and converted into workers for industrial capital, so the informed consent document 'frees' experimental subjects from being coerced guinea-pigs by providing them with the autonomous agency such a contract signifies. The concerns raised over ethical variability in global clinical trials are often premised on the notion that ethical enforcement is likely to be looser in the Third World than in the First. My attempt here has been to show that, on the contrary, it is precisely the global harmonization of ethical standards that provides the conditions of possibility for the experimental subjection of the 'merely risked' Third World subject; and further, that this harmonization of ethics goes hand-in-hand with the global harmonization of property regimes. These two parallel movements – the contractual codification of ethics and the exclusionary instruments of property – together provide global capital with the security to turn healthy Indian populations into experimental subjects, who are both merely risked and free to choose to be so.

The structural violence of clinical experimentation starts with the fact that it is a procedure that can only be set in motion by the risking of healthy subjects. Indeed, the very epistemology of clinical trials is risk-laden – both for the subjects experimented upon, and for the companies who invest huge amounts of money in a therapeutic molecule that may or may not eventually come to market. The structural violence of experimentation is then exacerbated by pre-existing global inequalities, which result in more bodies available for less cost in Third World locales. If the former violence is epistemic, the latter is historical. A third layer of structural violence is imposed in the form of the liberal contract, which frees the experimental subject to make his body available not just for experimentation, but for exploitation, since the clinical trial becomes a locus of surplus-health generation.

The question raised by this third layer of structural violence is one that was central for

Marx in his analysis of capital, and pertains to the conditions of possibility that ensure the availability of workers for capital – or in this case, of experimental subjects for clinical trials – in the first place. In 'The So-Called Primitive Accumulation', Marx shows that this availability is generated by pre-existing acts of violence that created a property-less proletariat. Such processes are historically specific, but they do show a consistency of form. Thus, for instance, subject recruitment into Phase I clinical trials in India occurs, on the face of it, through newspaper advertisements. The public face of trial recruitment does not, however, reveal the conditions that make it financially attractive for individuals to risk themselves as experimental subjects.

I have written elsewhere, for example, about Wellquest, which is located in the mill districts of Mumbai (Sunder Rajan 2005, 2006). I learned from scientists there that most of the trial subjects recruited by this CRO happened to be unemployed mill workers who had lost their jobs due to the progressive evisceration of the Mumbai textile industry over the last thirty years. The number of unemployed is over two hundred thousand, many of whom are still waiting for the payment of back wages. They are already, therefore, subjected to the violence of de-proletarianization that occurred following the demise of a sector of manufacturing capital. This violence is exacerbated by the fact that the textile mills are situated on prime land for property development, with former mill owners themselves turning to real-estate speculation as a far more lucrative source of capital investment. This means that the workers' tenements or *chawls*, mainly located close to the mills, are under threat of demolition, so that in addition to losing wage and livelihood, these workers are now in danger of losing their shelter as well. Demolition of the *chawls* was temporarily halted by a 2005 Bombay High Court verdict that stayed real-estate development in the mill districts, but this was overturned by the Indian Supreme Court in March 2006, making it legal to tear down the mills and *chawls* and build middle-class housing instead.

The violence of de-proletarianization and dispossession is a function of the dominance of speculative real estate, which has replaced textile manufacturing as a source of value-generation for capital. A number of unemployed mill workers have turned into street hawkers in order to earn a living, but there is an organized state and middle-class campaign against the hawkers, who are deemed noisy and polluting, and perhaps most importantly, accused of taking up valuable parking space. There is no way to understand the dynamics of clinical experimentation in the mill districts of Mumbai without taking into account all these prior moments of violence that provide the inducement to sign an informed consent form. First the mill workers are removed from their factories. Then they are removed from their dwellings. Then they are removed from the streets. Only thus do they acquire the freedom to become autonomous trial 'volunteers'.

Global connections

One way of understanding the situation of expropriation that I have described is in terms of neo-colonialism. [...] a deep historical and continuing inequality, whereby rich/First World/white subjects enrich their health – and often wealth – through the corporeal dispossession of subaltern/Third World/racially marked subjects. While sympathetic to the inequalities that such accounts describe, the accumulation by dispossession, [...] that I am trying to trace here is not agential but structural, where the one thing that accumulates as a consequence of 'merely risking' experimental subjects is not health – not even that of the advanced liberal subject – but value.

For this, it is important to turn to Dumit's (2006) account of surplus health in the United States. The therapeutic economy that Dumit traces in the US context is also not one of pastoral care, but rather therapeutic saturation. Dumit and I have indeed suggested that, considered from the perspective of pharmaceutical company logic, health in the US is not about healthiness either, but about expanding the market for therapeutics. Rising therapeutic consumption can be achieved either by increasing the number of people who take a particular drug – most effectively achieved by 'off-label use', i.e. prescribing drugs for treatments other

than those for which the drug was initially approved – or by increasing the timespan of the prescription, justified by reframing diseases as chronic states rather than events. Dumit observes that currently 'the average American is prescribed and purchases somewhere between nine and thirteen different prescription-only drugs per year.' He continues:

According to the pharmacy benefits companies and insurance companies, such as Express Scripts, sampling 3 million unique individuals in their plans, 11 per cent of Americans were prescribed cholesterol-lowering drugs last year, 40 per cent of all those over 50. More than 20 per cent of women over 40 were prescribed anti-depressants in 2002, almost 10 per cent of boys 10–14 were prescribed attention-deficit disorder drugs ... The growth rates for almost all classes of drugs have been in the low double digits for a decade, with prescription rates for children growing upwards of 30 per cent per year. Similarly, both the prevalence (the number of people on each drug) and the intensity (the size of the yearly prescription) are projected to continue to grow in all drug categories for the foreseeable future. The figures do match the fears, and according to many surveys, Americans are spending more time, more energy, more attention, and money on health. Health clearly is not simply a cost to the nation to be reduced; it is also a market to be grown.

Marx's analysis in Volume One of *Capital* is two-fold. First, the contemporary conditions of industrial capital that he traces are marked by exploitation materialized through surplus-value, a function of labour-power being always already greater than the labour remunerated by wage. Analogously to this, surplus health is a function of potential therapeutic consumption that is always already greater than that required to maintain healthiness. This excess therapeutic consumption is not harmless – indeed, it involves ever-greater medication of the American population, and has produced catastrophic and fatal side-effects such as those associated with the cox-2 inhibitor Vioxx. This therapeutic saturation also leads directly to biomedical rationalizations for the outsourcing of clinical trials, as it becomes increasingly difficult to test the effects of experimental drugs in populations who tend to be on many other drugs that interact with the molecules being tested.

But the conditions of possibility for exploitation through surplus-value generation are, as Marx shows, dependent on a prior expropriation, achieved through a form of violent accumulation that forces people into becoming workers for industrial capital in the first place. The two-fold movement of capital – violent dispossession followed by exploitation – is a temporal one in Marx's analysis. In the case of clinical trials, however, the violence is spatial, with Third World experimental subjects expropriated not so that First World consumer subjects become healthy, but so that they can be exploited. In both cases, the only value that is constantly preserved and increased is value itself.

Much of my argument rests on the fact that clinical experimentation in the Indian context is not linked to therapeutic access. It is, however, certainly possible to imagine such a situation; and if this linkage is not created either by the intervention of advocacy groups fighting for access to drugs, or by the state's insistence on a biopolitical rationale of public good and public health, it is most likely to be brought about by market mechanisms once India is perceived as a potential market for therapeutic consumption. In such a scenario, one can quite easily envisage the continued expropriation of experimental subjects – those who fall out of the market because they lack the purchasing power to buy drugs – side by side with exploitation of therapeutic consumers within India itself. Stefan Ecks has been studying psychiatric drug marketing by companies like Pfizer in India, and observed strategies not dissimilar to those employed in the US.

If we are to understand biocapital from the perspective of the pharmaceutical companies' logic, then what is at stake is not therapeutic access in the cause of health, but increasing therapeutic consumption in the cause of value. In parallel, from the perspective of CROs, the issue is not clinical trials in the cause of therapeutic access, but rather clinical trials in the cause of value. The global articulation of pharmaceutical and CRO logics of value-generation both structures and overdetermines an allegedly benign enterprise in terms of expropriation and exploitation. Other competing logics of capital also naturally come into play, most notably a logic of insurance that is particularly salient in the American context of managed care. It is also relevant to the European public-health context, where paying for increased therapeutic consumption is a burden, and the logic of value dictates an accent on disease prevention that is not mediated by therapeutic saturation.

It is important in every case to privilege the analysis of value, rather than assuming from the outset that the issue is one of biopolitics or pastoral care. At the same time there are many incongruities that are vital to note, not least the Indian state's hyper-attentiveness to ethics and its regulation of clinical practice. The structural violence of global clinical trials on the subcontinent is not due to a lack of ethics, but to the fact that value, captured by the logic of capital and mediated through the pharmaceutical and CRO industries, overdetermines the practices that emerge.

REFERENCES

Dumit, Joseph
   2006a "Drugs, Algorithms, Markets and Surplus Health." Presented at the Lively Capital workshop. University of California, Irvine.
Dumit, Joseph
   2006b "Living in the Aggregate: Accumulating Prognoses, Growing Markets, Experimental Subjects." Presented at the American Anthropological Association Annual Meetings. San Jose, CA.
Ecks, Stefan
   2006 "Global Citizenship Inc.: Big Pharma and 'Depression Awareness' in Urban India." Presented at the Asian Biotechnologies Workshop. Honolulu, HI.
Grace, Patricia
   1998 *Baby No-Eyes*. Honolulu.
Harvey, David
   2003 *The New Imperialism*. Oxford.
Jones, Jennifer and Alan Zuckerman
   "Clinical Research Trials: Creating Competitive and Financial Advantages." *Managing*

the Margin Newsletter. Available at www. hfma.org.

Kearney, A. T.
2006 "Make Your Move: Taking Clinical Trials to the Best Location." Available at www.atkearney.com

Marx, Karl
1976 *Capital: A Critique of Political Economy, Volume One.* Translated by Ben Fowkes. Harmondsworth.

NASSCOM
2002 *McKinsey Report.* Available at www. nasscom.in.

Padmanabhan, Manjula
2003 *Harvest.* London.

Petryna, Adriana
2005a "Ethical Variability: Drug Development and Globalizing Clinical Trials." *American Ethnologist* 32(2):183–97

Petryna, Adriana
2005b "Drug Development and the Ethics of the Globalized Clinical Trial." Princeton Institute for Advanced Study Occasional Paper 22.

Sunder Rajan, Kaushik
2005 "Subjects of Speculation: Emergent Life Sciences and Market Logics in the US and India." *American Anthropologist.* 107(1):19–30.

Sunder Rajan, Kaushik
2006 *Biocapital: The Constitution of Postgenomic Life.* Durham, NC: Duke.

Part VI

Global Health, Global Medicine

Introduction

For over half a century, anthropologists have been engaged in international health, becoming increasingly influential as scientific advisors, researchers and advocates in the modernist projects of public health and medicine, as well as scholars of these endeavors and of the social lives of the diseases that produced them. In the late twentieth century, HIV/AIDS and its global threat revolutionized the institutional, financial and political architecture of international health (Brown et al. 2006), culminating in a robust global health movement led in part by anthropologists who are also physician-activists. Essays in this part span nearly a half century; read together they represent diverse lineages, historical threads, and ethnographic engagements which have made the anthropology of global health one of the most vital empirical and theoretical domains in anthropology today.

Speaking in 1976 at a USAID workshop on international health planning, George Foster, then a leading anthropologist of international health at the University of California Berkeley, debunked simplistic notions that the cultures of "traditional peoples" are barriers to use of scientific medicine, arguing instead that *"economic* and *social* costs" and the cultures and interests of those responsible for delivering care are the greatest barriers. Foster's stance with the people to be served is a recognizable common thread evident in Paul Farmer's work and that of a great many anthropologists (cf. Nguyen 2005; Hyde 2007; Biehl 2008).

Craig Janes and Kitty Corbett's essay, originally published in the 2009 *Annual Review of Anthropology,* is a gift of references and a masterful tour through the vast riches of anthropological research in international health and recent writings on anthropology and global health (Adams et al. 2008; Nichter 2008). Although introducing an array of definitional components for global health, they argue that the anthropology of global health is constituted by health actions aimed at reducing global health inequalities and developing "salutogenic sociocultural, political, and economic systems." Four broad topics are discussed: (1) explaining health inequities;

(2) global technoscapes for the circulation of bioscience, biotechnologies, and biomedicine; (3) interrogating health policy, focusing on expert knowledge and its limits and the politics of policy-making; and (4) the roles of non-governmental organizations and consequences of their interventions. This essay offers many ideas to consider and readings to pursue.

Pimpawun Boonmongkon, Mark Nichter, and Jen Pylypa present a study of Thai women's concerns about their gynecological health, why it matters, and how health screening programs for cervical cancer can have unintended consequences. This abridged essay is a classic ethnographic study of the meaning of symptoms and the failures of policies and clinical services, the results of which illustrate the importance of the anthropological stance of listening to and acting on the concerns of patients. The Thai researcher's position at Thailand's leading medical university enabled the group to initiate changes in clinical services and screening programs based on women's concerns.

Paul Farmer's essay on medical ethics and social rights in a global era, from his book *Pathologies of Power,* may be read as a manifesto on how to insert social justice into a global era bioethics and as medicine's moral voice, invoking Virchow, social medicine's earliest charity physician, to serve "where pathology lies heaviest." As an MD/PhD, Farmer packs this essay with empirical examples exploring "ironies of inequalities." He cajoles readers to stand with the destitute sick. Farmer's stance with the weakest is anthropological; yet as an MD he is able to provide clinical care, as he has done over the past 25 years for thousands of poor patients, many suffering from HIV or TB in Haiti, Russia, Rwanda, and elsewhere. Farmer has energized generations of young people, and through their activities has launched a global health movement that has had profound effects. True to his liberation theology, Farmer calls supporters to commit to a global political agenda to make social and economic rights part of human rights, and quality health care a human right in the global medical commons.

Didier Fassin's essay on humanitarianism as a politics of life segues into the final section on postcolonial disorders. Fassin, an MD/PhD sociologist/anthropologist and physician, now at the Institute for Advanced Study at Princeton, is a former vice-president of Médecins Sans Frontières, France. He explores the moral and political complexities of humanitarian interventions and medical missions, the "radical inequality" in the "differentiation between lives to be saved" (the victims) and "lives to be risked" (the MSF teams). Fassin's thought-provoking discussion challenges interpretation or valuation of actions and interventions by medical NGOs such as MSF and other major organizational players who have benefited from and been strengthened by the flows of private and public money into global health.

This section represents what continues to be a critical domain of medical anthropology. Now linked to social medicine and the human rights tradition and responding to the emergent realities of global epidemics and treatable diseases too often left untreated in poor communities, medical anthropology has taken a leading role in the rise of a new global health movement.

REFERENCES

Adams, Vincanne, Thomas Novotny, and Hannah Leslie
  2008 "Global Health Diplomacy." *Medical Anthropology Quarterly* 27:315–23.
Biehl, Joao
  2008 *Will to Live*. Princeton: Princeton University Press.
Brown, T. M., M., Cueto, and E. Fee.
  2006 "The World Health Organization and the Transition form International to Global Public Health." *American Journal of Public Health* 96(1): 62–72.
Hyde, Sandra T.
  2007 *Eating Spring Rice: The Cultural Politics of AIDS in Southwest China*. Berkeley: University of California Press.
Nichter, Mark
  2008 *Global Health*. Tucson: University of Arizona Press.
Nguyen Vinh-Kim
  2005 "Antiretroviral Globalism, Biopolitics, and Therapeutic Citizenship." In Aihwa Ong and Stephen J. Collier, eds., *Global Assemblages*. Oxford: Blackwell Publishers, pp. 124–44.

31

Medical Anthropology and International Health Planning

George M. Foster

Introduction

On a number of occasions and in various settings during the last generation the Agency for International Development (and predecessor organizations) has brought together health personnel and behavioral scientists to explore the ways in which knowledge about the social organization and cultural forms of "target" groups, the recipients of health services, can assist in the planning and operation of these services. As early as 1951 the Institute of Inter-American Affairs contracted with the Smithsonian Institution for behavioral science assistance in a six-month long team evaluation of the first ten years of United States-assisted health programs in Latin America (Anonymous 1953; Servicio 1953). Subsequently the "Health Advisory Committee" of the Foreign Operations Administration included behavioral scientists as well as medical and administrative personnel. Over the years many formal and informal meetings have been held, all concerned with the problem that brings us together today: the ways in which knowledge of the social, cultural, and psychological factors in traditional societies that influence change can be used to improve health service planning and operations, including the search for new ways to make the most efficient use of scarce health resources.

A Sequence of Premises

While it may seem discouraging that the interrelationships between sociocultural and medical-health behavior phenomena are in danger of being rehashed once more, the terms of reference for this meeting are challenging in that they reflect a broader and more flexible approach to the basic problems than has been found in many earlier conferences. In order better to appreciate this flexibility it will be helpful briefly to review the changing premises, the underlying assumptions, that have characterized American-aided health programs in developing countries. Three major premises have appeared in chronological order:

(1) *The institutional forms and clinical practices of the medical systems of technologically-advanced nations are the appropriate models for the development of health services in all countries.* In early American attempts to help developing countries provide better health services for their citizens, program planners and field personnel operated on the basis of two seemingly obvious (to them) assumptions:

George M. Foster, "Medical Anthropology and International Health Planning," *Medical Anthropology Newsletter* 7/3 (1976): 12–18. Reproduced by permission of the American Anthropological Association from *Medical Anthropology Newsletter* 7/3 (1976), pp. 12–18, 1976. Not for sale or further reproduction.

First, the best and most advanced American preventive and curative medical practices, *and* the institutional framework that provides these services, are absolutes that work equally well in all socio-cultural and economic settings; and, second, the people in developing countries will immediately perceive the advantages accruing to them if they give up old medical practices and adopt new ones. (One wonders if smallpox immunization was taken as the universal model, for here indeed is a medical technique whose efficacy does not depend on culture; willingness to be vaccinated is, of course, another matter, and that *does* depend on cultural factors.)

These ethnocentric assumptions represented the prevailing view that American civilization was superior in all ways to other societies, and that given the opportunity people in "less fortunate" countries would clamor to adopt our ways. In the past, Western medical personnel have been, if anything, even more ethnocentric than the general public about the superiority of scientific medicine in all its ramifications, finding it difficult to believe that all peoples would not quickly accept it. Consequently, early workers in international health programs saw their task in simplistic, easily definable terms: transplant the American models, and health goals will be achieved. This philosophy underlay the work of the Rockefeller Foundation in its attempts to eradicate hookworm in Ceylon, 1916–22, and it was implicit in much of the work of the Institute of Inter-American Affairs beginning in 1942. Even today more than a few traces of this point of view are found in international health programs.

(2) *Medical and public health programs in developing countries will be more successful if in design and operation they take into consideration the social, cultural, and psychological characteristics of the target group.* By about 1950, American international health specialists began to realize that the successful delivery of improved health services required more than the silver platter approach. They began to appreciate that modernization is a social as well as a technological phenomenon, and that the people who modernize have cultures and values that strongly influence their decisions

in accepting or rejecting innovation. Small numbers of anthropologists came into international public health during the years following 1950, and they played an important role in promoting the "human factors in technological development" point of view, which postulates that the major problems in the development of traditional communities (including health services) are embedded in the society and culture of the target group. These people, it was now assumed, are anxious to enjoy better health, and they are willing to change their health behavior if they understand better the advantages in new ways. If the cultural, social, and psychological "barriers" that inhibit acceptance of new health programs could be identified, it was reasoned, health programs could be designed and presented in ways that conform to cultural expectations. Recognition of the importance of understanding sociocultural factors in designing and carrying out health programs represented a great step forward, and much progress has been made in the delivery of health services as a consequence of this awareness. Still, the fact that we are assembled here indicates that this assumption alone, valid as far as it goes, is insufficient to the task.

(3) *The most successful medical and public health programs in developing countries require knowledge about the social, cultural and psychological factors inherent in the innovating organizations and their professional personnel.* In other words, major "barriers" to improved health programs also are found in the cultures of bureaucracies, the assumptions of the medical profession, and in the psychological makeup of the specialists who participate in these programs. This assumption, regrettably, appears not to be widely accepted; it is, in fact, stoutly resisted by many. The second premise – that the principal barriers are in the target group – was easily accepted by international health personnel. It seemed to offer quick and easy answers to many problems that had seemed insoluble, and it defined the problem as "out there," among the people who were to be helped. The implications of premise three are, however, disquieting; it is much harder to point the finger at oneself and say, "A lot of the difficulty is right here."

Nevertheless, I am increasingly struck by the fact that many of the apparent resistances to acceptance of health services commonly attributed to villagers' apathy and their cultural barriers, are, in fact, the result of administrative and professional inadequacies. International health programs made significant strides when the importance of social, cultural and psychological factors in target group cultures was recognized. The next opportunity for comparable progress lies, first, in recognizing (or admitting) the limitations in present bureaucratic forms, and in many professional and individual assumptions found in all health programs; and second, in being willing to face up to these problems, even at the cost of professional discomfort.

Innovation in Health Behavior

Let us now ask a pair of questions that stem from premises two and three: (1) What have we learned about the sociocultural and psychological factors in traditional populations that enable us better to understand the process of accepting scientific medicine, and that suggest leads in future program planning? and (2) What do we know about health bureaucracies and health personnel, or what must be learned about them, in order to design and carry out more effective health programs?

In early analyses of the sociocultural factors that seemed to inhibit acceptance of scientific medicine by traditional peoples, anthropologists developed an "adversary" model to explain the resistances that occurred. It was postulated that scientific and traditional medicine were locked in battle, each trying to win (or hold on to) the allegiance of the community. The model postulated that traditional peoples divided illness into two categories: those that medical doctors understood and could cure; and those medical doctors did not know about, much less understand, and which therefore they could not treat. Acute, infectious diseases – those yielding to antibiotics – quickly fell into the first category; the medical doctor's competence here was easily demonstrated. Chronic illnesses, those with major psychological components, and those "magical" in nature (e.g.,

the evil eye) – illnesses marked by vague and shifting symptoms – tended to remain the provenience of the traditional curer. The task of the anthropologist was to help medical personnel find ways to demonstrate the superiority of scientific medicine, which little by little would move the illnesses in this second category into the first one, the illnesses routinely brought to the medical doctor.

This model is not without merit: independently it has been worked out in Latin America, South and southeast Asia, and other places as well. It was through this model that we learned the *pragmatic* quality of traditional reasoning processes, that if peasant and tribal peoples could *perceive* advantages resulting from changed behavior, they were willing to drop old and cherished beliefs and practices by the wayside. This dichotomous model – illnesses medical doctors can cure, and those they cannot cure – has proven to be simplistic, as will be pointed out a little farther along.

Obviously there are social, cultural, and psychological barriers to the full acceptance of modern medicine that are found in every traditional community. It would be foolish to deny the importance of these factors, examples of which are known to all of us. In parts of Latin America there is great resistance to withdrawal of blood for laboratory analyses, or for blood transfusions, because of the belief that blood is a non-renewable substance, and that a person is weakened permanently by such withdrawals (Adams 1955:446–7). In Africa where the belief in witchcraft is strong, resistance to the use of sanitary latrines has been noted. People are reluctant to concentrate their feces for the convenience of witches who may wish to work their magic on them (Kark 1962:26). In India it has often been reported that villagers are reluctant to vaccinate against smallpox because of the belief that this is a "sacred" disease sent by a Mother Goddess whose will should not be contravened. In other countries, pregnant women have given as their reason for refusing hospital delivery the fear that the placenta will not be given to the family for ritual disposal. All of these, and countless more examples, can be given of real "barriers" to full acceptance of available medical services.

Yet I am increasingly convinced that *economic* and *social costs* are more important in determining the use or nonuse of scientific medicine than is the belief-conflict between traditional and modern medicine. I now believe that the adversary model is appropriate for the initial contact period when traditional peoples for the first time have the alternative of consulting medical doctors. But the evidence is overwhelming that in countries where traditional peoples have had access to modern medicine for a generation or longer, and where this medicine has been of reasonably good quality, the battle has been won, and scientific medicine is the victor.

The first decision-making model to account for choice of medical help, worked out by anthropologists for developing countries, was a three-stage sequence: (1) home remedies, (2) indigenous curer, and (3) the medical doctor, but only after the first two choices failed to produce results. In 1945, this was true in Tzintzuntzan, Mexico, a peasant community I have studied since that date. Today, however, the sequence is the same as that followed by many Americans: (1) home remedy, (2) medical doctor, and (3) indigenous curer (or faith healer in the United States) only after the first two choices fail to produce results.

It may be argued that relatively few countries in the developing world have the resources of Mexico, and that general acceptance of scientific medicine will not come so readily in the rest of the world. Yet the evidence suggests the contrary. In India, Banerji and his colleagues have carried out studies that show the same trend. In a fairly extensive study they were surprised to find

that the response to the major medical care problems is very much in favour of the western ... system of medicine, irrespective of social, economic, occupational and regional considerations. *Availability of such services and capacity of patients to meet the expenses are the two major constraining factors* (Banerji 1974:6; emphasis added).

Further, while Banerji found numerous examples of consulting practitioners of indigenous or homeopathic medicine,

Among those who suffer from major illness, only a very tiny fraction preferentially adopt these practices by *positively rejecting* facilities of the western system of medicine which are more efficacious and which are easily available and accessible to them (1974:7)

The picture is the same in Thailand where, in a major study of doctor–patient relationships, it was found that "The decision to go to a hospital depends less on the gravity of the disease than on financial resources" (Hinderling 1973:74). The same study revealed that, while in rural areas far from hospitals physicians are sometimes seen as a last resort, in cities the order is reversed: "The modern doctor is the first to be consulted, and [only] if he is not successful, one of the quite fashionable [traditional] healers will be called upon" (Boesch 1972:34).

The Basis for Acceptance of Scientific Medicine

We now turn to the motivations and processes underlying innovation in medical practice. The first thing we note is that they are essentially the same as those that underlie innovation in all areas. I suggest that people will change traditional behavior, i.e., innovate:

1 if they perceive personal economic, social, psychological, health, or other advantages in so doing;
2 if they perceive change as a realistic possibility for them;
3 if the economic costs are within their capabilities;
4 if the social costs do not outweigh the perceived advantage.

In other words, people are remarkably pragmatic in evaluating and testing new alternatives, including health services. One can almost speak of a cost-benefit mode of analysis. When, on the basis of empirical evidence, traditional peoples see that scientific medicine is more effective than their own, and when they can have scientific medicine on terms they deem acceptable, they happily turn to it.

Speaking of the acceptance of curative medicine in Ecuador, Erasmus, many years ago
pointed out that, as far as tradition was
concerned, "folk beliefs in themselves are
offering no resistance to modern medical practices *in so far as those practices may be judged
by the folk on an empirical basis*"
(Erasmus 1952:418; emphasis added). In
contrast Erasmus found that preventive medicine was resisted because its comprehension is
essentially theoretical, not lending itself to easy
empirical verification.

The evidence clearly indicates that, as far as
individual decision making is concerned, curative medical services are embraced much more
readily than preventive services. The reason is
obvious: the results of scientific curative medicine are much more easily demonstrated than
the results of preventive medicine. Few people
suffering from yaws or other dangerous infections which have been cut short by an injection
of an antibiotic question that this is indeed
a miracle medicine much superior to any
they have previously known. Cause and effect
are easily comprehended when serious illness
gives way to no illness in a few hours or days.
Cause and effect are less easily seen when, as in
the case of immunization and environmental
sanitation programs, no disease is followed by
no disease. The implications that must be
drawn from this evidence is that the traditional
American separation of most clinical from
most preventive medical measures is, in other
parts of the world, counter-productive. Experience suggests that preventive measures
are more apt to be accepted if they are "blan-
keted in" with, or sold as a part of a "package
deal" along with curative medicine, whose advantages are so much more easily demonstrated.

But, however pragmatic people may be, this
quality is of little value unless innovation is
seen as a realistic aspiration for the individual.
A peasant farmer may be persuaded that
hybrid rice sown on a heavily fertilized irri-
gated field is agriculturally advantageous, but
if his marginal lands do not lend themselves to
this intensive approach, or if credit facilities are
inadequate, his planting practices are unlikely
to change. Similarly, changing health practices
may be perceived to be desirable but if for any
one or combination of reasons a person feels
the goal is unrealistic, change motivation will
be lacking.

"Free" Services

When traditional peoples attempt to determine
whether contemplated changes in their health
practices are in fact realistic, economic factors
appear to be the most important of all variables. While on the one hand token fees for
medical services have often been reported to
confer value on these services, and hence may
be desirable policy in some situations (e.g.,
Foster 1973:136–8), most improved medical
services for village peoples will have to be provided by the state, at little or no cost to the
consumers. Increasingly this is recognized, and
more and more "free" services are offered.
"Free" services, unfortunately, are often expensive by village standards. Ndeti, for example, in
a study of tuberculosis control in Kenya found
that the bus fare kept a large number of patients
from coming to the clinic (Ndeti 1972:408).

In Indonesia, family planning services,
"free" in the strict sense of the word, are sometimes underutilized because of social customs
requiring expenditures. Most mothers are
interested in birth control only after they have
had four or five children. Often they have no
one with whom to leave these children so that
when, in response to the urging of a family
planning worker, they decide to visit a clinic,
at least the younger children must trail along.
This usually means a bus fare for all. But a trip
on a bus is, by definition, an "outing," and on
such occasions people buy food snacks, to
which Indonesians are much addicted. So a
mother with three or four small children may
well spend a day's income on a simple visit to
the "free" family planning clinic.

Other kinds of costs may also make "free"
family planning services prohibitively expensive. In a village near Bandung, in western Java,
at the bottom of a steep valley reached only by
a poor dirt road, a woman seeking family planning help has to ascend to the health center in a
truck or old bus that requires nearly an hour
for the five-mile trip, paying 100 rupiahs fare
each way. There she finds that, prior to being

given pills or fitted with an IUD she must take a pregnancy test, which carries a laboratory fee of 150 rupiahs. The woman is asked to return three days later – again at a cost of 200 rupiahs for transportation – to learn the laboratory results. If the 200 rupiahs lost by absence from work for two days are added in, it costs a woman 750 rupiahs – more than a week's income – simply to find out if she is eligible for family planning. Small wonder that few of these women are interested in this kind of service (author's field notes).

Social Costs

Finally, we must take note of the "social" costs often involved in changing health behavior. A young woman may be convinced that the government health center in or near her village that offers pre- and post-natal care, and delivery services by a doctor and nurse-midwife team, is a more desirable alternative than is delivery with the aid of a village midwife. But if the midwife is her mother's sister, failure to turn to the aunt may be seen as a personal rejection, an act that may cause major family rifts. This kind of a "social" cost is sometimes seen by traditional peoples as too high a price to pay for perceived advantage. Major behavioral changes almost always produce, or require, major restructuring of traditional and valued social relationships. When the "social" costs of this restructuring – the conflict potential – are seen as outweighing the potential advantage, the decision will be against change.

Bureaucracies in Relation to Health Innovation

We now turn to the (frequently) unrecognized barriers to the best possible health services that are inherent in bureaucratic structures and in the premises of their personnel. The term "Bureaucracy" is used here, not in a pejorative sense, but rather to refer to an organization, an administrative structure, whose manifest functions are to meet formally-defined societal needs. As a university professor, I see myself as

much a bureaucrat as is a medical adviser sent abroad by AID. My manifest function is to contribute to higher education and research, formally-defined as a societal need.

My argument here is that if we are fully to appreciate the dynamics of the planned change process, in health practices and in all other fields, it is essential to study administrators, planners, and professional specialists as individuals and as members of professions and bureaucracies, in the same ways and for the same reasons that we study traditional societies or any other client group – for bureaucracies and their personnel can be studied in essentially the same fashion as a peasant village or the urban neighborhood served by a public health center. A bureaucracy, in its structural and dynamic aspects, is very much like a "natural" community such as, for example, a peasant village, in that it is a real society with a real culture. And, like a peasant village, most bureaucracies include members of both sexes of widely varying ages, organized in a hierarchy of authority, responsibility, obligations, and functional tasks. Bureaucracies have social structures that define the role relationships and statuses of their members, and they have devices to change these relationships, through promotion, horizontal shifts, by-passing manoeuvers and – rarely – demotion. Like all people in social units, the personnel of bureaucracies, and the bureaucracies themselves, operate on the basis of implicit and explicit assumptions which can be analyzed just as can those assumptions found in natural societies. Many of these assumptions are influential in the planning of developmental programs, as the following examples will show.

A bureaucracy, as we have seen, ostensibly exists to fulfill a need or needs in society; the manifest functions of bureaucracies are expressed in their charters or enabling legislation, and it is expected that they will fulfill these functions, normally defined in terms of a client group. Yet we all know that, in practice, the primary concern of every bureaucracy and of its personnel is the corporate survival and, if possible, the growth of the organization, and the simultaneous protection of the position of staff members. Only when these concerns are taken care of can a bureaucracy turn full attention to its client group; and on those occasions when corporate or individual survival are threatened, this group may receive short shrift.

A second premise characterizing most bureaucracies is that the convenience of personnel, their likes and dislikes, has priority over the convenience of clients. This is seen particularly clearly in hours of service. I speak from experience: in setting my major university lectures at eight o'clock in the morning I have uppermost in mind my own convenience. I realize this hour is not the choice of most members of my client group, the students, whose needs I am supposed to serve. They would prefer the more popular hour of ten o'clock; and were I to lecture at that time my client group would double. Similarly, hours of service of government offices, including health departments, in this country and in developing countries, are set for the convenience of personnel and not for clients. We have all observed instances where the services of government clinics have been badly underutilized, largely because official hours from eight in the morning until two in the afternoon are the least convenient time for village women. Moreover, frequent failure of health personnel to be available at these stipulated times means that long and expensive trips by patients may be in vain. Such casual attention to the needs and feelings of patients is at least as much a "barrier" to adoption of better health practices as are beliefs in the efficacy of traditional medicine, or the fear of disrupting family relationships by adopting new health customs.

time they change and evolve. Innovative programs and pilot projects designed to meet these changing definitions of purpose and need require that new skills and professional specialties be brought into the organization. Simultaneously the talents of some staff members which were of critical importance during an earlier period, or in the context of projects now closed out, may become less essential. To put it briefly, new priorities mean that new roles must be created, and some old roles given added importance, while other old roles diminish in importance, with loss of relative rank, authority, and privilege to the incumbents occupying these latter roles. But, just as the first concern of a bureaucracy is to ensure its survival and to protect itself against inroads from competing organizations, so is the first priority of the professional to protect his or her position within the organization. Like people in "natural" communities, we professionals jealously guard our traditional perquisites and privileges; we do not willingly surrender something except in exchange for something as good or better. All of us, as bureaucrats, rationalize our resistance to change that may leave us in a less desirable position by arguing – and usually genuinely believing – that what is good for us is also best for our institution, and for its clients. Consequently, we may go to extreme lengths, including back-biting, in-fighting, and bickering in effort to protect ourselves. The resulting social costs – lowered morale and intra-organizational friction – often seem to outweigh the advantages of greater responsiveness to new needs, and consequently most bureaucracies change very slowly.

Social Costs of Changes in Bureaucracies

The social cost of bureaucratic flexibility, of responsiveness to changing needs, are at least as great as are the social costs of new behavior in traditional communities. The problem lies in the inevitable changes in role relationships – changes that threaten the position of some of the members of the group – that accompany major restructuring in any society, a bureaucracy included. The societal needs that a major bureaucracy should meet are not static; over

Medical Role Perceptions as Barriers to Change

The underlying assumptions of medical personnel about their roles, responsibilities, and the structure of medical services sometimes constitute barriers to the development of health services best suited to the needs of developing countries. The traditional American division of health services into preventive and curative fields, for example, which developed in response to a variety of pressures and vested interests inherent in the American way of life, was assumed in early programs to be the "norm" for overseas development. The Rockefeller anti-hookworm campaign in Ceylon was very strictly a preventive program, and field personnel repeatedly were cautioned not to become involved in curative services. Yet one reason the project failed to eradicate hookworm was that to the Ceylonese the rationale of environmental sanitation to the exclusion of *their* health priorities made little sense.

> Some villagers were irritated by the concentration on hookworm disease in view of their other overwhelming medical needs. ... The villagers were more interested in having their wounds and abscesses dressed and their miscellaneous acute illnesses attended than continuing in the dull routines of anti-hookworm work (Phillips 1955:289).

Despite the home-office warnings not to scatter their energies by engaging in curative activities, field directors found they had to treat all kinds of complaints in order to gain support for the hookworm work.

Institute of Inter-American Affairs programs in Latin America in the 1940s also emphasized prevention rather than curing. This medical assumption has, in the past, proven to be one of the most serious of all barriers in building better health services in developing countries. Fortunately, few if any such countries today are planning their health services on other than a combined basis.

The mode of definition of health problems frequently limits medical organizations in searching for the most efficient ways of meeting health needs. As John Bryant has pointed out, a health problem is what is defined by the medical establishment (headed by medical doctors) as a health problem; consequently health priorities set by "medically qualified" people are the appropriate priorities. In exploring this phenomenon, we find that we are dealing not alone with the traditional wisdom of the medical profession, but also – frequently – with the ego structure of individual specialists. As professionals we are proud of our skills, and we derive satisfaction in demonstrating our competences to ourselves and our colleagues, *and* in having these competences acknowledged. If we are honest with ourselves, we

must admit that we crave recognition. Consequently, our ego-needs not in-frequently motivate us to search out and concentrate on special problems that are important, not so much to our client group as to ourselves, because of the opportunity they offer to demonstrate to our peers our exceptional capacities. All too often we confuse our psychological needs with the needs of our clients, and we assume that our personal priorities must also be those of the people we serve. In the planning and operation of health programs we must acknowledge that personal interests – even research hobbies – play an enormously important role in the final form of a service.

Finally, we must note an assumption of many medical doctors that is crucial to one of the main themes of this workshop, the possible role as sub-professional workers of indigenous medical personnel. John Bryant, in *Health and the Developing World*, has put the matter succinctly and sympathetically. A part of the greatness of the good physician, he says, is his acceptance of responsibility to give unstintingly of himself to those who need his help. But this is also the basis for his traditional reluctance to share his activities with others, to relinquish some of his tasks to less thoroughly trained personnel. To admit that many of the professional tasks he has been trained to perform can be carried out equally well by less well trained people apparently threatens the ego of many medical practitioners.

> A curious side of this concept [that only the physician can provide quality care] is the value the physician places on the particular acts of diagnosis and prescription of treatment. Physicians are anxious to use every level of health worker in furthering a health program ... but the words "diagnose" and "prescribe" evoke the strongest feelings of professional possessiveness (Bryant 1969:141–2).

The concept that the physician must attend personally to his patients actually determines the form of most health services, says Bryant, and it can obstruct efforts to change the design of health systems.

> Thus while logic tells us that the physician's role should be determined by the health needs of the entire population, implementation of

this logic is obstructed by the insistence of the medical profession that only physicians can evaluate and treat the sick. This stand of the medical profession has a paralyzing effect on the design and implementation of health services and is one of the most serious obstacles to the effective use of limited health resources" (1969:143).

Bryant's warning leads to my final point: possible roles for traditional healers in national health services.

Possible Roles for Traditional Healers

Paradoxically, the growing acceptance of Western medicine is creating a crisis in most developing countries. There are not now, nor will there be in the foreseeable future, sufficient fully-trained health personnel to meet all health needs. Auxiliary health workers have been and will continue to be used in almost all countries. In the former British and French colonies, local men were trained as "dressers" or "*infirmier auxiliaires*" to staff rural clinics and, depending on level of training, to perform a variety of therapeutic duties including simple laboratory analyses. Among the Navaho Indians the "health visitor" works under the supervision of the public health nurse, significantly extending her capacity to fulfill her role. In contemporary China, rural "barefoot doctors" offer a primary level of treatment in a referral system which sends seriously ill patients to more highly trained health personnel.

In these, and in other comparable instances, the sub-professional worker is (or was) a member of the formal health establishment, trained by qualified teachers, and paid by, and formally incorporated into colonial, tribal, or national health services. Because of the relative success of this approach in helping to solve health problems, and in the face of (almost certainly) permanent shortages of highly trained personnel, the question periodically is asked, should indigenous healers also be recognized as having something important to offer? Should they, in some way, be incorporated into the health services of a country? In

the development of national health programs based on Western medicine official attitudes toward traditional healers have ranged from neglect to outright opposition: they have been looked upon by most medical doctors as undesirable competitors, if not outright enemies to be vanquished. Only occasionally, as with Ayurvedic medicine in India, has an indigenous medical system and its practitioners been formally encouraged by government. Even in India the vast substratum of "folk" medicine not recognized as Ayurvedic is ignored by the government.

The question of recognition of traditional healers is important because, in addition to the manpower problem, the fact remains that no scientific medical system completely satisfies all health needs of a nation. Even in countries with highly developed health care systems many people, under certain conditions, will turn to non-establishment forms of medical help such as faith healers, herbal doctors and the like. "Alternate" forms of medical care fill social, psychological, and perhaps organic health needs which, at least for some people, remain unmet by physicians and associated care services. With respect to a formal policy, the answers are not easy. Viewing particularly the supportive sociopsychological functions of the indigenous curer, anthropologists have been impressed with the positive aspects of non-Western medicine. Medical doctors, on the other hand, point out that some traditional remedies are definitely dangerous, and that at the very least treatment by traditional curers may delay referral to medical doctors until routine treatment such as an appendectomy becomes vastly more complicated.

Harrison, in discussing the possible role of non-Western medical personnel in Nigeria found that most government personnel were skeptical of their value.

> One government official told me that they are untrainable because of their superstitious beliefs and because their practice is secret and difficult to evaluate. They view the delivery of babies as a supernatural process. Mothers are discouraged from using traditional healers because there are so many quacks among them (Harrison 1974–5:12).

This negative evaluation is reflected in most other countries.

In spite of this prevailing view, successful efforts have been made to incorporate indigenous midwives into formal medical services. Since most births are "normal," it is reasoned, the primary problem is (1) to encourage the midwife to practice hygienic methods and (2) to refer difficult cases to government health services. Since at least the early 1950s village midwives in El Salvador have been recognized and trained by government personnel, and among the Navajo Indians similar training has reduced infant and maternal mortality. More recently there are reports of this kind of training for indigenous midwives in Tanzania (Dunlop 1974–5:138) and Liberia (Dennis 1974–5:23).

Mental illness is a second area in which formal recognition of traditional healers seems potentially promising. Since patient expectation is an important element in therapy, it seems reasonable to expect that in the absence of organic dysfunction mental stress and illness can be alleviated by curers whose treatments have been seen to be successful in the past. Torrey believes that, in spite of the anecdotal nature of the evidence on the efficacy of therapists in other cultures, "It is almost unanimous in suggesting that witchdoctors get about the same therapeutic results as psychiatrists do" (Torrey 1973:119). In Nigeria, Maclean appears favorably impressed by many aspects of traditional treatment of mental illness, and not the least by rituals enacted to symbolize recovery at the end of a period of treatment. Dressed in the clothing worn during his illness, the patient is taken to a river where a dove is sacrificed over his head, and he is washed in its blood. Then his old clothing is removed and, with the carcass of the bird, thrown into the stream and carried away, while the priest-curer chants:

As the river can never flow backwards,
So may this illness never return.

The former patient now dresses in new clothes and meets his relatives who have assembled for a feast in honor of his newly-recovered health. Both patient and family benefit from this ritual: the former is reassured that his relatives welcome him back to his usual role, while the latter has the priest's assurance that he can be counted on to carry on with his normal activities. This is in striking contrast, says Maclean, to Western society where a former mental patient leaves the hospital with a stigma which may never disappear (Maclean 1971:79–80).

Whatever the potential merit of making formal use of the medical talents of indigenous curers, the idea has made little progress in practice. Perhaps the question will never need to be resolved, for it erroneously assumes that traditional healers will continue to be produced in the same numbers and with the same skills as in the past. But social, economic, and educational change is coming with such speed in all the world that most of tomorrow's traditional healers probably will have been trained in medical schools, schools of nursing, and other government health institutions. Consequently, I suspect that any increase in the formal use of traditional healers in the context of national health services will be at best no more than a transitional step, and that after relatively few years, the question of their possible utility will be moot.

REFERENCES

Adams, Richard N.
  1955   A Nutritional Research Program in Guatemala. In *Health, Culture and Community.* B. D. Paul, ed. New York: Russell Sage Foundation. pp. 435–458.
Anonymous
  [1953]   *10 Years of Cooperative Health Programs in Latin America: An Evaluation.* Washington, DC: Conducted by the Public Health Service, Department of Health, Education, and Welfare for The Institute of Inter-American Affairs.
Banerji, D.
  1974   *Health Behaviour of Rural Populations: Impact of Rural Health Services. A Preliminary Communication.* New Delhi: Jawaharlal Nehru University, Centre of Social Medicine and Community Health.
Boesch, Ernst E.
  1972   Communication Between Doctors and Patients in Thailand, Part I. Saarbrücken: University of the Saar, Socio-Psychological Research Centre on Development Planning.

Bryant, John
1969 *Health and the Developing World.* Ithaca & London: Cornell University Press.

Dennis, Ruth E.
1974–5 The Traditional Healer in Liberia. In *Traditional Healers: Use and Non-Use in Health Care Delivery.* I. E. Harrison and D. W. Dunlop, eds. East Lansing, MI: Michigan State University, The African Studies Center [Rural Africana No. 26]. pp. 17–23.

Dunlop, David W.
1974–5 Alternatives to "Modern" Health-Delivery Systems in Africa: Issues for Public Policy Consideration on the Role of Traditional Healers. In *Traditional Healers: Use and Non-Use in Health Care Delivery.* I. E. Harrison and D. W. Dunlop, eds. East Lansing, MI: Michigan State University, The African Studies Center [Rural Africana No. 26]. pp. 131–9.

Erasmus, Charles J.
1952 Changing Folk Beliefs and Relativity of Empirical Knowledge. *Southwestern Journal of Anthropology* 8:411–28.

Foster, George M.
1973 *Traditional Societies and Technological Change.* New York: Harper and Row.

Harrison, Ira E.
1974–5 Traditional Healers: A Neglected Source of Health Manpower. In *Traditional Healers: Use and Non-Use in Health Care Delivery.* I. E. Harrison and D. W. Dunlop, eds. East Lansing, MI: Michigan State University, The African Studies Center [Rural Africana, No. 26]. pp. 5–16.

Hinderling, Paul
1973 Communication Between Doctors and Patients in Thailand, Part III. Saarbrücken: University of the Saar, Socio-Psychological Research Centre on Development Planning.

Kark, Sidney, and Emily Kark
1962 A Practice of Social Medicine. Chapter 1 in *A Practice of Social Medicine: A South African Team's Experiences in Different African Communities.* S. L. Kark and G. E. Steuart, eds. Edinburgh & London: E. and S. Livingstone. pp. 3–40.

Maclean, Una
1971 *Magical Medicine: A Nigerian Case-Study.* Harmondsworth, Middlesex: Penguin Books.

Ndeti, K.
1972 Sociocultural Aspects of Tuberculosis Defalutation: A Case Study. *Social Science and Medicine* 6:397–412.

Philips, Jane
1955 The Hookworm Campaign in Ceylon. In *Hands Across Frontiers: Case Studies in Technical Cooperation.* H. M. Teaf, Jr. and P. G. Franck, eds. Ithaca, NY: Cornell University Press. pp. 265–305.

Servicio
1953 Ten Years of Operation of the Bilateral Health Programs of the Institute of Inter-American Affairs. *Public Health Reports* 68:829–57.

Torrey, E. Fuller
1973 *The Mind Game: Witchdoctors and Psychiatrists.* New York: Bantam Books. [First ed. 1972.]

32

Anthropology and Global Health

Craig R. Janes and Kitty K. Corbett

Defining Global Health

Defining global health in relation to anthropological research and practice is a challenge. Although in common use in a variety of disciplines, the term defies simple delineation. It frequently serves as a gloss signaling complexities inherent in linking health and accelerating and intensifying global processes, although it sometimes simply refers to work that has an international (read: poor country) dimension. In his recent book on the subject, Nichter (2008) suggests that anthropology intersects global health along a number of dimensions, ranging from the study of popular health culture and local perceptions as a way to both critique and improve international public health, to the study of ethics, governance, and emergent forms of biological citizenship. Cast in such a broad framework, though, these intersections could characterize much of the development of medical anthropology to the present, including, especially, much of the ethnographic applied research on local social and cultural factors linked to improving community health in developing countries (Foster 1976; Hahn & Inhorn 2009; Inhorn & Janes 2007; Nichter 1989, 1991; Paul 1955). To further complicate matters, until recently anthropologists have not typically invoked the term global health as a referent for a subdisciplinary domain of research or practice or in description of their own identity as scholars. Although a recent upsurge in publications and several recent editorials suggest that global health may at last be finding a home in anthropology, definitional clarity is needed (Adams et al. 2008; Erickson 2003; Inhorn 2007a; Nichter 2008; Pfeiffer & Nichter 2008; Whiteford & Manderson 2000).

As noted, global health is used to either supplant or mirror the longstanding conceptual domain of international health. This distinction is complicated by the fact that international health references a better-defined set of research and applied skills, many of which are derived from the disciplines that constitute public health and development studies (including anthropology; compare Nichter 2008). In contrast, global health remains a diffuse and highly diverse arena of scholarship and practice (Inst. Med. 2009; Macfarlane et al. 2008). The political scientist Kelley Lee, a prolific writer on global health, distinguishes the two by highlighting the construct of transnationalism. Lee argues that global health, as opposed to international health, should be a field of scholarship and practice that focuses on health issues that transcend the territorial

Craig R. Janes and Kitty K. Corbett, "Anthropology and Global Health," *Annual Review of Anthropology* 38 (2009): 167–83.

boundaries of states (Lee 2003c). International health becomes global health when the causes or consequences of ill health "circumvent, undermine, or are oblivious to the territorial boundaries of states, and thus beyond the capacity of states to address effectively through state institutions alone" (Lee et al. 2002, p. 5).

Lee (2003a,c) argues for a model that specifically positions health as an outcome of processes that have intensified human interaction, given that previous boundaries separating individuals and population groups "have become increasingly eroded and redefined, resulting in new forms of social organization and interaction across them" (Lee 2003a, p. 21). She identifies three such boundaries or dimensions of globalization: the spatial, the temporal, and the cognitive. As she and others note, in this sense global health has come to occupy a new and different kind of political space that demands the study of population health in the context of power relations in a world system (Brown et al. 2006; Kickbush 2003; Lee 2003c).

Lee's model merges with writing in anthropology and sociology that looks at globalization from the perspective of local, though not necessarily spatially bound, social contexts. Appadurai (1991, 1996), for example, has invoked the idea of "scapes" that have come to stand in place of older place-based divisions. Burawoy (2000), who with his graduate students developed a theoretical and methodological program to "ground globalization," observes that the "mishmash of migrations, capital flows, hostilities, and opportunities jostling within the hot signifier of globalization" (p. ix) can be sorted along three axes. These axes are global forces, including global economic and political processes as mediated by agents, institutions, and ideas; global connections, referring to the underlying social grids, networks, flows, and new forms of sociality; and the global imagination, which addresses the adoption of values and images that circulate globally.

Burawoy takes these abstractions of globalization and applies them to understand something local. Yet what constitutes the "local" in the context of globalization is contested (Ferguson 2005; Janes 2004; Morgan

2001; Ong & Collier 2005a). Although the concept of locality is worthy of extended analysis, we take a pragmatic approach: As ethnographers we study people-in-places or people-in-contexts. We thus prefer the definition advanced by Ginsburg & Rapp (1995b): "[T]he local is not defined by geographical boundaries but is understood as any small-scale arena in which social meanings are informed and adjusted" (p. 8).

What does this mean for understanding health? Both theoretically and methodologically the task is to understand how various assemblages of global, national, and subnational factors converge on a health issue, problem, or outcome in a particular local context. Ong & Collier (2005a) refer to these processes collectively as the "actual global," and they prefer the more fluid, irreducible, and emergent concept of the "global assemblage" to "the global": An assemblage "does not always involve new forms, but forms that are shifting, in formation, or at stake" (p. 12). These heterogeneous global assemblages interact with local institutions, social worlds, and cultural identities through unpredictable and uncertain processes (Whiteford & Manderson 2000). Consistent with Burawoy's (2000) approach to grounded globalization, anthropological work in global health thus requires a focus on the instantiation of global assemblages in local social arenas, however defined. Methodologically, Burawoy (2000) argues for the grounding of globalization through what he identifies as the extended case method: "extending from observer to participant, extending observations over time and place, extending from process to external forces, and extending theory" (p. 28). In so doing, the ethnographer is positioned to "construct perspectives on globalization from below" (p. 341).

With this information as a brief background, and for purposes of this exercise, we offer the following definition of global health as it pertains to anthropology: Global health is an area of research and practice that endeavours to link health, broadly conceived as a dynamic state that is an essential resource for life and well-being, to assemblages of global processes, recognizing that these assemblages are complex, diverse, temporally unstable, contingent, and often contested or resisted at different social scales. This includes work that focuses on health inequities; the distribution of resources intended to produce health and well-being, including science and technology; social identities related to health and biology; the development and local consequences of global health policy; the organization of health services; and the relationship of anthropogenic transformations of the biosphere to health. The ultimate goal of anthropological work in and of global health is to reduce global health inequities and contribute to the development of sustainable and salutogenic sociocultural, political, and economic systems.

Although global health conceptually includes all peoples regardless of social, economic, and political contexts, its ethical and moral commitment is to the most vulnerable. However, and given the impending and hitherto unprecedented scale of global catastrophe that environmental destruction, mass species extinction, and anthropogenic climate change presage, global health might benefit from redefining the vulnerable to include all of us (McMichael & Beaglehole 2003).

So defined, the anthropological project in global health can be arranged along several axes. Here we review what we consider key arenas of research and practice: ethnographic studies of health inequities in political and economic contexts; analysis of the impact on local worlds of the assemblages of science and technology that circulate globally; interrogation, analysis, and critique of international health programs and policies; and analysis of the health consequences of the reconfiguration of the social relations of international health development.

Explaining Health Inequities

The anthropological contribution to the study of health inequities has primarily been to ground globalization (as anticipated by Burowoy 2000 and Nichter 2008) through exposing processes by which people are constrained or victimized or resisting external forces in the context of local social worlds (Baer et al. 2003; Farmer 1997, 2003, 2004; Farmer et al. 1996; Kim et al. 2005; Maternowska 2006;

Pfeiffer & Nichter 2008; Scheper-Hughes 1993). This research encompasses different registers, mainly in the depth of engagement with local materials, the care by which the local is nested within higher-level social structures, and the degree to which the analysis is used as a platform for public health advocacy. However, this work tends to share a common, critical theoretical perspective that focuses on explicating or grounding health inequities in reference to upstream constellations of international political economy, regional history, and development ideology. It is closely linked with critical medical anthropology, a research tradition that seeks to identify the social origins of distress and disease, recognizing that these origins are ultimately located within the processes and contradictions inherent in the capitalist world system (Baer et al. 2003; Singer & Baer 1995). Farmer (2004) has used the concept of "structural violence" to explain this impact of political-economic regimes of oppression on the health of the poor.

Such work has contributed to redefining the concept of risk in epidemiology by redirecting attention from risky behaviors to structural factors that constrain or determine behavior. For example, early reports on the epidemiology of HIV/AIDS tended to focus on individual behaviors rather than on the impact of poverty and marginality that differentially affected men and women within particular populations and communities (Farmer et al. 1996, 2001; Simmons et al. 1996). Pointing to the tendency of some public health researchers to conflate poverty and cultural difference, Farmer and colleagues argued against "immodest claims of causality" and for a focus on, and mitigation of, the structural violence that produces ill being on a massive scale among the poor (Farmer 2003; Farmer et al. 2001; Simmons et al. 1996; Singer 1997). In similar fashion, anthropological research on infectious diseases, particularly HIV/AIDS, TB, and cholera, have contributed significantly to moving global public health away from a narrow focus on risk groups (Baer et al. 2003; Trostle 2005).

The social origins of infection with HIV are often bound up with or linked to a number of other threats to health and well-being, and in turn, the coexistence of two or more diseases may synergistically interact to produce a higher degree of pathogenesis (an example would be HIV and TB coinfection). Termed syndemics, these synergistic processes suggest a biosocial model of disease (Nichter 2008; Singer 2009; Singer & Clair 2003) that conceives "of disease both in terms of its interrelationships with noxious social conditions and social relationships, and as one form of expression of social suffering...it would make us more alert, as well, to the likelihood of multiple, interacting deleterious conditions among populations produced by the structural violence of social inequality" (Singer & Clair 2003, p. 434).

Many researchers experience a tension between a close rendering of the local and effective engagement with the global. Analytically and methodologically, how does one extend ethnographic work to incorporate globalization while portraying faithfully the rich human stories that bring voice to the poor and suffering, without conceptually flattening, simplifying, or objectifying one or the other (Butt 2002)? Farmer and his colleagues often juxtapose stories of individual suffering with political-economic givens, offering sometimes thin analyses of intervening processes and structures. Some have observed that the concept of structural violence is a black box, rarely unpacked (Bourgois & Scheper-Hughes 2004; Wacquant 2004). Future work on global health inequities might thus profitably employ ecosocial epidemiology (Krieger 2001) by addressing, for instance, the interplay among exposure, susceptibility, and adaptation at meso- and macroscales across the life course (Nichter 2008). Application within global health contexts of the construct of "intersectionality" also provides a way to unpack the concept of structural violence. Derived primarily from feminist studies, this theoretical and methodological perspective emphasizes the importance of simultaneously considering how different aspects of social location (e.g., gender, ethnicity, class, age, geography, sexual identity) interlock and the impact of systems and processes of oppression and domination (Hankivsky & Cormier 2009; Hulko 2009).

Whether explicitly identified as critical medical anthropology or not, a substantial body of scholarly work in anthropology seeks to link wider social, economic, and political forces to local experiences of sickness and suffering. We believe that this work is an important adjunct to the emerging scholarship on the social determinants of health that tends to focus more on patterns evident at population levels (Comm. Soc. Determinants Health 2008). A few examples include studies of extreme hunger and scarcity in northeastern Brazil (Scheper-Hughes 1993); the global circulation of tobacco and its impacts (Nichter & Cartwright 1991; Stebbins 1991); parasitic and infectious diseases (Briggs & Mantini-Briggs 2003; Farmer 1999; Feldman 2008; Ferguson 2005; Inhorn & Brown 1997; Kendall 2005; Manderson & Huang 2005; Whiteford & Hill 2005); reproductive health, fertility, and infertility (Inhorn 2003, 2007b; Janes & Chuluundorj 2004; Maternowska 2006; Morsy 1995); mental ill health (Desjarlais et al. 1995; Kleinman 1988); alcohol and drug use (Singer 2008); and life style transitions and noncommunicable diseases (Dressler & Bindon 2000, Evans et al. 2001, McElroy 2005).

Although anthropologists have engaged with many of the core themes of health equity studies in global public health, they lag in taking up some emerging concerns. Gaps are apparent in the domain of environmental change affecting and affected by global processes. Examples range from climate change broadly (Baer & Singer 2009; Guest 2005; McMichael & Beaglehole 2003; Patz et al. 2005) to specific problems such as microbial resistance (Orzech & Nichter 2008). Many of the models of human impacts of climate change point to the need for more research to identify factors that affect the vulnerabilities of local populations in the context of political economy (Intergov. Panel Climate Change 2007). We anticipate that in the next decade medical anthropology will begin to investigate more systematically the relationship of global environmental transformations to health.

Global Technoscapes

Invoking the term technoscape, Appadurai (1996) refers to the "global configuration ...

of technology, and the fact that technology, both high and low, both mechanical and information, now moves at high speeds across various kinds of previously impervious boundaries" (p. 34). The global technoscape as it pertains to health is comprised of an inextricable mix of things (e.g., medicines, medical devices, machines), techniques (e.g., medical procedures), and bundles of shared understandings and epistemological practices that together constitute science in the global north. Far from being a homogenizing influence, the global circulation of science and technology engages various localities as one component of a global assemblage (Ong & Collier 2005a). This assemblage of things, ideologies, and representations interacts with communities in diverse ways, both shaping and being transformed by local beliefs and practices. Questions central to investigation of global science concern how paradigms, practices, and results are negotiated and unfold far from their places of origin (Adams et al. 2005). As many scholars have noted, the products and purported benefits of science and technology are unevenly distributed; some sites and groups have greater access than others do (Ginsburg and Rapp 1995b; Inhorn 2003).

Examples of key works in this area include the local impact of biomedical research practices, such as those involving translation of the ethical principles of scientific research, especially clinical trials, in specific cultural contexts (Adams et al. 2005; Petryna 2005); the circulation of medicalized objectifications of body and behavior, such as those having to do with sexuality in this era of HIV (Parker 2000; Pigg & Adams 2005); the transformations of local beliefs and understandings about the body, life, and death that are entailed by the globalization of human organ replacement therapies (Lock 2001; Marshall & Daar 2000); local acceptances of and resistance to contraceptive technologies (Maternowska 2006; Rak & Janes 2004); the complex local/global dynamics of organ transplantation and medical tourism (Cohen 2005; Scheper-Hughes 2000, 2005), including the definitional exercises needed to create harvestable tissues and organs (Lock 2001; Marshall & Daar 2000); and cases illustrating complexities of corporate practices, medicalization, and the politics of biomedical knowledge through the interwoven dynamics of drug production, marketing, and sales practices, the classification of disease, and patterns of clinical practice (Applbaum 2006; Hayden 2007; Singer & Baer 2008).

A particularly robust area of research has focused on the globalization of reproductive and prenatal diagnostic technologies (Browner & Sargent 2009; Erikson 2003; Ginsburg & Rapp 1995a; Inhorn 2003, 2005, 2007b; Ong & Collier 2005b). Writing of the globalization of treatments for infertility, Inhorn (2003) observes that "[l]ocal considerations, be they cultural, social, economic, or political, shape and sometimes curtail the way in which these Western-generated technologies are both offered to and received by non-Western subjects" (p. 1844). Cultural or religious proscription of procedures such as donor insemination has led to increased global demand and rapid circulation of more expensive technologies such as in-vitro fertilization (Inhorn 2003). In Egypt, for example, men and women contending with infertility are confronted by constraints that are deeply embedded in local social and cultural contexts. These arenas of constraint include local understandings of reproductive biology, social and economic barriers to access, gender dynamics within marriage, and local understandings of Islam (Inhorn 2003, p. 1844, 2005, 2007b).

Globalization also sets into motion people, for example, the export of physicians and nurses (the "brain drain") from low-income countries to rich countries (Pfeiffer & Nichter 2008), and "medical tourists" and others who travel to places where desired technologies exist or are affordable (Kangas 2002). As noted above, it also enables the flow of organs, tissues, and genetic materials (Marshall & Daar 2000; Scheper-Hughes 2005). Described as an artifact of "second coming" capitalism, the worldwide spread of medical procedures and technologies has produced "strange markets and 'occult' economies" (Comaroff & Comaroff 2001, cited in Scheper-Hughes 2005, p. 149).

Bioscience is not the only set of ideas about bodies, physiology, and health that circulate globally. Countervailing creativities also exist, whereby what were formerly "local" and "non-western" engage both the imagination and the markets at the center of the world system. This is the case for Asian medicines, both brought by immigrants and practiced by immigrant communities, but also adopted by New Agers and others challenging the hegemony of conventional biomedicine. In their places of origin and their global circulation, the content and practice of these medical traditions are transformed (Alter 2005; Høg & Hsu 2002; Janes 2002). In many cases these processes of transformation involve at their core the commoditization of medicinal substances, which is in turn based on the reduction of complex systems of diagnosis, explanation, and healing to the exchange and consumption of medicinal substances (Janes 1999).

Medicines – *materia medica* – are at the heart of much of what we might define as "medical technologies." Although medicines, especially pharmaceuticals, were ignored as a focal topic more often than not by medical anthropologists in the first decades of the discipline, work by van der Geest and other anthropologists in the 1980s and 1990s initiated a florescence of research on their uses in the context of global influences and on factors affecting their production, distribution, demand, and consumption (Trostle 1996; van der Geest et al. 1988, 1996). This trend continues, spurred in part by the ethical and practical challenges represented by the need for people everywhere who live with HIV/AIDS to receive treatment (Farmer et al. 2001; Robins 2009; Whyte et al. 2006). Addressing access needs requires investigation into pharmaceutical governance, trade practices, patent protection, distribution channels, and alternative industries and markets, as well as local organizations and the cultural and ritual properties of medicines. Approaches to understanding how medicines function in society increasingly include attention to the context of global assemblages, including greater attention to formal and institutional sectors (Hayden 2007; Kim 2009; Mather 2006; Oldani 2004). As anthropologists reflect on medication use, including not just underuse but also overuse, inappropriate use, and errors in delivering appropriate medications to patients,

they increasingly situate these practices within global institutional and perceptual systems (Nichter 2008). Medicines, whether originating in local traditions or developed through the pharmaceutical pipeline, are global citizens.

One dimension of the global circulation of expert, biomedical knowledge on disease, therapeutic regimes, and prevention is the creation of novel social forms (Biehl 2007; Lee 2003a; Nguyen 2005; Rose & Novas 2005). In the context of HIV, notes Nguyen (2005), these groups are "more than social movements articulated around objectives" and are a "complex biopolitical assemblage, cobbled together from global flows of organisms, drugs, discourses, and technologies of all kinds" (p. 125). Nguyen is interested particularly in how the constellations of technoscientific understandings of prevention and treatment that together constitute the global AIDS industry are translated locally by groups and organizations to mobilize a response to the epidemic. Similarly, Petryna (2002) shows how the Chernobyl disaster and its impacts on health provided an avenue for affected individuals, joined by a biologically mediated identity, to make claims on the state for resources. The development of therapeutic groups is increasingly entangled with the industry of health development (Nguyen 2005, p. 125). This form of citizenship represents evolving subjectivities, politics, and ethics that result from the globalization of biomedical developments and discoveries (Ecks 2005; Rose & Novas 2005).

Interrogating Health Policy

Analysis of the formation, dissemination, and local consequences of expert knowledge forms the core of the anthropological critique of global public health policy (Castro & Singer 2004; Whiteford & Manderson 2000). This critique focuses on both the process and consequences of policymaking: ideological and political-economic relations that influence decision makers and the policymaking process and the impacts, intended or otherwise, of specific policies on the health and well-being of the intended beneficiaries. In regard to the latter, it is common for observers to report on the problems inherent in localizing global health policies (Whiteford & Manderson 2000). Central to the interrogation of health policy, an area only a few anthropologists have explored in any depth (e.g., Justice 1986), are the processes by and through which the substances of international health policymaking – knowledge, ideology, politics of representation, competing vested interests, processes of persuasion and advocacy, etc. – come to constitute it. In a pure and perhaps idealized form, policy represents translating knowledge into action. What are these processes of translation? Is it possible, thinking here in ethnographic terms, to expose these processes through careful analysis of global policymaking communities? And how might anthropologists proactively affect these translational processes?

Nichter (2008) suggests that policymakers tend to simplify and frame problems in ways that limit the thinking about possible solutions; these "key social representations" dominate health and development discourse as "master narratives" (p. 2). Lee & Goodman (2002) argue that the networks of so-called experts in global health tend to be fairly small but are positioned strategically to create and successfully advocate for solutions to key international agencies. Such networks comprise what are in international relations and globalization literatures termed epistemic communities (Adler & Haas 1992), loose networks of actors that develop common frameworks of knowledge, values, and beliefs that underlie configurations of public health policy and action. Although presumably oriented to technical matters, these epistemic communities are powerful because they, as representatives at least implicitly of the global capitalist class (Singer & Castro 2004), can set agendas, frame issues, identify problems, and propose solutions. These networks extend into major universities, especially in the fields of economics and public health (Lee & Goodman 2002) and are now at the core of global health governance (Adams et al. 2008).

Van der Geest (2006), in commenting about pharmaceutical matters, critiques an overemphasis in global health on policies as a solution, commenting about the lip service and culture of policy makers whose mandate is to produce planning reports and documents (e.g., about essential medicines, their distribution, etc.) but who are not invested in program implementation. Whyte & Birungi (2000) found that World Health Organization (WHO)-inspired model policies were ineffective in changing local-level and lay practices around inappropriate prescription and use of pharmaceutical medicines. Hardon (2005), also critical of policymakers, asserts that their work often entails a focus on "magic bullets." She notes that recent policy shifts reflect a growing acknowledgment in the policy sectors that people without economic resources or literacy can and do use HIV/AIDS treatments appropriately. Yet although many more people now have access to previously far too expensive treatments, the policies have had side effects. The prices of pharmaceuticals are still extremely high for people on the margins of the economy, and entire family networks may experience cash depletion and food insecurity as they shift the household economy to procure medicines for a family member who is ill (Whyte et al. 2006).

The global circulation of expert knowledge produces particular relations of power between policy makers and policy subjects. The collapse of the primary care initiatives fostered at Alma Ata in 1978, the resurgence of selective forms of primary care and vertical public health programs, and the ascendency of the World Bank as the principal health policymaking institution provide a glimpse of how these processes work themselves out (Janes 2004, 2009; Janes et al. 2005; Lee & Goodman 2002; Paluzzi 2004). Deploying a set of strategies to reframe health and health care in narrow technical terms (i.e., the development of the disability adjusted life year, or DALY) subject to the principles of classical economics, a relatively small group of individuals crafted an approach to health care that removed it from public governance and placed it largely in the hands of the market, complementing and bolstering processes of structural adjustment begun in the 1980s (Farmer 2003; Farmer & Castro 2004; Janes 2004; World Bank 1993). The result has been increasing inequities and contradictions at local levels, for example reforms that mandate selling medicines to poor people who cannot afford them (Keshavjee 2004). Although it is remarkable that the WHO is currently attempting to reclaim the discourse on health reform and reassert the principles of primary care (World Health Organ. 2008), it remains to be seen whether rights-based approaches will be able to trump the neoliberal orthodoxy that dominates health sector policy.

Population and reproductive policy is a significant area in which deeply held beliefs about the causes and consequences of poverty, and the role of scientific development and expert knowledge of demographic processes in remediating poverty, have come to drive health and social policy (Escobar 1995; Maternowska 2006). For example, in a series of works focusing on population policy in China, Greenhalgh (2005) has shown how the development of coercive family planning practices linked a version of Western population science with socialist planning and party-led community mobilization in order to achieve demographic modernity. Although the International Conference on Population Development held in Cairo in 1994 urged countries to move away from a narrow focus on fertility targets and to respect and protect women's rights to make an informed choice about their reproduction, in many contexts oppressive and coercive regimes of family planning have continued, directed primarily at poor women (Castro 2004; Greenhalgh 2005; Maternowska 2006; Morsy 1995). Other important works also focus on the problematic disjuncture between global reproductive health policy and the lived experiences of local women and men (Berry 2009; Browner & Sargent 2010; Castro 2004; Ginsburg & Rapp 1995a; Rak & Janes 2004; Towghi 2004).

The anthropological literature documenting the problematic implementation of international health development policy is vast. Other examples include, in addition to the above, work on child immunization (Justice 2000; Nichter 1995); implementation of therapeutic regimes for tuberculosis (DOTS) and treatment of multiple-drug-resistant forms of the disease (Farmer 2003; Kim et al. 2005; Nichter 2008); disaster management and resettlement (Whiteford & Tobin 2004); the globalization of bioethics and ethical issues, including especially

those arising in the context of organ transplantation and drug development (Marshall 2005; Marshall & Koenig 2004; Petryna 2005); the local impact of the global extension of regimes of monitoring and evaluation of public health programs, a variant of "audit cultures" (Nichter 2008; Strathern 2000); ideologies of community participation and political will in international health program planning (Janes 2004; Morgan 1989, 1997, 2001); and HIV/AIDS treatment and prevention policies (Bastos 1999; Biehl 2007; Desclaux 2004; Farmer 1999; Farmer et al. 2001).

An Unruly Mélange

Neoliberal development strategies initiated in the health sector since the 1980s have systematically reduced the size, scope, and reach of public health services. As a result, a number of private organizations, grouped collectively under the general heading of civil society, have become a cornerstone to health development. These include everything from small, local private organizations, to faith-based charities, to local offices of large international philanthropies. Favored as implementing agents by bilateral and international donors, including the major foundations and development banks, these agents of civil society have in many locales effectively supplanted government in the provision of primary health care. Often uncoordinated, competing with one another for donor and ministerial attention, duplicating efforts, and distorting local economies through the demands for food, housing, transportation, and entertainment by their expatriate staffs they comprise, as Buse & Walt (1997) note, an unruly mélange (Adams et al. 2008; Pfeiffer 2003, 2004).

Despite their prominence in health development, nongovernmental organizations (NGOs) have received relatively little attention as social and cultural phenomena in their own right (though see Abramson 1999; Markowitz 2001; Pfeiffer 2003, 2004; Redfield 2005). Pfeiffer (2003, 2004) has documented how in Mozambique the operation of NGOs, instead of strengthening health services, may have in fact had the opposite effect, undermining local control of health programs and contributing to the health human resource crisis by recruiting public-sector employees from public health service. Pfeiffer also gives us a glimpse of the social dynamics of NGOs, observing that in the interaction between the elite, educated technicians from the rich countries and community members living in extreme poverty, the exercise of power is laid bare: international NGOs intensify unequal social relations at the local level.

The expansion of NGOs is but one example of a growing number of transnational institutions that have become active in global health. Along with existing bilateral donors, intergovernmental institutions, and public private partnerships, these include economic interest groups, large philanthropic organizations, and multinational pharmaceutical companies. The effective practice of global health regardless of disciplinary background increasingly requires not just understanding of how to work effectively at a local level to improve health and well-being, but also skills to work across these many, and often competing, interest groups (Adams et al. 2008).

Conclusion: Reflections on the Economy of Knowledge in Global Health

A colleague of ours, reflecting on the virtual invasion of Africa by international researchers, suggested that the continent's new export was information for university-based researchers and pharmaceutical companies. In addition, academic programs in global health (like our own), located primarily in schools of public health in North America, send thousands of students abroad each year to complete global health practice placements. Presumably these students gain through these experiences the knowledge and skills they need to "do" global health. This experience raises the spectre of a new form of colonialism: extending uses of sites in the global south to study their disease burdens to satisfy the needs of science (particularly, these days, the AIDS industry) to find new subjects and explore new problems.

Citing his colleague, Jim Kim, Farmer (1999) has wryly observed that we are now in the midst of a global "Tuskegee experiment." We are mindful of the fact that global health, a field of exploding popularity largely in Europe and North America, is deeply involved in this manner of knowledge creation, exploitation, and exchange.

We argue that a central ethical problem for anthropologists, as for scholars of global health more generally, is consideration of the fairness of the terms of this exchange and whether their work contributes to social justice and the remediation of structural violence where it is the most severe. This problem provokes two questions: Are the products of anthropological scholarship in global health – conceptually, theoretically, methodologically, and pragmatically – relevant to those broadly interdisciplinary efforts to improve health and well-being? And, is anthropology, principally an academic discipline, prepared in the context of global health to engage in what we refer to here as principled engagement and intervention?

Partly in response to these questions, it is useful to reflect on anthropology's relevance to global health, which we have encapsulated into four main areas of research and practice. In the first of these, through ethnographic analysis of health inequities, anthropologists have added considerable depth to the project of identifying the social determinants of health (Comm. Soc. Determinants Health 2008). By specifying links among local life worlds and the global forces of neoliberal development, anthropologists have laid bare the lines of power, exploitation, and structural violence. Although more conceptual development is needed, this work has pointed to inherent flaws in health development programs that do not take poverty and environmental degradation, their root causes and consequences, as primary problems.

Second, and what now currently seems to be a popular avenue of research, is the study of global technoscience. Here anthropologists focus on the global circulation of technology and the bundles of meanings, representations, and understandings that together constitute biomedical science in the global north. The intent here is twofold: to unpack and explicate the cultural context of science and its products, and then to understand how science, as a social and cultural product, interacts with the local, where it is transformed and transforms, through being adopted, used, and resisted. Theoretically complex, this research area nevertheless has simple, direct, and profound implications for global health problems related to access to medicine and technology, the impact of western bioscience on conceptions of the body, ethical issues related to experimentation, the commoditization of body parts, identity and citizenship, and emerging processes of governance.

Third, an investigation of the globalization of western bioscience facilitates interrogation of entailed policies. How are policies made? Who makes these policies, and what ideologies, discourses, representations, and systems of knowledge do they draw on to craft decisions? How are policies made by global communities implemented, and to what effect, in highly variable local settings and contexts? Here, as with the study of the global technoscape, the focus is on examining the unintended consequences of policy for locals, reflecting on the fact that for the poor and vulnerable it is an unlevel playing field (Whiteford & Manderson 2000).

Fourth, it is clear from the analysis of global health policymaking that the institutional landscape in health development has been transformed. The proliferation of nonstate actors and neoliberal development practices that both constitute an engage civil society has produced a complex mix of groups and organizations at state and community levels. Successful health development entails both coordinating across this unruly mélange and understanding the social and cultural effects of their various operations. Yet there is much we do not understand about how civil society operates in global health. The principal questions appear to be when and how private organizations operating in parallel to the state foster, or compromise, positive health outcomes, and whether they in fact contribute to reducing, or increasing, health inequities.

Although clearly relevant, we have to ask whether anthropology has contributed, or is capable of contributing, in substantive ways to the kinds of engagement and interventions that promise to reduce health inequities, foster social justice, and address the challenges to global health presaged by global climate change, habitat destruction, and mass species extinction, as well as the global economic crisis? Here we are less sanguine. We have promising examples, and the work that many researchers have done lends itself clearly to concrete, appropriate policies, programs, and interventions. Like many, we are buoyed by the work of Farmer and his colleagues at Partners in Health in a variety of country and community settings, from poverty-stricken neighbourhoods in the United States to postgenocide Rwanda. We are also mindful of the several generations of anthropologists who, largely external to the academy, through hard work at community to policy levels, through clear and principled commitment to socially and culturally relevant public health efforts, have made a difference. These efforts are, in many ways, both the foundation and the backbone of current medical anthropology and constitute in large measure the substance of promise and hope that we hold out to our students. Nevertheless, we also recognize that many anthropologists continue to be reluctant to do work identified as "applied" or "public health," or, perhaps perceived as worse, glossed as "development" (Escobar 1995; Ferguson 1997).

Although writing of current work in pharmaceutical anthropology, van der Geest (2006) offers an opinion that is a cautionary note to other anthropologists working in global health:

Overcoming the "temptation" of just writing about the intriguing [pharmaceutical] nexus should be a first concern of medical anthropologists. We owe it to our informants to contribute to the actual improvement of distribution and use of pharmaceuticals. Ironically, however, that imperative of turning our paper medicines into medicines that cure and protect people is not exactly what mainstream anthropology encourages us to do. Applied medical anthropology is somewhat slighted as diluted anthropology and as too subservient to policy and medical science. My view, however, is that uncommitted ethnographers lack reflexivity and fail to see themselves in the nexus of pharmaceuticals and of culture in general. Their methodological innocence gives way to epistemological naïveté. (pp. 313–14)

To this we add simply that the problems living beings face globally are too vast and the assaults on social justice and the environment too egregious for us to worry overly much about the sullying effects of doing applied work. Commitment and action are sometimes messy; the fine points of theory and abstract conceptualization may appear irrelevant in the worlds of suffering, injustice, and environmental degradation that we face, and being a principled "public intellectual" is sometimes not enough. What we should be worried about, as we consider our disciplinary position as producers and consumers of knowledge in the global political economy, is the pressing question of "so what?" We are called to apply our tools and knowledge, to seek interdisciplinary and intersectoral partnerships, and to both propose and engage directly in potential solutions.

REFERENCES

Abramson D.
1999   A critical look at NGOs and civil society as a means to an end in Uzbekistan. *Hum. Organ.* 58:240–50.

Adams V, Miller S, Craig S, Samen A, Nyima, et al.
2005   The challenge of cross-cultural clinical trials research: case report from the Tibetan Autonomous Region, People's Republic of China. *Med. Anthropol. Q.* 19:267–89.

Adams V, Novotny TE, Leslie H.
2008   Global health diplomacy. *Med. Anthropol.* 27:315–23.

Adler E, Haas PM.
1992   Epistemic communities, world order, and the creation of a reflective research program. *Int. Organ.* 46:367–90.

Alter JS.
2005   *Asian Medicine and Globalization.* Philadelphia: Univ. Penn. Press.

Appadurai A.
1991   Global: notes and queries for a transnational anthropology. In *Recapturaing Anthropology: Working in the Present*, ed. RG Fox, pp. 191–210. Santa Fe, NM: New Sch. Am. Res. Press.

Appadurai A.
1996   *Modernity at Large: Cultural Dimensions of Globalization.* Minneapolis: Univ. Minn. Press.

Applbaum K.
2006   Educating for global mental health: the adoption of SSRIs in Japan. See Petryna et al. 2006, pp. 85–110.

Baer H, Singer M, Susser I, eds.
2003   *Medical Anthropology and the World System.* Westport, CT: Praeger.

Baer H, Singer M.
2009   *Global Warming and the Political Ecology of Health: Emerging Crises and Systemic Solutions.* Walnut Creek, CA: Left Coast Press.

Bastos C.
1999   *Global Responses to AIDS: Science in Emergency.* Bloomington: Indiana Univ. Press.

Berry NS.
2009   Making pregnancy safer for women around the world: the example of safe motherhood and maternal death in Guatemala. See Hahn & Inhorn 2009, pp. 422–46.

Biehl J.
2007   *Will to Live: AIDS Therapies and the Politics of Survival.* Princeton, NJ: Princeton Univ. Press.

Bourgois P, Scheper-Hughes N.
2004   Comment on "An anthropology of structural violence," by Paul Farmer. *Curr. Anthropol.* 45:317–18.

Briggs CL, Mantini-Briggs C.
2003   *Stories in a Time of Cholera: The Transnational Circulation of Bacteria and Racial Stigmata in a Venezuelan Epidemic.* Berkeley: Univ. Calif. Press.

Brown TM, Cueto M, Fee E.
2006   The World Health Organization and the transition from "international" to "global" public health. *Am. J. Public Health* 96:62–72.

Browner CH, Sargent CF.
2010   *Reproduction, Globalization, and the State.* Durham, NC: Duke Univ. Press. In press.

Burawoy M.
2000   Conclusion: grounding globalization. In *Global Ethnography: Forces, Connections, and Imaginations in a Postmodern World*, ed. M Burawoy, JA Blum, S George, Z Gille, T Gowan, et al., pp. 337–50. Berkeley: Univ. Calif. Press.

Buse K, Walt G.
1997   An unruly mélange? Coordinating external resources to the health sector: a review. *Soc. Sci. Med.* 45:449–63.

Butt L.
2002   The suffering stranger: medical anthropology and international morality. *Med. Anthropol.* 21:1–24.

Castro A.
2004   Contracepting and childbirth: the integration of reproductive health and population policies in Mexico. See Castro & Singer 2004, pp. 133–44.

Castro A, Singer M, eds.
2004   *Unhealthy Health Policy: A Critical Anthropological Examination.* Walnut Creek, CA: AltaMira.

Cohen L.
2005   Operability, bioavailability, and exception. See Ong & Collier 2005b, pp. 79–90.

Comaroff J, Comaroff J, eds.
2001   *Millenial Capitalism and the Culture of Neoliberalism.* Durham, NC: Duke Univ. Press.

Comm. Soc. Determinants Health.
2008   *Closing the Gap in a Generation: Health Equity Through Action on the Social Determinants of Health.* Geneva: World Health Organ.

Desclaux A.
2004   Equity in access to AIDS treatment in Africa. See Castro & Singer 2004, pp. 115–32.

Desjarlais R, Eisenberg L, Good B, Kleinman A.
1995   *World Mental Health: Problems and Priorities in Low-Income Countries.* Oxford: Oxford Univ. Press.

Dressler WW, Bindon JR.
2000   The health consequences of cultural consonance: cultural dimensions of lifestyle. *Am. Anthropol.* 102:244–60.

Ecks S.
2005   Pharmaceutical citizenship: antidepressant marketing and the promise of demarginalization in India. *Anthropol. Med.* 12:239–54.

Erickson PI.
2003   Medical anthropology and global health. *Med. Anthropol. Q.* 17:3–4.

Erikson SL.
2003   Post-diagnostic abortion in Germany: reproduction gone awry, again? *Soc. Sci. Med.* 56:1987–2001.

Escobar A.
1995   *Encountering Development: The Making and Unmaking of the Third World.* Princeton, NJ: Princeton Univ. Press.

Evans M, Sinclair RC, Fusimalohi C, Liava'a V.
2001   Globalization, diet, and health: an example from Tonga. *Bull. World Health Organ.* 79:856–62.

Farmer P.
1997   On suffering and structural violence: the view from below. In *Social Suffering,* ed. A Kleinman, V Das, M Lock, pp. 261–84. Berkeley: Univ. Calif. Press.

Farmer P.
1999   *Infections and Inequalities: The Modern Plagues.* Berkeley: Univ. Calif. Press.

Farmer P.
2003   *Pathologies of Power: Health, Human Rights, and the New War on the Poor.* Berkeley: Univ. Calif. Press.

Farmer P.
2004   An anthropology of structural violence. *Curr. Anthropol.* 45:305–17.

Farmer P, Castro A.
2004   Pearls of the Antilles? Public health in Haiti and Cuba. See Castro & Singer 2004, pp. 3–28.

Farmer P, Connors M, Simmons J, eds.
1996   *Women, Poverty, and Aids: Sex, Drugs, and Structural Violence.* Monroe, ME: Common Courage.

Farmer P, Léandre F, Mukherjee JS, Claude MS, Nevil P, et al.
2001   Community-based approaches to HIV treatment in resource-poor settings. *Lancet* 358:404–9.

Feldman DA, ed.
2008   *AIDS, Culture and Africa.* Gainesville: Univ. Press Fla.

Ferguson A.
2005   Water reform, gender, and HIV/AIDS: perspectives from Malawi. See Whiteford & Whiteford 2005, pp. 45–66.

Ferguson J.
1997   Anthropology and its evil twin: "development" in the constitution of a discipline. In *International Development and the Social Sciences: Essays on the History and Politics of Knowledge,* ed. F Cooper, R Packard, pp. 150–75. Berkeley: Univ. Calif. Press.

Foster GM.
1976   Medical anthropology and international health planning. *Med. Anthropol. Newsl.* 7:12–18.

Ginsburg F, Rapp R, eds.
1995a   *Conceiving the New World Order: The Global Politics of Reproduction.* Berkeley: Univ. Calif. Press.

Ginsburg F, Rapp R.
1995b   Introduction. See Ginsburg & Rapp 1995b, pp. 1–18

Greenhalgh S.
2005 Globalization and population governance in China. See Ong & Collier 2005b, pp. 354–72.

Guest G, ed.
2005 *Globalization, Health, and the Environment: An Integrated Perspective.* Lanham, MA: AltaMira.

Hahn RA, Inhorn MC.
2009 *Anthropology and Public Health: Bridging Differences in Culture and Society.* New York: Oxford Univ. Press. 2nd ed.

Hankivsky O, Cormier R.
2009 *Intersectionality: Moving Women's Health Research and Policy Forward.* Vancouver, BC: Women's Health Res. Netw., Simon Fraser Univ. http://www.whrn.ca

Hardon A.
2005 Confronting the HIV/AIDS epidemic in sub-Saharan Africa: policy versus practice. *Int. Soc. Sci. J.* 57:601–8.

Hayden C.
2007 A generic solution? Pharmaceuticals and the politics of the similar in Mexico. *Curr. Anthropol.* 4:475–95.

Høg E, Hsu E.
2002 Introduction to special issue: countervailing creativity: patient agency in the globalisation of Asian medicines. *Anthropol. Med.* 9:205–21.

Hulko W.
2009 The time- and context-contingent nature of intersectionality and interlocking oppressions. *Affilia* 24:44–55.

Inhorn MC.
2003 Global infertility and the globalization of new reproductive technologies: illustrations from Egypt. *Soc. Sci. Med.* 56:1837–51.

Inhorn MC.
2005 Gender, health, and globalization in the Middle East: male infertility, ICSI, and men's resistance. In *Globalization, Women, and Health in the Twenty-First Century*, ed. I Kickbush, KA Hartwig, JM List, pp. 113–25. New York: Palgrave Macmillan.

Inhorn MC.
2007a Medical anthropology at the intersections. *Med. Anthropol. Q.* 21:249–55.

Inhorn MC, ed.
2007b *Reproductive Disruptions: Gender, Technology, and Biopolitics in the New Millennium.* New York: Berghahn.

Inhorn MC, Brown PJ, eds.
1997 *The Anthropology of Infectious Disease: International Health Perspectives.* Amsterdam, The Neth.: Gordon and Breach.

Inhorn MC, Janes CR.
2007 The behavioral research agenda in global health: an advocate's legacy. *Global Public Health* 2:294–312.

Inst. Med.
2009 *The U.S. Commitment to Global Health: Recommendations for the New Administration.* Washington, DC: Natl. Acad. Press.

Intergov. Panel Climate Change.
2007 *Climate Change 2007 – Impacts, Adaptation and Vulnerability.* Contribution of Working Group II to the Fourth Assessment Report of the IPCC. Cambridge, UK: Cambridge Univ. Press, http://www.ipcc.ch/ipccreports/ar4-wg2.htm

Janes CR.
1999 The health transition and the crisis of traditional medicine: the case of Tibet. *Soc. Sci. Med.* 48:1803–20.

Janes CR.
2002 Buddhism, science, and market: the globalisation of Tibetan medicine. *Anthropol. Med.* 9:267–89.

Janes CR.
2004 Going global in century XXI: medical anthropology and the new primary health care. *Hum. Organ. J. Soc. Appl. Anthropol.* 63:457–71.

Janes CR.
2009 An ethnographic evaluation of post-Alma Ata health system reforms in Mongolia: lessons for addressing health inequities in poor communities. See Hahn & Inhorn 2009, pp. 652–80.

Janes CR, Chuluundorj O.
2004 Free markets and dead mothers: the social ecology of maternal mortality in postsocialist Mongolia. *Med. Anthropol. Q.* 18:102–29.

Janes CR, Chuluundorj O, Hilliard C, Rak K, Janchiv K.
2005 Poor medicine for poor people? Assessing the impact of neoliberal reform on health care equity in a postsocialist context. *Global Public Health* 1:5–30.

Justice J.
1986 *Policies, Plans and People: Foreign Aid and Health Development.* Berkeley: Univ. Calif. Press.

Justice J.
2000   The politics of child survival. See Whiteford & Manderson 2000a, pp. 23–38.

Kangas B.
2002   Therapeutic itineraries in a global world: Yemenis and their search for biomedical treatment abroad. *Med. Anthropol.* 21:35–78.

Kendall C.
2005   Waste not, want not: grounded globalization and global lessons for water use from Lima, Peru. See Whiteford & Whiteford 2005, pp. 85–106.

Keshavjee S.
2004   The contradictions of a revolving drug fund in post-Soviet Tajikistan: selling medicines to starving patients. See Castro & Singer 2004, pp. 97–114.

Kickbush I.
2003   Global health governance; some theoretical considerations on the new political space. See Lee 2003b, pp. 192–203.

Kim J.
2009   Transcultural medicine: a multi-sited ethnography on the scientific-industrial networking of Korean medicine. *Med. Anthropol.* 28:31–64.

Kim JY, Shakow A, Mate K, Vanderwarker C, Gupta R, Farmer P.
2005   Limited good and limited vision: multidrug-resistant tuberculosis and global health policy. *Soc. Sci. Med.* 61:847–59.

Kleinman A.
1988   *Social Origins of Distress and Disease: Depression, Neurasthenia, and Pain in Modern China.* New Haven, CT: Yale Univ. Press.

Krieger N.
2001   Theories for social epidemiology in the 21st century: an ecosocial perspective. *Int. J. Epidemiol.* 30:668–77.

Lee K.
2003a   *Globalization and Health: An Introduction.* New York: Palgrave Macmillan.

Lee K, ed.
2003b   *Health Impacts of Globalization: Towards Global Governance.* New York: Palgrave MacMillan.

Lee K.
2003c   Introduction. See Lee 2003b, pp. 1–12.

Lee K, Fustukian S, Buse K.
2002   An introduction to global health policy. In *Health Policy in a Globalizing World*, ed. SH Lees, K Buse, S Fustukian, pp. 3–17. Cambridge, UK: Cambridge Univ. Press.

Lee K, Goodman H.
2002   Global policy networks: the propagation of health care financing reform since the 1980s. In *Health Policy in a Globalising World*, ed. K Lee, K Buse, S Fustukian, pp. 97–119. Cambridge, UK: Cambridge Univ. Press.

Lock M.
2001   *Twice Dead: Organ Transplants and the Reinvention of Death.* Berkeley: Univ. Calif. Press

Macfarlane SB, Jacobs M, Kaaya EE.
2008   In the name of global health: trends in academic institutions. *J. Public Health Policy* 29:383–401.

Manderson L, Huang Y.
2005   Water, vectorborne disease, and gender: schistosomiasis in rural China. See Whiteford & Whiteford 2005, pp. 67–84.

Markowitz L.
2001   Finding the field: notes on the ethnography of NGOs. *Hum. Organ.* 60:40–6.

Marshall P, Koenig B.
2004   Accounting for culture in a globalized bioethics. *J. Law Med. Ethics* 32:252–66, 191.

Marshall PA.
2005   Human rights, cultural pluralism, and international health research. *Theor. Med. Bioeth.* 26:529–57.

Marshall PA, Daar A.
2000   Ethical issues in human organ replacement: a case study from India. See Whiteford & Manderson 2000a, pp. 205–30.

Maternowska MC.
2006   *Reproducing Inequities: Poverty and the Politics of Population in Haiti.* New Brunswick, NJ: Rutgers Univ. Press.

Mather C.
2006   Medical innovation, unmet medical need, and the drug pipeline. *Can. J. Clin. Pharmacol.* 13:e85–91.

McElroy A.
2005   Health ecology in Nunavut: Inuit elders' concepts of nutrition, health, and political change. See Guest 2005, pp. 107–32.

McMichael T, Beaglehole R.
2003   The global context for public health. In *Global Public Health: A New Era*, ed. R Beaglehole, pp. 1–23. New York: Oxford.

Morgan LM.
1989   "Political will" and community participation in Costa Rican primary health care. *Med. Anthropol. Q.* 3:232–45.

Morgan LM.
1997 *Community Participation in Health: The Politics of Primary Care in Costa Rica.* Cambridge, UK: Cambridge Univ. Press.

Morgan LM.
2001 Community participation in health: perpetual allure, persistent challenge. *Health Policy Plann.* 16:221–30.

Morsy SA.
1995 Deadly reproduction among Egyptian women: maternal mortality and the medicalization of population control. See Ginsburg & Rapp 1995b, pp. 162–76.

Nguyen VK.
2005 Antiretroviral globalism, biopolitics, and therepeutic citizenship. See Ong & Collier 2005b, pp. 124–44.

Nichter M.
1989 *Anthropology and International Health: South Asian Case Studies.* Dordrecht: Kluwer.

Nichter M.
1991 Use of social science research to improve epidemiologic studies of and interventions for diarrhea and dysentery. *Rev. Infect. Dis.* 13(Suppl. 4):S265–71.

Nichter M.
1995 Vaccinations in the Third World: a consideration of community demand. *Soc. Sci. Med.* 41:617–32.

Nichter M.
2008 *Global Health: Why Cultural Perceptions, Social Representations, and Biopolitics Matter.* Tucson: Univ. Ariz. Press.

Nichter M, Cartwright E.
1991 Saving the children for the tobacco industry. *Med. Anthropol. Q.* 5:236–56.

Oldani MJ.
2004 Thick prescriptions: toward an interpretation of pharmaceutical sales practices. *Med. Anthropol. Q.* 18:325–56.

Ong A, Collier SJ.
2005a Global assemblages, anthropological problems. See Ong & Collier 2005b, pp. 3–21.

Ong A, Collier SJ, eds.
2005b *Global Assemblages: Technology, Politics, and Ethics as Anthropological Problems.* Malden, MA: Blackwell.

Orzech KM, Nichter M.
2008 From resilience to resistance: political ecological lessons from antibiotic and pesticide resistance. *Annu. Rev. Anthropol.* 37:267–82.

Paluzzi JE.
2004 Primary health care since Alma Ata: lost in the Bretton Woods? See Castro & Singer 2004, pp. 63–78.

Parker R.
2000 Administering the epidemic: HIV/AIDS policy, models of development, and international health. See Whiteford & Manderson 2000a, pp. 39–56.

Patz JA, Campbell-Lendrum D, Holloway T, Foley JA.
2005 Impact of regional climate change on human health. *Nature* 438:310–17.

Paul B, ed.
1955 *Health, Culture and Community: Case Studies of Public Reactions to Health Programs.* New York: Sage.

Petryna A.
2002 *Life Exposed: Biological Citizens After Chernobyl.* Princeton, NJ: Princeton Univ. Press.

Petryna A.
2005 Ethical variability: drug development and globalizing clinical trials. *Am. Ethnol.* 32:183–97.

Petryna A, Lakoff A, Kleinman A, eds.
2006 *Global Pharmaceuticals: Ethics, Markets, Practices.* Durham, NC: Duke Univ. Press.

Pfeiffer J.
2003 International NGOs and primary health care in Mozambique: the need for a new model of collaboration. *Soc. Sci. Med.* 56:725–38.

Pfeiffer J.
2004 International NGOs in the Mozambique health sector: the "velvet glove" of privatization. See Castro & Singer 2004, pp. 43–62.

Pfeiffer J, Nichter M.
2008 What can critical medical anthropology contribute to global health? *Med. Anthropol. Q.* 22:410–15.

Pigg SL, Adams V.
2005 Introduction: the moral object of sex. In *Sex in Development: Science, Sexuality, and Morality in Global Perspective*, ed. V Adams, SL Pigg, pp. 1–38. Durham, NC: Duke Univ. Press.

Rak K, Janes CR.
2004 Reproductive health in post-transition Mongolia: global discourses and local realities. In *Globalization and Health*, ed. RL Harris, MJ Seid, pp. 171–96. Leiden, The Neth.: Brill.

Redfield P.
2005 Doctors, borders, and life in crisis. *Cult. Anthropol.* 20:328–61.

Robins S.
2009   Foot soldiers of global health: teaching and preaching AIDS science and modern medicine on the frontline. *Med. Anthropol.* 28:81–107.

Rose N, Novas C.
2005   Biological citizenship. See Ong & Collier 2005b, pp. 439–63.

Scheper-Hughes N.
1993   *Death Without Weeping: The Violence of Everyday Life in Brazil.* Berkeley: Univ. Calif. Press.

Scheper-Hughes N.
2000   The global traffic in human organs. *Curr. Anthropol.* 41:191–224.

Scheper-Hughes N.
2005   The last commodity: posthuman ethics and the global traffic in "fresh" organs. See Ong & Collier 2005b, pp. 145–68.

Simmons J, Farmer P, Schoepf BG.
1996   A global perspective. See Farmer et al. 1996, pp. 39–90

Singer M.
1997   *The Political Economy of AIDS.* Amityville, NY: Baywood.

Singer M.
2008   *Drugs and Development: Global Impact on Sustainable Growth and Human Rights.* Prospect Heights, IL: Waveland.

Singer M.
2009   *Introduction to Syndemics: A Systems Approach to Public and Community Health.* San Francisco, CA: Jossey-Bass.

Singer M, Baer H.
1995   *Critical Medical Anthropology.* Amityville, NY: Baywood.

Singer M, Baer H.
2008   *Killer Commodities: Public Health and the Corporate Production of Harm.* Lanham, MD: AltaMira/Roman Littlefield.

Singer M, Castro A.
2004   Introduction. Anthropology and health policy: a critical perspective. See Castro & Singer 2004, pp. xi–xx.

Singer M, Clair S.
2003   Syndemics and public health: reconceptualizing disease in bio-social context. *Med. Anthropol. Q.* 17:423–41.

Stebbins KR.
1991   Tobacco, politics and economics: implications for global health. *Soc. Sci. Med.* 33:1317–26.

Strathern M.
2000   *Audit Cultures: Anthropological Studies in Accountability, Ethics and the Academy.* London: Routledge.

Towghi F.
2004   Shifting policies toward traditional midwives: implications for reproductive health care in Pakistan. See Castro & Singer 2004, pp. 79–95.

Trostle J.
1996   Inappropriate distribution of medicines by professionals in developing countries. *Soc. Sci. Med.* 42:1117–20.

Trostle J.
2005   *Epidemiology and Culture.* New York: Cambridge Univ. Press.

Van Der Geest S.
2006   Anthropology and the pharmaceutical nexus. *Anthropol. Q.* 79:303–314.

Van Der Geest S, Hardon A, Whyte SR, eds.
1988   *The Context of Medicines in Developing Countries: Studies in Pharmaceutical Anthropology.* Dordrecht, The Neth.: Kluwer.

Van Der Geest S, Whyte SR, Hardon A.
1996   The anthropology of pharmaceuticals: a biographical approach. *Annu. Rev. Anthropol.* 25:153–78.

Wacquant L.
2004   Comment on: "An anthropology of structural violence," by Paul Farmer. *Curr. Anthropol.* 45:322.

Whiteford LM, Hill B.
2005   The political ecology of dengue in Cuba and the Dominican Republic. See Guest 2005, pp. 219–38.

Whiteford LM, Manderson L, eds.
2000a   *Global Health Policy, Local Realities: The Fallacy of the Level Playing Field.* Boulder, CO: Lynne Rienner.

Whiteford LM, Manderson L.
2000b   Introduction. See Whiteford & Manderson 2000a, pp. 1–22.

Whiteford LM, Tobin GA.
2004   Saving lives, destroying livelihoods: emergency evacuation and resettlement policies in Ecuador. See Castro & Singer 2004, pp. 189–202.

Whiteford LM, Whiteford S, eds.
2005   *Globalization, Water, and Health: Resource Management in Times of Scarcity.* Santa Fe, NM: Sch. Am. Res. Press.

Whyte SR, Birungi H.
    2000   The business of medicines and the polit-
    ics of knowledge. See Whiteford & Manderson
    2000a, pp. 127–50.
Whyte SR, Whyte MA, Meinert L, Kyaddondo B.
    2006   Treating AIDS: dilemmas of unequal access
    in Uganda. See Petryna et al. 2006, pp. 240–62.

World Bank.
    1993   *Investing in Health: World Develop-
    ment Report 1993*. New York: Oxford Univ.
    Press for the World Bank.
World Health Organ.
    Primary Health Care: Now More than Ever.
    Geneva: WHO.

33

Mot Luuk Problems in Northeast Thailand
Why Women's Own Health Concerns Matter as Much as Disease Rates

Pimpawun Boonmongkon, Mark Nichter, and Jen Pylypa

Introduction

Over the last decade, increased interest has been directed toward women's gynecological morbidity in developing countries, particularly reproductive tract infections (RTIs). Women's RTIs include infections of both the lower and upper reproductive tracts that can be sexually transmitted, endogenous (resulting from overgrowth of microorganisms normally present in the vagina), or iatrogenic (contracted during medical procedures) (Population Council, 1996). RTIs are a cause of pelvic inflammatory disease (PID), which can result in infertility, a contributing factor to low birth weight and premature delivery a risk factor for cervical cancer and AIDS, and in the case of some specific infections, a health problem experienced more often by users of particular forms of contraception. In addition to such issues, women's activist groups have become interested in RTIs as an important arena through which to expand the focus of women's health initiatives to include an emphasis on the poor quality of health services for women, and on women's sexual health as conceived more broadly than just their reproductive capacity.

Reproductive tract infections in women are a difficult area for both study and intervention. They are often asymptomatic, difficult to diagnose even in the presence of symptoms, frequently stigmatized and therefore not easily discussed in surveys or during history taking, and problematic for epidemiological data collection due to the invasiveness and personal discomfort associated with gynecological exams. One consequence of these difficulties is that data collected through various methods including surveys of self-reported symptoms, clinical examinations, and laboratory assessments each capture only partial information and therefore tend to result in different pictures of the scope and nature of women's health problems in a given population. Whereas

Pimpawun Boonmongkon, Mark Nichter, and Jen Pylypa, "*Mot Luuk* Problems in Northeast Thailand: Why Women's Own Health Concerns Matter as Much as Disease Rates," *Social Science Medicine* 53 (2004): 1095–112. © 2004 by Elsevier Science & Technology Journals. Reproduced with permission of Elsevier Science & Technology Journals in the format Textbook via Copyright Clearance Center.

epidemiological data may suggest that there is a low prevalence of major women's RTIs in a population (as in Northeast Thailand), self-reports may, in contrast, show gynecological complaints (defined as symptoms women associate with their reproductive system) to be a significant health concern for women. Such contrasts spark debates about the limitations and advantages of an evidence-based approach to health care planning versus a more humanistic and experiential approach to understanding health care needs.[1]

This study takes an ethnographic approach to the issue of gynecological complaints in Northeast Thailand, moving beyond the search for diagnostic accuracy and valid prevalence data to consider women's embodied experiences of these complaints and the degree to which these experiences influence their lives. We found that regardless of whether or not the symptoms women experienced were associated with clinically identifiable RTIs, symptoms that rural informants identified with their reproductive tract were such a significant concern for women that the resulting behaviors and fears were an important health issue in their own right. In-depth interviews revealed that symptoms that women associated with the 'uterus' (*mot luuk*) had a substantial impact on their health-seeking behavior, medication use, sexual relations, and state of mind. Some of the consequences of these symptoms included psychological suffering due to fears that such symptoms would progress to more severe illnesses, particularly cervical cancer, self-treatment practices which were biomedically ill-advised including the overuse of antibiotics, and frustrations as well as physical suffering due to unfulfilled expectations regarding treatment from health providers. The interventions that resulted from this study aim to address women's fears, felt and actual treatment needs, and antibiotic misuse, and to improve quality of care for women's health. We argue that formative research attentive to women's experiential health concerns is essential to improving health programs and to enhancing health communication and the quality of health services.

Background: Epidemiological vs. Experiential Approaches to Women's RTIs

The literature on women's reproductive tract infections encompasses three main types of studies: (1) community surveys that document women's self-reported symptoms and their patterns of consultation with practitioners, (2) clinic-based studies of disease prevalence based on practitioner diagnosis, pelvic exams and laboratory tests, and (3) community-based epidemiological studies employing physical examination and where feasible, pelvic exams and laboratory assessments. *Community surveys* have been used by activist scholars as a form of consciousness-raising and a means of drawing attention to the burden of women's ill health. These surveys are more easily conducted in some cultures than others, such as where gynecological symptoms are associated with infidelity or constitute a stigmatized condition. Even where women cooperate with such studies and surveys are attentive to local illness language, there is the problem of knowing when reported symptoms are denotative (pointing to particular bodily signs) versus connotative (indexical of more general health and/or life concerns). Many of those employing self-report methodology have focused attention on local illness terminology. [. . .] Many surveys, however, are not accompanied by intensive ethnographic research that investigates 'semantic illness networks' – that is, patterns of associations linked to illness terminology[2] (Good, 1977) – and how communication about symptoms (verbally and non-verbally) is responded to by significant others.

The biomedical validity of morbidity prevalence rates generated by surveys that rely on self-report data has been questioned by clinicians. Studies that have matched women's self-reported symptoms with diagnoses of RTIs based on clinical assessments have generally found a poor correlation between women's self-reports of common gynecological symptoms and clinical disease as determined by laboratory tests (Phan et al., 1998). Reasons for this include the under- and over-reporting of symptoms by women as well as the asymptomatic presence of disease. However, even where symptoms are present and accurately reported, the ability of specific signs and symptoms to predict the absence or presence of specific RTIs is poor. [...] It is not only women's self-reports of morbidity that turn out to be inaccurate measures of disease, but clinicians' presumptive diagnoses in the absence of laboratory tests. Over-diagnosis of RTIs (especially cervical infections) appears to be rampant in many clinical settings and is a cause for concern (Phan et al., 1998).

Clinic-based studies that rely on a review of patient records do not present an accurate picture of morbidity because women often do not feel comfortable presenting gynecological complaints to clinicians, either for fear of being reprimanded or stigmatized, or because of concerns relating to confidentiality. [...] Finally, well-sampled and carefully executed *community-based epidemiological studies* of RTIs have the potential for generating representative data on morbidity, but are invasive and difficult to carry out. [...] Epidemiological studies require careful rapport-building with community members (Bhatia, Cleland, Bhagavan, & Rao, 1997), and even under the best of conditions may reach only some segments of the female population (e.g., married women alone).

In sum, there are strengths and weaknesses associated with all three types of studies. The agendas of those employing different research methodologies differ and there are insights to be gained from each type of study. Unfortunately, communication between researchers engaged in these different forms of data collection is often limited and posturing at workshops on women's health is common. Women's activist groups continue to place emphasis on women's self-reports in order to attach a 'human face' to their suffering irrespective of disease rates, whereas clinicians and epidemiologists continue to focus on rates and reject the biomedical inaccuracy of self-reported symptoms as predictors of infection.

In contexts such as Thailand where women commonly consult government health staff for gynecological problems, there is a need to conduct research both on how gynecological complaints are being attended to in clinical settings and addressed by health education programs, and on what information is currently guiding thinking about health care planning. In middle-tier health care transition countries such as Thailand, health care officials are privy to an increasing amount of information on RTIs and STIs. They are briefed at national and international workshops about the findings of clinical and community-based epidemiological studies, providing them with a population-based perspective on disease distribution and the relative merits of various treatment regimens. Workshops feature well-trained biomedical researchers who call for a high standard of epidemiological research based on laboratory data to guide decision-making about the delivery of care. Women's activists attending these workshops as community representatives, in contrast, often call for better documentation of women's suffering through surveys relying on self-reported data as well as case studies. The latter is often met with ambivalence by influential doctors trained in obstetrics and gynecology or the treatment of sexually transmitted disease. It is not uncommon for such doctors to publicly question the relevance of self-report data, given the poor relationship between self-reported symptoms and laboratory diagnosis. Their argument resonates with the clinical experience of many regional Ministry of Public Health officials who once practiced as doctors in district hospitals.

Data on RTIs reflect on the government's public health commitment. In Thailand, rates of major STIs are down significantly from previous years (Hanenberg, Rojanapithayakorn, Kunasol, & Sokal, 1994). Current results of clinic- and community-based research on RTIs and STIs present a positive picture, speaking to the success of Thailand's efforts to control the spread of major STIs, including HIV. Surveys that show high rates of self-reported gynecological symptoms are perceived by some government officials as undermining this success story at a time when the eyes of the world are on Thailand's efforts to control STIs and AIDS. During workshops we have attended, data on the high prevalence of women's self-reported gynecological symptoms have been acknowledged, but explained away as either psychological in origin, a tool used by women to secure secondary gain, a generalized idiom of personal distress, or an expected inconvenience similar to the common cold. At one notable conference, a regional health official commented that 'the government cannot afford to attend to every runny nose or woman with vaginal discharge'.

In this paper, we enter the debate between advocates of epidemiological versus experiential approaches to assessing women's health care needs. This debate is representative of two streams of thought gaining visibility in clinical medicine and public health: evidence-based medicine, which focuses on the need for rational health care decision-making (but see Sackett et al., 1996:71) and a humanistic, narrative approach to understanding illness experience, which attends to the needs of patients and a desire to improve quality of care. Using our case study from Northeast Thailand, we illustrate why high-quality social science research on ethnogynecology and women's experiences of gynecological problems is a necessary complement to high-quality epidemiological research on RTIs and an evidence-based approach to care provision. The formative research we present and argue for in this paper extends far beyond conducting surveys that elicit self-reports of symptoms as some general index of women's ill health and well-being. We call for a broader-based research agenda leading to a more holistic understanding of gynecological illness experiences, including (1) women's recognition, perceptions and experience of symptoms, (2) local interpretations of health education messages about reproductive health, (3) women's self-medication and health care seeking patterns, (4) the ways in which symptoms are reported to health personnel and the style and content of health providers' communications with patients, (5) assumptions that influence practitioners' diagnoses and treatment of women's complaints, (6) factors that either predispose or complicate the use of illness as an 'idiom of distress' or a form of social commentary, and (7) ramifications of the pharmaceutical industry's responses to women's health concerns as a market niche to be exploited.

Methods

The fieldwork upon which this analysis is based took place from 1997 to 1998 among the rural, Lao-speaking (Isaan) population of Khon Kaen province, located in the impoverished Northeast of Thailand. The primary aim of the project was to document women's experiences of 'gynecological complaints', a term we use broadly to encompass (1) symptoms commonly associated with RTIs, and (2) pelvic, lower abdominal and back pains associated with hard manual labor, childbearing, menstruation, etc. as well as other symptoms linked to the 'uterus' (*mot luuk*) through cultural reasoning. We examined women's explanatory models about what ailed them, levels of concern associated with persistent complaints, forms of self-treatment, and patterns of health care seeking, as well as the types and quality of health services available to women. Women's reports of morbidity were initially captured on a survey of 1028 women in 16 villages employing local illness terminology previously documented during a short ethnographic pilot study. Illness experiences were then investigated during an intensive focused ethnographic study that aimed at achieving a more in-depth understanding of ethnogynecology, women's interpretations of symptoms and the progression of illness, physical and psychological suffering, and health seeking strategies.[3]

[...]

Ethnogynecology, Perceptions of Illness, and Illness Transformation

[...]

In Northeast Thailand, women's discussions of gynecological problems focus on an area of the body referred to as the *mot luuk*. Literally, the term *mot luuk* translates as 'uterus'; however, as locally conceived, *mot luuk* problems encompass a much wider array of symptoms broadly associated with the reproductive tract, abdominal and pelvic regions, and sometimes the urinary tract. Women frequently refer to symptoms ranging from abdominal and lower back pain to vaginal discharge, itching, odor and rash using the phrase *pen mot luuk* (literally: 'it's the uterus'). Pains, infections, or other health problems associated with the abdominal and pelvic regions that reference the *mot luuk* include pains associated with occupational health problems, such as muscle strains resulting from agricultural labor or weaving. Examples of such local illness terms include *jep mot luuk* ('pain in the uterus'), which is used to refer to abdominal pain of various etiologies, *mot luuk ak seep* ('inflammation/infection of the uterus'), an ambiguous term for *mot luuk* problems that is sometimes described as simply a more 'medical' term for *jep mot luuk*, and *mot luuk boo dii [mot luuk mai dii* ('bad uterus'), which refers to chronic uterine abnormalities with multiple possible causes.

Mot luuk problems are believed to have a wide range of causes [. . .] including many that Western medicine would not consider to be related to reproductive physiology. Many women with recurrent symptoms see their problems as ultimately resulting from some event earlier in life that either caused their ongoing symptoms or made them vulnerable to problems that emerged at a later point in time. Failing to follow the traditional postpartum practice of 'staying by the fire' (*yuu fai*) for a number of days following childbirth is one such past event; others include an injury or working very hard in youth, a complication or problem during a past pregnancy or abortion, pushing too hard during childbirth, and sterilization. [. . .] More than a quarter of the women interviewed who suffered from chronic or recurrent symptoms felt that their current problems were the result of an inadequate period of staying by the fire following childbirth, a practice that is believed to dry out the uterus and return it to its normal pre-pregnancy state. The increasing prevalence of hospital births has interfered with this custom, such that women are increasingly concerned about the ill health effects that its omission may cause (see also Mougne, 1978; Whittaker, 1995, 1996).

A number of women with recurrent or chronic symptoms see their illness as latent, that is, they feel that they experience recurrent symptoms because the disease or germs remain in their bodies and only manifest themselves at certain times, or because an 'ulcer' or 'wound' that exists inside the uterus persists without ever entirely healing. Hard work was the most commonly cited trigger that causes symptoms to reemerge; symptom recurrence is also associated with menstruation, tiredness, poor hygiene, or the sexual transmission of germs. [. . .]

Many women feared that if their symptoms were not treated or if they persisted for a long period of time, they would transform into a more severe illness. They engaged in a great deal of 'what if' speculation – what will happen if my symptoms persist, or if they get worse? Am I destined for a more severe or chronic illness? Some women [. . .] feared that their symptoms might turn into [. . .] a prolapsed uterus, a tumor, kidney stones, dysuria, or AIDS, while others expressed a non-specific concern that their illness could become 'something worse'. However, women's greatest concern by far (49 out of 50) was that their symptoms would 'become' cervical cancer (*maleng paak mot luuk*, or simply *maleng [mareng]*). [. . .] This perception was reiterated in interviews with health providers. [. . .] Health staff talked about women's infections transforming into 'pelvic inflammatory disease', a term they used very loosely during interviews with us and on patient records. Curiously, this term was not used in communications with patients and local women expressed no familiarity with it. [. . .] A few women imagined that gynecological complaints or sexually transmitted diseases might ultimately transform into AIDS, as has been reported elsewhere in Southeast Asia, such as in the Philippines (Nichter, 1996).

The connection that women draw between a wide range of abdominal and reproductive tract symptoms and cervical cancer can be explained by looking at their ethnomedical model of what is happening inside their bodies. From a biomedical perspective, women's complaints of *mot luuk* problems may include fungal, viral or bacterial infections that may be sexually transmitted as well as endogenous or iatrogenic in origin and muscle strain associated with hard manual labor. Each problem is different and requires specific treatment. Women in Northeast Thailand see things differently. They place a wide range of *mot luuk* problems on the same illness continuum as cervical cancer (see also Whittaker, 1996). The visual images of *mot luuk* problems that most women describe include the presence of a large ulcer, fungus, or collection of pus inside the uterus. They have a macroscopic, rather than microscopic image of the problem; that is, they imagine a large uterine anomaly that would be visible to the naked eye upon inspection during an internal exam. Cervical cancer is imagined as an extreme, life-threatening stage in the development of this uterine anomaly – the final common outcome of all untreated *mot luuk* problems. Ideas presented in health education materials distributed as part of a cervical cancer screening campaign in Khon Kaen Province have been appropriated by women and incorporated into these preexisting, ethnogynecological perceptions, and have thus come to inadvertently reinforce such local models (cf. Gregg 2000). One educational poster showing an enlarged photograph of advanced cervical cancer provides women with a macro-image of a microscopic anomaly; with no indication as to the scale of the photograph, the picture bears a striking resemblance to a large ulcer, fungus, or accumulation of pus. This image thus serves to reinforce the existing visual image of cervical cancer and perpetuates the link between cancer and the imagined manifestations of *mot luuk* problems (see Boonmongkon, Nichter, Pylypa, & Chantapasa, 1998).

Although it is clear that there are many different, and often ambiguous, ideas about how *mot luuk* symptoms can progress through subsequent stages and eventually become cervical cancer, the image of an ulcer, fungus/germ, pus, or 'infection' inside the uterus is a common theme. The specific pathways leading from women's own symptoms to cancer vary from woman to woman, but include certain common ideas. The initial symptoms are often described as 'pain in the uterus' (*jep mot luuk*), lower abdominal pain (*jep thoong nooi*), 'inflammation/ infection' of the uterus (*mot luuk ak seep*), a 'bad uterus' (*mot luuk boo dii [mot luuk mai dii]*), or vaginal discharge (*maat khaaw/tok khaaw*); in some cases, these problems lead directly to cancer, whereas in others they first cause a secondary set of symptoms, including discharge, fungus, itching, an ulcer or tumor, or infection, which then becomes cancer. [...] Similar variability in the perceived causes of cervical cancer has also been found to exist among Latina immigrants in the United States, one of the few populations for which such data exist (see Chavez, Hubbell, McMullin, Martinez, & Mishra, 1995; Hubbell, Chavez, Mishra, & Valdez, 1996).

Seven major pathways of illness transformation leading from other gynecological complaints to cervical cancer, identified during our ethnographic fieldwork, were presented to 10 women informants in villages and 10 in a nearby town who had not previously been interviewed, to see which of these models they recognized as common (see Table 33.1). These pathways were seen as possible ways in which illness could progress, not definitive routes of transformation. [...] Women suffering from chronic or recurrent *mot luuk* problems often maintained more than one explanatory model of illness causality and imagined multiple illness scenarios. Regardless of the particular series of intermediate stages, cervical cancer was recognized by all informants as the final common outcome.

Implications for Women's Suffering

Women who experience persistent or recurrent *mot luuk* problems, regardless of etiology, are often subject to both physical pain and psychological suffering. Many of the 50 women interviewed in-depth who suffer from chronic or recurrent *mot luuk* problems described the severity of their symptoms in functional terms. They often said that pain prevented them from sitting, walking, sleeping, or working. When asked how their symptoms affected their work, 60% of these 50 women stated that they had to alter their work activities significantly because of their illnesses. Some women spoke of their physical pain as intolerable and of vaginal itching severe enough to make them scratch until they bled or their skin burned. Many women

Table 33.1 *Explanatory models for maleng [mareng] paak mot luuk (cervical cancer): How many women recognize each pathway as common*

Model	Village (n = 10)	Town (n = 10)
Ulcer model: An ulcer inside of the *mot luuk* gets infected and full of pus, fungus/germs make the ulcer worse, discharge often occurs and the woman gets cancer.	10	8
Husband infects wife model: The husband has extramarital sex with a woman who is not clean and transfers fungus or germs to his wife who gets a *mot luuk* problem; discharge with bad odor occurs and sometimes itching. The woman develops *mot luuk ak seep* ('inflammation/infection of the uterus') and an ulcer and gets cancer.	7	8
Poor hygiene model: The *mot luuk* becomes infected from a woman working in a dirty place, dirt entering her body from a rice field or fish pond, not being able to wash after urination while working, or dirt transferred to her sexually from a man with poor hygiene. Fungus/germs cause itching and bad odor and discharge occurs. Cancer develops.	8	7
Hard work model: Hard work leads to lower abdominal pain; the woman gets *jep mot luuk* ('pain in the uterus') and/ or *mot luuk ak seep* ('inflammation/ infection of the uterus') which can become cancer.	5	5
IUD model: An IUD left inside for a long time causes an ulcer which becomes infected; discharge increases and the woman gets cancer.	4	3
Yuu fai model: After delivery of a child a woman does not stay by the fire (*yuu fai*) to dry out her *mot luuk*; discharge increases, fungus/germs develop and she can get cancer.	3	3
Sterilization model: Sterilization causes a woman to develop *mot luuk boo dii [mot luuk mai dii]* (a 'bad uterus'), which leads to cancer.	1	3

reported that they had suffered from chronic symptoms for years. One woman complained of having abnormally colored discharge, vaginal itching, and abdominal pain for 12 years; another woman suffered from discharge, itching, dysuria, and painful intercourse on an almost daily basis for 20 years. A local gynecologist who runs a private clinic reported that most of her patients had suffered from symptoms for at least 2 to 3 years. A review of patient histories kept by four private practitioners confirmed her impression.

Psychologically, the concerns about illness progression discussed above result in a great deal of worry and fear. First and foremost, women experiencing chronic or recurrent symptoms are concerned that their illness will culminate in cancer and death. The actual incidence of cervical cancer in Thailand is 28 cases per 100,000 women, but women in our study *perceived* the disease to be far more common. [. . .] This heightened fear of cervical

cancer has resulted from a combination of women's pre-existing, ethnogynecological models and the added effect of an intensive cervical cancer education and screening campaign conducted in the region. An unfortunate by-product of this well-intentioned campaign has been a situation in which women are convinced that cervical cancer is far more common than it really is. Enhanced awareness about cervical cancer has resulted in both higher Pap smear rates and a significant rise in women's anxiety and suffering related to fears of illness progression. Yet the great majority of these women most likely suffer from non-life threatening conditions such as recurrent bacterial or fungal infections that might be easily managed, if not cured.

The impact of educational activities was evident in in-depth interviews conducted with women who suffered from recurrent symptoms. One woman stated that from the health education messages dispersed over the village loudspeaker she learned how common cervical cancer is among women her age, and it made her so afraid of cancer that she suffers from insomnia. Several women reported going to the local health station to request sleeping pills because worrying about cancer kept them awake at night. One woman explicitly stated that her symptoms were not serious enough to prevent her from working as usual, but that she was still worried about them turning into cervical cancer *because they conducted a health education campaign in her village*. Another woman commented that "years ago people did not know about cervical cancer. Women had [vaginal] discharge and thought they had syphilis or gonorrhea. Now we think, cancer". In contrast to diseases such as syphilis and gonorrhea for which medications can be prescribed, cervical cancer is thought by many women to be incurable and is strongly associated with death.

The fear of cervical cancer among women suffering from recurrent *mot luuk* problems has reached extreme proportions. Many women spontaneously mentioned a fear of cancer and even a fear of dying when asked a general question about how their experience of *mot luuk* problems had affected their lives. One informant reported that when she saw two members of our research team coming to interview her, she feared that they were coming to tell her that she had cancer. In another village, a woman was diagnosed with cervical cancer after suffering from vaginal itching for a long time; now if women in this village experience vaginal itching for awhile, they worry about cancer. Psychological suffering from such worry and fear manifests itself as anxiety, insomnia, worry about chronic illness or death in the future, and concern over who will take care of children when chronic illness prevents the woman from fulfilling this role.

Sex is thought to hasten the onset of cervical cancer when one is suffering from *mot luuk* problems. Some women perceived sex to aggravate existing problems and others suspected that their husbands were in some way contaminating them with germs or impurities related to poor hygiene or extramarital sex. Wives thus faced a predicament: Should they continue sexual relations and place themselves at increased risk to cancer, or suspend sexual relations and risk losing their husbands to other women? In some instances wives did not have a choice, given the sexual demands of husbands and their own social powerlessness. In other cases, wives did suspend sexual relations with their husbands' consent, but worried that their husbands would eventually engage in extramarital relations. They feared that this would expose their husbands and themselves to sexually transmitted diseases and HIV/AIDS. In still other instances, wives with prolonged illnesses who maintained close relationships with their husbands suggested to their spouses that they take up sexual relations with local women who were sexually available, in lieu of visiting prostitutes. In three out of the fifty in-depth case histories we conducted with women experiencing chronic or recurrent *mot luuk* problems, wives sanctioned their husbands' extramarital sex in this manner, stating that it was too difficult for men to live without sex for more than a few months. [...] Our research suggests that in addition to general promiscuity, peer influence, and migration for work, *mot luuk* problems should be considered as a potentially significant influence on male extramarital relations.

Mot Luuk Problems as Idioms of Distress

Do women in Northeast Thailand commonly employ *mot luuk* complaints as "idioms of distress" (Nichter, 1981) and a means of securing secondary gain in the form of time off from work, social attention, or an acceptable excuse for refusing unwanted sexual relations? It may be recalled that this was an explanation offered by some outspoken clinicians and epidemiologists in Thailand for high rates of self-reported gynecological complaints. When investigating whether or not somatic complaints are being used as a means of articulating personal discontent, it is important to recognize when, in what contexts, and to whom such communication is being directed and whether feelings of discontent are recognized or acknowledged. It is also important to consider the ramifications of such communication and response to somatic complaints by others in both the short and long term.

Bearing in mind these issues: What is at stake for women in impoverished Northeast Thailand if they complain about gynecological problems as an 'idiom of distress'? In our study, we found that married women tended to inform both their close female friends and husbands about *mot luuk* problems, but did not wish others to learn about their symptoms. Gynecological problems are a source of gossip, especially when experienced by a woman whose husband has been absent or recently returned from migrant work. Knowledge of another's gynecological problems can be used against her to call into question the woman's or her husband's moral identity. These symptoms are associated with sexual impropriety and poor hygiene, in addition to a wide range of other causes. While women actively seek advice from close female friends and relatives about what kinds of medicine are effective for different *mot luuk* complaints and where they should go for treatment, confidentiality is important to them when they attend health stations and district hospitals.

Interviews with 10 husbands revealed that they acknowledged their wives' *mot luuk* complaints as both a consequence of hard work and a sign of women's vulnerability. However, they considered *mot luuk* complaints to be women's business and played little if any role in decision-making about treatment, aside from encouraging their wives to seek medical attention. Women reported that when medical attention was sought, they rarely requested their husbands' attendance at local clinics, and clinic staff complained that it is difficult to get husbands to take treatment along with their wives when it is suspected that the husband is the source of his wife's infection and re-infection. Health staff reported that if a husband is not presently experiencing symptoms, he is reluctant to engage in treatment, since his participation has the effect of fostering speculation about his responsibility for his wife's illness.

Women spoke of informing their husbands about the *mot luuk* pain they experienced, but they did not expect their husbands to pay special attention to them beyond offering assistance with work if requested. Some husbands requested that their wives not engage in strenuous work, but in most cases women attempted to return to work of their own accord. When impoverished women had to reduce or alter their work routines because of illness, they generally bemoaned the fact that they had less income and yet had to spend scarce resources on medical expenses. They saw no secondary gain from being able to earn less and eat less! Being able to relax and recuperate from an illness (secondary gain) was an upper class behavioral pattern that they were clearly not in a position to emulate. 'Cure me or give me better pain medication so I can work hard like before', one woman requested of a doctor. A cursory medical exam turned up nothing unusual and she was sent home with paracetamol. Later she complained to an interviewer, 'How can my family's welfare be good when I cannot work hard and there is less money? You ask me if my husband supports me and is sympathetic. How long can he afford to do so if work remains undone and his needs are unmet? When there is less money in the house there are more quarrels. When the children demand snacks, or items for school, I do not have money and I end up scolding them. Of course it is better to work!'

Women interviewed spoke of their powerlessness, need for money, and the ramifications of chronic *mot luuk* problems in terms of social risk (i.e., risk to valued social relationships). When we raised the possibility of amplifying (not inventing) *mot luuk* complaints as a means of communicating personal discontent, women spoke of having too much at stake to do such a thing. Complaining a lot about one's reproductive health and pain during sexual intercourse might lead a husband to take a minor wife (and feel he had a right to do so). Taking a minor wife (i.e., an established mistress) constitutes a threat not only to a woman, but also to her children, due to the economic ramifications of a husband spending family funds on his mistress. This is not to discount the possibility of individual women using *mot luuk* complaints as a means of avoiding sexual relations when social relations are strained, but to suggest that it is unlikely that this accounts for the vast majority of *mot luuk* complaints. Our research suggests that far more women suffer in silence by bearing physical pain during sexual relations, than complain of *mot luuk* problems to avoid sex.

During group discussions, women did occasionally speak of *mot luuk* pains in terms of women's difficult lot in life. At times it appeared that the experience of pain was linked to a woman's moral identity. Women who worked hard and sacrificed for the welfare of their families suffered pain, took medications, and kept on working. Could an association between being a virtuous woman, working hard, and bearing pain bias women's responses to survey questions about *mot luuk* complaints? Given that the symptoms in question are associated with hard work (lower back and abdominal pain), this possibility cannot be discounted. However, to argue that the majority of *mot luuk* complaints are related to identity management would be as misleading as to label such complaints as 'merely psychological' or a means to secondary gain. Little evidence supports this conclusion. On the contrary, there is compelling evidence to suggest that this is not the case.

Self-Treatment

How do Isaan women attempt to manage *mot luuk* complaints? What types of self-care and health care seeking are common, and how effective are they likely to be? When women initiate treatment, most engage in self-medication. Eighty percent of all women surveyed ($n = 1028$) reported self-medicating the last time they experienced a *mot luuk* problem. Three-quarters of these women purchased their medicines at village grocery shops, and almost two-thirds of them bought antibiotics. In our 50 in-depth case studies, women overwhelmingly reported treating their *mot luuk* problems – regardless of perceived etiology – with two popular brands of tetracycline (Kaanoo® and Hero®). Less commonly, they purchased penicillin. Case study interviews revealed that most women used inadequate doses of these antibiotics, taking between one and three pills only. Tetracycline, even when taken in the correct dosage, is medically inappropriate for many problems women classify as associated with

the *mot luuk*, such as muscle pain and fungal infections. Fungal infections are in fact exacerbated by the use of antibiotics. However, popular brands of tetracycline are widely believed to be 'good for *mot luuk* problems' in general and also capable of improving the condition of a 'bad uterus' (*mot luuk boo dii* [*mot luuk mai dii*]). These drugs were readily available in all villages surveyed, and were easily purchased without a medical prescription (see also Whittaker, 1996).

The idea of taking tetracycline for *mot luuk* problems is not merely a 'folk medical belief', for these medicines are marketed through poster and radio advertising as drugs to treat the uterus (see Boonmongkon, Nichter, Pylypa, & Chantapasa, 1998; Whittaker, 1996). Government bans on other drugs previously available in local provision shops have also likely contributed to the popularity of tetracycline. Self-medication is extremely common in both rural and urban Thailand – through the use of both brand name drugs, and unlabelled packets of a mixture of drugs assembled by drugstore staff according to non-standardized recipes (*yaa sut* [*yaa chut*]) that are commonly sold for particular complaints (Chantapasa & Nichter, 2001). The government has recently initiated campaigns against the sale of *yaa sut* drug packets at local grocery shops (but not at drug stores), and in the last few years fewer village grocery shops in the Northeast have been carrying *yaa sut* packets for women's problems. This has left a market niche open that companies selling tetracycline have been all too happy to exploit further through deceptive or ambiguous marketing.

What are women hoping to accomplish when they self-treat *mot luuk* problems with antibiotics? Some women interviewed about Kaanoo and Hero spoke of these drugs as a cure for common *mot luuk* problems, others as a means of preventing *mot luuk* problems from becoming worse, others as a prophylactic against the recurrence of problems they had experienced in the past, and still others as a pain killer for *mot luuk* problems. [...] Some women explicitly mentioned taking antibiotics so that they could continue to work, believing that Kaanoo would either reduce pain or prevent their problem from becoming worse. For many women, taking these medicines was no more noteworthy than taking stimulants or pain medications, drugs commonly consumed in rural Thailand to permit people to work longer hours (Sringernyuang, Hongvivatava, & Meeporn, 1991; Sringernyuang, Hongvivatava, & Pradabmuk, 1996). [...] Five of the 50 women [...] interviewed used some form of medication on an ongoing basis (daily, weekly, or monthly) in an attempt to either control or cure their illness.

Health Care Seeking

When self-medication fails to decrease the severity of *mot luuk* problems or a woman begins to worry that her symptoms are advancing to *maleng [mareng]* (cervical cancer), there are several sources of health care she may consult in both the public and private sector. Government health stations (*sathaanii anaamai*) staffed by nurses and/or midwives are found in most larger villages and within clusters of smaller adjoining villages. Their range and quality of services vary significantly by location. District hospitals are found in towns, and Khon Kaen city supports a regional hospital, a maternal and child health center, a university hospital, and a government clinic for the treatment sexually transmitted disease. Many government nurses and doctors [...] have private practices after hours, and in larger towns one finds other doctors in private practice as well as several drugstores that compete for clientele.

Most women in Northeast Thailand have contact with government health facilities. Nursing staff at local health stations and district hospitals see approximately three-quarters of all women in their service areas at least once per year. During our initial survey, 52% of informants reported visiting a local health station in the last six months and 37% had visited a district hospital. In the past year, 47% of women had visited a government health facility for some service related to obstetrics and gynecology (family planning, pre- or postnatal care, Pap smears, or *mot luuk* problems). When women seek out health services specifically for *mot luuk* problems, the vast majority of them consult government facilities first. [...]

Most of the women we interviewed spoke of visiting the health station primarily because it was convenient and inexpensive (particularly if they had government health cards), but expressed doubt that medicines obtained at the health station would cure their *mot luuk* problems. They went to the health station to get temporary relief from symptoms that they anticipated would return.

During the health service component of our research we documented that the vast majority of treatments offered to women at health stations for *mot luuk* problems were medically inappropriate (Chantapasa & Nichter, 2001). In one of the first clinic interactions we observed, a woman came and complained of pelvic and lower abdominal pain and demanded an injection so that she could return to work. She was given pills she recognized as common painkillers and was dissatisfied. She again requested an injection and was given a muscle relaxant in tablet form instead. "These types of demands are common," reported the nurse in charge, "We give them something to make them happy." A follow-up interview with the woman revealed that she and her neighbors commonly received injections for *jep mot luuk* ('pain in the uterus') at this health station. It appears that our presence had altered the treatment normally administered. In another health station, diazepam was administered for vague *mot luuk* complaints without any physical examination being performed or history taken. It was assumed that such complaints were psychological or work-related. In yet another health station, a woman complaining of vaginal itching and lower abdominal pain was given a painkiller and an antihistamine for her complaints of pelvic pain and excessive discharge. This was not her first time visiting the health station with this complaint. During an exit interview she spoke of her symptoms as annoying, but generally bearable, and the medicines she received as helping, but not curing her problem. She worried about cervical cancer because her problem did not seem to go away, and she wanted a physical examination and some reassurance that it was not transforming into a more serious condition.

Staff in health stations overwhelmingly reported feeling poorly trained and ill equipped to diagnose and treat patients with gynecological complaints. [...] During health staff training, far more emphasis is placed on the treatment of major STIs than on RTIs such as bacterial vaginosis and candidiasis, which health providers more commonly encounter. In the absence of clear treatment guidelines, the treatment offered to women presenting common gynecological symptoms was found to be inconsistent across health stations and often 'irrational' by biomedical criteria. [...] The limited set of drugs supplied to health stations by the provincial health service and the need to ration available drugs significantly influenced the treatment prescribed. Often, 3–5 days worth of an inappropriate antibiotic [...] is prescribed (Chantapasa & Nichter, forthcoming), and consultations are characterized by *ad hoc* 'diagnosis by response to treatment' in which diagnosis is retrospective, based on the efficacy, or lack thereof, of the treatment prescribed.

Women are generally referred from health stations to the district hospital when treatments are ineffective and ailments do not subside, or when the resident midwife or nurse does not feel comfortable treating them or has inadequate medicines to do so. Several women we interviewed took referrals to mean that they had a serious illness (such as cancer), when in fact they could just as easily have had a fungal infection treatable with appropriate medications. Other women (23 out of 50) traveled to district hospitals because they wanted an internal exam to set their minds at ease. [...]

An aggressive Pap smear campaign has been established in Northeast Thailand for the early detection of cervical cancer. District hospitals offer weekly Pap smear clinics. [...] Pap smears are generally conducted by nursing staff in the health promotion section of the hospital and in two out of three hospitals studied, reproductive tract infections are not treated by nursing staff conducting these exams. Thus, women experiencing symptoms are often recruited for cervical cancer screening but their immediate symptoms are not addressed. Furthermore, these women are poorly informed about the purpose of a Pap smear. Since women perceive of cancer as the most extreme manifestation on a continuum of *mot luuk* problems, they imagine that a Pap smear

is a procedure that identifies *any* gynecological disease. As they understand it, a Pap smear is a *diagnostic* procedure for all *mot luuk* problems (the worst of which is cancer), not a *screening* procedure for precursors of cervical cancer. Since many women think of cervical cancer as a large ulcer, fungus, or accumulation of pus that would be visible to the naked eye upon inspection, they expect to be immediately diagnosed when examined. However, instead of being informed by nursing staff about what they have seen, they are told to wait for laboratory results that often take up to 3 months to process. Thus, women's expectations for diagnosis and treatment are not met, and they go away worried, unsatisfied, and untreated.

The number of women attending Pap smear clinics in Northeast Thailand is at once a testimony to the success of this screening campaign, and a barometer for women's anxiety about *mot luuk* problems turning into cervical cancer. [...] Estimates by two nurses who routinely conduct Pap smears and data from exit interviews with dozens of women indicate that the vast majority of women who get Pap smears (over and above those recruited by health staff postpartum as a condition for receiving contraceptives) do so because they have vaginal discharge and fear cancer. These women want both treatment for their symptoms, and for the doctor 'to check and see if they have cancer'. [...]

Women visiting district hospitals for *mot luuk* problems by and large do not feel they receive enough information about their problems from staff. Exit interviews following Pap smears revealed that patients had several questions they wished to ask, but dared not for fear of being scolded or angering busy staff. Aside from wanting to be reassured that they did not have cancer, women wanted to know more about their health problems. Could their illness be cured or only managed? Why did the illness return, did it remain in the body, and what made it flare up? While patients had a lot to say to researchers about their *mot luuk* problems during exit interviews at hospitals, they were observed to volunteer little information to health staff and ask few questions. They provided only short answers to direct questions. Given the suffering that occurs as a result of misconceptions and miscommunication (as well as missed communication), addressing women's health concerns and providing answers to their questions needs to be identified as a priority.

Conclusions

Over the last decade, an evidence-based approach to health care priority setting has gained increasing prominence within international health circles (Murray & Lopez, 1997). Critics have questioned whether an approach that privileges epidemiological data, the cost-effectiveness of treatment, and impersonal measures of disability is adequate for determining local health care policy and practice. On the basis of this study, we argue that epidemiological data on the prevalence of RTIs and the effectiveness of treatment regimens are necessary but insufficient to guide women's health policy and clinical practice in Northeast Thailand. While we acknowledge that an evidence-based approach to health care rationing may be necessary in times of budgetary constraint, such an approach needs to be complemented by a humanistic appreciation of how illness is being experienced by local populations in different cultures. Health policy requires a consideration of more than just disease prevalence rates, for it is not diagnosable disease alone that is a cause of health concern, anxiety, and fear. At a time when disability-adjusted life years (DALYs) are being assigned to health problems by expert committees toward the end of health care planning (Murray & Lopez, 1996; World Bank, 1993), human suffering needs to be considered in context through an appreciation of the impact of illness on everyday life. Suffering entails more than the pain associated with complaints such as *jep mot luuk*, it involves several senses of loss: the loss of capacities, roles and relationships, of one's anticipated future and hopes for a better life, of peace of mind, and of one's very sense of coherence (Cassell, 1982, 1991).

In Northeast Thailand, women suffer from *mot luuk* problems, regardless of whether or not they have a disease that doctors classify as significant and worthy of treatment. Women's experiences of *mot luuk* problems are influenced by a complex of factors, including the burden of women's work, perceptions of illness causality that carry social significance, fears that sexual relations will aggravate symptoms and lead to cervical cancer, additional fears that they will lose their husbands to other women if sexual relations are suspended, inadequate information on *mot luuk* problems from clinics, and misinformation perpetuated by drug companies. Isaan women's responses to *mot luuk* problems emerge as significant health concerns in their own right — regardless of clinical diagnoses — when we consider their mental health ramifications as well as the iatrogenic consequences that may follow from inappropriate medication use and misguided care at the hands of primary health care staff.

The formative research described in this paper was used to inform a culturally sensitive women's health intervention. Following the collection of data in 1997–1998, an intervention was initiated that had both a clinic and a community based component. This intervention is presently in its second year. Thus far, education courses have been developed to teach health staff how to conduct culturally sensitive interviews and physical examinations with Isaan women, address local fears about cervical cancer, and treat routine RTI problems as well as muscle pain associated with work. The project has successfully lobbied the provincial government to develop treatment algorithms more relevant to local illness patterns and supply health stations in the intervention area with appropriate medicines not previously part of the standard set of drugs issued to health station staff. Women's health groups have been initiated and educational materials developed around questions women have about *mot luuk* problems. Local groups of health volunteers are being trained to conduct outreach programs using drama and to raise community consciousness about gender relations and illness transmission (reinfection, etc.). Village grocery shops have been targeted by a pharmacy school initiative to teach women about the harmful effects of using tetracycline for fungal infections. The extent to which these interventions will prove effective remains to be assessed. Our experience to date concurs with that of other scholar-activists working in the field of women's health: To truly meet the health needs of women, both the 'demand' side (women's health concerns) and 'supply' side (effective medical treatment) of health care provision need to be addressed simultaneously.

[…]

NOTES

1 Evidence-based medicine is advocated by the discipline of clinical epidemiology (Sackett, Maynes, & Tugwell, 1985, Sackett et al., 1996). Its application in the World Bank's (1993) report is driven by a political-economic agenda (Fox, 1999). The World Bank's agenda of cost-effectiveness in the context of health care rationing privileges measures of disease outcomes and representations of suffering such as disability-adjusted life years (DALYs), which attempt to make the burden of disease comparable across diseases, peoples, and locations (Murray & Lopez, 1996). As noted by critics (Arnesen & Nord, 1999, Kleinman & Kleinman, 1996) the DALY indicator relies on a simplified model of illness experience that discounts the cultural meaning of illness, gender and class differences in the illness experience, and the impact of how illness is experienced on individuals beyond the afflicted.

2 Good (1977) describes a 'semantic illness network' as 'the meaning of an illness which is constituted by its linking together in a potent image a complex of symbols, feelings, motives, and stresses'. An illness is thus understood as a 'syndrome' that indexes networks of cultural meanings and social interactions in society.

3 See Boonmongkon et al. (1998) for a complete published report of the study, including extensive notes on methods used.

REFERENCES

Arnesen, T., & Nord, E.
(1999) The value of DALY life: Problems and validity of disability adjusted life years. *British Medical Journal, 319*, 1423–5.

Bhatia, J. C., Cleland, J., Bhagavan, L., & Rao, N. S. N.
(1995) *Prevalence of gynecological morbidity among women in South India.* Indian Institute of Management-Bangalore. Bangalore: Unpublished paper.

Bhatia, J. C., Cleland, J., Bhagavan, L., & Rao, N. S. N.
(1997) Levels and determinants of gynecological morbidity in a district of South India. *Studies in Family Planning, 28*(2), 95–103.

Boonmongkon, P., Nichter, M., Pylypa, J., & Chantapasa, K.
(1998) *Understanding women's experience of gynecological problems: An ethnographic case study from Northeast Thailand.* Center for Health Policy Studies, Mahidol University, Nakornpathom, Thailand.

Boonmongkon, P., Pylypa, J., & Nichter, M.
(1999) Emerging fears of cervical cancer in Northeast Thailand. *Anthropology and Medicine, 16*(4), 359–80.

Cassell, E.
(1982) The nature of suffering and the goals of medicine. *New England Journal of Medicine, 306*(11), 639–45.

Cassell, E.
(1991) *The nature of suffering and the goals of medicine.* Oxford: Oxford University Press.

Chantapasa, K., & Nichter, M.
2001 *Treatment of gynecological complaints in Northeast Thailand: Practical logics and irrational practices.* forthcoming.

Chavez, L. R., Hubbell, F. A., McMullin, J. M., Martinez, R. G., & Mishra, S. I.
(1995) Structure and meaning in models of breast and cervical cancer risk factors: A comparison of perceptions among Latinas, Anglo women, and physicians. *Medical Anthropology Quarterly, 9*(1), 40–74.

Fox, D. M.
(1999) Epidemiology and the new political economy of medicine. *American Journal of Public Health, 89*, 493–6.

Good, B. J.
(1977) The heart of what's the matter. *Culture Medicine and Psychiatry, 1*(1), 25–58.

Gregg, J.
(2000) Mixed blessings: Cervical cancer screening in Recife, Brazil. *Medical Anthropology, 19*, 41–63.

Hanenberg, R. S., Rojanapithayakorn, W., Kunasol, P., & Sokal, D. C.
(1994) Impact of Thailand's HIV-control programme as indicated by the decline of sexually transmitted diseases. *Lancet, 344*, 243–6.

Hubbell, F. A., Chavez, L. R., Mishra, S. I., & Valdez, R. B.
(1996) Beliefs about sexual behavior and other predictors of Papanicolaou smear screening among Latinas and Anglo women. *Archives of Internal Medicine, 156*, 2353–8.

Kleinman, A., & Kleinman, J.
(1996) The appeal of experience, the dismay of images: Cultural appropriations of suffering in our times. *Daedalus, 125*, 1–23.

Mougne, C.
(1978) An ethnography of reproduction: Changing patterns of fertility in a northern Thaoi village. In P. A. Stott (Ed.), *Nature and Man in South East Asia* (pp. 68–106). London: SOAS, University of London.

Murray, C. J., & Lopez, A. D.
(1996) Evidence-based health policy – lessons from the Global Burden of Disease Study. *Science, 274*, 740–3.

Murray, C. J., & Lopez, A. D.
(1997) Global mortality, disability, and the contribution of risk factors: Global Burden of Disease Study. *Lancet, 349*, 1436–42.

Nichter, M.
(1981) Idioms of distress: Alternatives in the expression of psychosocial distress: A case study from South India. *Culture, Medicine and Psychiatry, 5*, 379–408.

Nichter, M.
(1989) The language of illness, contagion and symptom reporting, in anthropology and international health: South Asian case studies. (pp. 85–123), Dordrecht, The Netherlands: Kluwer Academic Publishers.

Nichter, M.
(1996) Self-medication and STD prevention. *Sexually Transmitted Diseases*, 353–6.

Olukoya, A. A., & Elias, C.
(1996) Perceptions of reproductive tract morbidity among Nigerian women and men. *Reproductive Health Matters, 7*, 56–65.

Phan, T. L., Elias, C., Uhrig, J., Nguyen, T. L., Bui, T. C., & Nguyen, H. P.

(1998) *The prevalence of reproductive tract infections at the MCH/FP Centre in Hue, Viet Nam: A cross-sectional descriptive study.* Draft Report.

Population Council
(1996) *Reproductive tract infection, lessons learned from the Field: Where do we go from here?* Report of a seminar presented under the auspices of the Population Council's Robert H. Ebert Program on Critical Issues in Reproductive Health and Population, February 6–7, 1995, New York, NY.

Sackett, D. L., Haynes, R. B., & Tugwell, P.
(1985) *Clinical epidemiology: A basic science for clinical medicine.* Boston: Little Brown, and Company.

Sackett, D. L., Rosenberg, W. M. C., Gray, J. A. M., Haynes, R. B., & Richardson, W. S.
(1996) Evidence based medicine: What it is and what it isn't. *British Medical Journal, 312*, 71–2.

Sringernyuang, L., Hongvivatava, T., & Meeporn, B.
(1991) *Socio-cultural aspects of painkillers use: A case of Thailand.* Paper presented at the International Conference on Social and Cultural Aspects of Pharmaceuticals, The Netherlands.

Sringernyuang, L., Hongvivatava, T., & Pradabmuk, P.
(1996) Where Thai villagers get their drugs. *Essential Drugs Monitor, 21*, 28.

Whittaker, A.
(1996) White blood and falling wombs: Ethnogynecology in Northeast Thailand. In P. L. Rice, & L. Manderson (Eds.), *Maternity and reproductive health in Asian societies* (pp. 207–25). Amsterdam: Harwood Academic Publishers.

Whittaker, A. M.
(1995) *Isaan women: Ethnicity, gender and health in Northeast Thailand.* Unpublished Ph.D. thesis. Tropical Health Program, University of Queensland, Brisbane.

34

The New Malaise
Medical Ethics and Social Rights in the Global Era

Paul Farmer

First, to what level of quality can medical ethics aspire, if it ignores callous discrimination in medical practice against large populations of the innocent poor? Second, how effective can such theories be in addressing the critical issues of medical and clinical ethics if they are unable to contribute to the closing of the gap of socio-medical disparity? (Marcio Fabri dos Anjos, "Medical Ethics in the Developing World: A Liberation Theology Perspective")

Far be it from me to make ethics tremble. I tremble even at the prospect that I will be found guilty of spreading the word that the pants of the great man are split. For that I have already prepared a defense aimed at exonerating me of all responsibility. . . . The result is that it will be very hard to identify the guilty party, to find anyone who is singularly responsible, if we are all rounded up by the police and charged with inciting a riot against ethics. (John Caputo, Against Ethics*)*

Double Standards of Medical "Ethics" for the Developing World

On March 30, 2000, while working in rural Haiti, I received an e-mail from a medical student. The subject line flashed by as the files reached me through the wonder of satellite technology. "More Tuskegee," it read.[1]

The Tuskegee Syphilis Study was conducted in Alabama by the US Public Health Service from 1932 to 1972. The researchers recorded the natural history of syphilis in an attempt to learn more about the disease by following six hundred men, of whom about four hundred had syphilis, throughout their lifetimes. All were African American, many were sharecroppers, and most lived in poverty. Despite the 1947 discovery of a cure for the disease – to this day, syphilis is treated with penicillin – subjects were never offered that very inexpensive drug, even though they had joined the study assuming that they would be treated. Nor were they informed of the study's real purpose.

Tuskegee ended in 1972 amid public outrage when the *Atlanta Constitution* and the *New York Times* ran front-page stories on the study. In a critical reassessment of Tuskegee, historian Allan Brandt notes, "The entire study had been predicated on nontreatment. Provision of effective medication would have violated the rationale of the experiment – to study the natural course of the disease until death."[2] It took the US government decades to acknowledge its wrongdoing; President Clinton's public apology came in 1997.

My student's e-mail message contained a Reuters story about a paper published the day before in the *New England Journal of Medicine*. Under his terse subject heading, he forwarded the story, without commentary:

Boston, March 29 – A study of more than 15,000 people in Uganda that has raised ethical questions about AIDS research in poor countries concluded that the risk of spreading AIDS through heterosexual sex rose and fell with the amount of virus in the blood.

The study, in Thursday's issue of the *New England Journal of Medicine*, also confirmed earlier research suggesting that circumcision guarded against the spread of *HIV*, the virus that causes AIDS.

The research was controversial, not because of its conclusions, but because of its methodology. Unlike studies of H.I.V. in developed countries, the volunteers in the Uganda study were not offered treatment, nor did doctors inform the healthy spouse of an infected person that his or her partner harbored the virus.

Instead, the team led by Dr. Thomas Quinn of the National Institute of Allergy and Infectious Diseases, tested the volunteers and tracked the spread of their illness.[3]

In brief, the randomized-control trial conducted between November 1994 and October 1998 examined the relationship between serum viral load, concurrent sexually transmitted diseases, and other known and putative HIV risk factors (for example, male circumcision and several sociodemographic and behavioral factors). The research team screened 15,127 individuals in a rural district of Uganda, of whom 415 were identified as HIV-positive with an initially HIV-negative

partner. The researchers then tracked these serodiscordant couples for thirty months, following the viral load of the infected partner and the rate of seroconversion among the previously uninfected partners. The study concludes that "viral load is the chief predictor of the risk of heterosexual transmission of HIV-I." Such a finding "raises the possibility that reductions in viral load brought about by the use of antiretroviral drugs could potentially reduce the rate of transmission." Quinn and colleagues called for *more research* "to develop and evaluate cost-effective methods, such as effective and inexpensive antiretroviral therapy or vaccines, for reducing viral load in HIV-infected persons."[4]

Already, the Ugandan study has occasioned a good deal of comment. Some of it appeared in the same issue of the *New England Journal of Medicine*: "Tragically," noted a researcher from another U.S. university, "results such as these could be obtained only in places with a very high incidence and prevalence of the virus and few practical or affordable means of preventing transmission . . . . The challenge now is to use these results *to develop prevention strategies* that can benefit everyone, especially those who participated in the research."[5]

Develop *prevention* strategies. This sounds eminently reasonable at first blush. But were more research and the development of prevention strategies the only real challenges emerging from this and other studies? I had just participated in a conference in rural Haiti – a conference attended mostly by women living in poverty, several of them also living with HIV – and the "challenge" as outlined in the paper or the accompanying commentary did not ring true to me. Prevention strategies had *already* failed those infected during the course of the Ugandan study; prevention strategies were hardly the "challenge" at hand for "those who participated in the research." The women at the meeting in rural Haiti had raised a very different set of challenges. As one asked, "What about those of us who already have HIV? Are we merely to wait for death?" Another participant said simply, "Treatment is important for sick people."

Commenting on the Ugandan study, others echoed my student. In the electronic magazine

Slate, one writer asked: "The 15,000 Ugandan volunteers in the sample were not offered treatment nor were their healthy sex partners informed that the research subjects were HIV positive. Excuse please, but why isn't this like the [*New England Journal of Medicine*] supporting the Tuskegee experiments?"[6]

Let us leave aside the fact that there were 415 serodiscordant couples in the study, not 15,000, and the facts that the *Journal* published rather than conducted the research and that its editor wrote a highly critical commentary.[7] The point here is that even though we might dismiss comments from outside the research community as inaccurate or tendentious or worse, an understanding of the social field that generates such commentary reminds us that we live in a peculiar age. Although historians and economists warn against simplistic use of the term "globalization," rapid developments in communications clearly are changing the way we understand, experience, and manage social inequality.[8] Surely it is a novel development that research published one day in the *New England Journal of Medicine* can, within twenty-four hours, trigger heated responses from around the globe.

These and other developments in communications are reminders that, increasingly, epidemics of disease are transnational ones.[9] Research universities and development agencies now also have global reach, and, just as epidemics are transnational, so too, increasingly, is research. But although pathogens readily cross borders, the fruits of research are often delayed in customs. For example, it seems to be easy enough to use First World diagnostics – in the Ugandan study, sophisticated assays of viral load were available – even though antiretroviral therapy is deemed unfeasible, too difficult, or "cost-ineffective." The most commonly encountered justification, though, is that antiretroviral therapy does not reflect "local standards of care." The devastation wrought by HIV in sub-Saharan Africa – AIDS is now far and away the leading cause of adult death across the continent and has already orphaned fourteen million children there – has brought the local-standard-of-care argument to the forefront of medical and public debate in the past few years.

A 1997 article by Peter Lurie and Sidney Wolfe triggered what have become increasingly vocal attacks on the AIDS clinical trials being conducted in developing countries – studies involving, for example, what many argue are unethical placebo controls in AZT trials attempting to develop a cheaper drug regimen to prevent mother-child transmission of HIV, Udo Schüklenk cast this argument in a different light:

In the real world there is no such thing as a fixed local standard of care. Rather, the local standard of care in, for example, India, is a standard of care determined by the prices set by Western pharmaceutical multinationals. The only reason why the [AZT placebo] trials took place at all is the pricing schedule set by the manufacturer of the drug. Glaxo-Wellcome therefore, more than anything else, determines what is described by bioethicists and clinical researchers as the "local standard of care."[10]

What does medical ethics have to say about such transnational research? The short answer: very little, so far. This in spite of the demands contained in the International Code of Medical Ethics, first drafted in Geneva in 1949, that physicians not only place the well-being of research subjects above the supposed benefits to science and society but also that they declare, "I will not permit considerations of religion, nationality, race, party politics or social standing to intervene between my duty and my patient."[11] But is it not precisely "social standing" and "nationality" that place Ugandans at risk for becoming AIDS research subjects *and* for receiving substandard medical care? By substandard, I mean lower than the care that the researchers would expect for themselves in the unlikely event that they were to contract HIV.

It is not my intention here to focus overmuch on one particular study. Indeed, Quinn and colleagues are likely not guilty of violating the ethical codes established by their university and by their Ugandan counterparts, as they were quick to protest. They pointed out that four institutional review boards in the United States and Uganda had approved the study and that a data safety and monitoring board from the National Institutes of Health, composed of

US and Ugandan representatives, monitored
their work. At no time was it recommended
that the researchers provide antiretrovirals to
the participants.[12] What I am suggesting is that
ethical codes and review boards are not always
helpful, to put it politely. They often share an
unacknowledged agreement that in fact all
humans are not created equal and that this
inequality accounts for both differential distribution of disease and differential standards
of care.

It is no exaggeration to say that the majority
of such international biomedical research has
inequality as its foundation. As Marcia Angell
has argued:

> Research in the Third World looks relatively
> attractive as it becomes better funded
> and regulations at home become more restrict-
> ive. Despite the existence of codes requiring that
> human subjects receive at least the
> same protection abroad as at home, they are
> still honored partly in the breach. The fact
> remains that many studies are done in the Third
> World that simply could not be done in the
> countries sponsoring the work. Clinical trials
> have become a big business, with many of the
> same imperatives. To survive, it is necessary to
> get the work done as quickly as possible, with a
> minimum of obstacles. When these consider-
> ations prevail, it seems as if we have not come
> very far from Tuskegee after all.[13]

These "ironies of inequality" are doubtless
the subject of much discussion among people
living in poverty – just as the absence of environmental or labor regulation in their home
countries, opening up ambiguous forms of "development," also spurs commentary. Any anthropologist could offer examples. But the
ironies are most pointed when ethical codes
developed in affluent countries are quickly
ditched as soon as affluent universities undertake research in poor countries. Then come a
series of efforts to develop alternative (read,
less stringent) codes "appropriate" to settings
of destitution. These revisions are termed
"sensible," "reasonable," "realistic." Those
who oppose such downgrades are branded as,
at best, "utopian" and "naïve" or, at worst,
"obstructionist" and even "irresponsible."

Inserting Social Justice Into Medical Ethics

The problem here, explored throughout this
book, is that our practice has not kept up with
our rhetoric. In arguing that health care is a
human right, one signs on to a lifetime of work
dedicated to erasing double standards for rich
and poor. Again, the question of social and
economic rights is raised, first and loudly by
the poor, and then timidly and reluctantly by
the rest of us. It has taken years for the sharp
critiques voiced by the poor to begin to work
their way into our medical journals and ethical
codes.

Without a social justice component, medical ethics risks becoming yet another strategy
for managing inequality. Within the field, however, promising developments have occurred.
Several years ago, an international working
group from varied professions gathered in
London (at Tavistock Square) to develop an
initial draft of a code of ethics for those who
work in health care. Members of this group
were convinced of the need for a moral framework that all health care professions could
relate to and that would encourage cooperation and mutual respect. The Tavistock
Group's "shared ethical principles for everybody in health care" is an attempt to recapture
the moral high ground of the position that
health is a human right, while avoiding the
relativism that has so far largely served the
interests of the nonpoor.[14] The bad news is that
the phrase "everybody in health care" refers to
expanding medical ethics to include nurses and
other health care *professionals* rather than to
include those who bear the brunt of disease.
The good news is that even though the poor are
not mentioned in the document, something just
as important is: the first of the ethical principles enumerated states that health care is a
human right.[15]

Of course, this has all been said before –
health care is certainly featured as a human
right in the Universal Declaration of Human
Rights – but the Tavistock document is a statement on *professional ethics* and, like most such
statements, was formulated by members of the
profession. What is the function of statements

of professional ethics? Writing about codes of medical ethics, Sohl and Bassford offer a polite definition that would be challenged by few:

While it is undeniable that a major motivation for desiring self-regulation is the pursuit of professional power, self-regulation carries with it an ethical component, and involves a moral commitment on the part of the profession. To see this one need only think of any of the occupational groups currently trying to be recognized as having professional status. One of their first acts is to formulate and publicize a code of ethics for their members.[16]

Codes of medical ethics exist in profusion, and though some are less self-serving than others, most have, as their implicit or avowed focus, the protection of the professionals. In the Tavistock document, we have something more novel: a code crafted by professionals that starts by asserting that health care is a human right.

In subsequent discussions, some have pushed this assertion even further, to argue that *quality* health care is a fundamental human right. In a very real way, such a redefinition would bring all those who comfortably agree with the Tavistock principles to the brink of the abyss. They would have to look down at the squalid misery endured by much of humanity, with its Sisyphean burden of readily treatable pathology, and ask how a decent physician or nurse (or other health professional) should act *ethically*. More specifically, what would the world's destitute sick, wherever they languish, have to say about the key tenets of the statement? And one could ask still harder questions: Do the invisible poor come into view only when they become research subjects or immigrants, or is the next step the inclusion of everyone under the rubric "everybody"? The inclusion of all humans under the rubric "human"? The inclusion of social and economic rights under the rubric "human rights"?

I pose these questions with trepidation. But they are, in my view, far and away the most important questions for medical ethics. I agree with Jon Sobrino and others who believe that "the poor and impoverished of the world, in

virtue of their very reality, constitute the most radical question of the truth of this world, as well as the most correct response to this question."[17] As a physician-anthropologist who serves the poor in Haiti, Boston, Peru, and Russia, I have no reason to back away from this stance in contemplating medical ethics, and every reason to cling to it ever more tightly. Our work – analysis and praxis – takes place at an invigorating intersection of medicine, social theory, philosophy, and political analysis. And these disciplines help us to see why it is so important to socialize ethics. As humans, we are all vulnerable to sickness; as physicians, we care for the vulnerable. But some groups are far more vulnerable than others, as every serious epidemiological study has shown. For the poor in affluent countries, it is possible to document the impact of services that are inferior to those offered the nonpoor. In many resource-poor countries, it is often possible to document a complete absence of modern medical care.[18] As other chapters in this book show, current trends are far from heartening.

A few decades ago, the impact of this injustice would have been significant, but not invariably a matter of life and death. That is, people lived and died, many of them unjustly, but even the well-to-do lived in fear of microbes that could kill them, as Nancy Tomes reminds us in her book about infectious diseases at the turn of the nineteenth century.[19] And although the nonpoor always did better than the poor, pneumococcal pneumonia and tuberculosis came with a high case-fatality rate, regardless of social station.

Everything is different now, in large part because medicine is indeed becoming the "youngest science," as Lewis Thomas has written.[20] Using the basic sciences to develop new therapies and the scientific method to evaluate their efficacy reminds us that the fight over equal access to leeches is certainly no longer one worth wasting time on. If the medical interventions in question are ineffective, or only marginally effective, lack of access to these interventions, though unfair, is of limited importance. But biomedicine can at last offer the sick truly revolutionary new therapies. In my own field, infectious disease, we have certainly seen a revolution. Antibiotics and vaccines can, for the fortunate few, virtually erase the risk of mortality from polio, tetanus, measles, pneumonia, staphylococcal and other bacterial infections, diarrheal disease, malaria, tuberculosis. Even HIV disease, the latest rebuke to undue optimism, has been rendered, for those with access to therapy, a readily treatable disease.

Then comes the obvious irony. In the areas where I work, most premature deaths are caused by precisely these pathologies.[21]

The Leading Ethical Question of Our Times

Into this irony comes bioethics. I have served on the ethics service of the Boston teaching hospital with which I am affiliated, and of course take each consult seriously. These consults are often enough about too much medical care. That is, we are called to explore cases in which care is painful, expensive, and prolonged well beyond the point of efficacy. This is termed "medical futility." But being a clinician who works in both a Harvard teaching hospital and rural Haiti, I can't help but make connections between the surfeit on one side – too much care – and the paucity on the other. As an infectious-disease consultant, I feel that my job in Haiti is to say, "Quickly, start the antibiotics," whereas my job in Boston often comes down to saying, "Stop the antibiotics." In Haiti I am called to explain, to those who come begging for assistance, that effective treatments for HIV are not "cost-effective," whereas in Boston I spend much of my time begging patients with AIDS – some of them originally from Haiti – to take these same medications. In Boston I might be alone in witnessing this painful irony, if not for the transnational Haitian janitors who keep the hospital clean.

What does bioethics have to say about this, the leading ethical question of our times? Almost nothing. Conventional medical ethics does a good job of erasing such obscene disparities, for at least four reasons. First, ethics draws strength from experience-distant disciplines such as philosophy, lending ethics debates

a curious, at times almost silly, tenor, as Larry Churchill has noted:

> Bioethical disputes – as measured by the debates in journals and conferences in the United States – often seem to be remote from the values of ordinary people and largely irrelevant to the decisions they encounter in health care. In this sense, philosophical theorizing might be considered harmless entertainment, which if taken too seriously would look ridiculous, as several Monty Python skits have successfully demonstrated.[22]

There have been few attempts to ground medical ethics in political economy, history, anthropology, sociology, and the other contextualizing disciplines (although each of these would have no doubt lent its own native silliness).[23]

Second, medical ethics has been to a large extent a phenomenon of industrialized nations. This has facilitated the process of erasing the poor, since most of them live elsewhere. Thus, the great majority of the world's ethical dilemmas – and, to my mind, the most serious ones – are not discussed by the very discipline claiming expertise in such matters. The third reason that medical ethics and bioethics have been mum on the leading ethical dilemma of our times is that experts have dominated public discourse on these matters, drowning out the voices of those who have far more direct experience. To again cite Churchill:

> Ethics, understood as the capacity to think critically about moral values and direct our actions in terms of such values, is a generic human capacity. Except for sociopaths, it is common to all of us, and skill in ethics does not lend itself easily to encapsulation in theoretical categories, core competencies, or a professional speciality.[24]

A fourth reason, in part an unavoidable one, is that in the hospital we are asked to address the "quandary ethics" of individual patients. In the affluent countries where bioethics has blossomed, these have often been elderly patients for whom further care is deemed futile, even though the machine of "care" grinds on, leaving family and providers feeling a bit ground up themselves.

As the Tavistock statement notes, "The personal experience of illness is generally the principal concern of individual patients; therefore, the principal focus of the health care delivery system must be individual patients and their families or support groups."[25] This priority is altogether appropriate and should not be changed. What should be changed, rather, is that millions are denied the chance to become patients and to have an "individual focus" trained on them. Beyond the administrative borders erected around catchment areas or states or nations, legions die – not of too much care or inappropriate care but rather of no care at all. One gets the sense, in attending ethics rounds and reading the now-copious ethics literature, that these have-nots are an embarrassment to the ethicists, for the problems of poverty and racism and a lack of national health insurance figure only rarely in a literature dominated by endless discussions of brain death, organ transplantation, xenotransplantation, and care at the end of life. When the end of life comes early – from death in childbirth, say, or from tuberculosis or infantile diarrhea – the scandal is immeasurably greater, but silence reigns in the medical ethics literature.

In an era of globalization and increased communication, this selective attention can become absurd. The world's poor already seem to have noticed that ethicists are capable of endlessly rehashing the perils of too much care, while each year millions die what the Haitians call "stupid deaths." The erasures are expedient for some, certainly, but the effaced are less easy to silence these days. One reason is that communications are different – and by and large better – in the global era. Another reason is the sheer burden of unnecessary suffering and premature death. A third is that the current trend is toward even further entrenchment of social inequality.

In the midst of all of this comes the second principle of the Tavistock document: "The care of individuals is at the center of health care delivery but must be viewed and practiced within the overall context of continuing work to generate the greatest possible health gains for groups and populations."[26] Here is a principle suited to our times. It contains its

own checks and balances. A principle such as this would lead us to push for public health but at the same time resist the prevailing conditions – conditions in which it is possible, indeed deemed reasonable, for physicians to contemplate the results of a study conducted among the destitute sick of Uganda and feel that the only challenge is "prevention." As the women participating in our conference in Haiti observed, prevention comes too late for people who are already sick and immiserated.

The self-appointed guardians of international health cannot *ethically* erase the tens of millions already sick with HIV disease. Even using their own, often punitive, analytic tools (for example, cost-effectiveness analysis), treatment of HIV should surely have its role among the destitute sick of southern Africa. As Evan Wood and colleagues argue, even "limited use of antiretrovirals could have an immediate and substantial impact on South Africa's AIDS epidemic."[27] Their assessment projected that the use of short-course prophylaxis would reduce perinatal transmission by 40 percent, preventing 110,000 infant HIV infections by 2005 – at a cost of less than 0.001 percent of the national per-person health expenditure. In a more costly scenario, triple-combination treatment for only 25 percent of the HIV-infected population would prevent both 430,000 incident AIDS cases and a 3.1-year decline in life expectancy.[28] Thus even without recourse to ethical reasoning – which would lead us to ask not "if" but rather "how" – we find the world revealed to us as it really is: a place in which the absolute majority of medical ethics violations go unremarked by experts in this field.

The millions already dying during childbirth or from diseases such as HIV and drug-resistant malaria and tuberculosis face other challenges beyond prevention.[29] If "the care of individuals is at the center of health care delivery," as the Tavistock statement argues, then concerns over equity won't simply go away. *In the global era, global health equity, more than ever before, must be a goal of any serious ethical charter.* Questions regarding social and economic rights are at the heart of what must become a new medical ethics.

Equity as the Fundamental Core of a New Medical Ethics

I conclude by asking questions that stem from serious contemplation of the first two principles of the Tavistock document.

If access to health care is considered a human right, who is considered human enough to have that right?

Looking back over the concept of human rights, we can see that social inequalities have always been used to deny some people status as fully human. When the French promoted the "rights of the citizen," they certainly did not – and do not, for that matter – confer citizenship lightly.[30] Thus human rights were, from the beginning, quite distinct from the rights of the human. And even supposedly subaltern voices could not be depended upon to believe in human rights: when the *gens de couleur* Ogé and Chavannes traveled from colonial Haiti to revolutionary France, they went to press for the rights of mulattoes to own slaves.[31] And so it has continued, with the poor, women, black people, those of low caste, people with disabilities, children, or "aliens" from other nations – you can fill in the blanks, depending to some extent on time and place – denied the full complement of human rights.

Many quests for the rights of the disenfranchised have in truth been quests for power sharing, a process not to be confused with the struggle for social justice for all. In an affluent country like the United States, the call to a unifying nationalism across lines of race and gender often leads to a struggle for the advancement of one group at the expense of others. The identity politics of our times has a troubling subtext: *I've been wronged in the past, and I want what's coming to me.* Wallerstein calls ours "the era of groupism – the construction of defensive groups, each of which asserts an identity around which it builds solidarity and struggles to survive alongside and against other such groups."[32] The fundamental unfairness of existing social structures can be made more palatable if those with access to resources, including medical care, include "historically underrepresented minorities." But cosmetic alterations will placate those at the bottom for only so long.

Nor, if we are going to honor our calling, can health care be considered a human right accorded only to citizens of *certain* nations. People may be erased by geographical chance, by the fact of living beyond the boundaries of an affluent nation-state, but they are erased nonetheless. Physicians who reject nationalism may move to an area with grotesque burdens of disease and find themselves chided for failing to serve those who may be less sick but who carry the same passport as they do.[33]

Can medical ethics, necessarily grounded in the dilemmas faced by patients, develop a broader view of who gets sick and why? Of who has access to care and why?

This is a critical question, in any inegalitarian social field, for a robust code of medical ethics. But the second principle of the Tavistock document demands that this exercise in social medicine figure prominently in our practice. This is in no way a call for clinicians to abandon a patient-focused view. When the push for broadening access, or for attacking only the perceived roots of excess disease, leads to lowering standards of individual patient care, this Luddite approach should be criticized in strong terms. Rather, this question is simply a call for mindfulness – as a moral and analytic stance – about the strikingly patterned pathways to both sickness and care. And yet medical ethics, in my experience, regards social ethics as somehow embarrassing and even inappropriate. Until we come to terms with this discomfort, we will be left with only half a principle.

Medical ethicists and physicians might reply that this is an exercise best left to epidemiologists and to those who study health care systems. But we should not pass this task on to other parties. First, we cannot always trust others to respect the rights of individual patients. Second, practitioners of many disciplines related to medicine have proven incapable of understanding the biosocial complexity that defines unequal health outcomes and health and human rights. Although disciplinary specialization has yielded great insights, the arguments in this book have tried to emphasize the cost of desocializing the concept of rights. Whether we consider Russian prisoners with drug-resistant tuberculosis, HIV-infected Cubans living within sanatoriums, Bostonians with AIDS living on the streets, or Haitians with AIDS detained on a US military base, the story is the same: a failure to understand social process leads to analytic failures, with significant implications for policy and practice.

How does the struggle for social and economic rights relate to, for example, a "Patient's Bill of Rights"?

Questions of erasure again loom large. Most charters of patients' rights seem unaware of the sick nonpatients who never get into the exclusive club of those who actually receive modern health care. In the broader social field in which the "bottom billion" have no access at all to modern medicine, the very real dilemmas of those who *do* have access to care have been the focus of most inquiry by medical ethicists. The right to health care would seem to be of little concern to modern medical ethics. By "modern," I mean the contemporary practice of medical ethics, which regards Nuremberg and Tuskegee as subjects of largely historical interest and ignores the Third World sick altogether, unless they happen to serve as research subjects. Thus, in discussions of medical ethics, global health equity has become the elephant in the room that no one mentions.

But whether we are talking about uninsured US citizens, hapless African research subjects, or prisoners with drug-resistant tuberculosis, charters proclaiming health care as a right take on their full power only when we add the clause "by the way, we *really* mean everybody." This could be dismissed as pie-in-the-sky, but it seems better to avoid erasure and set goals high than to sink to a "pragmatism" that leads inevitably to "ethical dilemmas" (to use the polite language of academic circles; the victims of such pragmatism do not mince words in this manner).

A charter such as the one proposed in Tavistock would mean that we would no longer be more comfortable talking about "patient autonomy" than about the right to receive care when sick. Such a charter would have a great deal to say about medical research conducted by First World universities in settings of Third World poverty. It's naïve to pretend that there are no competing agendas here. At the same time, the first half of the second principle reminds me to be focused on the individual patient. And it does not exhort me to treat only patients of a certain nationality.

What do the destitute sick have to say about medical ethics?

The short answer: plenty. And as a physician-anthropologist, I get an earful. After close to two decades of work in Haiti and much experience in poor neighborhoods of Lima and Boston, I suspect that the destitute sick are in many senses our most harsh and loyal critics. They are loyal in the sense that, even though we have served them poorly, the poor continue to come to our clinics and hospitals; they continue to offer critiques of our errors, if we are willing to listen. That their commentary has not figured prominently in discussions of medical ethics should raise eyebrows, at the very least. Why do we have an extensive literature on why it is not "cost-effective" or "feasible" (or "sustainable" or "appropriate technology") to treat poor people who have complicated diseases? This opinion represents, in the view of some, another slick ruse to distract us from the fundamental ethical problem of our era: the persistence of readily treatable maladies and the growth of both science and economic inequality. Since the poor are those put at risk of sickness and then denied access to care, they are in many ways those most affected by codes of medical ethics. Within and across national boundaries, the destitute sick should be the primary judges of any code of medical ethics. Applying a "perfect" ethical code in one country alone is an impossibility in the global era. Again, we are led back to global health equity as a necessary component of any discussion of medical ethics.

Should physicians be judged by a special calculus of accountability?

The short answer: of course. No other profession is accorded greater and more intimate access to the lives of the sick and suffering. With this great privilege comes responsibility. This is not a business contract. A fair amount has been written about the Nazi doctors, whose abuses of their professional authority led, in no small way, to the founding of modern medical ethics.[34] Although their crimes were perhaps no more heinous than those of other mid-range professionals in the machinery of the Third Reich, we judge them more harshly. Such murderous violations of the sacred contract between physician and patient are unlikely to find support in any quarter. Although these crimes are at the extreme end of the spectrum, there is room at that end to locate the Tuskegee experiments as well. Yet Tuskegee still has its defenders, some more vocal than others.[35] And the participation of US physicians in state-sponsored executions does not cause medical licenses to be revoked, since the death penalty is legal in the United States, and the law of the land seems to take precedence over moral codes and professional ethics.

To return to questions of accountability, I would also warn that the so-called "gray areas" of medical ethics are becoming more black and white with time. So it is with the challenge of the destitute sick. Do physicians have any special obligations to go where the pathology lies heaviest? Virchow thought so.[36] The liberation theologians think so. And the Tavistock statement makes it clear that, even within a code-generating professional body, the special obligation of the healer to the destitute sick must be respected if medicine is to merit the title "vocation."[37]

Human Rights in Medical Ethics – for Everybody

Perhaps the greatest challenge for medical ethics is to *resocialize the way we see ethical dilemmas in medicine*. Restoring to such problems their full social complexity is our best

vaccine against the erasures documented throughout this book. I don't feel uncomfortable doing an ethics consult in the intensive care unit of a Boston teaching hospital, because I don't believe a clinical ethics team is expected to discuss general social ethics in such a context any more than other clinicians are expected to discuss them during the course of a clinic visit. Of course, specific ethical and practical concerns relating to the patient's social and economic context often do – appropriately – crop up in clinical settings. But I do feel uncomfortable *writing* about these matters as if Haiti, Uganda, and Harlem belonged to a different world. They are part of the same world.

How often have we challenged the chicanery that leads us to forget that we are part of the same world? In the United States, the subtext of some ethical discussions has been, ironically enough, how best to manage our vast prosperity. And there is some truth in this; we are prosperous. I was en route from Moscow to the United States on the morning after President Clinton's State of the Union address in January 2000. In it, Clinton spoke proudly of our vast wealth and huge surpluses.[38] Yet I was still smarting after a bitter struggle over whether food supplements could be included in the budget of a project to treat tuberculosis within a Russian penitentiary system full to bursting with gaunt and coughing young men. The struggle was primarily with US and European technical consultants to the World Bank, which was proposing a loan to the Russian government as it seeks to respond to epidemic tuberculosis within its prisons. The Russian specialists wanted to include food supplements as part of the loan. The non-Russian Bank consultants countered that the drugs would work fine with or without malnutrition.

Was this food fight emblematic of an ethical dilemma? Does being human confer a right to survive?

We read in the Working Draft of the Tavistock statement: "Physicians and other clinicians should be advocates for their patients or the populations that they serve but should refrain from manipulating the system to obtain benefits for them to the substantial disadvantage of others."[39] I suspect that the writers' intention was to exhort physicians to refrain from exploiting some public-entitlement program in an affluent industrialized nation. But if Haiti and Uganda and Russia and Harlem are part of the same world, we could argue just as easily that conducting research in settings of great privation and excess burden of disease also runs the risk of "manipulating the system," with the system in question being the global web of connections that is increasingly visible to all of us. Much of this research would never be considered ethical within the country sponsoring the research; its approval by institutional review boards relies on the argument that the local standard of care – in the poor communities where the research subjects live and die—is no care at all. So too can we wonder, as the *Financial Times* estimates capital flight out of Russia at greater than $130 billion in seven years, if our failure to fight hard enough for food for prisoners with tuberculosis is merely a concession to far more powerful forces who are only too happy to "manipulate the system" to the substantial disadvantage of the poor.

The concept of human rights may at times be brandished as an all-purpose and "universal" tonic, but it was developed to protect the vulnerable. The true value of the human rights movement's central documents is revealed only when they serve to protect the rights of those who are most likely to have their rights violated. The proper beneficiaries of the Universal Declaration of Human Rights – however inexpedient this point might be in our age of individualism and affluence and relativism – are the poor and otherwise disempowered. The true value of the Tavistock statement is that it attempts to restore the language of rights to the arena of health care. Since the burden of disease is borne by the poor and otherwise marginalized, we are offered a chance, once again, to contemplate the lot of most of humanity and to ask, simply enough, if by "everybody" we truly mean everybody.

NOTES

1   For more on the Tuskegee study, including the role that racism played in its continuation, see

Brandt 1978 and Jones 1993. Rothman 1984 and Reverby 2000.

2   Brandt 1978, p. 27.

3   "Criticized Research Quantifies the Risk of AIDS Infection" 2000.

4   Quinn, Wawer, Sewankambo, et al. 2000, pp. 921, 927, 928.

5   Cohen 2000, p. 972; emphasis added.

6   Shuger 2000.

7   Angell 2000b.

8   Yach and Bettcher 1998b; Navarro 1998; and Kim, Millen, Irwin, and Gershman 2000.

9   See Farmer 1996c; Farmer 1999b; Farmer, Bayona, Becerra, et al. 1998; and Garrett 2000. For details on transnational cases of drug-resistant tuberculosis, for example, see Becerra, Farmer, and Kim 1999.

10   Schüklenk 2000, p. 973. Morsy 1993, Mintzes, Hardon, and Hanhart 1993.

11   World Medical Association 1983.

12   Gray, Quinn, Serwadda, et al. 2000.

13   Angell 1997a, p. 849.

14   The official title of the document, published simultaneously in several journals in early 1999, is "A Shared Statement of Ethical Principles for Those Who Shape and Give Health Care" (Benatar, Berwick, Bisognano, et al. 1999; Smith, Hiatt, and Berwick 1999a and 1999b). I had the good fortune to be involved in some of the follow-up discussions of the Tavistock Group, held in April 2000 at the American Academy of Arts and Sciences in Cambridge, Massachusetts. This meeting led to further clarification and expansion of the initial five principles into the following seven Tavistock principles:

> *Rights:* People have a right to health and health care
> *Balance:* Care of individual patients is central, but the health of populations is also our concern
> *Comprehensiveness:* In addition to treating illness, we have an obligation to ease suffering, minimise disability, prevent disease, and promote health
> *Cooperation:* Health care succeeds only if we cooperate with those we serve, each

other, and those in other
sectors

Improvement: Improving health care is
a serious and continuing
responsibility

Safety: Do no harm

Openness: Being open, honest, and
trustworthy is vital in
health care

(Berwick, Davidoff, Hiatt, et al. 2001, p.
616)

15 Benatar, Berwick, Bisognano, et al. 1999,
p. 145; Smith, Hiatt, and Berwick 1999a,
p. 250.

16 Sohl and Bassford 1986, p. 1175.

17 Sobrino 1988, p. 30.

18 World Bank 2001, pp. 98–100.

19 Tomes 1998.

20 Thomas 1983.

21 World Bank 2000.

22 Churchill 1999, p. 255. The medical anthropologist Arthur Kleinman received no small
amount of animus from medical ethicists
when he suggested, in the *Encyclopedia of
Bioethics,* that medical ethics was often quite
divorced from any tangible social reality
(Kleinman 1995).

23 For a discussion of the contributions anthropology could make to bioethics, see Marshall
and Koenig 1996.

24 Churchill 1999, p. 259.

25 Benatar, Berwick, Bisognano, et al. 1999, p.
146.

26 Ibid., p. 145.

27 Wood, Braitstein, Montaner, et al. 2000, p.
2095.

28 Ibid.

29 This point was made in reference to the chief
infectious causes of adult death (tuberculosis
and HIV) in a series of publications seeking
to cast treatment as a human right; see
Farmer 2001a; Farmer 2001b; and Farmer,
Léandre, Mukherjee, Claude, et al. 2001.

30 Perhaps one reason that France continues to
refer to the "rights of the citizen" is because
it expends no small amount of energy
denying some within its borders those rights
(Wallerstein 1995a).

31 See James 1963.

32 Wallerstein 1995a, pp. 6–7.

33 This liberal critique of physicians working
in another country when they "should
be" working in their own exposes another

fundamental hypocrisy of liberalism: that
concerning immigration. It's worth quoting
Wallerstein at some length:

Let us take a simple, very important, and
very immediately relevant issue: migration.
The political economy of the migration issue
is extremely simple. The world-economy is
more polarized than ever in two ways: socio-
economically and demographically. The gap
is yawning between North and South and
shows every sign of widening still further in
the next several decades. The consequence is
obvious. There is an enormous North-South
migratory pressure.

Look at this from the perspective of liberal
ideology. The concept of human rights
obviously includes the right to move about.
In the logic of liberalism, there should be no
passports and no visas. Everyone should be
allowed to work and settle everywhere, as is,
for example, true within the United States and
within most states today – certainly within
any state that pretends to be a liberal state.

In practice, of course, most people in the
North are literally aghast at the idea of
open frontiers (1995a, p. 160).

34 For considerations of the relationship between the Nuremberg code and American
bioethics, see Faden, Lederer, and Moreno.
1996; Moreno 1997; Moreno and Lederer
1996; Pellegrino 1997; Pellegrino and Thomasma 2000; Sidel 1996. See also Aly,
Chroust, and Pross 1994.

35 See, for example, White 2000.

36 Virchow was committed to improving the
health of the many, as opposed to just that of
the few. "For if medicine is really to accomplish its great task," he wrote, "it must intervene in political and social life. It must point
out the hindrances that impede the normal
social functioning of vital processes, and effect
their removal" (1849, p. 48). Navarro notes in
a letter published in the *Lancet:* "Public-
health institutions, including international
ones, too often ignore the analysis by one of
the founders of public health, Virchow, who
noted that 'medicine is not only a biological,
but also a social intervention and politics is
public health in the most profound sense' "
(1997, p. 1480). See also Eisenberg 1984.

37 Pellegrino makes a similar point: "One thing is
certain: if health care is a commodity, it is for

sale, and the physician is, indeed, a money-maker; if it is a human good, it cannot be for sale and the physician is a healer" (1999, p. 262).

38 Clinton 2000.
39 Benatar, Berwick, Bisognano, et al. 1999, p. 146.

BIBLIOGRAPHY

Aly, G., P. Chroust, and C. Pross
1994 *Cleansing the Fatherland: Nazi Medcine and Racial Hygiene.* Baltimore: Johns Hopkins University Press.
Angell, M.
1997a "The Ethics of Clinical Research in the Third World." *New England Journal of Medicine* 337 (12): 847–49.
Angell, M.
2000b "Investigators' Responsibilities for Hum an Subjects in Developing Countries." *New England Journal of Medicine* 342 (13): 967–69.
Becerra, M. C., P.E. Farmer, and J.Y. Kim
1999 "The Problem of Drug-Resistant Tuberculosis: An Overview." In *The Global Impact of Drug-Resistant Tuberculosis*, edited by Program in Infectious Disease and Social Change, pp. 1–38. Boston: Harvard Medical School and the Open Society Institute.
Benatar, S.R., D.M. Berwick, M. Bisognano, et al.
1999 "A Shared Statement of Ethical Principles for Those Who Shape and Give Health Care." *Annals of Internal Medicine* 130 (2): 144–47.
Berwick, D., F. Davidoff, H. Hiatt, et al.
2001 "Refining and Implementing the Tavistock Principles for Everybody in Health Care." *British Medical Journal* 323 (7313): 616–20.
Brandt, A.M.
1978 "Racism and Research: The Case of the Tuskegee Syphilis Study." *Hastings Center Report* 8 (6): 21–29.
Caputo, J.D.
1993 *Against Ethics: Contributions to a Poetics of Obligation with Constant Reference to Deconstruction.* Bloomington: Indiana University Press.
Churchill, L.R.
1997 "Bioethics in Social Context." In *The Social Medicine Reader,* edited by G.E. Henderson, N.M.P. King, R.P. Strauss, et al., pp. 310–20. Durham: Duke University Press.

Churchill, L.R.
1999 "Are We Professionals? A Critical Look at the Social Role of Bioethicists." *Daedalus* 128 (4): 253–74.
Clinton, W.J.
1997 Remarks by the President in Apology for Study Done in Tuskegee. 16 May. Available at *http://www.cdc.gov/nchstp/od/tuskegee/clintonp.htm.*
Clinton, W.J.
2000 State of the Union Address. 27 January. Available at *http://www.pbs.org/newshour/bb/white_house/jan-junoo/sotu4.html.*
Cohen, M.S.
2000 "Preventing Sexual Transmission of HIV – New Ideas from Sub-Saharan Africa." *New England Journal of Medicine* 342 (13): 970–72.
"Criticized Research Quantifies the Risk of AIDS Infection."
2000 *New York Times*, 30 March, p. A16.
Faden, R.R., S.E. Lederer, and J.D. Moreno
1996 "U.S. Medical Researchers, the Nuremberg Doctors Trial, and the Nuremberg Code: A Review of Findings of the Advisory Committee on Human Radiation Experiments." *Journal of the American Medical Association* 276 (20): 1667–71.
Farmer, P.E.
1996c "Social Inequalities and Emerging Infectious Diseases." *Emerging Infectious Diseases* 2 (4): 259–69.
Farmer, P.E.
1999b *Infections and Inequalities: The Modern Plagues.* Berkeley: University of California Press.
Farmer, P.E.
2001a *Infections and Inequalities: The Modern Plagues.* 2d ed., with a new preface. Berkeley: University of California Press.
Farmer, P.E.
2001b "The Major Infectious Diseases in the World—To Treat or Not to Treat?" *New England Journal of Medicine* 345 (3): 208–10.
Farmer, P.E., J. Bayona, M. Becerra, et al.
1998 "The Dilemma of MDR-TB in the Global Era." *International Journal of Tuberculosis and Lung Disease* 2 (11): 869–76.
Farmer, P.E., F. Léandre, J.S. Mukherjee, M.S. Claude, et al.
2001 "Community-Based Approaches to HIV Treatment in Resource-Poor Settings." *Lancet* 358 (9279): 404–9.

Garrett, L.
2000 *Betrayal of Trust: The Collapse of Global Public Health.* New York: Hyperion.

Gray, R.H., T.C. Quinn, D. Serwadda, et al.
2000 "The Ethics of Research in Developing Countries." *New England Journal of Medicine* 343 (5): 361–62.

James, C.L.R.
1963 *The Black Jacobins: Toussaint L'Ouverture and the San Domingo Revolution.* New York: Vintage Books.

Kim, J.Y., J.V. Millen, A. Irwin, and J. Gershman, eds
2000 *Dying for Growth: Global Inequality and the Health of the Poor.* Monroe, Maine: Common Courage Press.

Marshall, P.A., and B.A. Koenig
1996 "Bioethics in Anthropology: Perspectives on Culture, Medicine, and Morality." In *Medical Anthropology: Contemporary Theory and Method*, edited by C.F. Sargent and T.M. Johnson, pp. 349–73. Westport, Conn.: Praeger.

Moreno, J.D.
1997 "Reassessing the Influence of the Nuremberg Code on American Medical Ethics." *Journal of Contemporary Health Law and Policy* 13 (2): 347–60.

Moreno, J.D., and S.E. Lederer
1996 "Revising the History of the Cold War Research Ethics." *Kennedy Institute of Ethics Journal* 6(3): 223–37.

Navarro, V.
1998 "Whose Globalization?" *American Journal of Public Health* 88 (5): 742–43.

Pellegrino, E.
1997 "The Nazi Doctors and Nuremberg: Some Moral Lessons Revisited." *Annals of Internal Medicine* 127 (4): 307–8.

Pellegrino, E.
1999 "The Commodification of Medical and Health Care: The Moral Consequences of a Paradigm Shift from a Professional to a Market Ethic." *Journal of Medicine and Philosophy* 24 (3): 243–66.

Pellegrino, E.D., and D.C. Thomasma
2000 "Dubious Premises – Evil Conclusions: Moral Reasoning at the Nuremberg Trials." *Cambridge Quarterly of Health Care Ethics* 9 (2): 261–74.

Quinn, T.C., M.J. Wawer, N. Sewankambo, et al
2000 "Viral Load and Heterosexual Transmission of Human Immunodeficiency Virus Type I." *New England Journal of Medicine* 342 (13): 921–29.

Schüklenk, U.
2000 "Protecting the Vulnerable: Testing Times for Clinical Research Ethics." *Social Science and Medicine* 51 (6): 969–77.

Shuger, S.
2000 "Supreme Court Cover-Up." Today's Papers, *Slate*, 30 March. Available at *http://slate.msn.com/?id=1004976.*

Sidel, V.W.
1996 "The Social Responsibilities of Health Professionals: Lessons from Their Role in Nazi Germany." *Journal of the American Medical Association* 276 (20): 1679–81.

Smith, R., H. Hiatt, and D. Berwick
1999a "Shared Ethical Principles for Everybody in Health Care: A Working Draft from the Tavistock Group." *British Medical Journal* 318 (7178): 248–51.

Smith, R., H. Hiatt, and D. Berwick
1999b "A Shared Statement of Ethical Principles for Those Who Shape and Give Health Care: A Working Draft from the Tavistock Group." *Annals of Internal Medicine* 130 (2): 143–47.

Sobrino, J.
1988 *Spirituality of Liberation: Toward Political Holiness.* Maryknoll, N.Y.: Orbis Books.

Sohl, P., and H.A. Bassford
1986 "Codes of Medical Ethics: Traditional Foundations and Contemporary Practice." *Social Science and Medicine* 22 (II): 1175–79.

Thomas, L.
1983 *The Youngest Science: Notes of a Medicine-Watcher.* New York: Viking Press.

Tomes, N.
1998 *The Gospel of Germs: Men, Women, and the Microbe in American Life.* Cambridge, Mass.: Harvard University Press.

Virchow, R.L.K.
1849 *Die einheitsrebungen in der wissenschaftlichen medicin.* Berlin: Druck und Verlag von G. Reimer.

Wallerstein, I.
1995a *After Liberalism.* New York: The New Press.

White, R.M.
2000 "Unraveling the Tuskegee Study of Untreated Syphilis." *Archives of Internal Medicine* 160 (5): 585–98.

Wood, E., P. Braitstein, J.S. Schechter, et al.
  2000 "Extent to Which Low-Level Use of
  Antiretroviral Treatment Could Curb the AIDS
  Epidemic in Sub-Saharan Africa." *Lancet* 355
  (9221): 2095–100.
World Bank
  2000a *The Burden of Disease Among the
  Global Poor: Current Situation, Future Trends,
  and Implications for Strategy.* Washington, D.
  C.: World Bank.
World Bank
  2001 *World Development Indicators.* Table
  2.15. Washington, D.C.: International Bank.

World Medical Association
  1983 World Medical Association International Code of Medical Ethics. Amended by
  the Twenty-Second World Medical Assembly,
  Sydney, Australia, August 1968; and the
  Thirty-Fifth World Medical Assembly, Venice,
  Italy, October 1983. Available at *http://www.
  wma.net/e/policy/17-a_e.html.*
Yach, D., and D. Bettcher
  1998b "The Globalization of Public Health,
  II: The Convergence of Self-Interest and Altruism." *American Journal of Public Health* 88
  (5): 738–41.

35

Humanitarianism as a Politics of Life

Didier Fassin

Finally, this idea of man's sacredness gives grounds for reflection that what is here pronounced sacred was, according to ancient mythical thought, the marked bearer of guilt: life itself. (Walter Benjamin, "Critique of Violence")

On March 28, 2003, as on the last Friday of every month, the board of administrators of Médecins sans frontières (MSF; Doctors without Borders) met between five and eleven o'clock in the organization's head office on the first floor of a building in the eleventh arrondissement of Paris. On that particular evening a peculiar atmosphere of expectation and excitement reigned. There was of course the customary rapid overview of the situation in a number of "missions" in various parts of the world where the organization intervenes, followed by a more in-depth examination, with discussion of various specific topics concerning the running of the association and its humanitarian activities. The construction of the "international movement" was also raised: it referred to the network of sections in twenty countries, of which six are actually in a position to conduct operations, and which strives to ensure a coherence of identity and policy in the work of each national body beyond the details of local history and culture. The DNDi (Drugs for Neglected Diseases Initiative) program was another issue addressed: this is an original project that the organization had instigated two years earlier in order to establish, in international collaboration with private charitable foundations and public partners, a program of research and development similar to that of the pharmaceutical industry but dedicated to treatments deemed unprofitable because of the poverty of the Third World patients who need them.

The meeting of the board of administrators is open to the public. All members of the association have the right to participate, as do the employees who carry out the organization's bureaucratic and technical functions. In general, attendance gradually thins out as the evening wears on. But that evening many stayed, waiting for the last item on the agenda. The subject was the state of operations in Iraq. Eight days earlier, American and British troops had begun their bombardment of the country, ending the long run-up to a war that had been declared in a climate of growing international tension and division. MSF has a complex history with the Iraqi state, having refused to intervene during the period of the embargo so as not to succumb to what it considered to be the manipulation of international humanitarian sentiment by the criminal Baathist regime: bringing aid to the Iraqi population would have meant comforting Saddam Hussein's power. Nevertheless, the organization had

Didier Fassin, "Humanitarianism as a Politics of Life," *Public Culture* 19/3 (2007): 499–520.

recently changed its position and had started negotiating its presence with the Iraqi Ministry of Health, as the prospect of war was getting more and more obvious: a medical team of six was therefore present in Baghdad and, after long and difficult discussions in its executive committee, MSF had decided to stay.

The debate was now taking place publicly within the board of administrators. Should the medical team remain in Baghdad, given the danger it would face both from the cornered military of the Iraqi regime and from the predictable rain of American bombs, on the one hand, and given the likely limited efficacy of its presence, since the team was so small compared with the extensive health-care facilities and professionals available in Baghdad, on the other hand? Should the lives of aid workers be risked to save other lives among local populations? The discussion that arose around the presence of these members in Iraq was by all accounts the most intense debate the association has seen in the past few years. However, it avoided the most painful truth – the radical inequality that underlies this transaction in human lives.

I take this scene as a starting point for raising the question of humanitarian action as it constitutes one of the paradigmatic forms of a politics of life, by introducing this dialectic between lives to be saved and lives to be risked. What I call "politics of life" here are politics that give specific value and meaning to human life. They differ analytically from Foucauldian biopolitics, defined as "the regulation of population," in that they relate not to the technologies of power and the way populations are governed but to the evaluation of human beings and the meaning of their existence.[1] Humanitarian intervention is a biopolitics insofar as it sets up and manages refugee camps, establishes protected corridors in order to gain access to war casualties, develops statistical tools to measure malnutrition, and makes use of communication media to bear witness to injustice in the world. But humanitarian intervention is also a politics of life, as I suggest to phrase it, in that it takes as its object the saving of individuals, which presupposes not only risking others but also making a selection of which existences it is possible or legitimate to

save (e.g., by selecting AIDS patients to be given antiretroviral drugs for lack of resources, or deciding whether to provide assistance to people who have participated in massacres). And humanitarian intervention is also a politics of life in that it takes as its object the defense of causes, which presupposes not only leaving other causes aside but also producing public representations of the human beings to be defended (e.g., by showing them as victims rather than combatants and by displaying their condition in terms of suffering rather than the geopolitical situation). What sort of life is implicitly or explicitly taken into account in the political work of humanitarian intervention? This is the question that interests me.

In the first part, I differentiate lives to be saved and lives to be risked as a fundamental distinction between the mere physical and the fundamentally political dimensions of life, that based on the possibility of the subject to decide about it. This is what underlies the debate in MSF on whether or not to stay in Baghdad. In the second part, I discuss saving and risking the lives of others as a basic opposition between humanitarian and military politics of intervention in a supposedly clear separation of victims and enemies. This is what is meant by MSF team members who expose their own lives and the soldiers who expose the civil populations' lives. In the third part, I blur these lines by introducing a series of concrete situations unveiling more complex realities of the politics of life, revealing the aporia of risk taking, discriminating expatriates and nationals, and displacing lines from biological to biographical existences. This is what is implied by the final failure of MSF's mission in Baghdad with the abduction of its members and the departure from Iraq. The three configurations have a common moral background in which the sacred, as Walter Benjamin puts it, resides no longer in man as master of his existence but in "life itself."[2] However, the series of distinctions implied by the differentiation of lives on the battlefield indicates radical inequalities in the human condition.

To display these humanitarian politics of life I have thus chosen a classical dramaturgy with its unity of place, time, and action, because the social drama of the decision to stay seemed to me so emblematic of the tensions and contradictions within these politics. But there is another reason for me to concentrate on this episode: my personal implication in it, as I further discuss. In fact, I do not intend to present a detached examination, "to unveil and denounce truths and violations,"[3] but rather aim to enter, as it were, into the heart of humanitarian activity, to analyze the consequences of choices made and practices implemented – in short, to follow humanitarianism to its logical conclusion. I do it here on the basis of my experience and research primarily with MSF: experience as a member of the board of administrators for four years and research through a series of interviews with its personnel in Paris. The choice of studying this sole organization and moreover this specific event may seem to limit the scope, whereas humanitarianism increasingly appears as a language for states and international agencies as well. But although MSF is a unique organization, to which the award of the Nobel Peace Prize in 1999 nevertheless offered a certain exemplary value, I believe that the lessons from this case study can be applied much more widely, throwing light beyond the work of this particular organization onto the profound meaning and aporia of humanitarian politics of life.

Where It Hurts

During the months preceding the American invasion of Iraq, MSF, like many other aid organizations, undertook exploratory missions in Iraq and neighboring countries with the aim of predicting the consequences of military intervention, in terms both of injured and sick within Iraq and of refugees outside the country.[4] In particular, delicate negotiations were conducted with the Iraqi Ministry of Health and the Red Crescent in order to establish an official framework for the mission, so as to obtain the necessary residence permits and ensure independent operation. A memo of March 11, 2003, makes reference to two proposals that were agreed on by both sides, that is, the Iraqi regime and MSF: providing medical assistance in a hospital in the south of

Baghdad and taking responsibility for the care of a potential 20 million displaced people. But in the days following the signing of that agreement, the Iraqi authorities proved unwilling to keep their side of the bargain, forbidding the volunteers from entering hospitals to evaluate the health situation, on pain of expulsion: in this tense context, the humanitarian newcomers seemed suspect allies.

On March 18, George Bush issued a solemn appeal to Saddam Hussein, calling on him to leave Iraq within forty-eight hours. As the last flights evacuating expatriate staff of international and nongovernmental organizations were leaving Baghdad, and with three hundred of their members stationed in the country awaiting the strike from the Western armies, six members of MSF – including a surgeon, an anaesthesiologist, and a medical doctor – decided to stay despite the evident danger of the coming situation. They included one of MSF's most public figures, the president of the international movement. Other organizations made the same choice; in addition to the International Committee of the Red Cross, Première Urgence and Caritas maintained a skeleton presence. On March 20 the Americans and British launched their attack and the bombardment of the Iraqi capital began. Intense and intermittent, it lasted several days, during which the MSF team in Baghdad had very little chance of leaving its hotel. Several bombs fell nearby, a brutal reminder of how close the danger was. However, team members knew that the hospital where they had begun to work had received only a handful of patients with minor injuries, for which they supplied some surgical equipment. "At the moment the team feels that it is not very useful, but it is preparing for what may come," the desk officer in Paris commented.[5]

This period of looming danger and uncertainty formed the context for what the minutes of the administration board of March 28 call a "debate on the controversial decision to install a team in Baghdad."[6] There was lively discussion around the issue of the team's safety, as there had been a few days earlier, at the meeting of the executive committee that made the decision to stay in Iraq despite the imminence of the American intervention. Conflicting opinions were expressed and deep divisions emerged around whether it was justified to maintain a humanitarian presence in this context: the issues raised concerned both the evaluation of the danger and the anticipated efficacy of the team. As the president of the organization, who was himself in favor of the team's staying, remarked, the stake is the same in every situation involving humanitarian intervention: for those who are in the locality, once the conflict is under way, "there is no guaranteed emergency exit," and this was a question of "the occupational hazards of our profession." Staying in a country at war, he suggested, always has a cost, if not in actual human losses, then at least in terms of the possibility of casualties. Nevertheless, he concluded that "the level of risk we run in Baghdad does not seem any greater than in other places where we operate" and that "we have many teams in danger zones."[7] In the debate the issue of security was, however, overshadowed by another: what reasons were there for the team to remain? If the risks were high, what justified taking them? What use was a team on the spot, within the confined and endangered space where it found itself? It was the question of the usefulness of the mission that generated the most heated exchanges, but arguments on this point were quite contradictory.

Some believed, in effect, that wherever in the world MSF volunteers expose themselves to objective danger they do it to bring "real, concrete assistance," as one desk officer put it. In the case of Iraq, then, the potential contribution of a team of three health professionals was obviously modest compared with the hundreds of doctors, surgeons, and anaesthesiologists working in the thirty-five hospitals in Baghdad, or even, within the specific context of the team's intervention, compared with the sixty doctors, surgeons, and anaesthesiologists, with seventeen operating theaters, in the sole hospital where MSF workers aimed to offer their assistance. Nevertheless, efficacy was the officially accepted justification for the decision to stay. According to the organization's president, "The reason we have representatives in Baghdad is so that they can provide assistance. That is the criterion on which we based out decision." He was echoed by the executive

director: "We had no visibility, but we were aware that spaces could open if we were there." Some were not completely convinced by these responses, particularly given the small number of staff – six people, with only two possibly active in the operating room – relative to the Iraqi casualties that everyone anticipated. The vice president mused: "I have no view on whether it was right or not for the team to remain, but I nevertheless wonder why they decided to stay. It must be for some other reason than saving lives; it's not for their efficacy in terms of number of lives saved. I think we are not following the analysis through fully." One of the organization's founding members offered his own interpretation on this point: "It is part of our charter to be present in war zones – although we know that war surgery is inefficient because it saves only 10 percent more people than if there were no intervention. The question therefore is, to be there or not? If MSF was not there, I would ask why." An administrator retorted: "That's the whole point: the constant dialogue between the principles in our charter and genuine efficacy. Some people put more emphasis on the principles, some on efficacy; you often find that in teams." But the president insisted: "We send people when we think we can provide concrete assistance, not just in the name of an ideal! That should be really clear, unambiguous."[8] Finally, as the atmosphere of the discussion became increasingly tense, a young member of the Fundation Médecins sans frontières, the intellectual branch of the organization, attempted a synthesis between the logics of efficacy and principles: "It seems to me," he said, "that what Médecins sans frontières represents is an ethics in action; it's impossible to dissociate the two, and we are always aware of the limits of our activity. What is part of our principles is that each life saved counts, and that some actions save lives. I think that in Baghdad that space will be there very soon."[9] His analysis might have been correct, but unfortunately not his prediction: actually, events were to prove him wrong.

Four days after this meeting at MSF's Paris office, two members of the team that had remained in Baghdad were abducted. For over a week there was no news of them; the organization refrained from describing them as hostages or releasing their names, in order to avoid any additional risk. Anxiety mounted as Western troops approached. Conditions in the capital grew increasingly unsafe, and finally the hospital where the team had hoped to provide assistance was looted, leaving the four volunteers who were still free with no work. The desk officer for Iraq in Paris deplored the absurdity of the situation in a memo dated April 10: "Médecins sans frontières has had to suspend its activities at the very moment when Baghdad's hospitals are overrun with casualties."[10] After being held for nine days, the two members of the association were finally freed. They revealed that they had been taken by agents of the Iraqi intelligence service. Seventy-two hours later U.S. and British troops arrived in the center of Baghdad. For the team on the spot, which was now able to reach its hospital and get to work there, it seemed that the time had finally come when it could provide real assistance to the victims of the war. Moreover, aid was flooding in, especially from humanitarian organizations that had accumulated staff and equipment on the other side of the border in the expectation of refugees who never arrived, since the anticipated massive population movements had not occurred.

However, two weeks later, on April 28, the decision was made to interrupt the mission. The team was thus leaving Iraq before it had even started its aid operation. Having come to render assistance to "populations in danger," at a time when many had decided to leave a country deemed much too risky, MSF was therefore getting out of the country without having been able to intervene, just when most others, including the Belgian and Dutch sections of the association, were choosing to return or to stay. The team left a little disillusioned, not without criticism of the latecomers among humanitarian organizations who, it claimed, had been too ready to exaggerate the seriousness of the situation in order to sensitize their donors. "Desperately seeking humanitarian crisis," one former president of the association and the desk officer commented ironically, in a text published a few months later.[11] "No humanitarian crisis in Iraq," declared the current president in a French daily newspaper.[12] In order to

justify its surprising decision, MSF had to explain that its presence was henceforth unnecessary. At the end of this operation, although it conformed to both the spirit and the letter of the organization's charter, according to which members "bring aid to populations in distress" and "assess the risks and dangers of missions they carry out," MSF had certainly not shown the efficacy that had been the directors' justification for maintaining a team in Iraq, notably failing to "save lives" as they had hoped.[13] But what merits attention here, more than this failure, which was after all easily understood in the uncertain context of the war, is the strength of emotions aroused by this mission among the executive committee and the board of administrators.[14]

If one starts from the hypothesis that crisis in an institution arises when a situation touches directly on its core issues, then one needs to examine what underlies the conflict around the decision to stay in Iraq. The discussion among the board of administrators may be seen, in Weberian terms, as a confrontation between an ethics of conviction, represented by adherence to principles (to assist populations) regardless of the cost (to endanger aid workers), and an ethics of responsibility, identified with careful assessment of risk (if staying) in relation to the anticipated efficacy (by saving lives). The clash of ethics seems to be resolved in the final formulation of an "ethics in action" differentiating two constructions of life: the life that is saved, that of the victims, and the life that is risked, that of those intervening. Physically, there is no difference between them; philosophically, they are worlds apart. They illustrate the dualism that Giorgio Agamben derives from Aristotle's *Politics*, between the bare life that is to be assisted and the political life that is freely risked, between the *zoe* of "populations" who can only passively await the bombs and the aid workers and the *bios* of the "citizens of the world," the humanitarians who come to render them assistance.[15] Recognizing the inequality between these lives at the level of their meaning – even more than in terms of the threats they objectively face – is not to question either the justification for a specific humanitarian action undertaken in the name of the victims' rights or the good faith of individual humanitarian actors who defend those rights; it is rather to attempt to understand the anthropological configuration in which the two are located. Humanitarian workers have the freedom to sacrifice themselves for a good cause, whereas the Iraqi population shares the condition of those who can be sacrificed in a dirty war. In contemporary society this inequality is perhaps both the most ethically intolerable, in that it concerns the meaning of life itself, and the most morally tolerated, since it forms the basis for the principle of altruism.[16] And it is this truth that humanitarianism reveals.

The scene I describe above therefore has a general relevance. For me it also has a more personal resonance. As vice president of MSF at the time, I was one of the principal actors involved. And no doubt it holds a truth for me, too, since it was the last board of administrators meeting I attended. To understand the issues related to this tense discussion, one has to be reminded that in the humanitarian ethics the potential sacrifice of one's life reasserts the sacredness of others' lives, which is precisely denied by the military necessities. This is what I now explore.

Sacred Lives, Sacrificed Lives

Humanitarian intervention has become an important mode and even a dominant frame of reference for Western political intervention in global scenes of misfortune, both in cases of armed conflict and natural disasters and around their more or less direct consequences in the form of epidemics, famine, physical injury, and emotional trauma. No war is now without its humanitarian corridors and its humanitarian workers. And no Western military intervention into another country is now without its justification on humanitarian grounds.[17] Previously the province of nongovernmental organizations like the Red Cross, MSF, and many others in their wake and intergovernmental bodies, notably the United Nations High Commission for Refugees, humanitarian intervention has become a policy of nation-states, whether because governments are developing their own activity in the field (France, for example, has

had several ministers for humanitarian aid) or because they delegate it to paragovernmental agencies (such as the Oxford Committee for Famine Relief [Oxfam] in the United Kingdom). Whatever form it takes, what appears to be emerging is a humanitarian government at both the global and the local level, in the camps for displaced persons there and in the social services for illegal immigrants and asylum seekers here.[18] This is a government that defines itself through the introduction of morality into politics, in a so-called New World Order that appears to have succeeded the Realpolitik of the Cold War.

A common interpretation of this new situation tends to distinguish and to contrast politics and humanitarianism, declaring that the latter is gradually replacing the former or even announcing the advent of humanitarianism and the end of politics. "Humanitarianism is not a political issue and it should remain separate from political maneuvering," asserts Rony Brauman, a former president of MSF. Pointing to the renaissance of nongovernmental humanitarianism during the 1970s and 1980s, at a time when communism's star was waning, he even sees in this new configuration a sort of historical fluid mechanics based on the principle of the communicating vessels: "It is as if, during these periods when the ideological tide is going out, humanitarian action comes to occupy the space left vacant by politics."[19] Agamben offers a more radical version of this thesis, suggesting that "the separation of politics and humanitarianism that we are witnessing today represents the last phase of the separation of human rights from civil right." For the Italian philosopher, the image of the refugee becomes "the most significant sign of bare life in our era," and he sees the refugee camp as the "biopolitical paradigm." This being the case, humanitarianism, insofar as it distances itself from the figure of the nation-state, abandons the political field.[20] However, I believe that the contemporary world does not become more intelligible viewed in these terms, and one may doubt whether there exists, in one's own society or in any society, a space empty of politics or even a space outside politics – all the more given that these interpretations relegate the dominated and the excluded to this depoliticized space, leaving the political space to the dominant and the included. They are thus doubly problematic – first empirically, for all investigations show that on the contrary, forms of political life continue to arise even in the camps, and second ethically, since this reading appears to reinforce the domination and exclusion by denying the possibility of a political life to those who are subjected to them in practice.[21] Other avenues therefore need to be explored.

In fact everything suggests that rather than become separate, humanitarianism and politics are tending to merge – in governmental, inter-governmental, and nongovernmental spheres. In France at least three former presidents or vice presidents of MSF have become ministers; some have been elected to political office, others have entered the civil service at high levels – not only in the traditional aid sector, but also in health and social welfare. Conversely, former ministers of social affairs or of health have become presidents of Action contre la faim (Action Against Hunger) and the French Red Cross. Thus one is seeing a humanitarianization of national health and social policy and a politicization of humanitarian organizations. At the international level the process is even more marked, and one sees how, particularly since the Rwandan genocide, with the French army's belated Operation Turquoise, Western military action in arenas of disaster or conflict is conducted under the banner of humanitarianism, and increasingly insistent attempts are made to bring nongovernmental organizations on board.[22] When they intervened in Kosovo and Iraq, the governments allied to the North Atlantic Treaty Organization (NATO) and to the United States, respectively, spoke of the humanitarian imperative, thus confirming that the legitimacy of interventions was being displaced from the legal sphere (since they did not have the support of the United Nations) to the moral sphere (the defense of human rights and even, more restrictively and more specifically, the humanitarian right). Thus one can speak both of the humanitarianization of international crisis management and of the politicization of the nongovernmental humanitarian field. Rather than a dissociation, what one is actually seeing is increasingly a merging of politics and humanitarianism.

But what sort of humanitarian politics is being promoted? Bradol, president of MSF since June 2000, is probably the organization representative who expresses with the greatest force the founding ethic of humanitarian intervention – saving lives.[23] "By resisting the elimination of a particular sector of humanity, humanitarianism can create a way of life based on the satisfaction of offering unconditionally, to a person in danger of dying, the aid which enables him to survive," he writes. "It is on this condition that victories – always by definition provisional and partial – over this politics of the worst are possible." His moral geography of the world draws two opposing continents: that of the "established political powers" whose "role is to decide on human sacrifice, to divide the governed into those who must live and those who may die," and that of the "humanitarian project," which has "taken the arbitrary and radical stand of attempting to aid those sacrificed by society." The former relates to the "cannibal ideal" since "building the international order always requires its quota of victims." The latter derives from a "subversive dimension" since "humanitarian aid is offered as a priority to those whose need to live is threatened by the indifference or the overt hostility of others." Thus this binary world opposes a politics of death, that of the criminal states, to a politics of life, that of the humanitarian agents.[24] Politics is defined in moral terms: it consists of a new war of an axis of good against an axis of evil. By an astonishing paradox, at the very moment when some countries are throwing themselves into a moral crusade against their demonized enemies and appropriating the vocabulary and symbolism of humanitarianism, nongovernmental organizations are distancing themselves while nevertheless casting their discourse in the same rhetorical mold. This remarkable mimetism – which operates in both directions – should nevertheless not lead one into a form of relativism that would set warmongers and humanitarians on the same level. The fact that the rhetoric is reproduced does not mean that the politics are equivalent. While it may be fallacious to reduce the war makers to a consistently barbaric "necropolitics" and humanitarians to a purely altruistic "biopolitics," it is much more interesting to compare them in terms of the politics of life they effectively engender.[25]

The humanitarian politics of life is based on an entrenched standpoint in favor of the "side of the victims."[26] The world order, it supposes, is made up of the powerful and the weak. Humanitarian action takes place in the space between the two, being deployed among the weak as it denounces the powerful. It therefore relates to only one part of humanity – the one on the wrong side of life. It intervenes "in places where life is not worth a dollar."[27] It is aimed at those who are considered at risk of physical disappearance and incapable of maintaining their own existence. Admittedly, not all "survival" situations, as the humanitarian agents readily term them, are so dramatic; nor do they involve the same risks to life, but the scene is very much that of life under threat. The lives in question are those of refugees and displaced persons in camps (over there), and the homeless and asylum seekers at accommodation centers (over here), and it is largely the same organizations – like MSF and Médecins du monde – that look after them in an effort to challenge the boundaries between poor and rich countries, preferring to acknowledge the existence of "victims" in both.

This process essentializes the victims: against the thickness of biographies and the complexity of history, it draws a figure to which humanitarian aid is directed.[28] This construction is certainly necessary to justify humanitarianism, and it is also sufficient to it in that it has no need for the point of view of the persons in question. Moreover, in the configuration thus defined, these persons often willingly submit to the category assigned to them: they understand the logic of this construction, and they anticipate its potential benefits. The ontological principle of inequality finds its concrete manifestation in the act of assistance through which individuals identified as victims are established. They are those for whom the gift cannot imply a counter-gift, since it is assumed that they can only receive. They are the indebted of the world. In the system of Christian values that not only forms part of the history of the humanitarian movement but

also still informs the thinking of some of its members, there is no greater gift than that of one's own life. It is easy then to understand to what extent MSF's decision to go to Iraq plays on this ontology of inequality, by distinguishing those whose life is passively exposed, because they are at the mercy of the bombs, and those whose life can be freely sacrificed, because they have decided to stay.

This courageous decision – all the more courageous given that it was, as could be predicted from the moment it was made, of hardly any use – should moreover be understood from the point of view of the armed forces that intervene in present-day conflicts. In this respect, the ethical norms of the Western military establishment, clearly influenced by the general evolution of the value attached to human life, underwent a profound change over the course of the twentieth century: from the carnage of the World War I battlefields, the move was to a maximum avoidance of military losses among Western troops after the collective traumas of the Algerian war, for France, and above all of the Vietnam war, for the United States.

The corollary of the "zero death" doctrine, however, is the rhetoric of "collateral damage." Reducing the risks on one's own side implies increasing them on the enemy's side, including – in conflicts officially launched to "liberate" or "protect" populations – among civilians. When NATO intervened in Kosovo in 1999, not only did the strategic choice of an aerial operation make it possible to limit losses among the Allied forces, at the expense of the human casualties that a bombardment inevitably involves, but the tactical decision to have the planes fly at a high altitude in order to make them inaccessible to Serb weapons also necessarily brought with it a reduced level of ballistic precision: more than five hundred civilians were killed, but not one pilot.[29] When the United States invaded Iraq in 2003, in addition to the fact that there too the massive bombardment that had preceded and prepared the invasion had generated large numbers of casualties, including many civilians, the subsequent measures to ensure the security of American and British troops resulted in widespread preventive use of firearms, again in order to reduce the risk of soldiers being killed themselves. A year after military operations began, the army of occupation had suffered about a hundred deaths, compared to the one hundred thousand estimated by a British epidemiological investigation among the Iraqi population.[30] In both cases, the marked difference between the number of deaths on the two sides of the intervention offers an a posteriori measure of the implicit politics of an a priori differential evaluation of human beings: in Kosovo, sacrificing the life of several hundred is the condition of preserving the life of one individual; in Iraq, the life of one Western soldier is worth one thousand times the life of the inhabitants of a country in which the soldiers are intervening to "liberate" or "protect" them. One could however consider it moral progress that such a calculation is even possible: at the time of the first Gulf War, estimates of Iraqi deaths varied from a few thousand to several hundred thousand, but no attempt was made to count them either by the Allied troops or by the defeated regime. When no one counts deaths, it means that lives barely count.

In these conditions, the spectacular and controversial gesture of MSF members who decided to stay in Baghdad when the bombardment was about to begin issues a challenge to this politics of lives that do not count. By exposing themselves to danger, they opened up the question of the equality of lives in a concrete, immediate way: all lives become equal again, as vulnerable for Iraqis as for the humanitarian agents who are assisting them. The sacrifice to which they consented (risking being killed) shifted the radical inequality between the sacred life on one side (Western soldiers) and the sacrificed life on the other side (local civilians). By this heroic act long debated and weighed, the humanitarian politics of life offers a striking counterpoint to the military politics of life. At least it appears to.

Lives Valued, Lives Told

In effect this equality does not long withstand the test of the facts. The hostage taking during the first days of the U.S. intervention brought the humanitarian ideal back to harsh reality. The abduction of two team members paralyzed not only their four colleagues but also the entire organization, which initially halted all activity and then resolved to withdraw the mission.[31] On the Iraqi side, no life was saved; not one injured person was treated. Above all, it became clear that the organization itself could not countenance risking lives: when the danger shifted from the hypothetical to the real, the intervention was suspended in order to avoid risk to the staff abducted, and when the two members were released by their abductors, at a time when other aid organizations were setting to work in the vast arena of a far from pacified country, the French section of MSF left Iraq, arguing that the health situation did not after all give cause for concern and that conditions of operation could in no way be considered secure. The trauma of the abduction effectively highlighted the contradictions inherent in a declared politics of risking lives that did not hold up in the face of real danger. The case of Iraq is exemplary. Each time a member of a humanitarian organization has been taken hostage in recent years, in Colombia or the Caucasus, the mission in question has been wholly diverted from its initial goals and has concentrated on a single aim – saving the abducted companion. Moreover the protagonists in conflicts are well aware of the Western world's sensitivity to hostage taking and in some regions of the world take cynical advantage of it, unconcerned about the difference between soldiers and aid workers, private security guards and foreign journalists, and forcing states and nongovernmental organizations into protracted and difficult negotiations in which the value of the lives of those who have been abducted is assessed and translated into cash terms, often very specifically and precisely.[32] But even within this context, even among the members of humanitarian organizations, not all lives have the same value.

The most common distinction MSF makes in its missions (like all foreign organizations, whether involved in aid or development) is between "expatriates" and "nationals." Expatriates who come almost exclusively from Western countries are volunteers of the organization. Nationals are local agents who are considered as mere paid employees. This distinction, which is seen as simply an operational matter, not only involves huge differences in salary (and also contractual terms, since many local agents are recruited for limited periods, sometimes paid by the day) and in rights (particularly in decision and voting processes) but also has consequences regarding social and political protection. On the one hand, in the case of serious illness the medical coverage for expatriates is equivalent to that of the French system, while for nationals there is usually limited or no health insurance. Even when MSF was involved in an ambitious international program to promote antiretroviral drugs, its own local agents suffering from AIDS, particularly in Africa, were not receiving treatment.[33] On the other hand, when violent disturbances arose, while expatriates were usually spared, nationals enjoyed no institutional immunity. One inquiry reveals that almost six of every ten deaths among aid workers over the past twenty years were of local agents, but this is certainly a substantial underestimate, particularly with regard to Rwanda, as many of the locally employed staff did not appear on aid organizations' staff lists.[34] In other words, even within these institutions – as in development and cooperative organizations, too – distinctions are set up between foreign staff, almost always Western and white, and local employees. These distinctions, in addition to the material advantages conferred on foreign staff, are augmented by much more serious disadvantages that for the local staff, concern their very survival, whether they are endangered by illness or war. The AIDS epidemic on the one hand, and the Rwandan genocide on the other, cruelly exposed the workings of this process of exclusive categorization. Thus, within the humanitarian arena itself hierarchies of humanity are passively established but rarely identified for what they are – politics of life that at moments of crisis, result in the formation of two groups, those whose status protects their sacred character and those whom the institutions may sacrifice against their will. The protagonists in conflict are well aware of this distinction when they abduct people. They know that only foreigners have market value. Their compatriots are usually executed, as was

the case in August 2006 for seventeen Sri Lankan Action contre la faim humanitarian workers killed by military forces.

But the Iraq case unveils another truth. Until now, the hypothetical framework for analysis of humanitarianism has been that lives are saved by its intervention. This was of course the official reason given for maintaining a team in Baghdad. In actual fact the abduction, followed by the hasty withdrawal, meant that no Iraqi life was saved. This case is much less exceptional than has been suggested. Teams may arrive too late at disaster sites (where the civil security agents of large countries often arrive more quickly); they may not have the space to intervene with enough freedom and security (which the parties to conflict often refuse them); or local actors may take responsibility themselves for the injured and sick (when their health provision structures allow them to do so). This is where the second dimension of humanitarian action comes into play: providing assistance is of course important, but so is bearing witness.[35] Although testimony is an integral part of any humanitarian intervention, it takes on an even greater importance when the offer of assistance is late, impossible, or pointless – not only because it becomes the main focus of intervention, but also because it is then the only justification that can be given for it, either by agents or by populations. In Chechnya, where it is considered dangerous for humanitarian organizations to be present because of the abductions and murders, as in Palestine, where it seems pointless given the medical and surgical treatment available through local structures, bearing witness is a crucial activity. In the first case it is based on remotely controlled structures (from Moscow, where a number of missions have been established); in the second it uses the resources of psychiatry and psychology (making it possible to document the reality of trauma caused by the conflict).[36] And humanitarian testimony takes a particular form. Since, as has been seen, the organizations place themselves "on the side of the victims," provide assistance to them, and defend their cause, they produce one truth: that of the "victims."

By becoming their spokespersons, humanitarian organizations introduce another distinction into the public arena – the distinction between those who are subjects (the witnesses who testify to the misfortunes of the world) and those who can exist only as objects (the unfortunate whose suffering is testified to in front of the world). Of course, the humanitarian agents who collect accounts or carry out inquiries to reveal the violence or injustice suffered by oppressed or displaced or bombed populations base their testimony partly on what the victims of this violence or these injustices say about them. Their third-person testimony is grounded on first-person testimonies. However, the requirements of defending causes and the logic of their intervention lead them to what might be termed a humanitarian reduction of the victim. On the one hand, all that is retained of people's words is what contributes to a telling image in the public space: both the Chechen fighter and the Palestinian stone thrower become suffering beings who can only be described in terms of their physical injuries and psychological trauma. On the other hand, the individuals in question tend to conform to this portrait, knowing that it will have an impact on public opinion, and thus offer to the humanitarian agents the part of their experience that feeds the construction of them as human beings crushed by fate.

Of course, there is no single truth of their condition, and the narrative offered by victims to the exclusion of any other reality is just one of the possible truths through which their experience can be rendered intelligible, particularly given that by dint of being presented under this light of suffering, they end up perceiving themselves, too, at least in part, as victims. However, from the perspective of a politics of life and an ontology of inequality, the issue is not that the historical context and geopolitical dimensions of conflicts, the strategic games and contradictory interests, are erased by the representation of war situations given by those whose only interest is in the "insulted and humiliated," to use Brauman's formula. It is rather that if one believes that what distinguishes humans from other living beings is language and meaning and that what makes human life unique is therefore that it can be recounted, as Hannah Arendt asserts, then humanitarian testimony establishes two forms

of humanity and two sorts of life in the public space: there are those who can tell stories and those whose stories can be told only by others.[37] With this new dividing line, life is no longer, as it was before, biological (the life that is risked or sacrificed); it is henceforth biographical (the life that is lived but that others narrate). More tenuous and less visible, it is nevertheless essential to what constitutes beings insofar as they are human. At the very time when humanitarian action is shifting from bare life to qualified life, from physical survival to social existence, a new inequality is insinuating itself into humanitarian politics of life.

Humanitarian action by nongovernmental organizations, from the birth of the International Committee of the Red Cross to the emergence of the movement inaugurated by MSF, has historically been constructed in response to the inhumanity of war, a way of restoring the basic principles of humanity. Whether their origins are Christian, as among the charitable religious orders, or secular, with philanthropic societies, these principles have two aspects that refer back to the two senses of the word *humanity* itself. On the one hand, it is a concept that suggests that humanity, as a collective of human beings, is one and indivisible – a concept that, as one knows, is both recent and fragile. On the other hand, it is a sentiment that manifests an individual's gesture of humanity toward fellow humans who are suffering or in danger – a sentiment that gives a concrete sense of belonging to the human species. This paradigm has been established in contrast to others that either imply distinctions among human beings (through the idea of race, for example) or promote indifference to distant others (particularly by whipping up nationalist sentiment).

In contemporary conflicts the soldiers who intervene, in the name of either their country or higher concerns (leaving aside the question of whether this often largely rhetorical distinction is genuine), do not in theory negate the idea and sentiment of humanity; however, their practice calls it into question. The discourse of their governments and their officers generally leads them to construct the enemy as a category of humanity sufficiently distant to be killed in large numbers and without compassion. The inhumanity of contemporary war resides no longer in carnage shared roughly equally between the opposing sides but, rather, in the unequal value accorded to lives on the battlefield: the sacred life of the Western armies of intervention, in which each life lost is counted and honored, versus the expendable life of not only the enemy troops but also their civilian populations, whose losses are only roughly numbered and whose corpses end up in mass graves. In the face of these politics of life, both inhuman and inhumane, humanitarian organizations call for a politics of life that could reestablish solidarity among human beings and give equal value to all lives.

But neither the actors involved nor their usual commentators are sufficiently aware of the triple problematic of the humanitarian politics of life. First, it distinguishes lives that may be risked (humanitarian agents) from lives that can only be sacrificed (the populations among whom they intervene): this is illustrated by the Iraqi case. Second, within the movement itself it separates lives into those with higher value (expatriate humanitarian workers) and those that are accorded only limited protection (national staff): this is what the abductions starkly reveal. Third, it establishes a distinction between lives that can be narrated in the first person (those who intervene) and lives that are recounted only in the third person (the voiceless in the name of whom intervention is done): testimony, operating as an autobiographical account for the former and the construction of a cause for the latter, reveals this split. Thus as one gets deeper into humanitarianism a series of dimensions of what may be called a complex ontology of inequality unfolds that differentiates in a hierarchical manner the values of human lives. What I have shown here in relation to MSF holds in general for all humanitarian organizations, whether nongovernmental or supranational, whatever their different orientations, when one considers their ethics not through theoretical principles but in practical operations.

By describing these problems as an aporia, I intend to demonstrate that these contradictions are both constitutive of the humanitarian project and effectively insurmountable within the value systems of Western societies, particularly when considering the tension that exists between the claimed sacredness of life (which is no more viable in the context of wartime violence than in conditions of structural violence) and the expressed force of compassion (which makes it possible to maintain up to a certain point the thread of solidarity, even at the price of ontological inequality). Far from the ideological criticisms traditionally aimed at humanitarian organizations – which their agents in any case readily take up themselves – this critical perspective stresses the contradictions that exist in contemporary moral economies, well beyond the sphere of intervention of humanitarian organizations themselves, in what characterizes the political disorder of the world: the inequality of lives.

NOTES

Translated by Rachel Gomme

1 On the distinction between politics of life and biopolitics, see Didier Fassin, "La biopolitique n'est pas une politique de la vie" ("Biopolitics Is Not a Politics of Life"), *Sociologies et sociétés* 38 (2006): 35–48. For Michel Foucault, biopolitics correspond to the technologies defining, studying, counting, controlling, and, more generally, "normalizing" populations. See Michel Foucault, *The History of Sexuality: An Introduction* (New York: Vintage Books, 1990).

2 See Walter Benjamin, "Critique of Violence," in *Selected Writings*, vol. 1, *1913–1926* (1921: repr., Cambridge, Mass.: Harvard University Press, Belknap, 1996).

3 As formulated by Peter Redfield, "Doctors, Borders, and Life in Crisis," *Current Anthropology* 20 (2005): 328–61. Redfield's aim is rather to consider humanitarianism as "an array of particular embodied, situated practices emanating from the humanitarian desire to alleviate suffering of others" (330). I, however, think that critical thinking can and must emerge from within the analysis of these practices and this desire.

4 See, for instance, "Reflections on the U.S. Military's Provision of Assistance during and Immediately after Conflict with Iraq"

(draft internal paper, MSF, February 18, 2003).

5   From the minutes of the meeting of the administration board of the MSF, March 28, 2003 (hereafter cited as MSF minutes). These sessions are always recorded and afterward transcribed and summarized.

6   MSF minutes.

7   MSF minutes.

8   MSF minutes. Subsequently, however, in a retrospective evaluation of his organization's activity during this period, Jean-Hervé Bradol, president of MSF, was to comment: "On the whole, Iraq has been a small emergency for us" (Bradol's internal report: MSF, "Rapport moral 2003").

9   MSF minutes.

10 MSF, *Messages: Journal interne de Médecins sans frontières*, no. 124 (May 2003): 2.

11 Rony Brauman and Pierre Salignon, "Irak: La posture du missionnaire" ("Iraq: The Missionary Position"), in *A l'ombre des guerres justes* (*In the Shadow of Just Wars*), ed. Fabrice Weissman (Paris: Flammarion, 2003), 287.

12 References are taken from Brauman and Salignon, "Irak: La posture du missionnaire," 275–91; and from an interview with Bradol in *Le Figaro* on March 24, 2004. These comments may be contrasted with the analysis of the postwar situation by Médecins du monde (Doctors of the World), in "L'Irak en plein chaos" ("Iraq in Full Chaos"), *Médecins du monde: Le journal destiné aux donateurs* (September 2003): "Despite the end of the military conflict, Iraq finds itself in an alarming situation. The consequences of war are numerous: insecurity, shortages, risk of epidemics, technological backwardness. The international network of Médecins du monde has massively responded to the Iraqi emergency" (2).

13 MSF, "La charte de Médecins sans frontières" ("Charter of Médecins sans frontières"), www.paris.msf.org/site/site.nsf/pages/charte (accessed June 14, 2007).

14 The assessment of failure comes from the desk officer in charge of the program, Pierre Salignon, in an interview in *Le Monde* on May 8, 2003: "For those who have tried to achieve an independent humanitarian action, difficulties have been overwhelming and, in the end, we have failed."

15 See Giorgio Agamben, *Homo sacer: Le pouvoir souverain et la vie nue*, trans. Marilène Raiola (Paris: Seuil, 1997); published in English as *Homo Sacer: Sovereign Power and Bare Life*, trans. Daniel Heller-Roazen (Stanford, Calif.: Stanford University Press, 1998).

16 See Didier Fassin, "L'ordre moral du monde: Essai d'anthropologie de l'intolérable" ("The Moral Order of the World: Toward an Anthropology of the Intolerables"), in *Les constructions de l'intolérable* (*The Construction of the Intolerable*), ed. Didier Fassin and Patrice Bourdelais (Paris: La Découverte, 2005), 17–50.

17 Note the evolution from Michael Pugh, "Military Intervention and Humanitarian Action: Trends and Issues," *Disasters* 22 (1998): 339–51 (on the war in Bosnia), to Susan Woodward, "Humanitarian War: A New Consensus," *Disasters* 25 (2001): 331–44 (on the bombing of Kosovo).

18 On the notion of humanitarian government, see Didier Fassin, "Humanitarianism, a Non-governmental Government," in *Nongovernmental Politics*, ed. Michel Feher (New York: Zone Books, 2007), 149–59.

19 See Rony Brauman, *L'action humanitaire* (*Humanitarian Action*) (Paris: Flammarion, 2000), 61. He recognizes, however, that "humanitarianism cannot be considered apolitical" (61).

20 See Agamben, *Homo sacer: Le pouvoir souverain et la vie nue*, 145.

21 See Liisa Malkki, *Purity and Exile: Violence, Memory, and National Cosmology among Hutu Refugees in Tanzania* (Chicago: Chicago University Press, 1995); and Michel Agier, *Aux bords du monde, les réfugiés* (*Refugees at the Margins of the World*) (Paris: Flammarion, 2002).

22 See the testimony of Bernard Granjon, then in charge of Médecins du monde's mission in Rwanda, about his discussion with François Mitterrand, "Quatre-vingt minutes avec François Mitterand" ("Eighty Minutes with François Mitterrand"), in "Le génocide des Tutsis du Rwanda: Une abjection pour l'humanité, un échec pour les humanitaires" ("The Tutsi Genocide in Rwanda: Abjection for Humanity, Failure for Humanitarianism"), special issue, *Humanitaire: Enjeux, pratiques, débats*, no. 10(2004): 37–42.

23 See Jean-Hervé Bradol, "L'ordre international cannibale et l'action humanitaire" ("The Sacrificial International Order and Humanitarian Action"), in Weissman, *A l'ombre des guerres justes*, 32.

24 This dichotomy is of course destabilized when military and humanitarian agents become one, as described by Sherene Razack, *Dark Threats and White Knights: The Somalia Affair: Peacekeeping and the New Imperialism* (Toronto: University of Toronto Press, 2004).

25 "Necropolitics" is a concept proposed by Achille Mbembe as a corollary to Foucault's biopolitics; see Achille Mbembe, "Necropolitics," *Public Culture* 15 (2003): 11–40.

26 See Jean-Hervé Bradol, "Le camp des victimes" ("The Side of the Victims") in "1971–2001: 30 ans d'action humanitaire" ("1971–2001: Thirty Years of Humanitarian Action"), special issue, *Infos Médecins sans frontières* 89 (2001): 2.

27 See Laurence Hugues, "Liberia, là où la vie ne vaut pas une guinée" ("Liberia: Where Life Is Not Worth a Guinea"), *Messages: Journal interne de Médecins sans frontières*, no. 124 (2003): 3–4.

28 On the process of constructing victims, see Didier Fassin, "La cause des victimes" ("The Cause of the Victims"), *Les temps modernes*, no. 627 (2004): 73–91.

29 See the analysis proposed by Michael Ignatieff, "The New American Way of War," *New York Review of Books* 47, no. 12 (2000).

30 See the estimate suggested in Les Roberts, Riyadh Lafta, Richard Garfield, Jamal Khudhairi, and Gilbert Burnham, "Mortality before and after the 2003 Invasion of Iraq: Cluster Sample Survey," *Lancet* 364 (2004): 1857–64.

31 In the organization's internal critical journal, significantly called *DazibAG* (no. 125 [2003]: 27), François Calas, the head of the MSF team in Iraq and one of those who had been abducted by the Iraqi police, publicly expressed his frustration as the organization left the country: "The decision taken by the French section to leave Baghdad seemed to me very precipitate and has been justified after the fact on fallacious grounds. Rather than qualifying the crisis, we disqualified it. Ironically, one could say that we've come full

circle and because we failed to anticipate events, haste prevailed from beginning to end of our intervention."

32 The financial conditions of Arjan Erkel's release in Dagestan in 2004 have been publicly exposed, with the Dutch government claiming 1 million from the Swiss section of MSF to reimburse the ransom it paid to the kidnappers. See Philippe Ryfman, "Humanitarian Action on Trial," *Messages: Journal interne de Médecins sans frontières*, no. 137 (2005): 16.

33 The decision to give free antiretroviral drugs to national staff was finally reached by the board of directors in 2003. Nevertheless, Bradol notes that during his field visits, local staff members "were not usually aware of this decision." See MSF, "Rapport moral 2003."

34 The epidemiological study is Mani Sheik, Maria Isabel Gutierrez, Paul Bolton, Paul Spiegel, Michel Thieren, and Gilbert Burnham, "Deaths among Humanitarian Workers," *British Medical Journal* 321 (2000): 166–8. Between 1985 and 1998, 382 deaths were reported among staff of United Nations and nongovernmental bodies, of which almost a third occurred during the genocide in Rwanda. However, Bradol, who conducted a mission for MSF in 1994, comments: "If we asked humanitarian organizations for the list of their employees who died during the genocide, 90% would be unable to give it. And this gives an indication of what has or has not been done to help people when they really needed help." See Bradol, "La commémoration amnésique des humanitaires" ("The Amnesic Commemoration of Humanitarian Actors"), *Humanitaire: Enjeux, pratiques, débats*, no. 10 (2004): 12.

35 Historically, the emergence of the second age of humanitarianism, with the "French doctors" returning from the war in Biafra, was a reaction to the silence of the Red Cross, wedded to its principle of neutrality. Testimony in favor of the victims becomes, for MSF and even more for Médecins du monde, a key dimension of their action. See the six volumes of the series *Prises de parole publiques de MSF (Public Positions)*, ed. Laurence Binet (Paris: MSF, 2003–7), on Ethiopia 1984, El Salvador 1988, Rwanda 1994 and 1995, and refugees from Rwanda 1994–97.

36 On the testimony of MSF and Médecins du monde, compared with that of the local organizations Gaza Community Mental Health Programme (GCMHP) and Natal, the Israel Trauma Center for Victims of Terror and War, see Didier Fassin and Richard Rechtman, *L'empire du traumatisme: Enquête sur la condition de victime* (*The Empire of Trauma: Inquiry on the Condition of Victims*) (Paris: Flammarion, 2007), 281–319.

37 On life as "a story with enough coherence to be told," see Hannah Arendt, *The Human Condition* (Chicago: University of Chicago Press, 1958), 85.

Part VII

Postcolonial Disorders

Introduction

The final part of this reader groups a set of recent essays under the heading "Post-colonial Disorders." This phrase, taken from an edited collection by this title (M.-J. Good et al. 2008), refers both to emergent realities that have come increasingly to occupy medical anthropologists and to theoretical concerns and an emerging framework for writing about subjectivity in the early twenty-first century. These essays thus point to one of the possible futures for medical anthropology.

Postcolonial Disorders was conceived as an effort to re-think the nature of subjectivity – "everyday modes of experience, the social and psychological dimensions of individual lives, the psychological qualities of social life, the constitution of the subject, and forms of subjection" (B. Good et al. 2008:1) – found in the diverse places where anthropologists work today. At the beginning of a year long seminar which had long focused on "culture and mental health," we invited speakers to rethink some aspect of their work on subjectivity by replacing the common anthropological trope "culture" with the analytic category "postcoloniality" or "the postcolonial." What emerged from that project was a set of reflections on "disordered states," on political violence and the way it shapes individual lives (Aretxaga 2005); on labor migration and social displacement and the nature of subjectivity of those on the margins or borderlands; on the close linking of international health and political efforts to control pandemic infectious diseases and the resistances these efforts have produced in many postcolonial societies; on the complex space occupied by psychiatry in such settings; and on the haunting presence of colonial trauma and colonial memories associated with eruptions of social and psychological "disorders" and the diverse forms of humanitarian and medical responses. These are precisely the issues being addressed today by many medical anthropologists.

"Postcolonialism" was read broadly by many who presented to that Harvard seminar, suggesting relations between powerful political, economic, and state entities and those that are marginalized; recognition that anthropological knowledge categories are often resisted by those who experience research as reproducing colonial relations; and a critique of classic understandings of culture that allow the ghostly phantoms of colonial experience to remain beyond the reach of analysis. The book called for a broad project of investigating and theorizing subjects in postcolonial societies and situations, addressing "disorders" while taking seriously the special complexity of investigating social "pathologies" and "social suffering" (Kleinman et al. 1997; Das 2007). And it argued that medical and psychological anthropologists today carry out their work precisely among the dilemmas represented by this framing of the field. The essays in this final part of the reader, as well as a number of those in earlier sections of the book, can be read as contributing to this project, suggesting the benefits of conversations between medical anthropologists and those exploring postcolonial or political subjectivity and disordered states.

The section begins with a short essay by Byron and Mary-Jo Good that takes up "amok," an old category within medical anthropology, studies of "culture bound disorders" (e.g. Simons et al. 1985) and comparative psychiatry (e.g. Yap 1974). The Goods discovered that while most anthropological and psychiatric discussions of "amok" have focused on individual, dissociative violence, the Indonesian term *mengamuk*, to run amok, was often used by journalists during the repressive New Order regime of Indonesian president Suharto to describe unrest and threats of violence by Indonesian crowds, particularly during political campaigns. Analyzing sources for this use of *amuk* takes the reader back to British and Dutch colonial psychiatry with unexpected results. This reading opens a space for analyzing the political and psychological origins of the divide between "order" and "disorder" as deriving from Indonesia's terrifying "year of living dangerously," 1965–66, when between 600,000 and a million citizens were identified as Communists and killed.

The second essay, by Erica James, explores the political economy of "trauma" among Haitian women and men seeking restitution for the terrible violence enacted against them during the reign of terror following the ouster of legally elected President Jean-Bertrand Aristide. James analyzes the United States' perception of Haitians as threatening to "security" at precisely the time citizens were living the experience of insecurity. She introduces an analysis of the "occult economies of trauma" that led the humanitarian apparatus to "generate new forms of victimization" in the name of documenting and verifying human rights violations deserving of recompense, exploring the subjective effects of the production of "traumatic citizenship." And she argues that responses to Haitian politics cannot be understood outside of the historic imagination generated by an independence movement at the heart of New World slavery, and goes on to analyze how American foreign aid and humanitarian organizations reproduce colonial violence in the aftermath of recognized states of emergency.

These themes are picked up and extended in Mariella Pandolfi's analysis of the humanitarian apparatus in Albania and Kosovo. Pandolfi is one of a group of anthropologists developing critical analyses of the convergences between military and humanitarian forms of intervention, and the role of international organizations as "operators of a new military-humanitarian form of governance" (cf. Redfield 2005; Malkki 1996; Nordstrom 2005; Fassin and Rechtman 2009). Pandolfi draws together Foucault's analytics of biopolitics with Agamben's (1988) challenging formulation of "states of exception" to explore the logic of this emergent form of mobile sovereignty.

Sarah Willen shows that many of these issues are relevant to the political, juridical, bureaucratic, and humanitarian response to a group of 13,000 men, women and children who fled Darfur, Sudan, Eritrea, Somalia and the Ivory Coast, arriving at the border of Israel seeking protection. The resulting "unruly biopolitical drama" produced a complex hierarchy of humanitarian compassion, linked to an identification of some asylum seekers as having suffered a "holocaust," itself a highly contested claim, in contrast with others labeled as "labor infiltrators." This chaotic form of governmental "unruliness" may be contrasted with descriptions of powerful humanitarian governance, but these papers all sketch out ways in which institutions whose stated mission is to alleviate suffering "*generate,* rather than alleviate, violence," in Willen's terms. Taken together, these three essays raise questions about when humanitarian interventions reproduce colonial forms of governance and when they serve as crucial resources of marginalized populations; about the rise of the humanitarian impulse and the "dark side of virtue" (Kennedy 2004); and about the complex ethical space within which anthropologists inevitably operate when they are engaged in "postconflict" interventions or work with displaced persons.

Finally, Angela Garcia explores postcolonial subjectivity in a very different space – in a New Mexico "Hispano" community with the highest rates of heroin addiction in the United States. Members of this community are explicitly postcolonial, having been deprived of their land by multiple colonial regimes that controlled the American Southwest by turn, producing a melancholic legacy of loss and deprivation associated with "successive struggles over land expropriation and sociopolitical domination." Into this setting are introduced medical regimes that define addiction as chronic disease juxtaposed with a criminal apparatus that defines addiction as crime. Garcia, who herself grew up in a nearby community, writes a lyrical elegy for one of the women she came to know through her research. The exploration of Alma's subjectivity, her memories of her father's violent despair at the loss of ancestral lands, Alma's story of the loss of her sister and her account of her own "intolerable insomnia," serve as a basis for an extended elegy for the broader Hispano community of America's Southwest.

REFERENCES

Agamben, Giorgio
 1988   Homo Sacer: Sovereign Power and Bare Life. Stanford University Press.
Aretxaga, Begona
 2005   States of Terror: Begona Aretxaga's Essays. Reno: Center for Basque Studies, University of Nevada.
Das, Veena
 2007   Life and Words. Violence and the Descent into the Ordinary. Berkeley: University of California Press.
Fassin, Didier and Richard Rechtman
 2009   The Empire of Trauma: An Inquiry into the Condition of Victimhood. Princeton University Press.

Good, Byron, Mary-Jo DelVecchio Good, Sandra Teresa Hyde, and Sarah Pinto
  2008 Postcolonial Disorders: Reflection on Subjectivity in the Contemporary World. *In* M. Good, S. Hyde, S. Pinto, and B. Good, eds. Postcolonial Disorders. Berkeley: University of California Press.
Good, Mary-Jo DelVecchio, Sandra Teresa Hyde, Sarah Pinto, and Byron Good, eds.
  2008 Postcolonial Disorders. Berkeley: University of California Press.
Kennedy, David
  2004 The Dark Side of Virtue: Reassessing International Humanitarianism. Princeton University Press.
Kleinman, Arthur, Veena Das, and Margaret Lock, eds.
  1997 Social Suffering. Berkeley: University of California Press.
Malkki, Lisa
  1996 Speechless Emissaries: Refugees, Humanitarianism, and Dehistoricization. Cultural Anthropology 11: 377–404.
Nordstrom, Carolyn
  2005 Shadows of War: Violence, Power, and International Profiteering in the Twenty-First Century. Berkeley: University of California Press.
Redfield, Peter
  2005 Doctors, Borders, and Life in Crisis. Cultural Anthropology 20: 328–61.
Simons, Ronald C., and Charles C. Hughes, eds.
  1985 The Culture-Bound Syndromes: Folk Illnesses of Psychiatric and Anthropological Interest. Dordrecht: D. Reidel Publishing Co.
Yap, P. M.
  1974 Comparative Psychiatry: A Comparative Framework. Toronto: University of Toronto Press.

36

Amuk in Java
Madness and Violence in Indonesian Politics

Byron J. Good and Mary-Jo DelVecchio Good

It was 1997, and we were living in Yogyakarta, teaching at Gadjah Mada University with support from senior Fulbright lectureships and the American Indonesian Exchange Foundation. Although we were teaching and carrying out research on how culture shapes mental illness and its treatment, it was impossible not to attend to the political campaign that was underway. In April and May, "*konvois*" of youth on motorcycles or in trucks and automobiles, elaborately decorated in party colors and carrying banners, engines roaring and horns blaring rhythmically, took over urban streets throughout Indonesia, as part of the campaign leading up to what turned out to be the final national election before President Suharto was forced from office in May 1998. Although little real expression of opposition was allowed in Suharto's New Order elections, the *konvois* of *kampong* (local neighborhood) youth represented a substantial form of protest and class resistance, with the threat of violence always present. News reports of the campaign and of the rioting in several cities earlier in the year characterized the election as the most violent in Indonesian history.

Near the end of the campaign, an American journalist, another Fulbright scholar, was invited to Yogyakarta's Institute for Journalism (LPPPY) to discuss how her reporting on political campaigns in the United States compared with that in Indonesia. At the end of the talk, the moderator of the discussion asked for our observations. We commented simply that we were surprised by the near exclusive focus on campaign violence in the papers. We were surprised not that the violence would be reported, but that little else, including policy issues, was even mentioned in most news accounts. Every event seemed to be judged solely on where it lay along a continuum from order to disorder. The moderator asked whether we thought this was a "cultural" matter. We replied that it might have a cultural element, given Javanese values of polite comportment. But we suggested that this focus on order also seemed to have a "hegemonic" element, a quality of naturalizing order, treating nearly all mass political activity as disorder and potentially anarchic.

As we thought later about our spontaneous comments, we began to reflect on how political violence was often described in official discourse as a kind of madness and on the role of such language in pathologizing political protest. An experience of a tragedy involving a mentally ill man focused our attention on one aspect of this language.

We found a Javanese friend, a woman from a poor village outside Yogya who worked on the university staff, in tears one afternoon. The story was not yet clear, but a man from her village had gone mad, had been attacked by a group of village men who attempted to subdue him, and had been killed. Members of her family had been taken by the police for questioning. Over the next several days, the story began to emerge, as she and others in our neighborhood traveled back and forth to the village some two hours outside of Yogya. The man who had been killed was a man we had seen and caught on video several months earlier when we had visited an annual *slametan* (a communal feast involving the sharing of food) in our friend's village. He had participated in the dancing that day – which is why we had videotaped him – in a way we later learned was considered highly inappropriate. The whole village knew he had been mentally ill, though on that day he had been relatively healthy.

It turned out that this man had been periodically mad since the time, several years before, when he sold his house and land to the government as a site for a television relay station. As they began work on the station, tearing his house down, he had begun to go crazy. People speculated about the cause. Perhaps the "stress" of selling his land and seeing his house torn down had been too much and he had become crazy. Perhaps the spirits of the land, who had long gathered at this place, had been angered and had possessed him. Or perhaps the 45 million rupiah which he had received from selling his land had attracted jealousy and made him a target of black magic. Whatever the reason, this vigorous man in his 50s had begun, for the first time in his life, to suffer bouts of madness. He would become violent, threaten other villagers, chop down their trees and attack their agricultural plants, and resist their efforts to stop him. His family had sent him to a mental hospital for treatment several times. Each time he would return, suffer a relapse, and become violent again. Villagers were fed up; his family seemed helpless to control him, and the police had stopped responding to their complaints.

And then on a day in July he had become violent again, attacking another villager's tree with his machete. When the owner tried to stop him, the old man threatened him. The owner called a friend, but they were unable to subdue him. The two ran for help, found a group of forty village men working on a voluntary labor project, repairing a road, calling out "*mengamuk, mengamuk*." The whole group came running to stop him. When he threatened them, they picked up sticks and began beating him. When the incident was over, the old man was dead.

We were caught up in the affair, helping support our friend whose family members were being held for questioning, knowing that the family would have to pay the police to gain their release. The incident was reported in the local newspapers, and our attention was drawn to the wording of the news stories. One report included the sentence, "*Dalam keadaan emosinya memuncak itu Pawiro Rejo ngamuk dan mengancam penduduk yang berusaha mendekat.*" "At the culmination or peak of his emotional condition, Pawiro Rejo *ngamuk* (ran amok) and threatened those who tried to approach him." Each news report used the Javanese verbal form *ngamuk* or the Indonesian form *mengamuk* to describe his behavior.

These terms, more commonly in the noun form *amuk* (or "amok" as it is usually spelled in English), are well known to cultural psychiatrists – and have, of course, entered common parlance globally. Amok is a classic in the literature on "culture-bound syndromes," psychiatric conditions which seem to be unique to a particular culture or region of the world (Simons and Hughes 1985). Amok (Carr 1985) denotes an episode of dissociative violence, a behavioral syndrome of an individual, often from a Malay culture, who suddenly goes berserk, becomes wild and violent, attacking others and threatening to kill them, until he is subdued or killed by those he is threatening. Survivors are left with amnesia for their behaviors. The psychiatric literature treats amok as individual pathology, never as a form of mob violence by a group – the madness of the old man, not of the group who killed him. From the perspective of cultural psychiatry, the case of this villager was interesting because the term *mengamuk* was used for an individual with a much more chronic or persistent mental illness than usually described in this literature.

However, the case also drew our attention to the use of the term *mengamuk* in other news articles, particularly the newspaper stories and official pronouncements about campaign violence and riots that had been occurring earlier in 1997. *"Kenapa Massa Gampang Mengamuk?"* – "Why do the masses so easily run amok?" – the cover of a special issue of a weekly news magazine *Gatra* (31 Mei 1997), devoted entirely to this topic, read. *"Massa Mengamuk di Pekalongan"* – "The Masses Run Amok in Pekalongan" – was a headline in the national newspaper *Kompas*. And so it went: analyses of episodes of political violence were framed as the masses running amok, as *kerusuhan*, riots, as *anarkis* or *kebrutalan* – anarchy or brutality – of the masses. It was this conjunction that set us to thinking, and that suggests the value of reading these two literatures – the historical writing on amok (usually of individuals) and the news reports and analyses of mass political violence – against one another (cf. B. Good, Subandi, and M. Good 2007).

A few examples will indicate what a close reading of the historical writings might yield. Amok, in its restricted meaning as a psychiatric syndrome, was defined in 1951 by Dr. P. M. Yap, a leading cultural psychiatrist, as

an acute outburst of unrestrained violence, associated with homicidal attacks preceded by a period of brooding and ending with exhaustion and amnesia. (1951:41)

This view of amok as a culture-bound syndrome was based on widespread reports by travelers, colonial administrators, judges, and colonial psychiatrists, dating in particular from the nineteenth century, and is echoed by more recent accounts of anthropologists and psychologists. Case reports – from Malaysia, Singapore, Java, and Sumatra – of persons who "run amok," persons who would become depressed, brooding, and suddenly go on a homicidal rampage, ending only when they were subdued or were killed, but leaving the survivors with amnesia for the events, fascinated colonial observers and led to speculations on the causes

of this behavior. Explanations ranged from accounts of Malay culture and personality, to suggestions that such acute violence might result from infectious disease or the use of opium, to attempts to understand these cases as a specific form of mental illness or a distinctive form of committing suicide. For example, D.J. Galloway, a British psychiatrist who read a paper at the Fifth Congress of the Far Eastern Association of Tropical Medicine in Singapore in 1923, distinguished cases representing known forms of insanity from those he termed "true amoks." These included cases in which an individual was publicly shamed or humiliated, and after brooding retaliated, escalating to a rampage that ended in the death of the *pengamuk*, the person who had run amok. "The impress of the primitive mind lies brood over the whole series of events; the inflated self-esteem, the proportionate resentment at the wounding of it, the tendency of the resentment to pass uninhibited into action against the offender, the necessity of re-establishing his prestige ... the appeal to arms" – all of these explain the tendency for Malay natives to run amok (Galloway 1923:168, in Winzeler 1990: 109).

In another example, Van Loon, a Dutch psychiatrist in charge of the Batavia Hospital (outside present-day Jakarta), writing in the *British Journal of Medical Psychology* in 1928, combined a cultural and developmental view:

in the *malu* feeling (unbearable shame and embarrassment, especially when made ridiculous in public), in *mata gelap* (blind rage) and in the *bingung* reaction (losing one's head), etc., the Malay shows the same characteristic weakness, a *lack of resistance against sudden emotion*.

Following this reading over into the writing on political violence, it is easy to find similarities in the grammar of the discourse. Amok, in colonial psychiatry, is *pathological*, *impulsive* or *instinctual*, and *developmentally primitive*, a form of wild, uncontrolled – and exotic – antisocial behavior. And it is often seen to be caused by an overwhelming emotional response to frustration and humiliation. Analyses of the sources of mass violence in the news in 1997 often drew on a similar logic. Mass violence indexes lack of social, political, and intellectual development, a sign that the masses are not yet ready for democracy. It represents pathological, impulsive reactions to emotionally frustrating social conditions. The presence of the term *amuk* or *mengamuk* in the popular press reports on the violence associated with the campaign thus served to naturalize a reading of mass violence as pathology.

Although there are adequate data of this kind to support our hypothesis about how the term *amuk* functions in such reports, it would be a mistake to end the analysis at this point. As we have gone on to read the historical works, it is clear that the literature on *amuk* is a more complex resource for readings of commentaries on political violence in Indonesia.

The term amok in the colonial literature does not begin as a psychiatric term. The term apparently enters European languages in the mid-sixteenth century, referring to "groups of exceptionally courageous men who had taken a vow to sacrifice themselves in battle against an enemy" (Murphy 1973: 34). In the nineteenth century, use of the term *amuk* to refer to heroic acts of bravery on the part of warriors, *keris* (sacred dagger) in hand, was known but was said to be largely archaic, replaced by reports of individual pathological violence as the primary referent of the term. The attempt to define the "true amok," such as that we quoted from Galloway, was not however simply an attempt to distinguish heroic acts from pathology. It was rooted in a set of debates in colonial Malaysia and the Dutch Indies. First, it was rooted in legal debates about whether a person who committed murder while "running amok" should be held legally responsible for his acts. In a widely quoted ruling in 1846, Judge William Norris ruled that a man in Penang captured after killing eight persons was guilty, despite the defense that he had been grieving for his child who had died recently, had killed indiscriminately, and claimed he had no memory of killing anyone. Judge Norris found him guilty, sentenced him to be hanged and then to have his body "cut into pieces and cast into the sea or

into a ditch or scattered upon the ground" (Norris 1849: 462–3, quoted in Winzeler 1990: 101–2). This contrasted with the case of Bugis, a sailor on board ship in Singapore who had "suddenly picked up a dagger and slain a relative who was visiting him, then rushed on deck and began attacking and killing everyone in his vicinity," who was acquitted by reason of insanity (Earl 1837: 377–8, quoted in Winzeler 1990: 101). Psychiatrists' efforts to describe amok as a culture-bound psychiatric disorder were thus aimed less at portraying the exotic than at defending the *pengamuk* on grounds of madness, to build the case for an insanity plea based on a distinctive form of illness.

This debate opened onto a more general question of how the *pengamuk*, the person who runs amok, should be punished, and the linked speculation on its cause. As early as the end of the eighteenth century, William Marsden, in *The History of Sumatra* (1811 edn.), rejected the notion that opium caused the behavior, reporting that it is more likely caused by mistreatment of slaves or servants by colonialists. He reported a case he had personally observed of a slave, who "being treated by his mistress with extreme severity, for a trifling offence, vowed he would have revenge if she attempted to strike him again; and ran down the steps of the house, with a knife in each hand." When she cried out "mengamok!", the civil guard came and fired upon him. Marsden reports that in Batavia, where such persons "are broken on the wheel, with every aggravation of punishment that the most rigorous justice can inflict, the mucks happen in great frequency," proving the inefficacy of harsh punishment, in contrast to the "influence that mild government has upon the manners of people." Thus, Marsden contrasted detrimental responses to Dutch rule with the beneficial effects of English rule.

Our point is that while there were speculations about the causes of amok – whether it reflected Malay or Javanese character, whether it was linked to Islamic fanaticism, resulted from a constitution weakened by disease or from opium use, or represented a culturally distinctive form of suicide – these debates were formulated in the larger context of discussions of native violence in response to colonial rule. As with the colonial responses to cases of worker violence on the plantations of Sumatra (Stoler 1985, 1992), discussions of amok reflected concerns of order and disorder under the colonial regime, and included clear examples of resistance to harsh rule, even of the use of amok as an "instrument of social protest by individuals against rulers who abused their power" (Carr 1985: 202). The rejection of the psychiatrists' claim that amok was a local form of insanity, excusing the individual from punishment, and the vicious sentences given out suggest that in the colonial context some judges saw the act of running amok as heinous precisely because it was a form of violent protest against colonial rule, requiring extraordinary public displays of punishment.

Analyses by Indonesian intellectuals at the end of the New Order of why the masses of this period were "running amok" seemed to reflect a similar underlying logic. Intellectuals and journalists writing on outbreaks of violence associated with the run-up to the 1997 election often described these "riots" as resulting from frustration (*frustrasi*), "displaced aggression," "emotional illiteracy," "jealousy" associated with the gap between rich and poor, or the suggestibility of the masses. However, in what was often a remarkably open critique of the growing gap between rich and poor, corruption of the elite, and arrogance of government officials, writers in the Indonesian press of the mid-1990s, still under the censureship of the Suharto regime, carved out a space for social reflection and social critique. The special issue of Gatra, entitled *Kenapa Massa Gampang Mengamuk?*, described a poll they had undertaken of 787 university students and recent graduates; 57% of respondents agreed with the statement "riots can't be avoided in the process of democratization"; 49% agreed that "riots are important to stimulate change"; 93% agreed that violence reflects the growing social and economic gap, and 82% the ineffectiveness of political channels.

Intellectuals were often asked to write commentaries on the sources of violence. Arief Budiman criticized the lack of a "culture of tolerance" and the increasing place of violence in the language of politics, particularly in response to the growing role of the military in politics. "People have learned that if you want to play politics," he wrote (*Jakarta Post* May 15, 1997), "you have to use power and violence, not intellectual arguments." Berhanuddin, writing in *Kompas* (January 9, 1997), analyzed the growing differentiation of Indonesian society that has accompanied modernization, the loss of social and moral coherence, and the replacement of religious leaders with a background in the *pesantren* (Islamic boarding schools) and a closeness to the people with *kiyai* or religious leaders who are part of the alienated political elite. And so it goes: violence, described as masses running amok, served as a source for a critical reading of Indonesian society and politics and a site of at least covert contestation, and commentaries combine subscribing rational motives to the actors with a reading of violence as mad, mob action.

We have not attempted here to trace a direct historical linkage between colonial debates about amok and contemporary uses of *amuk* or *mengamuk*. However, our "reading together" of contemporary and historical uses of these terms suggests a strong resonance, indicating that the colonial, as well as resistance to the colonial, remain alive in the structure of contemporary discourses on both madness and violence.

In Java, the term *amuk* still has its primary grounding in psychopathology. Today there is little evidence of the kinds of dissociative episodes described by colonial psychiatrists. However, the term is used, primarily in verbal form, to describe the behavior of an individual suffering from schizophrenia or another psychotic illness who goes out of control, screaming or crying out, perhaps becoming violent or suddenly running out of the house into public spaces. *Mengamuk* thus references the loss of self-control and the concomitant breaking of social decorum, bringing madness into the public in a way that embarrasses families as well as the sufferer.

If *amuk* makes initial reference to the characteristics of an individual suffering mental illness, the broader uses of the term to stake a position on political violence open onto a long history of discussions of order, disorder, and resistance to colonial rule and oppression. Mikhail Bakhtin, Russian literary critic under the Stalinist regime, wrote:

> For the consciousness that lives in it, language is not an abstract system of normative forms but a concrete heterological opinion on the world. Every word gives off the scent of a profession, a genre, a current, a party, a particular work, a particular man, a generation, an era, a day, and an hour. Every word smells of the context and contexts in which it has lived its intense social life; all words and all forms are inhabited by intentions. (quoted in Todorov 1984: 56–7)

The word *amuk* reflects, even today, the "intense social life" of colonial psychiatry and colonial discussions of Malay peoples as impulsive, prone to violence, and subject to primitive emotions and rage. These figures have been taken up internally to offer "concrete heterological opinions" on contemporary political acts. Lt. Gen. Prabowo Subianto, who gained notoriety for human rights violations during the immediate post-Suharto *reformasi* times but has been rehabilitated as candidate for Vice President, running with Megawati Sukarnoputri in the 2009 elections, was reported in 2001 as acknowledging army excesses in East Timor, but as going on to defend the military, saying, "We do have a culture of violence, the tribes, the ethnic groups in Indonesia, the Indonesians will go very fast to violence. The word amok comes from the lingua franca of this archipelago, something we are aware of and that we do not like" (April 20, 2001, AFP). Gen. Zacky Anwar Makarim, who helped lead the Indonesian army in East Timor, said simply, "The character of the Indonesian people is indeed one that likes to go amuk" (Robinson 2001: 224). Such statements are classically hegemonic; they naturalize violence, obscure social and political responsibility by claiming violence to be in the character structure of Indonesians, and thus reflect the colonial (and now postcolonial) life of the term "amok."

The placing of political activities during the 1997 elections on a continuum from order to disorder, with which we began this essay, also reflected a deeper grammar of New Order politics. Suharto's New Order regime was born in a wave of violence unleashed by the military following the attempted coup of 30 September 1965. Supported by a virulent anti-Communist propaganda operation (Goodfellow 1995), over 500,000 Indonesians, only some of whom were formally associated with the Indonesian Communist Party (PKI), were arrested and imprisoned or summarily killed. During the 33 years of the New Order, Suharto's counter-coup was represented as the originating event that saved Indonesia from a Communist takeover, separating order and the New Order's authoritarian rule from disorder, associated with the "Communist menace," with nearly all forms of progressive political activities, and with hidden subversive forces. In this grammar, amok stands on the side of disorder. A wide range of explicit political activities, as well as occasional mob violence, were thus associated in New Order symbolic structures with subversion and the social evil to which Suharto's military authoritarianism was antidote.

At the same time, as we have suggested, the term *amuk* has had an alternative social life associated with colonial resistance and revolutionary violence, providing symbolic resources for a more complex and critical analysis of politics and modernity. Thus even official readings of history by New Order historiography represented heroic struggles against the Dutch – for example, a Balinese uprising led by the slave Untung Surapati (Ricklefs 1993: 82) – as resulting from the Balinese tendency to run amok (Degung Santikarma, personal communication). Amok also had the potential to describe violence as a powerful force for positive transformation, as when Sukarno was reported to say that "the Revolution runs amuck, rampages, sweeps people along like a tidal wave." During the first half of 1997, activists and intellectuals drew on these readings of *amuk* as resistance and sources of revolutionary change to provide analyses that subtly countered the official representations of mass violence as subversive disorder, examining labor disputes and perceived injustice by workers, ethnic and religious tensions in the society, and corruption and arrogance of the political elite as reasons for the masses running amok.

The debates we have been describing were specific to the New Order. With the fall of Suharto, and the ethnic and communal violence that followed, discussions of why the Indonesians so easily run amok took on new and urgent shape. Why had the reform failed to produce a more just society? Was it true that Indonesians required an authoritarian hand to maintain social order? Or were dark forces at work, promoting violence as a means of destabilizing the new democratic regime and pave the way for the return of military rule? In this setting, the image of mad violence and paranoia, reflected recursively in the actual experience of persons with psychotic illness, continued to haunt the nation. Intellectuals and artists – including Entang Wiharso with his massive *NusaAmuk* paintings (M. Good and B. Good 2008) – continued to reflect the nature of social order, even as the old grammar of the New Order regime continued to shape talk in ways largely out of consciousness. The colonial ghosts continue to haunt the present.

We have suggested elsewhere (B. Good et al. 2008) that the phrase "postcolonial disorders" captures an important dimension of the phenomena with which medical anthropologists are increasingly engaged today. Our goal here has been to indicate how amok, an old category from the so-called culture-bound disorders, might be analyzed when viewed from this perspective.

REFERENCES

Carr, John E.
  1985   Ethno-Behaviorism and the Culture-Bound Disorders: The Case of Amok. *In* R. Simons and C. Hughes, eds., The Culture-bound Syndromes. Dordrecht: D. Reidel Publishing Co., pp. 199–224.

Earl, G.
  1837 [1981]   The Eastern Seas. London: W. H. Allen and Co. reprinted Kuala Lampur: Oxford University Press.

Galloway, D. J.
  1923   On Amok. Transactions of the Fifth Congress of the Far-Eastern Association of Tropical Medicine, Singapore, pp. 162–71.

Good, Byron J., Mary-Jo DelVecchio Good, Sandra T. Hyde, and Sarah Pinto
  2008   Postcolonial Disorders: Reflections on Subjectivity in the Contemporary World. *In* M. Good, S. Hyde, S. Pinto, and B. Good, eds., Postcolonial Disorders. Berkeley: University of California Press, pp. 1–40.

Good, Byron J., Subandi, and Mary-Jo DelVecchio Good
  2007   The Subject of Mental Illness. Psychosis, Mad Violence, and Subjectivity in Indonesia. *In* João Biehl, Byron Good, and Arthur Klein, Subjectivity: Ethnographic Investigations. Berkeley: University of California Press, pp. 243–72.

Good, Mary-Jo DelVecchio, and Byron J. Good
  2008   Indonesia Sakit: Indonesian Disorders and the Subjective Experience and Interpretive Politics of Contemporary Indonesian Artists. *In* M. Good, S. Hyde, S. Pinto, and B. Good, eds., Postcolonial Disorders. Berkeley: University of California Press, pp. 62–108.

Goodfellow, Robert
  1995   Api Dalam Sekam: The New Order and the Ideology of Anti-Communism. Monash Working Papers No. 95. Clayton, Victoria: Monash University Press.

Marsden, William
  1811   The History of Sumatra. London: Longman, Hurst, Rees, Orme, and Brown.

Murphy, H. B. M.
  1973   History and the Evolution of Syndromes: The Striking Case of Latah and Amok. *In* M. Hammer, K. Salzinger, and S. Sutton, eds., Psychopathology: Contributions from the Social, Behavioral and Biological Sciences. New York: Wiley and Sons.

Norris, W.
  1849   Malay Amoks Referred to Mahomedanism. Journal of the Indian Archipelago and Eastern Asia 3:462–3.

Ricklefs, M. C.
  1993   A History of Modern Indonesia Since c.1300, 2nd edn. Stanford: Stanford University Press.

Robinson, Geoffrey
  2001   The Fruitless Search for a Smoking Gun: Tracing the Origins of Violence in East

Timor. *In* Freek Colobijn and Thomas Lindblad, eds., Roots of Violence in Indonesia. Leiden: KITLV.

Simons, Ronald C., and Charles C. Hughes, eds.
1985 The Culture-Bound Syndromes: Folk Illnesses of Psychiatric and Anthropological Interest. Dordrecht: D. Reidel Pub. Co.

Stoler, Ann Laura
1985 Perceptions of Protest: Defining the Dangerous in Colonial Sumatra. American Ethnologist 12:642–58.

Stoler, Ann Laura
1992 "In Cold Blood": Hierarchies of Credibility and the Politics of Colonial Narratives. Representations 37:151–89.

Todorov, Tzvetan
1984 Mikhail Bakhtin: The Dialogical Principle. Minneapolis: University of Minnesota Press.

Van Loon, F. G. H.
1928 Protopathic-Instinctive Phenomena in Normal and Pathological Malay Life. British Journal of Psychology 8:264–76.

Winzeler, Robert
1990 Amok: Historical, Psychological, and Cultural Perspectives. *In* Wazir Jahan Karim, ed., Emotions of culture: A Malay Perspective. Singapore: Oxford University Press.

Yap, P.M.
1951 Mental Diseases Peculiar to Certain Cultures. Journal of Mental Science 97:313–27.

37

The Political Economy of 'Trauma' in Haiti in the Democratic Era of Insecurity

Erica James

Where is the line between drawing attention to the suffering of others in order to assist them and appropriating the suffering of others for institutional or personal gain? This thorny question is emerging as the humanitarian assistance apparatus – assemblages (Deleuze 1988) of governmental and nongovernmental agencies – intervenes across and within national borders to assist traumatized "victims" of politically motivated and interpersonal violence, disasters, and the conflicts that arise within failed or failing states. As much as governmental and nongovernmental humanitarian interventions are motivated by compassion, they are also motivated by concerns for security: global political and economic security, as well as national, institutional, and "human" or "common" security – "the security of individuals [or groups] as an object of international policy" (Rothschild 1995: 54).

The definition of security has been extended in the post–Cold War era. From an initial, militaristic focus upon protecting the nation-state against other polities, current conceptions of security have shifted to encompass concerns for maintaining the integrity of the international system, promoting the security of groups and individuals, and concerns for the protection of the physical environment (Rothschild 1995: 55). As the definition of security has expanded, the imperative has been to determine the ways in which political, economic, social, or environmental factors impact "human security." In addition to this there has been an expansion of the locus of responsibility for promoting and protecting "human security" at a policy level. The institutions that adopt this humanitarian imperative include multilateral (international), national, and local governmental and nongovernmental institutions (among others) (Rothschild 1995: 55–56). In practice, however, both the conventional and expanded forms of security may be present within foreign policy initiatives of both governmental and nongovernmental institutions. One of the ways in which both traditional and expanded concerns for security have manifested, particularly since the reputed end of the Cold War, has been in international discourses of 'trauma' within the humanitarian assistance apparatus.

Erica James, "The Political Economy of 'Trauma' in Haiti in the Democratic Era of Insecurity," *Culture, Medicine and Psychiatry* 28 (2004): 127–49. With kind permission from Springer Science & Business Media: *Culture, Medicine and Psychiatry* 28 (2004), pp. 127–49.

In this article I explore the relationship between discourses of security – so prevalent in the West after the September 11, 2001, attacks – and discourses of 'trauma' or posttraumatic stress disorder (PTSD). Trauma and security issues intersected in fieldwork that I conducted with victims of organized violence over more than 27 months of residence in Haiti between 1995 and 2000. I worked at three institutions during this period in my capacity as an ethnographer, activist, and physical therapist: between 1996 and 1999 I worked at a privately funded women's clinic in Martissant – an urban area just southwest of the capital that was heavily targeted for violence during the recent 1991–94 coup years; from 1998 to 19991 participated in therapeutic sessions at an outpatient clinic at the Mars/Kline Center for Neurology and Psychiatry at the State University Medical Hospital located in the capital, Port-au-Prince; from 1997 to early 2000 I worked at a non-profit nongovernmental organization (NGO) funded by the United States Agency for International Development (USAID) that housed a rehabilitation program for victims of organized violence also located in Port-au-Prince.

The time period in which I conducted my research was considered to be a period of "democratic consolidation" after the US and UN Multinational Force restored democracy on October 15, 1994. Despite this military intervention, Haiti continued to be plagued by political and criminal violence, called *ensekirite* (insecurity) in everyday discourse. With its economic stagnation and ongoing instability there is a pervasive climate of fear and "nervousness" (Taussig 1992) within the Haitian social body, but it is both acute – with regularly high levels of fear and social paralysis – and chronic for *viktim*, those who claim to be the victims of state-sponsored violence from the recent 1991–94 coup years. Within this "insecure" environment I worked with *viktim* as they searched for assistance from a swarm of governmental and nongovernmental agencies that comprised the humanitarian assistance apparatus in Haiti at the time. I examined how the discourse of trauma is employed, and by whom, within the broader realm of governmental and nongovernmental humanitarian assistance in Haiti and the ways that deployment

engenders different linkages of power relations or forces from the local to international realms of social and political action (James 2003). At the same time I sought to understand and alleviate in some small measure the embodied suffering of my Haitian physical therapy clients at the clinic, and to witness how Haitian *viktim* articulated their trauma in therapy groups that I cofacilitated in the rehabilitation program. Despite the manifest struggle to cope with everyday *ensekirite* and the ongoing experience of "traumatic stress," a peculiar transformation of *viktim*'s subjective and intersubjective pain and despair occurred as they presented and were implicitly required to perform their suffering in order for it to be "recognized" in a variety of institutional and clinical contexts.

After a brief analysis of Western notions of trauma and their links to the recent shifts in security talk in political theory, I will analyze how historical stereotypes of Haitians and Haiti affect how Haitians are able to adopt subject positions within these discourses of security, suffering, hope, and despair. Through a discussion of the deployment of discourses of security and trauma during this period of research in Haiti, and their effects on the experience and tactics of *viktim*, I will show how these discourses can generate new economies based upon commodifications of suffering. Nonetheless, the ability to participate in these debates depends on positioning, whether geopolitical, communal, or individual. This piece is a meditation on how current concerns for safety and suffering are highly moral discourses that involve questions of compassion, ethics, obligation and action, and are inextricably linked to history and political economy.

Trauma in the 'Post–Cold War' Era

The post–Cold War era has been viewed by many sociopolitical theorists through the lens of "postmodernity," a term which signifies the breakdown of grand narratives of politics, economics, culture, and ideals of progress. According to theorists of postmodernism, the "symptoms" of the postmodern condition are also characterized by the experience of space and time as chaotic, fragmented, schizophrenic, or incoherent. This "postmodern condition" is indelibly marked by the disordering yet productive, or "titillating," effects of global capitalism (Harvey 1990: 39, 63; Jameson 1991; Lyotard 1984). While the content of geopolitical fears has changed since the end of the Cold War opposition between democracy, liberty, or capitalism and communism or socialism, the form or structure through which these discourses manifest continues to have a similar pattern – that of identifying threats to the security of the West or to "civilized nations," and resulting in some form of intervention. The continuation of these practices calls into question whether or not the Cold War has truly ended; however, the particular strategies by which current geopolitical threats are identified and managed are new. Against this perception of discontinuity or ruptures between modern and postmodern ideals and practices, I argue that the era begun by the end of the Cold War is *neo-modern* in character and hinges on security at the international, national, community, and individual levels.

Since the end of the Cold War, emerging proto-democracies – nations like Haiti that have struggled free from the shackles of dictatorship, socialism, or political conflict – have been targets of intervention. In some ways the modes of representation and practices of intervention in "transitional" states trace their genealogies at least as far back as the colonial era, but are not identical to interventions from that time. Nonetheless, the way in which the humanitarian assistance and development apparatus designs and attempts to implement social, political, and economic change in nations that are undergoing "transitions to democracy" or "post-conflict reconstruction" is unsettlingly familiar, but involves new bureaucratic technologies of suffering that are required to legitimize the activities of the intervener. With these practices the interveners establish their accountability to those whom they are responsible.

In describing this phenomenon I hesitate to use rhetorics of "neocolonialism," "neoliberalism," or "supracolonialism" (Pandolfi 2000) to describe what is currently happening in nations

like Haiti. That being said, the transnational efforts to rebuild post-conflict nations appeal to modernist or universalist languages of rights, civil society, law, and economic and human development in a manner reminiscent of the missions of colonial expansion. I will use the term "neo-modern," therefore, to refer to the neo-Enlightenment theories and practices of governance that arise in relationship to the crisis of the state in what has been called the post – Cold War era. In this formulation, both governmental and nongovernmental development and humanitarian assistance efforts engage in practices of intervention, social rehabilitation, and political and economic reformation. These interventions are designed to build "civil societies" that respect the "rule of law" and promote equality and citizenship for all of their members – aspects of "human security" – even as the states in which these assistance or development efforts are deployed open their markets to the unrestricted ebbs and flows of global capital. The technologies of intervention that arise in the effort to promote human security are reminiscent of what Foucault calls bio-power – *"techniques* of power present at every level of the social body and utilized by very diverse institutions (the family and the army, schools and the police, individual medicine and the administration of collective bodies), operated in the sphere of economic processes, their development, and the forces working to sustain them" (Foucault 1990: 141, emphasis in original).

In the neo-modern, post–Cold War era, the discourse of trauma permits the exercise of global bio-power by the humanitarian assistance apparatus as nations make the transition toward the respect for the rule of law, human rights, democracy, and capitalism. The responses to the traumatized victims of politically motivated violence become the meter by which states, criticized for their past predatory or negligent practices, are now measured in order to determine their competence and accountability toward their citizenry. This is also a manifestation of what Foucault calls the practice of "governmentality" (1991) – the discipline and management of populations through particular forms of government rationality. In the case of transnational humanitarian assistance the practices of governmentality often occur in place of the weak or failed state; however, this does not mean that they occur without challenge, resistance, or unintended consequences that belie the sovereignty of the intervening institution or polity.

Furthermore, in the neo-modern period a shift has occurred such that "toward the end of the 1980s, 'trauma' projects appear ... alongside food, health and shelter interventions" (Bracken and Petty 1998: 1). The emergence of trauma treatment programs reflects a growing familiarity with the concept within Western culture and a desire to tame the unimaginable:

> Over the course of the past two decades, the language of trauma has become part of the vernacular – it is accessible and familiar in contemporary Western culture. Thus, while a mass audience may find modern warfare, waged against ordinary civilians, almost unimaginable in its scale of brutality, when that experience is translated into the everyday language of stress, anxiety, and trauma, its character changes and becomes less challenging. (Bracken and Petty 1998: 1)

The discourse of trauma has been an organizing trope that has motivated new forms of technocratic practices designed to manage new categories of people within a social field – "victims of human rights violations" – whose shocking experiences of egregious and unspeakable forms of suffering evoke compassion, concern, anxiety, moral outrage, and fear in those who are proximal and distant witnesses.

The humanitarian apparatus has routinized or professionalized forms of response or intervention that targets the suffering of victims and transforms their experiences, identity, and "political subjectivity" (Aretxaga 1997). These acts of bureaucratized care can make of suffering and despair something productive; however, the unintended consequences of these acts can also engender what I am calling *occult economies* of trauma that generate new forms of victimization and reproduce sociopolitical inequalities at local, national, and international levels of engagement. For example, within the practice of humanitarian assistance

to victims of human rights violations, the suffering of the victim is confessed to physicians and psychiatrists, lawyers, activists, the clergy, and other human rights observers. These trauma narratives are documented in affidavits and other written testimonials and verified through physical examinations and psychological tests. The experience of suffering is appropriated or alienated from the subject and transformed (Das 1995; Kleinman and Kleinman 1991) into what I am calling the *trauma portfolio* – the aggregate of documentation and verification which "recognizes" or transubstantiates individuals, families, or collective sufferers into "victims" or "survivors" (Fraser 1995; Povinelli 2002; Taylor 1994).

This portfolio can be circulated within the global humanitarian market as currency (Kleinman 1995); however, portfolios are exchanged differently within local, national, and international humanitarian markets. At the level of the individual, the portfolio of trauma can resemble a portfolio of economic investments: it may become a symbolic index of worth or one's holdings, as well as a material representation of one's victim identity. Each document, photo, affidavit, or letter provided by local, national, and international institutions, or by individuals who have the political capital to affirm the authenticity of the individual's suffering, adds to the "value" of the portfolio relative to those of other sufferers once it is circulated within the humanitarian market.

At the community or collective level, *viktim* have joined together to form advocacy groups. Each member's portfolio adds to the strength of the group in having its needs met by local, national, and international institutions. With the best of intentions the governmental and nongovernmental humanitarian assistance apparatus assembles and collects these portfolios of suffering in order to fulfill their salvific missions of "doing good" (Fisher 1997). They collect them in order to support their interventions into nations, communities, and the minds and bodies of individuals. But they also collect and present them to acquire funding and political capital in order to promote their own institutional security even as they promote "human security" in their practices (James 2003).

As in the case of currencies that flow within the international monetary system, the trauma portfolios of some nations, communities, and individuals can be devalued. The question to be considered more generally is whose trauma – assuming that such a thing is universal—should be recognized as legitimate and why? What is at stake when we recognize others through the lens of their suffering and not through their political subjectivity? In what way do new forms of political recognition merely replicate the historical denials of humanity and sovereignty among formerly colonized nations?

Discourses of Trauma, Practices of Denial

In the early 1990s a tremendous amount of attention was given by the media to ethnic cleansing and genocidal rape in the Balkans, as well as to the psychological trauma or posttraumatic stress that the survivors of war were presumed to experience as a result of their victimization. Less present in the media at this time was the plight of Rwandans, whose two major ethnic groups were on a genocidal path of self-destruction. Even more obscure within the media was the suffering of Haitians who were caught in a "dirty war" perpetrated by the de facto military regime. On September 30, 1991, the first democratically elected president of Haiti, Jean-Bertrand Aristide, was ousted by a violent coup d'état after less than eight months in office. Subsequent to the coup a reign of terror was unleashed without constraint against the generally poor, pro-democracy *Lavalas* coalition members who supported Aristide. The perpetrators of this violence were several groups affiliated with the Forces Armées d'Haïti (FAD'H – the military/police), whose membership was seven thousand men. After the coup, tens of thousands of civilian, paramilitary attachés – armed and supported by FAD'H – joined with the military to control the population. The three years that followed the coup were years in which the extended military apparatus tortured, murdered, raped, and "disappeared" the *Lavalasyen* with impunity. Nearly three hundred thousand Haitians

were internally displaced, and tens of thousands fled by boat to other Caribbean nations, South America, and the United States. The majority of Haitian refugees who reached the United States were detained in prison-like conditions or sent back to Haiti, with the accusation that they were fleeing from poverty rather than politically motivated terror.

When reports were released by Haitian and international human rights organizations like the National Coalition for Haitian Refugees (now called the National Coalition for Haitian Rights), Human Rights Watch/Americas, Physicians for Human Rights, and others, outlining the increased use of brutal forms of repression as the coup regime sought to remain in control of the nation, some US government officials denied the reports and called them exaggerations. For example, a cable sent from the US Embassy in Port-au-Prince to Washington in April of 1994 states the following: "We are, frankly, suspicious of the sudden, high number of reported rapes, particularly in this culture, occurring at the same time that Aristide activists seek to draw a comparison between Haiti and Bosnia" (United States Embassy [Haiti] 1994). The use of systematic rape during the coup years was questioned and said to be part of Haitian culture rather than a strategy of war. The implication of this statement was that Haitian sexuality was naturally violent and depraved. The United States explicitly charged that the reports of human rights abuses were fabrications. The implicit message, however, was the incommensurability between the suffering of poor black men and women in Haiti with that of the embattled ethnic groups in the former Yugoslavia.

A further insinuation of this denial of experience is that Haitian men and women could not possibly suffer from trauma or traumatic memories in a culture in which political, criminal, and sexual violence are stereotyped as the norm. To some degree these US political officers evoked discourses of cultural, moral, emotional, and intellectual relativism that denied the recognition of Haitian humanity; however, this was not a new practice. Stereotypes of Haitian psychobiology have always been present as bio-political discourses (Foucault 1990, 1997) or rhetorics that accompany concerns for US and European political and economic security.

Since its successful achievement of independence in 1804, after the 12 years of the Saint-Domingue struggle for sovereignty, Haiti entered its postcolonial period as a political outcast within the slaveholding "international community." At the same time, however, the new nation was a source of inspiration and hope for enslaved blacks and colonized Africans throughout the world. Nevertheless, independent Haiti would be viewed continually as a threat to hemispheric and global security, and the "cancer of revolution" and the "contagion of black liberty" sparked numerous policies to secure American borders against the influx of Haitian revolutionaries (Jordan 1968: 375–402). Haiti would be denied political recognition of its sovereignty and right to exist for the next two hundred years.

Instead of receiving the same protections that the United States proclaimed in its Monroe Doctrine (1823), Haiti and Haitians were depicted as insane, highly sexed and syphilitic, deficient in both intellectual and moral capacity, superstitious, hysterical, and easily influenced by the charisma of *Vodou* priests and priestesses. Indeed, in the 19th century racialist works of Gobineau (1999), LeBon (1974), and Southern American physician Cartwright (1851), Haiti and Haitians became the case study to illustrate the genetic roots of black incapacity. For example, Cartwright defined *drapetomania* as a propensity for slaves to flee from the plantation. Using Haitians as evidence, he described *dysaesthesia Aethiopica* as a tendency for free blacks to suffer from "insensibility" that manifests as mischief due to stupidity, destruction of property and theft, diminished mental capacity and lassitude, and insensitivity to pain when subject to punishment for these actions. In this respect, Haitians were not viewed as having the capacity to feel, to love, or to reflect in a cognitive manner that would engender the moral capacity that was prerequisite for what one would categorize as "shell shock" or "trauma" at the turn of the 20th century.

From the 19th to the 20th century, stereotypes of Haitians as superstitious and sexually liberal continued to proliferate, especially during the 1915–34 American Occupation of Haiti (Craige 1933, 1934; Renda 2001) and more recently with the onset of the AIDS pandemic. In the early 1980s the CDC designated Haitians as vectors of HIV. As members of the infamous "4-H club," which also included hemophiliacs, heroin addicts, and homosexuals, Haitians as a racial and cultural group were labeled as a danger for the spread of infection (Farmer 1992; Sabatier 1988). While the sick or diseased have long been considered threats to the United States and other nations, those recognized as fleeing political repression have been given asylum. Nevertheless, as tens of thousands of Haitians fled to the United States in the 1980s and 1990s and were labeled "economic refugees," they were denied recognition as political subjects because of the potential threat that they represented. Upon analysis of the peculiarities with which Haitians have been treated in asylum cases and in US foreign policy (DeConde 1992; Lawyers Committee for Human Rights 1990; Miller 1984; Plummer 1992), it is possible to say to some degree that Haiti and Haitians continue to be symbols of horror, violence, pathology, and the chaos of a nation that the United States views as willfully refusing to follow a democratic path. Recurrent images of the violence of the Haitian Revolution and the ongoing negative stereotyping of the nation's people and leaders suggest that Haiti is an archetypal object of consciousness upon which the international imaginary remains fixated (Dash 1997; Freud 1997: 207; James 2003; 2008).

Beyond the screen of fantastic images, the reality is that Haiti remains infamous for being the poorest country in the Western Hemisphere and for its struggles toward democracy in the 21st century. While the accuracy of statistical measures may be questioned, the following figures are generally accepted as valid. Life expectancy in Haiti is estimated at 50.36 years for men and 52.92 years for women (Central Intelligence Agency 2004). Six percent of the entire population of Haiti is considered to be HIV positive; however, the infection rate may be as high as 13 percent in the Northwest Department (Dubuche 2002), which has been plagued with drought, food shortages, and heavy damage in the aftermath of Hurricanes

Georges and Mitch in the fall of 1998. The 2000 Human Development Report (United Nations Development Program 2000) affirms that 63 percent of the population lack access to safe water, 55 percent do not have access to health services, and 75 percent lack access to basic sanitation. Twenty-eight percent of children under age five are below normal weight. The infant mortality rate is 95 per 1,000 live births. Overall, at least 80 percent of the population lives in abject poverty (Central Intelligence Agency 2004). At the time of this writing the unemployment rate is believed to be nearly 70 percent. In terms of its economy, Haiti ranks a low 170th out of 206 countries, with a GNP of only US$460 per year (World Bank 2001).

Certainly, as a result of its dire poverty and political insecurity, many Haitians still attempt to flee Haiti in order to find a better future in the United States. While the anxiety that these hopeful migrants provoke continues to be acute, it inspired the most concern for the United States and its own bio-political security during the coup years of 1991–94, when Haitians were interdicted at sea and returned to Haiti's politically and economically insecure shores in the thousands without adequate hearings. Nonetheless, it is striking that what continues to be elided within national and international discourses of Haitian democracy is acknowledgment of the legacy of violence from the Duvalier dictatorships (1957–86) and the post-dictatorship period, as well as the egregious uses of torture and terror between 1991 and 1994. Just as the extremity of the violence has yet to receive thorough recognition and analysis in the manner that has been attempted in other "post-conflict" nations (Hayner 2001), the ongoing suffering of Haitian *viktim*, among the general population living in the climate of *ensekirite*, remains acute and nearly invisible.

What actually happened during the years of the coup d'état in Haiti, and how were victims of human rights abuses coping in the aftermath of conflict? Did they, in fact, suffer from 'post-traumatic stress' and how did this manifest according to gender? What assistance could be provided to help them rebuild their lives, and how could this be done successfully considering the ongoing crisis of insecurity in

Haiti's post-coup era? Given the crisis of the Haitian state and the ongoing international ambivalence toward assisting the nation, who or what institution or state should be held accountable for recognizing and repairing the legacy of egregious suffering in the recent and distant past?

Torture and its Consequences

Gender, sexuality, production, and reproduction were explicit factors in the mode of repression in Haiti during and after the coup d'état of 1991. This section is a general overview of the types of violence perpetrated during the coup years and is based upon my analysis of case files representing more than 2,000 *viktim*, my own documentation of cases in the field and physical therapy work at the clinic, and participation with *viktim* in discussion groups in a variety of settings. The majority of the poor who were targeted were designated *Lavalasyen* – supporters of Aristide. Just as Das and Nandy (1985) observed in their discussion of sacrificial and political violence in South Asia, there were differences in the particular "style" of violence employed to maintain the climate of terror in Haiti during these years. Men were attacked for their involvement in the popular democracy movement – whether as organizers or supporters. When apprehended, they may have been arrested or kidnapped, interrogated in a detention facility, beaten – at times with the intent to damage their sexual organs – whipped, derided, or humiliated. In order to ensure that they could never again perform manual labor or other work, they may have had a hand chopped off, or been cut in ways that left permanent physical damage. At times these attacks on the body and mind were accompanied by theft and destruction of property, livestock, or other possessions.

Women were also targeted for their active organizing role in the political domain, as well as in their roles as small-scale merchants; however, they were also victimized in place of their husbands, fathers, brothers, or spouses as surrogates – what Girard (1977) has called "sacrificial substitutes." They were often unable to go into hiding because of their responsibilities for their children and because their commercial activities bound them to local markets, so they were vulnerable to further attacks by the various military-affiliated groups. Although politically motivated rape occurred immediately after the coup, by late 1993 rape, repeated rapes, gang rapes, and even forced incest were tools of repression that were used systematically to terrorize families and communities generally, but women specifically.

The use of gendered and sexualized forms of torture and terror was intended to destroy the productivity and reproductivity of the individual victim, and to rupture the social bonds between the direct target of violence and his or her family and community through the use of physical pain, threats, and other coercive acts. As Scarry (1985) suggests, power and productivity were stripped from the targets of violence and transferred to the torturer(s), and to the coup apparatus as a whole as it sought to consolidate its hold over the nation. The efficacy of torture used in Haiti during this period, however, lay beyond its use against the "body" in the short-term. The forms of torture perpetrated were effective in controlling social space as well as the subjectivity of their targets over time. Beyond the initial attempt to extract legitimacy and power from victims' physical bodies through the use of pain, the purpose of these horrific acts was to inculcate what Patterson (1982) has described as "social death" of the victim and "natal alienation" from his or her social network of responsibility through the violation of moral norms. In this respect, the psychosocial sequelae of torture leave their traces on the individual psyche or self over time, as well as on the extended family and communities of *viktim*.

The Traumatic Sequelae of Torture: Social Death and Natal Alienation

In the aftermath of the coup years, the most common laments among *viktim* were feelings of shame, humiliation, powerlessness, and isolation or disconnection from their families and communities. These experiences and

articulations of suffering are also gendered. Women who had been raped were often abandoned by their partners or husbands and families and labeled as *fanm kadejak* – "the wives of the rapist." Alienated from their social group, they often fled to other areas in order to restart their lives. Many of these women were market vendors and had also lost their livelihoods at the time of the attack. In many cases, however, their only recourse for survival was to appropriate their own sexuality as a means to generate income, much as the coup apparatus appropriated power from their bodies during its reign of terror. Haitian women lamented their inability to care for their children – to send them to school, feed and clothe them – in accordance with cultural ideals of femininity and parenthood. Furthermore, women *viktim* and their children often suffered from tuberculosis, malaria, and malnutrition, as well as somatic forms of emotional distress arising from the imbalance of *san* (blood) in the body.

Haitian men who were victims of violence similarly articulated feelings of humiliation and shame at having been powerless to protect their families, and at having been subjected to abasing forms of torture. What they lamented most strongly in the therapy groups in which I participated was their rage and anger over the loss of their property, livestock, and public status – essential aspects of the ideals of masculinity. Indeed, the perceived loss of social status was among the greatest factors in the way that Haitian men experienced and narrated their trauma, depression, and anxiety. In many cases, however, the personal sense of shame, ongoing economic impotence, and failure to meet their expected social roles – fulfilling their domestic responsibilities to provide for their children and support their conjugal partners – culminated in the total abandonment of their families. The care and subsistence of the family was left to other relatives, or to no one, leaving women and children even more vulnerable.

Earlier in this paper I asked if PTSD manifested in Haiti following the coup years, and in what way. I can speak of "posttraumatic stress disorder" in Haiti, but only in a guarded sense. Many victims of organized violence in Haiti have suffered memory loss – not simply from dissociation in the psychological sense, but because of blunt trauma to the head. *Viktim* are generally hypervigilant and have feelings of detachment from others. Many expressed a "sense of a foreshortened future," or feelings of depersonalization – the sensation that their bodies did not feel like their own. But these "symptoms" do not capture the despair and social dislocation of people like Elsie, a 60-year-old grandmother who still searches for her son who has been missing since 1992. She spoke of him each time I saw her in the Martissant clinic. Her perpetual torment is not knowing if he is dead. If he is, her inability to lay his body to rest through proper funerary rites leaves her in a state of moral limbo in which she is vulnerable to haunting and persecution by the *zonbi*, an aspect of the disembodied soul of the deceased. But who or what institution or government is or should be responsible for repairing these moral cleavages?

Humanitarian Assistance, Security, and Bio-power

In the aftermath of the denials of gendered and sexualized forms of torture and the political motivation for acts of terror in Haiti in the early 1990s, a cacophony of dissent erupted from international and national human rights organizations and other supporters of the nation's fragile democracy against the US government. In response to the criticisms of its practices and the accusation that the United States was not a credible promoter of global human rights, the US government, through USAID, provided humanitarian assistance to *viktim* from the 1991–94 period. The vehicle for this aid was a rehabilitation program for victims of organized violence housed at a non-governmental organization. The program functioned in various incarnations from July of 1994 until February of 1995, and again from July of 1996 until May of 1999. During the early phase of 1994–95, the project provided complete medical care to *viktim*, including surgeries, trauma counseling, legal assistance, and stipends, to help alleviate suffering. Nonetheless, the attention to and promotion of

Haitian human security was not given without a simultaneous goal of protecting US national security and the US's own image in the international community: explicit within the draft documents for the first incarnation of this assistance project was the recognition that US credibility was low regarding supporting democracy and human rights in Haiti. Providing assistance to Haitians at this juncture was crucial to creating an image of the United States as accountable to its own citizenry and to the Haitian government and civil society whose democracy it intended to help consolidate; however, it can be debated whether this effort was successful.

The second phase of the project continued this assistance to victims of state-sponsored violence without restriction to time period, but required that beneficiaries be members of victims' associations or advocacy groups, or have a recommendation from a recognized institution like the Ministry of Justice, the Episcopal Justice and Peace Commission, local or international human rights groups, women's groups, or other formal institutions. The project continued to provide assistance to individuals and families until its untimely demise, when a series of attacks by disgruntled members of the victims' advocacy groups forced the rehabilitation program to close in order to preserve the security of its staff in May of 1999. During the suspension of services, however, individual members of the Democracy office of USAID/Haiti informed USAID/Washington that "there were no more victims in Haiti" and that funding for the program should be discontinued. This occurred at nearly the same moment as USAID/Washington's presentation of the Haitian rehabilitation project to Congress as an example of their success in providing relief to torture victims (US Congress 1999a, b).

In this field site the recognition of collective suffering by USAID was a security strategy for the US government: the rehabilitation project was viewed as a step toward building US credibility in Haitian civil society, legitimizing the impending US intervention into Haiti, as well as assisting individuals and families who might otherwise have lost their lives trying to reach asylum in the United States. The project was also viewed as useful in demonstrating the sincerity of US human rights practices overseas, as well as the US's own image as a humanitarian nation. Nevertheless, when this assistance became challenging or problematic and it was no longer necessary to maintain US authority or authenticity in this domain, the funding was discontinued and the existence of *viktim* denied once again. The abrupt withdrawal of aid left many individuals and families who were beneficiaries of the program with little time to find other resources to help them continue to rebuild their lives.

Within the privately funded humanitarian assistance apparatus, the political economy of trauma functioned in a different manner. I also worked at a women's clinic that had been established in Martissant by the joint efforts of two women's organizations, one Haitian and one US-based. One of the main goals of creating this space was to address concerns for the ongoing suffering of women who had been raped during the coup years. These women were encouraged to form survivors' organizations in addition to establishing their membership in the Haitian women's group that founded the clinic. They were provided with small business grants to help them recover financially, and many of them received subsistence supplies from the storehouse that the organizations maintained in the neighborhood. The US-based women's organization solicited funds on behalf of the clinic through its extended membership and frequently updated those on its mailing lists about the progress in assisting these "survivors." At times, however, those funds were slow to reach the clinic staff.

Over the course of my fieldwork, however, I learned that within the local community outside the clinic and the rehabilitation program, certain individuals acted as gatekeepers who facilitated or prevented the victims' access to either the Haitian or the international assistance organizations. In a country where as much as 70 percent of the population is illiterate, those who can read and write have tremendous power as mediators between the local and the international domain of charity, and are often sought as field assistants. In both of my field sites I became aware that outside of the institutions *viktim* were

often asked to pay the local representative or investigator who documented their cases and built their trauma portfolios before they were linked to the individuals and organizations that would assist them. In many cases, the dossiers were withheld until the ransom was paid to the investigator.

In some cases, those who could pay the local investigator would have false portfolios assembled for them. They might be recognized as victims locally, nationally, or internationally because of their purchased portfolio and their ability to perform a convincing tale of woe. Within the environment of poverty and insecurity that Haiti has experienced in the past decade, victim status – whether legitimate or purchased – offers the possibility for political recognition and economic assistance. In this respect, one of the social consequences of the intense international gaze placed upon trauma, rape, and victimization is the creation of what I am calling *trauma brokers* – gatekeepers to the humanitarian assistance apparatus who profit from the suffering of others and who supply the demands of consumers of performed suffering in the international humanitarian apparatus.

I remain haunted by my own part in this cycle of the appropriation, transformation, and commodification of suffering. I wonder how many voices have been silenced within or excluded from recognition within the discourses of trauma and victimization as they are currently conceived as originating from some past traumatic event. For example, I had been working at the women's clinic in Martissant for about a month when Louise came to ask me for a physical therapy session. I told her that my appointment book was full, as I had already arranged to work with rape survivors for the majority of my time at the clinic. Nevertheless, she came every day and waited for a chance that I might see her. Louise was not a member of any women's organization or human rights group. She was not a survivor of state-sponsored terror. In focusing on the trauma of systematic rape at this time I could not recognize her suffering. Nor did I recognize her need for a listening ear and a compassionate, nonthreatening touch.

I agreed to see her when one of my clients was unable to keep her appointment. We went back to the small room where the massage table stood in the center of an overflow waiting area. Mosquitoes buzzed near the floor and underneath a table in the room. We could hear the loud banter of some young boys in the neighborhood and the cries of the newest addition to the family who lived next door. Louise apologized to me because she did not have soap to bathe or to wash her clothes before coming to the clinic. Then she began to tell me her story. "I was almost raped," she said, as if to justify her worth in my eyes. "What happened?" I asked. "I'd been sleeping on the gallery of a house in Martissant. For the past year and a half I've had to sleep with men for money in order to feed my children and to try to send them to school. One of the men tried to rape me but I fought him off. Please don't tell anyone here at the clinic what I do."

I assured her that I would not. In preparation for the physical therapy session I asked her how she felt and she complained of intense low back pain. One night while she was "at work" on the gallery she had been drenched in a flash flood with water that flowed through the garbage and sewage that were dumped from each household onto the street in this neighborhood. She felt that the water had afflicted her with the pain in her back and pelvis. When I inquired further about her situation, Louise told me that often she had slept with ten men per night, accepting whatever they would give her in payment, which was often a slap in the face instead of money. She only used condoms with those who requested it. As she grimaced from pain with the effort to lie down on the table, I was reluctant to work with her before she had seen a doctor to determine what was the immediate cause of her physical pain. She misinterpreted my hesitation and said to me, "Don't worry. I'm not going to sleep with anyone after this massage. I still have two months before I have to pay the registration fee for school."

Ongoing Ethical Challenges

The global discourse of trauma is quickly becoming a language of entitlement in neo-modern discourses of human security that is deployed in the aftermath of each recognized state of emergency. It encodes the inequality between those who identify and label the suffering of others as disordered and those who have survived life-shattering circumstances and become 'victims,' 'rape survivors,' or 'patients.' In this era of *traumatic citizenship*, an era in which individuals and groups seek recognition, agency, political and economic power, and security through attempts to seek justice and restitution for past wrongs or experiences of victimization, we must ask ourselves what is at stake when we recognize and materially compensate others because of a single attribute – their suffering, their injury or trauma, their gender, or their race?

As Brown (1995) suggests, does this particular form of recognition perpetuate a second-class or underdeveloped status for those who are the objects of humanitarian intervention? Does the recognition of trauma in this manner perpetuate forms of bio-power that are rooted in the imperial past? In discussions of international security must the trauma and suffering of some nations be denied for fear that prolonged victim assistance may turn into forms of welfare or managed care without borders? Furthermore, when our compassion is fatigued or our gaze turns to other global terrors or dramatic forms of suffering that we witness from a distance (Boltanski 1999; Nussbaum 2003), what are the repercussions of withdrawing the "gift" of humanitarian aid?

Maurice Godelier has written the following on the "tyranny of the gift":

> Giving ... seems to establish a difference and an inequality of status between donor and recipient, which can in certain instances become a hierarchy: if this hierarchy already exists, then the gift expresses and legitimizes it. Two opposite movements are thus contained in a single act. The gift decreases the distance between the protagonists because it is a form of sharing, and it increases the social distance between them because one is now indebted to the other. ... It can be, simultaneously or successively, an act of generosity or of violence; in the latter case, however, the violence is disguised as a disinterested gesture, since it is committed by means of and in the form of sharing. (Godelier 1999: 12)

The development of the ethical economies outlined in Mauss' formulation of the gift (Mauss 1950) is extremely relevant to this discussion of suffering, security, reparations, and restitution, but also to the way in which violence may involve economies of appropriation and exchange in the form of taking. As I discussed in this article, the economies of extraction of suffering or trauma occur in different ways, depending on whether one examines the practices used during the repression of the coup years or the unintended generation of occult economies by the humanitarian assistance apparatus. Nonetheless, to examine these activities solely from the present without regard to history would be an error.

Haiti's infamous position as the "poorest country in the Western Hemisphere" has roots in colonial economies of violence, terror, and extraction of productivity from the bodies of slave laborers. Since its independence, the "state of extraction" remains linked to its current "state of pathology" (James 2003) – the perception on the part of international donors that the government of Haiti can neither arrest the political, criminal, and economic insecurity within its borders, nor consolidate its democracy according to their expectations. The dilemma remains that in nations like Haiti, where the state is incapable of meeting the needs of the poor majority, any means toward political recognition or assistance is crucial for its citizenry and may result in tragic tactics of survival, including transforming, appropriating, and circulating narratives of the suffering of victims as currency in the global political economy of trauma. In this respect trauma portfolios lie at the nexus of economies of compassion and terror (Nussbaum 2003) in which are linked local, national, and international forms of gift giving; security practices in insecure social and institutional environments; questions of global reparations; and quests for justice. The danger for the humanitarian assistance apparatus, however, is in assuming an obligation to a population that the state cannot or will not fulfill – and that the international community ignores or is reluctant to assume. While their actions are well-intended, even transnational nongovernmental organizations – that are not accountable to those they serve in local realms – may abuse their own power or contribute to occult economies of suffering.

There are no easy answers to the ethical and moral dilemmas that I have presented in this article, nor are the problems I describe new ones. The fact remains that the ubiquitous presence of human suffering caused by the pernicious acts of others, as well as the responses to it, is inextricably bound to local, national, and international histories, politics, economies, and cultures that are not easy to disentangle. In order to examine adequately issues of agency, causality, inequalities, prejudices, and oppression, questions of suffering, insecurity, and security will continue to require more complex analyses than can be encompassed by the conceptual frameworks of 'trauma,' 'human rights,' or even the trope of 'structural violence.' Thus the ethical task at hand is also not a new one.

Social theorists, activists, advocates, and other humanitarian actors involved in technologies of bio-power and knowledge production must still acknowledge and grapple with new forms of complexity in this neo-modern age, including our own unforeseen roles in perpetuating cycles of inequality and exclusion of those who would achieve equality and citizenship within the international community. In the domain of humanitarian assistance the challenge remains one of balancing the economy of gifts and exchanges and limiting dependencies and the perversion of aid (Terry 2002). The reality, however, is that for injured individuals and families who have no other recourse in these "cultures of insecurity" (Weldes et al. 1999) and uncertainty, the path of survival may lie in crime or the appropriation of others' suffering for personal gain. The remainder may risk death on the high seas to reach asylum on other shores, or may appropriate their own bodies and risk disease in order to survive. Those of us from cultures of relative security must acknowledge that while our intentions may be to "do good," there is always the potential that we who profit from the partial recognition of our subjects' humanity will perpetuate the cycle of global inequality. But perhaps this is a stepping-stone toward global inclusion – call it "trickle-down compassion," if you will.

REFERENCES

Allen, Irving M.
1996   PTSD Among African Americans. *In* Ethnocultural Aspects of Posttraumatic Stress Disorder: Issues, Research, and Clinical Applications. Anthony J. Marsella, Matthew J. Friedman, Ellen T. Gerrity, and Raymond M. Scurfield, eds., pp. 209–38. Washington, DC: American Psychological Association.

Aretxaga, Begoña
1997   Shattering Silence: Women, Nationalism, and Political Subjectivity in Northern Ireland. Princeton: Princeton University Press.

Boltanski, Luc
1999[1993]   Distant Suffering: Morality, Media and Politics. Graham Burchell, trans. Cambridge: Cambridge University Press.

Bracken, Patrick J., and Celia Petty, eds.
1998   Rethinking the Trauma of War. London and New York: Free Association Books.

Brown, Wendy
1995   States of Injury: Power and Freedom in Late Modernity. Princeton: Princeton University Press.

Cahill, Kevin M., ed.
2003   Traditions, Values, and Humanitarian Action. New York: Fordham University Press and the Center for International Health and Cooperation.

Cartwright, Samuel A.
1851   Report on the Diseases and Physical Peculiarities of the Negro Race. Part One. The New Orleans Medical and Surgical Journal 7 (May): 691–715.

Central Intelligence Agency
2004   The World Fact Book [Electronic document]. Retrieved March 18, 2004, from http://www.cia.gov/cia/publications/factbook/geos/ha.html#People.

Craige, John H.
1933   Black Bagdad. New York: Minton, Balch and Company.
1934   Cannibal Cousins. New York: Minton, Balch and Company.

Das, Veena
1995   Critical Events: An Anthropological Perspective on Contemporary India. Oxford: Oxford University Press.

Das, Veena, and Ashis Nandy
1985   Violence, Victimhood, and the Language of Silence. Contribution to Indian Sociology 19(1): 177–95.

Dash, J. Michael
1997   Haiti and the United States: Stereotypes and the Literary Imagination, 2nd edn. New York: St. Martin's Press.

DeConde, Alexander
1992   Ethnicity, Race, and American Foreign Policy. Boston: Northeastern University Press.

Deleuze, Gilles
1988   Foucault. Seán Hand, trans. Minneapolis: The University of Minnesota Press.

Dubuche, Georges
2002   Report on the MSH/HS-2004 project. Talk delivered at Management Sciences for Health headquarters, Boston, MA, May 22.

Farmer, Paul
1992   AIDS and Accusation: Haiti and the Geography of Blame. Berkeley and Los Angeles: University of California Press.

Fisher, William F.
1997   Doing Good? The Politics and Antipolitics of NGO Practices. Annual Review of Anthropology 26: 439–64.

Foucault, Michel
1990[1978]   The History of Sexuality, Vol. 1: An Introduction. Robert Hurley, trans. Vintage Books edition. New York: Random House.
1991   Governmentality. *In* The Foucault Effect: Studies in Governmentality. Graham Burchell, Colin Gordon, and Peter Miller eds., pp. 87–104. Chicago: The University of Chicago Press.
1997   Ethics: Subjectivity and Truth. Essential Works of Foucault 1954–1984, Vol. 1. Paul Rabinow, ed. Robert Hurley and others, trans. New York: The New Press.

Fraser, Nancy
1995   From Redistribution to Recognition? Dilemmas of Justice in a 'Post-Socialist' Age. New Left Review 212: 68–93.

Freud, Sigmund
1997[1927]   Fetishism. *In* Sexuality and the Psychology of Love. New York: Simon and Schuster.

Girard, René
1977[1972]   Violence and the Sacred. Patrick Gregory, trans. Baltimore: The Johns Hopkins University Press.

Gobineau, Arthur, comte de
  1999   The Inequality of Human Races. Adrian
  Collins, trans. New York: Howard Fertig, Inc.
Godelier, Maurice
  1999[1996]   The Enigma of the Gift. Chicago:
  The University of Chicago Press.
Harvey, David
  1990   The Condition of Postmodernity: An
  Enquiry Into the Origins of Cultural Change.
  Oxford: Blackwell.
Hayner, Priscilla B.
  2001   Unspeakable Truths: Confronting State
  Terror and Atrocity: How Truth Commissions
  Around the World Are Challenging the Past and
  Shaping the Future. New York and London:
  Routledge.
James, Erica Caple
  2003   The Violence of Misery: "Insecurity" in
  Haiti in the "Democratic" Era. Unpublished
  dissertation, Harvard University, Cambridge,
  MA: Harvard University.
  2008   Haunting Ghosts: Madness, Gender
  and *Ensekirite* in Haiti in the Democratic Era.
  In Postcolonial Disorders. Sandra Hyde and
  Mary-Jo DelVecchio Good, eds.
Jameson, Frederic
  1991   Postmodernism, or, The Cultural Logic of
  Late Capitalism. Durham: Duke University Press.
Jordan, Winthrop
  1968   White Over Black: American Attitudes
  Toward the Negro: 1550–1812. Chapel Hill:
  University of North Carolina Press.
Kleinman, Arthur
  1995   Writing at the Margin: Discourse Between
  Anthropology and Medicine. Berkeley and Los
  Angeles: University of California Press.
Kleinman, Arthur, and Joan Kleinman
  1991   Suffering and Its Professional Trans-
  formation: Toward an Ethnography of Inter-
  personal Experience. Culture, Medicine and
  Psychiatry 15(3): 275–301.
Lawyers Committee for Human Rights
  1990   Refugee Refoulement: The Forced
  Return of Haitians Under the U.S.–Haitian
  Interdiction Agreement. New York: Lawyers
  Committee for Human Rights.
LeBon, Gustave
  1974   The Psychology of Peoples. New York:
  Arno Press.
Lyotard, Jean-François
  1984[1979]   The Postmodern Condition: A
  Report on Knowledge. Minneapolis: University
  of Minnesota Press.

Mauss, Marcel
  1950   The Gift: The Form and Reason for
  Exchange in Archaic Societies. W.D. Halls,
  trans. New York and London: W.W. Norton.
Miller, Jake C.
  1984   The Plight of Haitian Refugees. New
  York: Praeger.
Nussbaum, Martha C.
  2003   Compassion and Terror. Daedalus 132
  (1): 10–26.
Pandolfi, Mariella
  2000   Une souveraineté mouvante et supracoloniale. Multitudes 3 [Electronic document].
  Available from http://multitudes.samizdat.net/
  article.php3?id_article=182.
Patterson, Orlando
  1982   Slavery and Social Death: A Comparative Study. Cambridge, MA and London: Harvard University Press.
Petryna, Adriana
  2002   Life Exposed: Biological Citizens after
  Chernobyl. Princeton, NJ: Princeton University
  Press.
Plummer, Brenda Gayle
  1992   Haiti and the United States: The Psychological Moment. Athens, GA: The University of Georgia Press.
Povinelli, Elizabeth A.
  2002   The Cunning of Recognition: Indigenous Alterity and the Making of Australian
  Multiculturalism. Durham and London: Duke
  University Press.
Renda, Mary A.
  2001   Taking Haiti: Military Occupation and
  the Culture of U.S. Imperialism, 1915–1940.
  Chapel Hill and London: The University of
  North Carolina Press.
Rieff, David
  2002   A Bed for the Night: Humanitarianism
  in Crisis. New York: Simon and Schuster.
Rothschild, Emma
  1995   What is Security? Daedalus 124(3): 53–98.
Sabatier, Renée
  1988   Blaming Others: Prejudice, Race and
  Worldwide AIDS. Philadelphia: The Panos
  Institute and New Society Publishers.
Scarry, Elaine
  1985   The Body in Pain: The Making and
  Unmaking of the World. Oxford: Oxford Uni-
  versity Press.
Taussig, Michael
  1992   The Nervous System. New York:
  Routledge.

Taylor, Charles
1994 The Politics of Recognition. *In* Multiculturalism: Examining the Politics of Recognition. Amy Gutmann, ed., pp. 25–73. Princeton, NJ: Princeton University Press.

Terry, Fiona
2002 Condemned to Repeat: The Paradox of Humanitarian Action. Ithaca, NY: Cornell University Press.

United Nations Development Program (UNDP)
1994 Human Development Report 1994. Oxford: Oxford University Press.
2000 Human Development Report 2000. New York: Oxford University Press.

United States Congress
1999a United States Policy Toward Victims of Torture. Hearing Before the Subcommittee on International Operations and Human Rights of the Committee on International Relations, House of Representatives. 106th Congress, First Session, June 29, 1999.
1999b U.S. Policy Toward Victims of Torture. Hearing before the Subcommittee on International Operations of the Committee on Foreign Relations, United States Senate. 106th Congress, First Session, July 30, 1999.

United States Embassy (Haiti)
1994 Haiti Human Rights Report. Unpublished U.S. State Department memorandum.

Weldes, Jutta, Mark Laffey, Hugh Gusterson, and Raymond Duvall
1999 Introduction. *In* Cultures of Insecurity: States, Communities, and the Production of Danger. Jutta Weldes, Mark Laffey, Hugh Gusterson, and Raymond Duvall, eds., pp. 1–33. Minneapolis: University of Minnesota Press.

World Bank
2001 World Development Report 2000/2001: Attacking Poverty. New York: Oxford University Press.

Young, Allan
1995 The Harmony of Illusions: Inventing Post-Traumatic Stress Disorder. Princeton, NJ: Princeton University Press.

38

Contract of Mutual (In)Difference
Governance and the Humanitarian Apparatus in Contemporary Albania and Kosovo

Mariella Pandolfi

Introduction

In his book *Le malheur des autres*, Bernard Kouchner, the founder of Médecins Sans Frontières and the former French Health Minister, wrote that "[h]umanitarian activities have become customary."[1] Kouchner's statement points to the new forms of globally organized power and expertise, located within new transnational regimes, humanitarian networks, non-governmental organizations (NGOs), and multi- and bilateral organizations that are now developing. These new transnational regimes, parallel to local forms of rule, constitute a mobile apparatus which I have defined as migrant sovereignties.[2]

With the explosive growth of NGOs of all scales and varieties that has occurred since 1945, we are witnessing a massive transformation in the nature of global governance.[3] Such growth has been fueled by the connected development of the UN system, and, more particularly, by the increasing global circulation and legitimization of discourse and politics of "human rights." Resolutions adopted by the UN Security Council and various international agencies and meetings show that new forms of sovereignty have come into place alongside older, territorialized forms. These new forms legitimize the right of interference and intervention, identifying a deterritorialized sovereignty that migrates around the globe to sites of "crisis" and humanitarian disaster.

At a time when international humanitarian processes are proliferating in militarized contexts the world over, it is imperative that we take time to reflect on the theoretical foundations, as well as the practical consequences, of such interventions. This is a perilous but necessary exercise, forcing us to consider the complex relationship between humanitarian organizations, international institutions, and specific segments of local élites. This paper addresses the ways in which the

Mariella Pandolfi, "Contract of Mutual (In)Difference: Governance and the Humanitarian Apparatus in Contemporary Albania and Kosovo," *Indiana Journal of Global and Legal Studies* 10 (2003): 369–80.

humanitarian-military apparatus constructs the logic behind its interventions, how interventions are carried out, and how they impact the local scene. It aims to identify the means by which institutional categories and interventions are transferred into this local political sphere and canonized as models of governance.

My work is specifically concerned with the post-war and post-communist Balkan territories and the assemblages that crisscross those territories.[4] From 1991 until the crucial months of the war, the international presence in Albania and Kosovo was active at various institutional levels. The true agents of military-economic-humanitarian action were the various international organizations, agencies, foundations, and NGOs, whose operations were shaped by a temporality of emergency. These agents espouse the legitimacy of the right of interference, the rhetoric of institution building, and a Western, neo-liberal, forced democratization of the southeastern European frontier. The power they wield is real, and is superimposed onto bureaucratic procedures and lengthy intergovernmental negotiations.[5]

The title of this paper – Contract of Mutual (In)Difference – seeks to draw attention to a central feature of our age that has gained prominence over the past ten years: the coexistence, within the same territorial perimeter, of two opposed modes of sovereignty. One of these is tied to a territorial configuration such as the nation-state, religion, or ethnicity. The other, which has resulted from the proliferation of non-territorialized forms of power and governance, such as the complex military-humanitarian apparatus, is deployed, legitimized, and imposed according to a planetary logic in "crisis" situations by an international "humanitarian" rule of law.

This discussion draws on fieldwork conducted in Albania and Kosovo since 1997, which has allowed me to travel behind the lines, so to speak, of the humanitarian apparatus. My argument is that military forces and multi- and bilateral organizations are transforming into a new form of transnational domination.[6]

I will begin by describing the convergence between military and humanitarian forms of intervention, and the role of NGOs as operators of a new military-humanitarian form of governance. I will show that the forms of governance that are expressed through NGOs can be understood as a new form of sovereignty, at the intersection of biopolitics[7] and "bare life," which is apparent in the way that international intervention manages bodies according to humanitarian categories. Finally, I will discuss how, in the aftermath of the humanitarian war in Kosovo, this new sovereignty has left behind a residue of humanitarian forms of governance, even as it moves to new sites of intervention.

I. Humanitarian Wars, the Culture of Intervention, and the Role of NGOs

Military and humanitarian intervention has a historical pedigree dating back to the face-off between European power and the Ottoman Empire in the nineteenth century. The first humanitarian war can be identified with the arrival of the French in Lebanon in 1860. This intervention aimed to protect Maronite Christians from Muslim attacks and occurred after 6,000 Maronites had been slaughtered by the Druses. I define the humanitarian apparatus as the entire complex of ideologies, organizational strategies, and actions that unfold due to pressure exerted by two elements: the right to interfere and the temporality of emergency. Proliferating through the twentieth century, NGOs have increasingly positioned themselves as a challenge to governments and occupied roles left vacant by government institutions. At other times, they have acted as a counterpoint to government actors, being much more agile at opening channels of intervention. By means of their own networks, international NGOs have created a direct and independent form of non-governmental diplomacy, allowing them to act in parallel to state governments.

Since 1993, the number of states that have appealed to NGOs as ad hoc experts in procedures and development of international agreements has increased tremendously. Their economic and intellectual resources, and their ability to manage information, have allowed a number of NGOs to acquire an authority that has often superseded that of state administrative bodies.[8] The increased relevance of their role vis-à-vis donors (nation-states and public institutions) is the result of their flexibility, mobility, and transnational expertise. This strategic capability allows them to intervene promptly in all corners of the globe, to maintain a transnational communication network, and finally to produce testimony.

In the "New World Order," crisis management integrates the roles of military and humanitarian aid. Veronique de Geoffroy discusses the military-humanitarian or civilian-military formula by noting that the vocabularies of these two realms are beginning to come together.[9] In both contexts, one speaks of an "area of responsibility" or of "projecting onto an area," and so forth – originally military expressions. Humanitarianism, as John Prendergast reminds us, cannot be viewed as a civil religion, or as an act of faith. In other words, it is a mode of historical action, which has social, economical and political consequences.[10]

Observing the diverse interpretations of humanitarian intervention, one soon discovers that the conventional discourse conceals a paradox. On the one hand, humanitarian aid is perceived as action that tends to consolidate state sovereignty, understood as a form of government in its multiple local and global political forms; on the other hand, humanitarian intervention is constructed as a measure of the progressive erosion of state sovereignty – in the name of the principles and practices of its own political organization – that extends over the whole planet. Both of these positions are projected onto a transnational scene in which relations and institutions distinct to each sovereign state are increasingly confused due to the more general pressure of globalization. The entire humanitarian apparatus legitimizes its presence in the name of an ethical and temporal rule that may be defined as the "culture of emergency."

II. Problematizing Sovereignty: Biopower and Bare Life

From varying perspectives, political scientists and international lawyers have identified four different ways of defining the concept of sovereignty today: (1) domestic sovereignty; (2) independent sovereignty; (3) Westphalian sovereignty; and (4) international legal sovereignty.[11] In contrast, over the last decade, anthropology has approached the problem of sovereignty ethnographically, "confronting" these typologies of sovereignty with a biopolitical notion of sovereignty. This work has drawn on theoretical concepts from the writings of Michel Foucault and, more recently, those of Giorgio Agamben.[12] Such displacement toward a "critical" zone of sovereignty – an intertwining of sovereignty and biopolitics – has allowed anthropology to adopt a more refined position than that of a mere accountant of different forms of sovereignty.

Foucault summarizes the formula for classical sovereignty as the prerogative to the right over life and death: the power to take life or let live in a given territory.[13] Biopolitics designates a reversal, or rather the contemporary metamorphosis, of this sovereign power, in that it is also exercised as the power to let die or to make live. Power, understood this way, implies an enormous expansion in its potential to dominate. While classical law reasoned about the individual and society, and the disciplines considered individuals and their bodies, biopolitics has as its focus entire populations, considered as biological and political problems.

In the case of the fall of traditional forms of sovereignty, there is also a collapse of official identity, which is what allows people to locate their lives at the juncture between the present situation within living humanity and one's belonging to the eternal human race. Politics is no longer geopolitics, and power no longer stops at the domination of subjects retained within real and institutional frontiers of States, or in the no-man's land of international relations. Power has become biopolitics.

The exercise of biopolitical sovereignty extends so far that the sovereign human being is stripped to the barest choice of life. In other words, the only choice left is located in what Primo Levi called "the gray zone," that is, the nonliving and the non-dying.[14] Agamben describes this space as Bare Life – the absolute political substance that, once isolated, allows the total definition of the subject's identity in demographic, ethnic, national or political terms.[15]

This slippage of our present age has occurred not only in order to legitimize ethnic cleansing and genocide, but also in the name of compassion, for the sake of protection and cure, in the name of what Fassin has defined as *la politique du vivant* (the politics of life).[16] This is the paradox that I want to address. The radical and central aspect of our democratic management – protecting victims, organizing health policies, codifying the new frontiers of genetics, intervening during "emergency" humanitarian catastrophes – assumes the logic of biopolitical technology.

Biopolitics thus reveals an inversion in the deployment of power – the reduction of subjective trajectories, of individuals, of men and women, to bodies. Such indistinct, displaced, and localized bodies come to be classified and defined as refugees, legal or illegal immigrants, or traumatized victims according to the diagnostic categories of humanitarian management.

I would thus locate the catalogue of human suffering inscribed by the deployment of "humanitarian" biopower at the juncture between two conceptual domains: that of "governmentality," which Foucault defined "as running through the totality constituted by instructions, procedures, analyses, tactics that allow the exercise of this very specific though extremely complex form of power, which has as its locus the population and as its essential technical instrument, security apparatuses,"[17] and that of the intersection of rights with biopower as developed by Agamben. The separation between humanitarianism and politics that we are experiencing today is the extreme phase of the separation of the rights of man from the rights of the citizen. In the final analysis, however, humanitarian organizations – which today are more and more supported by international commissions – can only grasp human life in the figure of bare or sacred life, and therefore, despite themselves, maintain a secret solidarity with the very powers they ought to fight.[18] Following Foucault, I view biopower as an articulation of the political with the biological; following Agamben, this

also means recognition of the paradox and the risk implied in the rule of law in modern democracies.

For Agamben there are two models of power, a juridical one focused on the problem of the legitimacy of Western power (the problem of sovereignty), and a non-juridical model centered on the problem of the effectiveness of Western power.[19] These two models meet in the dimension of exception.[20] Agamben writes:

> What is the place of sovereignty? If the sovereign, in the words of Carl Schmidt, is the one who may proclaim the state of exception and thus legally suspend the validity of law, then the space of sovereignty is a paradoxical space, as it lies both within and without the juridical order.
>
> What is an exception? It is a form of exclusion. It is a single case that is excluded from the general rule. But what characterizes the exception is that what is considered as excluded in reality maintains a relationship with the law, albeit in the form of a suspension.[21]

The fundamental operation of power is to isolate a bare life in each subject, a life that is irremediably exposed to sovereign decisions. Within the space of exception, a sovereign decision is exercised without mediation. Agamben observes and describes with ruthless sobriety the human destiny of the individual, the group, and the population at the moment in which it enters into this zone of arbitrariness.[22] In many areas of anthropological work, we are similarly confronted with the arbitrariness of rendering the human being no longer as a citizen, but as a bare life, a zoe.

III. "Bare Life" and Emergency in Kosovo and Albania

The places where the juridical state of suspension is activated may be refugee camps, or, as I have found in my research in Kosovo and Albania, the ambiguous setting-in-motion of the entire humanitarian apparatus. In all of these places individuals become a "population" to be numbered, ethnicized, and catalogued. In the process of humanitarian intervention, the state of exception is legitimized by the category of "emergency," which is a category of action recognized by law.

Determined as a temporal and temporary derogation in a precise context, the emergency category is "logically" opposed to the category of the ordinary. Paradoxically, emergency no longer constitutes an extraordinary or exceptional temporal category in humanitarian intervention. In the territories of humanitarian intervention, it has become the sole temporal modality of the new social contract, which includes the right of interference, temporality of emergency, and necessity of action.[23]

The occupation of space, the invasion of territory, and the crossing of borders are characterized by the need for mobility and speed in intervention; the humanitarian apparatus is in fact constructed on the logic of action. Responding to the priorities of international donors and bureaucratic frameworks, a thousand traces of action, often contradictory, propagate. They are performed by social actors concealing a profound ambivalence, if not hostility, toward the institutions that require action.[24] Humanitarian universalism bears an anti-state and anti-institutional current of rebellion, moving instead according to what Laïdi has more recently called planetary time.[25] The emotional components of the single humanitarian choice are also multiple and confused, and are often experienced in contradictory ways by single individuals, who may experience a mixture of pietas and cynicism, of the desire for adventure and the necessity to be present in the mediatized arena, of money and emergency, of bureaucracy and anti-ideology.

Edward Said has held that the discursive forms that feed a colonial power function not only as an instrumental form of consciousness, but also as an ambivalent protocol for imagination and desire.[26] Such recognition appears central for understanding how the humanitarian emergency constructs, feeds, and reinforces a power that under the guise of neutrality imposes rules of spatial and temporal compression.

The rhetoric of pietas, the one-dimensional construction of the enemy, and the "moral" necessity of simultaneous and fragmented action are discursive constructions that stifle any dissident or alternative voice. Witnessing is the central element in this regime of governmentality.

IV. Migrant Sovereignty in the Aftermath of Emergency

The overall feature present in most interviews of experts or aid workers active in the humanitarian apparatus is the trope of personal witnessing: "I saw, I was ..." is often rendered as "I did Bosnia, Albania, Kosovo, and I will surely do Macedonia and Afghanistan."[27]

As Rufin notes, the temptation to conceive all humanitarian matters as inherently innocent, so deep-seated in Western consciousness, is

> increasingly at variance with reality, because today humanitarianism has entered the era of high complexity ... which cannot accommodate either romantic tendencies or the desire to "naturalize" war, which forgets that conflicts are not engendered by some sort of barbarian absurdity born out of some kind of tribalism, or the result of an excess of extremist fury, but always have "political" origins.[28]

One cannot dispute the legitimacy of an intervention seeking to help victims on the ground or to rebuild a nation where massacres have taken place. Yet as soon as the media leave the scene of the "humanitarian disaster," the theater of generosity loses its actors.

In Albania, during the three-month-long war of 1999, the emergency provoked the deployment of an enormous apparatus of humanitarian organizations[29] to accommodate 500,000 refugees. In so doing, for the sake of efficiency and experience, it also interrupted negotiating activities with local institutions and with international diplomats present in Albania. Within twelve days, NATO, the international military force (AFOR[30]), and the bilateral and multilateral bodies active in Albania at the time had superseded the embassies and local government. The international organizations proposed that they administer ninety percent of the necessary aid themselves, with the remaining ten percent administered at the local level. Yet within two weeks, even this ten percent had been appropriated by the ad hoc intervention force. NATO's military logistical infrastructure was deployed with such "efficiency" that it had the whole territory under its control, assigning responsibilities and distributing roles. It was a global strategy of control that took advantage of economists, business consultants, and administrators who had earned their Masters' from the most prestigious American universities.

Wearing the badge of an international organization was enough to gain entry into the pyramid mausoleum built by Hoxha in the center of Tirana, which had become NATO headquarters, to view the maps – reports (updated every three hours) on the precise number of refugees, the situation of individuals displaced from one extremity to the other of the country, epidemics, the quantity of available drugs and where they were needed, the number of showers, how many toilets were needed in a specific location, and so forth. In short, it was an organizational strategy so pervasive that it immediately eliminated any possible alternative mode of intervention. All this, as I have said, in the name of the need to cure, nourish, and save "human lives."

The day after the war ended, in June 1999, I was still in Albania. Within a few days, the limelight of media compassion was turned off. Hotels were emptied of journalists, officials, and international aid workers; apartment leases were canceled. The transnational "army" was renting helicopters and cars to move on to another site of humanitarian compassion. At the same time, ethnic Albanians were quickly heading back to their homes in Kosovo. The end of the war and the mass return of the Kosovars resulted in the suppression of the "emergency" in Albania, which in a few days was to be displaced to the "liberated" territory of Kosovo. The result was that NGOs and international agencies active in Albania closed down their local operations and laid off their Albanian employees, leaving behind unused material which had not even been cleared by local customs. The emergency had moved elsewhere, and new operations, new logistics and apparatuses, had to be put in place in and for Kosovo.[31]

Three years later, projects that had been financed in Kosovo for the first year after the war have been put on hold because the "emergency" provisions have expired.[32] As a consequence, available funds can no longer be used. Moreover, the changed political situation in Serbia and the emergence of conflicts between KFOR, the UN mission in Kosovo, and the Albanian guerrillas in Macedonia have yet again displaced the focus of the "emergency."

Emergency and post-emergency are effects of suffering and violence that are consistent with categories recognized by international protocols. The line separating so-called "emergency" projects from "post-emergency" ones forces project directors constantly to revise their strategies at all levels in order to adopt the right rhetoric and thus be able to keep getting the funding necessary to keep their intervention afloat. Laïdi draws attention to the existence of a supply-effect of emergency. "As soon as emergency is professionalized, it tends to structure itself as social supply waiting for its demand. And if the demand does not exist, one tends to create it."[33] In other words, certain humanitarian organizations justify their existence with a circular logic: a state of emergency is legitimate because urgent action has to be taken.

The media-generated triangle of NATO, humanitarians, and refugees has eliminated the other social partners involved in the conflict from the game. At the same time, however, the "political" role that the humanitarian industry plays has become evident as certain sectors are developed while others are neglected, and as strategic priorities that go beyond the logic of defense, shelter, and protection are considered, constructing transnational priorities and weakening entire sectors of the local society that do not correspond to standards prioritized and recognized by the intervention.

A series of categories drawn from the discursive and operative strategies of humanitarianism is thus applied to the territory and to human beings. Such categories may be extended to the world system of potential and real donors, multilateral and bilateral accords, ad hoc UN agencies and, finally, to programs that are much less controllable – in terms of execution of project, budget, and so forth – if they are constructed and enacted in the period labeled as an "emergency."

The "do something syndrome" is the response adopted by governments, UN agencies, and international NGOs when confronted by the public's concern about a crisis. "Something must be done" is a powerful justification, particularly when further strengthened by the spectacle of distant suffering. Yet in the final analysis it shows the dangerous gap that exists between humanitarian "needs" and humanitarian "budgets."

It is a practice that constitutes subjects, both the operators of the intervention whose agency is cast within the humanitarian ideology, and those who would be their beneficiaries – the mute subjects whose dense sociality is reduced to thin descriptions in bureaucratic reports. Thus, in exemplary fashion, the bureaucratization of pietas, couched in the rhetoric of universalism, efficiency, good intentions, and the need to act, imbues and determines the stream of pamphlets and confidential reports that document the humanitarian universe.

The dimension of experience or previous individual and collective history is erased by the new categories in which human beings are pigeonholed; the terms "victim," "refugee," "trafficked woman," or "trauma case" do not relate to experiences of traumatic events, but are labels by means of which it is possible to activate procedures such as fundraising, protocols, the establishment of transversal and transnational institutions and, ultimately, of a business whose importance and amplitude is concealed by charitable pietas. A refugee is a completely exportable and generic category, whether from Bosnia or the Philippines; a trafficked woman enters into repatriation procedures whether she is in Kosovo or in Thailand; and demilitarization is accomplished with similar procedures whether in Africa or in South America.

Conclusion: The Kosovo "Exception" Now Exists for Better and Worse

In conclusion, let me draw the following points. First, all humanitarian action is legitimized by its humanitarian intentions, never by its defense of specific interests. The legitimacy of a humanitarian operation derives from its being conceived of as an end in itself, the expression of a humanitarian impulse. Such an operation should not be understood as an instrumental form of political action. Second, intervention most often occurs where there is the sudden breakdown of a pre-existing equilibrium. Humanitarian action is constructed out of such a "crisis," for it is here that it legitimates its operation. Yet the notion of the breakdown of a pre-existing equilibrium is ambiguous, as dramatic examples can testify. As underlined by the independent commission in Kosovo (August 1999–October 2000), we need a critical approach to the interpretation of emerging doctrine of humanitarian intervention. We need to shed light on the grey zone that lies between an extension of international law and a proposal for an international moral consensus where humanitarian interventions proliferate. In essence, this grey zone goes beyond strict ideas of legality to incorporate more flexible views of legitimacy. In a time characterized by "failing states" and "ethnic conflicts" – an explosion in the number of refugees and stateless persons – the humanitarian industry has emerged as an immensely powerful biopolitical force, effectively having power of life and death over millions the world over. It is time for this industry to be subjected to critical scrutiny.

NOTES

1 Bernard Kouchner, *Le Malheur des Autres* 313 (1991).

2 See Mariella Pandolfi, "L'industrie humanitaire: une souveraineté mouvante et supracoloniale. Réflexion sur l'expérience des Balkans." 3 *Multitudes* 97–105 (2000); see also Arjun Appadurai, "Sovereignty Without Territoriality: Notes for a Postnational Geography." *The Geography of Identity* 40–58 (Patricia Yaeger ed., 1996); Arjun Appadurai, *Modernity at Large: Cultural Dimensions of Globalisation* (1996). Drawing on Appadurai's notion of mobile sovereignty, we can define these transnational formations as migrant sovereignties which serve to link transnational forms of

domination over local political practices. The intricate network of the humanitarian political-economic-military complex that is superimposed as a migrant sovereignty upon Albanian society does not conceive any strategy of negotiation with its political, institutional, and social actors.

3 See generally Anne Marie Clark, "Non-Governmental Organisations and Their Influence on International Society." 48 *J. Int'l Aff.* 509–24 (1995).

4 See, e.g., Mariella Pandolfi, " 'Moral entrepreneurs' ", souverainetés mouvants et barbelés. Le bio-politique dans les Balkans post-communistes. 26 *Anthropologie et Societé* 29–51 (2002).

5 See Jean-Christophe Rufin, L'aventure humanitaire (1994); see also Jean-Christophe Rufin, "Pour l'humanitaire. Dépasser le sentiment d'échec." 105 *Le Débat* 4–21 (1999) [hereinafter Rufin, *Pour l'humanitaire*].

6 See generally Noam Chomsky, *The New Military Humanism: Lessons from Kosovo* (1999).

7 I use the term biopolitics in the manner developed by Michel Foucault to refer to the ensemble of administrative practices – schooling, policing, caring – that came to be used to administer populations with the rise of the modern state. See generally 1 Michel Foucault, *History of Sexuality* (Robert Hurley trans., 1978); see also 3, 4 Michel Foucault, *Dits et écrits: 1954–1988* (1994). Giorgio Agamben wrote "[a]ccording to Foucault, a society's 'threshold of biological modernity' is situated at the point at which the species and the individual as a simple living body become what is at stake in a society's political strategies." Giorgio Agamben, *Homo Sacer: Sovereign Power and Bare Life* (Daniel Heller-Roazen trans., 1998) [hereinafter *Homo Sacer*]. Michael Hardt and Toni Negri have further developed this concept to examine how these practices produce regimes of rule in the contemporary world that are radically limited to the management of life in the barest terms, as in concentration or refugee camps or in capitalist production. See generally Michael Hardt & Antonio Negri, *Empire* (2000).

8 After Bosnia, the humanitarian industry has constructed its own legitimacy to intervene, even militarily. Yet Bosnia was not the first time the industry intervened; in 1992, when Somalia witnessed Operation Restore Hope, forty international NGOs were present in that country. The second example of this type of mobilization was in November 1993, when seventy-six NGOs were set up in Rwanda.

9 See Veronique de Geoffroy, "Militaro-humanitaire ou civilo-militaire?." 12 *Mouvements* 49–54 (2000).

10 See generally John Prendergast, *Crisis Response: Humanitarian Band-Aids in Sudan and Somalia* 3 (1997).

11 Stephen D. Krasner, *Sovereignty: Organized Hypocrisy* 3 (1999).

12 See generally Giorgio Agamben, *The Coming Community* (Michael Hardt trans., 1993) [hereinafter *The Coming Community*]; *Homo Sacer, supra* note 7; Giorgio Agamben, *Means Without End: Notes on Politics* (Vincenzo Binetti & Cesare Casarino trans., 2000) [hereinafter *Means Without End*].

13 Foucault develops the term classical sovereignty at length, expressing classical sovereignty most succinctly as the power of life or death exercised by the sovereign ruler over his subjects: the King can condemn to death, or allow to live, anyone in the territory he rules. See generally Michel Foucault, *Il faut défendre la société: cours au Collège de France 1975–1976* (1997).

14 See Primo Levi, *The Drowned and the Saved* 20, 42–3 (Raymond Rosenthal trans., 1988) (1986).

15 The notion of bare life is more fully developed in *Homo Sacer, supra* note 7.

16 Didier Fassin, "Entre politiques du vivant et politiques de la vie. Pour une anthropologiede la santé." 1 *Les Notes de recherché du Cresp* 13 (2000), available at www.inserm.fr/cresp/cresp.nsf.

17 Michel Foucault, "La gouvernementalité." 54 *Actes* 10, 18 (1986).

18 *Homo Sacer, supra* note 7, at 133.

19 *Id.* at 5.

20 See generally *Homo Sacer, supra* note 7; *Means Without End, supra* note 12; *The Coming Community, supra* note 12; Giorgio Agamben, "Politica dell'esilio." 16 *Derivee Approdi* 25–27 (1998) [hereinafter Agamben, "Politica dell'esilio"].

21 Agamben, "Politica dell'esilio;" *supra* note 20, at 25 (author translation).

22   See generally Giorgio Agamben, *Remnants of Auschwitz: The Witness and the Archive* (Daniel Heller-Roazen trans., 1999).

23   Many protagonists of the humanitarian scene belong to the generation of 1968, which has always been mistrustful of institutions and local and national governments.

24   See generally Giorgio Agamben, *Means Without End: Notes on Politics* (Vincenzo Binetti & Cesare Casarino trans., 2000); see also generally Michael Hardt & Thomas Dumm, "Sovereignty, Multitudes, Absolute Democracy: A Discussion Between Michael Hardt and Thomas Dumm About Hardt and Negri's Empire." 4 *Theory & Event* (2000), at http://muse.jhu.edu/journals/theory_and_event/v004/4.3 hardt.html.

25   Zaki Laïdi, "L'urgence ou la dévalorisation-culturelle de l'avenir." *Urgence, souffrance, misère: Lutte humanitaire ou politique sociale?* 43–59 (Marc-Henry Soulet ed., 1998).

26   See generally Edward W. Said, *Orientalism* (1978).

27   The "confidential" report is a key cultural facet of the humanitarian world connecting press officers, general managers, officers-in-charge, local elites, intellectuals, and especially journalists. Anyone who possesses, transmits, or receives a confidential report immediately increases his or her own credibility within the local context of humanitarian operations. During the war in Kosovo, strictly "confidential" documents from Brussels, Washington, the World Bank, and other strategic studies' think-tanks circulated widely in Tirana. The effect of confidential reports, then, is two-fold. On one level, they produce a discourse on the locals which is taken up in the international circuit. On another level, their channels of circulation serve to create a bipolar society within the local with, at one end, the élites who lavishly display their access to information and, at the other, those who are constructed as passive objects of knowledge. In this sense we can speak of a machine for producing hierarchies and top-down power flows. On one side, one finds the sectors of society in an implicit partnership with transnational values and agencies maintained through continuous dialogue and collaboration. On the other side, one finds a passive marginalized sector of the local society, which may also include those government representatives who have failed to become part of the international organization circuit. Humanitarian intervention introduces a wedge within local societies, splitting them into two separate parts.

28   Rufin, "Pour l'humanitaire," *supra* note 5, at 10, 20.

29   In Albania from April to July 1999, AFOR had 19 nationalities in its ranks, over 7,000 NATO soldiers, 4 groups of observers, including two from the Organisation for Cooperation and Security in Europe (OCSE), and a dozen people from Western special government missions. During the Kosovo conflict, 180 international NGOs were present in Albania. The result in Kosovo, one year after the conflict: 40,000 soldiers from KFOR (a NATO-led, international security force), and 20,000 civilians (working for UNMIK, United Nations Mission in Kosovo, and international NGOs).

30   Albanian United Nations Military Forces.

31   These observations are culled from two years of fieldwork from 1998 to 2000, during which I interviewed key officials, politicians, and civil society actors before, during, and after the conflict in Kosovo.

32   I observed from my interviews that the "emergency" period was an administrative definition that allowed loosening the rules for the allocation and distribution of resources, regardless of the actual situation on the ground.

33   Laïdi, *supra* note 24, at 57.

39

Darfur through a Shoah Lens
Sudanese Asylum Seekers, Unruly Biopolitical Dramas, and the Politics of Humanitarian Compassion in Israel

Sarah S. Willen

The calamity of the rightless is not that they are deprived of life, liberty, and the pursuit of happiness, or of equality before the law and freedom of opinion – formulas which were designed to solve problems within given communities – but that they no longer belong to any community whatsoever. (Hannah Arendt)

... as one gets deeper into humanitarianism a series of dimensions of what may be called a complex ontology of inequality unfolds that differentiates in a hierarchical manner the values of human lives. (Didier Fassin)

Compassion begins from where we are, from the circle of our cares and concerns. It will be felt only toward those things and persons we see as important, and of course most of us most of the time ascribe importance in a very uneven and inconstant way. (Martha Nussbaum)

In this essay, I explore how people seeking refuge and political asylum become engulfed in fraught biopolitical dramas that expose the inconsistencies, the contradictions, and even the violence that lurk within contemporary forms of humanitarian compassion. Ethnographically, I focus on the governmental unruliness and the hierarchy of suffering that emerged when more than 13,000 people – among them men, women, and children fleeing Darfur, the civil war in South Sudan, Eritrea, Somalia

and the Ivory Coast – trekked through the Sinai desert and across the long, porous Egyptian-Israeli border in 2007–2008. Those who arrived on Israel's southern doorstep seeking protection are far from alone; they join a growing population of more than 16 million refugees and asylum seekers worldwide (UNHCR 2009). And like many of these millions, their flight has not thrust them into an open-armed human rights-based or humanitarian embrace, but rather flung them against rigid

Sarah S. Willen, "Darfur through a Shoah Lens: Sudanese Asylum Seekers, Unruly Biopolitical Dramas, and the Politics of Humanitarian Compassion in Israel." Substantially modified version of a piece that appeared in French in *Cultures & Conflits* n°72, autumn 2008, as "L'hyperpolitique du 'Plus jamais ça!': demandeurs d'asile soudanais, turbulence gouvernementale et politiques de contrôle des réfugiés en Israël."

walls – some metaphoric and some quite literal – of exclusion, denial, and dehumanization. Despite any moral obligations that may cling to (or exude from) imperial histories, lingering postcolonial ties, or contemporary neocolonial imbrications, countries in the Global North – especially Western Europe, North America, Australia, and now Israel – have been loath to accept or integrate refugees from the Global South. At times, however, historical memory and "political emotions" (Hage 2009) are invoked in ways that mitigate these exclusionary attitudes. Here I draw upon fieldwork conducted in Israel in 2007 to explore one such instance, which challenges us to ask: How ought a country built, to a great extent, by refugees fleeing genocide respond to a contemporary influx of refugees escaping similar circumstances?

Given the volatile politics of refugee claims-making around the globe, it should come as no surprise that the unanticipated influx of over 10,000 African refugees into Israel generated an almost instantaneous wave of public attention, political controversy, and grassroots activism. Although these anxious Israeli reactions echoed similar concerns in other Northern refugee destinations, they bore a decidedly local cast. In one sense, public discussion and debate were framed by the country's demographically inflected self-definition as a "Jewish and democratic state" and infused with a sense of "demographic trepidation" concerning the possibility that a much larger wave of refugees from distressed African countries would soon follow. Interrupting this xenophobic chorus, however, was a separate array of voices focusing on the small group of asylum seekers who had survived horrors that evoked collective Jewish-Israeli memories of the Shoah, or Holocaust: those fleeing what the international community described as genocide in Darfur. According to the leaders and citizen-activists who publicized this morally freighted historical analogy, Israeli Jews and refugees from Darfur are bound together in what one newspaper called a "kinship of genocide" (Burston 2008). This analogy also spurred a high profile grassroots campaign led by Jewish communities in the United States under the slogan, "Save Darfur." Driving these

novel kinship formulations was the ubiquitous refrain, if not the central organizing principle, of contemporary Jewish identity: "Never again!"[1] Thus the slogans of one refugee experience were adapted to evoke humanitarian compassion for other refugees – but not without friction and conflict.

The localized biopolitical drama that ensued reveals new layers of complexity in the contemporary politics of international human rights and refugee migration. First, it intersects with the already complicated refugee stories of both Israelis (not only from Europe, but also from North Africa, Yemen, Iraq, Iran, and elsewhere) and Palestinians (in the West Bank and Gaza and in the wider Middle Eastern and global diaspora). Second, it shows how Israel has become a fortified way-station on the outer perimeter of "Fortress Europe"; now, its new "detention centers" must be added to similar carceral apparatuses in Turkey, North Africa, and Eastern Europe.

In analyzing the ideological, performative, and emotional dynamics of Israeli reactions to this particular refugee influx, I aim to shed light on both the power and the danger embedded within contemporary configurations of humanitarian sentiment including, in particular, those motivated by symbolic (mis)identification and political emotion. I begin by exploring the governmental "unruliness" that resulted when thousands of asylum seekers made their way through the Sinai desert and across the border into Israel. Unruliness, here, has two referents, both applicable far beyond the particularities of the present case: first, the legal, political, and administrative disorder faced by asylum seekers and all those who interact with them on the ground; and second, the failings and failures of the "international refugee regime" (Malkki 1995) and its local counterparts which, although purportedly anchored in rules, rights and laws, often do not deliver on their promise. I then turn to questions of rhetoric and representation to explore how a stunningly diverse array of Israeli activists quickly took up the "kinship of genocide" analogy and cast themselves as legitimate "trauma brokers" (James 2004) on behalf of Sudanese asylum seekers from Darfur. In analyzing the power and the limits of this potent historical analogy,

I explore how different stakeholders respond to contemporary processes of asylum seeking, and to the forms of state violence that can arise in response, by reasoning through history in markedly different ways.

In probing the dynamics of this unruly biopolitical drama, my broader goal is to explore three problems that complicate contemporary enactments of humanitarian compassion. First, this ethnographic case clearly reveals the lability and arbitrariness of the terms used not only by states but also by humanitarian actors to classify and, in effect, to rank candidates for empathy and compassion. Not only are terms like "asylum seeker," "refugee," "illegal immigrant," and "infiltrator" implicated within broader techniques of governmentality, but they also reduce the "subjective trajectories" of individual men, women, and children to "indistinct, displaced, and localized bodies" (Pandolfi 2003: 374) – that is, to a form of what Agamben (1998) calls "bare life," or biological life stripped of agency or political voice (cf. Arendt 1973). When subjectivity and political identity are sheared away, human distinctiveness and dignity are deactivated and suppressed; they are "erased by the new categories in which human beings are pigeonholed" (Pandolfi 2003: 381). Once such unique, subjective trajectories have been annulled, it is only through suffering that humanitarian biopolitics can make room for compassion (Ticktin 2006). Such biopolitical operations beg important questions, both ethical and ethnographic, among them: "What is at stake when we recognize others through the lens of their suffering and not through their political subjectivity?" (James 2004: 132; cf. Biehl this volume, Ticktin this volume).

Not all suffering is equal, and this brings us to the second troubling dimension of humanitarian compassion. In the growing literature on migrants and refugees within local and global economies of humanitarian concern, three characteristics are particularly noteworthy. Suffering that engenders a particularly strong humanitarian response typically (1) bears the marks of trauma; (2) can be "proven" and packaged convincingly (Fassin and D'Halluin 2007; Giordano 2008; McKinney 2007; Ticktin 2006); and crucially (3) tends to map closely onto the moral agendas and concerns of those who are empowered to bestow, withhold, or withdraw the "gift" of humanitarian compassion (Fassin 2005, 2007; James 2004; Nussbaum 2003; Pandolfi 2003). In other words, humanitarian economies of concern are not neutral; they are always and inevitably shot through with politics, ideology, and historical consciousness.

What happens, then, to those who have endured the "wrong kind" of suffering? The answer to this question reveals a third paradox: humanitarianism's not-so-hidden potential to generate, rather than alleviate, violence (James 2004; Nyers 2000; Ticktin 2006). In the present case, two groups have become casualties of this derivative form of humanitarian violence. First, the vast majority of African asylum seekers in Israel are not from Darfur; as a result, they rank much lower in the local "hierarchy of suffering" that has emerged (Farmer 2003: 29–30, see also Fassin 2007). Second, the everyday struggles of another, nearby refugee population are thundering in their absence from public and political conversation: Palestinians in the West Bank and Gaza who are caught in the brutal gridlock of Israeli occupation. I return to the roots and implications of this glaring absence in the article's conclusion. First, we must situate this biopolitical drama in ethnographic context.

Refugee Migration Against the Backdrop of a Globalizing Labor Market

The recent influx of African asylum seekers into Israel arrived at a tumultuous time – although it is always a tumultuous time in the region of Israel-Palestine – but nonetheless, it began just as the Israeli government and the Israeli public were finally, if reluctantly, beginning to acknowledge the country's new status as a destination for transnational migration from the global South. From 1993 to 2000, between 200,000 and 300,000 transnational migrant workers arrived in Israel, about half unauthorized and the other half unauthorized, and by 2000 they comprised over 10 percent of the country's labor force (Kemp and Raijman

2008; Willen 2007e). In the same time period, small numbers of asylum seekers, mostly from unstable African countries including Liberia, Sierra Leone, Ivory Coast, Ethiopia, and most recently Sudan and Eritrea, entered the country as well (Adout 2007; Anteby-Yemini 2009; Ben-Dor and Kagan 2007).

In 2002, ostensibly in response to rising unemployment, the Israeli government initiated a costly, heavily mediatized, and occasionally violent mass deportation campaign targeting the country's non-Jewish, non-Arab residents (Willen 2007b, 2007d). Although "illegal" migrant workers were the campaign's primary targets, others – including asylum seekers – were occasionally caught in its dragnet (Willen 2010). More than 140,000 unauthorized residents were "distanced" from Israel, to employ the Immigration Police's sanitizing euphemism, including about 50,000 who were arrested and forcibly deported and thousands of others who were "encouraged" – that is, regularly and systematically intimidated – into leaving "voluntarily." Meanwhile, Israel has continued to recruit "legal" transnational workers to perform work that Israelis won't, and Palestinians now can't, perform.

Although the larger story of Israel's encounter with transnational labor migration lies beyond the scope of this discussion (but see Kemp and Raijman 2008; Willen 2007c), it is important to emphasize that the smoldering conflict between the Israelis and the Palestinians, the recent globalization of Israel's labor force (partly in response to the conflict), and the harsh government crackdown on burgeoning populations of transnational labor migrants all contribute to the overall "unruliness" animating Israel's response to this new wave of African refugees. So, too, do persistent memories of the Shoah, Israel's "founding trauma" (LaCapra 2001), as I will elaborate momentarily.

The Lability of Labels and the Arbitrary Deployment of Juridical Categories

Another, broader factor contributing to this governmental unruliness is the epistemological and classificatory confusion associated with newly arrived border-crossers, whom the state resists describing as either asylum seekers or refugees, instead calling them "infiltrators" (*mistanenim*). More precisely, the Israeli government, military, and police have been reluctant to distinguish between economically motivated migrants, like the "illegal migrant workers" the state has invested heavily in rounding up and expelling since 2002, and "asylum seekers" or "refugees" fleeing war, political conflict, or government repression. By mid-2008, national politicians had fused their parallel accusations of unlawful entry and unlawful work-seeking into a new term altogether: "labor infiltrators" (*mistanenei avoda*).

The state's reluctance to proclaim Israel a destination for legitimate asylum seeking stems from two facets of the "demographic trepidation" noted earlier: first, an explicit desire to limit the number of non-Jews arriving in the country from the global South, and second, a concomitant desire to avoid acknowledging any debts – material or otherwise – to Palestinian refugees. As a result, Israel has avoided developing any national asylum legislation, any systematic procedure for reviewing asylum petitions, or any infrastructure to accommodate or protect asylum seekers. Instead, it has studiously avoided precedent-setting moves, resulting in a "juridical void" (Akoka 2006, cited in Anteby-Yemini 2009) that severely impedes the translation of international legal statutes into national-level practice. One way the state has evaded these internationally defined legal obligations is by simply calling asylum seekers by another name. The strategic redefinition of new arrivals using a creative neologism, "labor infiltrators," is consistent with the state's habitual rejection of potential immigrants who do not arrive via the "Law of Return," the law that grants virtually automatic Israeli citizenship to anyone of Jewish heritage while denying it to almost all others.

Despite the state's vigorous resistance to recognizing asylum or refugee claims, two forms of protection are nonetheless available in Israel: "temporary protected status" (TPS) and formal refugee status. Petitioners from a group facing danger in their country of origin can apply to UNHCR (not to the Israeli government) for TPS as "humanitarian refugees."

Bearers of this provisional form of status receive a letter declaring their temporary immunity to deportation and, in some instances, granting them authorization to work. Importantly, bearers of TPS are not entitled to any social rights or benefits. In contrast to TPS petitions, applications for permanent refugee status must be filed individually. Although Israel has made limited use of TPS provisions to grant temporary protection to small groups of asylum seekers – just over 500 people as of 2005, mostly from Congo, Liberia, Sierra Leone and Ivory Coast – it has been much more conservative in its allocation of recognized refugee status (Kritzman 2007). For instance, Israel granted refugee status to 12 of 922 petitioners in 2004, 11 of 909 in 2005, 3 of 832 in 2007, and just one of 1586 in 2008.[2]

Sudanese Asylum Seekers: A "Kinship of Genocide," "Enemy Nationals," or a New Captive Labor Force?

The recent influx of African refugees into Israel has proven particularly prone to ideologically motivated redefinition. The event that precipitated this wave of border-crossing was the violent dispersal of a peaceful demonstration at a protest camp of about 2,500 Sudanese men, women, and children outside the offices of the United Nations High Commissioner on Refugees (UNHCR) in Cairo. Refugees had established the camp in September 2005 to demonstrate against their harsh living conditions in Egypt and UNHCR's failure to attend to their petitions for refugee status and resettlement. After three months of fruitless protest, the Egyptian police dispersed the camp in December 2005 using tear gas, water cannons, and live ammunition. Twenty-seven Sudanese demonstrators were killed, and hundreds of others were arrested, interrogated, and in some cases tortured by the Egyptian police (Azzam 2006). In the wake of these events, the numbers of Sudanese men, women, and children fleeing Cairo and heading toward the Israeli border increased – among them Muslims from Darfur and Christians from South Sudan – as did the numbers of non-Sudanese refugees from Eritrea and several other African countries.

Unlike asylum seekers from other troubled African countries, those from Sudan were initially denied the opportunity to apply for TPS in Israel. Instead, Sudanese asylum seekers were classified by the Israeli state as "enemy nationals" – i.e., as citizens of a state with which Israel has no diplomatic relations – and detained without judicial review (Ben-Dor and Kagan 2007). Importantly, many Sudanese asylum seekers had fled because of violence inflicted upon them by Sudan itself – as had Jews fleeing Nazi persecution in the 1940s. In effect, Israel's policy of detaining refugees from Darfur as "enemy nationals" is tantamount to World War II-era British (and, in some cases, American) policies of detaining German Jews who fled the Nazi regime on the basis of their German citizenship (see Ilan 2006). (As an historical note, the fledgling Israeli state worked with the International Refugee Organization, predecessor of UNHCR, to sponsor an article in the Fourth Geneva Convention exempting refugees from classification as "enemy nationals" (Ben-Dor and Kagan 2007).)

In a savvy rhetorical move, attorneys at Tel Aviv University's Refugee Rights Legal Clinic called attention to this Nazi-era analogy in an effort to bolster their legal argument that detention of Sudanese asylum seekers as "enemy nationals" violates international law. On several key occasions, their arguments proved persuasive in court. For instance, in an August 2006 decision to release four Sudanese from Darfur who had been imprisoned without judicial review, the deciding judge determined that their situation

> is not qualitatively different from the fate of tens of thousands of German Jews who felt their very souls were threatened when they fled from the Nazi regime and arrived in England seeking refuge. These refugees were first treated as enemies and were put in custody, but the British authorities realized pretty soon the ... moral injustice and changed their attitude in favour of the refugees of the Nazi regime. (Ibid.)

Rather than relying only upon codified law, the judge's decision tapped into deep wells of political emotion that lie beneath, and on occasion substantively influence, the Israeli legal system. Building upon court decisions like this one, and working in close collaboration with local human rights NGOs, lawyers at the Refugee Rights Clinic succeeded in convincing the courts to release first dozens and later hundreds of Sudanese (and eventually other African) refugees from detention through what are described as "alternative to imprisonment" arrangements.

These "alternative" arrangements typically involved the release of a small number of detainees from prison into the hands of an employer – at either an agricultural settlement (kibbutz or moshav) or a hotel – who has agreed to provide them, and sometimes their families, with housing, food, and other basic needs in exchange for their labor. Significantly, these employment conditions, in which detainee/employees are bound to a single employer and place of residence, were strikingly similar to the "binding arrangement" (hesder ha'kvila) that governed the employment of "legal" migrant workers until it was struck down by Israel's High Court in 2006 as a form of "modern slavery" following a lengthy battle waged by local human rights groups.

Indeed, these "alternative" arrangements were riddled with legal, political, and moral problems. First, they were coordinated neither by the state nor the courts, but rather on an ad hoc basis – ironically, by the very human rights groups that spent years fighting for the abolition of the "binding arrangement." Second, it is particularly striking that these human rights groups' efforts to "free" refugees from detention put them in cahoots with private commercial interests that benefited financially from the state's willingness to transform detained asylum seekers into a new captive labor force. Third, the release of detainees to such work arrangements has created a "revolving door" in jails, which have now become spaces of circulation; as more detainees are released, space becomes available to arrest and detain others. Fourth, reports quickly emerged about the exploitation and abuse of newly released refugee workers, especially in agricultural settings. Overall, these "alternative to imprisonment" arrangements – fragile, haphazardly organized, sporadically

implemented, and imbued with practical and moral dilemmas – further exemplify the growing unruliness characterizing Israel's response to this new refugee influx.

Inter-agency Bickering and Growing Governmental Unruliness

Another facet of this unruliness involves the inter-agency tensions that erupted as the number of asylum seekers arriving daily began to climb in spring 2007. At first, the army threw up its hands and declared asylum seekers the responsibility of the Immigration Police, which originally was created in 2002 to deport unauthorized migrant workers. The military reserve units stationed on the border initiated an informal policy of bringing asylum seekers – sometimes one or two, sometimes entire busloads – to the southern city of Beersheva with the intention of handing them over to the Immigration Police. The police, however, refused responsibility as well, declaring their "detention centers" full to capacity with unauthorized migrant workers slated for deportation. As a result, hundreds of asylum seekers were left – effectively dumped – on the streets of Beersheva: on one occasion near the central bus station, on another near the train station, and on another outside of City Hall (Bereshovsky 2007; Grinberg 2007b, 2007d).

These jurisdictional disputes became both lighting rods for public attention and clear illustrations of growing governmental unruliness. On one occasion in June 2007, for instance, a busload of refugees was dropped off by the army at a local police station – and then promptly transported back to the regional military command center by the police. The military spokesperson issued an indignant response:

Does the army know how to provide formula and diapers to children of refugees? Does the army deal with registration and giving medical examinations? Someone forgot what the role of the IDF [Israel Defense Forces] is along the Israel-Egypt border. ... This is an absurd situation. Where is the Immigration Administration [i.e., the Immigration Police]? (Azoulay 2007)

A representative of that administration turned the blame around, declaring that,

> The IDF should close down the border with Egypt hermetically so refugees will not be able to enter Israel. If the Immigration Administration would have to deal with these refugees, in a week all the holding areas would be full and they will stay that way for more than a decade – because it will not be possible to send them back to their countries. (ibid.)

Sometimes these disputes became emotionally charged public spectacles involving a long and varied cast of characters. On a separate occasion in May 2007, for instance, more than three dozen refugees from Darfur who had been detained on a military base were dropped off by the army at district police headquarters in Beersheva. An article in Ha'aretz newspaper traced the inter-agency chaos that ensued:

> The police refused to take custody of the refugees and they were left in the street as welfare and military authorities scrambled to find a solution for them. Eventually they were transferred to a military housing facility in the city.
>
> Media reports of the refugees prompted the prime minister's adviser for social and welfare affairs ... to intervene. It was decided that Be'er Sheva's welfare authority would take care of the Sudanese families in a few days.
>
> *The remaining refugees will be held by the police as illegal aliens.*
>
> The reserve soldiers who had brought the refugees to the police headquarters drove off, leaving the refugees – men, women and children – in the street, surrounded by the media.
>
> [...]
>
> A Southern District Police spokesman said that the bus transporting the refugees was sent back to IDF Southern Command because "police deal with criminals, and this isn't the case." (Grinberg 2007b, emphasis added)

Jurisdictional disputes like this one are highly revealing. First, they highlight the profound and ongoing tension between two constructions of asylum seekers: either as criminal infiltrators to be detained and, if possible, expelled, or as vulnerable people who must be protected. While the military and the police have tended to espouse the former construction and leave the latter to civil society organizations (or

municipal welfare departments), often the distinction is less clear-cut.

Second, this dispute throws the arbitrary nature of governmental detention practices into stark relief. In the absence of systematic laws or policies, the decision to detain or not to detain often hinges not on the substance of a petitioner's case – a matter of little concern to either the military or the police – but rather on two separate factors: the availability of space within a detention facility, and inter-agency dynamics. If space is available when a group of asylum seekers is arrested, they will likely be detained. If not, they may find themselves "dumped" in a manner that forces another state agency – i.e. the police or a local municipality – to take responsibility for them. In this particular incident, perhaps because of the concentrated media attention, the municipal welfare department was called in to provide a default option. But when space in their housing facilities ran out, it was no secret that, "The remaining refugees [would] be held by the police as illegal aliens." It would be difficult to find a clearer illustration of the arbitrary deployment of juridical categories than this.

Strange Bedfellows: The Emerging Refugee Advocacy Movement

This generalized atmosphere of non-policy and governmental chaos soon yielded a corollary effect; it catalyzed a new, highly energized branch of Israel's migrant and refugee advocacy movement[3] under the impassioned but largely inexperienced leadership of a group of social work students in Beersheva. The students quickly forged ties with diverse organizations and individuals as they sought temporary accommodation for refugees who had been abandoned unceremoniously on the streets of their city. Within a few short months, a hodgepodge of initiatives, organizations, and "strange bedfellows" coalitions had sprung up, including student groups; veteran human rights organizations; Zionist immigrant aid organizations; and religious groups including the movement for Reform Judaism, a Muslim organization in southern Israel, the International Christian Embassy (founded to support Jews' return to the biblical Holy Land), and congregations of Messianic Jews, or "Jews for Jesus." Some groups collected food, clothing, and toiletries; others organized housing, medical care, or Hebrew language lessons; and still others helped asylum seekers navigate the UNHCR and Israeli legal systems. Although motivated by good intentions, this broad-based, patchwork movement has not only struggled with, but also contributed to the overall atmosphere of unruliness.

Five events propelled this movement forward. First, then-Prime Minister Ehud Olmert's controversial policy of "hot return" provoked considerable public debate. According to Olmert, the arrangement had been coordinated with Egyptian President Hosni Mubarak, and individuals deported to Egypt would be safe from further deportation to Sudan (*refoulement*). Mubarak, however, publicly denied the existence of any such agreement.

Second, in an effort to pressure the state to develop a coherent policy response, the municipality of Beersheva transported several busloads of asylum seekers to Jerusalem for a staged demonstration in the Rose Garden outside the Knesset (Parliament). Although the Prime Minister's office paid little attention, the demonstration attracted a great deal of local media attention and captured the interest of still more local organizations and Israeli citizens.

A third key development involved reports of Egyptian police brutality at the border. In late July, Egyptian police officers shot and killed a Sudanese woman from Darfur (Grinberg 2007a). A few weeks later, in a TV news interview, several Israeli military reservists described a scuffle at the border in which three asylum seekers trying to cross into Israel were shot dead by Egyptian police and a fourth, who jumped onto the wire fence in an attempt to cross, was dragged back and bludgeoned to death by the Egyptians in view of the Israeli soldiers on the other side. These and other reports of Egyptian police violence weakened Olmert's argument that immediate deportation to Egypt – which Israeli human rights organizations insist is a clear violation of international law – could take place without endangering lives.

These brutal events precipitated a strong case of what Erica James (2004) has called

"do something syndrome." Within a day or so of this final incident, a majority of Israeli parliament members – 63 of a total 120 – had, indeed, done something; they signed a petition asking the government not to deport any more Sudanese asylum seekers to Egypt. The MPs signing the petition represented a stunning cross-section of the Israeli political spectrum including not just the left-center Labor party and the center-right Likud, but also the National Religious Party, which represents right-wing Jewish settlers in the Occupied Territories, and the mixed Jewish-Arab Communist party. According to the petition's "kinship of genocide" logic, "The refugees need protection and sanctuary, and the Jewish people's history as well as the values of democracy and humanity pose a moral imperative for us to give them that shelter" (Grinberg 2007c). Despite this lofty rhetoric, a group of more than 50 refugees, most of them from Darfur, were deported to Egypt just a few weeks later.

Fifth, in late summer, the government announced a decision to grant Israeli citizenship to 498 refugees from Darfur already residing in the country. A newspaper article reporting on the decision employed the same reasoning as the petition; Israel cannot ignore the refugees' fate because of the history of the Jewish people. The same article reiterated Olmert's earlier declaration that anyone attempting to cross the southern border would be deported immediately to Egypt (Mualem 2007).

As this chaotic situation unfolded, I interviewed representatives of ten organizations involved in responding to the refugee influx; attended several key public meetings and policy conferences; interviewed several refugees; and visited two impromptu shelters. Two themes dominated these meetings and encounters: first, generalized state of governmental unruliness, and second, the Shoah/Darfur analogy and "kinship of genocide" logic.

"Founding Trauma," "Political Emotion," and Grassroots Activism

To begin making sense of the privileged position of Sudanese from Darfur within Israel's emerging local hierarchy of suffering, we must consider the particular forms of "political emotion" evoked by the Shoah/Darfur analogy. This historical analogy clearly activates what Dominick LaCapra (2001) calls a "founding trauma" for Jewish Israel: a collective memory of mass trauma that can be reactivated when a group feels threatened. In some instances, the reactivation of a "founding trauma" might catalyze violence and destruction; indeed, some would argue that this process explains (or partly explains) the tone and tenor of Israel's occupation of the West Bank and Gaza.

Yet a founding trauma might offer the seeds of not only violence and destruction, but also their inverse. In the present case, for instance, numerous Israeli leaders and groups quickly began to invoke the "never again" analogy as an ethical injunction, first, to remember an episode of violence, destruction, and trauma in Jewish-Israeli history, and second, to translate that collective memory into a beneficent ethical imperative. Sharp-tongued Israeli politician and Holocaust survivor Yosef (Tommy) Lapid, for instance, said, "I don't think that the Jewish people can look the other way when such a horrible genocide is being conducted. It is our obligation to be of as much help as we can" (in Kraft 2007). In a similar vein, Chairman of the Yad Vashem National Holocaust Memorial in Jerusalem said that,

> As Jews who have the memory of the Holocaust embedded in us, we cannot stand by as refugees from the genocide in Darfur knock on our doors. The memory of the past, and the Jewish values that underpin our existence, require us to show humanitarian solidarity with the persecuted. (quoted in Uchitelle-Pierce 2007)

Even some religious leaders, like the politically conservative Chief Rabbi of Tel Aviv-Jaffa Yisrael Lau, joined in this chorus of sentiment. In a letter to the Prime Minister, Lau described aid to the Sudanese refugees as "our moral obligation as a Jewish state" (Ma'ariv 2007). Emotionally laden comments like these were remarkably common in spring and summer 2007. Indeed, when a student petition protesting the deportation of Sudanese refugees began to circulate in May 2007, an article in the conservative Jerusalem Post accurately observed

that, "the growing number of signatories exemplifies a unity rare in Israel's heterogeneous society" (Gerver and Klass 2007). Yet this ostensible unity masks a much deeper matter: the degree to which Darfuri refugees in Israel, like refugees the world over, quickly become a kind of discursive blank canvas upon which diverse actors begin to project their own moral values and political emotions.

Clearly the trope of "never again" has become hyper-politicized in ways that beg ethnographic investigation. One might be tempted to write off such invocations as hollow rhetoric, political correctness, or cynical exploitation of a searing historical analogy, and it would be easy enough to find support for any of these arguments. And yet, I contend, invocations of "never again" must be taken quite seriously as both an appeal to and an expression of what Ghassan Hage (2009) describes as "political emotion." For some Israelis who witness the arrival of refugees from Darfur and hear politicians or rabbis saying "never again," the analogy is a form of banal, hollow, or cynical rhetoric. For others, like Dov Lior, chief rabbi of the radical right-wing Jewish settlement in the West Bank city of Hebron, the parallel must be wholly rejected as a kind of mis-remembering. According to Lior and other militant Zionists, the "refugees" who matter are the Jewish settlers who were forcibly removed from Gaza by the Israeli military during its withdrawal in 2005 (Wagner 2007). But for many mainstream and left-leaning Israelis, the Shoah/Darfur analogy holds powerful resonance. For some newly minted refugee advocates, it represents a deeply felt political emotion that demands immediate translation into social practice. For savvier, more seasoned activists, it is a political emotion to be strategically mobilized – one might say manipulated – in support of certain forms of action and practice (including fundraising).

Not surprisingly, such appeals to political emotion bore substantial and immediate consequences. Existing organizations grew quickly in strength; organizations that emerged virtually overnight quickly ballooned in size, staff, and stature; and the groups listed earlier were literally overwhelmed with offers of food, clothing, volunteer energy, and money. Yet these grassroots efforts – well-intentioned but completely uncoordinated, unsupervised, and even on occasion working at cross-purposes – also contributed to the overall atmosphere of unruliness.

"The Genocide Issue" and "the Heart of Israelis"

According to Ilana Weisman,[4] a seasoned public health nurse in her early 50s whose small, upper-middle class community in the Jerusalem hills provided temporary shelter to 21 Sudanese refugees for nearly a month in the summer of 2007, the "kinship of genocide" logic is the primary cause of this upwelling of public energy and concern.

At the July demonstration outside the Knesset, some refugee advocates began to suspect a government plan to arrest and detain Sudanese demonstrators en masse. In response, they quickly began searching for temporary housing arrangements for refugees. A member of Ilana's community agreed to take in several families and house them in the community's kindergarten, which was vacant for the summer. When a local human rights organization placed 21 refugees in their community, among them 14 adults and 7 children ranging in age from 10 months to 6 years, it had virtually no concrete assistance to offer. As a result, Ilana, one of only two community members who spoke any Arabic, along with another neighbor, Michal, took on the formidable task of attending to all 21 of their guests' basic needs, including food, shelter, and health care. "The organization that brought them here didn't organize anything," she told me.

Nothing. Not food, not health care, not shelter, nothing. I called the organization when I realized there would be babies and asked them to send diapers and formula ... and they did, but that was it. That's what we received from them in two weeks time.

Initially the refugees' presence generated objections from community members but, as Ilana explained, their efforts gradually came together and sentiments shifted.

Everything else the community organized on its own and, I must say, the community really warmed even though initially there was a lot of objection to them being here. ... [R]eally I can't tell you the extent to which people came forward to help them and – I'm really proud of this community.

Despite the initial objections, Ilana and Michal were quickly overwhelmed with offers from neighbors who wanted to help, including some who later called to apologize for their earlier reluctance. "In the end it turned out that I had to rack my brain every day to think of things for people to do to help because they so wanted to help."

When I asked Ilana about her motivations, and her neighbors', for providing asylum seekers with temporary shelter, she turned immediately to the Shoah/Darfur analogy. "Did it matter that these people were Sudanese?" I asked. "Would it have mattered if they were from another African country?" "I am absolutely convinced it does make a difference," she responded unequivocally.

People are more likely here to come forward to help people from Darfur because of the whole Holocaust issue ... people identify with their plight. I myself am a child of [Holocaust] survivors, and I'm sure that has something to do with why I was basically willing to do another shift every day in addition to my regular job. ... I think that the genocide issue particularly speaks to the heart of Israelis.

Alongside her sharp criticisms of both the government's chaotic actions and the refugee advocacy groups' lack of coordination, Ilana spoke proudly of her small community's achievements. She was especially glad that in welcoming these 21 asylum seekers into their community "under the radar" of the authorities, she and her neighbors had succeeded in preventing their arrest and detention. Indeed, the very morning after these families moved into their vacant kindergarten, the authorities had descended upon the Rose Garden, arrested the remaining Sudanese demonstrators – men, women, and children – and bussed them to the detention camp in the southern Negev desert.

The "kinship of genocide" logic that moved Ilana and many other Israeli refugee advocates hinged on a choice to recognize, and identify with, a very specific kind of pain and suffering and, in effect, to ignore others. Ilana addressed this issue obliquely in explaining why she was willing to turn her life upside down, even for a month, to aid the Sudanese refugees who had arrived on her doorstep.

[W]hile I completely recognize the fact that hunger and the other issues and AIDS that are plaguing Africa are incredibly important, I think that the rest of the world can also do something about those issues, but I think that it's very very important for Israel as a nation based on our history to address issues of geno-cide. It's even more important for us than issues of hunger or ... other sorts of issues.

Speaking from her practical experience as a public health nurse, Ilana argued that no indi-vidual, community, or country can solve all of the world's humanitarian problems; instead, it is necessary to prioritize. In her view, such priorities should be influenced by two factors: first, a realistic understanding of available re-sources and capacities, and second, a carefully reasoned moral calculus. In the present in-stance, she proposed, this moral calculus should take into account both history and col-lective experience – or, put differently, "founding trauma" and "political emotion."[5]

On one hand, a "kinship of genocide" logic has emerged as an important impetus for di-verse forms of ethically informed social prac-tice, including the efforts of Ilana and her neighbors. On the other hand, however, the Shoah/Darfur analogy and its implicit logic of selective compassion also can have powerful negative, even violent, consequences. The recent deployment of "never again" discourse in Israel offers a clear illustration of how exceptionalist forms of humanitarian logic, al-though motivated by compassion or empathy, can conceal not-so-hidden forms of violence.

The Violence of Humanitarianism

What forms can such violence take? One such form is the production of what Paul Farmer (2003) calls hierarchies of suffering. As anthro-pologist Kelly McKinney observes, choosing to acknowledge the suffering of some asylum seekers but not others involves squeezing social reality into a "grid of victimization" in which "psychological, moral, and political ambiguity and complexity are eliminated" (2007: 285). The "never again" paradigm, I contend, in-volves precisely such a grid of victimization. Implicitly, it creates the possibility of express-ing a certain kind of political emotion – we might call it empathy – toward a group whose suffering is deemed analogous to collective memories of Jewish suffering. Those whose suffering fails to map onto the grid, however, are ignored or, in the extreme case, abandoned.

Veena Das has suggested that, "we need to think of pain as asking for acknowledgment and recognition; denial of the other's pain is not about the failings of the intellect but the failings of the spirit" (Das 1997: 88). In his response to Das, Stanley Cavell writes that in facing another's pain,

You are ... not at liberty to believe or disbe-lieve ... at your leisure. You are forced to respond, either to acknowledge it in return or to avoid it; *the future between us is at stake.* ... Not to respond to such a claim, when it is you to whom it is addressed, is to deny its existence, and hence is an act of violence (however momentary, mostly unnoticeable); as it were, the lack of response is a silence that perpetuates the violence of pain itself. (Cavell 1997: 94, emphasis added)

In choosing to respond to or avoid another's pain, Cavell writes, "the future between us is at stake"; to acknowledge or not to acknowledge another's pain in the first instance will inevit-ably shape how any subsequent relationship unfolds. I take Cavell's comment to mean that mobilizing political emotions through the rallying cry of "never again" offers both the possibility of recognition, of intersubjective engagement, and of justice and, at the same time, the possibility of doing further violence to others whose pain continues to go unrecog-nized. In the present context, choosing to rec-ognize the pain of Sudanese survivors from Darfur by refracting their experiences through this political-emotional lens involves avoiding or denying the pain of other refugees, including South Sudanese, Eritreans, and other African asylum seekers – not to mention the Palestinian refugees living under Israeli occupation and military gridlock. This avoidance and this denial constitute what we might call, following Miriam Ticktin (2006), "the violence of humanitarianism" (see also Nyers 2000).

"A Very Arbitrary Distinction"

The privileged place of Sudanese from Darfur within Israel's local hierarchy of suffering emerged with stark clarity in an interview I conducted with Boaz Friedman,[6] spokesman for the most publicity-savvy organizational coalition working on behalf of Darfuri refugees in Israel. The coalition was, by all measures, a "strange bedfellows" endeavor involving human rights NGOs, liberal religious leaders, and two rather different celebrity members: a renowned senior Holocaust scholar, and Boaz. A slick public relations agent and local celebrity, Boaz became famous after winning an Israeli "reality TV" competition that garnered him the opportunity to spend a year touring United States college campuses and communities promoting Israel's public image. Staff members at several coalition organizations – all sharp-tongued human rights activists I knew through my earlier fieldwork with "illegal" migrant workers – strongly encouraged me to interview him even as their measured words revealed varying degrees of disagreement with his personal agenda.

I began to understand these reservations the moment Boaz began articulating his goals for the coalition, which diverged markedly from those of the human rights activists I knew well. The coalition's primary objective, he explained in the unapologetic language of a public relations strategist, is "to distance the refugee issue from the issue of migrant workers at the level of [public] consciousness. It's to call it by a different name so people will like it more." As our conversation continued, the chasm between Boaz's own goals and those of his coalition partners came into sharp focus. "Personally," he said,

I am not here to help migrant workers. I'm here to help refugees fleeing genocide. I'm working on behalf of [refugees] from Sudan. I'm not working on behalf of [refugees] from Eritrea ... In objective terms, it's a very arbitrary distinction. Someone who came here

from Congo hasn't suffered less than someone who's come here from Sudan, maybe more.

Particularly given his partners' history of insistently human rights-based advocacy for both migrant workers and refugees, Boaz' explicitly humanitarian commitment to Sudanese refugees alone – not to refugees from Eritrea or Congo, not to migrant workers – was a major bone of contention within the coalition.

For the human rights advocates, all asylum seekers possess legal rights and moral entitlements that the state is legally and politically obligated to ensure. For humanitarian advocates like Boaz, history and collective memory – experiences of "founding trauma" and "political emotion" – produce a moral obligation that both individual citizens and the state ought, but are not obligated, to fulfill. As Ticktin observes, "Humanitarianism is about the exception rather than the rule, [and] about generosity rather than entitlement", whereas, "Rights entail a concept of justice, which includes standards of obligation and implies equality between individuals" (2006: 45). A humanitarian logic hinges not on intrinsic properties of asylum seekers as rights-bearing human beings, but on the cultivation of an adequately compelling rhetorical or symbolic relationship between provider and recipient of compassion or aid (cf. Nussbaum 2003). It is the arbitrary and contingent nature of this relationship-building process that inflicts violence upon those who, although equally "deserving," are abandoned by those whose primary intention is to "do good" (Fisher 1997). Within the refugee rights coalition, such differences of opinion were of great consequence, not least because the line Boaz drew profoundly affected the sort of public statements he was prepared to make, the forms of aid he would coordinate or support, and the messages he would bring to the Knesset and to the Israeli public.

Conclusion: Political Emotions, Governmental Unruliness, and the Politics of Humanitarian Compassion

Israeli responses to this unanticipated influx of asylum seekers reveal much about the contemporary politics of humanitarian compassion, which often functions not only as a salve for a wide array of postcolonial disorders (Good et al. 2008), but also as a catalyst for new forms of dis-order. First, Israel's haphazard use of classificatory labels highlights the arbitrary and fluid nature of terms now used to characterize people who move, generally with complicated motives and personal stories, across political borders. When three dozen Sudanese asylum seekers were abandoned on the streets of Beersheva by the Israeli military, for example, some eventually were granted protection by the municipal welfare authority, who consented to view them as vulnerable persons whom the state is obligated to protect and assist.[7] And yet, as Ha'aretz newspaper reported, "The remaining refugees" were to be "held by the police as illegal aliens." Depending upon who is doing the labeling, the same border-crossers may be cast as "asylum seekers," "refugees," "illegal migrant workers," or even, in the Israeli government's accusatory neologism, "labor infiltrators." Clearly these "new categories in which human beings are pigeonholed" (Pandolfi 2003: 381) are only marginally grounded in the circumstances of individual lives. They strip away individuality, subjectivity, and dignity, leaving only faceless, often defenseless masses of people whose last shred of hope for eliciting humanitarian compassion or reestablishing a meaningful political identity may hinge on their ability to successfully market their suffering.

Moreover, as a growing body of scholarship reveals, one must have endured the "right" kind of suffering in order to make a successful claim within prevailing economies of humanitarian sentiment. Suffering with the strongest currency is that which is traumatic, verifiable, and/or significant – for reasons supported by ideology or political emotion – in the eyes of those empowered to grant, refuse, or revoke the "gift" of compassion. How are such determinations made? In order to achieve humanitarian subjecthood, one's suffering must map onto the locally salient "grid of victimization." In the present instance, and within the emerging hierarchy of suffering based on the Shoah/Darfur analogy and the arresting rhetorical power of the slogan, "never again," there are clear winners and losers. Sudanese from Darfur, in a perverse, provisional sense, have "won," and other refugees – South Sudanese, Eritreans, and African refugees already living in the country, among others – have "lost." As Boaz put forth unapologetically, success or failure is a function of rhetorical power and discursive prowess – not of asylum seekers themselves, but of self-appointed "trauma brokers" (James 2004) like Boaz himself, along with diverse others including Ilana Weisman, the Chief Rabbi of Tel Aviv, the judge in the "enemy nationals" case, and even Boaz's skeptical (but complicit) human rights partners.

These trauma brokers' analogical mode of reasoning through history is clearly double-edged. Although it does create possibilities for the expansive cultivation of empathy and ethically motivated intervention, these political emotions do not necessarily translate into humanitarian gestures of practical, legal, or moral consequence. Asylum seekers from Darfur have come to inhabit a privileged position within Israel's local hierarchy of suffering on the basis of their trauma brokers' – and, at times, their own – skillful and strategic representation of their experiences of suffering and trauma. Yet this infelicitous status offers no real guarantee of protection. Even as a small number of Darfuris have been promised the state's greatest gift – the gift of full political and social recognition in the form of Israeli citizenship – many others have been detained and expelled, and those who persist in attempting to enter Israeli territory are immediately deported (Ravid et al. 2007). Humanitarian gestures, divorced from any standard of law or justice, clearly can be strategically enacted, discursively manipulated – and refused, revoked, or terminated at will.

This local hierarchy of suffering has also played another, more hidden role in framing public and political conversations about the recent refugee influx in Israel. Throughout this unruly biopolitical drama, there has been virtually no discussion of Israel's obligations to another refugee population: Palestinians living under Israeli occupation. This is no coincidence; the logic of humanitarian exception has made it possible for the state to respond with calculated beneficence toward a small, hyper-politicized group of refugees in response to pressing popular demand while continuing to ignore its responsibilities toward Palestinians whose lives it regulates, constrains, and controls. Only a tiny handful of Israeli refugee advocates have commented upon this link. Groups that that have, most of them established human rights organizations with multipronged agendas, take pains to keep their struggles separate, largely because it is so much easier to mobilize political emotion in support of the former struggle than the latter. Thus the logic of humanitarian exception – charity-based, discretionary, and subject to ideological manipulation – has proven particularly expedient, especially from the state's point of view.

Overall, the key features of the Israeli state's response to this refugee influx – dubious and ideologically motivated modes of classification, including the failure to operationalize the distinction between economic migrants and political refugees; bureaucratic and administrative disorder; the mixing of policymaking and political emotion – are in no way unique to Israel. Rather, they are all features of a much broader, global pattern of classificatory and moral "unruliness" regarding the status, rights, and entitlements of asylum seekers and other border-crossing populations. In the absence of systematic or enforceable rules or laws, states, including those that proudly proclaim their commitment to human rights, effectively are free to respond however they wish. In some cases, irregular migrants' presence is simply ignored. In other instances, irregular entrants are systematically arrested and deported, and those who try to enter are banished to liminal spaces of exception like "detention centers" at airports (in France, Israel, and other countries); on remote islands (like the Italian island of Lampedusa or the independent island of Nauru near Australia); or in desolate desert regions (in Australia and now in southern Israel). This unruliness can have deeply repressive, and even violent, consequences. Yet even repressive and violent governmental techniques like mass detention and expulsion are proving ineffectual as means of containing or preventing "irregular" migration flows.

Cavell observes that the choice to either acknowledge or avoid the pain of another has weighty and far-reaching consequences; in

making that choice, he contends, "the future between us is at stake." As the events analyzed here would suggest, such futures are always, perhaps inevitably imprinted with lingering, potent, often hyper-politicized traces of emotion, of elsewhere, and of the past.

NOTES

1 For an incisive critique of the contemporary Jewish preoccupation with the Shoah, see Burg 2008.
2 Data from the Knesset Research and Information Center, and UNHCR-Israel, provided by the TAU Refugee Rights Clinic (personal communication).
3 For more on this movement, see Kemp and Raijman 2004; Willen 2005, 2007a.
4 Pseudonym.
5 Ilana's comments echo those of Martha Nussbaum, quoted in the epigraph above.
6 Pseudonym.
7 On July 1, 2009, the Israeli government reorganized the Immigration Police and initiated a new expulsion campaign with a declared target of 200,000 deportees. Asylum seekers and refugees, as well as Israeli-born children of unauthorized migrants, were among the explicit targets of the campaign. At the same time, the Knesset passed the first reading of a legislative bill that would allow not only for the immediate expulsion of newly arrived asylum seekers and refugees, but also the imprisonment of individuals who assist them.

REFERENCES

Adout, R.
   2007 Trafficked Women and Political Asylum Seekers, in Transnational Migration to Israel in Global Comparative Context. Edited by S. S. Willen. Lanham, MD: Lexington Books.
Agamben, G.
   1998 Homo Sacer: Sovereign Power and Bare Life. Stanford: Stanford University Press.
Akoka, K.
   2006 La demande d'asile en Israel: Vers la "nationalization" de la procedure de prise en charge.

Anteby-Yemini, L.
2009 Les "réfugiés soudanais" en Israël: discours, représentations, mobilizations. Maghreb-Machrek, Spring 199: 71–84.

Arendt, H.
1973 The Decline of the Nation-State and the End of the Rights of Man, in The Origins of Totalitarianism. New York: Harcourt Brace Jovanovich.

Azoulay, Y.
2007 Refugees spur tension between IDF, police, immigration officials, in Ha'aretz newspaper. June 25.

Azzam, F. ed.
2006 A Tragedy of Failures and False Expectations: Report on the Events Surrounding the Three-month Sit-in and Forced Removal of Sudanese Refugees in Cairo, September–December 2005 Cairo: Forced Migration and Refugee Studies Program, American University in Cairo.

Ben-Dor, A., and M. Kagan
2007 The Refugee from My Enemy is My Enemy: The Detention and Exclusion of Sudanese Refugees in Israel, at the Minerva Center for Human Rights Biannual Conference for Human Rights in Israel.

Bereshovsky, A.
2007 Sudanese refugees left outside Beersheba city hall. July 3, in Ynet.com.

Burg, A.
2008 The Holocaust Is Over; We Must Rise From Its Ashes. New York: Palgrave Macmillan.

Burston, B.
2008 A kinship of genocide, in Ha'aretz newspaper. November 23.

Cavell, S.
1997 Comments on Veena Das's Essay "Language and Body: Transactions in the Construction of Pain," in Social Suffering. Edited by A. Kleinman, V. Das, and M. Lock. Berkeley: University of California.

Das, V.
1997 Language and Body: Transactions in the Construction of Pain, in Social Suffering. Edited by A. Kleinman, V. Das, and M. Lock. Berkeley: University of California.

Farmer, P.
2003 Pathologies of Power. Berkeley: University of California Press.

Fassin, D.
2005 Compassion and Repression: The Moral Economy of Immigration Policies in France. Cultural Anthropology 20:362–87.

Fassin, D.
2007 Humanitarianism as a Politics of Life. Public Culture 19:499–520.

Fassin, D., and E. D'Halluin
2007 Critical Evidence: The Politics of Trauma in French Asylum Policies. Ethos 35:300–29.

Fisher, W. F.
1997 Doing Good? The Politics and Antipolitics of NGO Practices. Annual Review of Anthropology 26:439–64.

Gerver, M. and O. Klass
2007 "Never again" means what?, in Jerusalem Post. May 16.

Giordano, C.
2008 Practices of Translation and the Making of Migrant Subjectivities in Contemporary Italy. American Ethnologist 35:588.

Good, B., M.-J. D. Good S. T., Hyde, and S. Pinto
2008 Postcolonial Disorders: Reflections on Subjectivity in the Contemporary World, in Postcolonial Disorders. Edited by M. J. D. Good S. T Hyde, S. Pinto, and B. Good. Berkeley: University of California Press.

Grinberg, M.
2007a Egyptian police kill Darfur woman en route to Israel, in Ha'aretz newspaper. July 22.

Grinberg, M.
2007b IDF leaves 37 refugees stranded in downtown Be'er Sheva, in Ha'aretz newspaper. May 9.

Grinberg, M.
2007c MKs oppose deporting Darfur refugees to Egypt, in Ha'aretz newspaper. August 3.

Grinberg, M.
2007d Prisons Service: No more space to absorb Sudanese refugees, in Ha'aretz newspaper. December 1.

Hage, G.
2009 Hating Israel in the Field: On Ethnography and Political Emotions. Anthropological Theory 9:59–79.

Ilan, S.
2006 A Genocide is Not Much Less than a Holocaust, in Ha'aretz newspaper. May 13.

James, E.
2004 The Political Economy of "Trauma" in Haiti in the Democratic Era of Insecurity. Culture, Medicine and Psychiatry 28:127–49.

Kemp, A., and R. Raijman
2004 "Tel Aviv Is Not Foreign to You": Urban Incorporation Policy on Labor Migrants in Israel. International Migration Review 38:26–51.

Kemp, A., and R. Raijman
2008 Migrants and Workers: The Political Economy of Labor Migration in Israel. Tel Aviv: Van Leer Jerusalem Institute and Hakibbutz Hameuchad [Hebrew].

Kraft, D.
2007 Sudanese in Israel Hope They Have Found a Home, in New York Times. March 18.

Kritzman, T.
2007 Israel as a State of Temporary Asylum, presented at the Association for Israel Studies Annual Meeting. Ra'anana, Israel.

LaCapra, D.
2001 Writing History, Writing Trauma. Baltimore: Johns Hopkins University Press.

Ma'ariv
2007 Lau to Olmert: Free the Sudanese. Maariv – NRG. May 22.

Malkki, L.
1995 Refugees and Exile: From "Refugee Studies" to the National Order of Things. Annual Review of Anthropology 24:495–523.

McKinney, K.
2007 "Breaking the Conspiracy of Silence": Testimony, Traumatic Memory, and Psychotherapy with Survivors of Political Violence. Ethos 35:265–99.

Mualem, M.
2007 Israel to grant citizenship to hundreds of Darfur refugees, in Ha'aretz newspaper. September 5.

Nussbaum, M. C.
2003 Compassion and Terror. Daedalus 132:10–26.

Nyers, P.
2000 On Humanitarian Violence: "Humanity" and the Logic of Sovereignty, in (Dis)Placing Security: Critical Re-evaluations of the Boundaries of Security Studies. Edited by S. Arnold and J. M. Beier. Toronto: Centre for International and Security Studies.

Pandolfi, M.
2003 Contract of Mutual (In)Difference: Governance and the Humanitarian Apparatus in Contemporary Albania and Kosovo. Indiana Journal of Global and Legal Studies 10:369–380.

Ravid, B., M. Grinberg, Y. Hai, Ha'aretz correspondents, and Associated Press
2007 Government: Darfur refugees will be refused entry into Israel. Ha'aretz newspaper. August 20.

Ticktin, M.
2006 Where Ethics and Politics Meet: The Violence of Humanitarianism in France. American Ethnologist 33:33–49.

Uchitelle-Pierce, B.
2007 Darfur refugees establish bond of suffering in Yad Vashem visit, in Jerusalem Post. March 12.

UNHCR
2009 2008 Global Trends. Accessed July 1, 2009, at http://www.unhcr.org/pages/49c3646c4d6.html.

Wagner, M.
2007 "Israel is not obligated to aid refugees," in Jerusalem Post. June 6.

Willen, S. S.
2005 Birthing "Invisible" Children: State Power, NGO Activism, and Reproductive Health among Undocumented Migrant Workers in Tel Aviv, Israel. Journal of Middle East Women's Studies 1:55–88.

Willen, S. S.
2007a "Flesh of our Flesh"? Undocumented Migrants' Search for Meaning in the Wake of a Suicide Bombing, in Transnational Migration to Israel in Global Comparative Context. Edited by S. S. Willen. Lanham, MD: Lexington.

Willen, S. S.
2007b "Illegality," Mass Deportation and the Threat of Violent Arrest: Structural Violence and Social Suffering in the Lives of Undocumented Migrant Workers in Israel, in Trauma and Memory: Reading, Healing, and Making Law. Edited by A. Sarat, M. Alberstein, and N. Davidovitch, pp. 168–203. Stanford: Stanford University Press.

Willen, S. S.
2007c Introduction, in Transnational Migration to Israel in Global Comparative Perspective. Edited by S. S. Willen. Lanham, MD: Lexington Books.

Willen, S. S.
2007d Toward a Critical Phenomenology of "Illegality": State Power, Criminalization, and Abjectivity among Undocumented Migrant Workers in Tel Aviv, Israel. International Migration 45:8–36.

Willen, S. S. ed.
2007e Transnational Migration to Israel in Global Comparative Context. Lanham, MD: Lexington Books.

Willen, S. S.
  2010 Citizens, "Real" Others, and "Other" Others: The Biopolitics of Otherness and the Deportation of Undocumented Migrant Workers from Tel Aviv, Israel, in The Deportation Regime: Sovereignty, Space, and the Freedom of Movement. Edited by N. De Genova and N. Peutz. Durham, NC: Duke University Press.
Willen, S. S. (under review)
  Do "Illegal" Migrants have a "Right to Health"? Engaging Ethical Theory as Social Practice at a Tel Aviv Open Clinic.

40

The Elegiac Addict
History, Chronicity, and the Melancholic Subject

Angela Garcia

For Alma.

On the cusp of her 29th birthday, Alma Gallegos was covered lying in the parking lot near the emergency room (ER) entrance at Española Hospital. Like many patients that present at this particular ER, she was anonymously dumped by acquaintances that likely feared she might die or was already dead. In fact, Alma was close to death: her breath was shallow; her heart rate barely discernible; and, despite the intense summer heat, her skin cold to the touch. On quick inspection of her swollen limbs, the attending physician determined that Alma had overdosed on heroin, and she was treated with Naloxone, an opioid antidote that, if administered in time, revives the body's central nervous and respiratory systems. Alma's vitals were soon stabilized, and she remained in the hospital until the local drug court mandated that she be transferred to the very drug treatment facility that she had recently discharged herself from.

Four days after her overdose, Alma emerged from the facility's women's dormitory. Having privately suffered through the initial torments of heroin withdrawal, it was now expected that she begin putting addictive experience into a social and linguistic frame – an exercise central to the clinic's therapeutic process. It was in my capacity as a patient attendant at the detoxification clinic that I observed Alma that morning. She pulled at her hair uncomfortably; her body twitched and pebbles of sweat collected on her brow. For several minutes, she looked around the counselor's small, windowless office and then asked in the Hispano manner (that is, more statement than question): "Yo estuve aquí una vez, no?" [I've been here before, haven't I?].[1]

Indeed, it was Alma's second admission to the detoxification clinic in a year, and her sixth admission to a drug recovery program in just five years. Addicted to heroin for half her life, Alma's affective world – from her embodied pains, to her cravings, to the quietude she experiences during a heroin high – were as familiar to her as the institutions intermittently charged to apprehend and/or care for her. It was a familiarity achieved through certain recurring fractures, indexed by long stretches of heroin use, arrest, mandatory treatment, and an eventual and ongoing return to heroin use, arrest, and treatment.

Angela Garcia, "The Elegiac Addict: History, Chronicity, and the Melancholic Subject," *Cultural Anthropology* 23/4 (2009): 718–46. Reproduced by permission of the American Anthropological Association from *Cultural Anthropology* 23/4 (2009), pp. 718–46. Not for sale or further reproduction.

In clinical parlance, Alma's return to detox was a "relapse." Such a determination was in accordance to the logic of contemporary public health and addiction medicine, which understands and treats drug addiction primarily as a "chronic health problem, not a moral failing or a social problem" (McLellan et al. 2000:1689). But Alma understood her presence at the clinic as less a "relapse" – which connotes a period of remission – and more a "return"; a return to living "once more and innumerable times more" (Nietzsche 2000:274) this particular aspect of Hispano life: these weary limbs, this room, this familiar and anticipated question now posed to her by the drug counselor: what happened?

Alma plainly answered that nothing happened. She said, "Es que lo que tengo no termina" [It's just that what I have has no end]. Almost two years later, Alma was again rushed to the same hospital ER, where she was pronounced dead after overdosing on heroin.

This essay considers heroin addiction and overdose in northern New Mexico's Española Valley as a vexing condition marked by both the impossibility and the inevitability of an end. It reflects on observations and interviews I conducted with Alma between 2004 and 2006 and gives a sense of her struggle to reconcile this condition's inherent contradictions. As a frontline clinical staff member at the region's drug treatment facility and an anthropologist, I closely followed Alma as she moved within and between institutional and intimate domains, including the clinic, drug courts, "picaderos" (shooting galleries), home, and church. As the discursive forms and practices associated with these domains worked toward constituting Alma as "recovering" or not, a presupposition of return emerged. Outside of the clinic, Alma was a part of a local world that readily used heroin to "treat" the recurring pains associated with the ongoing history of loss and displacement that had come to characterize Hispano life. Within the clinic, she was expected to prepare the grounds for her "recovery," even if the biomedical model of chronicity, on which the clinic's practices were based, alleged that her condition was, by definition, unending.

Embedded in these simultaneously opposed and conspiring worlds, Alma struggled to confirm her existence against their shared presupposition of inevitable return: a return to certain historically situated pains, to using heroin, to the clinic. It is the central argument of this essay that the interplay of these biomedical and local discourses compelled the very dynamics of "endlessness" that Alma felt herself prisoner of, and set the groundwork for her fatal overdose.

In this essay, I stress the political and psychoanalytic and link the experience of heroin addiction to certain historical and discursive refrains. As a critical phenomenology of heroin addiction, it evokes what I call the "elegiac" nature of heroin addiction in the Hispano milieu, while also accounting for the generative matrices that produce these affects (see, e.g., Das 1996; Desjarlais 1997; O'Nell 1996; Scheper-Hughes 1992). My particular concern here is with how forms of historical loss, the embodied complexity of addiction, and local and biomedical logics of chronicity tragically coincided in Alma's life.

There is, Alma once told me, no way out – "no hay salida" [no exit]. With her words in mind, the larger goal of this essay is to understand how loss and return is experienced across the Hispano landscape, how they emerged, and how they led Alma to decide that her life was not worth living.

The Melancholic Subject

The Española Valley is a rural network of poor, Spanish-speaking villages, at the center of a triangle whose points are the tourist meccas of Santa Fe and Taos and the technomilitary complex of Los Alamos. It encompasses the site of the first Spanish colonial settlement in the Southwest, where present-day Española resides, and evolved out of a historical context of successive struggles over land expropriation and sociopolitical domination – first by Spain, then Mexico, and, finally, by the United States (Gonzales-Berry and Maciel 2000; Rodríguez 1987). Since 1848, when New Mexico became a U.S. territory, generations of land grant heirs have struggled to retain ancestral lands. This conflict persists, intensified by real estate speculation, in-migration, and labor magnets such as Los Alamos, Santa Fe, and Albuquerque. Today, many Hispanos resist further displacement through strategies of cultural preservation and memoralization. In the realm of tradition, for example, there are yearly re-enactments of the Hispano colonial past, including the arrival of 16th-century Spanish settler Don Juan de Oñate. Agricultural practices with Spanish colonial roots, such as the community-based system of irrigation and water governance known as acequias, remain vital to the economic survival of some villages, and are the locus of cultural preservation. And language itself speaks to the past, as the unique Spanish dialect of Hispanos is still peppered with archaisms that date back to the original *pobladores*, or townsfolk. But these traditions and practices, which Hispanos claim have been around "forever," are also being abandoned. Many have surrendered claims to their ancestral land and language and, by extension, the life they represent. Indeed, many younger Hispanos poignantly refer to themselves as "heirs of nothing."

Since the 1990s, the Española Valley has had the highest rate of heroin overdose and heroin-induced death in the country. With just over 30,000 residents, nearly 70 people died from heroin overdose in one recent 18-month period. The social and emotional wake of these deaths reverberates with the still tender wounds of recent history, such as the ongoing dispossession of land, and the consequent fragmentation of social order and intimate life. These constitute a recurring experience of loss that, if not directly assimilable, is nevertheless familiar – familiar in the sense of the very structure of recurrence, and in the sense of the close connection this structure has to forms of loss: the loss of a tradition, a village, a daughter, a friend. My concern here is about these experiences of loss and memories of it, how intersecting forms of history come to bear on the present, and how heroin use – and overdose in particular – exposes the painful recognition that the future has been swallowed up by the past.

In "Mourning and Melancholia" Sigmund Freud defines mourning as "the reaction to the loss of a loved person, or to the loss of some abstraction" (1989:586). It designates a psychic process to loss where the mourner is able to gradually work through grief, reaching a definite conclusion whereby the lost object or ideal is let go and the mourner able to move on. Melancholy, by contrast, designates mourning without end. It entails an incorporation of the lost person or ideal as a means to keep it alive. Regarding its somatic features, Freud describes the sleeplessness of the melancholic, suggesting that it attests to the steadfastness of the condition. "The complex of melancholia," he writes, "behaves like an open wound" (1989:589).

In Freud's conception, the melancholic's sustained devotion to what is lost is pathological. He warns that the intensity of the "self-tormenting" condition can culminate in suicide (1989:588). More recent efforts to examine Freud's exploration of melancholia are critical of his understanding of it as pathology and offer important modifications to his theory (see Butler 2004; Cheng 2001; Eng and Kazanjian 2003; Muñoz 1997). But here, I pursue Freud's original suggestion regarding the danger to life melancholy may pose. In *The Ego and the Id* (1960), Freud writes that the unrelenting nature of melancholy transforms the subject into one who mourns – transforms her, first and foremost, into a melancholic subject. But what if we conceive the subject of melancholy not simply as the one who suffers but, rather, as the recurring historical refrains through which sentiments of "endless" suffering arise? How to attend to these wounds?

The melancholic subject that the title of this essay refers is thus about Alma, and about the structures in which her fatal overdose took root. And it refers to the all-too-familiar experiences of loss, articulated now as addiction, which have been shaped, in part, by the kinds of attachments that the logic of chronicity assumes. The recent work of anthropologists show us how medical and technical forms of knowledge and intervention shape the experience and course of illness, and more broadly affect subjectivity (Biehl 2005; Cohen 1999; Petryna 2002; Young 1997). In the context of addiction, chronicity as knowledge and practice has become the ground for a new form of melancholic subjectivity, one that recasts a long-standing ethos of Hispano suffering into a succession of recurring institutional interactions. As Michael Fischer describes, "We are embedded, ethically, as well as existentially and materially, in technologies and technological prostheses" and these take us into new models of ethics in which "our older moral traditions have little guidance or experience to offer" (2003:51). In the context of emerging technologies, Fischer aptly describes us as being "*thrown* ... to new forms of social life" (2003:51, emphasis added). I want to suggest that the Hispano ethos of suffering is a social referent for addiction's recent biomedical turn, and the disparate technologies in which this turn is embedded (drug treatment centers, research conferences, NA meetings, and so on) deepens this ethos of suffering in unexpected, even dangerous, ways. In the context of its preceding Hispano forms, I examine how these technologies not so much throw us, but bury us beneath the weight of that which does not end.

A Work of Mourning

Anthropology has shown how following the life history of a single person can illuminate the complex intimate and structural relations that constitute a life, a community, and a social world (Biehl 2005; Das and Kleinman 2000; Desjarlais 2003; Pandolfo 1998). I also engage in this form of inquiry, while recognizing that there are many elements of Alma's story that I do not know, and other elements that could be told in the voice of Bernadette, Yvette, Johnny, Marcus, or the many other subjects I followed during the course of my research. They were all caught within the same cycle of trying to live their lives without heroin and succumbing their lives to it. I thus present Alma as embodying a condition that is more than hers alone.

While there are certain refrains in Alma's experience that belong to Hispanos more broadly, one of my goals here is to convey Alma as she appeared to me — generous, reflective, and deeply engaged in trying to find a way to live. In rendering Alma's life, and in trying to account for her death, I undertake a kind of "work of mourning." This differs from

recent anthropological works on violence and subjectivity, which examine discursive practices that seek to make possible the repair of injury and of the everyday (see Das and Kleinman 2000, 2001; Seremetakis 1991). This work of mourning is in another tradition, the Hispano tradition, which commemorates the singularity of death while insisting on the inevitable repetition of it. It is a tradition that includes the creation of memorials called "descansos" (resting places) that are publicly placed at or near the site of death. The descanso does not seek to reinhabit the site of loss, or repair the everyday, but insists on death's essential relationship to life. Over the years, heroin-related descansos have gathered on the Hispano landscape. Frequently adorned with the used syringes that contained the lethal dose of drug, they highlight just how enmeshed heroin has become in physical space and everyday life, and pose the question of whether and how "mourning as repair" is possible or even desired in the face of unrelenting loss. Rising along the edges of dirt roads and scattered among the Valley's juniperdotted hills, the undisturbed presence of the descansos constitute a kind of ethical commitment to that which was lost; they keep vigil over it; they coexist.

One day, while sitting together in my parked car in front of the Española Public Library, a certain memory flashed up for Alma, urgent and unannounced. It was a cold afternoon, already dark despite the early hour. I turned on the car's ignition and was ready to return Alma to the halfway house in which she resided following 30 days of heroin detoxification. To my surprise, Alma grabbed my hand and told me to wait; she wasn't ready to go back. For a few moments we stared quietly at the library's iron-barred windows, our breath visible in the chilly air. Alma broke the silence and said that her older sister Ana, whom she never mentioned to me before, loved to read. Ana ... killed by a drunk driver four years before. She had been on her way to work, Alma recalled, driving along the windy, two-lane highway that connects Española to the village of Chimayó.

Following local custom, the Gallegos family put up a handmade descanso in the spot that Ana was killed. Alma told me that afternoon that it still marks her sister's death, and asked if I'd seen it. She described the plastic yellow flowers and the fading family portrait that adorned Ana's wooden cross. I knew the descanso and offered to drive her there. Alma shook her head no, adding that for years she would have to turn her head and look away every time she passed the cross on her way to Chimayó to meet her dealer. She confessed that she still turned her head away, but was able to conjure the image of the descanso in her mind. "Ahí está," she said, "mirándome" [There it is, looking at me].

In his examination of the English elegy, Peter Sacks notes that the traditional forms and figures of the genre relate to an experience of loss and the search for a consolation (1985). The passage from grief to consolation is often presented in the form of repetition – through the recurrence of certain words and refrains. According to Sacks, the elegy's repetitive structure functions to separate the living from the dead and forces the bereaved to accept a loss that she might otherwise refuse. In this way, the repetition creates a rhythm of lament that allows grief to be simultaneously conjured forth and laid to rest. But what if the structure of repetition creates not a working through of grief, but its intensification? How might the structure of repetition become constitutive of a kind of endless mourning?

Passing her sister's roadside memorial on her way to score heroin, Alma created her own rhythm of lament: a counterpoint of yesterday and today, memory and forgetting, death and life. Like her sister's descanso, the elegiac character of Alma's narrative offers a continuous double-take on thinking about the relationship between history of loss and the present: what is lost remains. In Alma's words, it is "sin fin" (without end) forging the patterns of her experience.

The Entanglements of Time

In thinking about the temporal dimensions of loss and sentiment, I have found Raymond Williams's concept of "structure of feeling" particularly useful. Structures of feeling are actively felt sensibilities derived from lived, material histories. According to Williams, at any given time, there are multiple structures of feeling in operation, corresponding roughly to the generations living at that time. Each generation creates its own structure of feeling in response to the world it inherits – taking up or abandoning the sensibilities of its predecessors. His way of thinking about "the living substance of perceptions and relationships" thus has a temporal dimension that helps elucidate the interlocking nature of experience and affect (1977:34).

Consider, for instance, expressions often repeated among elder Hispanos: "Todo es historia" [History is everything]. It is a saying that simultaneously acknowledges the loss of times past and the longing for continuity in a precarious and changing world. Another: "La historia es una herida" [History is a wound] which is frequently evoked in the context of expressing the material and cultural losses that resulted from the region's past. And another, repeated by the addicted: "Chiva es el remedio para todo" [Heroin cures everything]. Thus, while elders worry that the younger generation is all too willing to forget the past, the young are just as likely to understand the heroin problem as a contemporary consequence of it, while still offering heroin as a remedy for the pain that accompanies the past. In this way, young and old insist that to meaningfully address the heroin problem, one must also address the region's deep historical scars.

There are other kinds of scars, such as those on the skin. The needle marks and abscesses that mapped Alma's body – open wounds in the literal sense – powerfully attested to how addiction is also a historical formation and immanent experience. These are wounds in which the future, the present, and the past commingle through the force of recurring need: the need to score heroin, to get high, to find a vein. Alma once described it to me like this:

The thing about being hooked is you're always thinking ahead, thinking about your next fix, how you're going to get the money, where it's going to come from. It goes on and on. ... And now, I've been using so long, nothing ever lasts. The high ... it's over before you know it and you're back to it, thinking about the next fix, making calls. It never stops.

Byron Good notes that in illness narratives, the autobiographical narrator tells a story that is not yet finished – there is more than one temporality woven together in a narrative (1994). Indeed, in talking about her addiction, Alma could express all of the following: the experience of past heroin use, the vicissitudes of her current condition, and the inevitability of further heroin use. Such entanglements show how time and the Hispano trope of endlessness are reworked through the experience of addiction. This point begs a larger question, which relates to addiction's physiological dimensions and to what extent the structure of endlessness is embedded within it.

From the point at which heroin enters the bloodstream, the physiological effects – the rush – occurs very quickly, usually within 20 seconds to a minute. Affected are the central nervous, cardiovascular, respiratory, endocrine, gastrointestinal and genitourinary systems, as well the skin. Morphine, the psychoactive ingredient in heroin, causes the state of euphoria, analgesia, and sedation associated with a heroin high. Over time, increasingly larger and more frequent doses of heroin are needed to achieve this state. Using becomes less about achieving a high and more about staving off withdrawal. Heroin is medicine – it relieves the pain its use creates. There is a complex, even geometrical, relationship between the Hispano trope of endlessness and the physiological experience of heroin addiction. And it is made more complex through the explanatory model of chronicity.

Briefly, the model of chronicity likens addiction to a lifelong disease. It is enduring and relapses are an expected occurrence. Treatment is lifelong and partially effective (Appel and Kott 2000; Brewer 1998). The chronicity model emerged in the 1960s, partly as a response to the high incidence of repeated relapse seen among addicts who entered publicly funded treatment programs. It was intended to dispel the long-held assumption that heroin addicts were innately psychopathic and irredeemable (see Acker 2002). Underpinning this rescripting of addiction was the explosion of

drug use in new economic and social settings – out of the "shadows" and into the white, middle-class mainstream. New constellations of disciplinary interests emerged that reexamined addiction. This turn culminated with the introduction of methadone maintenance in the 1960s.

The concept and practice of "maintenance" ushered in a new addiction research agenda for the behavioral and biosciences. Recent developments in bioscientific knowledge point to the genetic and neurological basis of addiction, usually described in terms of "adaptive changes" or "habituation" (Camí 2003; McLellan et al. 2000). Mediated by a new set of medical and scientific translations, the current vision of addiction as "chronic" bears contradictions that are both enabling and disabling. It can indeed counter old, reductionist explanations of behavior or culture and potentially relieve the moral repercussions of "relapse." But such a framing risks obfuscating other, perhaps more vital dimensions that encompass a local sense of what it is to suffer from an unending condition.

The ideologies and practices associated with addiction's biomedical turn, and the institutions in which they are embedded, have generated new affects and narratives of those struggling with addiction. Heroin addicts frequently express that they had little or no chance of recovery, and often explain their pessimism in biological terms. Their addiction, they say, is in the blood, like a virus, something they could not eradicate or recover from, even if they wanted to. But this local understanding of addiction differs from the medicoscientific view. In the Hispano milieu, the family is often the primary domain of heroin use, and heroin is frequently shared between fathers and sons or mothers and daughters. Heroin addiction is conceived of as a kind of contemporary "inheritance" – an intergenerational and intersubjective experience that accesses, literally, the bloodline. Thus, while addicts emphasize the biological language of "chronicity," particularly when talking about their "lifelong struggle" with heroin, their experiences reveal profound differences in the symbolic ordering of addiction and time, whereby the "lifelong" struggles of an addict may exceed that which is traditionally conceived of as "a life." Here, "lifelong" may represent several, related lives, entangled together in ways that make a strictly biologized and individualized approach to treatment futile.

Despite the increasing reliance on metaphors of chronic disease, practically speaking, the motivating factor behind drug recovery is invariably understood in terms of personal choice or will. This is largely because of two factors: first, the prevailing "Twelve Step" model of recovery, which emphasizes personal power over addiction (made possible through the sustained reflection over past behaviors – what is described as a "moral inventory" – as well as the personal act of "surrender" to a "higher power"); and, second, the ever-expanding punitive approach to addiction, which emphasizes the addict's capacity to reason and, therefore, control her drug-using behavior. Both the Twelve-Step and the juridical institutions draw their justification and legitimacy from liberalism, which purports personal autonomy of each rational agent and, correspondingly, treats individuals as responsible for their freely chosen actions. There are clear tensions between these arguments and institutional practices and the biomedical model of addiction. Whereas from a biomedical perspective relapse is understandable and even expected, from a juridical perspective the relapsed addict is ultimately assigned the blame for relapse and is seen as lacking the will to recover.

Increasingly, the mechanism through which addicts enter publicly funded treatment is through the drug courts, which leverage the threat of imprisonment if the "offending addict" does not comply with treatment. Here, the traditional boundaries between the therapeutic impetus of medical and social services, and the state's authority to control "criminal" individuals and populations, are further blurred, even eradicated. Nearly all of the addicts I encountered during my research were court-appointed, or sentenced, to detox and treatment – a finding that mirrors national statistics of publicly funded treatment programs.[2] Those with the highest rates of "relapse" were eventually incarcerated one or more times as a consequence of not complying with prior treatment sentences. Alma, for

example, spent a total of 18 months at a women's detention center for two separate sentences relating to drug possession charges. At the time of her death, she was awaiting her court date for "offenses" relating to her failure to comply with an earlier round of court-appointed treatment. The great irony is that her relapse was expected, even innocent, at least from a medical perspective. From the juridical perspective, however, it represented a failure of will and was to be reckoned – either through a sentence for further treatment, incarceration, or both.

How have the seemingly incompatible discourses of "chronicity" and "choice" supplanted alternative ways of understanding and treating addiction? What are the psychic effects of these discourses, particularly for those that have been through repeated cycles of recovery and relapse? How do medical and juridical responses to addiction lock addicts into an incommensurate "medical-moral identity" (Young 2006) in which the outcome of relapse is not only expected, but produced?

Jean Jackson has written of the uncertain ontological status of the chronically ill (2005). She describes how this status provokes stigma, and forces the patient into deeper modes of suffering. Many of the heroin addicts I interviewed – addicts who, in today's lingo would be described as chronically ill – told not of uncertainty, but of fixity. Alma, for instance, described her life and the struggles and losses that defined it as being without end. She echoed the sentiments of many addicts I spoke with when she told me that the only way she could exit this cycle of endlessness was through a heroin high. Alma once said to me, "The only time I feel really ok is when I don't feel *anything*. When I'm high, it's like … it's hard to explain, but just for a little while everything goes away. But that feeling of nothing … It's gone before you know it."

Hoy–Today

Hoy Recovery is a publicly funded, community-based drug program located on the outskirts of Española. Established in the early 1970s, Hoy, which means "today" in Spanish, initially provided peer support for male alcoholics, many of who were returning from the war in Vietnam. Former clients and staff recall those early years of operation as fraternal. "It was like a house," one staff member remembered. "We all lived together and helped each other out. We were like family." Over time, there was an increasing number of younger men seeking services for heroin addiction. In the 1980s, heroin addicts were being transferred to Hoy on release from the local hospital or the county jail. The facility became cramped, and the waiting list to gain entrance to it grew. In 1998, a support group was established for women, and they began accessing Hoy's limited services. With the rising caseload, the recovery home took on an increasingly institutional feel. A thick, Plexiglas wall was added in the lobby, separating staff "on the inside" from the increasing needs of addicts "afuera" [on the outside]. Most addicts stayed for only a few days; many returned within months; still others died on release from the program or died waiting to get in.

In 2004, Hoy established a medically monitored detoxification clinic, which focused on the unique and growing needs of heroin addiction. Located in the nearby village of Velarde, Hoy's detox program was comprised of a group of small adobe houses that surround a larger building. The detoxification clinic was once a state mental institution for Hispanic adolescents called Piñon Hills. For years, the facility sat vacant, its exterior walls scorched by the fire that led to the facility's closure. County officials considered condemning the building, but a 1999 special congressional hearing on the region's heroin problem identified it as a potential site for a much needed drug treatment center. Five years later, Hoy's Detoxification Clinic opened its doors.

The clinic signified certain cultural, economic, and medical advancements in a historically impoverished and drug-weary region. It was the first facility in the region specifically for heroin addiction. It was also the first to promote a medical model for detoxification by offering antiopioid medications in a "clinical setting." At the opening, musicians performed traditional rancheras as journalists and state politicians toured the facility. County officials spoke movingly about the opportunity to reduce heroin overdoses and many recounted their own struggles with addiction. A prayer for healing was murmured. With the cutting of the yellow ribbon, the troubled memory of Piñon Hills was laid to rest and Hoy Recovery was born.

The year of Hoy's opening, there were 40 fatal heroin overdoses in the Española Valley.

I had just been hired as a detox attendant at the newly opened facility and was on duty the morning Alma was admitted. She was in a state of acute heroin withdrawal. Alma immediately began to beg for medications to ease the pains in her stomach and limbs. The male counselor on duty explained that she needed to undergo a drug search before she could receive a dose of a Robaxin, a muscle relaxant. As the only female attendant on duty, I was instructed to lead Alma to the women's dormitory and perform the routine search.

I had observed drug searches in the past, but this was the first I would carry out. We stood in a room the size of a school bus, beside one of six narrow beds that would briefly become Alma's. She was familiar with the procedure and began removing her clothes. I hastily combed through her sweaty garments – my fingers tracing the inside seams of her jeans, her tank top, the crotch of her panties, the underwire of her bra. When I was finished, I told Alma that I could arrange to have personal belongings delivered to the recovery center. Alma responded that she had none.

She would sleep in that bed for only a fraction of her "drug sentence," leaving early on her third morning because she said there were mice in the women's dormitory, and she did not feel safe when there were no women on duty. I asked the head counselor if he knew where Alma went. He responded with a shrug and added that he knew Alma; she'd be back soon enough. I was struck by the counselor's sense of the inevitability of her return, which I came to understand as similar to the hopelessness and "burnout" that many clinicians and mental health professionals feel, particularly those who work in resource-poor hospitals with high caseloads (see Raviola et al. 2002). Mental health professionals working at Hoy seemed to succumb to a kind of moral detachment that results from working too long in an environment of mounting need and repeated loss. I worried about how the discourse of chronicity strengthened the assumption of return that was expressed, and perhaps fostered, by caregivers.

In fact, I did see Alma again a few months later, during the counseling session recounted at the beginning of this essay. She had just been readmitted to the detox clinic following an overdose, for which she was hospitalized less than 24 hours, and then transferred to Hoy, as directed by her parole officer. According to her patient file, Alma's heroin overdose was labeled an "accidental poisoning," the circumstances of which remained unclear. The attending physician recommended that she begin a regimen of antidepressants to treat what was described as "underlying emotional issues," the nature of which also remained unclear. I shuffled through the other papers in Alma's patient file, and learned that she was 29 years old, married, and had no reported children. Her mother was listed as her emergency contact, and her permanent address was located in Tierra Amarilla, the county seat about 70 miles north of Española.

I began to see Alma regularly in the evenings, at the start of my shift. She would linger around my "station" – a desk positioned at the crux of a L-shaped hallway that led to the patient dormitories, which were separated by gender. As a detox attendant, my primary duties were to watch and record the activities of patients between the hours of 6 p.m. and 8 a.m., details which might become significant in case of any legal issues, which were common. I also dispensed medications, supposedly according to the orders of a clinic nurse, but there was no such nurse – the clinic could not afford to maintain one.

During her second stint at the detox clinic, Alma would lean on my desk and fill me in on the details of the day's events – which patients walked out, which got kicked out – stressing, it seems, the hard-won fact that she had made it, she had stayed. She became, in a way, my friend. Each time I would return to the clinic and find that she was still there, I felt something akin to relief. She grew uncomfortable, though, if I commended her in any way for

staying, or if I asked her about "la vida afuera" [life outside]. "I don't like thinking about that," she would say, referring to her future, to what existed beyond the clinic walls. Or, "Don't throw me a party yet!" suggesting that, any day, she might just lose it. In the end, Alma remained in detox for 30 days. She was then transferred to Hoy Recovery Program's 90-day "Community Integration Program" – a kind of halfway house where she would begin the process of "finding one's feet," to use the language of the program's mission. Alma liked to joke that, after 15 years of heroin use, she had no feet, only collapsed veins.

The Community Integration Program was a chaotic, run-down facility on the outskirts of Española. There were more bodies than beds, and residents spent most of their days watching television, usually one of the many *Cops*-like reality-based programs, or Court TV, both programs in which clients essentially saw themselves criminalized on screen. Alma and I saw each other only occasionally during this time – sometimes over lunch, sometimes during shopping trips to the Super Wal-Mart, where she briefly worked while a resident of the program. Built in 1999, the Española Super Wal-Mart is now the second-largest employer in the Valley, after Los Alamos National Laboratories. Most employees are part time and earn less than seven dollars an hour. Onsite drug testing is a mandatory requirement for employment. Alma once described her dark blue work smock as reminiscent of her former prison attire.

During my visits with Alma during this time, it was apparent to me that she was growing demoralized and anxious. Her days at the residency program were long and monotonous, just as they were at work. Her only respite, she told me, was the mile-long walk down Railroad Avenue, an industrial artery that connects Hoy's residency program to Española's Riverside Drive, where Wal-Mart is located. During her walks to and from work, Alma considered her options. Stick out the rest of her treatment sentence with no real promise of a different future; move back into the trailer she had shared with her estranged husband; or return to the family home back in Tierra Amarilla. None of these options appealed to her. She didn't know what to do.

Yellow Earth

Sometimes I shoot up and I'm sure it's gonna be the last time. The needle'll be in me and I'll be pushing the plunger in thinking, *this is it! Se acabó!* [It's over!]. But I wake up all sick and life for me ... [pause] it doesn't stop. Even when it should, you know? There's no reason to live a life like this. Not one like this.

It was 2:45 in the morning when I recorded these words. Shortly after our afternoon at the public library, Alma went on a four-day heroin binge. She was passed out in an Española laundromat, where she had sought shelter from the cold, and was arrested for heroin possession. After two nights at the county jail in Tierra Amarilla, Alma returned to the detoxification clinic – her final opportunity, as her parole officer put it, to "straighten up." It was Alma's third admission to Hoy in 14 months. On admission, the intake counselor asked why she "sabotaged" her recovery yet again. Alma responded that there wasn't anything to sabotage, that this was her life.

On her second night back, Alma remained with me in the clinic's common room. Plagued by memories, she couldn't sleep. I suggested her sleeplessness was related to heroin withdrawal and, in the absence of more effective medications, suggested a warm bath. Alma shook her head no, said it was the thoughts "messing with" her head, thoughts she needed to get out lest she would explode.

And it was a tangle of thought and memory that she related to me that night. She talked about her home in Tierra Amarilla, the village where her family has lived "forever," and where she had just spent two nights at the County Jail, trembling alone in a windowless cell. She left her village when she was 17 years old, a year short of high school graduation, because she said she was choking on the memories of her elders, particularly her father's violent despair over the loss of ancestral lands. Her retreat from their memories, she said, was drugs.

Several weeks later, I began the process of transcribing Alma's recorded narrative. She spoke of her sister, of Tierra Amarilla, of memories that were her own and memories that she had inherited. At one point in the recording,

she paused for a long time, and then she said, "It all keeps me awake at night." And, minutes later: "it weighs heavy on my heart." Alma repeated the phrase "it weighs heavy on my heart" throughout the recorded narrative. Detective-like, I kept rewinding the recording and replaying it, trying to locate all the events that explained such heaviness. But Alma's admission of feeling was temporally disconnected from specific recollections of the past. Throughout her recorded narrative, such phrases of pain dangled precariously, isolated utterances that seemed to speak, as it were, for themselves. Whatever the reason for the apparent disconnectedness between feeling and event, one of the themes that Alma kept returning to in her narrative was the sense that nothing changes, that life and its ensuing pain is unalterable – "without end" [sin termina]. Indeed, it was within such terms that she explained her relapse, and at one point acknowledged that she knew she would return to the clinic, as if her relapse and readmission were simply part of the order of things, cause and effect. Referring to the so-called responsibility and challenge of staying clean – which is stressed by counselors at the clinic – Alma said, "It's not that I wasn't *ready* ... it's that there's nothing to be ready *for*."

Shortly after transcribing Alma's narrative, I drove up Highway 84 to Tierra Amarilla. It was fall and the cottonwoods along the Chama River were in full yellow bloom. As I climbed higher into the San Juan Mountains, tall, full-bodied ponderosa pines flanked the road. Set back from the highway were clusters of adobe houses and trailers and, adjacent to these, neat stacks of firewood ready for the coming chill of winter.

As I entered Tierra Amarilla, Alma's words began to echo in my mind. I imagined that she were in the passenger seat beside me, accompanying me with her memories. What memories might she have of that empty lot, or the burned-out trailer next to it? Did she know who scratched out Reies Lopez Tijerina's name on the historic marker that welcomes visitors to the infamous mountain village? Only a generation ago, the residents of this village worked on the land – in ranching, farming, and forestry. Now, each weekday morning, the village empties out and becomes a virtual ghost town as locals make the 85-mile drive to Los Alamos or Española for work. Among the abandoned lumber mills, dilapidated corrals, and boarded-up houses, I imagined events Alma might have participated in or witnessed: parties, marriages ... overdoses, deaths. She had spoken to me of some of these things that night at the detox clinic and told me, for instance, about the suicide of a trusted schoolteacher who had tutored her in reading. "She slashed her wrists in the woods and didn't leave a note," Alma said. "My brother's friends found her when they were out partying. The only thing we could think is that her son died in Desert Storm."

Tierra Amarilla: "Yellow Earth." Perhaps more than any other *norteño* (northern) New Mexican village, it is the symbolic ground of the Hispano history of dispossession and longing for land and times past that has inspired decades of political struggle – by turns mainstream and underground, through means violent and not. Tierra Amarilla was first settled as a land grant in the mid-1600s. Like all land grants in northern New Mexico, Spanish and, later, Mexican settlers were allotted land for an individual home; an irrigable plot for personal farming; and the right to share common land with other settlers for pasture, timber, and hunting. According to the deeds, personal allotments could be sold as private property, but common lands could not. The commons were just that – collective property – and were to be used and preserved for the community's wellbeing.

Since 1848, when New Mexico became part of the United States, generations of land-grant heirs have found themselves struggling to regain lost lands. Even today, they continue to argue that the United States broke the Treaty of Guadalupe Hidalgo, which was intended to protect titles secured before the war, thereby preserving the economic and cultural integrity of Hispano people. The heirs of the Tierra Amarilla land grant, which include Alma, alone lost over half a million acres, much of it now part of the Carson National Forest.

Here, the idea that the land was "lost" is no mere exercise in nostalgia; over generations it has given rise to a constant stream of rebellion, most famously in Tierra Amarilla 40 years ago when Reies Lopez Tijerina and a group of armed insurgents stormed the local courthouse, a symbol of an "outsider" authority that drove a wedge between the people and the land. The "Courthouse Raid" – as it is now known – prompted the governor to activate the National Guard and send in tanks to suppress the rebellion. A five-day manhunt by 500 law enforcement agents ensued. The rebellion was successful in symbolizing how deep passions run on the issue of the land and who has rights to it. In an interview following the raid, Tijerina exclaimed, "These people will always remember how they lost the land ... they have not forgotten after hundreds of years ... they will never forget" (Kosek 2006:344). Indeed, memories and sentiments regarding land loss remain powerful tropes, particularly among elders. The ultimate irony is that which was "lost" is still *there* for Hispanos to see – it's all around them in the mountains, rivers, mesas, and buttes. One wonders how Freud's conception of melancholy can be extended to address such material losses, losses like land that remain present but out of reach, particularly in a context where land is constituent to cultural identity and economic survival.

As I drove through Tierra Amarilla on that fall day – through the plaza anchored by the infamous courthouse – Alma's narrative was fresh on my mind. I couldn't help but wonder what role "the land" plays in memories of women like Alma: women who, in her words "didn't exist" during the most militant phase of the land grant movement; women whose lives have been dominated not by the loss of land, but by the loss of people. Certainly these forms of loss intersect in powerful ways. Alma's insistence that there is "nothing there ... nothing but memory" speaks to tragedies of earlier generations that are indelibly linked to the present. And the material legacy of land loss in northern New Mexico is the very stage for losses associated with heroin use. Indeed, the first time Alma shot up was deep in the forest, in a crumbling adobe on a large parcel of land that once belonged to "la familia Mascaranes," a shepherding family who lost land-use rights when much of the common land were designated a National Forest, a transformation that erased their livelihood. Their old adobe remains locked in the forest and is the site of many of Alma's heroin-related memories, including the first time Alma witnessed a heroin overdose.

I wanted to talk to the Mascaranes family, but I didn't know how to find them. I thought of asking a clerk at the general store, but the general store no longer existed; it was boarded up. I drove to the County Offices – a newer complex painted the color of adobe and the only building in the plaza that wasn't in a state of complete disrepair. Despite being a weekday afternoon, even it was closed.

As I drove home, I thought of Alma's words. "There's nothing up there no more. Nothing but memories."

Intolerable Insomnia

Alma left the heroin detox clinic three days after our predawn interview. According to the detox attendant on duty at the time of her departure, she simply walked out at approximately two in the morning. I asked to see her discharge papers, which patients are required to sign in acknowledgment that they had received counseling on the potential consequences – legal and not – of leaving detox before "successful completion." Alma signed her name in bubbly, childlike script. In response to the question "Reason for Self-Discharge," she wrote, "CANT SLEEP."

Jorge Luis Borges writes of the "unbearable lucidity of insomnia" (1998:98). He describes sleep as a state in which one is able to forget oneself. When one awakens, however, time, places, and people return – the self returns. One of the many words in Spanish for "to awaken" and which Borges regularly employs is *recordarse*, which translates literally to "remember oneself." In this sense, when one awakens, one remembers oneself; in the absence of sleep, the self never leaves, never forgets, and, thus, remains vigilant over itself and its memories. Borges understood that this vigilance leads one to a state of despair. In his

short story "The Circular Ruins," a man who suffers from insomnia walks miles through a jungle in hopes of tiring himself, losing himself to sleep. "In his perpetual state of wakefulness," Borges writes, "tears of anger burned the old man's eyes" (1998:98).

According to the attendant who was on duty the night of Alma's departure, no one picked her up at the clinic, suggesting that she would have had to walk 15 miles of dark highway to reach Española. I called the only phone number that I had for Alma, which was for the trailer that she shared with her on-again, off-again husband. There was no response. Over the next week I tried calling again and again. Eventually, a recorded voice answered, curtly informing me that the number I was trying to reach had been disconnected.

Several weeks after my visit to Tierra Amarilla, Alma called me. She wanted me to know that she was okay and that, although she knew what people must have thought regarding her discharge, she hadn't "screwed things up yet." Her tone was casual, even happy. She lived alone, worked at the local Subway sandwich shop, and was attending services at Rock Christian Fellowship – a growing evangelical church in Española. Like Victory Outreach, the church's faith-based activism is embedded within a larger ideological framework of drug recovery and tries to ensure that recovering converts are kept busy with activities so as to be able to "save" their lives. Indeed, the Rock's pastor preaches regularly about his own struggle with drugs, including heroin, and appeals to his congregants to "get clean" through rebirth, spiritual training, and evangelizing. It was a message that appealed to Alma. I wondered how Alma's transition from Catholicism to Evangelicalism might be understood as a reflection of her complicated relationship not only with drugs but also with her past and of a desire to forget.

The following afternoon I drove to the trailer that Alma had shared with her husband. Although it was still light outside, it was almost completely dark inside the trailer. Alma invited me in, informing me as she did that her home currently lacked phone service and electricity. But she quickly added that she was confident that her utilities would be reinstalled within the week, thanks to help from the Fellowship. I asked Alma if she was warm enough, worried that winter was on its way and the trailer would get terribly cold. Did she need anything? Alma told me that she was okay and laughed that her recent weight gain – a benefit from quitting heroin and eating on the job – was helping to keep her warm.

Votive candles flickered on a small coffee table in the living room where I waited for Alma to change out of her work clothes. Aside from a threadbare couch, the coffee table, and a large wall hanging depicting the Virgin de Guadalupe, the living room was completely bare. I wondered if this was a consequence of her husband's departure or if it was simply amplified by the absence of heat and light. I looked at the votives and the Virgin de Guadalupe. It seemed to me that Alma had not entirely yet let go of her Catholic roots, her ties to the past. I was curious about her foray into Evangelicalism and wondered about her desire to be "born again," for a future.

Positioned between a discount grocery store and a mobile home showroom, the Rock Christian Fellowship is a sprawling cinderblock complex located in the center of Española. Its presence can be spotted from some distance by an enormous neon billboard depicting the face of Jesus and which reads, "Rock Christian Fellowship: Making Disciples." In addition to traditional church services, the Fellowship offers a childcare center, a men's recovery home, a "spiritual university," and a restaurant. The Solid Rock Café sits on the northern edge of the complex. Alma suggested we go there for a light dinner. When we arrived, the café was nearly empty. We sat at a small table near the window and watched the evening rush hour traffic gather along Riverside Drive. To my surprise, Alma pulled out two Subway sandwiches from a backpack. I ordered each of us a soft drink and we ate our sandwiches – which had grown soggy with time – in comfortable silence.

Alma told me that the Fellowship was helping her and added that she didn't know what she would do without it. I asked her

about the night she left the clinic. She told me that it was a mistake to have been sent back – that the clinic didn't work because its focus on the past made life unbearable. "They want you to always be thinking about what you did, why you did it, how you're always gonna be an addict and you got to stay clean, fight the temptation. You're always 'ceptible to heroin and there's no cure ... [that's why] I like it here [the Fellowship]. They're not always looking back, you know? Pastor Naranjo talks about the future; he says that's what counts. The future – so you can be blessed and go to heaven." Alma continued,

> At Hoy, with 12 Steps ... it's like with Luis [her husband], always reminding me of the fuck-ups, you know? The things I've done. It's like, you don't have to keep reminding me! I know better than anyone else what I've done and where I've been. I can't forget. But don't keep pushing me down there, you know? I have a hard enough time dealing with it.

Alma's account of being "pushed" into remembering that she is at perpetual risk of relapsing into "past" addictive behavior provides a powerful critique of the model of chronicity, an approach that began, in part, as a well-meaning attempt to dispel the moral implications of being a drug addict. But Alma's framing suggests that there are, in fact, moral and psychological repercussions to approaching addiction as a chronic, unending process. Anthropologists have described how the uncertain ontological status of the chronically ill – be they depressed, asthmatic, or addicted – can provoke stigmatizing reactions in others (Jackson 2005; Luhmann 2007). This is true in Alma's experience, although I would add that the idea that her addiction is chronic – that is, its chronicity, it's unendingness – may provoke other, perhaps more dangerous, responses, including a deep sense of hopelessness. And while some might read Alma's appeal for "the system" and her husband to stop "pushing [her] down there" as "denial," an alternative reading may be that it is a genuine plea for a new understanding and approach to addiction. I began to understand Alma's turn toward Evangelicalism as an attempt to carve out such a response. "I don't want to go through this anymore," she said of the seemingly perpetual cycle of treatment and relapse. Perhaps it was in Evangelicalism, and through the promise of being "born again" that Alma was able to envision putting an end to chronicity as such and to seek for herself a true and lasting recovery.

Indeed, that evening in the restaurant, Alma quietly swore to me that she hadn't used heroin since she left the clinic, crediting the Fellowship and her new, forward-looking perspective with her sobriety. The only problem, she said, was that she still couldn't sleep. I could see by her eyes that this was true. Bloodshot and watery, Alma's eyes conveyed the culmination of too many sleepless nights. She told me she hated nighttime because she worried, even before getting into bed, that sleep would not come. I asked her how many nights it had been since she slept. "Nights!" she laughed. It had been so long since she'd slept that she didn't even remember what it felt like.

True insomnia is not merely tossing and turning on a bad night. Rather, it is sleeplessness night after night, a mind and a body in revolt against itself. Alma described wanting sleep like a hungry person wanting food; her insomnia was a kind of starvation, or another kind of withdrawal. It had gotten to a point where normal patterns of wakefulness and sleep no longer made sense or seemed permanently unavailable to her. During the hours that preceded her departure from the clinic, Alma said her mind started "playing tricks":

I kept going over things in my mind, you know? I'd tell myself to stop but I couldn't. My thoughts were like separate. I can't control it. It's always been like this for me.

[That night at the clinic] I was thinking about my parents and how they're getting old and are probably going to die. How I messed things up and, like, my mom hates me now and she's up there in T. A. [Tierra Amarilla] and I don't go there no more. I don't. I don't even like to call. But mostly, I kept thinking about Ana and how fucked up everything is, how she died. Did she, like, *know* she was going to die? Did she feel it?

This is what I kept thinking that night.

"Insomnia," the Romanian philosopher Emil Cioran writes, "enlarges the slightest vexation and converts it into a blow of fate, stands vigil over our wounds and keeps them from flagging" (1992:140). Night after night, the same thoughts appeared to Alma. She asked me why that is – asked me why, during the day, she was able to get by, but why at night the same thoughts and memories swelled up, always in the same way.

Alma asked the social services coordinator at the Fellowship for help – hoping that she would be referred to a physician who could write her a legitimate prescription for a sleep aid. Her request was denied. She admitted to me that she resorted to buying prescription meds – mostly tranquilizers – off the street. But it was too expensive, costing up to ten dollars a pill, and the effect too temporary. The thoughts, Alma told me, always returned. They were, in her words, without end.

The only time I can sleep is with *chiva* (heroin). That's the only time and it's the best sleep, before you forget everything. There's nothing, just this quiet. I can't explain it to you. It's the best medicine.

I asked Alma that evening whether she was worried that she'd start using again – if her insomnia would cause her to return to heroin. "Yes ... always," she said. It was always on her mind.

Perpetual Peace

Last Christmas, Alma's estranged husband found her lying on her couch, alone and unresponsive. Within minutes, she arrived at the Española Hospital, a short distance from the trailer they once shared, and was pronounced dead. A toxicology examination performed by the Office of the Medical Investigator determined her cause of death to be a lethal combination of heroin and the prescription medication diazepam (valium). Her death was classified an "accidental poisoning," the standard classification given to an overdose with no corroborating evidence of intent.

However, an overdose surveillance report examining the characteristics and intent of overdose events at the Española Hospital ER between 2004–05 suggests otherwise (Shah 2006). It found overdoses resulting from a combination of prescription medications (i.e., benzodiazepine, diazepam) and heroin – overdoses like Alma's – to be the routine presentation in the emergency department. Nearly half (47 percent) of these overdoses were determined to be attempted suicide, with female gender being the most significant covariate among those who attempted suicide via overdose. Alma's death might have been a suicide.

There is an overwhelming sense of despair staff at the Española Hospital feels, witnessing the same men and women cycling in and out of the ER; several have described to me their terrible premonitions that the next time would be the last for this or that individual (in such a sparsely populated region, staff and patients were likely as not to be friends or family). Some clinicians ask overdose patients whether they "meant to do it," a question meant to begin the process of rewriting the script of the "accidental overdose." At the same time, the clinicians acknowledge that the intermittent triage care they provide, or even answering the question of intentionality, in and of themselves do not constitute even the possibility of recovery. Collecting this data merely ensures that some intentional overdoses will be recognized as such. The clinicians thus partake in their own work of mourning – one that does not suppose it can heal the inevitable recurrence of these events, but that is nevertheless committed to marking them as they occur, seemingly without end. They, too, keep vigil over loss.

Since Freud, there remains an implicit understanding that the melancholic subject is trapped in affect and incapable of sublimating the pain of past loss so as to live meaningfully in the present. Even melancholia's contemporary interlocutors tend to agree that such sublimation can occur only through the process of narrativization, such as in elegy, through which the past is resurrected, but only with the intent to vitalize the present (Ruti 2005; Silverman 2000). To tend to the past as such, to remain loyal to it without this presentist perspective, is to remain its prisoner and to live a life as a partially realized subject.

Alma's past remained a fundamental force in her everyday experience, and it was not a force that was "appropriated" in the goal of defining a future, or for learning how to self-actualize, or even heal. Rather, her past, which was undeniably filled with the sorrow of loss, was experienced as such: painful, heavyhearted, and seemingly endless. Does it mean that to be passionately engaged with the past on its own terms, one necessarily sacrifices the potential for a present, and even sacrifices the self? Can one live a melancholy life that is meaningful on its own terms?

Before her death, I believed so. I believed that seeing and experiencing the world and the past as painful – and to not forget or sublimate this pain for other purposes – is likewise a way of living in the world. In other words, there is meaning in melancholia, meaning in wounds that haven't, and perhaps may never, heal. But I am left wondering whether Alma believed this, for it seems to me now that she wanted to forget, wanted to heal – and desperately so. That is, above all, what heroin offered her: an ahistorical frame in which to finally sleep. But the various relational, historical, and institutional processes in which she was embedded kept reminding her of the past; that the painful moment *would* return and disturb whatever momentary peace she achieved.

There is nothing accidental about Alma's death. It was forged out of the forms of endlessness in which she lived.

Alma's descanso is not in Española but, instead, in the Carson National Forest, on the land to which she was heir. Her memorial is a cross that is made of tree branches, woven together with bits of rusted wire. Overlaying the wooden cross is another – this one made of intersecting syringes. Alma's father made the cross of wood and etched into it her name, the day of her death, and the command, "no te olvides" [Never forget]. Her husband later added the cross of intersecting syringes, expressing her need to forget. Standing beside a towering spruce, Alma's descanso voices the losses of her ancestors and her parents – losses she inherited, and reaffirms, in death.

In this essay, I have tried to show how Alma's need to forget was made to cohere through a multiplicity of losses, memories, injections, places, institutions, and practices. This multiplicity produced a new dimension of chronic in which Alma felt herself irrevocably tied. The connection between feelings of endlessness, medical notions of chronicity and relapse, and juridical categories and responses to recidivism are more than metaphorical. They are coconstitutive. Here, feelings of endlessness give rise to heroin use, which lead to forms of intervention premised on return. Alma struggled to find a way out, but the promise of rebirth, like the work of "recovery," was undermined by the powerful presupposition of return that was always already in place.

NOTES

1 In this essay, I use the term *Hispano* to refer to the Spanish-speaking people of northern New Mexico, many of whom trace their ancestrics back to the region's original Spanish settlers. They thus consider themselves Hispano or Spanish.

2 See Office of Applied Studies, U.S. Department of Health and Human Services 2005. Treatment Episode Data Set (TEDS): 2002. Discharges from Substance Abuse Treatment Services (DASIS Series S-25, DHHS Publication No. (SMA) 04–3967). Rockville, MD: Substance Abuse Mental Health Services Administration. Retrieved on 10/10/07 from http://wwwdasis.samhsa.gov/teds02/ 2002_teds_rpt_d.pdf.

REFERENCES

Acker, Caroline Jean
    2002 Creating the American Junkie: Addiction Research in the Classic Era of Narcotics Control. Baltimore: Johns Hopkins University Press.
Appel, P. W., and Joseph H. Kott
    2000 Causes and Rates of Death among Methadone Maintenance Patients. Mount Sinai Journal of Medicine 66:444–51.
Biehl, João
    2005 Vita: Life in a Zone of Social Abandonment. Berkeley: University of California Press.
Borges, Jorge Luis
    1998 Collected Fictions. New York: Penguin Putnam.
Brewer, D. D.
    1998 Drug Use Predictors of Partner Violence in Opiate Dependent Women. Violence Vice 13 (2):107–15.
Butler, Judith
    2004 Precarious Life: The Powers of Mourning and Violence. London: Verso.
Camí, Jordi
    2003 Drug Addiction. New England Journal of Medicine 348(10):375–86.
Cheng, Anne Anlin
    2001 The Melancholy of Race. New York: Oxford University Press.
Cioran, Emil M.
    1992 Anathemas and Admiration. London: Quartet.
Cohen, Lawrence
    1999 Where It Hurts: Indian Material for an Ethics of Organ Transplantation. Special Issue, "Bioethics and Beyond," Daedalus 128 (4):135–65.
Das, Veena
    1996 Language and Body: Transactions in the Construction of Pain. Daedalus 125:67–92.
Das, Veena, and Arthur Kleinman
    2000 The Act of Witnessing: Violence, Poisonous Knowledge, and Subjectivity. In Violence and Subjectivty. Veena Das, Arthur Kleinman, Mamphela Ramphele, and Pamela Reynolds, eds. Pp. 205–55. Berkeley: University of California Press.
    2001 Introduction. In Remaking a World: Violence, Social Suffering, and Recovery. Veena Das, Arthur Kleinman, Mamphela Ramphele, and Pamela Reynolds, eds. Pp. 1–30. Berkeley: University of California Press.
Desjarlas, Robert
    1997 Shelter Blues: Selfhood and Sanity among the Homeless. Philadelphia: University of Pennsylvania Press.
    2003 Sensory Biographies: Lives and Deaths among Depal's Yolmo Buddhists. Berkeley: University of California Press.
DWI Resource Center
    2005 DWI Problem Statement Publication, Rio Arriba County. DWI Resource Center, Albuquerque, New Mexico. Electronic document,

http://www.dwiresourcecenter.org/downloads/highlights/RioArriba_Highlights_Mar05. pdf, accessed November 15, 2007.

Ebright, Malcolm
1994 Land Grants and Law Suits in Northern New Mexico. Albuquerque: University of New Mexico Press.

Eng, David L., and David Kazanjian
2003 Loss: The Politics of Mourning. Berkeley: University of California Press.

Fischer, Michael M. J.
2003 Emergent Forms of Life and the Anthropological Voice. Durham, NC: Duke University Press.

Ford, Michael
1994 Addiction in Action: Drugs, Addiction, Liberalism and the Law. In Beyond the Pleasure Dome: Writing and Addiction from the Romantics. Sue Vice, Matthew Campbell, and Tim Armstrong, eds. Pp. 62–81. Sheffield: Sheffield Academic Press.

Freud, Sigmund
1960 The Ego and the Id. New York: W. W. Norton.
1989 Mourning and Melancholia. In The Freud Reader. Peter Gay, ed. Pp. 584–5. New York: W. W. Norton.

Gardner, Richard
1970 Grito!! Reies Tijerina and the New Mexico Land Grant War of 1967. New York: Harper Colophon.

Good, Byron
1994 Medicine, Rationality and Experience. Cambridge: Cambridge University Press.

Gonzales, Phillip
2003 Struggle for Survival: The Hispanic Land Grants of New Mexico, 1848–2001. Agricultural History 77(2):293–324.

Gonzales-Berry, Erlinda, and David Maciel
2000 The Contested Homeland: A Chicano History of Northern New Mexico. Albuquerque: University of New Mexico Press.

Huyssen, Andreas
2000 Present Pasts: Media, Politics, Amnesia. Public Culture 12(1):21–38.

Jackson, Jean
2005 Stigma, Liminality, and Chronic Pain: Mind-Body Borderlands. American Ethnologist 32(3):332–53.

Jenkins, Henry
2006 "People from that Part of the World": The Politics of Dislocation. Cultural Anthropology 21(3):469–86.

Klingemann, Harald
2001 The Time Game: Temporal Perspectives of Patients and Staff in Alcohol and Drug Treatment. Time and Society 10:303–28.

Kosek, Jake
2006 Understories: The Political Life of Forests in Northern New Mexico. Durham, NC: Duke University Press.

Lipsitz, George
2006 Learning from New Orleans: The Social Warrant of Hostile Privatism and Competitive Consumer Citizenship. Cultural Anthropology 21(3):451–68.

Luhmann, T. M.
2007 Social Defeat and the Culture of Chronicity: Or Why Schizophrenia Does So Well over There and Badly Here. Culture, Medicine, Psychiatry 31(2):135–72.

Masco, Joseph
2004 Mutant Ecologies: Radioactive Life in Post–Cold War New Mexico. Cultural Anthropology 19(4):517–50.

McLellan, J., A. Thomas, David C. Lewis, Charles P. O'Brien, Herbert D. Kleber.
2000 Drug Dependence: A Chronic Medical Illness: Implications for Treatment, Insurance, and Outcomes Evaluation. Journal of the American Medical Association 284: 1689–95.

Muñoz, José E.
1997 Photographies of Mourning: Melancholia and Ambivalence in Van Der Zee, Mapplethorpe, and Looking for Langston. In Race and the Subject of Masculinities. Harry Stecopoulos and Michael Uebel, eds. Pp. 337–60. Durham, NC: Duke University Press.

Nabokov, Peter
1970 Tijerina and the Courthouse Raid. Palo Alto: Ramparts.

Nietzsche, Friedrich
2000 The Gay Science. Cambridge: Cambridge University Press.

Office of Applied Studies, U.S. Department of Health and Human Services
2005 Treatment Episode Data Set (TEDS): 2002. Discharges from Substance Abuse Treatment Services (DASIS Series S-25, DHHS PublicationNo. (SMA) 04–3967). Substance Abuse Mental Health Services Administration. Electronic document, http://wwwdasis.samhsa.gov/teds02/2002_teds_rpt_d.pdf, accessed October 10, 2007.

O'Nell, DeLeane Theresa
1996 Disciplined Hearts: History, Identity, and Depression in an American Indian Community. Berkeley: University of California Press.

Pandolfo, Stephania
1998 Impasse of Angels: Scenes from a Moroccan Space of Memory. Chicago: University of Chicago Press.

Petryna, Adriana
2002 Life Exposed: Biological Citizens after Chernobyl. Princeton: Princeton University Press.

Preble, Ed, and John Casey Jr.
1969 Taking Care of Business: The Heroin User's Life on the Street. International Journal of the Addictions 4(1):1–24.

Raviola, Giuseppe, M'Imunya Machoki, Esther Mwaikambo, and Mary-Jo DelVecchio Good
2002 HIV, Disease Plague, Demoralization and "Burnout": Resident Experience of the Medical Profession in Nairobi, Kenya. Culture, Medicine, Psychiatry 26(1):55–86.

Rodríguez, Sylvia
1987 Land, Water and Ethnic Identity in Taos. In Land, Water and Culture: New Perspectiveson Hispanic Land Grants. Charles Briggs and John Van Ness, eds. Pp. 313–403. Albuquerque: University of New Mexico Press.

Ruti, Mari
2005 From Melancholia to Meaning: How to Live the Past in the Present. Psychoanalytic Dialogues 15(5):637–60.

Sacks, Peter
1985 The English Elegy: Studies in the Genre from Spencer to Yeats. Baltimore: Johns Hopkins University Press.

Savage, Seddon
2008 Challenges in Using Opioids to Treat Pain in Persons with Substance Abuse Disorders. Addiction Science and Clinical Practice 4(2):4–25.

Scheper-Hughes, Nancy
1992 Death without Weeping: The Violence of Everyday Life in Brazil. Berkeley: University of California Press.

Serematakis, Nadia
1991 The Last Word: Women, Death, and Divination in Inner Mani. Chicago: University of Chicago Press.

Shah, Nina
2006 Overdose Surveillance in Hospital Departments in Northern New Mexico: A Pilot Study. New Mexico Epidemiology 2006 (3):1–4.

Silverman, K.
2000 World Spectators. Stanford: Stanford University Press.

U.S. Senate
1999 Rio Arriba County Strategy to Combat Heroin Addiction. Hearing before a Subcommittee of the Committee on Appropriations, United States Senate, One Hundred Sixth Congress, First Session. Special Hearing (Espanola, New Mexico, March 30, 1999). Washington, DC: U.S. Government Printing Office.

Young, Allan
1997 The Harmony of Illusions: Inventing Post-Traumatic Stress Disorder. Princeton: Princeton University Press.

Young, Allan
2006 America's Transient Mental Illness: A Brief History of the Self-Traumatized Perpetrator. In Subjectivity: Ethnographic Investigations. João Biehl, Byron Good, and Arthur Kleinman, eds. Pp. 155–178. Berkeley: University of California Press.

Williams, Raymond
1977 Marxism and Literature. Oxford: Oxford University Press.

Index

Page numbers in *italics* denote tables and figures